About Pearson

Pearson is the world's learning company, with presence across 70 countries worldwide. Our unique insights and world-class expertise comes from a long history of working closely with renowned teachers, authors and thought leaders, as a result of which, we have emerged as the preferred choice for millions of teachers and learners across the world.

We believe learning opens up opportunities, creates fulfilling careers and hence better lives. We hence collaborate with the best of minds to deliver you class-leading products, spread across the Higher Education and K12 spectrum.

Superior learning experience and improved outcomes are at the heart of everything we do. This product is the result of one such effort.

Your feedback plays a critical role in the evolution of our products and you can reachus@pearson.com. We look forward to it.

Financial Markets and Institutions

EIGHTH EDITION

Financial Markets and Institutions

EIGHTH EDITION

Frederic S. Mishkin
Graduate School of Business, Columbia University

Stanley G. Eakins
East Carolina University

Tulsi Jayakumar
S.P. Jain Institute of Management & Research

R.K. Pattnaik
S.P. Jain Institute of Management & Research

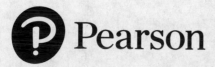 Pearson

Authorized adaptation from the United States edition, entitled *Financial Markets and Institutions,* *8th edition*, ISBN 978-0-13-34-2362-4, by Frederic S. Mishkin and Stanley Eakins, published by Pearson Education, Inc, Copyright © 2015.

Indian Subcontinent Adaptation

ISBN 978-93-325-8552-2

First Impression, 2017
Third Impression, 2018
Fourth Impression, 2019

This edition is manufactured in India and is authorized for sale only in India, Bangladesh, Bhutan, Pakistan, Nepal, Sri Lanka and the Maldives. Circulation of this edition outside of these territories is UNAUTHORIZED.

Published by Pearson India Education Services Pvt. Ltd, CIN: U72200TN2005PTC057128.

Head Office: 15th Floor, Tower-B, World Trade Tower, Plot No. 1, Block-C, Sector-16, Noida 201 301, Uttar Pradesh, India
Registered Office: 4th Floor, Software Block, Elnet Software City, TS-140, Block 2 & 9, Rajiv Gandhi Salai, Taramani, Chennai 600 113, TamilNadu, India.
Fax: 080-30461003, Phone: 080-30461060
Website : in.pearson.com , Email: companysecretary.india@pearson.com

Printed in India by Sai Printo Pack Pvt. Ltd.

Testimonials

As someone who until recently was closely involved with regulation and development of the financial markets in India I find the publication extremely useful handbook of theories and practices relating to the markets in India.

The authors have addressed the developments in a very clear, concise and comprehensive manner. The publication of a book of this nature and scope is very timely when the financial markets in India are in the cusp of transformational changes.

The book will thus be a valuable reference point for students, academician's practitioners.

Harun R Khan
Former Deputy Governor of Reserve Bank of India
Currently Non-executive Chairman, the National Securities
and Clearing Corporation of India (NSCCL)
and senior Adviser, KPMG India

The landscape of India›s financial markets has undergone a sea change in the last two and a half decades. Both RBI and SEBI have been instrumental in spearheading these changes and I am happy to have been associated with both these prestigious institutions in the area of market development and regulation. There has always been an acutely felt need for an authentic book to trace these developments in India. This long pending vacuum has finally been filled by this book, which gives an excellent treatise of India's markets and institutions. I am sure that this book will vet the appetite for knowledge and research of one and all—students, researchers as well as practitioners.

G. Mahalingam
Former Executive Director (RBI)
Currently Wholetime Member (SEBI)

It is indeed gratifying to note that Dr. Pattnaik and Dr. Jayakumar's adaptation of Mishkin and Eakins' classic text on financial markets retains all its successful ingredients that made it such a hit, but with an Indian flavour. Not just the lucid text, detailed real-world case studies, up-to-date material and extensive illustrative, India-specific examples, particularly in this post-GFC (Global Financial Crisis) world, but retaining a strong, unbroken connection throughout, with the theoretical underpinnings of Finance and its key principles.

Markets in India share many similarities, but also have institutions and features that differentiate them from those in the West, and a book that relates to the theory and practice of finance from an Indian perspective is uniquely suited for anyone studying this US$2trn economy, be they academics or practitioners.

Dr. Tirthankar Patnaik
Chief India Strategist, Mizuho Bank

The best books on economics combine rigorous theory with the institutional structures in which the analytical framework operates. This is wonderful and much needed addition to fill a gap in India's economic textbook space. The authors' backgrounds enable them to jointly provide a rich content, which will be particularly useful for students in learning economics and finance through an analytical lens that they can apply to India's policy developments.

Saugata Bhattacharya
Chief Economist and Senior Vice President
Axis Bank

To My Dad
>—F. S. M.

To My Wife, Laurie
>—S. G. E.

To My Husband, Jay
& Daughter, Radhika
>—T. J.

To My Parents
>—R. K. P.

Contents in Brief

Contents in Detail

PART FOUR   CENTRAL BANKING AND THE CONDUCT OF MONETARY POLICY

Chapter 9   Central Banks and the Reserve Bank of India (RBI)

PART SIX THE FINANCIAL INSTITUTIONS INDUSTRY

Chapter 16 Banking and the Management of Financial Institutions

Chapter 17 Financial Regulation

Contents on the Web

**The following updated chapters appendices are available
on our Website at www.pearsonhighered.com/mishkin_eakins.**

CHAPTER APPENDICES

Preface

A Note from Frederic Mishkin

When I took leave from Columbia University in September 2006 to take a position as a member (governor) of the Board of Governors of the Federal Reserve System, I never imagined how exciting—and stressful—the job was likely to be. How was I to know that, as Alan Greenspan put it, the world economy would be hit by a "once-in-a-century credit tsunami," the global financial crisis of 2007–2009? When I returned to Columbia in September 2008, the financial crisis had reached a particularly virulent stage, with credit markets completely frozen and some of our largest financial institutions in very deep trouble. The global financial crisis, which has been the worst financial crisis the world has experienced since the Great Depression, has completely changed the nature of financial markets and institutions.

Given what has happened, the study of financial markets and institutions has become particularly exciting. I hope that students reading this book will have as much fun learning from it as we have had in writing it.

August 2013

What's New in the Eighth Edition

In addition to the expected updating of all data through 2013 whenever possible, there is major new material in every part of the text.

New Material on Financial Markets and Institutions

In light of ongoing research and changes in financial markets and institutions, we have added the following material to keep the text current:

- A new Case box on the Over th Counter Exchange in India (OTCEI) and a new case box on the Government securities market in India (Chapter 2)
- A new Minicase box on Deep Discount Bonds in India and Inflation Indexed Bonds in India (Chapter 3)
- A new case on Municipal Bonds in India (Chapter 5)
- A new Mini-Case box on Raj Rajaratnam and the Galleon insider trading scandal (Chapter 6)

- A new section on why the efficient markets hypothesis does not imply that financial markets are efficient (Chapter 6)
- A new mini case on Indian companies and Internal Control Requirements (Chapter 7)
- A new Mini-Case box on collateralized debt obligations (CDOs) (Chapter 8)
- A new Global box on the European Sovereign Debt Crisis (Chapter 8)
- A new case on Financial Crisis: Past, Present and Future and India: Lessons from the Financial Crisis (Chapter 8)

The chapters pertaining to the Money Markets (Chapter 11), Bond Markets (Chapter 12)and large sections of Chapter 13 and 14 pertaining to the Stock Market and Foreign Exchange Market respectively have been completely re-written from the Indian perspective.

- A new case on India's Balance of Payments (Chapter 15)
- A new Case on India and the Policy Trilemma (Chapter 15)
- A new discussion of India's Balance of payments using the BPM 6 format (Chapter 15 A)
- A new section on Balance Sheets of Scheduled Commercial Banks in India (Chapter 16)
- A section on DICGC in India, RBI and Prompt Corrective Action Framework for commercial banks, macro-prudential framework in India and other sections pertaining to financial regulation in India (Chapter 17)
- A completely rewritten chapter on Banking Industry: Structure and competition from the Indian perspective (Chapter 18)
- A new case on NBFCs in India (Chapter 18)
- A new section on macroprudential versus microprudential supervision (Chapter 18)
- A new section on too-big-to-fail and future regulation (Chapter 18)
- A new case on the Interest Rate Risk in Banking Book in India (Chapter 19)
- A new section on Interest Rate derivatives in India (Chapter 20)
- A new Case Box on Business in the Futures & Options segment in India (Chapter 20)
- A new case box on India and the Global Financial Crisis (Chapter 21)
- A new Web chapter on financial crisis in emerging market economies that provides a much more extensive treatment of financial crisis in these countries

New Material on Monetary Policy

In the aftermath of the global financial crisis, there have been major changes in the way central banks conduct monetary policy. Chapters 9 and 10, as also Chapter 10(A) have been completely rewritten to give the Indian perspective and the functioning of the Reserve Bank of India. This has involved a substantial rewriting of Chapter 10, along with the following new material.

- A complete discussion on the history, structure and functions of the RBI (Chapter 9)
- A new section on the role of the Governor and the most recent developments in the constitution of a Monetary Policy Committee (Chapter 9)
- A new section on the RBI's balance sheet (Chapter 10)

- A new section on monetary policy tools in India (Chapter 10)
- A new section on Goals of Monetary policy (Chapter 10)
- A new case on Inflationary Targeting: The Indian experience (Chapter 10)
- A new section on Liquidity vs. Monetary Management (Chapter 10 A new section on evolution of monetary policy in India and the current monetary policy framework (Chapter 10)
- A new section on Transmission of Monetary Policy and impediments to such transmission (Chapter 10)
- A detailed discussion of the RBI's assets and liabilities (Chapter 10 A)
- A discussion of the new monetary policy tool, changing the interest paid on reserves (Chapter 10)
- A new "Inside the Fed" box on why the Fed pays interest on reserves (Chapter 10)
- A new section on nonconventional monetary policy tools and quantitative easing (Chapter 10)
- A new Inside the Fed box on Fed lending facilities during the global financial crisis (Chapter 10)
- A new Inside the Fed box on Ben Bernanke and the Federal Reserve Adoption of Inflation Targeting (Chapter 10)
- A more extensive discussion of the debate over whether central banks should try to pop bubbles (Chapter 10)
- A new section on the policy trilemma (Chapter 16)
- A new section on monetary unions (Chapter 16)
- A Mini-Case on whether the Euro will survive

Appendices on the Web

The Web site for this book, **www.pearsonhighered.com/mishkin_eakins**, has allowed us to retain and add new material for the book by posting content online. The appendices include:

Chapter 4: Models of Asset Pricing

Chapter 4: Applying the Asset Market Approach to a Commodity Market: The Case of Gold

Chapter 4: Loanable Funds Framework

Chapter 4: Supply and Demand in the Market for Money: The Liquidity Preference Framework

Chapter 10: RBI's Assets and Liabilities

Chapter 14: The Interest Parity Condition

Chapter 15: The Balance of Payments Account

Chapter 17: Evaluating FDICIA and Other Proposed Reforms of the Bank Regulatory System

Chapter 17: Banking Crisis Throughout the World

Chapter 20: More on Hedging with Financial Derivatives

Instructors can either use these appendices in class to supplement the material in the textbook or recommend them to students who want to expand their knowledge of the financial markets and institutions field.

Hallmarks

Although this text has undergone a major revision, it retains the basic hallmarks that make it the best-selling textbook on financial markets and institutions. The eighth edition of *Financial Markets and Institutions* is a practical introduction to the workings of today's financial markets and institutions. Moving beyond the descriptions and definitions provided by other textbooks in the field, *Financial Markets and Institutions* encourages students to understand the connection between the theoretical concepts and their real-world applications. By enhancing students' analytical abilities and concrete problem-solving skills, this textbook prepares students for successful careers in the financial services industry or successful interactions with financial institutions, whatever their jobs.

To prepare students for their future careers, *Financial Markets and Institutions* provides the following features:

- A unifying analytic framework that uses a few basic principles to organize students' thinking. These principles include:
  Asymmetric information (agency) problems
  Conflicts of interest
  Transaction costs
  Supply and demand
  Asset market equilibrium
  Efficient markets
  Measurement and management of risk
- "The Practicing Manager" sections include nearly 20 hands-on applications that emphasize the financial practitioner's approach to financial markets and institutions.
- A careful step-by-step development of models enables students to master the material more easily.
- A high degree of flexibility allows professors to teach the course in the manner they prefer.
- International perspectives are completely integrated throughout the text.
- "Following the Financial News" is a feature that encourages the reading of a financial newspaper.
- Numerous cases increase students' interest by applying theory to real-world data and examples.
- The text focuses on the impact of electronic (computer and telecommunications) technology on the financial system. The text makes extensive use of the Internet with Web exercises, Web sources for charts and tables, and Web references in the margins. It also features special "E-Finance" boxes that explain how changes in technology have affected financial markets and institutions.

Flexibility

There are as many ways to teach financial markets and institutions as there are instructors. Thus, there is a great need to make a textbook flexible in order to satisfy the diverse needs of instructors, and that has been a primary objective in writing this book. This textbook achieves this flexibility in the following ways:

- Core chapters provide the basic analysis used throughout the book, and other chapters or sections of chapters can be assigned or omitted according to instructor preferences. For example, Chapter 2 introduces the financial system and basic concepts such as transaction costs, adverse selection, and moral hazard. After covering Chapter 2, an instructor can decide to teach a more detailed treatment of financial structure and financial crisis using chapters in Part 3 of the text, or cover specific chapters on financial markets or financial institutions in Parts 4 or 5 of the text, or the instructor can skip these chapters and take any of a number of different paths.

- The approach to internationalizing the text using separate, marked international sections within chapters and separate chapters on the foreign exchange market and the international monetary system is comprehensive yet flexible. Although many instructors will teach all the international material, others will choose not to. Instructors who want less emphasis on international topics can easily skip Chapter 15 (on the foreign exchange market) and Chapter 16 (on the international financial system).

- "The Practicing Manager" applications, as well as Part 7 on the management of financial institutions, are self-contained and so can be skipped without loss of continuity. Thus, an instructor wishing to teach a less managerially oriented course, who might want to focus on public policy issues, will have no trouble doing so. Alternatively, Part 7 can be taught earlier in the course, immediately after Chapter 17 on bank management.

The course outlines listed next for a semester teaching schedule illustrate how this book can be used for courses with a different emphasis. More detailed information about how the text can offer flexibility in your course is available in the *Instructor's Manual.*

> *Financial markets and institutions emphasis:* Chapters 1–5, 7–8, 11–13, 17–19, and a choice of five other text chapters
> *Financial markets and institutions with international emphasis:* Chapters 1–5, 7–8, 11–13, 15–19, and a choice of three other text chapters
> *Managerial emphasis:* Chapters 1–5, 17–19, 23–24, and a choice of eight other text chapters
> *Public policy emphasis:* Chapters 1–5, 7–10, 17–18, and a choice of seven other text chapters

Pedagogical Aids

A textbook must be a solid motivational tool. To this end, we have incorporated a wide variety of pedagogical features.

1. **Chapter Previews** at the beginning of each chapter tell students where the chapter is heading, why specific topics are important, and how they relate to other topics in the book.
2. **Cases** demonstrate how the analysis in the book can be used to explain many important real-world situations.
3. **"The Practicing Manager"** is a set of special cases that introduce students to real-world problems that managers of financial institutions have to solve.
4. **Numerical Examples** guide students through solutions to financial problems using formulas, time lines, and calculator key strokes.
5. **"Following the Financial News" boxes** introduce students to relevant news articles and data that are reported daily in financial news sources and explain how to read them.

6. **"Inside the RBI" boxes** give students a feel for what is important in the operation and structure of the Federal Reserve System.

7. **"Global" boxes** include interesting material with an international focus.

8. **"E-Finance" boxes** relate how changes in technology have affected financial markets and institutions.

9. **"Conflicts of Interest" boxes** outline conflicts of interest in different financial service industries.

10. **"Mini-Case" boxes** highlight dramatic historical episodes or apply the theory to the data.

11. **Summary Tables** are useful study aids for reviewing material.

12. **Key Statements** are important points that are set in boldface type so that students can easily find them for later reference.

13. **Graphs** with captions, numbering over 60, help students understand the interrelationship of the variables plotted and the principles of analysis.

14. **Summaries** at the end of each chapter list the chapter's main points.

15. **Key Terms** are important words or phrases that appear in boldface type when they are defined for the first time and are listed at the end of each chapter.

16. **End-of-Chapter Questions** help students learn the subject matter by applying economic concepts and feature a special class of questions that students find particularly relevant, titled "Predicting the Future."

17. **End-of-Chapter Quantitative Problems**, numbering over 250, help students to develop their quantitative skills.

18. **Web Exercises** encourage students to collect information from online sources or use online resources to enhance their learning experience.

19. **Web Sources** report the URL source of the data used to create the many tables and charts.

20. **Marginal Web References** point the student to Web sites that provide information or data that supplement the text material.

21. **Glossary** at the back of the book defines all the key terms.

22. **Full Solutions to the Questions and Quantitative Problems** appear in the *Instructor's Manual* and on the Instructor's Resource Center at **www.pearsonhighered.com/irc**. Professors have the flexibility to share the solutions with their students as they see fit.

Supplementary Materials

The eighth edition of *Financial Markets and Institutions* includes the most comprehensive program of supplementary materials of any textbook in its field. These items are available to qualified domestic adopters but in some cases may not be available to international adopters. These include the following items:

For the Professor

1. **Online Instructor's Manual:** This manual, prepared by the authors, includes chapter outlines, overviews, teaching tips, and complete solutions to questions and problems in the text.

2. **Online PowerPoint:** Prepared by John Banko (University of Florida). The presentation, which contains lecture notes and the complete set of figures and tables from the textbook, contains more than 1,000 slides that comprehensively outline the major points covered in the text.

3. **Online Test Item File:** Updated and revised for the eighth edition, the **Test Item File** comprises over 2,500 multiple-choice, true-false, and essay questions. All of the questions from the Test Item File are available in computerized format for use in the TestGen software. The TestGen software is available for both Windows and Macintosh systems.

Acknowledgments

As always in so large a project, there are many people to thank. Our special gratitude goes to Bruce Kaplan, former economics editor at HarperCollins; Donna Battista, my former finance editor; Adrienne D'Ambrosio, my current finance editor at Pearson; and Jane Tufts and Amy Fleischer, our former development editors. We also have been assisted by comments from my colleagues at Columbia and from my students.

In addition, we have been guided in this edition and its predecessors by the thoughtful comments of outside reviewers and correspondents. Their feedback has made this a better book. In particular, we thank:

Ibrahim J. Affanen, Indiana University of Pennsylvania
Vikas Agarwal, Georgia State University
Senay Agca, George Washington University
Aigbe Akhigbe, University of Akron
Ronald Anderson, University of Nevada–Las Vegas
Bala G. Arshanapalli, Indiana University Northwest
Christopher Bain, Ohio State University
James C. Baker, Kent State University
John Banko, University of Central Florida
Mounther H. Barakat, University of Houston–Clear Lake
Joel Barber, Florida International University
Thomas M. Barnes, Alfred University
Marco Bassetto, Northwestern University
Dallas R. Blevins, University of Montevallo
Matej Blusko, University of Georgia
Paul J. Bolster, Northeastern University
Lowell Boudreaux, Texas A&M University–Galveston
Deanne Butchey, Florida International University
Mitch Charklewicz, Central Connecticut State University
Yea-Mow Chen, San Francisco State University
N. K. Chidambaran, Tulane University
Wan-Jiun Paul Chiou, Shippensburg University
Jeffrey A. Clark, Florida State University
Robert Bruce Cochran, San Jose State University
William Colclough, University of Wisconsin–La Crosse
Elizabeth Cooperman, University of Baltimore
Brian Davis, Pennsylvania State University
Carl Davison, Mississippi State University
Cris de la Torre, University of Northern Colorado
Erik Devos, Ohio University at SUNY Binghamton
Alan Durell, Dartmouth College
Franklin R. Edwards, Columbia University
Marty Eichenbaum, Northwestern University
Elyas Elyasiani, Temple University
Edward C. Erickson, California State University–Stanislaus
Kenneth Fah, Ohio Dominican College
J. Howard Finch, Florida Gulf Coast University

E. Bruce Fredrikson, Syracuse University
Cheryl Frohlich, University of North Florida
James Gatti, University of Vermont
Paul Girma, State University of New York–New Paltz
Susan Glanz, St. John's University
Gary Gray, Pennsylvania State University
Wei Guan, University of South Florida–St. Petersburg
Charles Guez, University of Houston
Beverly L. Hadaway, University of Texas
John A. Halloran, University of Notre Dame
Billie J. Hamilton, East Carolina University
John H. Hand, Auburn University
Jeffery Heinfeldt, Ohio Northern University
Don P. Holdren, Marshall University
Adora Holstein, Robert Morris College
Sylvia C. Hudgins, Old Dominion University
Jerry G. Hunt, East Carolina University
Boulis Ibrahim, Heroit-Watt University
William E. Jackson, University of North Carolina–Chapel Hill
Joe James, Sam Houston State University
Melvin H. Jameson, University of Nevada–Las Vegas
Kurt Jessewein, Texas A&M International University
Jack Jordan, Seton Hall University
Tejendra Kalia, Worcester State College
Taeho Kim, Thunderbird: The American Graduate School of International Management
Taewon Kim, California State University–Los Angeles
Elinda Kiss, University of Maryland
Glen A. Larsen, Jr., University of Tulsa
James E. Larsen, Wright State University
Rick LeCompte, Wichita State University
Baeyong Lee, Fayetteville State University
Boyden E. Lee, New Mexico State University
Adam Lei, Midwestern State University
Kartono Liano, Mississippi State University
John Litvan, Southwest Missouri State
Richard A. Lord, Georgia College

Robert L. Losey, American University
Anthony Loviscek, Seton Hall University
James Lynch, Robert Morris College
Judy E. Maese, New Mexico State University
William Mahnic, Case Western Reserve University
Inayat Mangla, Western Michigan University
William Marcum, Wake Forest University
David A. Martin, Albright College
Lanny Martindale, Texas A&M University
Joseph S. Mascia, Adelphi University
Khalid Metabdin, College of St. Rose
Robert McLeod, University of Alabama
David Milton, Bentley College
A. H. Moini, University of Wisconsin–Whitewater
Russell Morris, Johns Hopkins University
Chee Ng, Fairleigh Dickinson University
Srinivas Nippani, Texas A&M Commerce
Terry Nixon, Indiana University
William E. O'Connell, Jr., The College of William and Mary
Masao Ogaki, Ohio State University
Sam Olesky, University of California–Berkeley
Evren Ors, Southern Illinois University
Coleen C. Pantalone, Northeastern University
Scott Pardee, University of Chicago
James Peters, Fairleigh Dickinson University
Fred Puritz, State University of New York–Oneonta
Mahmud Rahman, Eastern Michigan University
Anoop Rai, Hofstra University

Mitchell Ratner, Rider University
David Reps, Pace University–Westchester
Terry Richardson, Bowling Green State University
Jack Rubens, Bryant College
Charles B. Ruscher, James Madison University
William Sackley, University of Southern Mississippi
Kevin Salyer, University of California–Davis
Siamack Shojai, Manhattan College
Javadi Siamak, Oklahoma University
Donald Smith, Boston University
Kenneth Smith, University of Texas–Dallas
Sonya Williams Stanton, Ohio State University
Michael Sullivan, Florida International University
Rick Swasey, Northeastern University
Anjan Thackor, University of Michigan
Janet M. Todd, University of Delaware
James Tripp, Western Illinois University
Carlos Ulibarri, Washington State University
Emre Unlu, University of Nebraska–Lincoln
John Wagster, Wayne State University
Bruce Watson, Wellesley College
David A. Whidbee, California State University–Sacramento
Arthur J. Wilson, George Washington University
Shee Q. Wong, University of Minnesota–Duluth
Criss G. Woodruff, Radford University
Tong Yu, University of Rhode Island
Dave Zalewski, Providence College

Finally, I want to thank my wife, Sally, my son, Matthew, and my daughter, Laura, who provide me with a warm and happy environment that enables me to do my work, and my father, Sydney, now deceased, who a long time ago put me on the path that led to this book.

Frederic S. Mishkin

I would like to thank Rick Mishkin for his excellent comments on my contributions. By working with Rick on this text, not only have I gained greater skill as a writer, but I have also gained a friend. I would also like to thank my wife, Laurie, for patiently reading each draft of this manuscript and for helping make this my best work. Through the years, her help and support have made this aspect of my career possible.

Stanley G. Eakins

I would like to thank my husband, Jay and daughter, Radhika, who provide me the strength and security to put long hours at work of the sort this book required. I also owe it to my parents, who instilled in me the passion to go after my dreams.

Tulsi Jayakumar

I would like to thank my parents who inspired me to give my best.

R. K. Pattnaik

About the Authors

Frederic S. Mishkin is the Alfred Lerner Professor of Banking and Financial Institutions at the Graduate School of Business, Columbia University. From September 2006 to August 2008, he was a member (governor) of the Board of Governors of the Federal Reserve System.

He is also a research associate at the National Bureau of Economic Research and past president of the Eastern Economics Association. Since receiving his Ph.D. from the Massachusetts Institute of Technology in 1976, he has taught at the University of Chicago, Northwestern University, Princeton University, and Columbia University. He has also received an honorary professorship from the People's (Renmin) University of China. From 1994 to 1997, he was executive vice president and director of research at the Federal Reserve Bank of New York and an associate economist of the Federal Open Market Committee of the Federal Reserve System.

Professor Mishkin's research focuses on monetary policy and its impact on financial markets and the aggregate economy. He is the author of more than 20 books, including *Macroeconomics: Policy and Practice, Second Edition* (Pearson, 2015); *The Economics of Money, Banking and Financial Markets*, Tenth Edition (Pearson, 2013); *Monetary Policy Strategy* (MIT Press, 2007); *The Next Great Globalization: How Disadvantaged Nations Can Harness Their Financial Systems to Get Rich* (Princeton University Press, 2006); *Inflation Targeting: Lessons from the International Experience* (Princeton University Press, 1999); *Money, Interest Rates, and Inflation* (Edward Elgar, 1993); and *A Rational Expectations Approach to Macroeconometrics: Testing Policy Ineffectiveness and Efficient Markets Models* (University of Chicago Press, 1983). In addition, he has published more than 200 articles in such journals as *American Economic Review*, *Journal of Political Economy*, *Econometrica*, *Quarterly Journal of Economics*, *Journal of Finance*, *Journal of Applied Econometrics*, *Journal of Economic Perspectives*, and *Journal of Money Credit and Banking*.

Professor Mishkin has served on the editorial board of the *American Economic Review* and has been an associate editor at the *Journal of Business and Economic Statistics*, *Journal of Applied Econometrics*, *Journal of Economic Perspectives*, *Journal of Money, Credit and Banking*, and *Journal of International Money and Finance*; he also served as the editor of the Federal Reserve Bank of New York's *Economic Policy Review*. He is currently an associate editor (member of the editorial board) at five academic journals, including *International Finance*; *Finance India*; *Emerging Markets, Finance and Trade*; *Review of Development Finance*, and *Borsa Economic Review*. He has been a consultant to the Board of Governors of the Federal Reserve System, the World Bank, and the International Monetary Fund, as well as to many central banks throughout the world. He was also a member of the International Advisory Board to the Financial Supervisory Service of South Korea and an adviser to the Institute for Monetary and Economic Research at the Bank of Korea. Professor Mishkin has also served as a senior fellow at the Federal Deposit Insurance Corporation's Center for Banking Research and as an academic consultant to and member of the Economic Advisory Panel of the Federal Reserve Bank of New York.

Stanley G. Eakins has notable experience as a financial practitioner, serving as vice president and comptroller at the First National Bank of Fairbanks and as a commercial and real estate loan officer. A founder of the Denali Title and Escrow Agency, a title insurance company in Fairbanks, Alaska, he also ran the operations side of a bank and was the chief finance officer for a multimillion-dollar construction and development company.

Professor Eakins received his Ph.D. from Arizona State University. He is the Dean for the College of Business at East Carolina University. His research is focused primarily on the role of institutions in corporate control and how they influence investment practices. He is also interested in integrating multimedia tools into the learning environment and has received grants from East Carolina University in support of this work.

A contributor to journals such as the *Quarterly Journal of Business and Economics*, the *Journal of Financial Research*, and the *International Review of Financial Analysis*, Professor Eakins is also the author of *Corporate Finance Online (CFO)* (Pearson, 2014), a multimedia online text designed from the ground up for electronic delivery.

Dr. Tulsi Jayakumar is Professor (Economics) at S. P. Jain Institute of Management and Research, Mumbai. An alumnus of the Delhi School of Economics, she has a rich experience of 25 years of teaching across the country. She regularly contributes to business newspapers including Mint, Hindu Business Line, Free Press Journal and Financial Express etc. Her cases and articles have been published by reputed national and international journals and case repositories and her cases have won international acclaim.

Dr. R. K. Pattnaik is Professor (Economics) at S. P. Jain Institute of Management and Research, Mumbai. He is a PhD from IIT Mumbai and a central banker, with 2 1/2 decades of experience with the Reserve Bank of India. He was actively involved in the financial reform process and with policy initiatives and regulations pertaining to the financial markets. His articles in the press and in journals have been widely acclaimed.

1

CHAPTER

Why Study Financial Markets and Institutions?

> PREVIEW

On the evening news you have just heard that the bond market has been booming. Does this mean that interest rates will fall so that it is easier for you to finance the purchase of a new computer system for your small retail business? Will the economy improve in the future so that it is a good time to build a new building or add to the one you are in? Should you try to raise funds by issuing stocks or bonds, or instead go to the bank for a loan? If you import goods from abroad, should you be concerned that they will become more expensive?

This book provides answers to these questions by examining how financial markets (such as those for bonds, stocks, and foreign exchange) and financial institutions (banks, insurance companies, mutual funds, and other institutions) work. Financial markets and institutions not only affect your everyday life but also involve huge flows of funds— crores of rupees—throughout our economy, which in turn affect business profits, the production of goods and services, and even the economic well-being of other countries. What happens to financial markets and institutions is of great concern to politicians and can even have a major impact on elections. The study of financial markets and institutions will reward you with an understanding of many exciting issues. In this chapter we provide a road map of the book by outlining these exciting issues and exploring why they are worth studying.

Why Study Financial Markets?

Parts 2 and 5 of this book focus on **financial markets,** markets in which funds are transferred from people who have an excess of available funds to people who have a shortage. Financial markets, such as bond and stock markets, are crucial to promoting greater economic efficiency by channeling funds from people who do not have a productive use for them to those who do. Indeed, well-functioning financial markets are a key factor in producing high economic growth, and poorly performing financial markets are one reason that many countries in the world remain desperately poor. Activities in financial markets also have direct effects on personal wealth, the behavior of businesses and consumers, and the cyclical performance of the economy.

Debt Markets and Interest Rates

A **security** (also called a *financial instrument*) is a claim on the issuer's future income or **assets** (any financial claim or piece of property that is subject to ownership). A **bond** is a debt security that promises to make payments periodically for a specified period of time.[1] Debt markets, also often referred to generically as the *bond* market, are especially important to economic activity because they enable corporations and governments to borrow in order to finance their activities; the bond market is also where interest rates are determined. An **interest rate** is the cost of borrowing or the price paid for the rental of funds (usually expressed as a percentage of the rental of ₹100 per year). Many types of interest rates are found in the economy—mortgage interest rates, car loan rates, and interest rates on many types of bonds.

Interest rates are important on a number of levels. On a personal level, high interest rates could deter you from buying a house or a car because the cost of financing it would be high. Conversely, high interest rates could encourage you to save because you can earn more interest income by putting aside some of your earnings as savings. On a more general level, interest rates have an impact on the overall health of the economy because they affect not only consumers' willingness to spend or save but also businesses' investment decisions. High interest rates, for example, might cause a corporation to postpone building a new plant that would provide more jobs.

Because changes in interest rates have important effects on individuals, financial institutions, businesses, and the overall economy, it is important to explain fluctuations in interest rates that have been substantial over the past 20 years. For example, the interest rate on 91-Day Treasury bills peaked at over 12.5% in 1995–96. This interest rate fell to 4.5% in 2003–04, and then rose to above 7% in 2007–08. It then fell to 3.5% in 2009–10, rose to 8.9% in 2013–14 and then remained above 8% in 2014–15.

Because different interest rates have a tendency to move in unison, economists frequently lump interest rates together and refer to "the" interest rate. As Figure 1.1 shows, however, interest rates on several types of bonds can differ substantially. The interest rate on 91-day Treasury bills, for example, fluctuates more than the other interest rates and is lower, on an average. The interest rates on AAA corporate

GO ONLINE
http://dbie.rbi.org.in/DBIE/ dbie.rbi?site=home
The Reserve Bank of India's database provides access to daily, weekly, monthly, quarterly, and annual releases and historical data for selected interest rates, foreign exchange rates and so on.

---

[1]The definition of *bond* used throughout this book is the broad one in common use by academics, which covers both short- and long-term debt instruments. However, some practitioners in financial markets use the word *bond* to describe only specific long-term debt instruments such as corporate bonds or Indian dated government securities.

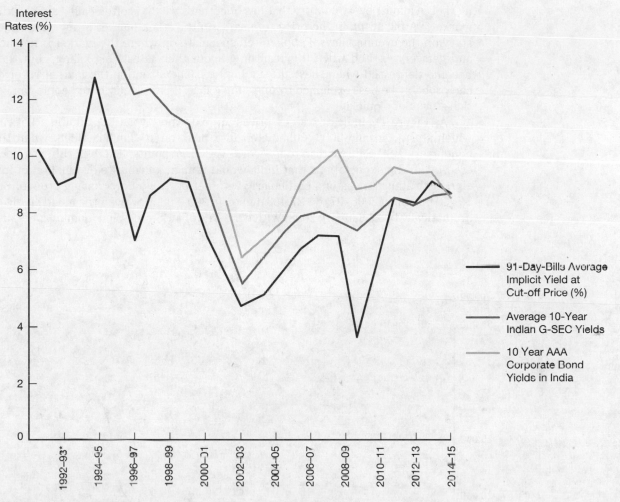

FIGURE 1.1 Interest Rates on Selected Bonds, 1992–2014

Although different interest rates have a tendency to move in unison, they do often differ substantially and the spreads between them fluctuate.

Source: Reserve Bank of India, Bloomberg, Reuters.

bonds are higher, on an average, than the other interest rates, and the spreads also vary. The spreads surged during the period 2007–2009, before they narrowed again.

In Chapters 2, 11 and 12 we study the role of debt markets in the economy, and in Chapters 3 through 5 we examine what an interest rate is, how the common movements in interest rates come about, and why the interest rates on different bonds vary.

The Stock Market

A **common stock** (typically just called a **stock**) represents a share of ownership in a corporation. It is a security that is a claim on the earnings and assets of the corporation. Issuing stock and selling it to the public is a way for corporations to raise funds to finance their activities. The stock market, in which claims on the earnings of corporations (shares of stock) are traded, is the most widely followed financial market in almost every country that has one; that's why it is often called simply "the market." A big swing in the prices of shares in the stock market is always a major story on the evening news. People often speculate on where the market is heading and get very excited when they can brag about their latest "big killing," but they become depressed when they suffer a big loss. The attention the market receives can probably be best explained by one simple fact: It is a place where people can get rich—or poor—quickly.

As Figure 1.2 indicates, stock prices are extremely volatile. A bull market run which started in mid-2003, culminated in a peak on 10 January 2008, when the benchmark BSE Sensex rose to a record 21,206.77 points. The bull-run was powered by strong expectations that India would remain a favourite destination of foreign institutional investors, particularly with net portfolio flows having grown from $7060 million in 2006–07 to $27,433 million in 2007–08. However, the mood changed dramatically by 21 January 2008. With concerns of a US recession looming large, the

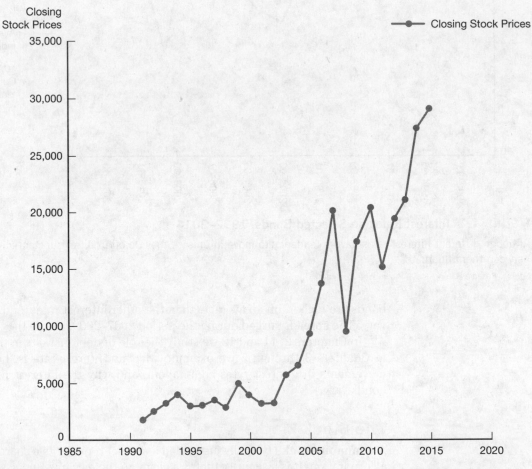

FIGURE 1.2 **Stock Prices as Measured by the S&P BSE Sensex, 1990–2015**

Stock prices are extremely volatile.

Source: BSE India, http://www.bseindia.com/indices/indexarchivedata.aspx.

BSE Sensex experienced its biggest single day decline ever on that day, plummeting 7.4%. In 2008, the BSE Sensex fell sharply by over 50% of its value in 2007, and stood at about 9,647 in 2008. By 2010, it again crossed the 20,000 mark, followed by another dip in 2011. The Sensex then rose, with a bull rally commencing in September 2013 in a run up to India's general elections. Between September 2013 and January 2015, the BSE Sensex surged by 47%. On 22 January 2015, the Sensex rose above the psychologically important 29,000-point mark buoyed by optimistic sentiments regarding economic recovery that could lead to strong inflows of funds. These considerable fluctuations in stock prices affect the size of people's wealth, and as a result, may affect their willingness to spend.

The stock market is also an important factor in business investment decisions because the price of shares affects the amount of funds that can be raised by selling newly issued stock to finance investment spending. A higher price for a firm's shares means that it can raise a larger amount of funds, which can be used to buy production facilities and equipment.

In Chapter 2 we examine the role that the stock market plays in the financial system, and we return to the issue of how stock prices behave and respond to information in the marketplace in Chapters 6 and 13.

The Foreign Exchange Market

For funds to be transferred from one country to another, they have to be converted from the currency in the country of origin (say, rupees) into the currency of the country they are going to (say, dollars). The **foreign exchange market** is where this conversion takes place, so it is instrumental in moving funds between countries. It is also important because it is where the **foreign exchange rate,** the price of one country's currency in terms of another's, is determined.

Figure 1.3 shows the exchange rate of the Indian rupee vis-à-vis the US dollar from 1991 to 2013. The Indian rupee was on a fixed rate regime from Independence. In 1991, when India faced a serious Balance of Payments crisis, the Reserve Bank of India devalued the currency to ₹17.9 against the dollar. The rupee was allowed to float from 1993 and to be determined by market sentiments, with the provision that the central bank would intervene in situations of extreme volatility.

Since 1998, the rupee remained in the 40-50 band. In 2007, it had appreciated to 41. After 2011, however, the rupee depreciated sharply and remained weak based on external sector developments, as also domestic policy uncertainties. In 2013-14, with the US Fed indicating a gradual withdrawal of the Quantitative Easing (QE) program on 22 May 2013, there was a repricing of risk and concomitant capital outflows from several Emerging Market and Developing Economies (EMDEs), including India. Between May and September 2013, India witnessed a net outflow of FII investments of about $16.6 billion. The rupee depreciated sharply and reached a historical low of ₹68.80 to a dollar on 28 August 2013. With the government and the Reserve Bank undertaking various measures to stem the capital outflows, as also the Fed's decision to maintain the pace of QE, the rupee appreciated in October 2013.

What have these fluctuations in the exchange rate meant to the Indian public and businesses? A change in the exchange rate has a direct effect on Indian consumers because it affects the cost of imports. In 1991, when the dollar was worth around ₹23, 100 dollars of American goods (say, American wine) cost ₹2,300. When the rupee subsequently weakened, raising the cost of a dollar to ₹59 in

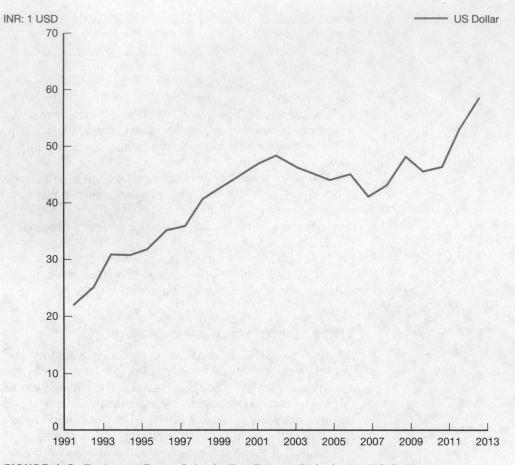

FIGURE 1.3 **Exchange Rate of the Indian Rupee vis-à-vis the US Dollar (Calendar Year-Annual Average), 1991–2013**

The value of the Indian rupee has depreciated relative to the US dollar over the years.

Source: Reserve Bank of India, http://dbie.rbi.org.in/DBIE/dbie.rbi?site=publications#!2.

2013; the same 100 dollars of wine now cost ₹5,900. Thus, a weaker rupee leads to more expensive foreign goods, makes vacationing abroad more expensive, and raises the cost of indulging your desire for imported delicacies. When the value of the rupee drops, Indians decrease their purchases of foreign goods and increase their consumption of domestic goods.

Conversely, a strong rupee means that Indian goods exported abroad will cost more in foreign countries, and hence foreigners will buy fewer of them. A strong rupee would benefit Indian consumers by making foreign goods cheaper but hurt Indian businesses and eliminate some jobs by cutting both domestic and foreign sales of their products. Fluctuations in the foreign exchange markets thus have major consequences for the Indian economy.

In Chapter 14 we study how exchange rates are determined in the foreign exchange market, in which dollars are bought and sold for foreign currencies.

Why Study Financial Institutions?

The second major focus of this book is financial institutions. Financial institutions are what make financial markets work. Without them, financial markets would not be able to move funds from people who save to people who have productive investment opportunities. They thus play a crucial role in improving the efficiency of the economy.

Structure of the Financial System

The financial system is complex, comprising many types of private-sector financial institutions, including banks, insurance companies, mutual funds, finance companies, and investment banks— all of which are heavily regulated by the government. If you wanted to make a loan to IBM or General Motors, for example, you would not go directly to the president of the company and offer a loan. Instead, you would lend to such companies indirectly through **financial intermediaries,** institutions such as commercial banks, savings and loan associations, mutual savings banks, insurance companies, mutual funds, pension funds, and finance companies that borrow funds from people who have saved and in turn make loans to others.

Why are financial intermediaries so crucial to well-functioning financial markets? Why do they give credit to one party but not to another? Why do they usually write complicated legal documents when they extend loans? Why are they the most heavily regulated businesses in the economy?

We answer these questions by developing a coherent framework for analyzing financial structure both in India and in the rest of the world in Chapter 7.

Financial Crisis

At times, the financial system seizes up and produces **financial crisis,** major disruptions in financial markets that are characterized by sharp declines in asset prices and the failures of many financial and nonfinancial firms. Financial crisis have been a feature of capitalist economies for hundreds of years and are typically followed by the worst business cycle downturns. From 2007 to 2009, the U.S. economy was hit by the worst financial crisis since the Great Depression. Defaults in subprime residential mortgages led to major losses in financial institutions, not only producing numerous bank failures but also leading to the demise of Bear Stearns and Lehman Brothers, two of the largest investment banks in the United States. The result of the crisis was the worst recession since World War II, which is now referred to as the "Great Recession."

Why these crisis occur and why they do so much damage to the economy is discussed in Chapter 8.

Central Banks and the Conduct of Monetary Policy

GO ONLINE
http://www.rbi.org.in/home.aspx
Access general information on the banking system, RBI data and monetary policy.

The most important financial institution in the financial system is the **central bank**, the government agency responsible for the conduct of monetary policy, which in India is the **Reserve Bank of India** (called the **RBI**). **Monetary policy** involves the management of interest rates and the quantity of **money,** also referred to as the **money supply** (defined as anything that is generally accepted in payment for goods and services or in the repayment of debt). Because monetary policy affects interest rates, inflation, and business cycles, all of which have a major impact on financial markets and institutions, we study how monetary policy is conducted by central banks in both India and abroad in Chapters 9 and 10.

The International Financial System

The tremendous increase in capital flows between countries means that the international financial system has a growing impact on domestic economies. Whether a country fixes its exchange rate to that of another is an important determinant of how monetary policy is conducted. Whether there are capital controls that restrict mobility of capital across national borders has a large effect on domestic financial systems and the performance of the economy. What role international financial institutions such as the International Monetary Fund should play in the international financial system is very controversial. All of these issues are explored in Chapter 16.

Banks and Other Financial Institutions

Banks are financial institutions that accept deposits and make loans. Banks are the financial intermediaries that the average person interacts with most frequently. A person who needs a loan to buy a house or a car usually obtains it from a local bank. Many Indians keep their financial wealth in banks in the form of checking accounts, savings accounts, or other types of bank deposits. Because banks are the largest financial intermediaries in our economy, they deserve careful study. However, banks are not the only important financial institutions. Indeed, in recent years, other financial institutions such as insurance companies, finance companies, pension funds, mutual funds, and investment banks have been growing at the expense of banks, and so we need to study them as well. We study banks and all these other institutions in Parts 6 and 7.

Financial Innovation

In the good old days, when you took cash out of the bank or wanted to check your account balance, you got to say hello to a friendly human. Nowadays, you are more likely to interact with an automatic teller machine (ATM) when withdrawing cash and to use your home computer to check your account balance. **Financial innovation,** the development of new financial products and services, can be an important force for good by making the financial system more efficient. Unfortunately, as we will see in Chapter 8, financial innovation can have a dark side: It can lead to devastating financial crisis. In Chapter 19 we study why and how financial innovation takes place, with particular emphasis on how the dramatic improvements in information technology have led to new financial products and the ability to deliver financial services electronically, in what has become known as **e-finance.** We also study financial innovation because it shows us how creative thinking on the part of financial institutions can lead to higher profits but can sometimes result in financial disasters. By seeing how and why financial institutions have been creative in the past, we obtain a better grasp of how they may be creative in the future. This knowledge provides us with useful clues about how the financial system may change over time and will help keep our understanding about banks and other financial institutions from becoming obsolete.

Managing Risk in Financial Institutions

In recent years, the economic environment has become an increasingly risky place. Interest rates have fluctuated wildly, stock markets have crashed both here and abroad, speculative crisis have occurred in the foreign exchange markets, and failures of financial institutions have reached levels unprecedented since the Great Depression. To avoid wild swings in profitability (and even possibly failure) resulting from this environment, financial institutions must be concerned with how to cope with increased risk. We look at techniques that these institutions use when they engage in risk management in Chapter 23. Then in Chapter 24, we look at how these institutions make use of new financial instruments, such as financial futures, options, and swaps, to manage risk.

Applied Managerial Perspective

Another reason for studying financial institutions is that they are among the largest employers in the country and frequently pay very high salaries. Hence, some of you have a very practical reason for studying financial institutions: It may help you get a good job in the financial sector. Even if your interests lie elsewhere, you should still care about how financial institutions are run because there will be many times in your life, as an individual, an employee, or the owner of a business, when you will interact with these institutions. Knowing how financial institutions are managed may help you get a better deal when you need to borrow from them or if you decide to supply them with funds.

This book emphasizes an applied managerial perspective in teaching you about financial markets and institutions by including special case applications headed "The Practicing Manager." These cases introduce you to the real-world problems that managers of financial institutions commonly face and need to solve in their day-to-day jobs. For example, how does the manager of a financial institution come up with a new financial product that will be profitable? How does a manager of a financial institution manage the risk that the institution faces from fluctuations in interest rates, stock prices, or foreign exchange rates? Should a manager hire an expert to help discern where monetary policy might be going in the future?

Not only do "The Practicing Manager" cases, which answer these questions and others like them, provide you with some special analytic tools that you will need if you make your career at a financial institution, but they also give you a feel for what a job as the manager of a financial institution is all about.

How We Will Study Financial Markets and Institutions

Instead of focusing on a mass of dull facts that will soon become obsolete, this textbook emphasizes a unifying, analytic framework for studying financial markets and institutions. This framework uses a few basic concepts to help organize your thinking about the determination of asset prices, the structure of financial markets, bank management, and the role of monetary policy in the economy. The basic concepts are equilibrium, basic supply and demand analysis to explain behavior in financial markets, the search for profits, and an approach to financial structure based on transaction costs and asymmetric information.

The unifying framework used in this book will keep your knowledge from becoming obsolete and make the material more interesting. It will enable you to learn what *really* matters without having to memorize material that you will forget soon after the final exam. This framework will also provide you with the tools needed to understand trends in the financial marketplace and in variables such as interest rates and exchange rates.

To help you understand and apply the unifying analytic framework, simple models are constructed throughout the text in which the variables held constant are carefully delineated, each step in the derivation of the model is clearly and carefully laid out, and the models are then used to explain various phenomena by focusing on changes in one variable at a time, holding all other variables constant.

To reinforce the models' usefulness, this text also emphasizes the interaction of theoretical analysis and empirical data in order to expose you to real-life events and data. To make the study of financial markets and institutions even more relevant and to help you learn the material, the book contains, besides "The Practicing Manager" cases, numerous additional cases and mini-cases that demonstrate how you can use the analysis in the book to explain many real-world situations.

To function better in the real world outside the classroom, you must have the tools to follow the financial news that appears in leading financial publications and on the Web. To help and encourage you to read the financial section of the newspaper, this book contains two special features. The first is a set of special boxed inserts titled "Following the Financial News" that provide detailed information and definitions you need to evaluate the data that are discussed frequently in the media. This book also contains nearly 400 end-of-chapter questions and problems that ask you to apply the analytic concepts you have learned to other real-world issues. Particularly relevant is a special class of problems headed "Predicting the Future." These questions give you an opportunity to review and apply many of the important financial concepts and tools presented throughout the book.

Exploring the Web

The World Wide Web has become an extremely valuable and convenient resource for financial research. We emphasize the importance of this tool in several ways. First, wherever we use the Web to find information to build the charts and tables that appear throughout the text, we include the source site's URL. These sites often contain additional information and are updated frequently. Second, we have added Web exercises to the end of each chapter. These exercises prompt you to visit sites related to the chapter and to work with real-time data and information. We have also supplied Web references to the end of each chapter that list the URLs of sites related to the material being discussed. Visit these sites to further explore a topic you find of particular interest. Web site URLs are subject to frequent change. We have tried to select stable sites, but we realize that even government URLs change. The publisher's Web site (www.pearsonhighered.com/mishkin_eakins) will maintain an updated list of current URLs for your reference.

Collecting and Graphing Data

The following Web exercise is especially important because it demonstrates how to export data from a Web site into Microsoft Excel for further analysis. We suggest you work through this problem on your own so that you will be able to perform this activity when prompted in subsequent Web exercises whenever you want to collect data from the Web and apply it to particular situations.

Web Exercise

You have been hired by Risky Ventures, Inc., as a consultant to help the company analyze interest-rate trends from the beginning of 2012 to the present. Your employers are initially interested in determining the relationship between long- and short-term interest rates in that year. The biggest task you must immediately undertake is collecting market interest-rate data. You know the best source of this information is the Web.

1. You decide that your best indicator of long-term interest rates is that on 10-year government securities. Your first task is to gather historical data. Go to the RBI website at http://www.rbi.org.in/home.aspx, a terrific resource for economic data.

   Go into Database ⟶ Database on Indian Economy ⟶ Statistics Financial Markets ⟶ Government Securities Market ⟶ Monthly Yield of SGL Transactions in Government Dated Securities for Various Maturities. The data is available for period 1 April 1996 to 31 December 2014 (at the time of writing the book). The site should look like Figure 1.4.

2. Now that you have located an accurate source of historical interest-rate data, the next step is choosing the sample period and getting it onto a spreadsheet.

   Go into Document ⟶ Save report to my computer as ⟶ Excel.

   The downloaded document should look like Figure 1.5.

3. You now want to analyze the interest rates by first graphing them. Put headings such as "10-Year maturity yields (interest rates)" and "1-Year

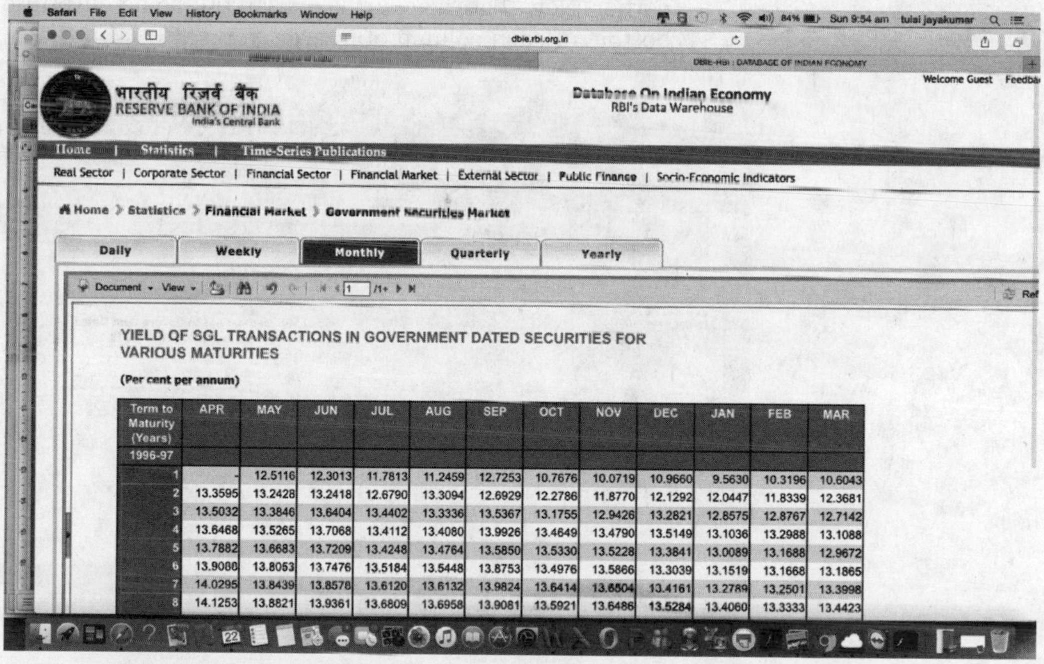

Term to Maturity (Years)	APR	MAY	JUN	JUL	AUG	SEP	OCT	NOV	DEC	JAN	FEB	MAR
1996-97												
1	-	12.5116	12.3013	11.7813	11.2459	12.7253	10.7676	10.0719	10.9660	9.5630	10.3196	10.6043
2	13.3595	13.2428	13.2418	12.6790	13.3094	12.6929	12.2786	11.8770	12.1292	12.0447	11.8339	12.3681
3	13.5032	13.3846	13.6404	13.4402	13.3336	13.5367	13.1755	12.9426	13.2821	12.8575	12.8767	12.7142
4	13.6468	13.5265	13.7068	13.4112	13.4080	13.9926	13.4649	13.4790	13.5149	13.1036	13.2988	13.1088
5	13.7882	13.6683	13.7209	13.4248	13.4764	13.5850	13.5330	13.5228	13.3841	13.0089	13.1688	12.9672
6	13.9080	13.8053	13.7476	13.5184	13.5448	13.8753	13.4976	13.5866	13.3039	13.1519	13.1668	13.1865
7	14.0295	13.8439	13.8578	13.6120	13.6132	13.9824	13.6414	13.6504	13.4161	13.2789	13.2501	13.3998
8	14.1253	13.8821	13.9361	13.6809	13.6958	13.9081	13.5921	13.6486	13.5284	13.4060	13.3333	13.4423

FIGURE 1.4 Reserve Bank of India Database

Courtesy: The Reserve Bank of India (RBI), http://dbie.rbi.org.in/DBIE/dbie.rbi?site=statistics, as accessed on 12 May 2016 at 12pm.

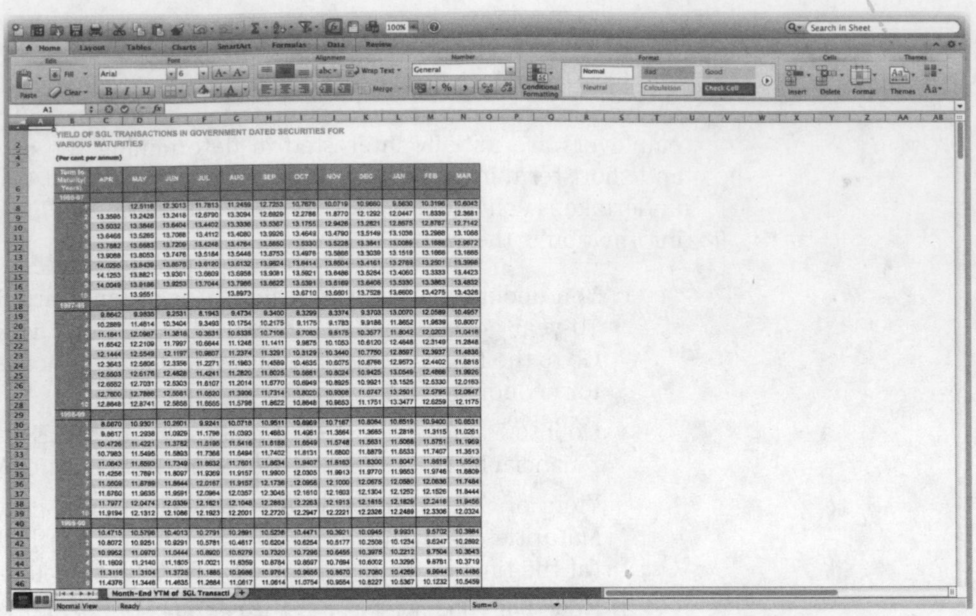

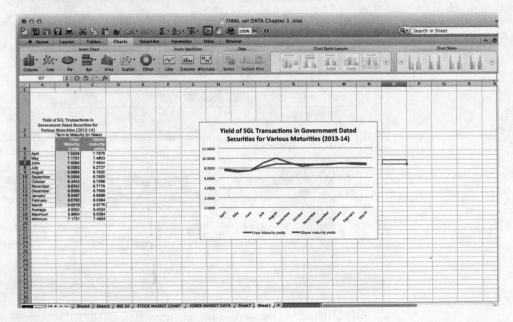

FIGURE 1.5 Excel Spreadsheet with Interest-Rate Data

Microsoft Office 2013, copyright © 2013 Microsoft Corporation.

maturity yields" at the top of each column of data. Highlight the two columns of interest-rate data you just created in Excel, including the headings. Click on "Insert" on the toolbar. Select the Line chart type that is in the top left corner. Now that the chart is drawn, put some descriptive statistics at the bottom of each column of interest rates. Click on the f_x icon on the Excel

FIGURE 1.6 Excel Graph of Interest-Data

Microsoft Office 2013, copyright © 2013 Microsoft Corporation.

tool bar, click on "Average" in the Insert Function Box, and click "OK." Highlight the dates for the series from April 2013 to March 2014 and click "OK." Similarly, add the Maximum and Minimum of each interest rate over the period. You should now see Figure 1.6.

Concluding Remarks

The field of financial markets and institutions is an exciting one. Not only will you develop skills that will be valuable in your career, but you will also gain a clearer understanding of events in financial markets and institutions you frequently hear about in the news media. This book will introduce you to many of the controversies that are hotly debated in the current political arena.

SUMMARY

1. Activities in financial markets have direct effects on individuals' wealth, the behavior of businesses, and the efficiency of our economy. Three financial markets deserve particular attention: the bond market (where interest rates are determined), the stock market (which has a major effect on people's wealth and on firms' investment decisions), and the foreign exchange market (because fluctuations in the foreign exchange rate have major consequences for the Indian economy).

2. Because monetary policy affects interest rates, inflation, and business cycles, all of which have an important impact on financial markets and institutions, we need to understand how monetary policy is conducted by central banks in the India and abroad.

3. Banks and other financial institutions channel funds from people who might not put them to productive use to people who can do so and thus play a crucial role in improving the efficiency of the economy. When the financial system seizes up and produces a financial crisis, financial firms fail, which causes severe damage to the economy.

4. Understanding how financial institutions are managed is important because there will be many times in your life, as an individual, an employee, or the owner of a business, when you will interact with them. "The Practicing Manager" cases not only provide special analytic tools that are useful if you choose a career with a financial institution but also give you a feel for what a job as the manager of a financial institution is all about.

5. This textbook emphasizes an analytic way of thinking by developing a unifying framework for the study of financial markets and institutions using a few basic principles. This textbook also focuses on the interaction of theoretical analysis and empirical data.

KEY TERMS

assets, p. 2
banks, p. 8
bond, p. 2
central bank, p. 7
common stock (stock), p. 3
e-finance, p. 8

Reserve Bank of India (RBI), p. 7
financial crisis, p. 7
financial innovation, p. 8
financial intermediaries, p. 7
financial markets, p. 2
foreign exchange market, p. 5

foreign exchange rate, p. 5
interest rate, p. 2
monetary policy, p. 7
money (money supply), p. 7
security, p. 2

QUESTIONS

1. Why are financial markets important to the health of the economy?

2. When interest rates rise, how might businesses and consumers change their economic behavior?

3. How can a change in interest rates affect the profitability of financial institutions?

4. Is everybody worse off when interest rates rise?

5. What effect might a fall in stock prices have on business investment?

6. What effect might a rise in stock prices have on consumers' decisions to spend?

7. How does a decline in the value of the dollar affect Indian consumers?

8. How does an increase in the value of the dollar affect American businesses?

9. How can changes in foreign exchange rates affect the profitability of financial institutions?

10. Looking at Figure 1.3, in what years would you have chosen to visit Disneyland in USA rather than the Taj Mahal in Agra?

11. What is the basic activity of banks?

12. What are the other important financial intermediaries in the economy besides banks?

13. Can you think of any financial innovation in the past 10 years that has affected you personally? Has it made you better or worse off? In what way?

14. What types of risks do financial institutions face?

15. Why do managers of financial institutions care so much about the activities of the Reserve Bank of India?

QUANTITATIVE PROBLEMS

1. The following table lists foreign exchange rates between Indian rupees and US dollars for the month of December 2014. For an Indian exporter who has received dollars, which day would have been the best to convert $200 into rupees? Which day would be the worst? What would be the difference in rupees?

12/31/2014	63.3315
12/30/2014	63.7498
12/29/2014	63.6539
12/26/2014	63.6355
12/24/2014	63.4614
12/23/2014	63.4475
12/22/2014	63.1757
12/19/2014	63.0670
12/18/2014	63.3161

12/17/2014	63.5813
12/16/2014	63.4135
12/15/2014	62.6529
12/12/2014	62.4422
12/11/2014	62.2059
12/10/2014	61.9500
12/09/2014	61.8750
12/08/2014	61.9253
12/05/2014	61.8535
12/04/2014	61.8771
12/03/2014	61.8866
12/02/2014	61.9255
12/01/2014	62.1377

Source: Reserve Bank of India, http://dbie.rbi .org.in/DBIE/dbie.rbi?site=home.

WEB EXERCISES

Working with Financial Market Data

1. In this exercise we will practice collecting data from the Web and graphing it using Excel. Use the example on pages 10–12 as a guide. Go to **www.forecasts .org/data/index.htm**, click on "Data" at the top of the page, click on "Stock Index Data," and choose the "U.S. Stock Indices—Monthly" option. Finally, choose the "Dow Jones Industrial Average" option.

   a. Using the method presented here in this chapter, move the data into an Excel spreadsheet.

   b. Using the data from step a, prepare a chart. Use the Chart Wizard to properly label your axes.

2. In Web Exercise 1 you collected and graphed the Dow Jones Industrial Average. This same site reports forecast values of the DJIA. Go to **www.forecasts.org/ data/index.htm**. Click the Dow Jones Industrials link under "6 Month Forecasts" in the far-left column.

   a. What is the Dow forecast to be in six months?

   b. What percentage increase is forecast for the next six months?

Overview of the Financial System

➤ PREVIEW

Suppose that you want to start a business that manufactures a recently invented low-cost robot that cleans the house (even does windows), mows the lawn, and washes the car, but you have no funds to put this wonderful invention into production. Walter has plenty of savings that he has inherited. If you and Walter could get together so that he could provide you with the funds, your company's robot would see the light of day, and you, Walter, and the economy would all be better off: Walter could earn a high return on his investment, you would get rich from producing the robot, and we would have cleaner houses, shinier cars, and more beautiful lawns.

Financial markets (bond and stock markets) and financial intermediaries (banks, insurance companies, and pension funds) have the basic function of getting people such as you and Walter together by moving funds from those who have a surplus of funds (Walter) to those who have a shortage of funds (you). More realistically, when Apple invents a better iPod, it may require funds to bring it to market. Similarly, when a local government needs to build a road or a school, it may need more funds than local property taxes provide. Well-functioning financial markets and financial intermediaries are crucial to our economic health.

To study the effects of financial markets and financial intermediaries on the economy, we need to acquire an understanding of their general structure and operation. In this chapter we learn about the major financial intermediaries and the instruments that are traded in financial markets.

This chapter offers a preliminary overview of the fascinating study of financial markets and institutions. We will return to a more detailed treatment of the regulation, structure, and evolution of financial markets and institutions in Parts 3 through 7.

Function of Financial Markets

Financial markets perform the essential economic function of channeling funds from households, firms, and governments that have saved surplus funds by spending less than their income to those that have a shortage of funds because they wish to spend more than their income. This function is shown schematically in Figure 2.1. Those who have saved and are lending funds, the lender-savers, are at the left and those who must borrow funds to finance their spending, the borrower-spenders, are at the right. The principal lender-savers are households, but business enterprises and the government (particularly state and local government), as well as foreigners and their governments, sometimes also find themselves with excess funds and so lend them out. The most important borrower-spenders are businesses and the government (particularly the Central government), but households and foreigners also borrow to finance their purchases of cars, furniture, and houses. The arrows show that funds flow from lender-savers to borrower-spenders via two routes.

In *direct finance* (the route at the bottom of Figure 2.1), borrowers borrow funds directly from lenders in financial markets by selling them *securities* (also called *financial instruments*), which are claims on the borrower's future income or assets. Securities are assets for the person who buys them, but they are **liabilities** (IOUs or debts) for the individual or firm that sells (issues) them.

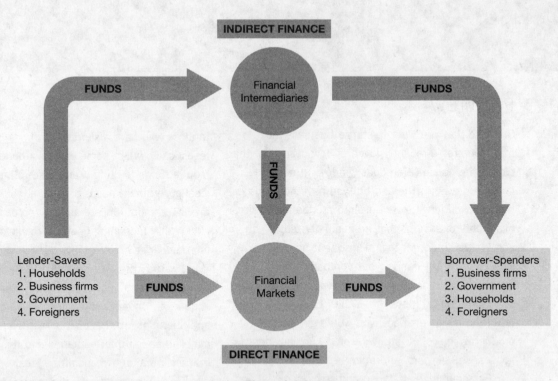

FIGURE 2.1 Flows of Funds Through the Financial System

The arrows show that funds flow from lender-savers to borrower-spenders via two routes: *direct finance*, in which borrowers borrow funds directly from financial markets by selling securities, and *indirect finance*, in which a financial intermediary borrows funds from lender-savers and then uses these funds to make loans to borrower-spenders.

For example, if Tata Motors needs to borrow funds to pay for a new factory to manufacture electric cars, it might borrow the funds from savers by selling them a *bond*, a debt security that promises to make payments periodically for a specified period of time, or a *stock*, a security that entitles the owner to a share of the company's profits and assets.

Why is this channeling of funds from savers to spenders so important to the economy? The answer is that the people who save are frequently not the same people who have profitable investment opportunities available to them, the entrepreneurs. Let's first think about this on a personal level. Suppose that you have saved ₹ 1,000 this year, but no borrowing or lending is possible because no financial markets are available. If you do not have an investment opportunity that will permit you to earn income with your savings, you will just hold on to the ₹ 1,000 and will earn no interest. However, Manoj the carpenter has a productive use for your ₹ 1,000: He can use it to purchase a new tool that will shorten the time it takes him to build a house, thereby earning an extra ₹ 200 per year. If you could get in touch with Manoj, you could lend him the ₹ 1,000 at a rental fee (interest) of ₹ 100 per year, and both of you would be better off. You would earn ₹ 100 per year on your ₹ 1,000, instead of the zero amount that you would earn otherwise, while Manoj would earn ₹ 100 more income per year (the ₹ 200 extra earnings per year minus the ₹ 100 rental fee for the use of the funds).

In the absence of financial markets, you and Manoj the carpenter might never get together. You would both be stuck with the status quo, and both of you would be worse off. Without financial markets, it is hard to transfer funds from a person who has no investment opportunities to one who has them. Financial markets are thus essential to promoting economic efficiency.

The existence of financial markets is beneficial even if someone borrows for a purpose other than increasing production in a business. Say that you are recently married, have a good job, and want to buy a house. You earn a good salary, but because you have just started to work, you have not saved much. Over time, you would have no problem saving enough to buy the house of your dreams, but by then you would be too old to get full enjoyment from it. Without financial markets, you are stuck; you cannot buy the house and must continue to live in your tiny apartment.

If a financial market were set up so that people who had built up savings could lend you the funds to buy the house, you would be more than happy to pay them some interest so that you could own a home while you are still young enough to enjoy it. Then, over time, you would pay back your loan. If this loan could occur, you would be better off, as would the persons who made you the loan. They would now earn some interest, whereas they would not if the financial market did not exist.

Now we can see why financial markets have such an important function in the economy. They allow funds to move from people who lack productive investment opportunities to people who have such opportunities. Financial markets are critical for producing an efficient allocation of **capital** (wealth, either financial or physical, that is employed to produce more wealth), which contributes to higher production and efficiency for the overall economy. Indeed, as we will explore in Chapter 8, when financial markets break down during financial crisis, as they did during the recent global financial crisis, severe economic hardship results, which can even lead to dangerous political instability.

Well-functioning financial markets also directly improve the well-being of consumers by allowing them to time their purchases better. They provide funds to young people to buy what they need and can eventually afford without forcing them to wait until they have saved up the entire purchase price. Financial markets that are operating efficiently improve the economic welfare of everyone in the society.

Structure of Financial Markets

Now that we understand the basic function of financial markets, let's look at their structure. The following descriptions of several categorizations of financial markets illustrate the essential features of these markets.

Debt and Equity Markets

A firm or an individual can obtain funds in a financial market in two ways. The most common method is to issue a debt instrument, such as a bond or a mortgage, which is a contractual agreement by the borrower to pay the holder of the instrument fixed rupee amounts at regular intervals (interest and principal payments) until a specified date (the maturity date), when a final payment is made. The **maturity** of a debt instrument is the number of years (term) until that instrument's expiration date. A debt instrument is **short-term** if its maturity is less than a year and **long-term** if its maturity is 10 years or longer. Debt instruments with a maturity between one and 10 years are said to be **intermediate-term.**

The second method of raising funds is by issuing **equities,** such as common stock, which are claims to share in the net income (income after expenses and taxes) and the assets of a business. If you own one share of common stock in a company that has issued one million shares, you are entitled to 1 one-millionth of the firm's net income and 1 one-millionth of the firm's assets. Equities often make periodic payments (**dividends**) to their holders and are considered long-term securities because they have no maturity date. In addition, owning stock means that you own a portion of the firm and thus have the right to vote on issues important to the firm and to elect its directors.

The main disadvantage of owning a corporation's equities rather than its debt is that an equity holder is a *residual claimant*; that is, the corporation must pay all its debt holders before it pays its equity holders. The advantage of holding equities is that equity holders benefit directly from any increases in the corporation's profitability or asset value because equities confer ownership rights on the equity holders. Debt holders do not share in this benefit because their rupee payments are fixed. We examine the pros and cons of debt versus equity instruments in more detail in Chapter 7, which provides an economic analysis of financial structure.

Primary and Secondary Markets

A **primary market** is a financial market in which new issues of a security, such as a bond or a stock, are sold to initial buyers by the corporation or government agency borrowing the funds. A **secondary market** is a financial market in which securities that have been previously issued can be resold.

The primary markets for securities are not well known to the public because the selling of securities to initial buyers often takes place behind closed doors. An important financial institution that assists in the initial sale of securities in the primary market is the **investment bank.** It does this by **underwriting** securities: It guarantees a price for a corporation's securities and then sells them to the public.

The New Stork Exchange, NASDAQ, BSE and NSE (National Stock Exchange), in which previously issued stocks are traded, are the best known examples of secondary markets. Other examples of secondary markets are foreign exchange markets, futures markets, and options markets. Securities brokers and dealers are crucial to a well-functioning secondary market. **Brokers** are agents of investors who match buyers with sellers of securities; **dealers** link buyers and sellers by buying and selling securities at stated prices.

When an individual buys a security in the secondary market, the person who has sold the security receives money in exchange for the security, but the corporation that issued the security acquires no new funds. A corporation acquires new funds only when its securities are first sold in the primary market. Nonetheless, secondary markets serve two important functions. First, they make it easier and quicker to sell these financial instruments to raise cash; that is, they make the financial instruments more **liquid.** The increased liquidity of these instruments then makes them more desirable and thus easier for the issuing firm to sell in the primary market. Second, they determine the price of the security that the issuing firm sells in the primary market. The investors who buy securities in the primary market will pay the issuing corporation no more than the price they think the secondary market will set for this security. The higher the security's price in the secondary market, the higher the price that the issuing firm will receive for a new security in the primary market, and hence the greater the amount of financial capital it can raise. Conditions in the secondary market are therefore the most relevant to corporations issuing securities. For this reason books like this one, which deal with financial markets, focus on the behavior of secondary markets rather than primary markets.

Exchanges and Over-the-Counter Markets

Secondary markets can be organized in two ways. One method is to organize **exchanges,** where buyers and sellers of securities (or their agents or brokers) meet in one central location to conduct trades. The New York and American Stock Exchange, the Bombay Stock Exchange and National Stock Exchange, the Chicago Board of Trade for Commodities and the Multi Commodity Exchange of India Limited (MCX) are examples of organized exchanges.

The other method of organizing a secondary market is to have an **over-the-counter (OTC) market,** in which dealers at different locations who have an inventory of securities stand ready to buy and sell securities "over the counter" to anyone who comes to them and is willing to accept their prices. Because over-the-counter dealers are in contact via computers and know the prices set by one another, the OTC market is very competitive and not very different from a market with an organized exchange.

Many common stocks are traded over the counter, although a majority of the largest corporations have their shares traded at organized stock exchanges. Government securities, in many countries of the world, are traded over-the-counter. The U.S. government bond market for example, with a larger trading volume than the New York Stock Exchange, is set up as an over-the-counter market. Forty or so dealers establish a "market" in these securities by standing ready to buy and sell U.S. government bonds. Other over-the-counter markets include those that trade

CASE

OVER THE COUNTER EXCHANGE OF INDIA (OTCEI)

OTCEI was incorporated in 1990 as a Section 25 company under the Companies Act 1956 and is recognized as a stock exchange under Section 4 of the Securities Contracts Regulation Act, 1956. The Exchange was set up to aid enterprising promoters in raising finance for new projects in a cost effective manner and to provide investors with a transparent & efficient mode of trading.

Modelled along the lines of the NASDAQ market of USA, OTCEI introduced many novel concepts to the Indian capital markets such as screen-based nation-wide trading, sponsorship of companies, market making, and scripless trading. The Exchange today has 115 listings and has assisted in providing capital for enterprises that have gone on to build successful brands.

Source: http://www.otcei.net/about/, as accessed on 12 March 2016 at 12pm.

other types of financial instruments such as negotiable certificates of deposit and foreign exchange.

In India, government securities can be traded in the secondary market either over the counter (OTC) or through the Negotiated Dealing System (NDS), Negotiated Dealing System-Order Matching (NDS-OM) or through stock exchanges. (See Box: Market for Government Securities in India).

In 2013, the RBI permitted trading in G-Secs through a nationwide, anonymous, order-driven screen-based trading system on stock exchanges, in the same manner in which trading takes place in equities. This was done with a view to encourage wider participation of all classes of investors, including retail, in G-Secs. Accordingly, trading of dated G-Sec in demat form was allowed on automated order driven system of the National Stock Exchange (NSE) of India, the Bombay Stock Exchange Ltd., Mumbai (BSE), the Over the Counter Exchange of India (OTCEI) and the MCX Stock Exchange. This trading facility was in addition to the reporting/trading facility in the NDS.[1]

Money and Capital Markets

Another way of distinguishing between markets is on the basis of the maturity of the securities traded in each market. The **money market** is a financial market in which only short-term debt instruments (generally those with original maturity of less than one year) are traded; the **capital market** is the market in which longer-term debt (generally with original maturity of one year or greater) and equity instruments are traded. Money market securities are usually more widely traded than longer-term securities and so tend to be more liquid. In addition, as we will see in Chapter 3, short-term securities have smaller fluctuations in prices than long-term securities, making them safer investments. As a result, corporations and

---

[1] https://www.rbi.org.in/scripts/BS_ViewMasCirculardetails.aspx?id=8175#f7, as accessed on 12 March 2016 at 12pm.

MARKETS FOR GOVERNMENT SECURITIES IN INDIA

Government securities in India are traded in an active secondary market. The securities can be bought / sold in the secondary market either (i) Over the Counter (OTC) or (ii) through the Negotiated Dealing System (NDS) or (iii) the Negotiated Dealing System-Order Matching (NDS-OM) or (iv) the stock exchanges

Over the Counter (OTC)/ Telephone Market In this market, a participant, who wants to buy or sell a government security, may contact a bank / Primary Dealer / financial institution either directly or through a broker registered with SEBI and negotiate for a certain amount of a particular security at a certain price. Such negotiations are usually done on telephone and a deal may be struck if both counterparties agree on the amount and rate. All trades undertaken in OTC market are reported on the secondary market module of the Negotiated Dealing System (NDS).

Negotiated Dealing System The Negotiated Dealing System (NDS) for electronic dealing and reporting of transactions in government securities was introduced in February 2002. It facilitates the members to submit electronically, bids or applications for primary issuance of Government Securities when auctions are conducted. NDS also provides an interface to the Securities Settlement System (SSS) of the Public Debt Office, RBI, Mumbai thereby facilitating settlement of transactions in Government Securities (both outright and repos) conducted in the secondary market. Membership to the NDS is restricted to members holding Subsidiary General Ledger (SGL) and/or Current Account with the RBI, Mumbai.

Negotiated Dealing System Order Matching (NDS-OM) In August 2005, RBI introduced an anonymous screen-based order matching module on NDS, called NDS-OM. This is an order-driven electronic system, where the participants can trade anonymously by placing their orders on the system or accepting the orders already placed by other participants. NDS-OM is operated by the Clearing Corporation of India Ltd. (CCIL) on behalf of the RBI. Direct access to the NDS-OM system is currently available only to select financial institutions like Commercial Banks, Primary Dealers, Insurance Companies, Mutual Funds, etc. Other participants can access this system through their custodians, i.e., with whom they maintain Gilt Accounts. The custodians place the orders on behalf of their customers like the urban co-operative banks. The advantages of NDS-OM are price transparency and better price discovery

Gilt Account holders have been given indirect access to NDS through custodian institutions. A member (who has the direct access) can report on the NDS the transaction of a Gilt Account holder in government securities. Similarly, Gilt Account holders have also been given indirect access to NDS-OM through the custodians. However, currently two gilt account holders of the same custodian are not permitted to undertake repo transactions between themselves.

Stock Exchanges Facilities are also available for trading in Government securities on stock exchanges (NSE, BSE) which cater to the needs of retail investors.

Source: https://www.rbi.org.in/Scripts/FAQView.aspx?Id=79#8, as accessed on 12 March 2016 at 12pm.

banks actively use the money market to earn interest on surplus funds that they expect to have only temporarily. Capital market securities, such as stocks and long-term bonds, are often held by financial intermediaries such as insurance companies and pension funds, which have little uncertainty about the amount of funds they will have available in the future.

The Call Money market, Treasury bill market and commercial bill market are the main constituents of the money markets in India. Capital markets comprise of the primary, secondary and derivative markets[2].

Internationalization of Financial Markets

The growing internationalization of financial markets has become an important trend. Before the 1980s, U.S. financial markets were much larger than those outside the United States, but in recent years the dominance of U.S. markets has been disappearing. The extraordinary growth of foreign financial markets has been the result of both large increases in the pool of savings in foreign countries such as Japan and the deregulation of foreign financial markets, which has enabled foreign markets to expand their activities. A look at international bond markets and world stock markets will give us a picture of how this globalization of financial markets is taking place.

International Bond Market, Eurobonds, and Eurocurrencies

The traditional instruments in the international bond market are known as foreign bonds. **Foreign bonds** are sold in a foreign country and are denominated in that country's currency. For example, if the German automaker Porsche sells a bond in the United States denominated in U.S. dollars, it is classified as a foreign bond. Foreign bonds have been an important instrument in the international capital market for centuries. In fact, a large percentage of U.S. railroads built in the nineteenth century were financed by sales of foreign bonds in Britain.

A more recent innovation in the international bond market is the **Eurobond,** a bond denominated in a currency other than that of the country in which it is sold—for example, a bond denominated in U.S. dollars sold in London. Currently, over 80% of the new issues in the international bond market are Eurobonds, and the market for these securities has grown very rapidly. As a result, the Eurobond market is now larger than even the U.S. corporate bond market.

A variant of the Eurobond is **Eurocurrencies,** which are foreign currencies deposited in banks outside the home country. The most important of the Eurocurrencies are **Eurodollars,** which are U.S. dollars deposited in foreign banks outside the United States or in foreign branches of U.S. banks. Because these short-term deposits earn interest, they are similar to short-term Eurobonds. American

---

[2] BSE launched the first Exchange-traded Index Derivative Contract in India i.e. futures on the capital market benchmark index—the BSE Sensex, on 9 June 2000. In sequence of product innovation, BSE commenced trading in Index Options on Sensex on 1 June 2001, Stock Options were introduced on 31 stocks on 9 July 2001 and Single Stock Futures were launched on 9 November 2002.
http://www.bseindia.com/markets/Derivatives/DeriReports/introduction.aspx?expandable=5.

banks borrow Eurodollar deposits from other banks or from their own foreign branches, and Eurodollars are now an important source of funds for American banks. Note that the euro, the currency used by countries in the European Monetary System, can create some confusion about the terms *Eurobond, Eurocurrencies,* and *Eurodollars.* A bond denominated in euros is called a Eurobond only *if it is sold outside the countries that have adopted the euro.* In fact, most Eurobonds are not denominated in euros but are instead denominated in U.S. dollars. Similarly, Eurodollars have nothing to do with euros, but are instead U.S. dollars deposited in banks outside the United States.

GO ONLINE
www.stockcharts.com
This site contains historical stock market index charts for many countries around the world.

GO ONLINE
http://quote.yahoo.com/m2?u
Access major world stock indexes, with charts, news, and components.

World Stock Markets

Until recently, the U.S. stock market was by far the largest in the world, but foreign stock markets have been growing in importance, with the United States not always number one.

The internationalization of financial markets is also leading the way to a more integrated world economy in which flows of goods and technology between countries are more commonplace. In later chapters, we will encounter many examples of the important roles that international factors play in our economy (see the Following the Financial News box).

> FOLLOWING THE FINANCIAL NEWS

Indian and Foreign Stock Market Indexes

Foreign stock market indexes are published daily in newspapers and Internet sites such as www.finance.yahoo.com.

The two most important stock market indexes in India are:

S&P BSE Sensex The S&P Bombay Stock Exchange Sensitive Index, also-called the BSE 30 or simply the SENSEX, is a free-float market-weighted stock market index of 30 well-established and financially sound companies listed on Bombay Stock Exchange. The oldest stock market index, it is regarded as the pulse of the domestic stock markets in India.

NIFTY The NSE S&P CNX Nifty 50 or the NIFTY, as it is commonly known, is the prime index of the National Stock exchange (NSE) and the second most important stock index of India (other than the SENSEX). The CNX Nifty is a well-diversified 50 stock index accounting for 22 sectors of the economy. It is used for a variety of purposes such as benchmarking fund portfolios, index based derivatives and index funds.

The important foreign stock indexes are:

Dow Jones Industrial Average (DJIA) An index of the 30 largest publicly traded corporations in the United States maintained by the Dow Jones Corporation.

S&P 500 An index of 500 of the largest companies traded in the United States maintained by Standard & Poor's.

Nasdaq Composite An index for all the stocks that trade on the Nasdaq stock market, where most of the technology stocks in the United States are traded.

FTSE 100 An index of the 100 most highly capitalized UK companies listed on the London Stock Exchange.

DAX An index of the 30 largest German companies trading on the Frankfurt Stock Exchange.

CAC 40 An index of the largest 40 French companies traded on Euronext Paris.

Hang Seng An index of the largest companies traded on the Hong Kong stock markets.

Strait Times An index of the largest 30 companies traded on the Singapore Exchange.

Function of Financial Intermediaries: Indirect Finance

As shown in Figure 2.1 (p. 16), funds also can move from lenders to borrowers by a second route called *indirect finance* because it involves a financial intermediary that stands between the lender-savers and the borrower-spenders and helps transfer funds from one to the other. A financial intermediary does this by borrowing funds from the lender-savers and then using these funds to make loans to borrower-spenders. For example, a bank might acquire funds by issuing a liability to the public (an asset for the public) in the form of savings deposits. It might then use the funds to acquire an asset by making a loan to Tata Motors or by buying a Government bond in the financial market. The ultimate result is that funds have been transferred from the public (the lender-savers) to Tata Motors or the Indian Government (the borrower-spender) with the help of the financial intermediary (the bank).

The process of indirect finance using financial intermediaries, called **financial intermediation,** is the primary route for moving funds from lenders to borrowers. Indeed, although the media focus much of their attention on securities markets, particularly the stock market, financial intermediaries are a far more important source of financing for corporations than securities markets are. This is true not only for India, but also for the United States and other industrialized countries (see the Global box on p. 25). Why are financial intermediaries and indirect finance so important in financial markets? To answer this question, we need to understand the role of transaction costs, risk sharing, and information costs in financial markets.

Transaction Costs

Transaction costs, the time and money spent in carrying out financial transactions, are a major problem for people who have excess funds to lend. As we have seen, Manoj the carpenter needs ₹1,000 for his new tool, and you know that it is an excellent investment opportunity. You have the cash and would like to lend him the money, but to protect your investment, you have to hire a lawyer to write up the loan contract that specifies how much interest Manoj will pay you, when he will make these interest payments, and when he will repay you the ₹1,000. Obtaining the contract will cost you ₹500. When you figure in this transaction cost for making the loan, you realize that you can't earn enough from the deal (you spend ₹500 to make perhaps ₹100) and reluctantly tell Manoj that he will have to look elsewhere.

This example illustrates that small savers like you or potential borrowers like Manoj might be frozen out of financial markets and thus be unable to benefit from them. Can anyone come to the rescue? Financial intermediaries can.

Financial intermediaries can substantially reduce transaction costs because they have developed expertise in lowering them and because their large size allows them to take advantage of **economies of scale,** the reduction in transaction costs per rupee of transactions as the size (scale) of transactions increases. For example, a bank knows how to find a good lawyer to produce an airtight loan contract, and this contract can be used over and over again in its loan transactions, thus lowering the legal cost per transaction. Instead of a loan contract (which may not be all that well written) costing ₹500, a bank can hire a topflight lawyer for ₹5,000 to draw up an airtight loan contract that can be used for 2,000 loans at a cost of ₹2.50 per loan.

The Importance of Financial Intermediaries Relative to Securities Markets: An International Comparison

Patterns of financing corporations differ across countries, but one key fact emerges: Studies of the major developed countries, including the United States, Canada, the United Kingdom, Japan, Italy, Germany, and France, show that when businesses go looking for funds to finance their activities, they usually obtain them indirectly through financial intermediaries and not directly from securities markets.* Even in the United States and Canada, which have the most developed securities markets in the world, loans from financial intermediaries are far more important for corporate finance than securities markets are. The countries that have made the least use of securities markets are Germany and Japan; in these two countries, financing from financial intermediaries has been almost 10 times greater than that from securities markets. However, after the deregulation of Japanese securities markets in recent years, the share of corporate financing by financial intermediaries has been declining relative to the use of securities markets.

Although the dominance of financial intermediaries over securities markets is clear in all countries, the relative importance of bond versus stock markets differs widely across countries. In the United States the bond market is far more important as a source of corporate finance: On average, the amount of new financing raised using bonds is 10 times the amount raised using stocks. By contrast, countries such as France and Italy make more use of equities markets than of the bond market to raise capital.

*See, for example, Colin Mayer, "Financial Systems, Corporate Finance, and Economic Development," in *Asymmetric Information, Corporate Finance, and Investment*, ed. R. Glenn Hubbard (Chicago: University of Chicago Press, 1990), pp. 307–332.

At a cost of ₹2.50 per loan, it now becomes profitable for the financial intermediary to lend Manoj the ₹1,000.

Because financial intermediaries are able to reduce transaction costs substantially, they make it possible for you to provide funds indirectly to people like Manoj with productive investment opportunities. In addition, a financial intermediary's low transaction costs mean that it can provide its customers with **liquidity services,** services that make it easier for customers to conduct transactions. For example, banks provide depositors with checking accounts that enable them to pay their bills easily. In addition, depositors can earn interest on checking and savings accounts and yet still convert them into goods and services whenever necessary.

Risk Sharing

Another benefit made possible by the low transaction costs of financial institutions is that they can help reduce the exposure of investors to **risk**—that is, uncertainty about the returns investors will earn on assets. Financial intermediaries do this through the process known as **risk sharing:** They create and sell assets with risk characteristics that people are comfortable with, and the intermediaries then use the funds they acquire by selling these assets to purchase other assets that may have far more risk. Low transaction costs allow financial intermediaries to share risk at low cost, enabling them to earn a profit on the spread between the returns they earn on risky assets and the payments they make on the assets they have sold. This process of risk sharing is also sometimes referred to as **asset transformation** because, in a sense, risky assets are turned into safer assets for investors.

Financial intermediaries also promote risk sharing by helping individuals to diversify and thereby lower the amount of risk to which they are exposed.

Diversification entails investing in a collection (**portfolio**) of assets whose returns do not always move together, with the result that overall risk is lower than for individual assets. (Diversification is just another name for the old adage, "You shouldn't put all your eggs in one basket.") Low transaction costs allow financial intermediaries to do this by pooling a collection of assets into a new asset and then selling it to individuals.

Asymmetric Information: Adverse Selection and Moral Hazard

The presence of transaction costs in financial markets explains, in part, why financial intermediaries and indirect finance play such an important role in financial markets. An additional reason is that in financial markets, one party often does not know enough about the other party to make accurate decisions. This inequality is called **asymmetric information.** For example, a borrower who takes out a loan usually has better information about the potential returns and risks associated with the investment projects for which the funds are earmarked than the lender does. Lack of information creates problems in the financial system both before and after the transaction is entered into.[3]

Adverse selection is the problem created by asymmetric information *before* the transaction occurs. Adverse selection in financial markets occurs when the potential borrowers who are the most likely to produce an undesirable (*adverse*) outcome—the bad credit risks—are the ones who most actively seek out a loan and are thus most likely to be selected. Because adverse selection makes it more likely that loans might be made to bad credit risks, lenders may decide not to make any loans even though good credit risks exist in the marketplace.

To understand why adverse selection occurs, suppose that you have two aunts to whom you might make a loan—Aunt Leela and Aunt Sheila. Aunt Leela is a conservative type who borrows only when she has an investment she is quite sure will pay off. Aunt Sheila, by contrast, is an inveterate gambler who has just come across a get-rich-quick scheme that will make her a millionaire if she can just borrow ₹1,000 to invest in it. Unfortunately, as with most get-rich-quick schemes, the probability is high that the investment won't pay off and that Aunt Sheila will lose the ₹1,000.

Which of your aunts is more likely to call you to ask for a loan? Aunt Sheila, of course, because she has so much to gain if the investment pays off. You, however, would not want to make a loan to her because the probability is high that her investment will turn sour and she will be unable to pay you back.

If you knew both your aunts very well—that is, if your information were not asymmetric—you wouldn't have a problem because you would know that Aunt Sheila is a bad risk and so you would not lend to her. Suppose, though, that you don't know your aunts well. You are more likely to lend to Aunt Sheila than to Aunt Leela because Aunt Sheila would be hounding you for the loan. Because of the possibility of adverse selection, you might decide not to lend to either of your aunts, even though there are times when Aunt Leela, who is an excellent credit risk, might need a loan for a worthwhile investment.

Moral hazard is the problem created by asymmetric information *after* the transaction occurs. Moral hazard in financial markets is the risk (*hazard*) that the

---

[3] Asymmetric information and the adverse selection and moral hazard concepts are also crucial problems for the insurance industry.

borrower might engage in activities that are undesirable (*immoral*) from the lender's point of view because they make it less likely that the loan will be paid back. Because moral hazard lowers the probability that the loan will be repaid, lenders may decide that they would rather not make a loan.

As an example of moral hazard, suppose that you made a ₹1,000 loan to another relative, Uncle Melvin, who needs the money to purchase a computer so that he can set up a business typing students' term papers. Once you have made the loan, however, Uncle Melvin is more likely to slip off to the track and play the horses. If he bets on a 20-to-1 long shot and wins with your money, he is able to pay back your ₹1,000 and live high off the hog with the remaining ₹19,000. But if he loses, as is likely, you don't get paid back, and all he has lost is his reputation as a reliable, upstanding uncle. Uncle Melvin therefore has an incentive to go to the track because his gains (₹19,000) if he bets correctly are much greater than the cost to him (his reputation) if he bets incorrectly. If you knew what Uncle Melvin was up to, you would prevent him from going to the track, and he would not be able to increase the moral hazard. However, because it is hard for you to keep informed about his whereabouts—that is, because information is asymmetric—there is a good chance that Uncle Melvin will go to the track and you will not get paid back. The risk of moral hazard might therefore discourage you from making the ₹1,000 loan to Uncle Melvin, even if you were sure that you would be paid back if he used it to set up his business.

The problems created by adverse selection and moral hazard are significant impediments to well-functioning financial markets. Again, financial intermediaries can alleviate these problems.

With financial intermediaries in the economy, small savers can provide their funds to the financial markets by lending these funds to a trustworthy intermediary—say, the Honest John Bank—which in turn lends the funds out either by making loans or by buying securities such as stocks or bonds. Successful financial intermediaries have higher earnings on their investments than do small savers because they are better equipped than individuals to screen out bad credit risks from good ones, thereby reducing losses due to adverse selection. In addition, financial intermediaries have high earnings because they develop expertise in monitoring the parties they lend to, thus reducing losses due to moral hazard. The result is that financial intermediaries can afford to pay lender-savers interest or provide substantial services and still earn a profit.

As we have seen, financial intermediaries play an important role in the economy because they provide liquidity services, promote risk sharing, and solve information problems, thereby allowing small savers and borrowers to benefit from the existence of financial markets. Financial intermediaries play a key role in improving economic efficiency because they help financial markets channel funds from lender-savers to people with productive investment opportunities. Without a well-functioning set of financial intermediaries, it is very hard for an economy to reach its full potential. We will explore further the role of financial intermediaries in the economy in Parts 5 and 6.

Economies of Scope and Conflicts of Interest

Another reason why financial intermediaries play such an important role in the economy is that by providing multiple financial services to their customers, such as offering them bank loans or selling their bonds for them, they can also achieve

economies of scope; that is, they can lower the cost of information production for each service by applying one information resource to many different services. An investment bank, for example, can evaluate how good a credit risk a corporation is when making a loan to the firm, which then helps the bank decide whether it would be easy to sell the bonds of this corporation to the public.

Although the presence of economies of scope may substantially benefit financial institutions, it also creates potential costs in terms of **conflicts of interest.** Conflicts of interest are a type of moral hazard problem that arise when a person or institution has multiple objectives (interests) and, as a result, has conflicts between those objectives. Conflicts of interest are especially likely to occur when a financial institution provides multiple services. The potentially competing interests of those services may lead an individual or firm to conceal information or disseminate misleading information. We care about conflicts of interest because a substantial reduction in the quality of information in financial markets increases asymmetric information problems and prevents financial markets from channeling funds into the most productive investment opportunities. Consequently, the financial markets and the economy become less efficient. We will discuss conflicts of interest in financial markets in more detail in Parts 3 and 6.

Types of Financial Intermediaries

We have seen why financial intermediaries have such an important function in the economy. Now we look at the principal financial intermediaries themselves and how they perform the intermediation function. They fall into three categories: depository institutions (banks), contractual savings institutions, and investment intermediaries. Table 2.1 provides a guide to the discussion of the financial intermediaries that fit into these three categories by describing their primary liabilities (sources of funds) and assets (uses of funds). The relative size of these intermediaries in India is indicated in Table 2.2, which lists the amount of their assets at the end of 2014.

Depository Institutions

Depository institutions (for simplicity, we refer to these as *banks* throughout this text) are financial intermediaries that accept deposits from individuals and institutions and make loans. In India, these institutions include commercial banks, cooperative banks and Regional Rural Banks (RRBs).

Commercial Banks　These financial intermediaries raise funds primarily by issuing checkable deposits (deposits on which checks can be written), savings deposits (deposits that are payable on demand but do not allow their owner to write checks), and time deposits (deposits with fixed terms to maturity). They then use these funds to make commercial, consumer, and mortgage loans and to buy government securities. The commercial banking sector in India comprises 26 public sector banks, 25 private banks and 43 foreign banks. The public sector banks comprise the 'State Bank of India' and its seven associate banks and 19 other banks owned by the government and account for almost three fourth of the banking sector. The Government of India has majority shares in these public sector banks.

TABLE 2.1   Primary Assets and Liabilities of Financial Intermediaries

Type of Intermediary	Primary Liabilities	Primary Assets
Depository institutions (banks)		
Commercial banks	Deposits	Business and consumer loans, mortgages, government securities
Cooperative banks	Deposits	Investments, loans and advances, bills receivable
Regional rural banks	Deposits	Loans and advances, investments
Contractual savings institutions		
Life insurance companies	Premiums from policies	Corporate bonds and mortgages
Non-life (General) insurance companies	Premiums from policies	Corporate bonds and stock, government securities
Pension funds	Employee and employer contributions	Corporate bonds and stock
Investment intermediaries		
Finance companies	Commercial paper, stocks, bonds	Consumer and business loans
Mutual funds	Shares	Stocks, bonds
Money market mutual funds	Shares	Money market instruments

References: https://www.rbi.org.in/scripts/PublicationsView.aspx?id=16505; http://financialservices.gov.in/banking/
Consolidated%20Review%20RRB.pdf; IRDA Annual Report 2014-15, https://www.irdai.gov.in/ADMINCMS/
cms/frmGeneral_Layout.aspx?page=PageNo2733&flag=1; http://www.pfrda.org.in//MyAuth/Admin/showimg
.cshtml?ID=459; http://www.moneycontrol.com/mutual-funds/amc assets-monitor, as accessed on 12 March 2016
at 12.30pm.

Cooperative Banks and RRBs   The cooperative banking sector in India comprises 1,589 urban cooperative banks and 93,550 rural cooperative banks, in addition to cooperative credit institutions. There are 56 regional rural banks.

Contractual Savings Institutions

Contractual savings institutions, such as insurance companies and pension funds, are financial intermediaries that acquire funds at periodic intervals on a contractual basis. Because they can predict with reasonable accuracy how much they will have to pay out in benefits in the coming years, they do not have to worry as much as depository institutions about losing funds quickly. As a result, the liquidity of assets is not as important a consideration for them as it is for depository institutions, and they tend to invest their funds primarily in long-term securities such as corporate bonds, stocks, and mortgages.

Life Insurance Companies   Life insurance companies insure people against financial hazards following a death and sell annuities (annual income payments upon retirement). They acquire funds from the premiums that people pay to keep their

TABLE 2.2   Principal Financial Intermediaries and Value of Their Assets

Type of Intermediary	Value of Assets (Amount in INR crore) as at 31 March 2014
Depository institutions (banks)	
Commercial banks	109,634.75[†]
Cooperative banks	3,372[**, †]
Regional rural banks	332,858
Contractual savings institutions	
Life insurance companies	328,101.14[*]
Non-life (General) insurance companies	84,684.28[*]
Pension funds	48,136
Investment intermediaries	
Mutual funds	900,753

*Figures pertain to 2014–15
**Figures pertain to 2013 for Urban Cooperative Banks.
[†]This figure is in INR billion
References: https://www.rbi.org.in/scripts/PublicationsView.aspx?id=16505; http://financialservices.gov.in/banking/Consolidated%20Review%20RRB.pdf; IRDA Annual Report 2014-15, https://www.irdai.gov.in/ADMINCMS/cms/frmGeneral_Layout.aspx?page=PageNo2733&flag=1; http://www.pfrda.org.in//MyAuth/Admin/showimg.cshtml?ID=459; http://www.moneycontrol.com/mutual-funds/amc-assets-monitor as accessed on 12 March 2016 at 12.35pm.

policies in force and use them mainly to buy corporate bonds and mortgages. They also purchase stocks but are restricted in the amount that they can hold. Currently, there are 24 life insurance companies registered with the Insurance Regulatory Development Authority of India (IRDAI). Among the life insurers, Life Insurance Corporation (LIC) is the sole public sector company.

Non-Life Insurance Companies   These companies insure their policyholders against loss from theft, fire, and accidents. They are very much like life insurance companies, receiving funds through premiums for their policies, but they have a greater possibility of loss of funds if major disasters occur. There are 28 non-life insurance companies in India, of which there are six public sector insurers, which include two specialised insurers namely Agriculture Insurance Company Ltd for crop insurance and Export Credit Guarantee Corporation of India for credit insurance. Moreover, there are five private sector insurers, registered to underwrite policies exclusively in health, personal accident and travel insurance segments.

Pension Funds and Government Retirement Funds   Private pension funds and state and local retirement funds provide retirement income in the form of annuities to employees who are covered by a pension plan. Funds are acquired by contributions from employers and from employees, who either have a contribution automatically deducted from their paychecks or contribute voluntarily. In India, the National Pension System (NPS) is administered and regulated by the Pension Fund Regulatory and Development Authority (PFRDA) created by an Act of Parliament. Besides the NPS, some mutual funds and insurance companies also offer pension plan or retirement plan, which are not under the jurisdiction of PFRDA.

The National Pension System (NPS) is a voluntary, defined contribution retirement savings scheme designed to enable the subscribers to make optimum decisions regarding their future through systematic savings during their working life. NPS seeks to inculcate the habit of saving for retirement amongst the citizens. It is an attempt towards finding a sustainable solution to the problem of providing adequate retirement income to every citizen of India.

Under the NPS, individual savings are pooled in to a pension fund, which are invested by PFRDA-regulated professional fund managers as per the approved investment guidelines in to the diversified portfolios comprising of government bonds, bills, corporate debentures and shares.

Investment Intermediaries

This category of financial intermediaries includes finance companies, mutual funds, money market mutual funds, and investment banks.

Finance Companies   Finance companies raise funds by selling commercial paper (a short-term debt instrument) and by issuing stocks and bonds. They lend these funds to consumers (who make purchases of such items as furniture, automobiles, and home improvements) and to small businesses. Some finance companies are organized by a parent corporation to help sell its product. For example, Bajaj Finance Limited is a part of the Bajaj Group and provides different types of loans like home loans, gold loans, personal loans, doctor loans etc.

Mutual Funds   These financial intermediaries acquire funds by selling shares to many individuals and use the proceeds to purchase diversified portfolios of stocks and bonds. Mutual funds allow shareholders to pool their resources so that they can take advantage of lower transaction costs when buying large blocks of stocks or bonds. In addition, mutual funds allow shareholders to hold more diversified portfolios than they otherwise would. Shareholders can sell (redeem) shares at any time, but the value of these shares will be determined by the value of the mutual fund's holdings of securities. Because these fluctuate greatly, the value of mutual fund shares do, too; therefore, investments in mutual funds can be risky.

Money Market Mutual Funds   These financial institutions have the characteristics of a mutual fund but also function to some extent as a depository institution because they offer deposit-type accounts. Like most mutual funds, they sell shares to acquire funds that are then used to buy money market instruments that are both safe and very liquid. The interest on these assets is paid out to the shareholders.

Investment Banks   Despite its name, an investment bank is not a bank or a financial intermediary in the ordinary sense; that is, it does not take in deposits and then lend them out. Instead, an investment bank is a different type of intermediary that helps a corporation issue securities. First it advises the corporation on which type of securities to issue (stocks or bonds); then it helps sell (underwrite) the securities by purchasing them from the corporation at a predetermined price and reselling them in the market. Investment banks also act as deal makers and earn enormous fees by helping corporations acquire other companies through mergers or acquisitions.

Regulation of the Financial System

GO
ONLINE
http://www.sebi.gov.in/
sebiweb/
Access the Securities and
Exchange Board of India
home page.

The financial system is among the most heavily regulated sectors of any economy, including India. The government regulates financial markets for two main reasons: to increase the information available to investors and to ensure the soundness of the financial system. We will examine how these two reasons have led to the present regulatory environment. As a study aid, the principal regulatory agencies of the Indian financial system are listed in Table 2.3.

Increasing Information Available to Investors

Asymmetric information in financial markets means that investors may be subject to adverse selection and moral hazard problems that may hinder the efficient operation of financial markets. Risky firms or outright crooks may be the most eager to sell securities to unwary investors, and the resulting adverse selection problem may keep investors out of financial markets. Furthermore, once an investor has bought a security, thereby lending money to a firm, the borrower may have incentives to engage in risky activities or to commit outright fraud. The presence of this moral hazard problem may also keep investors away from financial markets. Government

TABLE 2.3   Principal Regulatory Agencies of the Indian Financial System

Regulatory Agency	Subject of Regulation	Nature of Regulation
Reserve Bank of India	All scheduled commercial banks	Apex monetary authority of India
Securities and Exchange Board of India (SEBI)	Securities market	Regulates the securities market through its independent powers
Insurance Regulatory and Development Authority (IRDA)	The Insurance industry in India	Protects the interests of the policyholders, regulates, promotes and ensures orderly growth of the insurance industry
Forward Market Commission (FMC)	Commodity futures markets	This Commission allows commodity trading in 22 exchanges in India, out of which three are national level.
Pension Fund Regulatory and Development Authority (PFRDA)	Pension regulatory authority	Promotes and ensures orderly growth of the National Pension System and the schemes to which this system applies and protects the interests of the subscribers to various schemes of pension funds and related matters.

regulation can reduce adverse selection and moral hazard problems in financial markets and enhance the efficiency of the markets by increasing the amount of information available to investors.

Ensuring the Soundness of Financial Intermediaries

Asymmetric information can lead to the widespread collapse of financial intermediaries, referred to as a **financial panic.** Because providers of funds to financial intermediaries may not be able to assess whether the institutions holding their funds are sound, if they have doubts about the overall health of financial intermediaries, they may want to pull their funds out of both sound and unsound institutions. The possible outcome is a financial panic that produces large losses for the public and causes serious damage to the economy.

SUMMARY

1. The basic function of financial markets is to channel funds from savers who have an excess of funds to spenders who have a shortage of funds. Financial markets can do this either through direct finance, in which borrowers borrow funds directly from lenders by selling them securities, or through indirect finance, which involves a financial intermediary that stands between the lender savers and the borrower-spenders and helps transfer funds from one to the other. This channeling of funds improves the economic welfare of everyone in society. Because they allow funds to move from people who have no productive investment opportunities to those who have such opportunities, financial markets contribute to economic efficiency. In addition, channeling of funds directly benefits consumers by allowing them to make purchases when they need them most.

2. Financial markets can be classified as debt and equity markets, primary and secondary markets, exchanges and over-the-counter markets, and money and capital markets.

3. An important trend in recent years is the growing internationalization of financial markets. Eurobonds, which are denominated in a currency other than that of the country in which they are sold, are now the dominant security in the international bond market and have surpassed U.S. corporate bonds as a source of new funds. Eurodollars, which are U.S. dollars deposited in foreign banks, are an important source of funds for American banks.

4. Financial intermediaries are financial institutions that acquire funds by issuing liabilities and, in turn, use those funds to acquire assets by purchasing securities or making loans. Financial intermediaries play an important role in the financial system because they reduce transaction costs, allow risk sharing, and solve problems created by adverse selection and moral hazard. As a result, financial intermediaries allow small savers and borrowers to benefit from the existence of financial markets, thereby increasing the efficiency of the economy. However, the economies of scope that help make financial intermediaries successful can lead to conflicts of interest that make the financial system less efficient.

5. The principal financial intermediaries fall into three categories: a) banks—commercial banks, cooperative banks and Regional Rural Banks b) contractual savings institutions—Life Insurance companies, non-life insurance companies and pension funds; and c) investment intermediaries—finance companies, mutual funds, money market mutual funds, and investment banks.

6. The government regulates financial markets and financial intermediaries for two main reasons: to increase the information available to investors and to ensure the soundness of the financial system. Regulations include requiring disclosure of information to the public, restrictions on who can set up a financial intermediary, restrictions on the assets financial intermediaries can hold, the provision of deposit insurance, limits on competition, and restrictions on interest rates.

KEY TERMS

adverse selection, p. 26
asset transformation, p. 25
asymmetric information, p. 26
brokers, p. 19
capital, p. 17
capital market, p. 20
conflicts of interest, p. 28
dealers, p. 19
diversification, p. 26
dividends, p. 18
economies of scale, p. 24
economies of scope, p. 28
equities, p. 18
Eurobond, p. 22

Eurocurrencies, p. 22
Eurodollars, p. 22
exchanges, p. 19
financial intermediation, p. 24
financial panic, p. 33
foreign bonds, p. 22
intermediate-term, p. 18
investment bank, p. 19
liabilities, p. 16
liquid, p. 19
liquidity services, p. 25
long-term, p. 18
maturity, p. 18
money market, p. 20

moral hazard, p. 26
Negotiated Dealing System (NDS),
    p. 21
Negotiated Dealing System–Order
    Matching (NDS-OM), p. 21
over-the-counter (OTC)
    market, p. 19
portfolio, p. 26
primary market, p. 18
risk, p. 25
risk sharing, p. 25
secondary market, p. 18
short-term, p. 18
transaction costs, p. 24
underwriting, p. 19

QUESTIONS

1. Why is a share of Microsoft common stock an asset for its owner and a liability for Microsoft?

2. If I can buy a car today for ₹5,000 and it is worth ₹10,000 in extra income next year to me because it enables me to get a job as a traveling anvil seller, should I take out a loan from Larry the loan shark at a 90% interest rate if no one else will give me a loan? Will I be better or worse off as a result of taking out this loan? Can you make a case for legalizing loan-sharking?

3. Some economists suspect that one of the reasons that economies in developing countries grow so slowly is that they do not have well-developed financial markets. Does this argument make sense?

4. The U.S. economy borrowed heavily from the British in the nineteenth century to build a railroad system. What was the principal debt instrument used? Why did this make both countries better off?

5. "Because corporations do not actually raise any funds in secondary markets, they are less important to the economy than primary markets." Comment.

6. If you suspect that a company will go bankrupt next year, which would you rather hold, bonds issued by the company or equities issued by the company? Why?

7. How can the adverse selection problem explain why you are more likely to make a loan to a family member than to a stranger?

8. Think of one example in which you have had to deal with the adverse selection problem.

9. Why do loan sharks worry less about moral hazard in connection with their borrowers than some other lenders do?

10. If you are an employer, what kinds of moral hazard problems might you worry about with your employees?

11. If there were no asymmetry in the information that a borrower and a lender had, could there still be a moral hazard problem?

12. "In a world without information and transaction costs, financial intermediaries would not exist." Is this statement true, false, or uncertain? Explain your answer.

13. Why might you be willing to make a loan to your neighbor by putting funds in a savings account earning a 5% interest rate at the bank and having the bank lend her the funds at a 10% interest rate rather than lend her the funds yourself?

14. How does risk sharing benefit both financial intermediaries and private investors?

15. Discuss some of the manifestations of the globalization of world capital markets.

WEB EXERCISES

The Financial System

1. One of the best sources of information about financial institutions is the U.S. Flow of Funds report produced by the Federal Reserve. This document contains data on most financial intermediaries. Go to **www.federalreserve.gov/releases/Z1/**. Go to the most current release. You may have to install Acrobat Reader if your computer does not already have it; the site has a link to download it for free. Go to the Level Tables and answer the following questions.

   a. What percentage of assets do commercial banks hold in loans? What percentage of assets are held in mortgage loans?

   b. What percentage of assets do savings and loans hold in mortgage loans?

   c. What percentage of assets do credit unions hold in mortgage loans and in consumer loans?

2. The most famous financial market in the world is the New York Stock Exchange. Go to **www.nyse.com**.

   a. What is the mission of the NYSE?

   b. Firms must pay a fee to list their shares for sale on the NYSE. What would be the fee for a firm with five million common shares outstanding?

CHAPTER

3

What Do Interest Rates Mean and What is Their Role in Valuation?

> PREVIEW

Interest rates are among the most closely watched variables in the economy. Their movements are reported almost daily by the news media because they directly affect our everyday lives and have important consequences for the health of the economy. They affect personal decisions such as whether to consume or save, whether to buy a house, and whether to purchase bonds or put funds into a savings account. Interest rates also affect the economic decisions of businesses and households, such as whether to use their funds to invest in new equipment for factories or to save their money in a bank.

Before we can go on with the study of financial markets, we must understand exactly what the phrase *interest rates* means. In this chapter, we see that a concept known as the *yield to maturity* is the most accurate measure of interest rates; the yield to maturity is what financial economists mean when they use the term *interest rate*. We discuss how the yield to maturity is measured on credit market instruments and how it is used to value these instruments. We also see that a bond's interest rate does not necessarily indicate how good an investment the bond is because what it earns (its rate of return) does not necessarily equal its interest rate. Finally, we explore the distinction between real interest rates, which are adjusted for changes in the price level, and nominal interest rates, which are not.

Although learning definitions is not always the most exciting of pursuits, it is important to read carefully and understand the concepts presented in this chapter. Not only are they continually used throughout the remainder of this text, but a firm grasp of these terms will give you a clearer understanding of the role that interest rates play in your life as well as in the general economy.

Measuring Interest Rates

GO ONLINE
http://dbie.rbi.org.in/DBIE/
dbie.rbi?site=home
Under "Key Rates", you can
access information on key
interest rates in India.

Different debt instruments have very different streams of cash payments to the holder (known as **cash flows**), with very different timing. Thus, we first need to understand how we can compare the value of one kind of debt instrument with another before we see how interest rates are measured. To do this, we use the concept of *present value*.

Present Value

The concept of **present value (or present discounted value)** is based on the commonsense notion that a rupee of cash flow paid to you one year from now is less valuable to you than a rupee paid to you today: This notion is true because you can deposit a rupee in a savings account that earns interest and have more than a rupee in one year. Economists use a more formal definition, as explained in this section.

Let's look at the simplest kind of debt instrument, which we will call a **simple loan.** In this loan, the lender provides the borrower with an amount of funds (called the *principal*) that must be repaid to the lender at the *maturity date*, along with an additional payment for the interest. For example, if you made your friend Jyoti a simple loan of ₹100 for one year, you would require her to repay the principal of ₹100 in one year's time along with an additional payment for interest, say, ₹10. In the case of a simple loan like this one, the interest payment divided by the amount of the loan is a natural and sensible way to measure the interest rate. This measure of the so-called *simple interest rate, i,* is

$$i = \frac{₹10}{₹100} = 0.10 = 10\%$$

If you make this ₹100 loan, at the end of the year you would have ₹110, which can be rewritten as:

$$₹100 \times (1 + 0.10) = ₹110$$

If you then lent out the ₹110, at the end of the second year you would have:

$$₹110 \times (1 + 0.10) = ₹121$$

or, equivalently,

$$₹100 \times (1 + 0.10) \times (1 + 0.10) = ₹100 \times (1 + 0.10)^2 = ₹121$$

Continuing with the loan again, at the end of the third year you would have:

$$₹121 \times (1 + 0.10) = ₹100 \times (1 + 0.10)^3 = ₹133$$

Generalizing, we can see that at the end of n years, your ₹100 would turn into:

$$₹100 \times (1 + i)^n$$

The amounts you would have at the end of each year by making the ₹100 loan today can be seen in the following timeline:

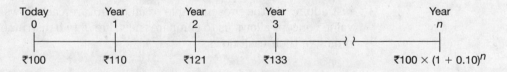

This timeline immediately tells you that you are just as happy having ₹100 today as having ₹110 a year from now (of course, as long as you are sure that Jyoti will pay you back). Or that you are just as happy having ₹100 today as having ₹121 two years from now, or ₹133 three years from now, or ₹100 × (1 + 0.10)^n in n years from now. The timeline tells us that we can also work backward from future amounts to the present. For example, ₹133 = ₹100 × (1 + 0.10)^3 three years from now is worth ₹100 today, so that:

$$₹100 = \frac{₹133}{(1 + 0.10)^3}$$

The process of calculating today's value of rupees received in the future, as we have done above, is called *discounting the future*. We can generalize this process by writing today's (present) value of ₹100 as PV, the future cash flow of ₹133 as CF, and replacing 0.10 (the 10% interest rate) by i. This leads to the following formula:

$$PV = \frac{CF}{(1 + i)^n} \tag{1}$$

Intuitively, what Equation 1 tells us is that if you are promised ₹1 of cash flow for certain 10 years from now, this rupee would not be as valuable to you as ₹1 is today because if you had the ₹1 today, you could invest it and end up with more than ₹1 in 10 years.

EXAMPLE 3.1

Simple Present Value

What is the present value of ₹250 to be paid in two years if the interest rate is 15%?

> **Solution**

The present value would be ₹189.04. Using Equation 1:

$$PV = \frac{CF}{(1 + i)^n}$$

where

CF = cash flow in two years = ₹250

i = annual interest rate   = 0.15

n = number of years   = 2

Thus,

$$PV = \frac{₹250}{(1 + 0.15)^2} = \frac{₹250}{1.3225} = ₹189.04$$

Today 0	Year 1	Year 2

₹250

₹189.04 ◄

The concept of present value is extremely useful because it enables us to figure out today's value of a credit market instrument at a given simple interest rate i by just adding up the present value of all the future cash flows received. The present value concept allows us to compare the value of two instruments with very different timing of their cash flows.

Four Types of Credit Market Instruments

In terms of the timing of their cash flows, there are four basic types of credit market instruments.

1. A simple loan, which we have already discussed, in which the lender provides the borrower with an amount of funds, which must be repaid to the lender at the maturity date along with an additional payment for the interest. Many money market instruments are of this type, for example, commercial loans to businesses.

2. A **fixed-payment loan** (also called a **fully amortized loan**) in which the lender provides the borrower with an amount of funds, which must be repaid by making the same payment every period (such as a month), consisting of part of the principal and interest for a set number of years. For example, if you borrowed ₹1,000, a fixed-payment loan might require you to pay ₹126 every year for 25 years. Installment loans (such as auto loans) and home loans are frequently of the fixed-payment type.

3. A **coupon bond** pays the owner of the bond a fixed interest payment (coupon payment) every year until the maturity date, when a specified final amount (**face value** or **par value**) is repaid. The coupon payment is so named because the bondholder used to obtain payment by clipping a coupon off the bond and sending it to the bond issuer, who then sent the payment to the holder. On all but the oldest bonds, it is no longer necessary to send in coupons to receive these payments. A coupon bond with ₹1,000 face value, for example, might pay you a coupon payment of ₹100 per year for 10 years, and at the maturity date repay you the face value amount of ₹1,000. (The face value of a bond is usually in ₹1,000 increments.)

   A coupon bond is identified by three pieces of information. First is the corporation or government agency that issues the bond. Second is the maturity date of the bond. Third is the bond's **coupon rate,** the rupee amount of the yearly coupon payment expressed as a percentage of the face value of the bond. In our example, the coupon bond has a yearly coupon payment of ₹100 and a face value of ₹1,000. The coupon rate is then ₹100/₹1,000 − 0.10, or 10%. Capital market instruments such as 10 Year-Government of India securities and notes and corporate bonds are examples of coupon bonds.

4. A **discount bond** (also called a **zero-coupon bond**) is bought at a price below its face value (at a discount), and the face value is repaid at the maturity date. Unlike a coupon bond, a discount bond does not make any interest payments; it just pays off the face value. Zero coupon bonds called Deep discount bonds in India were preferred by retail investors during the early 1990s. Examples of such bonds include the Narmada Bond launched in 1993, which on an investment of ₹3,600 promised to give ₹1.10 lakhs in 20 years, thus offering an attractive rate of interest of 18%. The ICICI Children's Bond at a 16% interest rate promised ₹1 lakh on an investment of ₹7,000, 18 years after 1995. Other than facilitating long term planning, such bonds offered very good guaranteed returns as well. However, when the market interest rates dropped to below 10% in the year 2000, most of these bonds were called back for early redemption by the issuers. This left the investors in the bonds ending up being paid much earlier than the maturity dates, as also having no other option for similar guaranteed returns in the market. The Government of India issued such bonds in the nineties, but has not issued them after that.

NABARD'S DEEP DISCOUNT BOND

The National Bank for Agricultural and Rural Development (NABARD) launched a Deep discount bond—the Bhavishya Nirman Bond on 23 March 2010, a first of sorts for this decade. The NABARD Deep Discount Bond is the latest Zero Coupon Bond introduced in India. The bond was issued at ₹9,750 for a maturity value of ₹20,000 after 10 years, giving it a return of 7.45%. The bond offered investors the advantage of being open for trading on the Bombay Stock Exchange, thus allowing the bond-holder the opportunity to make some capital gains in case the interest rate during the period dropped below 7.45%. With indexation benefits on the capital gains, the tax liability of the capital gains was much lesser. Further, on maturity, NABARD would not withhold TDS, which was positive, particularly for senior citizens.

These four types of instruments require payments at different times: Simple loans and discount bonds make payment only at their maturity dates, whereas fixed-payment loans and coupon bonds have payments periodically until maturity. How would you decide which of these instruments would provide you with more income? They all seem so different because they make payments at different times. To solve this problem, we use the concept of present value, explained earlier, to provide us with a procedure for measuring interest rates on these types of instruments.

Yield to Maturity

Of the several common ways of calculating interest rates, the most important is the **yield to maturity,** the interest rate that equates the present value of cash flows received from a debt instrument with its value today. Because the concept behind the calculation of the yield to maturity makes good economic sense, financial economists consider it the most accurate measure of interest rates.

To understand the yield to maturity better, we now look at how it is calculated for the four types of credit market instruments. The key in all these examples to understanding the calculation of the yield to maturity is equating today's value of the debt instrument with the present value of all of its future cash flow payments.

Simple Loan   With the concept of present value, the yield to maturity on a simple loan is easy to calculate. For the one-year loan we discussed, today's value is ₹100, and the cash flow in one year's time would be ₹110 (the repayment of ₹100 plus the interest payment of ₹10). We can use this information to solve for the yield to maturity i by recognizing that the present value of the future payments must equal today's value of a loan.

EXAMPLE 3.2

Simple Loan

If Pete borrows ₹100 from his sister and next year she wants ₹110 back from him, what is the yield to maturity on this loan?

> **Solution**
The yield to maturity on the loan is 10%.

$$PV = \frac{CF}{(1 + i)^n}$$

where

PV = amount borrowed = ₹100

CF = cash flow in one year = ₹110

n = number of years = 1

Thus,

$$₹100 = \frac{₹110}{(1 + i)}$$

$$(1 + i)₹100 = ₹110$$

$$(1 + i) = \frac{₹110}{₹100}$$

$$i = 1.10 - 1 = 0.10 = 10\%$$

Today
0

Year
1

├──────────────────────────────┤

₹100

₹110

────────→ $i = 10\%$ ◄────────

This calculation of the yield to maturity should look familiar because it equals the interest payment of ₹10 divided by the loan amount of ₹100; that is, it equals the simple interest rate on the loan. An important point to recognize is that *for simple loans, the simple interest rate equals the yield to maturity*. Hence the same term i is used to denote both the yield to maturity and the simple interest rate.

Fixed-Payment Loan Recall that this type of loan has the same cash flow payment every year throughout the life of the loan. On a fixed-rate mortgage, for example, the borrower makes the same payment to the bank every month until the maturity date, when the loan will be completely paid off. To calculate the yield to maturity for a fixed-payment loan, we follow the same strategy we used for the simple loan—we equate today's value of the loan with its present value. Because the fixed-payment loan involves more than one cash flow payment, the present value of the fixed-payment loan is calculated as the sum of the present values of all cash flows (using Equation 1).

Suppose the loan is ₹1,000 and the yearly cash flow payment is ₹85.81 for the next 25 years. The present value is calculated as follows: At the end of one year, there is a ₹85.81 cash flow payment with a PV of ₹85.81/(1 + i); at the end of two years, there is another ₹85.81 cash flow payment with a PV of ₹85.81/(1 + i)²; and so on until at the end of the 25th year, the last cash flow payment of ₹85.81 with a PV of ₹85.81/(1 + i)²⁵ is made. Making today's value of the loan (₹1,000) equal to the sum of the present values of all the yearly cash flows gives us

$$₹1,000 = \frac{₹85.81}{1 + i} + \frac{₹85.81}{(1 + i)^2} + \frac{₹85.81}{(1 + i)^3} + \ldots + \frac{₹85.81}{(1 + i)^{25}}$$

More generally, for any fixed-payment loan,

$$LV = \frac{FP}{1 + i} + \frac{FP}{(1 + i)^2} + \frac{FP}{(1 + i)^3} + \cdots + \frac{FP}{(1 + i)^n} \tag{2}$$

where

LV = loan value
FP = fixed yearly cash flow payment
n = number of years until maturity

For a fixed-payment loan amount, the fixed yearly payment and the number of years until maturity are known quantities, and only the yield to maturity is not. So we can solve this equation for the yield to maturity i. Because this calculation is not easy, many pocket calculators have programs that allow you to find i given the loan's numbers for LV, FP, and n. For example, in the case of the 25-year loan with yearly payments of ₹85.81, the yield to maturity that solves Equation 2 is 7%. Real estate brokers always have a pocket calculator that can solve such equations so that they can immediately tell the prospective house buyer exactly what the yearly (or monthly) payments will be if the house purchase is financed by a mortgage.

EXAMPLE 3.3

Fixed-Payment Loan

You decide to purchase a new home and need a ₹100,000 mortgage. You take out a loan from the bank that has an interest rate of 7%. What is the yearly payment to the bank to pay off the loan in 20 years?

> **Solution**

The yearly payment to the bank is ₹9,439.29.

$$LV = \frac{FP}{1 + i} + \frac{FP}{(1 + i)^2} + \frac{FP}{(1 + i)^3} + \cdots + \frac{FP}{(1 + i)^n}$$

where

LV = loan value amount   = ₹100,000
i = annual interest rate = 0.07
n = number of years   = 20

Thus,

$$₹100,000 = +\frac{FP}{1 + 0.07} + \frac{FP}{(1 + 0.07)^2} + \frac{FP}{(1 + 0.07)^3} + \cdots + \frac{FP}{(1 + 0.07)^{20}}$$

To find the yearly payment for the loan using a financial calculator:

n = number of years   = 20
PV = amount of the loan (LV)   = –100,000
FV = amount of the loan after 20 years = 0
i = annual interest rate   = .07

Then push the *PMT* button = fixed yearly payment (FP) = ₹9,439.29.

Coupon Bond   To calculate the yield to maturity for a coupon bond, follow the same strategy used for the fixed-payment loan: Equate today's value of the bond with its present value. Because coupon bonds also have more than one cash flow payment, the present value of the bond is calculated as the sum of the present values of all the coupon payments plus the present value of the final payment of the face value of the bond.

The present value of a ₹1,000 face value bond with 10 years to maturity and yearly coupon payments of ₹100 (a 10% coupon rate) can be calculated as follows: At the end of one year, there is a ₹100 coupon payment with a PV of ₹100/$(1 + i)$; at the end of two years, there is another ₹100 coupon payment with a PV of ₹100/$(1 + i)^2$; and so on until at maturity, there is a ₹100 coupon payment with a PV of ₹100/$(1 + i)^{10}$; plus the repayment of the ₹1,000 face value with a PV of ₹1,000/$(1 + i)^{10}$. Setting today's value of the bond (its current price, denoted by P) equal to the sum of the present values of all the cash flows for this bond gives

$$P = \frac{₹100}{(1 + i)} + \frac{₹100}{(1 + i)^2} + \frac{₹100}{(1 + i)^3} + \cdots + \frac{₹100}{(1 + i)^{10}} + \frac{₹1,000}{(1 + i)^{10}}$$

More generally, for any coupon bond,[1]

$$P = \frac{C}{(1 + i)} + \frac{C}{(1 + i)^2} + \frac{C}{(1 + i)^3} + \cdots + \frac{C}{(1 + i)^n} + \frac{F}{(1 + i)^n} \qquad (3)$$

where

P = price of coupon bond
C = yearly coupon payment
F = face value of the bond
n = years to maturity date

In Equation 3, the coupon payment, the face value, the years to maturity, and the price of the bond are known quantities, and only the yield to maturity is not. Hence we can solve this equation for the yield to maturity i.[2] As in the case of the fixed-payment loan, this calculation is not easy, so business-oriented software and calculators have built-in programs that solve this equation for you.

EXAMPLE 3.4

Coupon Bond

Find the price of a 10% coupon bond with a face value of ₹1,000, a 12.25% yield to maturity, and eight years to maturity.

➤ Solution
The price of the bond is ₹889.20. To solve using a financial calculator,

n	= years to maturity	= 8
FV	= face value of the bond	= 1,000
i	= annual interest rate	= 12.25%
PMT	= yearly coupon payments	= 100

Then push the PV button = price of the bond = ₹889.20.

---

[1]Most coupon bonds actually make coupon payments on a semiannual basis rather than once a year as assumed here. The effect on the calculations is only very slight and is ignored here.
[2]In other contexts, it is also called the *internal rate of return*.

TABLE 3.1   Yields to Maturity on a 10% Coupon Rate Bond Maturing in 10 Years (Face Value = ₹1,000)

Price of Bond (₹)	Yield to Maturity (%)
1,200	7.13
1,100	8.48
1,000	10.00
900	11.75
800	13.81

Table 3.1 shows the yields to maturity calculated for several bond prices. Three interesting facts emerge:

1. When the coupon bond is priced at its face value, the yield to maturity equals the coupon rate.
2. The price of a coupon bond and the yield to maturity are negatively related; that is, as the yield to maturity rises, the price of the bond falls. If the yield to maturity falls, the price of the bond rises.
3. The yield to maturity is greater than the coupon rate when the bond price is below its face value.

These three facts are true for any coupon bond and are really not surprising if you think about the reasoning behind the calculation of the yield to maturity. When you put ₹1,000 in a bank account with an interest rate of 10%, you can take out ₹100 every year and you will be left with the ₹1,000 at the end of 10 years. This process is similar to buying the ₹1,000 bond with a 10% coupon rate analyzed in Table 3.1, which pays a ₹100 coupon payment every year and then repays ₹1,000 at the end of 10 years. If the bond is purchased at the par value of ₹1,000, its yield to maturity must equal the interest rate of 10%, which is also equal to the coupon rate of 10%. The same reasoning applied to any coupon bond demonstrates that if the coupon bond is purchased at its par value, the yield to maturity and the coupon rate must be equal.

It is straightforward to show that the valuation of a bond and the yield to maturity are negatively related. As i, the yield to maturity, rises, all denominators in the bond price formula must necessarily rise. Hence a rise in the interest rate as measured by the yield to maturity means that the value and therefore the price of the bond must fall. Another way to explain why the bond price falls when the interest rises is that a higher interest rate implies that the future coupon payments and final payment are worth less when discounted back to the present; hence the price of the bond must be lower.

The third fact, that the yield to maturity is greater than the coupon rate when the bond price is below its par value, follows directly from facts 1 and 2. When the yield to maturity equals the coupon rate, then the bond price is at the face value; when the yield to maturity rises above the coupon rate, the bond price necessarily falls and so must be below the face value of the bond.

One special case of a coupon bond that is worth discussing because its yield to maturity is particularly easy to calculate is called a **perpetuity**, or a **consol;** it is a perpetual bond with no maturity date and no repayment of principal that makes

GO ONLINE
www.teachmefinance.com
Access a review of the key financial concepts: time value of money, annuities, perpetuities, and so on.

fixed coupon payments of ₹C forever. The formula in Equation 3 for the price of a perpetuity, P_c, simplifies to the following:[3]

$$P_c = \frac{C}{i_c}$$ (4)

where
P_c = price of the perpetuity (consol)
C = yearly payment
i_c = yield to maturity of the perpetuity (consol)

One nice feature of perpetuities is that you can immediately see that as i_c goes up, the price of the bond falls. For example, if a perpetuity pays ₹100 per year forever and the interest rate is 10%, its price will be ₹1,000 = ₹100/0.10. If the interest rate rises to 20%, its price will fall to ₹500 = ₹100/0.20. We can also rewrite this formula as

$$i_c = \frac{C}{P_c}$$ (5)

EXAMPLE 3.5

Perpetuity

What is the yield to maturity on a bond that has a price of ₹2,000 and pays ₹100 annually forever?

> **Solution**
The yield to maturity would be 5%.

$$i_c = \frac{C}{P_c}$$

where

C = yearly payment = ₹100

P_c = price of perpetuity (consol) = ₹2,000

Thus,

$$i_c = \frac{₹100}{₹2,000}$$

$$i_c = 0.05 = 5\%$$

---

[3] The bond price formula for a perpetuity is

$$P_c = \frac{C}{1 + i_c} + \frac{C}{(1 + i_c)^2} + \frac{C}{(1 + i_c)^3} + \ldots$$

which can be written

$$P_c = C(x + x^2 + x^3 + \ldots)$$

in which $x = 1/(1 + i)$. From your high school algebra you might remember the formula for an infinite sum:

$$1 + x + x^2 + x^3 + \ldots = \frac{1}{1 - x} \quad \text{for } x < 1$$

and so

$$P_c = C\left(\frac{1}{1 - x} - 1\right) = C\left[\frac{1}{1 - 1/(1 + i_c)} - 1\right]$$

which by suitable algebraic manipulation becomes

$$P_c = C\left(\frac{1 + i_c}{i_c} - \frac{i_c}{i_c}\right) = \frac{C}{i_c}$$

The formula in Equation 5, which describes the calculation of the yield to maturity for a perpetuity, also provides a useful approximation for the yield to maturity on coupon bonds. When a coupon bond has a long term to maturity (say, 20 years or more), it is very much like a perpetuity, which pays coupon payments forever. This is because the cash flows more than 20 years in the future have such small present discounted values that the value of a long-term coupon bond is very close to the value of a perpetuity with the same coupon rate. Thus, i_c in Equation 5 will be very close to the yield to maturity for any long-term bond. For this reason, i_c, the yearly coupon payment divided by the price of the security, has been given the name **current yield** and is frequently used as an approximation to describe interest rates on long-term bonds.

Discount Bond   The yield-to-maturity calculation for a discount bond is similar to that for the simple loan. Let's consider a discount bond such as a 364-day Indian government T-bill, which pays a face value of ₹1,000 in one year's time. If the current purchase price of this bill is ₹900, then equating this price to the present value of the ₹1,000 received in one year, using Equation 1, gives

$$\text{₹}900 = \frac{\text{₹}1{,}000}{1 + i}$$

and solving for i,

$$(1 + i) \times \text{₹}900 = \text{₹}1{,}000$$

$$\text{₹}900 + \text{₹}900i = \text{₹}1{,}000$$

$$\text{₹}900i = \text{₹}1{,}000 - \text{₹}900$$

$$i = \frac{\text{₹}1{,}000 - \text{₹}900}{\text{₹}900} = 0.111 = 11.1\%$$

More generally, for any one-year discount bond, the yield to maturity can be written as

$$i = \frac{F - P}{P} \tag{6}$$

where F = face value of the discount bond
                  P = current price of the discount bond

In other words, the yield to maturity equals the increase in price over the year $F - P$ divided by the initial price P. In normal circumstances, investors earn positive returns from holding these securities and so they sell at a discount, meaning that the current price of the bond is below the face value. Therefore, $F - P$ should be positive, and the yield to maturity should be positive as well. However, this is not always the case, as extraordinary events in Japan indicated (see the Global box on p. 48).

An important feature of this equation is that it indicates that for a discount bond, the yield to maturity is negatively related to the current bond price. This is the same conclusion that we reached for a coupon bond. For example, Equation 6 shows that a rise in the bond price from ₹900 to ₹950 means that the bond will have a smaller increase in its price over its lifetime, and the yield to maturity falls from 11.1% to 5.3%. Similarly, a fall in the yield to maturity means that the price of the discount bond has risen.

Summary The concept of present value tells you that a rupee in the future is not as valuable to you as a rupee today because you can earn interest on this rupee. Specifically, a rupee received n years from now is worth only ₹$1/(1 + i)^n$ today. The present value of a set of future cash flows on a debt instrument equals the sum of the present values of each of the future cash flows. The yield to maturity for an instrument is the interest rate that equates the present value of the future cash flows on that instrument to its value today. Because the procedure for calculating the yield to maturity is based on sound economic principles, this is the measure that financial economists think most accurately describes the interest rate.

Our calculations of the yield to maturity for a variety of bonds reveal the important fact that *current bond prices and interest rates are negatively related: When the interest rate rises, the price of the bond falls, and vice versa*.

The Distinction Between Real and Nominal Interest Rates

So far in our discussion of interest rates, we have ignored the effects of inflation on the cost of borrowing. What we have up to now been calling the interest rate makes no allowance for inflation, and it is more precisely referred to as the **nominal interest rate.** We distinguish it from the **real interest rate,** the interest rate that is adjusted by subtracting expected changes in the price level (inflation) so that it more accurately reflects the true cost of borrowing. This interest rate is more precisely referred to as the *ex ante real interest rate* because it is adjusted for *expected* changes in the price level. The *ex ante* real interest rate is most important to economic decisions, and typically it is what financial economists mean when they make reference to the "real" interest rate. The interest rate that is adjusted for *actual* changes in the price level is called the *ex post real interest rate*. It describes how well a lender has done in real terms *after the fact*.

The real interest rate is more accurately defined by the *Fisher equation*, named for Irving Fisher, one of the great monetary economists of the twentieth century. The Fisher equation states that the nominal interest rate i equals the real interest rate i_r plus the expected rate of inflation π^e.[4]

$$i = i_r + \pi^e \tag{7}$$

Rearranging terms, we find that the real interest rate equals the nominal interest rate minus the expected inflation rate:

$$i_r = i - \pi^e \tag{8}$$

---

[4]A more precise formulation of the Fisher equation is

$$i = i_r + \pi^e + (i_r \times \pi^e)$$

because

$$1 + i = (1 + i_r)(1 + \pi^e) = 1 + i_r + \pi^e + (i_r \times \pi^e)$$

and subtracting 1 from both sides gives us the first equation. For small values of i_r and π^e, the term $i_r \times \pi^e$ is so small that we ignore it.

Negative T-Bill Rates? It Can Happen

We normally assume that the yield to maturity must always be positive. A negative yield to maturity would imply that you are willing to pay more for a bond today than you will receive for it in the future (as our formula for yield to maturity on a discount bond demonstrates). A negative yield to maturity therefore seems like an impossibility because you would do better by holding cash that has the same value in the future as it does today.

Events in Japan in the late 1990s and in the United States during the 2008 global financial crisis have demonstrated that this reasoning is not quite correct. In November 1998, the yield to maturity on Japanese six-month Treasury bills became negative, at −0.004%. In September 2008, the yield to maturity on three-month U.S. T-bills fell very slightly below zero for a very brief period.

While negative yields on short-term debts was essentially unheard of prior to the global financial crisis of 2008, the phenomenon of negative Treasury-Bill rates has been witnessed in various countries of the world. For instance, yields on some U.S. bills have persisted to be negative since 2011 reflecting extraordinarily expansive central-bank policy and anemic growth in much of the world. Similarly, two-year yields had fallen below zero in Denmark, Finland, Belgium and the Netherlands in 2014.

Negative interest rates are an extremely unusual event. How could this happen?

As we will see in Chapter 4, the weakness of the economy and a flight to quality during a financial crisis can drive interest rates to low levels, but these two factors can't explain the negative yield to maturity. The answer is that large investors found it more convenient to hold these Treasury bills as a store of value rather than holding cash because the bills are denominated in larger amounts and can be stored electronically. For that reason, some investors were willing to hold them, despite their negative yield to maturity, even though in monetary terms the investors would be better off holding cash. Clearly, the convenience of T-bills goes only so far, and thus the yield to maturity can drop only a little bit below zero.

To see why this definition makes sense, let us first consider a situation in which you have made a one-year simple loan with a 5% interest rate ($i = 5\%$) and you expect the price level to rise by 3% over the course of the year ($\pi^e = 3\%$). As a result of making the loan, at the end of the year you expect to have 2% more in **real terms,** that is, in terms of real goods and services you can buy.

EXAMPLE 3.6

Real and Nominal Interest Rates

What is the real interest rate if the nominal interest rate is 8% and the expected inflation rate is 10% over the course of a year?

> Solution

The real interest rate is −2%. Although you will be receiving 8% more rupees at the end of the year, you will be paying 10% more for goods. The result is that you will be able to buy 2% fewer goods at the end of the year, and you will be 2% worse off in real terms.

$$i_r = i - \pi^e$$

where

i = nominal interest rate = 0.08

π^e = expected inflation rate = 0.10

Thus,

$$i_r = 0.08 - 0.10 = -0.02 = -2\%$$

In this case, the interest rate you expect to earn in terms of real goods and services is 2%; that is,

$$i_r = 5\% - 3\% = 2\%$$

as indicated by the Fisher definition.

As a lender, you are clearly less eager to make a loan in Example 3.6 because in terms of real goods and services you have actually earned a negative interest rate of 2%. By contrast, as the borrower, you fare quite well because at the end of the year, the amounts you will have to pay back will be worth 2% less in terms of goods and services—you as the borrower will be ahead by 2% in real terms. *When the real interest rate is low, there are greater incentives to borrow and fewer incentives to lend.*

The distinction between real and nominal interest rates is important because the real interest rate, which reflects the real cost of borrowing, is likely to be a better indicator of the incentives to borrow and lend. It appears to be a better guide to how people will be affected by what is happening in credit markets. Figure 3.1 presents estimates of the real and nominal interest rates on weighted average deposit rates from 2000–01 to 2013–14. It can be seen that nominal and real interest rates do not move together.

In particular, high nominal rates of interest were accompanied by extremely low real interest rates, as witnessed especially in the post 2010 period. By the standard of nominal interest rates, you would have thought that credit market conditions were tight in this period because it was expensive to borrow. However, the estimates of the real interest rates indicate that you would have been mistaken. In real terms, the cost of borrowing was quite low.

The Distinction Between Interest Rates and Returns

Many people think that the interest rate on a bond tells them all they need to know about how well off they are as a result of owning it. If Ravi the investor thinks he is better off when he owns a long-term bond yielding a 10% interest rate and the interest rate rises to 20%, he will have a rude awakening: As we will shortly see, Ravi has lost his shirt! How well a person does by holding a bond or any other security over a particular time period is accurately measured by the **return,** or, in more precise terminology, the **rate of return.** The concept of return discussed here is extremely important because it is used continually throughout the book. Make sure that you understand how a return is calculated and why it can differ from the interest rate. This understanding will make the material presented later in the book easier to follow.

For any security, the rate of return is defined as the payments to the owner plus the change in its value, expressed as a fraction of its purchase price. To make this definition clearer, let us see what the return would look like for a ₹1,000-face-value coupon bond with a coupon rate of 10% that is bought for ₹1,000, held for one year, and then sold for ₹1,200. The payments to the owner are the yearly coupon payments of ₹100, and the change in its value is ₹1,200 – ₹1,000 = ₹200. Adding these together and expressing them as a fraction of the purchase price of ₹1,000 gives us the one-year holding-period return for this bond:

$$\frac{₹100 + ₹200}{₹1,000} = \frac{₹300}{₹1,000} = 0.30 = 30\%$$

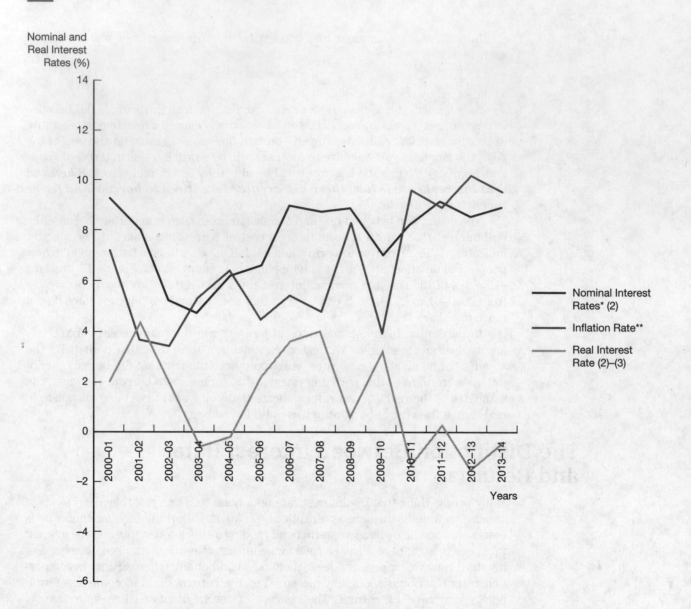

FIGURE 3.1   Real and Nominal Interest Rates (Weighted Average Deposit Rate), 2000–01 to 2013–14

Nominal and real interest rates often do not move together. When nominal rates were high in the post–2010 period, real interest rates in India were actually extremely low-often, even negative.

Sources: Nominal interest rates are measured with reference to weighted average deposit rates. Data on deposit rates relate to five major Public Sector Banks up to 2003–04. For subsequent years, the data relate to five major banks. Data prior to 2012–2013 pertains to inflation measured by the Consumer Price Index Industrial Workers (CPIIW). Post 2012–2013, the measure of inflation used in India is the Consumer Price Index (Combined). Nominal interest rates are taken from the Reserve Bank of India's Database for the Indian economy: https://rbidocs.rbi.org.in/rdocs/Publications/PDFs/074T_SHE130914L.pdf; The data on India's inflation is collected from : http://dbie.rbi.org.in/DBIE/dbie.rbi?site=statistics; https://www.rbi.org.in/Scripts/AnnualReportPublications.aspx?Id=265, as accessed on 12 March 2016 at 1.30pm.

Inflation Indexed Bonds in India

With high inflation rates, the real returns in India, especially in the post 2008 period had been very low or even negative (See Figure 3.1). This had led to investors turning to real estate or gold, which promised higher returns. The high appetite for gold had led to wider Current Account Deficit (CAD) and pressure on the rupee.

In September 2013, Governor Raghuram Rajan announced the launch of Inflation Indexed Bonds (IIBs). This was an initiative to counter the impact of inflation on savings and investment by Indians. These bonds were meant to offer lucrative positive real rates of return, yet safe investment options, especially for investors lured by traditional options such as gold, and protect both principal and interest repayments. An earlier version of such bonds had been the Capital Indexed bonds issued in 1997.

The bonds sought to protect the principal through adjusting it for an inflation component (by multiplying the principal with the index ratio (IR)), and paying the adjusted principal or the face value, whichever was higher at the time of redemption. The interest rate was protected against inflation by paying a fixed coupon rate on the principal adjusted against inflation.

Initially, the RBI launched bonds linked to the Wholesale Price Index (WPI). These bonds offered a yield of 1.44% over the WPI. Later, in December 2013, the RBI launched bonds linked to the Consumer Price Index (CPI) for retail investors. Interest on such bonds was fixed with reference to the final Consumer Price Index–Combined (CPI-C) used with a three-month lag, at 1.5% higher than the latter. For example, if inflation as measured by CPI-C were 8%, these bonds would pay an interest of 9.5%, and if inflation went up to 8.5%, the bonds would pay 10%. The inflation-linked bonds were being sold through only a few banks, including State Bank of India, HDFC Bank Ltd, ICICI Bank Ltd, and Axis Bank Ltd.

However, in June 2014, these bonds were declared "unsuccessful" and their sale was discontinued. Analysts blamed poor marketing and high taxes as reasons for their failure.

Sources: https://rbi.org.in/Scripts/FAQView.aspx?Id=91; https://in.finance.yahoo.com/news/basics-explained--whayt-are-inflation-indexed-bonds--044304348.html; http://blogs.wsj.com/indiarealtime/2014/06/17/what-went-wrong-with-rajans-inflation-bonds/

You may have noticed something quite surprising about the return that we have just calculated: It equals 30%, yet as Table 3.1 indicates, initially the yield to maturity was only 10%. This discrepancy demonstrates that **the return on a bond will not necessarily equal the interest rate on that bond**. We now see that the distinction between interest rate and return can be important, although for many securities the two may be closely related.

More generally, the return on a bond held from time t to time $t + 1$ can be written as

$$R = \frac{C + P_{t+1} - P_t}{P_t} \qquad (9)$$

where
R = return from holding the bond from time t to time $t + 1$
P_t = price of the bond at time t
P_{t+1} = price of the bond at time $t + 1$
C = coupon payment

EXAMPLE 3.7

Rate of Return

What would the rate of return be on a bond bought for ₹1,000 and sold one year later for ₹800? The bond has a face value of ₹1,000 and a coupon rate of 8%.

> **Solution**
The rate of return on the bond for holding it one year is –12%.

$$R = \frac{C + P_{t+1} - P_t}{P_t}$$

where

C = coupon payment = ₹1,000 × 0.08 = ₹80

P_{t+1} = price of the bond one year later = ₹800

P_t = price of the bond today = ₹1,000

Thus,

$$R = \frac{₹80 + (₹800 - ₹1,000)}{₹1,000} = \frac{-120}{1,000} = -0.12 = -12\%$$

A convenient way to rewrite the return formula in Equation 9 is to recognize that it can be split into two terms:

$$R = \frac{C}{P_t} + \frac{P_{t+1} - P_t}{P_t}$$

The first term is the current yield i_c (the coupon payment over the purchase price):

$$\frac{C}{P_t} = i_c$$

The second term is the **rate of capital gain,** or the change in the bond's price relative to the initial purchase price:

$$\frac{P_{t+1} - P_t}{P_t} = g$$

where g = rate of capital gain. Equation 9 can then be rewritten as

$$R = i_c + g \qquad (10)$$

which shows that the return on a bond is the current yield i_c plus the rate of capital gain g. This rewritten formula illustrates the point we just discovered. Even for a bond for which the current yield i_c is an accurate measure of the yield to maturity, the return can differ substantially from the interest rate. Returns will differ from the interest rate especially if the price of the bond experiences sizeable fluctuations, which then produce substantial capital gains or losses.

To explore this point even further, let's look at what happens to the returns on bonds of different maturities when interest rates rise. Using Equation 10 above, Table 3.2 calculates the one-year return on several 10% coupon rate bonds all purchased at par when interest rates on all these bonds rise from 10% to 20%. Several key findings in this table are generally true of all bonds:

TABLE 3.2   One-Year Returns on Different-Maturity 10% Coupon Rate Bonds When Interest Rates Rise from 10% to 20%

(1) Years to Maturity When Bond Is Purchased	(2) Initial Current Yield (%)	(3) Initial Price (₹)	(4) Price Next Year* (₹)	(5) Rate of Capital Gain (%)	(6) Rate of Return (2 + 5) (%)
30	10	1,000	503	−49.7	−39.7
20	10	1,000	516	−48.4	−38.4
10	10	1,000	597	−40.3	−30.3
5	10	1,000	741	−25.9	−15.9
2	10	1,000	917	−8.3	+ 1.7
1	10	1,000	1,000	0.0	+10.0

*Calculated with a financial calculator using Equation 3.

- The only bond whose return equals the initial yield to maturity is one whose time to maturity is the same as the holding period (see the last bond in Table 3.2).
- A rise in interest rates is associated with a fall in bond prices, resulting in capital losses on bonds whose terms to maturity are longer than the holding period.
- The more distant a bond's maturity, the greater the size of the price change associated with an interest-rate change.
- The more distant a bond's maturity, the lower the rate of return that occurs as a result of the increase in the interest rate.
- Even though a bond has a substantial initial interest rate, its return can turn out to be negative if interest rates rise.

At first, it frequently puzzles students that a rise in interest rates can mean that a bond has been a poor investment (as it puzzles poor Ravi the investor). The trick to understanding this is to recognize that a rise in the interest rate means that the price of a bond has fallen. A rise in interest rates therefore means that a capital loss has occurred, and if this loss is large enough, the bond can be a poor investment indeed. For example, we see in Table 3.2 that the bond that has 30 years to maturity when purchased has a capital loss of 49.7% when the interest rate rises from 10% to 20%. This loss is so large that it exceeds the current yield of 10%, resulting in a negative return (loss) of −39.7%. If Ravi does not sell the bond, the capital loss is often referred to as a "paper loss." This is a loss nonetheless because if he had not bought this bond and had instead put his money in the bank, he would now be able to buy more bonds at their lower price than he presently owns.

Maturity and the Volatility of Bond Returns: Interest-Rate Risk

The finding that the prices of longer-maturity bonds respond more dramatically to changes in interest rates helps explain an important fact about the behavior of bond markets: **Prices and returns for long-term bonds are more volatile than those for shorter-term bonds.** Price changes of +20% and −20% within a year, with corresponding variations in returns, are common for bonds more than 20 years away from maturity.

We now see that changes in interest rates make investments in long-term bonds quite risky. Indeed, the riskiness of an asset's return that results from interest-rate changes is so important that it has been given a special name, **interest-rate risk.** Dealing with interest-rate risk is a major concern of managers of financial institutions and investors, as we will see in later chapters (see also the Mini-Case box "Helping Investors select Desired Interest-Rate Risk").

Although long-term debt instruments have substantial interest-rate risk, short-term debt instruments do not. Indeed, bonds with a maturity that is as short as the holding period have no interest-rate risk.[6] We see this for the coupon bond at the bottom of Table 3.2, which has no uncertainty about the rate of return because it equals the yield to maturity, which is known at the time the bond is purchased. The key to understanding why there is no interest-rate risk for *any* bond whose time to maturity matches the holding period is to recognize that (in this case) the price at the end of the holding period is already fixed at the face value. The change in interest rates can then have no effect on the price at the end of the holding period for these bonds, and the return will therefore be equal to the yield to maturity known at the time the bond is purchased.

Reinvestment Risk

Up to now, we have been assuming that all holding periods are short and equal to the maturity on short-term bonds and are thus not subject to interest-rate risk. However, if an investor's holding period is longer than the term to maturity of the bond, the investor is exposed to a type of interest-rate risk called **reinvestment risk.** Reinvestment risk occurs because the proceeds from the short-term bond need to be reinvested at a future interest rate that is uncertain.

To understand reinvestment risk, suppose that Ravi the investor has a holding period of two years and decides to purchase a ₹1,000 one-year, 10% coupon rate bond at face value and then purchase another one at the end of the first year. If the initial interest rate is 10%, Ravi will have ₹1,100 at the end of the year. If the interest rate on one-year bonds rises to 20% at the end of the year, as in Table 3.2, Ravi will find that buying ₹1,100 worth of another one-year bond will leave him at the end of the second year with ₹1,100 × (1 + 0.20) = ₹1,320. Thus, Ravi's two-year return will be (₹1,320 − ₹1,000)/₹1,000 = 0.32 = 32%, which equals 14.9% at an annual rate. In this case, Ravi has earned more by buying the one-year bonds than if he had initially purchased the two-year bond with an interest rate of 10%. Thus, when Ravi has a holding period that is longer than the term to maturity of the bonds he purchases, he benefits from a rise in interest rates. Conversely, if interest rates on one-year bonds fall to 5% at the end of the year, Ravi will have only ₹1,155 at the end of two years:

---

[6]The statement that there is no interest-rate risk for any bond whose time to maturity matches the holding period is literally true only for discount bonds and zero-coupon bonds that make no intermediate cash payments before the holding period is over. A coupon bond that makes an intermediate cash payment before the holding period is over requires that this payment be reinvested at some future date. Because the interest rate at which this payment can be reinvested is uncertain, there is some uncertainty about the return on this coupon bond even when the time to maturity equals the holding period. However, the riskiness of the return on a coupon bond from reinvesting the coupon payments is typically quite small, and so the basic point that a coupon bond with a time to maturity equaling the holding period has very little risk still holds true.

₹1,100 × (1 + 0.05). Thus, his two-year return will be (₹1,155 − ₹1,000)/₹1,000 = 0.155 = 15.5%, which is 7.2% at an annual rate. With a holding period greater than the term to maturity of the bond, Ravi now loses from a fall in interest rates.

We have thus seen that when the holding period is longer than the term to maturity of a bond, the return is uncertain because the future interest rate when reinvestment occurs is also uncertain—in short, there is reinvestment risk. We also see that if the holding period is longer than the term to maturity of the bond, the investor benefits from a rise in interest rates and is hurt by a fall in interest rates.

Summary

The return on a bond, which tells you how good an investment it has been over the holding period, is equal to the yield to maturity in only one special case: when the holding period and the maturity of the bond are identical. Bonds whose term to

> **MINI-CASE**
>
> ## Helping Investors Select Desired Interest-Rate Risk
>
> Because many investors know how much interest rate risk they are exposed to, some mutual fund companies try to educate investors about the perils of interest-rate risk, as well as to offer investment alternatives that match their investors' preferences.
>
> The UTI Mutual Fund in India , for instance helps investors understand their risk tolerance based on their investment objective, viz. capital preservation, income generation and capital appreciation. Such an objective will further be based on the investor's age and personality. The investment plan will thus adhere to the investor's age, his objective and the personality. Such investment needs can be catered to by options, including bank deposits (savings as well as fixed deposit accounts), Real estate, gold etc., at the same time, mutual funds to address such objectives would include cash funds, debt funds and equity funds.
>
> The Fund advises investors to choose from Aggressive Plans, Moderate Plans and Conservative Plans, based on different combinations of investments in growth schemes, income schemes, money market schemes and balanced schemes.
>
> The Aggressive Plan leans towards more risk and suits investors who are in their prime earning years and are willing to take the risk. It is a plan that renders more growth in a long-term. The Moderate Plan suits investors who wish moderate growth and moderate income, and who desire growth as well as stability. It has a preponderance of balanced schemes. The Conservative Plan suits investors who are retired and wish for capital preservation. It has a preponderance of income schemes.
>
> The below chart depicts an example of the best fund suited for investors desirous of Aggressive Plans.
>
> **Aggressive Plan**
>
> | Fund Name | 1 Year Return in % | 1 Year Rank | 3 Year Return in % | 3 Year Rank | 5 Year Return in % | 5 Year Rank |
> |---|---|---|---|---|---|---|
> | A | 119.59 | 42/219 | 27.7 | 1/162 | 10.30 | 87/96 |
> | B | 12.093 | 40/219 | 24.6 | 2/162 | 13.45 | 43/96 |
> | C | 165.72 | 1/219 | 21.71 | 3/162 | 28.20 | 3/96 |
> | D | 89.02 | 130/219 | 21.48 | 4/162 | 23.25 | 26/96 |
> | E | 113.90 | 58/219 | 21.26 | 5/162 | 26.26 | 17/96 |
>
> Looking at the above chart, Fund C seems to be the most consistent.
>
> Source: http://www.utimf.com/learningcentre/Pages/choosing-the-right-fund.aspx, as accessed on 12 March 2016 at 1.45pm.

maturity is longer than the holding period are subject to interest-rate risk: Changes in interest rates lead to capital gains and losses that produce substantial differences between the return and the yield to maturity known at the time the bond is purchased. Interest-rate risk is especially important for long-term bonds, where the capital gains and losses can be substantial. This is why long-term bonds are not considered to be safe assets with a sure return over short holding periods. Bonds whose term to maturity is shorter than the holding period are also subject to reinvestment risk. Reinvestment risk occurs because the proceeds from the short-term bond need to be reinvested at a future interest rate that is uncertain.

THE PRACTICING MANAGER

Calculating Duration to Measure Interest-Rate Risk

Earlier in our discussion of interest-rate risk, we saw that when interest rates change, a bond with a longer term to maturity has a larger change in its price and hence more interest-rate risk than a bond with a shorter term to maturity. Although this is a useful general fact, in order to measure interest-rate risk, the manager of a financial institution needs more precise information on the actual capital gain or loss that occurs when the interest rate changes by a certain amount. To do this, the manager needs to make use of the concept of **duration,** the average lifetime of a debt security's stream of payments.

The fact that two bonds have the same term to maturity does not mean that they have the same interest-rate risk. A long-term discount bond with 10 years to maturity, a so-called zero-coupon bond, makes all of its payments at the end of the 10 years, whereas a 10% coupon bond with 10 years to maturity makes substantial cash payments before the maturity date. Since the coupon bond makes payments earlier than the zero-coupon bond, we might intuitively guess that the coupon bond's *effective maturity*, the term to maturity that accurately measures interest-rate risk, is shorter than it is for the zero-coupon discount bond.

Indeed, this is exactly what we find in Example 3.8.

EXAMPLE 3.8

Rate of Capital Gain

Calculate the rate of capital gain or loss on a 10-year zero-coupon bond for which the interest rate has increased from 10% to 20%. The bond has a face value of ₹1,000.

> Solution
The rate of capital gain or loss is –49.7%.

$$g = \frac{P_{t+1} - P_t}{P_t}$$

where

$$P_{t+1} = \text{price of the bond one year from now} = \frac{₹1,000}{(1 + 0.20)^9} = ₹193.81$$

$$P_t = \text{price of the bond today} = \frac{₹1,000}{(1 + 0.10)^{10}} = ₹385.54$$

Thus,

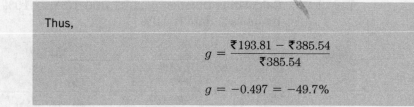

$$g = \frac{₹193.81 - ₹385.54}{₹385.54}$$

$$g = -0.497 = -49.7\%$$

But as we have already calculated in Table 3.2, the capital gain on the 10% 10-year coupon bond is –40.3%. We see that interest-rate risk for the 10-year coupon bond is less than for the 10-year zero-coupon bond, so the effective maturity on the coupon bond (which measures interest-rate risk) is, as expected, shorter than the effective maturity on the zero-coupon bond.

Calculating Duration

To calculate the duration or effective maturity on any debt security, Frederick Macaulay, a researcher at the National Bureau of Economic Research, invented the concept of duration more than half a century ago. Because a zero-coupon bond makes no cash payments before the bond matures, it makes sense to define its effective maturity as equal to its actual term to maturity. Macaulay then realized that he could measure the effective maturity of a coupon bond by recognizing that a coupon bond is equivalent to a set of zero-coupon discount bonds. A 10-year 10% coupon bond with ₹1,000 face value has cash payments identical to the following set of zero-coupon bonds: a ₹100 one-year zero-coupon bond (which pays the equivalent of the ₹100 coupon payment made by the ₹1,000 10-year 10% coupon bond at the end of one year), a ₹100 two-year zero-coupon bond (which pays the equivalent of the ₹100 coupon payment at the end of two years), . . . , a ₹100 10-year zero-coupon bond (which pays the equivalent of the ₹100 coupon payment at the end of 10 years), and a ₹1,000 10-year zero-coupon bond (which pays back the equivalent of the coupon bond's ₹1,000 face value). This set of coupon bonds is shown in the following timeline:

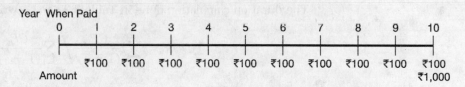

Year When Paid

| 0 | 1 | 2 | 3 | 4 | 5 | 6 | 7 | 8 | 9 | 10 |

Amount: ₹100 ₹100 ₹100 ₹100 ₹100 ₹100 ₹100 ₹100 ₹100 ₹100 / ₹1,000

This same set of coupon bonds is listed in column (2) of Table 3.3, which calculates the duration on the 10-year coupon bond when its interest rate is 10%.

To get the effective maturity of this set of zero-coupon bonds, we would want to sum up the effective maturity of each zero-coupon bond, weighting it by the percentage of the total value of all the bonds that it represents. In other words, the duration of this set of zero-coupon bonds is the weighted average of the effective maturities of the individual zero-coupon bonds, with the weights equaling the proportion of the total value represented by each zero-coupon bond. We do this in several steps in Table 3.3. First we calculate the present value of each of the zero-coupon bonds when the interest rate is 10% in column (3). Then in column (4) we divide each of these present values by ₹1,000, the total present value of the set of zero-coupon bonds, to get the percentage of the total value of all the bonds that

TABLE 3.3 Calculating Duration on a ₹1,000 10-Year 10% Coupon Bond When Its Interest Rate Is 10%

(1) Year	(2) Cash Payments (Zero-Coupon Bonds) (₹)	(3) Present Value (PV) of Cash Payments (i = 10%) (₹)	(4) Weights (% of total PV = PV/₹1,000) (%)	(5) Weighted Maturity (1 × 4)/100 (years)
1	100	90.91	9.091	0.09091
2	100	82.64	8.264	0.16528
3	100	75.13	7.513	0.22539
4	100	68.30	6.830	0.27320
5	100	62.09	6.209	0.31045
6	100	56.44	5.644	0.33864
7	100	51.32	5.132	0.35924
8	100	46.65	4.665	0.37320
9	100	42.41	4.241	0.38169
10	100	38.55	3.855	0.38550
10	1,000	385.54	38.554	3.85500
Total		1,000.00	100.000	6.75850

each bond represents. Note that the sum of the weights in column (4) must total 100%, as shown at the bottom of the column.

To get the effective maturity of the set of zero-coupon bonds, we add up the weighted maturities in column (5) and obtain the figure of 6.76 years. This figure for the effective maturity of the set of zero-coupon bonds is the duration of the 10% 10-year coupon bond because the bond is equivalent to this set of zero-coupon bonds. In short, we see that *duration is a weighted average of the maturities of the cash payments*.

The duration calculation done in Table 3.3 can be written as follows:

$$DUR = \sum_{t=1}^{n} t\frac{CP_t}{(1 + i)^t} \bigg/ \sum_{t=1}^{n} \frac{CP_t}{(1 + i)^t} \qquad (11)$$

where DUR = duration
t = years until cash payment is made
CP_t = cash payment (interest plus principal) at time t
i = interest rate
n = years to maturity of the security

This formula is not as intuitive as the calculation done in Table 3.3, but it does have the advantage that it can easily be programmed into a calculator or computer, making duration calculations very easy.

If we calculate the duration for an 11-year 10% coupon bond when the interest rate is again 10%, we find that it equals 7.14 years, which is greater than the 6.76 years for the 10-year bond. Thus, we have reached the expected conclusion: *All else being equal, the longer the term to maturity of a bond, the longer its duration.*

TABLE 3.4 Calculating Duration on a ₹1,000 10-Year 10% Coupon Bond When Its Interest Rate Is 20%

(1) Year	(2) Cash Payments (Zero-Coupon Bonds) (₹)	(3) Present Value (PV) of Cash Payments (i = 20%) (₹)	(4) Weights (% of total PV = PV/ ₹580.76) (%)	(5) Weighted Maturity (1 × 4)/100 (Years)
1	100	83.33	14.348	0.14348
2	100	69.44	11.957	0.23914
3	100	57.87	9.965	0.29895
4	100	48.23	8.305	0.33220
5	100	40.19	6.920	0.34600
6	100	33.49	5.767	0.34602
7	100	27.91	4.806	0.33642
8	100	23.26	4.005	0.32040
9	100	19.38	3.337	0.30033
10	100	16.15	2.781	0.27810
10	1,000	161.51	27.808	2.78100
Total		580.76	100.000	5.72204

You might think that knowing the maturity of a coupon bond is enough to tell you what its duration is. However, that is not the case. To see this and to give you more practice in calculating duration, in Table 3.4 we again calculate the duration for the 10-year 10% coupon bond, but when the current interest rate is 20% rather than 10% as in Table 3.3. The calculation in Table 3.4 reveals that the duration of the coupon bond at this higher interest rate has fallen from 6.76 years to 5.72 years. The explanation is fairly straightforward. When the interest rate is higher, the cash payments in the future are discounted more heavily and become less important in present-value terms relative to the total present value of all the payments. The relative weight for these cash payments drops as we see in Table 3.4, and so the effective maturity of the bond falls. We have come to an important conclusion: ***All else being equal, when interest rates rise, the duration of a coupon bond falls***.

The duration of a coupon bond is also affected by its coupon rate. For example, consider a 10-year 20% coupon bond when the interest rate is 10%. Using the same procedure, we find that its duration at the higher 20% coupon rate is 5.98 years versus 6.76 years when the coupon rate is 10%. The explanation is that a higher coupon rate means that a relatively greater amount of the cash payments is made earlier in the life of the bond, and so the effective maturity of the bond must fall. We have thus established a third fact about duration: ***All else being equal, the higher the coupon rate on the bond, the shorter the bond's duration***.

One additional fact about duration makes this concept useful when applied to a portfolio of securities. Our examples have shown that duration is equal to the weighted average of the durations of the cash payments (the effective maturities of the corresponding zero-coupon bonds). So if we calculate the duration for two different securities, it should be easy to see that the duration of a portfolio of the two securities is just the weighted average of the durations of the two securities, with the weights reflecting the proportion of the portfolio invested in each.

EXAMPLE 3.9

Duration

A manager of a financial institution is holding 25% of a portfolio in a bond with a five-year duration and 75% in a bond with a 10-year duration. What is the duration of the portfolio?

> Solution

The duration of the portfolio is 8.75 years.

$$(0.25 \times 5) + (0.75 \times 10) = 1.25 + 7.5 = 8.75 \text{ years}$$

We now see that *the duration of a portfolio of securities is the weighted average of the durations of the individual securities, with the weights reflecting the proportion of the portfolio invested in each.* This fact about duration is often referred to as the *additive property of duration*, and it is extremely useful because it means that the duration of a portfolio of securities is easy to calculate from the durations of the individual securities.

To summarize, our calculations of duration for coupon bonds have revealed four facts:

1. The longer the term to maturity of a bond, everything else being equal, the greater its duration.
2. When interest rates rise, everything else being equal, the duration of a coupon bond falls.
3. The higher the coupon rate on the bond, everything else being equal, the shorter the bond's duration.
4. Duration is additive: The duration of a portfolio of securities is the weighted average of the durations of the individual securities, with the weights reflecting the proportion of the portfolio invested in each.

Duration and Interest-Rate Risk

Now that we understand how duration is calculated, we want to see how it can be used by the practicing financial institution manager to measure interest-rate risk. Duration is a particularly useful concept because it provides a good approximation, particularly when interest-rate changes are small, for how much the security price changes for a given change in interest rates, as the following formula indicates:

$$\%\Delta P \approx -DUR \times \frac{\Delta i}{1 + i} \qquad (12)$$

where
$\%\Delta P = (P_{t+1} - P_t)/P_t$ = percentage change in the price of the security from t to $t + 1$ = rate of capital gain.
DUR = duration.
i = interest rate.

EXAMPLE 3.10

Duration and Interest-Rate Risk

A pension fund manager is holding a 10-year 10% coupon bond in the fund's portfolio, and the interest rate is currently 10%. What loss would the fund be exposed to if the interest rate rises to 11% tomorrow?

> Solution

The approximate percentage change in the price of the bond is –6.15%.

As the calculation in Table 3.3 shows, the duration of a 10-year 10% coupon bond is 6.76 years.

$$\%\Delta P \approx -DUR \times \frac{\Delta i}{1 + i}$$

where

DUR = duration $\qquad\qquad$ = 6.76

Δi = change in interest rate = 0.11 − 0.10 = 0.01

i = current interest rate = 0.10

Thus,

$$\%\Delta P \approx -6.76 \times \frac{0.01}{1 + 0.10}$$

$$\%\Delta P \approx -0.0615 = -6.15\%$$

EXAMPLE 3.11

Duration and Interest-Rate Risk

Now the pension manager has the option to hold a 10-year coupon bond with a coupon rate of 20% instead of 10%. As mentioned earlier, the duration for this 20% coupon bond is 5.98 years when the interest rate is 10%. Find the approximate change in the bond price when the interest rate increases from 10% to 11%.

> Solution

This time the approximate change in bond price is −5.4%. This change in bond price is much smaller than for the higher duration coupon bond.

$$\%\Delta P \approx DUR \times \frac{\Delta i}{1 + i}$$

where

DUR = duration $\qquad\qquad$ = 5.98

Δi = change in interest rate = 0.11 − 0.10 = 0.01

i = current interest rate = 0.10

Thus,

$$\%\Delta P \approx -5.98 \times \frac{0.01}{1 + 0.10}$$

$$\%\Delta P \approx -0.054 = -5.4\%$$

The pension fund manager realizes that the interest-rate risk on the 20% coupon bond is less than on the 10% coupon, so he switches the fund out of the 10% coupon bond and into the 20% coupon bond.

Examples 3.10 and 3.11 have led the pension fund manager to an important conclusion about the relationship of duration and interest-rate risk: ***The greater the duration of a security, the greater the percentage change in the market value of the security for a given change in interest rates. Therefore, the greater the duration of a security, the greater its interest-rate risk***.

This reasoning applies equally to a portfolio of securities. So by calculating the duration of the fund's portfolio of securities using the methods outlined here, a pension fund manager can easily ascertain the amount of interest-rate risk the entire fund is exposed to. As we will see in Chapter 23, duration is a highly useful concept for the management of interest-rate risk that is widely used by managers of banks and other financial institutions.

SUMMARY

1. The yield to maturity, which is the measure most accurately reflecting the interest rate, is the interest rate that equates the present value of future cash flows of a debt instrument with its value today. Application of this principle reveals that bond prices and interest rates are negatively related: When the interest rate rises, the price of the bond must fall, and vice versa.

2. The real interest rate is defined as the nominal interest rate minus the expected rate of inflation. It is both a better measure of the incentives to borrow and lend and a more accurate indicator of the tightness of credit market conditions than the nominal interest rate.

3. The return on a security, which tells you how well you have done by holding this security over a stated period of time, can differ substantially from the interest rate as measured by the yield to maturity. Long-term bond prices have substantial fluctuations when interest rates change and thus bear interest-rate risk. The resulting capital gains and losses can be large, which is why long-term bonds are not considered to be safe assets with a sure return. Bonds whose maturity is shorter than the holding period are also subject to reinvestment risk, which occurs because the proceeds from the short-term bond need to be reinvested at a future interest rate that is uncertain.

4. Duration, the average lifetime of a debt security's stream of payments, is a measure of effective maturity, the term to maturity that accurately measures interest-rate risk. Everything else being equal, the duration of a bond is greater the longer the maturity of a bond, when interest rates fall, or when the coupon rate of a coupon bond falls. Duration is additive: The duration of a portfolio of securities is the weighted average of the durations of the individual securities, with the weights reflecting the proportion of the portfolio invested in each. The greater the duration of a security, the greater the percentage change in the market value of the security for a given change in interest rates. Therefore, the greater the duration of a security, the greater its interest-rate risk.

KEY TERMS

cash flows, p. 37
coupon bond, p. 39
coupon rate, p. 39
current yield, p. 46
discount bond (zero-coupon bond), p. 39
duration, p. 56

face value (par value), p. 39
fixed-payment loan (fully amortized loan), p. 39
interest-rate risk, p. 54
nominal interest rate, p. 47
perpetuity (consol), p. 44
present value (present discounted value), p. 37

rate of capital gain, p. 52
real interest rate, p. 47
real terms, p. 48
reinvestment risk, p. 54
return (rate of return), p. 49
simple loan, p. 37
yield to maturity, p. 40

QUESTIONS

1. Write down the formula that is used to calculate the yield to maturity on a 20-year 10% coupon bond with ₹1,000 face value that sells for ₹2,000.

2. If there is a decline in interest rates, which would you rather be holding, long-term bonds or short-term bonds? Why? Which type of bond has the greater interest-rate risk?

3. A financial adviser has just given you the following advice: "Long-term bonds are a great investment because their interest rate is over 20%." Is the financial adviser necessarily right?

4. If mortgage rates rise from 5% to 10%, but the expected rate of increase in housing prices rises from 2% to 9%, are people more or less likely to buy houses?

QUANTITATIVE PROBLEMS

1. Calculate the present value of a ₹1,000 zero-coupon bond with five years to maturity if the yield to maturity is 6%.

2. A lottery claims its grand prize is ₹10 million, payable over 20 years at ₹500,000 per year. If the first payment is made immediately, what is this grand prize really worth? Use an interest rate of 6%.

3. Consider a bond with a 7% annual coupon and a face value of ₹1,000. Complete the following table.

Years to Maturity	Yield to Maturity	Current Price
3	5	
3	7	
6	7	
9	7	
9	9	

What relationships do you observe between maturity and discount rate and the current price?

4. Consider a coupon bond that has a ₹1,000 par value and a coupon rate of 10%. The bond is currently selling for ₹1,150 and has eight years to maturity. What is the bond's yield to maturity?

5. You are willing to pay ₹15,625 now to purchase a perpetuity that will pay you and your heirs ₹1,250 each year, forever, starting at the end of this year. If your required rate of return does not change, how much would you be willing to pay if this were a 20-year, annual payment, ordinary annuity instead of a perpetuity?

6. What is the price of a perpetuity that has a coupon of ₹50 per year and a yield to maturity of 2.5%? If the yield to maturity doubles, what will happen to its price?

7. Property taxes in DeKalb County are roughly 2.66% of the purchase price every year. If you just bought a ₹100,000 home, what is the *PV* of all the future property tax payments? Assume that the house remains worth ₹100,000 forever, property tax rates never change, and that a 9% interest rate is used for discounting.

8. Assume you just deposited ₹1,000 into a bank account. The current real interest rate is 2%, and inflation is expected to be 6% over the next year. What nominal rate would you require from the bank over the next year? How much money will you have at the end of one year? If you are saving to buy a stereo that currently sells for ₹1,050, will you have enough to buy it?

9. A 10-year, 7% coupon bond with a face value of ₹1,000 is currently selling for ₹871.65. Compute your rate of return if you sell the bond next year for ₹880.10.

10. You have paid ₹980.30 for an 8% coupon bond with a face value of ₹1,000 that matures in five years. You plan on holding the bond for one year. If you want to earn a 9% rate of return on this investment, what price must you sell the bond for? Is this realistic?

11. Calculate the duration of a ₹1,000, 6% coupon bond with three years to maturity. Assume that all market interest rates are 7%.

12. Consider the bond in the previous question. Calculate the expected price change if interest rates drop to 6.75% using the duration approximation. Calculate the actual price change using discounted cash flow.

13. The duration of a ₹100 million portfolio is 10 years. ₹40 million in new securities are added to the portfolio, increasing the duration of the portfolio to 12.5 years. What is the duration of the ₹40 million in new securities?

14. A bank has two 3-year commercial loans with a present value of ₹70 million. The first is a ₹30 million loan that requires a single payment of ₹37.8 million in three years, with no other payments till then. The second loan is for ₹40 million. It requires an annual interest payment of ₹3.6 million. The principal of ₹40 million is due in three years.

a. What is the duration of the bank's commercial loan portfolio?

b. What will happen to the value of its portfolio if the general level of interest rates increases from 8% to 8.5%?

15. Consider a bond that promises the following cash flows. The yield to maturity is 12%.

Year	0	1	2	3	4
Promised Payments	160	160	170	180	230

You plan to buy this bond, hold it for 2.5 years, and then sell the bond.

a. What total cash will you receive from the bond after the 2.5 years? Assume that periodic cash flows are reinvested at 12%.

b. If immediately after you buy this bond all market interest rates drop to 11% (including your reinvestment rate), what will be the impact on your total cash flow after 2.5 years? How does this compare to part (a)?

c. Assuming all market interest rates are 12%, what is the duration of this bond?

Understanding Interest Rates

1. Investigate the data available from the Reserve Bank of India database at **http://dbie.rbi.org.in/ DBIE/dbie.rbi?site=publications**. (Enter the RBI website at rbi.org.in and choose 'Statistics'. Under Statistics, choose 'Database on the Indian Economy'. Choose 'Time Series Publications', then choose 'Ratios and Rates'. You can view the key ratios and rates in the Indian context on a weekly basis).

Then answer the following questions:

a. Prepare a chart to understand how the interest rates on 91-day, 182-day, 364-day Treasury bill yields have moved over the last 10 weeks.

b. What has been the movement in the 10-year government securities yield over the same period?

c. For the same period, plot the term deposit rates (> 1year) and Base rates of banks.

4

Why Do Interest Rates Change?

> PREVIEW

In this chapter we examine why the overall level of *nominal* interest rates (which we refer to simply as "interest rates") changes and the factors that influence their behavior. We learned in Chapter 3 that interest rates are negatively related to the price of bonds, so if we can explain why bond prices change, we can also explain why interest rates fluctuate. Here we will apply supply-and-demand analysis to examine how bond prices and interest rates change.

Determinants of Asset Demand

An **asset** is a piece of property that is a store of value. Items such as money, bonds, stocks, art, land, houses, farm equipment, and manufacturing machinery are all assets. Facing the question of whether to buy and hold an asset or whether to buy one asset rather than another, an individual must consider the following factors:

1. **Wealth**, the total resources owned by the individual, including all assets
2. **Expected return** (the return expected over the next period) on one asset relative to alternative assets
3. **Risk** (the degree of uncertainty associated with the return) on one asset relative to alternative assets
4. **Liquidity** (the ease and speed with which an asset can be turned into cash) relative to alternative assets

Wealth

When we find that our wealth has increased, we have more resources available with which to purchase assets and so, not surprisingly, the quantity of assets we demand increases.[1] Therefore, the effect of changes in wealth on the quantity demanded of an asset can be summarized as follows: ***Holding everything else constant, an increase in wealth raises the quantity demanded of an asset.***

Expected Returns

In Chapter 3 we saw that the return on an asset (such as a bond) measures how much we gain from holding that asset. When we make a decision to buy an asset, we are influenced by what we expect the return on that asset to be. If an Exxon-Mobil bond, for example, has a return of 15% half of the time and 5% the other half, its expected return (which you can think of as the average return) is 10%. More formally, the expected return on an asset is the weighted average of all possible returns, where the weights are the probabilities of occurrence of that return:

$$R^e = p_1 R_1 + p_2 R_2 + \ldots + p_n R_n \tag{1}$$

where

R^e = expected return
n = number of possible outcomes (states of nature)
R_i = return in the ith state of nature
p_i = probability of occurrence of the return R_i

---

[1]Although it is possible that some assets (called *inferior assets*) might have the property that the quantity demanded does not increase as wealth increases, such assets are rare. Hence we will always assume that demand for an asset increases as wealth increases.

EXAMPLE 4.1

Expected Return

What is the expected return on the Exxon-Mobil bond if the return is 12% two-thirds of the time and 8% one-third of the time?

> Solution

The expected return is 10.68%.

$$R^e = p_1R_1 + p_2R_2$$

where

p_1 = probability of occurrence of return 1 $= \frac{2}{3} = 0.67$

R_1 = return in state 1 $= 12\% = 0.12$

p_2 = probability of occurrence return 2 $= \frac{1}{3} = 0.33$

R_2 = return in state 2 $= 8\% = 0.08$

Thus,

$$R^e = (.67)(0.12) + (.33)(0.08) = 0.1068 \doteq 10.68\%$$

If the expected return on the Exxon-Mobil bond rises relative to expected returns on alternative assets, holding everything else constant, then it becomes more desirable to purchase it, and the quantity demanded increases. This can occur in either of two ways: (1) when the expected return on the Exxon-Mobil bond rises while the return on an alternative asset—say, stock in IBM—remains unchanged or (2) when the return on the alternative asset, the IBM stock, falls while the return on the Exxon-Mobil bond remains unchanged. To summarize, *an increase in an asset's expected return relative to that of an alternative asset, holding everything else unchanged, raises the quantity demanded of the asset.*

Risk

The degree of risk or uncertainty of an asset's returns also affects demand for the asset. Consider two assets, stock in Fly-by-Night Airlines and stock in Feet-on-the-Ground Bus Company. Suppose that Fly-by-Night stock has a return of 15% half of the time and 5% the other half of the time, making its expected return 10%, while stock in Feet-on-the-Ground has a fixed return of 10%. Fly-by-Night stock has uncertainty associated with its returns and so has greater risk than stock in Feet-on-the-Ground, whose return is a sure thing.

To see this more formally, we can use a measure of risk called the **standard deviation.** The standard deviation of returns on an asset is calculated as follows. First you need to calculate the expected return, R^e; then you subtract the expected return from each return to get a deviation; then you square each deviation and multiply it by the probability of occurrence of that outcome; finally, you add up all these weighted squared deviations and take the square root. The formula for the standard deviation, σ, is thus:

$$\sigma = \sqrt{p_1(R_1 - R^e)^2 + p_2(R_2 - R^e)^2 + \ldots + p_n(R_n - R^e)^2} \qquad (2)$$

The higher the standard deviation, σ, the greater the risk of an asset.

EXAMPLE 4.2

Standard Deviation

What is the standard deviation of the returns on the Fly-by-Night Airlines stock and Feet-on-the Ground Bus Company, with the same return outcomes and probabilities described above? Of these two stocks, which is riskier?

> **Solution**

Fly-by-Night Airlines has a standard deviation of returns of 5%.

$$\sigma = \sqrt{p_1(R_1 - R^e)^2 + p_2(R_2 - R^e)^2}$$
$$R^e = p_1R_1 + p_2R_2$$

where

p_1 = probability of occurrence of return 1 $= \frac{1}{2} = 0.50$

R_1 = return in state 1 $= 15\% = 0.15$

p_2 = probability of occurrence of return 2 $= \frac{1}{2} = 0.50$

R_2 = return in state 2 $= 5\% = 0.05$

R^e = expected return $= (.50)(0.15) + (.50)(0.05) = 0.10$

Thus,

$$\sigma = \sqrt{(.50)(0.15 - 0.10)^2 + (.50)(0.05 - 0.10)^2}$$
$$\sigma = \sqrt{(.50)(0.0025) + (.50)(0.0025)} = \sqrt{0.0025} = 0.05 = 5\%$$

Feet-on-the-Ground Bus Company has a standard deviation of returns of 0%.

$$\sigma = \sqrt{p_1(R_1 - R^e)^2}$$
$$R^e = p_1R_1$$

where

p_1 = probability of occurrence of return 1 $= 1.0$

R_1 = return in state 1 $= 10\% = 0.10$

R^e = expected return $= (1.0)(0.10) = 0.10$

Thus,

$$\sigma = \sqrt{(1.0)(0.10 - 0.10)^2}$$
$$= \sqrt{0} = 0 = 0\%$$

Clearly, Fly-by-Night Airlines is a riskier stock because its standard deviation of returns of 5% is higher than the zero standard deviation of returns for Feet-on-the-Ground Bus Company, which has a certain return.

A *risk-averse* person prefers stock in the Feet-on-the-Ground (the sure thing) to Fly-by-Night stock (the riskier asset), even though the stocks have the same expected return, 10%. By contrast, a person who prefers risk is a *risk preferer* or *risk lover*. Most people are risk-averse, especially in their financial decisions: Everything else being equal, they prefer to hold the less risky asset. Hence, ***holding*** *everything else constant, if an asset's risk rises relative to that of alternative assets, its quantity demanded will fall.*[2]

Liquidity

Another factor that affects the demand for an asset is how quickly it can be converted into cash at low cost—its liquidity. An asset is liquid if the market in which it is traded has depth and breadth, that is, if the market has many buyers and sellers. A house is not a very liquid asset because it may be hard to find a buyer quickly; if a house must be sold to pay off bills, it might have to be sold for a much lower price. And the transaction costs in selling a house (broker's commissions, lawyer's fees, and so on) are substantial. A Government of India Treasury bill, by contrast, is a highly liquid asset. It can be sold in a well-organized market with many buyers, so it can be sold quickly at low cost. *The more liquid an asset is relative to alternative assets, holding everything else unchanged, the more desirable it is, and the greater will be the quantity demanded.*

Theory of Portfolio Choice

All the determining factors we have just discussed can be assembled into the **theory of portfolio choice,** which tells us how much of an asset people want to hold in their portfolio. It states that, holding all the other factors constant:

1. The quantity demanded of an asset is usually positively related to wealth, with the response being greater if the asset is a luxury than if it is a necessity.
2. The quantity demanded of an asset is positively related to its expected return relative to alternative assets.
3. The quantity demanded of an asset is negatively related to the risk of its returns relative to alternative assets.
4. The quantity demanded of an asset is positively related to its liquidity relative to alternative assets.

These results are summarized in Table 4.1.

Supply and Demand in the Bond Market

We approach the analysis of interest-rate determination by studying the supply of and demand for bonds. Because interest rates on different securities tend to move together, in this chapter we will act as if there is only one type of security and a single interest rate in the entire economy. In Chapter 5, we will expand our analysis to look at why interest rates on different securities differ.

The first step is to use the analysis to obtain a **demand curve,** which shows the relationship between the quantity demanded and the price when all other economic variables are held constant (that is, values of other variables are taken as

---

[2]Diversification, the holding of many risky assets in a portfolio, reduces the overall risk an investor faces. If you are interested in how diversification lowers risk and what effect this has on the price of an asset, you can look at an appendix to this chapter that describes models of asset pricing and is on the book's Web site at http://www.pearsoned.co.in/FredericSMishkin/.

TABLE 4.1   **Response of the Quantity of an Asset Demanded to**
SUMMARY   **Changes in Wealth, Expected Returns, Risk, and Liquidity**

Variable	Change in Variable	Change in Quantity Demanded
Wealth	↑	↑
Expected return relative to other assets	↑	↑
Risk relative to other assets	↑	↓
Liquidity relative to other assets	↑	↑

Note: Only increases in the variables are shown. The effect of decreases in the variables on the change in quantity demanded would be the opposite of those indicated in the far-right column.

given). You may recall from previous finance and economics courses that the assumption that all other economic variables are held constant is called *ceteris paribus*, which means "other things being equal" in Latin.

Demand Curve

To clarify our analysis, let's consider the demand for one-year discount bonds, which make no coupon payments but pay the owner the ₹1,000 face value in a year. If the holding period is one year, then as we have seen in Chapter 3, the return on the bonds is known absolutely and is equal to the interest rate as measured by the yield to maturity. This means that the expected return on this bond is equal to the interest rate i, which, using Equation 6 in Chapter 3, is

$$i = R^e = \frac{F - P}{P}$$

where
i = interest rate = yield to maturity
R^e = expected return
F = face value of the discount bond
P = initial purchase price of the discount bond

This formula shows that a particular value of the interest rate corresponds to each bond price. If the bond sells for ₹950, the interest rate and expected return are

$$\frac{₹1,000 - ₹950}{₹950} = 0.053 = 5.3\%$$

At this 5.3% interest rate and expected return corresponding to a bond price of ₹950, let us assume that the quantity of bonds demanded is ₹100 billion, which is plotted as point A in Figure 4.1.

At a price of ₹900, the interest rate and expected return are

$$\frac{₹1,000 - ₹900}{₹900} = 0.111 = 11.1\%$$

Because the expected return on these bonds is higher, with all other economic variables (such as income, expected returns on other assets, risk, and liquidity) held

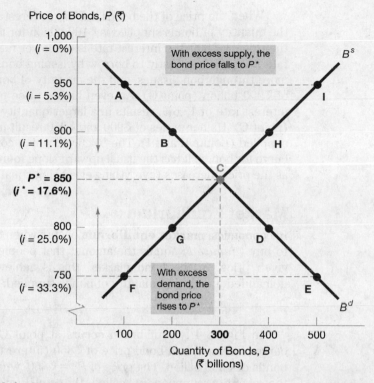

FIGURE 4.1 Supply and Demand for Bonds

Equilibrium in the bond market occurs at point C, the intersection of the demand curve B^d and the bond supply curve B^s. The equilibrium price is $P^* = ₹850$, and the equilibrium interest rate is $i^* = 17.6\%$.

constant, the quantity demanded of bonds will be higher as predicted by the theory of portfolio choice. Point B in Figure 4.1 shows that the quantity of bonds demanded at the price of ₹900 has risen to ₹200 billion. Continuing with this reasoning, we see that if the bond price is ₹850 (interest rate and expected return = 17.6%), the quantity of bonds demanded (point C) will be greater than at point B. Similarly, at the lower prices of ₹800 (interest rate = 25%) and ₹750 (interest rate = 33.3%), the quantity of bonds demanded will be even higher (points D and E). The curve B^d, which connects these points, is the demand curve for bonds. It has the usual downward slope, indicating that at lower prices of the bond (everything else being equal), the quantity demanded is higher.[3]

Supply Curve

An important assumption behind the demand curve for bonds in Figure 4.1 is that all other economic variables besides the bond's price and interest rate are held constant. We use the same assumption in deriving a **supply curve,** which shows the relationship between the quantity supplied and the price when all other economic variables are held constant.

---

[3]Although our analysis indicates that the demand curve slopes downward, it does not imply that the curve is a straight line. For ease of exposition, however, we will draw demand curves and supply curves as straight lines.

When the price of the bonds is ₹750 (interest rate = 33.3%), point F shows that the quantity of bonds supplied is ₹100 billion for the example we are considering. If the price is ₹800, the interest rate is the lower rate of 25%. Because at this interest rate it is now less costly to borrow by issuing bonds, firms will be willing to borrow more through bond issues, and the quantity of bonds supplied is at the higher level of ₹200 billion (point G). An even higher price of ₹850, corresponding to a lower interest rate of 17.6%, results in a larger quantity of bonds supplied of ₹300 billion (point C). Higher prices of ₹900 and ₹950 result in even greater quantities of bonds supplied (points H and I). The B^s curve, which connects these points, is the supply curve for bonds. It has the usual upward slope found in supply curves, indicating that as the price increases (everything else being equal), the quantity supplied increases.

Market Equilibrium

In economics, **market equilibrium** occurs when the amount that people are willing to buy (*demand*) equals the amount that people are willing to sell (*supply*) at a given price. In the bond market, this is achieved when the quantity of bonds demanded equals the quantity of bonds supplied:

$$B^d = B^s \tag{3}$$

In Figure 4.1, equilibrium occurs at point C, where the demand and supply curves intersect at a bond price of ₹850 (interest rate of 17.6%) and a quantity of bonds of ₹300 billion. The price of $P^* = ₹850$, where the quantity demanded equals the quantity supplied, is called the *equilibrium*, or *market-clearing*, price. Similarly, the interest rate of $i^* = 17.6\%$ that corresponds to this price is called the equilibrium, or market-clearing, interest rate.

The concepts of market equilibrium and equilibrium price or interest rate are useful because the market tends to head toward them. We can see that it does in Figure 4.1 by first looking at what happens when we have a bond price that is above the equilibrium price. When the price of bonds is set too high, at, say, ₹950, the quantity of bonds supplied at point I is greater than the quantity of bonds demanded at point A. A situation like this, in which the quantity of bonds supplied exceeds the quantity of bonds demanded, is called a condition of **excess supply.** Because people want to sell more bonds than others want to buy, the price of the bonds will fall, which is why the downward arrow is drawn in the figure at the bond price of ₹950. As long as the bond price remains above the equilibrium price, an excess supply of bonds will continue to be available, and the price will continue to fall. This decline will stop only when the price has reached the equilibrium price of ₹850, where the excess supply of bonds has been eliminated.

Now let's look at what happens when the price of bonds is below the equilibrium price. If the price of the bonds is set too low, at, say, ₹750, the quantity demanded at point E is greater than the quantity supplied at point F. This is called a condition of **excess demand.** People now want to buy more bonds than others are willing to sell, so the price of bonds will be driven up, as illustrated by the upward arrow drawn in the figure at the bond price of ₹750. Only when the excess demand for bonds is eliminated by the price rising to the equilibrium level of ₹850 is there no further tendency for the price to rise.

We can see that the concept of equilibrium price is a useful one because it indicates where the market will settle. Because each price on the vertical axis of Figure 4.1 corresponds to a particular value of the interest rate, the same diagram also shows that the interest rate will head toward the equilibrium interest rate of 17.6%. When the interest rate is below the equilibrium interest rate, as it is when it is at 5.3%, the price of the bond is above the equilibrium price, and an excess supply of bonds will result. The price of the bond then falls, leading to a rise in the interest rate toward the equilibrium level. Similarly, when the interest rate is above the equilibrium level, as it is when it is at 33.3%, an excess demand for bonds occurs, and the bond price will rise, driving the interest rate back down to the equilibrium level of 17.6%.

Supply-and-Demand Analysis

Our Figure 4.1 is a conventional supply-and-demand diagram with price on the vertical axis and quantity on the horizontal axis. Because the interest rate that corresponds to each bond price is also marked on the vertical axis, this diagram allows us to read the equilibrium interest rate, giving us a model that describes the determination of interest rates. It is important to recognize that a supply-and-demand diagram like Figure 4.1 can be drawn for *any type* of bond because the interest rate and price of a bond are *always* negatively related for all kinds of bond, whether a discount bond or a coupon bond.

An important feature of the analysis here is that supply and demand are always in terms of *stocks* (amounts at a given point in time) of assets, not in terms of *flows*. The **asset market approach** to understanding behavior in financial markets—which emphasizes stocks of assets rather than flows in determining asset prices—is the dominant methodology used by economists because correctly conducting analyses in terms of flows is very tricky, especially when we encounter inflation.[4]

Changes in Equilibrium Interest Rates

We will now use the supply-and-demand framework for bonds to analyze why interest rates change. To avoid confusion, it is important to make the distinction between *movements along* a demand (or supply) curve and *shifts in* a demand (or supply) curve. When quantity demanded (or supplied) changes as a result of a change in the price of the bond (or, equivalently, a change in the interest rate), we have a *movement along* the demand (or supply) curve. The change in the quantity demanded when we move from point A to B to C in Figure 4.1, for example, is a movement along a demand curve. A *shift in* the demand (or supply) curve, by contrast, occurs when the quantity demanded (or supplied) changes *at each given price (or interest rate)* of the bond in response to a change in some other factor besides the bond's price or interest rate. When one of these factors changes, causing a shift in the demand or supply curve, there will be a new equilibrium value for the interest rate.

In the following pages, we will look at how the supply and demand curves shift in response to changes in variables, such as expected inflation and wealth, and what effects these changes have on the equilibrium value of interest rates.

---

[4]The asset market approach developed in the text is useful in understanding not only how interest rates behave but also how any asset price is determined. A second appendix to this chapter, which is on this book's Web site at http://www.pearsoned.co.in/FredericSMishkin/, shows how the asset market approach can be applied to understanding the behavior of commodity markets, and in particular, the gold market. The analysis of the bond market that we have developed here has another interpretation that uses a different terminology and framework involving the supply and demand for loanable funds. This loanable funds framework is discussed in a third appendix to this chapter, which is also on the book's Web site.

Shifts in the Demand for Bonds

The theory of portfolio choice which we developed at the beginning of the chapter provides a framework for deciding which factors cause the demand curve for bonds to shift. These factors include changes in four parameters:

1. Wealth
2. Expected returns on bonds relative to alternative assets
3. Risk of bonds relative to alternative assets
4. Liquidity of bonds relative to alternative assets

To see how a change in each of these factors (holding all other factors constant) can shift the demand curve, let's look at some examples. (As a study aid, Table 4.2 summarizes the effects of changes in these factors on the bond demand curve.)

Wealth   When the economy is growing rapidly in a business cycle expansion and wealth is increasing, the quantity of bonds demanded at each bond price (or interest rate) increases, as shown in Figure 4.2. To see how this works, consider point B on the initial demand curve for bonds B_1^d. With higher wealth, the quantity of bonds demanded at the same price must rise, to point B′. Similarly, for point D the higher wealth causes the quantity demanded at the same bond price to rise to point D′. Continuing with this reasoning for every point on the initial demand curve B_1^d, we can see that the demand curve shifts to the right from B_1^d to B_2^d as is indicated by the arrows.

The conclusion we have reached is that *in a business cycle expansion with growing wealth, the demand for bonds rises and the demand curve for bonds shifts to the right.* With the same reasoning applied, *in a recession, when income and wealth are falling, the demand for bonds falls, and the demand curve shifts to the left.*

Another factor that affects wealth is the public's propensity to save. If households save more, wealth increases and, as we have seen, the demand for bonds rises and the demand curve for bonds shifts to the right. Conversely, if people save less, wealth and the demand for bonds will fall and the demand curve shifts to the left.

Expected Returns   For a one-year discount bond and a one-year holding period, the expected return and the interest rate are identical, so nothing besides today's interest rate affects the expected return.

For bonds with maturities of greater than one year, the expected return may differ from the interest rate. For example, we saw in Chapter 3, Table 3.2, that a rise in the interest rate on a long-term bond from 10% to 20% would lead to a sharp decline in price and a very large negative return. Hence, if people began to think that interest rates would be higher next year than they had originally anticipated, the expected return today on long-term bonds would fall, and the quantity demanded would fall at each interest rate. *Higher expected interest rates in the future lower the expected return for long-term bonds, decrease the demand, and shift the demand curve to the left.*

By contrast, a revision downward of expectations of future interest rates would mean that long-term bond prices would be expected to rise more than originally anticipated, and the resulting higher expected return today would raise the quantity demanded at each bond price and interest rate. *Lower expected interest rates in the future increase the demand for long-term bonds and shift the demand curve to the right* (as in Figure 4.2).

TABLE 4.2 **Factors That Shift the Demand Curve for Bonds**
SUMMARY

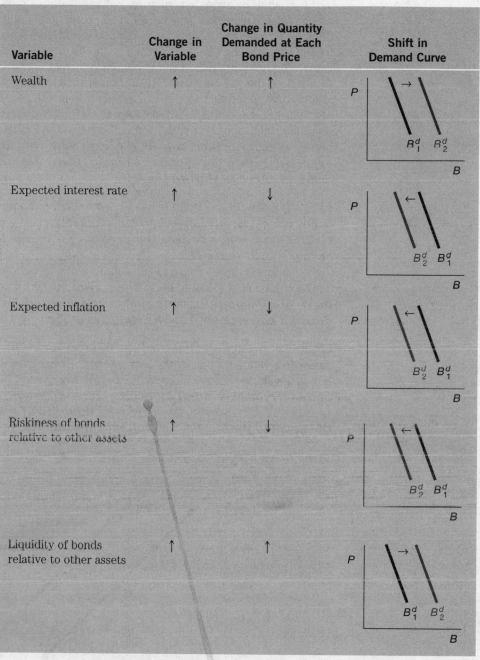

Variable	Change in Variable	Change in Quantity Demanded at Each Bond Price	Shift in Demand Curve
Wealth	↑	↑	
Expected interest rate	↑	↓	
Expected inflation	↑	↓	
Riskiness of bonds relative to other assets	↑	↓	
Liquidity of bonds relative to other assets	↑	↑	

Note: Only increases in the variables are shown. The effect of decreases in the variables on the change in demand would be the opposite of those indicated in the remaining columns.

Changes in expected returns on other assets can also shift the demand curve for bonds. If people suddenly became more optimistic about the stock market and began to expect higher stock prices in the future, both expected capital gains and expected returns on stocks would rise. With the expected return on bonds held constant, the expected return on bonds today relative to stocks would fall, lowering the demand for bonds and shifting the demand curve to the left.

A change in expected inflation is likely to alter expected returns on physical assets (also called *real assets*) such as automobiles and houses, which affect the demand for bonds. An increase in expected inflation, say, from 5% to 10%, will lead to higher prices on cars and houses in the future and hence higher nominal capital gains. The resulting rise in the expected returns today on these real assets will lead to a fall in the expected return on bonds relative to the expected return on real assets today and thus cause the demand for bonds to fall. Alternatively, we can think of the rise in expected inflation as lowering the real interest rate on bonds, and the resulting decline in the relative expected return on bonds will cause the demand for bonds to fall. *An increase in the expected rate of inflation lowers the expected return for bonds, causing their demand to decline and the demand curve to shift to the left.*

Risk   If prices in the bond market become more volatile, the risk associated with bonds increases, and bonds become a less attractive asset. *An increase in the riskiness of bonds causes the demand for bonds to fall and the demand curve to shift to the left.*

Conversely, an increase in the volatility of prices in another asset market, such as the stock market, would make bonds more attractive. *An increase in the riskiness of alternative assets causes the demand for bonds to rise and the demand curve to shift to the right* (as in Figure 4.2).

Liquidity   If more people started trading in the bond market, and as a result it became easier to sell bonds quickly, the increase in their liquidity would cause the quantity of bonds demanded at each interest rate to rise. *Increased liquidity of bonds results in an increased demand for bonds, and the demand curve shifts to the right* (see Figure 4.2). *Similarly, increased liquidity of alternative assets lowers the demand for bonds and shifts the demand curve to the left.*

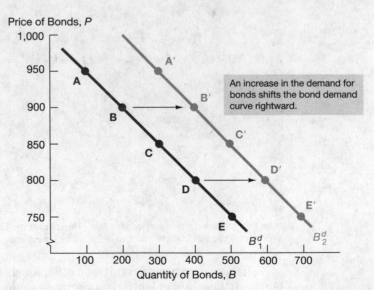

FIGURE 4.2 Shift in the Demand Curve for Bonds
When the demand for bonds increases, the demand curve shifts to the right as shown.

Shifts in the Supply of Bonds

Certain factors can cause the supply curve for bonds to shift. Among these are:

1. Expected profitability of investment opportunities
2. Expected inflation
3. Government budget

We will look at how the supply curve shifts when each of these factors changes (all others remaining constant). (As a study aid, Table 4.3 summarizes the effects of changes in these factors on the bond supply curve.)

Expected Profitability of Investment Opportunities   The more profitable plant and equipment investments that a firm expects it can make, the more willing it will be to borrow to finance these investments. When the economy is growing rapidly, as in a business cycle expansion, investment opportunities that are expected to be profitable abound, and the quantity of bonds supplied at any given bond price will increase (see Figure 4.3). ***Therefore, in a business cycle expansion, the supply of bonds increases, and the supply curve shifts to the right. Likewise, in a***

TABLE 4.3   Factors That Shift the Supply of Bonds
SUMMARY

Variable	Change in Variable	Change in Quantity Supplied at Each Bond Price	Shift in Supply Curve
Profitability of investments	↑	↑	
Expected inflation	↑	↑	
Government deficit	↑	↑	

Note: Only increases in the variables are shown. The effect of decreases in the variables on the change in supply would be the opposite of those indicated in the remaining columns.

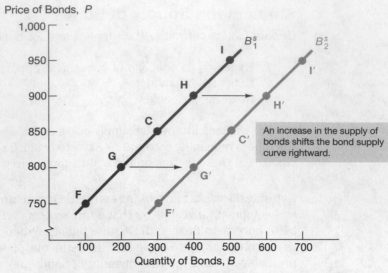

FIGURE 4.3 Shift in the Supply Curve for Bonds

When the supply of bonds increases, the supply curve shifts to the right.

recession, when far fewer profitable investment opportunities are expected, the supply of bonds falls, and the supply curve shifts to the left.

Expected Inflation As we saw in Chapter 3, the real cost of borrowing is more accurately measured by the real interest rate, which equals the (nominal) interest rate minus the expected inflation rate. For a given interest rate (and bond price), when expected inflation increases, the real cost of borrowing falls; hence the quantity of bonds supplied increases at any given bond price. *An increase in expected inflation causes the supply of bonds to increase and the supply curve to shift to the right* (see Figure 4.3).

Government Budget The activities of the government can influence the supply of bonds in several ways. The Government of India issues bonds to finance government deficits, the gap between the government's expenditures and its revenues. When these deficits are large, the Government of India sells more bonds, and the quantity of bonds supplied at each bond price increases. *Higher government deficits increase the supply of bonds and shift the supply curve to the right* (see Figure 4.3). *On the other hand, government surpluses, decrease the supply of bonds and shift the supply curve to the left.*

State and local governments and other government agencies also issue bonds to finance their expenditures, and this can affect the supply of bonds as well. We now can use our knowledge of how supply-and-demand curves shift to analyze how the equilibrium interest rate can change. The best way to do this is to pursue several case applications. In going through these applications, keep two things in mind:

1. When you examine the effect of a variable change, remember we are assuming that all other variables are unchanged; that is, we are making use of the *ceteris paribus* assumption.

2. Remember that the interest rate is negatively related to the bond price, so when the equilibrium bond price rises, the equilibrium interest rate falls. Conversely, if the equilibrium bond price moves downward, the equilibrium interest rate rises.

CASE

Changes in the Interest Rate Due to Expected Inflation: The Fisher Effect

☁ **GO ONLINE**

https://www.rbi.org.in/
Scripts/PublicationsView.
aspx?id=16679
https://www.rbi.org.in/
Scripts/PublicationsView.
aspx?id=16680

Historical information for inflation can be accessed from RBI websites. Till 2012, India measured inflation using the Wholesale Price Index (WPI). The Consumer Price Index Industrial Workers (CPI-IW) may be used as a proxy for inflation as well.

We have already done most of the work to evaluate how a change in expected inflation affects the nominal interest rate, in that we have already analyzed how a change in expected inflation shifts the supply and demand curves. Figure 4.4 shows the effect of an increase in expected inflation on the equilibrium interest rate.

Suppose that expected inflation is initially 5% and the initial supply and demand curves B_1^s and B_1^d intersect at point 1, where the equilibrium bond price is P_1. If expected inflation rises to 10%, the expected return on bonds relative to real assets falls for any given bond price and interest rate. As a result, the demand for bonds falls, and the demand curve shifts to the left from B_1^d to B_2^d. The rise in expected inflation also shifts the supply curve. At any given bond price and interest rate, the real cost of borrowing has declined, causing the quantity of bonds supplied to increase, and the supply curve shifts to the right, from B_1^s to B_2^s.

When the demand and supply curves shift in response to the change in expected inflation, the equilibrium moves from point 1 to point 2, the intersection of B_2^d and B_2^s. The equilibrium bond price has fallen from P_1 to P_2, and because the bond price is negatively related to the interest rate, this means that the interest rate has risen. Note that Figure 4.4 has been drawn so that the equilibrium quantity of bonds remains the same for both point 1 and point 2. However, depending on the size of the shifts in the supply and demand curves, the equilibrium quantity of bonds could either rise or fall when expected inflation rises.

Our supply-and-demand analysis has led us to an important observation: **When expected inflation rises, interest rates will rise.** This result has been named

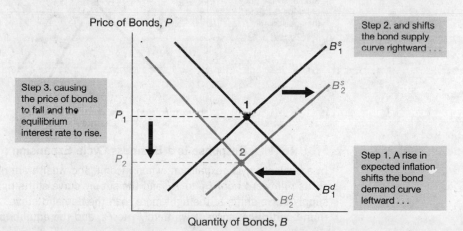

FIGURE 4.4 Response to a Change in Expected Inflation

When expected inflation rises, the supply curve shifts from B_1^s to B_2^s, and the demand curve shifts from B_1^d to B_2^d. The equilibrium moves from point 1 to point 2, with the result that the equilibrium bond price falls from P_1 to P_2 and the equilibrium interest rate rises.

the **Fisher effect,** after Irving Fisher, the economist who first pointed out the relationship of expected inflation to interest rates. In the Indian context, recent studies have pointed to the absence of the Fisher effect.[5]

Changes in the Interest Rate Due to a Business Cycle Expansion

Figure 4.5 analyzes the effects of a business cycle expansion on interest rates. In a business cycle expansion, the amounts of goods and services being produced in the economy increase, so national income rises. When this occurs, businesses are more willing to borrow because they are likely to have many profitable investment opportunities for which they need financing. Hence at a given bond price, the quantity of bonds that firms want to sell (that is, the supply of bonds) will increase. This means that in a business cycle expansion, the supply curve for bonds shifts to the right (see Figure 4.5) from B_1^s to B_2^s .

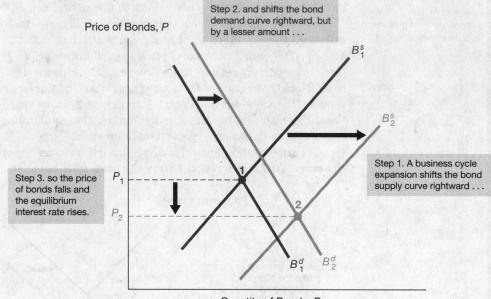

Step 2. and shifts the bond demand curve rightward, but by a lesser amount . . .

Price of Bonds, P

B_1^s

B_2^s

Step 1. A business cycle expansion shifts the bond supply curve rightward . . .

Step 3. so the price of bonds falls and the equilibrium interest rate rises.

P_1

P_2

B_1^d B_2^d

Quantity of Bonds, B

FIGURE 4.5 Response to a Business Cycle Expansion

In a business cycle expansion, when income and wealth are rising, the demand curve shifts rightward from B_1^d to B_2^d and the supply curve shifts rightward from B_1^s to B_2^s. If the supply curve shifts to the right more than the demand curve, as in this figure, the equilibrium bond price moves down from P_1 to P_2, and the equilibrium interest rate rises.

---

[5]Pattanaik, S., Behera, H. and Kavediya, R. (2013), "Real Interest rate Impact on Investment and Growth: What The Empirical Evidence for India Suggests?", *Reserve Bank of India*, pp. 1–43. Available at https://rbidocs.rbi.org.in/rdocs/Publications/PDFs/IDGSR08082013.pdf, as accessed on 12 March 2016 at 2pm.

Expansion in the economy will also affect the demand for bonds. As the business cycle expands, wealth is likely to increase, and the theory of portfolio choice tells us that the demand for bonds will rise as well. We see this in Figure 4.5, where the demand curve has shifted to the right, from B_1^d to B_2^d.

Given that both the supply and demand curves have shifted to the right, we know that the new equilibrium reached at the intersection of B_2^d and B_2^s must also move to the right. However, depending on whether the supply curve shifts more than the demand curve, or vice versa, the new equilibrium interest rate can either rise or fall.

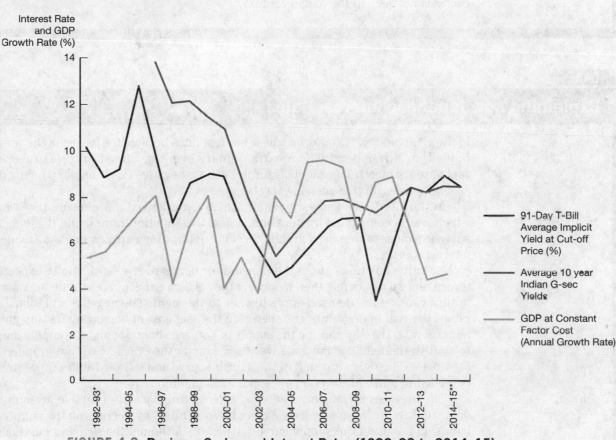

FIGURE 4.6 Business Cycles and Interest Rates (1992–93 to 2014–15)

The Indian case does not depict a one-to-one relationship between interest rates and business cycles.

In the Indian case, interest rates were administered with a captive market in government bonds and absence of an active debt management policy by the government till 1992–93. Subsequently, interest rates were market-related. However, due to the private placement and devolvement by the RBI in the primary issuance market, market rates were not truly market determined till 2005–06. Effective, 1 April 2006, with the adherence to Fiscal Responsibility and Budgetary Management Act (FRBM) Borrowing Rule, the RBI is prohibited from participating in the primary issuance market as the debt manager. This development, in some sense, facilitated true price discovery and resulted in market determined interest rates.

Source: Reserve Bank of India database https://www.rbi.org.in.

The supply-and-demand analysis used here gives us an ambiguous answer to the question of what will happen to interest rates in a business cycle expansion. Figure 4.5 has been drawn so that the shift in the supply curve is greater than the shift in the demand curve, causing the equilibrium bond price to fall to P_2, leading to a rise in the equilibrium interest rate. The reason the figure has been drawn so that a business cycle expansion and a rise in income lead to a higher interest rate is that this is the outcome we actually see in the data. Figure 4.6 plots the movement of short-term and long-term interest rates in India as depicted by the 91-day T-bill rates and the 10 year Government security (G-sec) yields between 1992–93 and 2014–15. As seen, the one-to-one relationship between interest rates and business cycles is not seen in the Indian context.

CASE

Explaining Low Japanese Interest Rates

In the 1990s and early 2000s, Japanese interest rates became the lowest in the world. Indeed, in November 1998 an extraordinary event occurred: Interest rates on Japanese six-month Treasury bills turned slightly negative (see Chapter 3). Why did Japanese rates drop to such low levels?

In the late 1990s and early 2000s, Japan experienced a prolonged recession, which was accompanied by deflation, a negative inflation rate. Using these facts, analysis similar to that used in the preceding application explains the low Japanese interest rates.

Negative inflation caused the demand for bonds to rise because the expected return on real assets fell, thereby raising the relative expected return on bonds and in turn causing the demand curve to shift to the right. The negative inflation also raised the real interest rate and therefore the real cost of borrowing for any given nominal rate, thereby causing the supply of bonds to contract and the supply curve to shift to the left. The outcome was then exactly the opposite of that graphed in Figure 4.4: The rightward shift of the demand curve and leftward shift of the supply curve led to a rise in the bond price and a fall in interest rates.

The business cycle contraction and the resulting lack of profitable investment opportunities in Japan also led to lower interest rates, by decreasing the supply of bonds and shifting the supply curve to the left. Although the demand curve also would shift to the left because wealth decreased during the business cycle contraction, we have seen in the preceding application that the demand curve would shift less than the supply curve. Thus, the bond price rose and interest rates fell (the opposite outcome to that in Figure 4.5).

Usually, we think that low interest rates are a good thing because they make it cheap to borrow. But the Japanese example shows that just as a fallacy is present in the adage, "You can never be too rich or too thin" (maybe you can't be too rich, but you can certainly be too thin and damage your health), a fallacy is present in always thinking that lower interest rates are better. In Japan, the low and even negative interest rates were a sign that the Japanese economy was in real trouble, with falling prices and a contracting economy. Only when the Japanese economy returns to health will interest rates rise back to more normal levels.

Profiting from Interest-Rate Forecasts

Given the importance of interest rates, the media frequently report interest-rate forecasts, as the Following the Financial News box on page 83 indicates. Because changes in interest rates have a major impact on the profitability of financial institutions, financial managers care a great deal about the path of future interest rates. Managers of financial institutions obtain interest-rate forecasts either by hiring their staff economists to generate forecasts or by purchasing forecasts from other financial institutions or economic forecasting firms.

Several methods are used to produce interest-rate forecasts. One of the most popular is based on the supply and demand for bonds framework described here, and it is used by financial institutions.[6] Using this framework, analysts predict what will happen to the factors that affect the supply of and demand for bonds—factors such as the strength of the economy, the profitability of investment opportunities, the expected inflation rate, and the size of government deficits and borrowing. They then use the supply-and-demand analysis outlined in the chapter to come up with their interest-rate forecasts.

Forecasting done with the supply and demand for bonds framework often does not make use of formal economic models but rather depends on the judgment or "feel" of the forecaster. An alternative method of forecasting interest rates makes use of **econometric models,** models whose equations are estimated with statistical procedures using past data. These models involve interlocking equations that, once input variables such as the behavior of government spending and monetary policy are plugged in, produce simultaneous forecasts of many variables including interest rates. The basic assumption of these forecasting models is that the estimated relationships among variables will continue to hold up in the future. Given this assumption, the forecaster makes predictions of the expected path of the input variables and then lets the model generate forecasts of variables such as interest rates.

> FOLLOWING THE FINANCIAL NEWS

Forecasting Interest Rates

Forecasting interest rates is a time-honored profession. Financial economists are hired (sometimes at very high salaries) to forecast interest rates because businesses need to know what the rates will be in order to plan their future spending, and banks and investors require interest-rate forecasts in order to decide which assets to buy. Interest-rate forecasters predict what will happen to the factors that affect the supply and demand for bonds and for money—factors such as the strength of the economy, the profitability of investment opportunities, the expected inflation rate, and the size of government budget deficits and borrowing. They then use the supply-and-demand analysis we have outlined here to come up with their interest-rate forecasts.

For the US economy, the *Wall Street Journal* reports interest-rate forecasts by leading prognosticators twice a year (early January and July) on its Web site.

In India, the website of *Trading Economics* provides interest rate forecasts, as also the estimates of future annual GDP growth rates, inflation rates and unemployment rates.[7]

---

[6]Another framework used to produce forecasts of interest rates, developed by John Maynard Keynes, analyzes the supply and demand for money and is called the *liquidity preference framework*. This framework is discussed in a fourth appendix to this chapter, which can be found on the book's Web site at http://www.pearsoned.co.in/FredericSMishkin/.

[7]See http://www.tradingeconomics.com/india/interest-rate/forecast; http://www.tradingeconomics.com/india/gdp-growth-annual/forecast; http://www.tradingeconomics.com/india/inflation-cpi/forecast; http://www.tradingeconomics.com/india/unemployment-rate/forecast, as accessed on 13 March 2016 at 3pm.

Many of these econometric models are quite large, involving hundreds and sometimes over a thousand equations, and consequently require computers to produce their forecasts.

Managers of financial institutions rely on these forecasts to make decisions about which assets they should hold. A manager who believes the forecast that long-term interest rates will fall in the future would seek to purchase long-term bonds for the asset account because, as we have seen in Chapter 3, the drop in interest rates will produce large capital gains. Conversely, if forecasts say that interest rates are likely to rise in the future, the manager will prefer to hold short-term bonds or loans in the portfolio in order to avoid potential capital losses on long-term securities.

Forecasts of interest rates also help managers decide whether to borrow long-term or short-term. If interest rates are forecast to rise in the future, the financial institution manager will want to lock in the low interest rates by borrowing long-term; if the forecasts say that interest rates will fall, the manager will seek to borrow short-term in order to take advantage of low interest-rate costs in the future.

Clearly, good forecasts of future interest rates are extremely valuable to the financial institution manager, who, not surprisingly, would be willing to pay a lot for accurate forecasts. Unfortunately, interest-rate forecasting is a perilous business, and even the top forecasters, to their embarrassment, are frequently far off in their forecasts.

SUMMARY

1. The theory of portfolio choice tells us that the quantity demanded of an asset is (a) positively related to wealth, (b) positively related to the expected return on the asset relative to alternative assets, (c) negatively related to the riskiness of the asset relative to alternative assets, and (d) positively related to the liquidity of the asset relative to alternative assets.

2. Diversification (the holding of more than one asset) benefits investors because it reduces the risk they face, and the benefits are greater the less returns on securities move together.

3. The supply-and-demand analysis for bonds provides a theory of how interest rates are determined. It predicts that interest rates will change when there is a change in demand because of changes in income (or wealth), expected returns, risk, or liquidity, or when there is a change in supply because of changes in the attractiveness of investment opportunities, the real cost of borrowing, or government activities.

KEY TERMS

asset, p. 66
asset market approach, p. 73
demand curve, p. 69
econometric models, p. 83
excess demand, p. 72

excess supply, p. 72
expected return, p. 66
Fisher effect, p. 80
liquidity, p. 66
market equilibrium, p. 72

risk, p. 66
standard deviation, p. 67
supply curve, p. 71
theory of portfolio choice, p. 69
wealth, p. 66

QUESTIONS

1. Explain why you would be more or less willing to buy a share of Polaroid stock in the following situations:

   a. Your wealth falls.

   b. You expect it (Polaroid stock) to appreciate in value.

   c. The bond market becomes more liquid.

   d. You expect gold to appreciate in value.

   e. Prices in the bond market become more volatile.

2. Explain why you would be more or less willing to buy a house under the following circumstances:

   a. You just inherited ₹100,000.

b. Real estate commissions fall from 6% of the sales price to 4% of the sales price.

c. You expect Polaroid stock to double in value next year.

d. Prices in the stock market become more volatile.

e. You expect housing prices to fall.

3. "The more risk-averse people are, the more likely they are to diversify." Is this statement true, false, or uncertain? Explain your answer.

4. I own a professional football team, and I plan to diversify by purchasing shares in either a company that owns a pro basketball team or a pharmaceutical company. Which of these two investments is more likely to reduce the overall risk I face? Why?

5. "No one who is risk-averse will ever buy a security that has a lower expected return, more risk, and less liquidity than another security." Is this statement true, false, or uncertain? Explain your answer.

For items 6–13, answer each question by drawing the appropriate supply-and-demand diagrams.

6. An important way in which the RBI decreases the money supply is by selling bonds to the public. Using a supply-and-demand analysis for bonds, show what effect this action has on interest rates.

7. Using the supply-and-demand for bonds framework, show why interest rates are procyclical (rising when the economy is expanding and falling during recessions).

8. What effect will a sudden increase in the volatility of gold prices have on interest rates?

9. How might a sudden increase in people's expectations of future real estate prices affect interest rates?

10. Explain what effect a large fiscal deficit might have on interest rates.

11. In the aftermath of the global financial crisis, U.S. government budget deficits increased dramatically, yet interest rates on U.S. Treasury debt fell sharply and stayed low for many years. Does this make sense? Why or why not?

12. Using a supply-and-demand analysis for bonds, show what the effect is on interest rates when the riskiness of bonds rises.

13. Will there be an effect on interest rates if brokerage commissions on stocks fall? Explain your answer.

Predicting the Future

14. The Prime Minister of India announces in a press conference that he will fight the higher inflation rate with a new anti-inflation program. Predict what will happen to interest rates if the public believes him.

15. The Governor of the RBI announces that interest rates will rise sharply next year, and the market believes him. What will happen to today's interest rate on AT&T bonds, such as the $8\frac{1}{8}$ of 2022?

16. Predict what will happen to interest rates if the public suddenly expects a large increase in stock prices.

17. Predict what will happen to interest rates if prices in the bond market become more volatile.

QUANTITATIVE PROBLEMS

1. You own a ₹1,000-par zero-coupon bond that has five years of remaining maturity. You plan on selling the bond in one year and believe that the required yield next year will have the following probability distribution:

Probability	Required Yield (%)
0.1	6.60
0.2	6.75
0.4	7.00
0.2	7.20
0.1	7.45

a. What is your expected price when you sell the bond?

b. What is the standard deviation of the bond price?

2. Consider a ₹1,000-par junk bond paying a 12% annual coupon with two years to maturity. The issuing company has a 20% chance of defaulting this year, in which case the bond would not pay anything. If the company survives the first year, paying the annual coupon payment, it then has a 25% chance of defaulting in the second year. If the company defaults in the second year, neither the final coupon payment nor par value of the bond will be paid.

a. What price must investors pay for this bond to expect a 10% yield to maturity?

b. At that price, what is the expected holding period return and standard deviation of returns? Assume that periodic cash flows are reinvested at 10%.

3. Last month, corporations supplied ₹250 billion in one-year discount bonds to investors at an average market rate of 11.8%. This month, an additional ₹25 billion in one-year discount bonds became available, and market rates increased to 12.2%. Assuming that the demand curve remained constant, derive a linear equation for the demand for bonds, using prices instead of interest rates.

4. An economist has concluded that, near the point of equilibrium, the demand curve and supply curve for one-year discount bonds can be estimated using the following equations:

$$B^d: \text{Price} = \frac{-2}{5}\text{Quantity} + 940$$

$$B^s: \text{Price} = \text{Quantity} + 500$$

   a. What is the expected equilibrium price and quantity of bonds in this market?

   b. Given your answer to part (a), which is the expected interest rate in this market?

5. The demand curve and the supply curve for one-year discount bonds were estimated using the following equations:

$$B^d: \text{Price} = \frac{-2}{5}\text{Quantity} + 940$$

$$B^s: \text{Price} = \text{Quantity} + 500$$

Following a dramatic increase in the value of the stock market, many retirees started moving money out of the stock market and into bonds. This resulted in a parallel shift in the demand for bonds, such that the price of bonds at all quantities increased ₹50. Assuming no change in the supply equation for bonds, what is the new equilibrium price and quantity? What is the new market interest rate?

6. The demand curve and the supply curve for one-year discount bonds were estimated using the following equations:

$$B^d: \text{Price} = \frac{-2}{5}\text{Quantity} + 990$$

$$B^s: \text{Price} = \text{Quantity} + 500$$

As the stock market continued to rise, the RBI felt the need to increase the interest rates. As a result, the new market interest rate increased to 19.65%, but the equilibrium quantity remained unchanged. What are the new demand and supply equations? Assume parallel shifts in the equations.

WEB EXERCISES

Interest Rates and Inflation

1. One of the largest influences on the level of interest rates is inflation. A number of sites report inflation over time. Go to **https://www.rbi.org.in/Scripts/ PublicationsView.aspx?id=8248**. Calculate the inflation rate from 1970–71 to 1984–85. Next for the inflation rate from 1984–85 onwards, go to https://www.rbi.org.in/Scripts/PublicationsView. aspx?id=16680. Review the CPI-IW data available, and the CPI-C since 2012–13. What has been the average rate of inflation since 1970, 1980, 1990, 2000, 2010, 2015? Which year had the lowest inflation? Which year had the highest inflation?

2. Increasing prices erode the purchasing power of the rupee. It is interesting to compute what goods would have cost at some point in the past after adjusting for inflation. Go to **http://minneapolisfed.org/ Research/data/us/calc/**. What would a car that cost ₹22,000 today have cost the year that you were born?

3. One of the points made in this chapter is that inflation erodes investment returns. Go to **www .moneychimp.com/articles/econ/inflation_ calculator.htm** and review how changes in inflation alter your real return. What happens to the adjusted value of an investment compared with its inflation-adjusted value as

   a. inflation increases?

   b. the investment horizon lengthens?

   c. expected returns increase?

WEB APPENDICES

Please visit our Web site at **http://www.pearsoned .co.in/FredericSMishkin/** to read the Web appendices to Chapter 4:

- **Appendix 1:** Models of Asset Pricing

- **Appendix 2:** Applying the Asset Market Approach to a Commodity Market: The Case of Gold

- **Appendix 3:** Loanable Funds Framework

- **Appendix 4:** Supply and Demand in the Market for Money: The Liquidity Preference Framework

How Do Risk and Term Structure Affect Interest Rates?

> PREVIEW

In our supply-and-demand analysis of interest rate behavior in Chapter 4, we examined the determination of just one interest rate. Yet we saw earlier that there are enormous numbers of bonds on which the interest rates can and do differ. In this chapter we complete the interest-rate picture by examining the relationship of the various interest rates to one another. Understanding why they differ from bond to bond can help businesses, banks, insurance companies, and private investors decide which bonds to purchase as investments and which ones to sell.

We first look at why bonds with the same term to maturity have different interest rates. The relationship among these interest rates is called the **risk structure of interest rates,** although risk, liquidity, and income tax rules all play a role in determining the risk structure. A bond's term to maturity also affects its interest rate, and the relationship among interest rates on bonds with different terms to maturity is called the **term structure of interest rates.** In this chapter we examine the sources and causes of fluctuations in interest rates relative to one another and look at a number of theories that explain these fluctuations.

Risk Structure of Interest Rates

Figure 5.1 shows the yields to maturity for several categories of long-term bonds from 2002–03 to 2014–15. It shows us two important features of interest-rate behavior for bonds of the same maturity: Interest rates on different categories of bonds differ from one another in any given year, and the spread (or difference) between the interest rates varies over time. The interest rates on 10-year AAA corporate bonds in India, for example, are the average 10-year Indian Government security (G-sec) yields throughout the period 2002–2003 to 2014–15. However, the spread between these interest rates vary over time, being greater in certain years than others. Thus, the spread between the corporate bonds and Indian G-sec yields was very large during the years of the Global Financial Crisis (2008–09) and then reduced subsequently. In 2014–15, with the corporate bond yields falling below that of the Indian government securities, the spread in fact became negative. Which factors are responsible for these phenomena?

Default Risk

One attribute of a bond that influences its interest rate is its risk of **default,** which occurs when the issuer of the bond is unable or unwilling to make interest payments when promised or to pay off the face value when the bond matures. A corporation

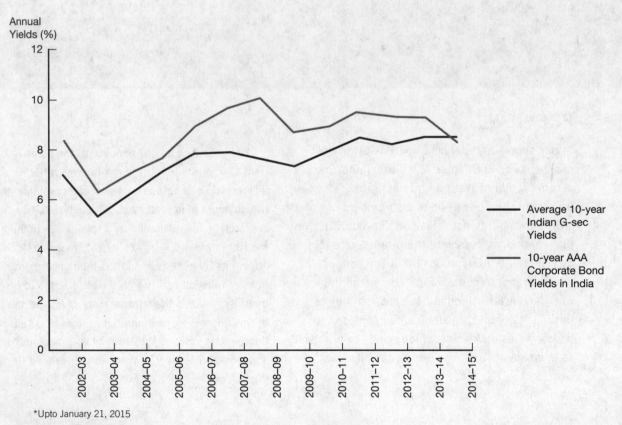

*Upto January 21, 2015

FIGURE 5.1 **Long-Term Bond Yields in India: 2002–2015**

Interest rates on different types of bonds differ from one another in any given year, andthe spread (or difference) between the interest rates varies over time.

Source: http://dbie.rbi.org.in/DBIE/dbie.rbi?site=statistics, as accessed on 13 March 2016 at 3.30pm.

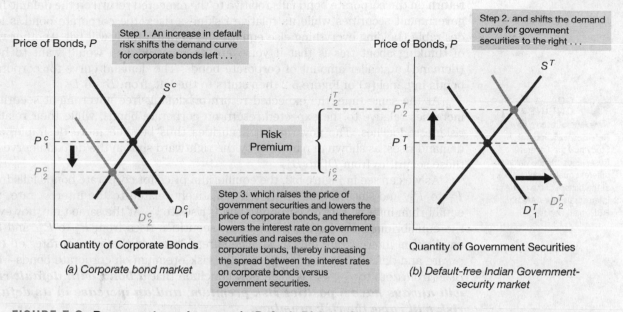

FIGURE 5.2 Response to an Increase in Default Risk on Corporate Bonds

Initially $P_1^c = P_1^T$ and the risk premium is zero. An increase in default risk on corporate bonds shifts the demand curve from D_1^c to D_2^c. Simultaneously, it shifts the demand curve for government securities from D_1^c to D_2^c. The equilibrium price for corporate bonds falls from P_1^c to P_2^c, and the equilibrium interest rate on corporate bonds rises to i_2^c. In the Government security market, the equilibrium bond price rises from P_1^T to P_2^T and the equilibrium interest rate falls to i_2^T. The brace indicates the difference between i_2^c and i_2^T, the risk premium on corporate bonds. (Note that because P_2^c is lower than P_2^c, i_2^c is greater than i_2^T.)

suffering big losses, such as the major airline companies like Deccan, Kingfisher and Sahara might be more likely to suspend interest payments on its bonds. The default risk on its bonds would therefore be quite high. By contrast, Indian Government securities have usually been considered to have no default risk because the central government can always increase taxes to pay off its obligations. Bonds like these with no default risk are called **default-free bonds.** The spread between the interest rates on bonds with default risk and default-free bonds, both of the same maturity, called the **risk premium,** indicates how much additional interest people must earn to be willing to hold that risky bond. Our supply-and-demand analysis of the bond market in Chapter 4 can be used to explain why a bond with default risk always has a positive risk premium and why the higher the default risk is, the larger the risk premium will be.

To examine the effect of default risk on interest rates, let's look at the supply-and-demand diagrams for the default-free (Indian government securities) and corporate long-term bond markets in Figure 5.2. To make the diagrams somewhat easier to read, let's assume that initially corporate bonds have the same default risk as Indian government securities. In this case, these two bonds have the same attributes (identical risk and maturity); their equilibrium prices and interest rates will initially be equal ($P_1^c = P_1^T$ and $i_1^c = i_1^T$), and the risk premium on corporate bonds ($i_1^c - i_1^T$) will be zero.

If the possibility of a default increases because a corporation begins to suffer large losses, the default risk on corporate bonds will increase, and the expected return on these bonds will decrease. In addition, the corporate bond's return will be more uncertain. The theory of portfolio choice predicts that because the expected return on the corporate bond falls relative to the expected return on the default-free government securities while its relative riskiness rises, the corporate bond is less desirable (holding everything else equal), and demand for it will fall. Another way of thinking about this is that if you were an investor, you would want to hold (demand) a smaller amount of corporate bonds. The demand curve for corporate bonds in panel (a) of Figure 5.2 then shifts to the left, from D_1^c to D_2^c.

At the same time, the expected return on default-free government securities increases relative to the expected return on corporate bonds, while their relative riskiness declines. The government securities thus become more desirable, and demand rises, as shown in panel (b) by the rightward shift in the demand curve for these securities from D_1^T to D_2^T.

As we can see in Figure 5.2, the equilibrium price for corporate bonds falls from P_1^c to P_2^c, and since the bond price is negatively related to the interest rate, the equilibrium interest rate on corporate bonds rises to i_2^c. At the same time, however, the equilibrium price for the government securities rises from P_1^T to P_2^T, and the equilibrium interest rate falls to i_2^T. The spread between the interest rates on corporate and default-free bonds—that is, the risk premium on corporate bonds—has risen from zero to $i_2^c - i_2^T$. We can now conclude that ***a bond with default risk will always have a positive risk premium, and an increase in its default risk will raise the risk premium.***

Because default risk is so important to the size of the risk premium, purchasers of bonds need to know whether a corporation is likely to default on its bonds. This information is provided by **credit-rating agencies,** investment advisory firms that rate the quality of corporate and **municipal bonds** in terms of the probability of default. Table 5.1 provides the ratings and their description for the two largest

GO ONLINE
www.federalreserve.gov/ Releases/h15/update/ Study how the Federal Reserve reports the yields on different quality bonds. Look at the bottom of the listing of interest rates for AAA- and BBB-rated bonds.

TABLE 5.1   Bond Ratings by Moody's and Standard and Poor's

Moody's	Rating Standard and Poor's	Descriptions	Examples of Corporations with Bonds Outstanding in 2013
Aaa	AAA	Highest quality (lowest default risk)	Microsoft, Johnson & Johnson, Mobil Corp.
Aa	AA	High quality	Shell Oil, Sanofi, General Electric
A	A	Upper-medium grade	Bank of America, Intel Corp., McDonald's, Inc.
Baa	BBB	Medium grade	Hewlett-Packard, FedEx, Harley Davidson
Ba	BB	Lower-medium grade	Charter Communications, Netflix, Best Buy
B	B	Speculative	Rite Aid, United Airlines, Delta Airlines
Caa	CCC, CC	Poor (high default risk)	Western Express, RadioShack, J.C. Penney
C	D	Highly speculative	American Airlines

credit-rating agencies, Moody's Investor Service and Standard and Poor's Corporation. Bonds with relatively low risk of default are called *investment-grade* securities and have a rating of Baa (or BBB) and above. Bonds with ratings below Baa (or BBB) have higher default risk and have been aptly dubbed speculative-grade or **junk bonds.** Because these bonds always have higher interest rates than investment-grade securities, they are also referred to as high-yield bonds.

Next let's look at Figure 5.1 at the beginning of the chapter and see if we can explain the relationship between interest rates on corporate and Indian Government securities. Corporate bonds always have higher interest rates than Indian Government securities because they always have some risk of default, whereas Indian Government securities do not. Again, as expected, both default risks and risk premiums for corporate bonds rose especially during the financial crisis, widening the spread between interest rates on corporate bonds and those on government securities.

Liquidity

Another attribute of a bond that influences its interest rate is its liquidity. As we learned in Chapter 4, a liquid asset is one that can be quickly and cheaply converted into cash if the need arises. The more liquid an asset is, the more desirable it is (holding everything else constant). Indian Government securities are the most liquid of all long-term bonds; because they are so widely traded, they are the easiest to sell quickly and the cost of selling them is low. Corporate bonds are not as liquid

---

CASE

The Global Financial Crisis and the Baa-Treasury Spread in the United States

Starting in August 2007, the collapse of the subprime mortgage market led to large losses in financial institutions (which we will discuss more extensively in Chapter 8). As a consequence of the subprime collapse and the subsequent global financial crisis, many investors began to doubt the financial health of corporations with low credit ratings such as Baa and even the reliability of the ratings themselves. The perceived increase in default risk for Baa bonds made them less desirable at any given interest rate, decreased the quantity demanded, and shifted the demand curve for Baa bonds to the left. As shown in panel (a) of Figure 5.2, the interest rate on Baa bonds should have risen, which is indeed what happened. Interest rates on Baa bonds rose by 280 basis points (2.80 percentage points) from 6.63% at the end of July 2007 to 9.43% at the most virulent stage of the global financial crisis in mid-October 2008. But the increase in perceived default risk for Baa bonds in October 2008 made default-free US Treasury bonds relatively more attractive and shifted the demand curve for these securities to the right—an outcome described by some analysts as a "flight to quality." Just as our analysis predicts in Figure 5.2, interest rates on Treasury bonds fell by 80 basis points, from 4.78% at the end of July 2007 to 3.98% in mid-October 2008. The spread between interest rates on Baa and Treasury bonds rose by 360 basis points, from 1.85% before the crisis to 5.45% afterward.

because fewer bonds for any one corporation are traded; thus, it can be costly to sell these bonds in an emergency because it might be hard to find buyers quickly.

How does the reduced liquidity of the corporate bonds affect their interest rates relative to the interest rate on government securities? We can use supply-and-demand analysis with the same figure that was used to analyze the effect of default risk, Figure 5.2, to show that the lower liquidity of corporate bonds relative to government securities increases the spread between the interest rates on these two bonds. Let's start the analysis by assuming that initially corporate and government bonds are equally liquid and all their other attributes are the same. As shown in Figure 5.2, their equilibrium prices and interest rates will initially be equal: $P_1^c = P_1^T$ and $i_1^c - i_1^T$. If the corporate bond becomes less liquid than the government securities because it is less widely traded, then (as the theory of portfolio choice indicates) demand for it will fall, shifting its demand curve from D_1^c to D_2^c as in panel (a). The government security now becomes relatively more liquid in comparison with the corporate bond, so its demand curve shifts rightward from D_1^T to D_2^T as in panel (b). The shifts in the curves in Figure 5.2 show that the price of the less liquid corporate bond falls and its interest rate rises, while the price of the more liquid government security rises and its interest rate falls.

The result is that the spread between the interest rates on the two bond types has increased. Therefore, the differences between interest rates on corporate bonds and government securities (that is, the risk premiums) reflect not only the corporate bond's default risk but also its liquidity. This is why a risk premium is more accurately a "risk and liquidity premium," but convention dictates that it is called a *risk premium*.

Income Tax Considerations

A third factor explaining the risk structure of interest rates is income tax considerations. Such considerations explain why bonds such as municipal bonds in the United States carry even lower interest rates than the U.S. Treasury bonds. These bonds are not default-free. State and local governments have defaulted on the municipal bonds they have issued in the past, particularly during the Great Depression and even more recently in San Bernardino, Mammoth Lakes, Stockton (all in California); Jefferson Country, Alabama; Harrisburg, Pennsylvania; Central Falls, Rhode Island; and Boise Country, Idaho. Also, municipal bonds are not as liquid as U.S. Treasury bonds.

Why is it, then, that these bonds have had lower interest rates than U.S. Treasury bonds for at least 40 years? The explanation lies in the fact that interest payments on municipal bonds are exempt from federal income taxes, a factor that has the same effect on the demand for municipal bonds as an increase in their expected return. Municipal bonds are a new phenomenon in India (see Box). The Government of India has allowed municipalities to issue tax-free municipal bonds since 2001.

To understand income tax considerations as determining the spreads between interest rates, let's imagine that you have a high enough income to put you in the 35% income tax bracket, where for every extra rupee of income you have to pay 35 paise to the government. If you own a ₹1,000-face-value Indian government security that sells for ₹1,000 and has a coupon payment of ₹100, you get to keep only ₹65 of the payment after taxes. Although the security has a 10% interest rate, you actually earn only 6.5% after taxes.

Suppose, however, that you put your savings into a ₹1,000-face-value municipal bond that sells for ₹1,000 and pays only ₹80 in coupon payments. Its interest rate is only 8%, but because it is a tax-exempt security, you pay no taxes on the ₹80 coupon payment, so you earn 8% after taxes. Clearly, you earn more on the municipal bond after taxes, so you are willing to hold the riskier and less liquid municipal bond even though it has a lower interest rate than the Indian government security.

CASE

MUNICIPAL BONDS IN INDIA

A Municipal Corporation is a local government body that administers a city of population 200,000 or more, is administratively a part of a district in which it is located but interacts directly with the state government. Some of the large Municipal Corporations in India are Mumbai, Delhi, Kolkata, Bangalore etc.

The Constitution (74th Amendment) Act, 1992 empowered the Urban Local Bodies (ULBs) to mobilize resources independent of the State Governments for the provision, operation and maintenance of urban services as listed in twelfth schedule.

The major sources of revenue to the ULBs are property tax, profession tax, advertisement, user charges, fees / charges for usage of municipal assets and facilities, assigned revenues like share of entertainment tax, stamp duty etc., and devolution and grants-in-aid.

Traditionally, ULBs have relied on the grants and subsidized funds provided by the Central and State Government for providing the basic urban services. In addition, ULBs borrow funds from development financial institutions, multilateral and bilateral funding agencies, through Central and State Government. ULBs are also entitled to borrow through issuance of Municipal Bonds.

Municipal bonds were seen as a means of financing the growing needs of urban infrastructure, especially in the context of the developemnt of 'Smart Cities' as announced in the Union Budget of 2014-15.

The constraints in the municipal bond market in India existed both, on the supply and demand side. The constraints on the supply side inhibited ULBs from issuing bonds and those on the demand side limited investors (individual and institutional) from investing in the municipal bond market.

The Bangalore Municipal Corporation was the first municipal corporation to issue a municipal bond of ₹1250 million with a state guarantee in 1997. However, the access to capital market commenced in January 1998, when the Ahmedabad Municipal Corporation (AMC) issued the first municipal bonds in the country without state government guarantee for financing infrastructure projects in the city. AMC had raised ₹1,000 million by the said public issue. It was followed by more issues through private placement.

The debt market in India for municipal securities had grown considerably since the issuance of Ahmedabad bonds. Since 1998, other cities had accessed the capital markets through municipal bonds without state government guarantee including Nashik, Nagpur, Ludhiana, and Madurai. In most cases, bond proceeds had been used to fund water and sewerage schemes or road projects. India's city governments had thus mobilized about ₹4,450 million from the domestic capital market through taxable municipal bonds. The last issuance was done by Greater Vishakhapatnam Municipal Corporation for ₹30 Crores in 2010.

The Government of India, in order to boost the municipal bond market, allowed the municipalities to issue tax-free municipal bonds in February 2001.

On March 22, 2015, India's market regulator, Securities and Exchange Board of India (SEBI) allowed municipal bodies in India to issue debt securities which could also be listed. According to SEBI, its regulations relating to municipality bonds will provide a "framework governing the issuance and listing of bonds by municipalities and will enable the investors to make an informed investment decision before investing in the bonds issued by such entities".

SEBI regulations also set disclosure rules for these bonds and could also facilitate listing of privately placed municipal bonds. These regulations confirm to the government's guidelines for issuing tax-free bonds by municipalities.

As per SEBI rules, all municipal bonds should have a mandatory credit rating, which should be of investment grade in case of public issuances, these bonds should have a three-year tenure and banks or financial institutions should be appointed as monetary agencies which will prepare periodic reports on the issuer. Further, the funds raised from public issue of debt securities shall be used only for projects that are specified under objects in the offer document.

Source: http://www.sebi.gov.in/cms/sebi_data/attachdocs/1419931499189.pdf, as accessed on 13 March 2016 at 3.34pm.

EXAMPLE 5.1

Income Tax Considerations

Suppose you had the opportunity to buy either a tax-exempted municipal bond or a corporate bond, both of which have a face value and purchase price of ₹1,000. The municipal bond has coupon payments of ₹60 and a coupon rate of 6%. The corporate bond has coupon payments of ₹80 and an interest rate of 8%. Which bond would you choose to purchase, assuming a 40% tax rate?

> **Solution**

You would choose to purchase the municipal bond because it will earn you ₹60 in coupon payments and an interest rate after taxes of 6%. Since municipal bonds are tax-exempt, you pay no taxes on the ₹60 coupon payments and earn 6% after taxes. However, you have to pay taxes on corporate bonds. You will keep only 60% of the ₹80 coupon payment because the other 40% goes to taxes. Therefore, you receive ₹48 of the coupon payment and have an interest rate of 4.8% after taxes. Buying the municipal bond would yield you higher earnings.

Another way of understanding why municipal bonds have lower interest rates than Treasury bonds in the United States is to use the supply-and-demand analysis depicted in Figure 5.3. We assume that municipal and Treasury bonds have identical attributes and so have the same bond prices as drawn in the figure: $P_1^m = P_1^T$ and the same interest rates. Once the municipal bonds are given a tax advantage that raises their after-tax expected return relative to Treasury bonds and makes them more desirable, demand for them rises, and their demand curve shifts to the right, from D_1^m to D_2^m. The result is that their equilibrium bond price

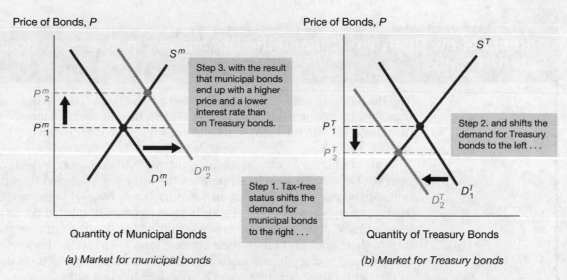

(a) Market for municipal bonds   **(b) Market for Treasury bonds**

FIGURE 5.3   Interest Rates on Municipal and Treasury Bonds in the United States

When the municipal bond is given tax-free status, demand for the municipal bond shifts rightward from D_1^m to D_2^m and demand for the Treasury bond shifts leftward from D_1^T to D_2^T. The equilibrium price of the municipal bond rises from P_1^m to P_2^m so its interest rate falls, while the equilibrium price of the Treasury bond falls from P_1^T to P_2^T and its interest rate rises. The result is that municipal bonds end up with lower interest rates than those on Treasury bonds.

rises from P_1^m to P_2^m and their equilibrium interest rate falls. By contrast, Treasury bonds have now become less desirable relative to municipal bonds; demand for Treasury bonds decreases, and D_1^T shifts to D_2^T. The Treasury bond price falls from P_1^T to P_2^T, and the interest rate rises. The resulting lower interest rates for municipal bonds and higher interest rates for Treasury bonds explain why municipal bonds can have interest rates below those of Treasury bonds.[1]

Summary

The risk structure of interest rates (the relationship among interest rates on bonds with the same maturity) is explained by three factors: default risk, liquidity, and the income tax treatment of a bond's interest payments. As a bond's default risk increases, the risk premium on that bond (the spread between its interest rate and the interest rate on a default-free Treasury bond) rises. The greater liquidity of Treasury bonds also explains why their interest rates are lower than those on less liquid bonds. If a bond has a favorable tax treatment, as do municipal bonds, whose interest payments are exempt from Central income taxes, its interest rate will be lower.

---

[1]In contrast to corporate bonds, Treasury bonds are exempt from state and local income taxes. Using the analysis in the text, you should be able to show that this feature of Treasury bonds provides an additional reason why interest rates on corporate bonds are higher than those on Treasury bonds.

CASE

Effects of the Bush Tax Cut and the Obama Tax Increase on Bond Interest Rates

The Bush tax cut passed in 2001 scheduled a reduction of the top income tax bracket from 39% to 35% over a 10-year period. What is the effect of this income tax decrease on interest rates in the municipal bond market relative to those in the Treasury bond market?

Our supply-and-demand analysis provides the answer. A decreased income tax rate for wealthy people means that the after-tax expected return on tax-free municipal bonds relative to that on Treasury bonds is lower because the interest on Treasury bonds is now taxed at a lower rate. Because municipal bonds now become less desirable, their demand decreases, shifting the demand curve to the left, which lowers their price and raises their interest rate. Conversely, the lower income tax rate makes Treasury bonds more desirable; this change shifts their demand curve to the right, raises their price, and lowers their interest rates.

Our analysis thus shows that the Bush tax cut raised the interest rates on municipal bonds relative to the interest rate on Treasury bonds.

With the Obama tax increase that repealed the Bush tax cuts for high-income tax payers in 2013, the analysis would be reversed. The Obama tax increase raises the after-tax expected return on tax-free municipal bonds relative to Treasury bonds. Demand for municipal bonds would increase, shifting the demand curve to the right, which raises their price and lowers their interest rate. Conversely, the higher tax rate would make Treasury bonds less desirable, shifting their demand curve to the left, lowering their price, and raising their interest rate. The higher tax rates for high-income households would thus result in lower interest rates on municipal bonds relative to the interest rate on Treasury bonds.

Term Structure of Interest Rates

GO ONLINE

http://stockcharts.com/charts/YieldCurve.html
Go to http://stockcharts.com/freecharts/yieldcurve.php to look at the dynamic yield curve. This chart shows the relationship between interest rates and stocks over time.

To see Government of India 10 Year securities yield curve, go to: http://www.bloomberg.com/quote/GIND10YR:IND.

We have seen how risk, liquidity, and tax considerations (collectively embedded in the risk structure) can influence interest rates. Another factor that influences the interest rate on a bond is its term to maturity: Bonds with identical risk, liquidity, and tax characteristics may have different interest rates because the time remaining to maturity is different. A plot of the yields on bonds with differing terms to maturity but the same risk, liquidity, and tax considerations is called a **yield curve,** and it describes the term structure of interest rates for particular types of bonds, such as government bonds. The Following the Financial News box on page 96 shows several yield curves for Government of India dated securities that are published in the RBI database. Yield curves can be classified as upward-sloping, flat, and downward-sloping (the last sort is often referred to as an **inverted yield curve**). When yield curves slope upward, the most usual case, the long-term interest rates are above the short-term interest rates; when yield curves are flat, short- and long-term interest rates are the same; and when yield curves are inverted, long-term interest rates are below short-term interest rates. Yield curves can also have more complicated shapes in which they first slope up and then down, or vice versa as in the Following the Financial News box. Why do we usually see upward slopes of the yield curve but sometimes other shapes?

Besides explaining why yield curves take on different shapes at different times, a good theory of the term structure of interest rates must explain the following three important empirical facts:

1. As we see in Figure 5.4, interest rates on bonds of different maturities move together over time.
2. When short-term interest rates are low, yield curves are more likely to have an upward slope; when short-term interest rates are high, yield curves are more likely to slope downward and be inverted.
3. Yield curves almost always slope upward.

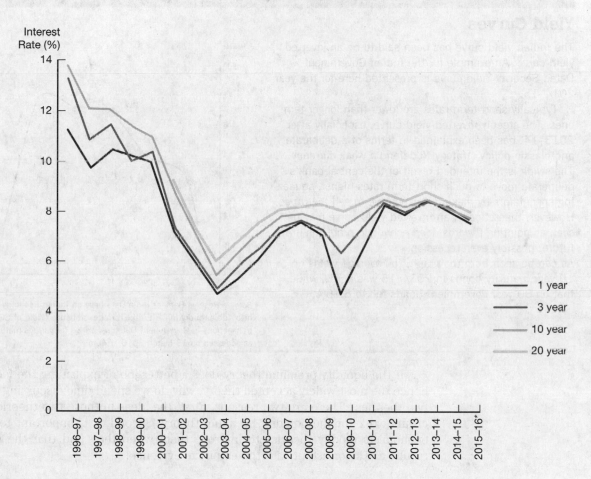

*Data pertains to April 2015 to November 2015

FIGURE 5.4 Movements Over Time of Interest Rates on Indian Government Securities with Different Maturities

Interest rates on bonds of different maturities move together over time.

Source: Reserve Bank of India Data base on Indian Economy http://dbie.rbi.org.in/DBIE/dbie.rbi?site=statistics, (Yield of SGL transactions in Government Dated securities for various maturities), as accessed on 13 March 2016 at 3.45pm.

Three theories have been put forward to explain the term structure of interest rates—that is, the relationship among interest rates on bonds of different maturities reflected in yield curve patterns: (1) the expectations theory, (2) the market segmentation theory, and (3) the liquidity premium theory, each of which is described in the following sections. The expectations theory does a good job of explaining the first two facts on our list, but not the third. The market segmentation theory can account for fact 3 but not the other two facts, which are well explained by the expectations theory. Because each theory explains facts that the other cannot, a natural way to seek a better understanding of the term structure is to combine features of both theories, which leads us to the liquidity premium theory, which can cover all three facts.

> FOLLOWING THE FINANCIAL NEWS

Yield Curves

The Indian yield curve has been said to be an inverted yield-curve. An example for the Indian Government Dated Security Yield curve is presented here for the year 2014–15.

Typically short-term rates are lower than longer-term ones. The steeply inverted yield curve, especially after 2013–14, has been explained in terms of a deliberate and classic policy strategy to defend a weak currency. The swing is the intended result of the central bank's deliberate move to push short-term rates higher, squeezing speculators by making it expensive to sell the rupee. However, theoretically, an inverted yield curve may be seen as pointing towards deep economic problems in the future, possibly even recession.

As can be seen from the graph, the average yields on 10-year maturity bonds in 2014–15 was 8.3%, while that on 30-year government bonds fell to 8.16%.

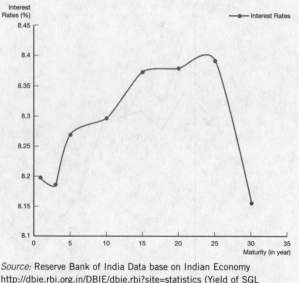

Source: Reserve Bank of India Data base on Indian Economy http://dbie.rbi.org.in/DBIE/dbie.rbi?site=statistics (Yield of SGL transactions in Government Dated securities for various maturities), as accessed on 13 March 2016 at 4pm.

If the liquidity premium theory does a better job of explaining the facts and is hence the most widely accepted theory, why do we spend time discussing the other two theories? There are two reasons. First, the ideas in these two theories lay the groundwork for the liquidity premium theory. Second, it is important to see how economists modify theories to improve them when they find that the predicted results are inconsistent with the empirical evidence.

Expectations Theory

The **expectations theory** of the term structure states the following commonsense proposition: The interest rate on a long-term bond will equal an average of the short-term interest rates that people expect to occur over the life of the long-term bond. For example, if people expect that short-term interest rates will be 10% on average over the coming five years, the expectations theory predicts that the interest rate on bonds with five years to maturity will be 10%, too. If short-term interest rates were expected to rise even higher after this five-year period, so that the average short-term interest rate over the coming 20 years is 11%, then the interest rate on 20-year bonds would equal 11% and would be higher than the interest rate on five-year bonds. We can see that the explanation provided by the expectations theory for why interest rates on bonds of different maturities differ is that short-term interest rates are expected to have different values at future dates.

The key assumption behind this theory is that buyers of bonds do not prefer bonds of one maturity over another, so they will not hold any quantity of a bond if its expected return is less than that of another bond with a different maturity. Bonds that have this characteristic are said to be *perfect substitutes*. What this means in practice is that if bonds with different maturities are perfect substitutes, the expected return on these bonds must be equal.

To see how the assumption that bonds with different maturities are perfect substitutes leads to the expectations theory, let's consider the following two investment strategies:

1. Purchase a one-year bond, and when it matures in one year, purchase another one-year bond.
2. Purchase a two-year bond and hold it until maturity.

Because both strategies must have the same expected return if people are holding both one- and two-year bonds, the interest rate on the two-year bond must equal the average of the two one-year interest rates.

Expectations Theory

The current interest rate on a one-year bond is 9%, and you expect the interest rate on the one-year bond next year to be 11%. What is the expected return over the two years? What interest rate must a two-year bond have to equal the two one-year bonds?

> Solution

The expected return over the two years will average 10% per year ([9% + 11%]/2 = 10%). The bondholder will be willing to hold both the one- and two-year bonds only if the expected return per year of the two-year bond equals 10%. Therefore, the interest rate on the two-year bond must equal 10%, the average interest rate on the two one-year bonds. Graphically, we have:

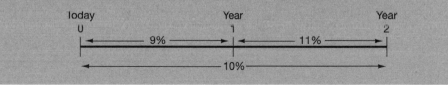

We can make this argument more general. For an investment of ₹1, consider the choice of holding, for two periods, a two-period bond or two one-period bonds. Using the definitions

i_t = today's (time t) interest rate on a one-period bond

i_{t+1}^e = interest rate on a one-period bond expected for next period (time $t + 1$)

i_{2t} = today's (time t) interest rate on the two-period bond the expected return over the two periods from investing ₹1 in the two-period bond and holding it for the two periods can be calculated as

$$(1 + i_{2t})(1 + i_{2t}) - 1 = 1 + 2i_{2t} + (i_{2t})^2 - 1 = 2i_{2t} + (i_{2t})^2$$

After the second period, the ₹1 investment is worth $(1 + i_{2t})(1 + i_{2t})$. Subtracting the ₹1 initial investment from this amount and dividing by the initial ₹1 investment gives the rate of return calculated in the previous equation. Because $(i_{2t})^2$ is extremely small—if $i_{2t} = 10\% = 0.10$, then $(i_{2t})^2 = 0.01$—we can simplify the expected return for holding the two-period bond for the two periods to

$$2i_{2t}$$

With the other strategy, in which one-period bonds are bought, the expected return on the ₹1 investment over the two periods is

$$(1 + i_t)(1 + i_{t+1}^e) - 1 = 1 + i_t + i_{t+1}^e + i_t(i_{t+1}^e) - 1 = i_t + i_{t+1}^e + i_t(i_{t+1}^e)$$

This calculation is derived by recognizing that after the first period, the ₹1 investment becomes $1 + i_t$, and this is reinvested in the one-period bond for the next period, yielding an amount $(1 + i_t)(1 + i_{t+1}^e)$. Then subtracting the ₹1 initial investment from this amount and dividing by the initial investment of ₹1 gives the expected return for the strategy of holding one-period bonds for the two periods. Because $i_t(i_{t+1}^e)$ is also extremely small—if $i_t = i_{t+1}^e = 0.10$, then $i_t(i_{t+1}^e) = 0.01$—we can simplify this to

$$i_t + i_{t+1}^e$$

Both bonds will be held only if these expected returns are equal—that is, when

$$2i_{2t} = i_t + i_{t+1}^e$$

Solving for i_{2t} in terms of the one-period rates, we have

$$i_{2t} = \frac{i_t + i_{t+1}^e}{2} \tag{1}$$

which tells us that the two-period rate must equal the average of the two one-period rates. Graphically, this can be shown as

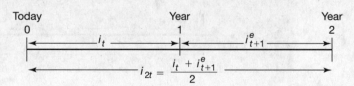

We can conduct the same steps for bonds with a longer maturity so that we can examine the whole term structure of interest rates. Doing so, we will find that the interest rate of i_{nt} on an n-period bond must be

$$i_{nt} = \frac{i_t + i_{t+1}^e + i_{t+2}^e + \ldots + i_{t+(n-1)}^e}{n} \tag{2}$$

Equation 2 states that the n-period interest rate equals the average of the one-period interest rates expected to occur over the n-period life of the bond. This is a restatement of the expectations theory in more precise terms.[2]

EXAMPLE 5.3

Expectations Theory

The one-year interest rates over the next five years are expected to be 5%, 6%, 7%, 8%, and 9%. Given this information, what are the interest rates on a two-year bond and a five-year bond? Explain what is happening to the yield curve.

> Solution

The interest rate on the two-year bond would be 5.5%.

$$i_{nt} = \frac{i_t + i^e_{t+1} + i^e_{t+2} + \ldots + i^e_{t+(n-1)}}{n}$$

where

i_t = year 1 interest rate = 5%

i^e_{t+1} = year 2 interest rate = 6%

n = number of years = 2

Thus,

$$i_{2t} = \frac{5\% + 6\%}{2} = 5.5\%$$

The interest rate on the five-year bond would be 7%.

$$i_{nt} = \frac{i_t + i^e_{t+1} + i^e_{t+2} + \ldots + i^e_{t+(n-1)}}{n}$$

where

i_t = year 1 interest rate = 5%

i^e_{t+1} = year 2 interest rate = 6%

i^e_{t+2} = year 3 interest rate = 7%

i^e_{t+3} = year 4 interest rate = 8%

i^e_{t+4} = year 5 interest rate = 9%

n = number of years = 5

Thus,

$$i_{5t} = \frac{5\% + 6\% + 7\% + 8\% + 9\%}{5} = 7.0\%$$

Using the same equation for the one-, three-, and four-year interest rates, you will be able to verify the one-year to five-year rates as 5.0%, 5.5%, 6.0%, 6.5%, and 7.0%, respectively. The rising trend in short-term interest rates produces an upward-sloping yield curve along which interest rates rise as maturity lengthens.

---

[2]The analysis here has been conducted for discount bonds. Formulas for interest rates on coupon bonds would differ slightly from those used here but would convey the same principle.

The expectations theory is an elegant theory that explains why the term structure of interest rates (as represented by yield curves) changes at different times. When the yield curve is upward-sloping, the expectations theory suggests that short-term interest rates are expected to rise in the future, as we have seen in our numerical example. In this situation, in which the long-term rate is currently higher than the short-term rate, the average of future short-term rates is expected to be higher than the current short-term rate, which can occur only if short-term interest rates are expected to rise. This result is what we see in our numerical example. When the yield curve is inverted (slopes downward), the average of future short-term interest rates is expected to be lower than the current short-term rate, implying that short-term interest rates are expected to fall, on average, in the future. Only when the yield curve is flat does the expectations theory suggest that short-term interest rates are not expected to change, on average, in the future.

The expectations theory also explains fact 1, which states that interest rates on bonds with different maturities move together over time. Historically, short-term interest rates have had the characteristic that if they increase today, they will tend to be higher in the future. Hence a rise in short-term rates will raise people's expectations of future short-term rates. Because long-term rates are the average of expected future short-term rates, a rise in short-term rates will also raise long-term rates, causing short- and long-term rates to move together.

The expectations theory also explains fact 2, which states that yield curves tend to have an upward slope when short-term interest rates are low and are inverted when short-term rates are high. When short-term rates are low, people generally expect them to rise to some normal level in the future, and the average of future expected short-term rates is high relative to the current short-term rate. Therefore, long-term interest rates will be substantially higher than current short-term rates, and the yield curve would then have an upward slope. Conversely, if short-term rates are high, people usually expect them to come back down. Long-term rates would then drop below short-term rates because the average of expected future short-term rates would be lower than current short-term rates, and the yield curve would slope downward and become inverted.[3]

The expectations theory is an attractive theory because it provides a simple explanation of the behavior of the term structure, but unfortunately it has a major shortcoming: It cannot explain fact 3, which says that yield curves usually slope upward. The typical upward slope of yield curves implies that short-term interest rates are usually expected to rise in the future. In practice, short-term interest rates are just as likely to fall as they are to rise, and so the expectations theory suggests that the typical yield curve should be flat rather than upward-sloping.

---

[3]The expectations theory explains another important fact about the relationship between short-term and long-term interest rates. As you can see in Figure 5.4, short-term interest rates are more volatile than long-term rates. If interest rates are *mean-reverting*—that is, if they tend to head back down after they are at unusually high levels or go back up when they are at unusually low levels—then an average of these short-term rates must necessarily have less volatility than the short-term rates themselves. Because the expectations theory suggests that the long-term rate will be an average of future short-term rates, it implies that the long-term rate will have less volatility than short-term rates.

Market Segmentation Theory

As the name suggests, the **market segmentation theory** of the term structure sees markets for different-maturity bonds as completely separate and segmented. The interest rate for each bond with a different maturity is then determined by the supply of and demand for that bond, with no effects from expected returns on other bonds with other maturities.

The key assumption in market segmentation theory is that bonds of different maturities are not substitutes at all, so the expected return from holding a bond of one maturity has no effect on the demand for a bond of another maturity. This theory of the term structure is at the opposite extreme to the expectations theory, which assumes that bonds of different maturities are perfect substitutes.

The argument for why bonds of different maturities are not substitutes is that investors have strong preferences for bonds of one maturity but not for another, so they will be concerned with the expected returns only for bonds of the maturity they prefer. This might occur because they have a particular holding period in mind, and if they match the maturity of the bond to the desired holding period, they can obtain a certain return with no risk at all.[4] (We have seen in Chapter 3 that if the term to maturity equals the holding period, the return is known for certain because it equals the yield exactly, and no interest-rate risk exists.) For example, people who have a short holding period would prefer to hold short-term bonds. Conversely, if you were putting funds away for your young child to go to college, your desired holding period might be much longer, and you would want to hold longer-term bonds.

In market segmentation theory, differing yield curve patterns are accounted for by supply-and-demand differences associated with bonds of different maturities. If, as seems sensible, investors desire short holding periods and generally prefer bonds with shorter maturities that have less interest-rate risk, market segmentation theory can explain fact 3, which states that yield curves typically slope upward. Because in the typical situation the demand for long-term bonds is relatively lower than that for short-term bonds, long-term bonds will have lower prices and higher interest rates, and hence the yield curve will typically slope upward.

Although market segmentation theory can explain why yield curves usually tend to slope upward, it has a major flaw in that it cannot explain facts 1 and 2. First, because it views the market for bonds of different maturities as completely segmented, there is no reason for a rise in interest rates on a bond of one maturity to affect the interest rate on a bond of another maturity. Therefore, it cannot explain why interest rates on bonds of different maturities tend to move together (fact 1). Second, because it is not clear how demand and supply for short- versus long-term bonds change with the level of short-term interest rates, the theory cannot explain why yield curves tend to slope upward when short-term interest rates are low and to be inverted when short-term interest rates are high (fact 2).

Because each of our two theories explains empirical facts that the other cannot, a logical step is to combine the theories, which leads us to the liquidity premium theory.

---

[4]The statement that there is no uncertainty about the return if the term to maturity equals the holding period is literally true only for a discount bond. For a coupon bond with a long holding period, some risk exists because coupon payments must be reinvested before the bond matures. Our analysis here is thus being conducted for discount bonds. However, the gist of the analysis remains the same for coupon bonds because the amount of this risk from reinvestment is small when coupon bonds have the same term to maturity as the holding period.

Liquidity Premium Theory

The **liquidity premium theory** of the term structure states that the interest rate on a long-term bond will equal an average of short-term interest rates expected to occur over the life of the long-term bond plus a liquidity premium (also referred to as a term premium) that responds to supply-and-demand conditions for that bond.

The liquidity premium theory's key assumption is that bonds of different maturities are substitutes, which means that the expected return on one bond *does* influence the expected return on a bond of a different maturity, but it allows investors to prefer one bond maturity over another. In other words, bonds of different maturities are assumed to be substitutes but not perfect substitutes. Investors tend to prefer shorter-term bonds because these bonds bear less interest-rate risk. For these reasons, investors must be offered a positive liquidity premium to induce them to hold longer-term bonds. Such an outcome would modify the expectations theory by adding a positive liquidity premium to the equation that describes the relationship between long- and short-term interest rates. The liquidity premium theory is thus written as

$$i_{nt} = \frac{i_t + i_{t+1}^e + i_{t+2}^e + \ldots + i_{t+(n-1)}^e}{n} + l_{nt} \tag{3}$$

where l_{nt} is the liquidity (term) premium for the n-period bond at time t, which is always positive and rises with the term to maturity of the bond, n.[5]

The relationship between the expectations theory and the liquidity premium theory is shown in Figure 5.5. There we see that because the liquidity premium is always positive and typically grows as the term to maturity increases, the yield curve implied by the liquidity premium theory is always above the yield curve implied by the expectations theory and generally has a steeper slope. (Note that for simplicity we are assuming that the expectations theory yield curve is flat.)

EXAMPLE 5.4

Liquidity Premium Theory

As in Example 3, let's suppose that the one-year interest rates over the next five years are expected to be 5%, 6%, 7%, 8%, and 9%. Investors' preferences for holding short-term bonds have the liquidity premiums for one-year to five-year bonds as 0%, 0.25%, 0.5%, 0.75%, and 1.0%, respectively. What is the interest rate on a two-year bond and a five-year bond? Compare these findings with the answer from Example 3 dealing with the pure expectations theory.

---

[5]Closely related to the liquidity premium theory is the **preferred habitat theory,** which takes a somewhat less direct approach to modifying the expectations hypothesis but comes to a similar conclusion. It assumes that investors have a preference for bonds of one maturity over another, a particular bond maturity (preferred habitat) in which they prefer to invest. Because they prefer bonds of one maturity over another, they will be willing to buy bonds that do not have the preferred maturity (habitat) only if they earn a somewhat higher expected return. Because investors are likely to prefer the habitat of short-term bonds over that of longer-term bonds, they are willing to hold long-term bonds only if they have higher expected returns. This reasoning leads to the same Equation 3 implied by the liquidity premium theory, with a term premium that typically rises with maturity.

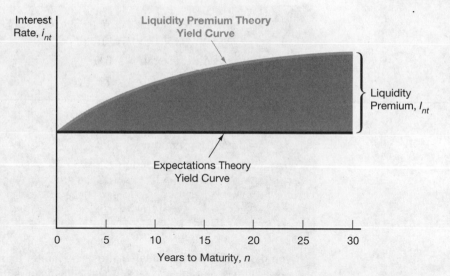

FIGURE 5.5 The Relationship Between the Liquidity Premium and Expectations Theories

Because the liquidity premium is always positive and grows as the term to maturity increases, the yield curve implied by the liquidity premium theory is always above the yield curve implied by the expectations theory and has a steeper slope. For simplicity, the yield curve implied by the expectations theory is drawn under the scenario of unchanging future one-year interest rates.

> **Solution**

The interest rate on the two-year bond would be 5.75%.

$$i_{nt} = \frac{i_t + i^e_{t+1} + i^e_{t+2} + \ldots + i^e_{t+(n-1)}}{n} + l_{nt}$$

where

i_t = year 1 interest rate = 5%

i^e_{t+1} = year 2 interest rate = 6%

l_{nt} = liquidity premium = 0.25%

n = number of years = 2

Thus,

$$i_{2t} = \frac{5\% + 6\%}{2} + 0.25\% = 5.75\%$$

The interest rate on the five-year bond would be 8%.

$$i_{nt} = \frac{i_t + i^e_{t+1} + i^e_{t+2} + \ldots + i^e_{t+(n-1)}}{n} + l_{nt}$$

where

i_t = year 1 interest rate = 5%

i_{t+1}^e = year 2 interest rate = 6%

i_{t+2}^e = year 3 interest rate = 7%

i_{t+3}^e = year 4 interest rate = 8%

i_{t+4}^e = year 5 interest rate = 9%

l_{2t} = liquidity premium = 1%

n = number of years = 5

Thus,

$$i_{5t} = \frac{5\% + 6\% + 7\% + 8\% + 9\%}{5} + 1\% = 8.0\%$$

If you did similar calculations for the one-, three-, and four-year interest rates, the one-year to five-year interest rates would be as follows: 5.0%, 5.75%, 6.5%, 7.25%, and 8.0%, respectively. Comparing these findings with those for the pure expectations theory, we can see that the liquidity preference theory produces yield curves that slope more steeply upward because of investors' preferences for short-term bonds.

Let's see if the liquidity premium theory is consistent with all three empirical facts we have discussed. They explain fact 1, which states that interest rates on different-maturity bonds move together over time: A rise in short-term interest rates indicates that short-term interest rates will, on average, be higher in the future, and the first term in Equation 3 then implies that long-term interest rates will rise along with them.

They also explain why yield curves tend to have an especially steep upward slope when short-term interest rates are low and to be inverted when short-term rates are high (fact 2). Because investors generally expect short-term interest rates to rise to some normal level when they are low, the average of future expected short-term rates will be high relative to the current short-term rate. With the additional boost of a positive liquidity premium, long-term interest rates will be substantially higher than current short-term rates, and the yield curve will then have a steep upward slope. Conversely, if short-term rates are high, people usually expect them to come back down. Long-term rates will then drop below short-term rates because the average of expected future short-term rates will be so far below current short-term rates that despite positive liquidity premiums, the yield curve will slope downward.

The liquidity premium theory explains fact 3, which states that yield curves typically slope upward, by recognizing that the liquidity premium rises with a bond's maturity because of investors' preferences for short-term bonds. Even if short-term interest rates are expected to stay the same on average in the future, long-term interest rates will be above short-term interest rates, and yield curves will typically slope upward.

How can the liquidity premium theory explain the occasional appearance of inverted yield curves if the liquidity premium is positive? It must be that at times

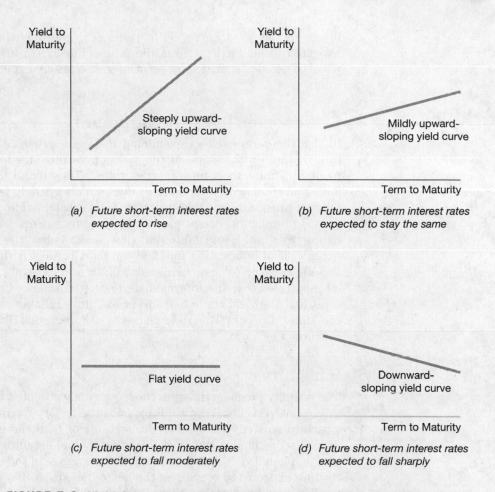

FIGURE 5.6 Yield Curves and the Market's Expectations of Future Short-Term Interest Rates According to the Liquidity Premium Theory

A steeply rising yield curve, as in panel (a) indicates that short-term interest rates are expected to rise in the future. A moderately steep yield curve, as in panel (b), indicates that short-term interest rates are not expected to rise or fall much in the future. A flat yield curve, as in panel (c), indicates that short-term rates are expected to fall moderately in the future. Finally, an inverted yield curve, as in panel (d), indicates that short-term interest rates are expected to fall sharply in the future.

short-term interest rates are expected to fall so much in the future that the average of the expected short-term rates is well below the current short-term rate. Even when the positive liquidity premium is added to this average, the resulting long-term rate will still be lower than the current short-term interest rate.

As our discussion indicates, a particularly attractive feature of the liquidity premium theory is that it tells you what the market is predicting about future short-term interest rates just from the slope of the yield curve. A steeply rising yield curve, as in panel (a) of Figure 5.6, indicates that short-term interest rates are expected to rise in the future. A moderately steep yield curve, as in panel (b), indicates that short-term interest rates are not expected to rise or fall much in the future. A flat yield curve, as in panel (c), indicates that short-term rates are expected to fall moderately in the future. Finally, an inverted yield curve, as in panel (d), indicates that short-term interest rates are expected to fall sharply in the future.

Evidence on the Term Structure

In the 1980s researchers examining the term structure of interest rates questioned whether the slope of the yield curve provides information about movements of future short-term interest rates.[6] They found that the spread between long- and short-term interest rates does not always help predict future short-term interest rates, a finding that may stem from substantial fluctuations in the liquidity (term) premium for long-term bonds. More recent research using more discriminating tests now favors a different view. It shows that the term structure contains quite a bit of information for the very short run (over the next several months) and the long run (over several years) but is unreliable at predicting movements in interest rates over the intermediate term (the time in between).[7] Research also finds that the yield curve helps forecast future inflation and business cycles (see the Mini-Case box "The Yield Curve as a Forecasting Tool for Inflation and the Business Cycle").

Summary

The liquidity premium theory is the most widely accepted theory of the term structure of interest rates because it explains the major empirical facts about the term structure so well. It combines the features of both the expectations theory and market segmentation theory by asserting that a long-term interest rate will be the sum of a liquidity (term) premium and the average of the short-term interest rates that are expected to occur over the life of the bond.

The liquidity premium theory explains the following facts:

1. Interest rates on bonds of different maturities tend to move together over time.
2. Yield curves usually slope upward.
3. When short-term interest rates are low, yield curves are more likely to have a steep upward slope, whereas when short-term interest rates are high, yield curves are more likely to be inverted.

The theory also helps us predict the movement of short-term interest rates in the future. A steep upward slope of the yield curve means that short-term rates are

[6]Robert J. Shiller, John Y. Campbell, and Kermit L. Schoenholtz, "Forward Rates and Future Policy: Interpreting the Term Structure of Interest Rates," *Brookings Papers on Economic Activity* 1 (1983): 173–217; N. Gregory Mankiw and Lawrence H. Summers, "Do Long-Term Interest Rates Overreact to Short-Term Interest Rates?" *Brookings Papers on Economic Activity* 1 (1984): 223–242.

[7]Eugene Fama, "The Information in the Term Structure," *Journal of Financial Economics* 13 (1984): 509–528; Eugene Fama and Robert Bliss, "The Information in Long-Maturity Forward Rates," *American Economic Review* 77 (1987): 680–692; John Y. Campbell and Robert J. Shiller, "Cointegration and Tests of the Present Value Models," *Journal of Political Economy* 95 (1987): 1062–1088; John Y. Campbell and Robert J. Shiller, "Yield Spreads and Interest Rate Movements: A Bird's Eye View," *Review of Economic Studies* 58 (1991): 495–514.

› MINI-CASE

The Yield Curve as a Forecasting Tool for Inflation and the Business Cycle

Because the yield curve contains information about future expected interest rates, it should also have the capacity to help forecast inflation and real output fluctuations. To see why, recall from Chapter 4 that rising interest rates are associated with economic booms and falling interest rates with recessions. When the yield curve is either flat or downward-sloping, it suggests that future short-term interest rates are expected to fall and, therefore, that the economy is more likely to enter a recession. Indeed, the yield curve is found to be an accurate predictor of the business cycle.[a]

In Chapter 3, we also learned that a nominal interest rate is composed of a real interest rate and expected inflation, implying that the yield curve contains information about both the future path of nominal interest rates and future inflation. A steep upward-sloping yield curve predicts a future increase in inflation, while a flat or downward-sloping yield curve forecasts a future decline in inflation.[b]

The ability of the yield curve to forecast business cycles and inflation is one reason why the slope of the yield curve is part of the toolkit of many economic forecasters and is often viewed as a useful indicator of the stance of monetary policy, with a steep yield curve indicating loose policy and a flat or downward-sloping yield curve indicating tight policy.

---

[a]For example, see Arturo Estrella and Frederic S. Mishkin, "Predicting U.S. Recessions: Financial Variables as Leading Indicators," *Review of Economics and Statistics* 80 (February 1998): 45–61.
[b]Frederic S. Mishkin, "What Does the Term Structure Tell Us About Future Inflation?" *Journal of Monetary Economics* 25 (January 1990): 77–95; and Frederic S. Mishkin, "The Information in the Longer-Maturity Term Structure About Future Inflation," *Quarterly Journal of Economics* 55 (August 1990): 815–828.

expected to rise, a mild upward slope means that short-term rates are expected to remain the same, a flat slope means that short-term rates are expected to fall moderately, and an inverted yield curve means that short-term rates are expected to fall sharply.

CASE

Interpreting Yield Curves, 1980–2013

Figure 5.7 illustrates several yield curves that have appeared for U.S. government bonds in recent years. What do these yield curves tell us about the public's expectations of future movements of short-term interest rates?

The steep inverted yield curve that occurred on January 15, 1981, indicated that short-term interest rates were expected to decline sharply in the future. For longer-term interest rates with their positive liquidity premium to be well below the short-term interest rate, short-term interest rates must be expected to decline so sharply that their average is far below the current short-term rate. Indeed, the public's expectations of sharply lower short-term interest rates evident in the yield curve were realized soon after January 15; by March, three-month Treasury bill rates had declined from the 16% level to 13%.

The steep upward-sloping yield curve on March 28, 1985, and June 20, 2013, indicated that short-term interest rates would climb in the future. The long-term

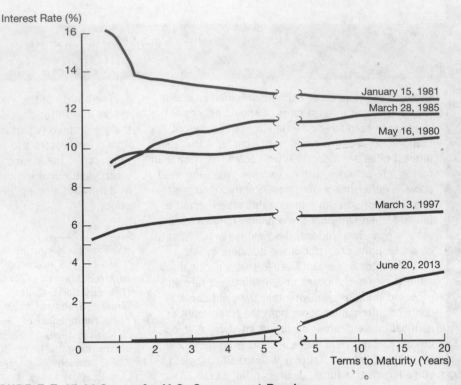

FIGURE 5.7 Yield Curves for U.S. Government Bonds

Yield curves for U.S. government bonds for different dates from 1981 to 2013.

Sources: Federal Reserve Bank of St. Louis; FRED database, http://research.stlouisfed.org/fred2/; *Wall Street Journal*, various dates.

interest rate is higher than the short-term interest rate when short-term interest rates are expected to rise because their average plus the liquidity premium will be higher than the current short-term rate. The moderately upward-sloping yield curves on May 16, 1980, and March 3, 1997, indicated that short-term interest rates were expected neither to rise nor to fall in the near future. In this case, their average remains the same as the current short-term rate, and the positive liquidity premium for longer-term bonds explains the moderate upward slope of the yield curve.

Using the Term Structure to Forecast Interest Rates

As was discussed in Chapter 4, interest-rate forecasts are extremely important to managers of financial institutions because future changes in interest rates have a significant impact on the profitability of their institutions. Furthermore, interest-rate forecasts are needed when managers of financial institutions have to set interest rates on loans that are promised to customers in the future. Our discussion of the term structure of interest rates has indicated that the slope of the yield curve provides general information about the market's prediction of the future path of interest rates. For example, a steeply upward-sloping yield curve indicates that short-term interest rates are predicted to rise in the future, and a downward-sloping yield curve indicates that short-term interest rates are predicted to fall. However, a financial institution manager needs much more specific information on interest-rate forecasts than this. Here we show how the manager of a financial institution can generate specific forecasts of interest rates using the term structure.

To see how this is done, let's start the analysis using the approach we took in developing the pure expectations theory. Recall that because bonds of different maturities are perfect substitutes, we assumed that the expected return over two periods from investing ₹1 in a two-period bond, which is $(1 + i_{2t})(1 + i_{2t}) - 1$, must equal the expected return from investing ₹1 in one-period bonds, which is $(1 + i_t)(1 + i_{t+1}^e) - 1$. This is shown graphically as follows:

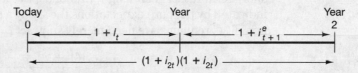

In other words,

$$(1 + i_t)(1 + i_{t+1}^e) - 1 = (1 + i_{2t})(1 + i_{2t}) - 1$$

Through some tedious algebra we can solve for i_{t+1}^e:

$$i_{t+1}^e = \frac{(1 + i_{2t})^2}{1 + i_t} - 1 \qquad (4)$$

This measure of i_{t+1}^e is called the **forward rate** because it is the one-period interest rate that the pure expectations theory of the term structure indicates is expected to prevail one period in the future. To differentiate forward rates derived from the term structure from actual interest rates that are observed at time t, we call these observed interest rates **spot rates.**

Going back to Example 3, which we used to discuss the pure expectations theory earlier in this chapter, at time t the one-year interest rate is 5% and the two-year rate is 5.5%. Plugging these numbers into Equation 4 yields the following estimate of the forward rate one period in the future:

$$i_{t+1}^e = \frac{(1 + 0.055)^2}{1 + 0.05} - 1 = 0.06 = 6\%$$

Not surprisingly, this 6% forward rate is identical to the expected one-year interest rate one year in the future that we used in Example 3. This is exactly what we should find, as our calculation here is just another way of looking at the pure expectations theory.

We can also compare holding the three-year bond against holding a sequence of one-year bonds, which reveals the following relationship:

$$(1 + i_t)(1 + i_{t+1}^e)(1 + i_{t+2}^e) - 1 = (1 + i_{3t})(1 + i_{3t})(1 + i_{3t}) - 1$$

and plugging in the estimate for i_{t+1}^e derived in Equation 4, we can solve for i_{t+2}^e:

$$i_{t+2}^e = \frac{(1 + i_{3t})^3}{(1 + i_{2t})^2} - 1$$

Continuing with these calculations, we obtain the general solution for the forward rate n periods into the future:

$$i_{t+n}^e = \frac{(1 + i_{n+1t})^{n+1}}{(1 + i_{nt})^n} - 1 \qquad (5)$$

Our discussion indicated that the pure expectations theory is not entirely satisfactory because investors must be compensated with liquidity premiums to induce them to hold longer-term bonds. Hence we need to modify our analysis, as we did when discussing the liquidity premium theory, by allowing for these liquidity premiums in estimating predictions of future interest rates.

Recall from the discussion of those theories that because investors prefer to hold short-term rather than long-term bonds, the n-period interest rate differs from that indicated by the pure expectations theory by a liquidity premium of l_{nt}. So to allow for liquidity premiums, we need merely subtract l_{nt} from i_{nt} in our formula to derive i_{t+n}^e:

$$i_{t+n}^e = \frac{(1 + i_{n+1t} - l_{n+1t})^{n+1}}{(1 + i_{nt} - l_{nt})^n} - 1 \qquad (6)$$

This measure of i_{t+n}^e is referred to, naturally enough, as the *adjusted forward-rate forecast*.

In the case of i_{t+1}^e, Equation 6 produces the following estimate:

$$i_{t+1}^e = \frac{(1 + i_{2t} - l_{2t})^2}{1 + i_t} - 1$$

Using Example 4 in our discussion of the liquidity premium theory, at time t the l_{2t} liquidity premium is 0.25%, $l_{1t} = 0$, the one-year interest rate is 5%, and the two-year interest rate is 5.75%. Plugging these numbers into our equation yields the following adjusted forward-rate forecast for one period in the future:

$$i_{t+1}^e = \frac{(1 + 0.0575 - 0.0025)^2}{1 + 0.05} - 1 = 0.06 = 6\%$$

which is the same as the expected interest rate used in Example 3, as it should be.

Our analysis of the term structure thus provides managers of financial institutions with a fairly straightforward procedure for producing interest-rate forecasts. First they need to estimate l_{nt}, the values of the liquidity premiums for various n. Then they need merely apply the formula in Equation 6 to derive the market's forecasts of future interest rates.

EXAMPLE 5.5

Forward Rate

A customer asks a bank if it would be willing to commit to making the customer a one-year loan at an interest rate of 8% one year from now. To compensate for the costs of making the loan, the bank needs to charge one percentage point more than the expected interest rate on a Treasury bond with the same maturity if it is to make a profit. If the bank manager estimates the liquidity premium to be 0.4%, and the one-year Treasury bond rate is 6% and the two-year bond rate is 7%, should the manager be willing to make the commitment?

> **Solution**

The bank manager is unwilling to make the loan because at an interest rate of 8%, the loan is likely to be unprofitable to the bank.

$$i_{t+n}^e = \frac{(1 + i_{n+1t} - l_{n+1t})^{n+1}}{(1 + i_{nt} - l_{nt})^n} - 1$$

where

i_{n+1t}	= two-year bond rate	= 0.07
l_{n+1t}	= liquidity premium	= 0.004
i_{nt}	= one-year bond rate	= 0.06
l_{1t}	= liquidity premium	= 0
n	= number of years	= 1

Thus,

$$i_{t+1}^e = \frac{(1 + 0.07 - 0.004)^2}{1 + 0.06} - 1 = 0.072 = 7.2\%$$

The market's forecast of the one-year Treasury bond rate one year in the future is therefore 7.2%. Adding the 1% necessary to make a profit on the one-year loan means that the loan is expected to be profitable only if it has an interest rate of 8.2% or higher.

As we will see in Chapter 6, the bond market's forecasts of interest rates may be the most accurate ones possible. If this is the case, the estimates of the market's forecasts of future interest rates using the simple procedure outlined here may be the best interest-rate forecasts that a financial institution manager can obtain.

SUMMARY

1. Bonds with the same maturity will have different interest rates because of three factors: default risk, liquidity, and tax considerations. The greater a bond's default risk, the higher its interest rate relative to other bonds; the greater a bond's liquidity, the lower its interest rate; and bonds with tax-exempt status will have lower interest rates than they otherwise would. The relationship among interest rates on bonds with the same maturity that arise because of these three factors is known as the *risk structure of interest rates*.

2. Several theories of the term structure provide explanations of how interest rates on bonds with different terms to maturity are related. The expectations

theory views long-term interest rates as equaling the average of future short-term interest rates expected to occur over the life of the bond. By contrast, the market segmentation theory treats the determination of interest rates for each bond's maturity as the outcome of supply and demand in that market only. Neither of these theories by itself can explain the fact that interest rates on bonds of different maturities move together over time and that yield curves usually slope upward.

3. The liquidity premium theory combines the features of the other two theories, and by so doing is able to explain the facts just mentioned. It views long-term interest rates as equaling the average of future short-term interest rates expected to occur over the life of the bond plus a liquidity premium. This theory allows us to infer the market's expectations about the movement of future short-term interest rates from the yield curve. A steeply upward-sloping curve indicates that future short-term rates are expected to rise; a mildly upward-sloping curve that short-term rates are expected to stay the same; a flat curve that short-term rates are expected to decline slightly; and an inverted yield curve that a substantial decline in short-term rates is expected in the future.

KEY TERMS

credit-rating agencies, p. 90
default, p. 88
default-free bonds, p. 89
expectations theory, p. 98
forward rate, p. 111
inverted yield curve, p. 96

junk bonds, p. 91
liquidity premium theory, p. 104
market segmentation theory, p. 103
municipal bonds, p. 90
preferred habitat theory, p. 104

risk premium, p. 89
risk structure of interest rates, p. 87
spot rate, p. 111
term structure of interest rates, p. 87
yield curve, p. 96

QUESTIONS

1. Which should have the higher risk premium on its interest rates, a corporate bond with a Moody's Baa rating or a corporate bond with a C rating? Why?

2. Why do Indian Treasury bills have lower interest rates than large-denomination negotiable bank CDs?

3. Risk premiums on corporate bonds are usually anticyclical; that is, they decrease during business cycle expansions and increase during recessions. Why is this so?

4. "If bonds of different maturities are close substitutes, their interest rates are more likely to move together." Is this statement true, false, or uncertain? Explain your answer.

5. If yield curves, on average, were flat, what would this say about the liquidity premiums in the term structure? Would you be more or less willing to accept the pure expectations theory?

6. If a yield curve looks like the one shown here, what is the market predicting about the movement of future short-term interest rates? What might the yield curve indicate about the market's predictions about the inflation rate in the future?

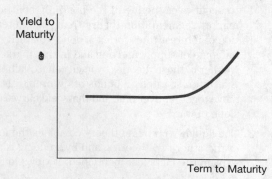

7. If a yield curve looks like the one below, what is the market predicting about the movement of future short-term interest rates? What might the yield curve indicate about the market's predictions about the inflation rate in the future?

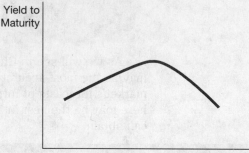

8. What effect would reducing income tax rates have on the interest rates of municipal bonds? Would interest rates of Government securities be affected and, if so, how?

Predicting the Future

9. Predict what will happen to interest rates on a corporation's bonds if the Indian government guarantees today that it will pay creditors if the corporation goes bankrupt in the future. What will happen to the interest rates on Treasury securities?

10. Predict what would happen to the risk premiums on corporate bonds if brokerage commissions were lowered in the corporate bond market.

11. If the income tax exemption on municipal bonds were abolished, what would happen to the interest rates on these bonds? What effect would it have on Indian 10 year G-sec yields?

QUANTITATIVE PROBLEMS

1. Assuming that the expectations theory is the correct theory of the term structure, calculate the interest rates in the term structure for maturities of one to five years, and plot the resulting yield curves for the following series of one-year interest rates over the next five years:

   a. 5%, 7%, 7%, 7%, 7%

   b. 5%, 4%, 4%, 4%, 4%

   How would your yield curves change if people preferred shorter-term bonds over longer-term bonds?

2. Government economists have forecasted one-year T-bill rates for the following five years, as follows:

Year	1-Year Rate (%)
1	4.25
2	5.15
3	5.50
4	6.25
5	7.10

   You have a liquidity premium of 0.25% for the next two years and 0.50% thereafter. Would you be willing to purchase a four-year T-bond at a 5.75% interest rate?

3. How does the after-tax yield on a ₹1,000,000 municipal bond with a coupon rate of 8% paying interest annually compare with that of a ₹1,000,000 corporate bond with a coupon rate of 10% paying interest annually? Assume that you are in the 25% tax bracket.

4. Consider the decision to purchase either a five-year corporate bond or a five-year municipal bond. The corporate bond is a 12% annual coupon bond with a par value of ₹1,000. It is currently yielding 11.5%. The municipal bond has an 8.5% annual coupon and a par value of ₹1,000. It is currently yielding 7%. Which of the two bonds would be more beneficial to you? Assume that your marginal tax rate is 35%.

5. Debt issued by Southeastern Corporation currently yields 12%. A municipal bond of equal risk currently yields 8%. At what marginal tax rate would an investor be indifferent between these two bonds?

6. One-year T-bill rates are expected to steadily increase by 150 basis points per year over the next six years. Determine the required interest rate on a three-year T-bond and a six-year T-bond if the current one-year interest rate is 7.5%. Assume that the expectations hypothesis for interest rates holds.

7. The one-year interest rate over the next 10 years will be 3%, 4.5%, 6%, 7.5%, 9%, 10.5%, 13%, 14.5%, 16%, and 17.5%. Using the expectations theory, what will be the interest rates on a three-year bond, a six-year bond, and a nine-year bond?

8. Using the information from the previous question, assume that investors prefer holding short-term bonds. A liquidity premium of 10 basis points is required for each year of a bond's maturity. What will be the interest rates on a three-year bond, a six-year bond, and a nine-year bond?

9. Which bond would produce a greater return if the expectations theory were to hold true, a two-year bond with an interest rate of 15% or two one-year bonds with sequential interest payments of 13% and 17%?

10. Little Monsters, Inc., borrowed ₹1,000,000 for two years from NorthernBank, Inc., at an 11.5% interest rate. The current risk-free rate is 2%, and Little Monsters' financial condition warrants a default risk premium of 3% and a liquidity risk premium of 2%. The maturity risk premium for a two-year loan is 1%, and inflation is expected to be 3% next year. What does this information imply about the rate of inflation in the second year?

11. One-year T-bill rates are 2% currently. If interest rates are expected to go up after three years by 2% every year, what should be the required interest rate on a 10-year bond issued today? Assume that the expectations theory holds.

12. One-year T-bill rates over the next four years are expected to be 3%, 4%, 5%, and 5.5%. If four-year T-bonds are yielding 4.5%, what is the liquidity premium on this bond?

13. At your favorite bond store, Bonds-R-Us, you see the following prices:

    One-year ₹100 zero selling for ₹90.19

    Three-year 10% coupon ₹1,000 par bond selling for ₹1,000

    Two-year 10% coupon ₹1,000 par bond selling for ₹1,000

    Assume that the expectations theory for the term structure of interest rates holds, no liquidity premium exists, and the bonds are equally risky. What is the implied one-year rate two years from now?

14. You observe the following market interest rates, for both borrowing and lending:

    One-year rate = 5%

Two-year rate = 6%

One-year rate one year from now = 7.25%

How can you take advantage of these rates to earn a riskless profit? Assume that the expectations theory for interest rates holds.

15. If the interest rates on one- to five-year bonds are currently 4%, 5%, 6%, 7%, and 8%, and the term premiums for one- to five-year bonds are 0%, 0.25%, 0.35%, 0.40%, and 0.50%, predict what the one-year interest rate will be two years from now.

WEB EXERCISES

The Risk and Term Structures of Interest Rates

1. The amount of additional interest investors receive due to the various risk premiums changes over time. Sometimes the risk premiums are much larger than at other times. For example, the default risk premium was very small in the late 1990s when the economy was so healthy that business failures were rare. This risk premium increases during recessions.

   Go to the Federal Reserve Bank of St. Louis FRED database at **http://research.stlouisfed.org/fred2/** and find the interest-rate listings for AAA- and Baa-rated bonds at three points in time: the most recent; June 1, 1995; and June 1, 1992. Prepare a graph that shows these three time periods (see Figure 5.1 for an example). Are the risk premiums stable or do they change over time?

2. Figure 5.7 shows a number of yield curves at various points in time. Go to **www.bloomberg.com**, and click on "Markets Data" at the top of the page. Find the Treasury yield curve. Does the current yield curve fall above or below the most recent one listed in Figure 5.7? Is the current yield curve flatter or steeper than the most recent one reported in Figure 5.7?

3. Investment companies attempt to explain to investors the nature of the risk the investor incurs when buying shares in their mutual funds. For example, go to **https://www.amfiindia.com**.

   a. Select the bond fund you would recommend to an investor who has a very low tolerance for risk. Justify your answer.

   b. Select the bond fund you would recommend to an investor who has a higher tolerance for risk and a long investment horizon. Justify your answer.

6

Are Financial Markets Efficient?

> PREVIEW

Throughout our discussion of how financial markets work, you may have noticed that the subject of expectations keeps cropping up. Expectations of returns, risk, and liquidity are central elements in the demand for assets; expectations of inflation have a major impact on bond prices and interest rates; expectations about the likelihood of default are the most important factor that determines the risk structure of interest rates; and expectations of future short-term interest rates play a central role in determining the term structure of interest rates. Not only are expectations critical in understanding behavior in financial markets, but as we will see later in this book, they are also central to our understanding of how financial institutions operate.

To understand how expectations are formed so that we can understand how securities prices move over time, we look at the efficient market hypothesis. In this chapter we examine the basic reasoning behind the efficient market hypothesis in order to explain some puzzling features of the operation and behavior of financial markets. You will see, for example, why changes in stock prices are unpredictable and why listening to a stockbroker's hot tips may not be a good idea.

Theoretically, the efficient market hypothesis should be a powerful tool for analyzing behavior in financial markets. But to establish that it is in reality a useful tool, we must compare the theory with the data. Does the empirical evidence support the theory? Though mixed, the available evidence indicates that for many purposes, this theory is a good starting point for analyzing expectations.

The Efficient Market Hypothesis

To understand how expectations affect securities prices, we need to look at how information in the market affects these prices. To do this we examine the **efficient market hypothesis** (also referred to as the **theory of efficient capital markets**), which states that prices of securities in financial markets fully reflect all available information. But what does this mean?

You may recall from Chapter 3 that the rate of return from holding a security equals the sum of the capital gain on the security (the change in the price) plus any cash payments, divided by the initial purchase price of the security:

$$R = \frac{P_{t+1} - P_t + C}{P_t} \tag{1}$$

where
R = rate of return on the security held from time t to time $t + 1$ (say, the end of 2014 to the end of 2015)

P_{t+1} = price of the security at time $t + 1$, the end of the holding period

P_t = the price of the security at time t, the beginning of the holding period

C = cash payment (coupon or dividend payments) made in the period t to $t + 1$

Let's look at the expectation of this return at time t, the beginning of the holding period. Because the current price and the cash payment C are known at the beginning, the only variable in the definition of the return that is uncertain is the price next period, P_{t+1}.[1] Denoting the expectation of the security's price at the end of the holding period as P_{t+1}^e, the expected return R^e is

$$R^e = \frac{P_{t+1}^e - P_t + C}{P_t}$$

The efficient market hypothesis views expectations as equal to optimal forecasts using all available information. What exactly does this mean? An optimal forecast is the best guess of the future using all available information. This does not mean that the forecast is perfectly accurate, but only that it is the best possible given the available information. This can be written more formally as

$$P_{t+1}^e = P_{t+1}^{of}$$

which in turn implies that the expected return on the security will equal the optimal forecast of the return:

$$R^e = R^{of} \tag{2}$$

Unfortunately, we cannot observe either R^e or P_{t+1}^e, so the equations above by themselves do not tell us much about how the financial market behaves. However,

---

[1]There are cases in which C might not be known at the beginning of the period, but that does not make a substantial difference to the analysis. We would in that case assume that not only price expectations but also the expectations of C are optimal forecasts using all available information.

if we can devise some way to measure the value of R^e, these equations will have important implications for how prices of securities change in financial markets.

The supply-and-demand analysis of the bond market developed in Chapter 4 shows us that the expected return on a security (the interest rate in the case of the bond examined) will have a tendency to head toward the equilibrium return that equates the quantity demanded to the quantity supplied. Supply-and-demand analysis enables us to determine the expected return on a security with the following equilibrium condition: The expected return on a security R^e equals the equilibrium return R^*, which equates the quantity of the security demanded to the quantity supplied; that is,

$$R^e = R^* \tag{3}$$

The academic field of finance explores the factors (risk and liquidity, for example) that influence the equilibrium returns on securities. For our purposes, it is sufficient to know that we can determine the equilibrium return and thus determine the expected return with the equilibrium condition.

We can derive an equation to describe pricing behavior in an efficient market by using the equilibrium condition to replace R^e with R^* in Equation 2. In this way we obtain

$$R^{of} = R^* \tag{4}$$

This equation tells us that *current prices in a financial market will be set so that the optimal forecast of a security's return using all available information equals the security's equilibrium return.* Financial economists state it more simply: A security's price fully reflects all available information in an efficient market.

EXAMPLE 6.1

The Efficient Market Hypothesis

Suppose that a share of Microsoft had a closing price yesterday of ₹90, but new information was announced after the market closed that caused a revision in the forecast of the price for next year to go to ₹120. If the annual equilibrium return on Microsoft is 15%, what does the efficient market hypothesis indicate the price will go to today when the market opens? (Assume that Microsoft pays no dividends.)

> **Solution**
The price would rise to ₹104.35 after the opening.

$$R^{of} = \frac{P^{of}_{t+1} - P_t + C}{P_t} = R^*$$

where
R^{of} = optimal forecast of the return = 15% = 0.15
R^* = equilibrium return = 15% = 0.15
P^{of}_{t+1} = optimal forecast of price next year = ₹120
P_t = price today after opening
C = cash (dividend) payment = 0

Thus,

$$0.15 = \frac{₹120 - P_t}{P_t}$$

$$P_t \times 0.15 = ₹120 - P_t$$

$$P_t(1.15) = ₹120$$

$$P_t = ₹104.35$$

Rationale Behind the Hypothesis

To see why the efficient market hypothesis makes sense, we make use of the concept of **arbitrage,** in which market participants (*arbitrageurs*) eliminate **unexploited profit opportunities,** meaning returns on a security that are larger than what is justified by the characteristics of that security. Arbitrage is of two types: *pure arbitrage*, in which the elimination of unexploited profit opportunities involves no risk, and the type of arbitrage we discuss here, in which the arbitrageur takes on some risk when eliminating the unexploited profit opportunities. To see how arbitrage leads to the efficient market hypothesis, suppose that, given its risk characteristics, the normal return on a security, say, Exxon-Mobil common stock, is 10% at an annual rate, and its current price P_t is lower than the optimal forecast of tomorrow's price P_{t+1}^e so that the optimal forecast of the return at an annual rate is 50%, which is greater than the equilibrium return of 10%. We are now able to predict that, on average, Exxon-Mobil's return would be abnormally high, so there is an unexpected profit opportunity. Knowing that, on average, you can earn such an abnormally high rate of return on Exxon-Mobil because $R^{of} > R^*$, you would buy more, which would in turn drive up its current price relative to the expected future price P_{t+1}^e, thereby lowering R^{of}. When the current price had risen sufficiently so that R^{of} equals R^* and the efficient market condition (Equation 4) is satisfied, the buying of Exxon-Mobil will stop, and the unexploited profit opportunity will have disappeared.

Similarly, a security for which the optimal forecast of the return is –5% while the equilibrium return is 10% ($R^{of} < R^*$) would be a poor investment because, on average, it earns less than the equilibrium return. In such a case, you would sell the security and drive down its current price relative to the expected future price until R^{of} rose to the level of R^* and the efficient market condition is again satisfied. What we have shown can be summarized as follows:

$$\left. \begin{array}{l} R^{of} > R^* \rightarrow P_t \uparrow \rightarrow R^{of} \downarrow \\ R^{of} < R^* \rightarrow P_t \downarrow \rightarrow R^{of} \uparrow \end{array} \right\} \text{until } R^{of} = R^*$$

Another way to state the efficient market condition is this: ***In an efficient market, all unexploited profit opportunities will be eliminated.***

An extremely important factor in this reasoning is that ***not everyone in a financial market must be well informed about a security for its price to be driven to the point at which the efficient market condition holds.*** Financial markets are structured so that many participants can play. As long as a few (who are often referred to as "smart money") keep their eyes open for unexploited profit opportunities, they will eliminate the profit opportunities that appear because in so doing, they make a profit. The efficient market hypothesis makes sense because it does not require everyone in a market to be cognizant of what is happening to every security.

Evidence on the Efficient Market Hypothesis

Early evidence on the efficient market hypothesis was quite favorable to it, but in recent years deeper analysis of the evidence suggests that the hypothesis may not always be entirely correct. Let's first look at the earlier evidence in favor of the hypothesis and then examine some of the more recent evidence that casts some doubt on it.

Evidence in Favor of Market Efficiency

Evidence in favor of market efficiency has examined the performance of investment analysts and mutual funds, whether stock prices reflect publicly available information, the random-walk behavior of stock prices, and the success of so-called technical analysis.

Performance of Investment Analysts and Mutual Funds   We have seen that one implication of the efficient market hypothesis is that when purchasing a security, you cannot expect to earn an abnormally high return, a return greater than the equilibrium return. This implies that it is impossible to beat the market. Many studies shed light on whether investment advisers and mutual funds (some of which charge steep sales commissions to people who purchase them) beat the market. One common test that has been performed is to take buy and sell recommendations from a group of advisers or mutual funds and compare the performance of the resulting selection of stocks with the market as a whole. Sometimes the advisers' choices have even been compared to a group of stocks chosen by putting a copy of the financial page of the newspaper on a dartboard and throwing darts. The *Wall Street Journal*, for example, used to have a regular feature called "Investment Dartboard" that compared how well stocks picked by investment advisers did relative to stocks picked by throwing darts. Did the advisers win? To their embarrassment, the dartboard beat them as often as they beat the dartboard. Furthermore, even when the comparison included only advisers who had been successful in the past in predicting the stock market, the advisers still didn't regularly beat the dartboard.

Consistent with the efficient market hypothesis, mutual funds are also not found to beat the market. Mutual funds not only do not outperform the market on average, but when they are separated into groups according to whether they had the highest or lowest profits in a chosen period, the mutual funds that did well in the first period did not beat the market in the second period.[2]

---

[2]An early study that found that mutual funds do not outperform the market is Michael C. Jensen, "The Performance of Mutual Funds in the Period 1945–64," *Journal of Finance* 23 (1968): 389–416. More recent studies on mutual fund performance are Mark Grimblatt and Sheridan Titman, "Mutual Fund Performance: An Analysis of Quarterly Portfolio Holdings," *Journal of Business* 62 (1989): 393–416; R. A. Ippolito, "Efficiency with Costly Information: A Study of Mutual Fund Performance, 1965–84," *Quarterly Journal of Economics* 104 (1989): 1–23; J. Lakonishok, A. Shleifer, and R. Vishny, "The Structure and Performance of the Money Management Industry," *Brookings Papers on Economic Activity, Microeconomics* (1992); and B. Malkiel, "Returns from Investing in Equity Mutual Funds, 1971–1991," *Journal of Finance* 50 (1995): 549–572.

The conclusion from the study of investment advisers and mutual fund performance is this: ***Having performed well in the past does not indicate that an investment adviser or a mutual fund will perform well in the future.*** This is not pleasing news to investment advisers, but it is exactly what the efficient market hypothesis predicts. It says that some advisers will be lucky and some will be unlucky. Being lucky does not mean that a forecaster actually has the ability to beat the market. (An exception that proves the rule is discussed in the Mini-Case box, "An Exception That Proves the Rule: Raj Rajaratnam and Galleon".)

Do Stock Prices Reflect Publicly Available Information?   The efficient market hypothesis predicts that stock prices will reflect all publicly available information. Thus, if information is already publicly available, a positive announcement about a company will not, on average, raise the price of its stock because this information is already reflected in the stock price. Early empirical evidence also confirmed this conjecture from the efficient market hypothesis: Favorable earnings announcements or announcements of stock splits (a division of a share of stock into multiple shares, which is usually followed by higher earnings) do not, on average, cause stock prices to rise.[3]

Random-Walk Behavior of Stock Prices   The term **random walk** describes the movements of a variable whose future changes cannot be predicted (are random) because, given today's value, the variable is just as likely to fall as to rise. An important implication of the efficient market hypothesis is that stock prices should approximately follow a random walk; that is, ***future changes in stock prices***

MINI-CASE

An Exception That Proves the Rule: Raj Rajaratnam and Galleon

The efficient market hypothesis indicates that investment advisers should not have the ability to beat the market. Yet that is exactly what Raj Rajaratnam and his Galleon Group were able to do until 2009, when he was charged by the Securities and Exchange Commission with making unfair profits (estimated to be on the order of ₹60 million) by trading on inside information. Rajaratnam was convicted in May of 2011 of insider trading and was sentenced to 11 years in prison and a fine of ₹150 million. If the stock market is efficient, can the SEC legitimately claim that Rajaratnam was able to beat the market? The answer is yes.

Rajaratnam and his Galleon Group made millions in profits for himself and his clients by investing in the stocks of firms on which he allegedly received inside information—from Rajat Gupta and Anil Kumar of McKinsey and Company, Robert Moffat of IBM, and Rajiv Goel and Roomy Khan of Intel Capital—about outside investments and other activities at specific firms. Rajaratnam and Galleon Group's ability to make millions year after year in the 2000s is an exception that proves the rule that financial analysts cannot continually outperform the market; yet it supports the efficient markets claim that only information unavailable to the market enables an investor to do so. Rajaratnam profited from knowing about inside information before the rest of the market; this information was known to him but unavailable to the market.

[3]Ray Ball and Philip Brown, "An Empirical Evaluation of Accounting Income Numbers," *Journal of Accounting Research* 6 (1968): 159–178; Eugene F. Fama, Lawrence Fisher, Michael C. Jensen, and Richard Roll, "The Adjustment of Stock Prices to New Information," *International Economic Review* 10 (1969): 1–21.

should, for all practical purposes, be unpredictable. The random-walk implication of the efficient market hypothesis is the one most commonly mentioned in the press because it is the most readily comprehensible to the public. In fact, when people mention the "random-walk theory of stock prices," they are in reality referring to the efficient market hypothesis.

The case for random-walk stock prices can be demonstrated. Suppose that people could predict that the price of Happy Feet Corporation (HFC) stock would rise 1% in the coming week. The predicted rate of capital gains and rate of return on HFC stock would then be over 50% at an annual rate. Since this is very likely to be far higher than the equilibrium rate of return on HFC stock ($R^{of} > R^*$), the efficient market hypothesis indicates that people would immediately buy this stock and bid up its current price. The action would stop only when the predictable change in the price dropped to near zero so that $R^{of} = R^*$.

Similarly, if people could predict that the price of HFC stock would fall by 1%, the predicted rate of return would be negative and less than the equilibrium return ($R^{of} < R^*$), and people would immediately sell. The current price would fall until the predictable change in the price rose back to near zero, where the efficient market condition again holds. The efficient market hypothesis suggests that the predictable change in stock prices will be near zero, leading to the conclusion that stock prices will generally follow a random walk.[4]

Financial economists have used two types of tests to explore the hypothesis that stock prices follow a random walk. In the first, they examine stock market records to see if changes in stock prices are systematically related to past changes and hence could have been predicted on that basis. The second type of test examines the data to see if publicly available information other than past stock prices could have been used to predict changes. These tests are somewhat more stringent because additional information (money supply growth, government spending, interest rates, corporate profits) might be used to help forecast stock returns. Early results from both types of tests generally confirmed the efficient market view that stock prices are not predictable and follow a random walk.[5]

Technical Analysis A popular technique used to predict stock prices, called technical analysis, is to study past stock price data and search for patterns such as trends and regular cycles. Rules for when to buy and sell stocks are then established on the basis of the patterns that emerge. The efficient market hypothesis suggests

---

[4]Note that the random-walk behavior of stock prices is only an *approximation* derived from the efficient market hypothesis. It would hold exactly only for a stock for which an unchanged price leads to its having the equilibrium return. Then, when the predictable change in the stock price is exactly zero, $R^{of} = R^*$.
[5]The first type of test, using only stock market data, is referred to as a test of *weak-form efficiency* because the information that can be used to predict stock prices is restricted solely to past price data. The second type of test is referred to as a test of *semistrong-form efficiency* because the information set is expanded to include all publicly available information, not just past stock prices. A third type of test is called a test of *strong-form efficiency* because the information set includes insider information, known only to the owners of the corporation, as when they plan to declare a high dividend. Strong-form tests do sometimes indicate that insider information can be used to predict changes in stock prices. This finding does not contradict the efficient markets theory because the information is not available to the market and hence cannot be reflected in market prices. In fact, there are strict laws against using insider information to trade in financial markets. For an early survey on the three forms of tests, see Eugene F. Fama, "Efficient Capital Markets: A Review of Theory and Empirical Work," *Journal of Finance* 25 (1970): 383–416.

CASE

Should Foreign Exchange Rates Follow a Random Walk?

Although the efficient market hypothesis is usually applied to the stock market, it can also be used to show that foreign exchange rates, like stock prices, should generally follow a random walk. To see why this is the case, consider what would happen if people could predict that a currency would appreciate by 1% in the coming week. By buying this currency, they could earn a greater than 50% return at an annual rate, which is likely to be far above the equilibrium return for holding a currency. As a result, people would immediately buy the currency and bid up its current price, thereby reducing the expected return. The process would stop only when the predictable change in the exchange rate dropped to near zero so that the optimal forecast of the return no longer differed from the equilibrium return. Likewise, if people could predict that the currency would depreciate by 1% in the coming week, they would sell it until the predictable change in the exchange rate was again near zero. The efficient market hypothesis therefore implies that future changes in exchange rates should, for all practical purposes, be unpredictable; in other words, exchange rates should follow random walks. This is exactly what empirical evidence finds.[*]

[*]See Richard A. Meese and Kenneth Rogoff, "Empirical Exchange Rate Models of the Seventies: Do They Fit Out of Sample?" *Journal of International Economics* 14 (1983): 3–24.

that technical analysis is a waste of time. The simplest way to understand why is to use the random-walk result derived from the efficient market hypothesis that holds that past stock price data cannot help predict changes. Therefore, technical analysis, which relies on such data to produce its forecasts, cannot successfully predict changes in stock prices.

Two types of tests bear directly on the value of technical analysis. The first performs the empirical analysis described earlier to evaluate the performance of any financial analyst, technical or otherwise. The results are exactly what the efficient market hypothesis predicts: Technical analysts fare no better than other financial analysts; on average, they do not outperform the market, and successful past forecasting does not imply that their forecasts will outperform the market in the future. The second type of test takes the rules developed in technical analysis for when to buy and sell stocks and applies them to new data.[6] The performance of these rules is then evaluated by the profits that would have been made using them. These tests also discredit technical analysis: It does not outperform the overall market.

[6]Sidney Alexander, "Price Movements in Speculative Markets: Trends or Random Walks?" *Industrial Management Review*, May 1961, pp. 7–26; and Sidney Alexander, "Price Movements in Speculative Markets: Trends or Random Walks? No. 2" in *The Random Character of Stock Prices*, ed. Paul Cootner (Cambridge, MA: MIT Press, 1964), pp. 338–372. More recent evidence also seems to discredit technical analysis, for example, F. Allen and R. Karjalainen, "Using Genetic Algorithms to Find Technical Trading Rules," *Journal of Financial Economics* (1999) 51: 245–271. However, some other research is more favorable to technical analysis, e.g., P. Sullivan, A. Timmerman, and H. White, "Data-Snooping, Technical Trading Rule Performance and the Bootstrap," Centre for Economic Policy Research Discussion Paper No. 1976, 1998.

Evidence Against Market Efficiency

All the early evidence supporting the efficient market hypothesis appeared to be overwhelming, causing Eugene Fama, a prominent financial economist, to state in his famous 1970 survey of the empirical evidence on the efficient market hypothesis, "The evidence in support of the efficient markets model is extensive, and (somewhat uniquely in economics) contradictory evidence is sparse."[7] However, in recent years, the theory has begun to show a few cracks, referred to as anomalies, and empirical evidence indicates that the efficient market hypothesis may not always be generally applicable.

Small-Firm Effect   One of the earliest reported anomalies in which the stock market did not appear to be efficient is called the *small-firm effect*. Many empirical studies have shown that small firms have earned abnormally high returns over long periods of time, even when the greater risk for these firms has been taken into account.[8] The small-firm effect seems to have diminished in recent years, but it is still a challenge to the theory of efficient markets. Various theories have been developed to explain the small-firm effect, suggesting that it may be due to rebalancing of portfolios by institutional investors, tax issues, low liquidity of small-firm stocks, large information costs in evaluating small firms, or an inappropriate measurement of risk for small-firm stocks.

January Effect   Over long periods of time, stock prices have tended to experience an abnormal price rise from December to January that is predictable and hence inconsistent with random-walk behavior. This so-called **January effect** seems to have diminished in recent years for shares of large companies but still occurs for shares of small companies.[9] Some financial economists argue that the January effect is due to tax issues. Investors have an incentive to sell stocks before the end of the year in December because they can then take capital losses on their tax return and reduce their tax liability. Then when the new year starts in January, they can repurchase the stocks, driving up their prices and producing abnormally high returns. Although this explanation seems sensible, it does not explain why institutional investors such as private pension funds, which are not subject to income taxes, do not take advantage of the abnormal returns in January and buy stocks in December, thus bidding up their price and eliminating the abnormal returns.[10]

---

[7]Eugene F. Fama, "Efficient Capital Markets: A Review of Theory and Empirical Work," *Journal of Finance* 25 (1970): 383–416.

[8]For example, see Marc R. Reinganum, "The Anomalous Stock Market Behavior of Small Firms in January: Empirical Tests of Tax Loss Selling Effects," *Journal of Financial Economics* 12 (1983): 89–104; Jay R. Ritter, "The Buying and Selling Behavior of Individual Investors at the Turn of the Year," *Journal of Finance* 43 (1988): 701–717; and Richard Roll, "Vas Ist Das? The Turn-of-the-Year Effect: Anomaly or Risk Mismeasurement?" *Journal of Portfolio Management* 9 (1988): 18–28.

[9]For example, see Donald B. Keim, "The CAPM and Equity Return Regularities," *Financial Analysts Journal* 42 (May–June 1986): 19–34.

[10]Another anomaly that makes the stock market seem less than efficient is the fact that the *Value Line Survey*, one of the most prominent investment advice newsletters, has produced stock recommendations that have yielded abnormally high returns on average. See Fischer Black, "Yes, Virginia, There Is Hope: Tests of the Value Line Ranking System," *Financial Analysts Journal* 29 (September–October 1973): 10–14, and Gur Huberman and Shmuel Kandel, "Market Efficiency and Value Line's Record," *Journal of Business* 63 (1990): 187–216. Whether the excellent performance of the *Value Line Survey* will continue in the future is, of course, a question mark.

Market Overreaction   Recent research suggests that stock prices may over-react to news announcements and that the pricing errors are corrected only slowly.[11] When corporations announce a major change in earnings, say, a large decline, the stock price may overshoot, and after an initial large decline, it may rise back to more normal levels over a period of several weeks. This violates the efficient market hypothesis because an investor could earn abnormally high returns, on average, by buying a stock immediately after a poor earnings announcement and then selling it after a couple of weeks when it has risen back to normal levels.

Excessive Volatility   A closely related phenomenon to market overreaction is that the stock market appears to display excessive volatility; that is, fluctuations in stock prices may be much greater than is warranted by fluctuations in their fundamental value. In an important paper, Robert Shiller of Yale University found that fluctuations in the S&P 500 stock index could not be justified by the subsequent fluctuations in the dividends of the stocks making up this index. There has been much subsequent technical work criticizing these results, but Shiller's work, along with research that finds that there are smaller fluctuations in stock prices when stock markets are closed, has produced a consensus that stock market prices appear to be driven by factors other than fundamentals.[12]

Mean Reversion   Some researchers have also found that stock returns display **mean reversion:** Stocks with low returns today tend to have high returns in the future, and vice versa. Hence stocks that have done poorly in the past are more likely to do well in the future because mean reversion indicates that there will be a predictable positive change in the future price, suggesting that stock prices are not a random walk. Other researchers have found that mean reversion is not nearly as strong in data after World War II and so have raised doubts about whether it is currently an important phenomenon. The evidence on mean reversion remains controversial.[13]

---

[11]Werner F. M. De Bondt and Richard Thaler, "Further Evidence on Investor Overreaction and Stock Market Seasonality," *Journal of Finance* 62 (1987): 557–580.

[12]Robert Shiller, "Do Stock Prices Move Too Much to Be Justified by Subsequent Changes in Dividends?" *American Economic Review* 71 (1981): 421–436, and Kenneth R. French and Richard Roll, "Stock Return Variances: The Arrival of Information and the Reaction of Traders," *Journal of Financial Economics* 17 (1986): 5–26.

[13]Evidence for mean reversion has been reported by James M. Poterba and Lawrence H. Summers, "Mean Reversion in Stock Prices: Evidence and Implications," *Journal of Financial Economics* 22 (1988): 27–59; Eugene F. Fama and Kenneth R. French, "Permanent and Temporary Components of Stock Prices," *Journal of Political Economy* 96 (1988): 246–273; and Andrew W. Lo and A. Craig MacKinlay, "Stock Market Prices Do Not Follow Random Walks: Evidence from a Simple Specification Test," *Review of Financial Studies* 1 (1988): 41–66. However, Myung Jig Kim, Charles R. Nelson, and Richard Startz, "Mean Reversion in Stock Prices? A Reappraisal of the Evidence," *Review of Economic Studies* 58 (1991): 515–528, question whether some of these findings are valid. For an excellent sum-mary of this evidence, see Charles Engel and Charles S. Morris, "Challenges to Stock Market Efficiency: Evidence from Mean Reversion Studies," Federal Reserve Bank of Kansas City *Economic Review*, September–October 1991, pp. 21–35. See also N. Jegadeesh and Sheridan Titman, "Returns to Buying Winners and Selling Losers: Implications for Stock Market Efficiency," *Journal of Finance* 48 (1993): 65–92, which shows that mean reversion also occurs for individual stocks.

New Information Is Not Always Immediately Incorporated into Stock Prices Although it is generally found that stock prices adjust rapidly to new information, as is suggested by the efficient market hypothesis, recent evidence suggests that, inconsistent with the efficient market hypothesis, stock prices do not instantaneously adjust to profit announcements. Instead, on average stock prices continue to rise for some time after the announcement of unexpectedly high profits, and they continue to fall after surprisingly low profit announcements.[14]

Overview of the Evidence on the Efficient Market Hypothesis

As you can see, the debate on the efficient market hypothesis is far from over. The evidence seems to suggest that the efficient market hypothesis may be a reasonable starting point for evaluating behavior in financial markets. However, there do seem to be important violations of market efficiency that suggest that the efficient market hypothesis may not be the whole story and so may not be generalizable to all behavior in financial markets.

THE PRACTICING MANAGER

Practical Guide to Investing in the Stock Market

The efficient market hypothesis has numerous applications to the real world. It is especially valuable because it can be applied directly to an issue that concerns managers of financial institutions (and the general public as well): how to make profits in the stock market. A practical guide to investing in the stock market, which we develop here, provides a better understanding of the use and implications of the efficient market hypothesis.

How Valuable Are Published Reports by Investment Advisers?

Suppose that you have just read in the "Heard on the Street" column of the *Wall Street Journal* that investment advisers are predicting a boom in oil stocks because an oil shortage is developing. Should you proceed to withdraw all your hard-earned savings from the bank and invest it in oil stocks?

The efficient market hypothesis tells us that when purchasing a security, we cannot expect to earn an abnormally high return, a return greater than the equilibrium return. Information in newspapers and in the published reports of investment advisers is readily available to many market participants and is already reflected in market prices. So acting on this information will not yield abnormally high returns, on average. As we have seen, the empirical evidence for the most part confirms that recommendations from investment advisers cannot help us outperform the general market. Indeed, as the Mini-Case "Should you Hire an Ape as Your Investment Adviser?" suggests, human investment advisers in San Francisco do not on average even outperform an orangutan!

---

[14]For example, see R. Ball and P. Brown, "An Empirical Evaluation of Accounting Income Numbers," *Journal of Accounting Research* (1968) 6: 159–178; L. Chan, N. Jegadeesh, and J. Lakonishok, "Momentum Strategies," *Journal of Finance* (1996) 51: 1681–1713; and Eugene Fama, "Market Efficiency, Long-Term Returns and Behavioral Finance," *Journal of Financial Economics* (1998) 49: 283–306.

Should You Hire an Ape as Your Investment Adviser?

The *San Francisco Chronicle* came up with an amusing way of evaluating how successful investment advisers are at picking stocks. They asked eight analysts to pick five stocks at the beginning of the year and then compared the performance of their stock picks to those chosen by Jolyn, an orangutan living at Marine World/Africa USA in Vallejo, California. Consistent with the results found in the "Investment Dartboard" feature of the *Wall Street Journal*, Jolyn beat the investment advisers as often as they beat her. Given this result, you might be just as well off hiring an orangutan as your investment adviser as you would hiring a human being!

Probably no other conclusion is met with more skepticism by students than this one when they first hear it. We all know or have heard of somebody who has been successful in the stock market for a period of many years. We wonder, how could someone be so consistently successful if he or she did not really know how to predict when returns would be abnormally high? The following story, reported in the press, illustrates why such anecdotal evidence is not reliable.

A get-rich-quick artist invented a clever scam. Every week, he wrote two letters. In letter A, he would pick team A to win a particular football game, and in letter B, he would pick the opponent, team B. A mailing list would then be separated into two groups, and he would send letter A to the people in one group and letter B to the people in the other. The following week he would do the same thing but would send these letters only to the group who had received the first letter with the correct prediction. After doing this for 10 games, he had a small cluster of people who had received letters predicting the correct winning team for every game. He then mailed a final letter to them, declaring that since he was obviously an expert predictor of the outcome of football games (he had picked winners 10 weeks in a row) and since his predictions were profitable for the recipients who bet on the games, he would continue to send his predictions only if he were paid a substantial amount of money. When one of his clients figured out what he was up to, the con man was prosecuted and thrown in jail!

What is the lesson of the story? Even if no forecaster is an accurate predictor of the market, there will always be a group of consistent winners. A person who has done well regularly in the past cannot guarantee that he or she will do well in the future. Note that there will also be a group of persistent losers, but you rarely hear about them because no one brags about a poor forecasting record.

Should You Be Skeptical of Hot Tips?

Suppose that your broker phones you with a hot tip to buy stock in the Happy Feet Corporation (HFC) because it has just developed a product that is completely effective in curing athlete's foot. The stock price is sure to go up. Should you follow this advice and buy HFC stock?

The efficient market hypothesis indicates that you should be skeptical of such news. If the stock market is efficient, it has already priced HFC stock so that its expected return will equal the equilibrium return. The hot tip is not particularly valuable and will not enable you to earn an abnormally high return.

You might wonder, though, if the hot tip is based on new information and would give you an edge on the rest of the market. If other market participants have gotten this information before you, the answer is no. As soon as the information hits the street, the unexploited profit opportunity it creates will be quickly eliminated. The stock's price will already reflect the information, and you should expect to realize only the equilibrium return. But if you are one of the first to know the new information (as Raj Rajaratnam was—see the Mini-Case box on page 122), it can do you some good. Only then can you be one of the lucky ones who, on average, will earn an abnormally high return by helping eliminate the unexploited profit opportunity by buying HFC stock.

Do Stock Prices Always Rise When There Is Good News?

If you follow the stock market, you might have noticed a puzzling phenomenon: When good news about a stock, such as a particularly favorable earnings report, is announced, the price of the stock frequently does not rise. The efficient market hypothesis and the random-walk behavior of stock prices explain this phenomenon.

Because changes in stock prices are unpredictable, when information is announced that has already been expected by the market, the stock price will remain unchanged. The announcement does not contain any new information that should lead to a change in stock prices. If this were not the case and the announcement led to a change in stock prices, it would mean that the change was predictable. Because that is ruled out in an efficient market, **stock prices will respond to announcements only when the information being announced is new and unexpected.** If the news is expected, there will be no stock price response. This is exactly what the evidence that we described earlier suggests will occur—that stock prices reflect publicly available information.

Sometimes a stock price declines when good news is announced. Although this seems somewhat peculiar, it is completely consistent with the workings of an efficient market. Suppose that although the announced news is good, it is not as good as expected. HFC's earnings may have risen 15%, but if the market expected earnings to rise by 20%, the new information is actually unfavorable, and the stock price declines.

Efficient Markets Prescription for the Investor

What does the efficient market hypothesis recommend for investing in the stock market? It tells us that hot tips, investment advisers' published recommendations, and technical analysis—all of which make use of publicly available information—cannot help an investor outperform the market. Indeed, it indicates that anyone without better information than other market participants cannot expect to beat the market. So what is an investor to do?

The efficient market hypothesis leads to the conclusion that such an investor (and almost all of us fit into this category) should not try to outguess the market by constantly buying and selling securities. This process does nothing but boost the income of brokers, who earn commissions on each trade.* Instead, the investor

---

*The investor may also have to pay the government capital gains taxes on any profits that are realized when a security is sold—an additional reason why continual buying and selling does not make sense.

should pursue a "buy and hold" strategy—purchase stocks and hold them for long periods of time. This will lead to the same returns, on average, but the investor's net profits will be higher because fewer brokerage commissions will have to be paid.**

It is frequently a sensible strategy for a small investor, whose costs of managing a portfolio may be high relative to its size, to buy into a mutual fund rather than individual stocks. Because the efficient market hypothesis indicates that no mutual fund can consistently outperform the market, an investor should not buy into one that has high management fees or that pays sales commissions to brokers but rather should purchase a no-load (commission-free) mutual fund that has low management fees.

As we have seen, the evidence indicates that it will not be easy to beat the prescription suggested here, although some of the anomalies to the efficient market hypothesis suggest that an extremely clever investor (which rules out most of us) may be able to outperform a buy-and-hold strategy.

**The investor can also minimize risk by holding a diversified portfolio. The investor will be better off by pursuing a buy-and-hold strategy with a diversified portfolio or with a mutual fund that has a diversified portfolio.

Why the Efficient Market Hypothesis Does Not Imply That Financial Markets Are Efficient

Many financial economists take the efficient market hypothesis one step further in their analysis of financial markets. Not only do they believe that expectations in financial markets are rational—that is, equal to optimal forecasts using all available information—but they also add the condition that prices in financial markets reflect the true fundamental (intrinsic) value of the securities. In other words, all prices are always correct and reflect **market fundamentals** (items that have a direct impact on future income streams of the securities) and so financial markets are efficient.

This stronger view of market efficiency has several important implications in the academic field of finance. First, it implies that in an efficient capital market, one investment is as good as any other because the securities' prices are correct. Second, it implies that a security's price reflects all available information about the intrinsic value of the security. Third, it implies that security prices can be used by managers of both financial and nonfinancial firms to assess their cost of capital (cost of financing their investments) accurately and hence that security prices can be used to help them make the correct decisions about whether a specific investment is worth making. This stronger version of market efficiency is a basic tenet of much analysis in the finance field.

The efficient markets hypothesis may be misnamed, however. It does not imply the stronger view of market efficiency but rather just that prices in markets like the stock market are unpredictable. Indeed, as the following application suggests, the existence of market crashes and **bubbles,** in which the prices of assets rise well above their fundamental values, cast serious doubt on the stronger view that financial markets are efficient but provide less of an argument against the basic lessons of the efficient markets hypothesis.

What Do Stock Market Crashes Tell Us About the Efficient Market Hypothesis?

On October 19, 1987, dub' ed "Black Monday," the Dow Jones Industrial Average declined more than 20%, the largest one-day decline in U.S. history. The collapse of the high-tech companies' share prices from their peaks in March 2000 caused the heavily tech-laden NASDAQ index to fall from about 5,000 in March 2000 to about 1,500 in 2001 and 2002, for a decline of well over 60%. These stock market crashes have caused many economists to question the validity of the efficient market hypothesis. They do not believe that an efficient market could have produced such massive swings in share prices. To what degree should these stock market crashes make us doubt the validity of the efficient market hypothesis?

Nothing in the efficient market hypothesis rules out large changes in stock prices. A large change in stock prices can result from new information that produces a dramatic decline in optimal forecasts of the future valuation of firms. However, economists are hard pressed to come up with fundamental changes in the economy that can explain the Black Monday and tech crashes. One lesson from these crashes is that factors other than market fundamentals probably have an effect on asset prices. Indeed, as we will explore in Chapters 8 and 9, there are good reasons to believe that there are impediments to financial markets working well. Hence these crashes have convinced many economists that the stronger version of the efficient market hypothesis, which states that asset prices reflect the true fundamental (intrinsic) value of securities, is incorrect. They attribute a large role in determination of asset prices to market psychology and to the institutional structure of the marketplace. However, nothing in this view contradicts the basic reasoning behind the weaker version of the efficient market hypothesis—that market participants eliminate unexploited profit opportunities. Even though stock market prices may not always solely reflect market fundamentals, as long as stock market crashes are unpredictable, the basic lessons of the efficient markets hypothesis hold.

However, other economists believe that market crashes and bubbles suggest that unexploited profit opportunities may exist and that the efficient market hypothesis might be fundamentally flawed. The controversy over the efficient market hypothesis continues.

Behavioral Finance

Doubts about the efficiency of financial markets, particularly after the stock market crash of 1987, led to a new field of study, **behavioral finance,** which applies concepts from other social sciences, such as anthropology, sociology, and particularly psychology, to understand the behavior of securities prices.[15]

---

[15]Surveys of this field can be found in Hersh Shefrin, *Beyond Greed and Fear: Understanding of Behavioral Finance and the Psychology of Investing* (Boston: Harvard Business School Press, 2000); Andrei Shleifer, *Inefficient Markets* (Oxford: Oxford University Press, 2000); and Robert J. Shiller, "From Efficient Market Theory to Behavioral Finance," Cowles Foundation Discussion Paper No. 1385 (October 2002).

As we have seen, the efficient market hypothesis assumes that unexploited profit opportunities are eliminated by "smart money." But can smart money dominate ordinary investors so that financial markets are efficient? Specifically, the efficient market hypothesis suggests that smart money sells when a stock price goes up irrationally, with the result that the stock falls back down to what is justified by fundamentals. However, for this to occur, smart money must be able to engage in **short sales,** in which they borrow stock from brokers and then sell it in the market, with the hope that they earn a profit by buying the stock back again ("covering the short") after it has fallen in price. However, work by psychologists suggests that people are subject to loss aversion: That is, they are more unhappy when they suffer losses than they are happy from making gains. Short sales can result in losses way in excess of an investor's initial investment if the stock price climbs sharply above the price at which the short sale is made (and these losses have the possibility of being unlimited if the stock price climbs to astronomical heights). Loss aversion can thus explain an important phenomenon: Very little short selling actually takes place. Short selling may also be constrained by rules restricting it because it seems unsavory that someone would make money from another person's misfortune. The fact that there is so little short selling can explain why stock prices sometimes get overvalued. Not enough short selling can take place by smart money to drive stock prices back down to their fundamental value.

Psychologists have also found that people tend to be overconfident in their own judgments (just as in "Lake Wobegon," everyone believes they are above average). As a result, it is no surprise that investors tend to believe they are smarter than other investors. These "smart" investors not only assume the market often doesn't get it right, but they are willing to trade on the basis of these beliefs. This can explain why securities markets have so much trading volume, something that the efficient market hypothesis does not predict.

Overconfidence and social contagion provide an explanation for stock market bubbles. When stock prices go up, investors attribute their profits to their intelligence and talk up the stock market. This word-of-mouth enthusiasm and the media then can produce an environment in which even more investors think stock prices will rise in the future. The result is then a so-called positive feedback loop in which prices continue to rise, producing a speculative bubble, which finally crashes when prices get too far out of line with fundamentals.[16]

The field of behavioral finance is a young one, but it holds out hope that we might be able to explain some features of securities markets' behavior that are not well explained by the efficient market hypothesis.

---

[16]See Robert J. Shiller, *Irrational Exuberance* (New York: Broadway Books, 2001).

SUMMARY

1. The efficient market hypothesis states that current security prices will fully reflect all available information because in an efficient market, all unexploited profit opportunities are eliminated. The elimination of unexploited profit opportunities necessary for a financial market to be efficient does not require that all market participants be well informed.

2. The evidence on the efficient market hypothesis is quite mixed. Early evidence on the performance of investment analysts and mutual funds, whether stock prices reflect publicly available information, the random-walk behavior of stock prices, or the success of so-called technical analysis, was quite favorable to the efficient market hypothesis. However, in recent years, evidence on the small-firm effect, the January effect, market overreaction, excessive volatility, mean reversion, and that new information is not always incorporated into stock prices suggests that the hypothesis may not always be entirely correct. The evidence seems to suggest that the efficient market hypothesis may be a reasonable starting point for evaluating behavior in financial markets, but it may not be generalizable to all behavior in financial markets.

3. The efficient market hypothesis indicates that hot tips, investment advisers' published recommendations, and technical analysis cannot help an investor outperform the market. The prescription for investors is to pursue a buy-and-hold strategy—purchase stocks and hold them for long periods of time. Empirical evidence generally supports these implications of the efficient market hypothesis in the stock market.

4. The existence of market crashes and bubbles have convinced many financial economists that the stronger version of the efficient market hypothesis, which states that asset prices reflect the true fundamental (intrinsic) value of securities, is not correct. It is far less clear that the stock market crashes show that the efficient market hypothesis is wrong. Even if the stock market were driven by factors other than fundamentals, the crashes do not clearly demonstrate that many of the basic lessons of the efficient market hypothesis are no longer valid as long as the crashes could not have been predicted.

5. The new field of behavioral finance applies concepts from other social sciences, such as anthropology, sociology, and particularly psychology, to understand the behavior of securities prices. Loss aversion, overconfidence, and social contagion can explain why trading volume is so high, stock prices get overvalued, and speculative bubbles occur.

KEY TERMS

arbitrage, p. 120
behavioral finance, p. 131
bubbles, p. 130
efficient market hypothesis, p. 118

January effect, p. 125
market fundamentals, p. 130
mean reversion, p. 126
random walk, p. 122

short sales, p. 132
theory of efficient capital markets, p. 118
unexploited profit opportunities, p. 120

QUESTIONS

1. "Forecasters' predictions of inflation are notoriously inaccurate, so their expectations of inflation cannot be optimal." Is this statement true, false, or uncertain? Explain your answer.

2. "Whenever it is snowing when Joe Commuter gets up in the morning, he misjudges how long it will take him to drive to work. Otherwise, his expectations of the driving time are perfectly accurate. Considering that it snows only once every 10 years where Joe lives, Joe's expectations are almost always perfectly accurate." Are Joe's expectations optimal? Why or why not?

3. If a forecaster spends hours every day studying data to forecast interest rates, but his expectations are not as accurate as predicting that tomorrow's interest rates will be identical to today's interest rates, are his expectations optimal?

4. "If stock prices did not follow a random walk, there would be unexploited profit opportunities in the market." Is this statement true, false, or uncertain? Explain your answer.

5. Suppose that increases in the money supply lead to a rise in stock prices. Does this mean that when you see that the money supply has had a sharp rise in the past week, you should go out and buy stocks? Why or why not?

6. If I read in the *Economic Times* that the "smart money" on Dalal Street expects stock prices to fall, should I follow that lead and sell all my stocks?

7. If my broker has been right in her five previous buy and sell recommendations, should I continue listening to her advice?

8. Can a person with optimal expectations expect the price of Google to rise by 10% in the next month?

9. "If most participants in the stock market do not follow what is happening to the monetary aggregates, prices of common stocks will not fully reflect information about them." Is this statement true, false, or uncertain? Explain your answer.

10. "An efficient market is one in which no one ever profits from having better information than the rest." Is this statement true, false, or uncertain? Explain your answer.

11. If higher money growth is associated with higher future inflation and if announced money growth turns out to be extremely high,but is still less than the market expected, what do you think would happen to long-term bond prices?

12. "Foreign exchange rates, like stock prices, should follow a random walk." Is this statement true, false, or uncertain? Explain your answer.

13. Can we expect the value of the dollar to rise by 2% next week if our expectations are optimal?

14. "Human fear is the source of stock market crashes, so these crashes indicate that expectations in the stock market cannot be optimal." Is this statement true, false, or uncertain? Explain your answer.

QUANTITATIVE PROBLEMS

1. A company has just announced a 3-for-1 stock split, effective immediately. Prior to the split, the company had a market value of ₹5 billion with 100 million shares outstanding. Assuming that the split conveys no new information about the company, what is the value of the company, the number of shares outstanding, and price per share after the split? If the actual market price immediately following the split is ₹17.00 per share, what does this tell us about market efficiency?

2. If the public expects a corporation to lose ₹5 a share this quarter and it actually loses ₹4, which is still the largest loss in the history of the company, what does the efficient market hypothesis say will happen to the price of the stock when the ₹4 loss is announced?

WEB EXERCISES

The Efficient Market Hypothesis

1. Visit **http://www.moneycontrol.com/stocks/hist-stock.php; http://www.nseindia.com; http://www.bseindia.com; http://www.sebi.com**. Review the indices for S & P BSE Sensex, CNX Midcap Index-NSE and the Nifty Midcap 50. Which Index appears most volatile? In which index would you have rather invested in 2000 if the investment had been allowed to compound until now?

2. The Internet is a great source of information on stock prices and stock price movements. Go to **http://finance.yahoo.com** and click on "Investing," then "Market Overview," and then on the DOW ticker to view current data on the Dow Jones Industrial Average. Click on the chart to manipulate the different variables. Change the time range, and observe the stock trend over various intervals. Have stock prices been going down over the last day, week, three months, and year?

CHAPTER

7

Why Do Financial Institutions Exist?

> PREVIEW

A healthy and vibrant economy requires a financial system that moves funds from people who save to people who have productive investment opportunities. But how does the financial system make sure that your hard-earned savings get channeled to those with productive investment opportunities?

This chapter answers that question by providing a theory for understanding why financial institutions exist to promote economic efficiency. The theoretical analysis focuses on a few simple but powerful economic concepts that enable us to explain features of our financial markets, such as why financial contracts are written as they are, and why financial intermediaries are more important than securities markets for getting funds to borrowers.

Basic Facts About Financial Structure Throughout the World

The financial system is complex in both structure and function throughout the world. It includes many types of institutions: banks, insurance companies, mutual funds, stock and bond markets, and so on—all of which are regulated by government. The financial system channels trillions of dollars per year from savers to people with productive investment opportunities. If we take a close look at financial structure all over the world, we find eight basic facts, some of which are quite surprising, that we need to explain to understand how the financial system works.

The bar chart in Figure 7.1 shows how American businesses financed their activities using external funds (those obtained from outside the business itself) in the period 1970–2000 and compares U.S. data with those of Germany, Japan, and Canada. The Bank Loans category is made up primarily of loans from depository institutions; Nonbank Loans is composed primarily of loans by other financial intermediaries; the Bonds category includes marketable debt securities such as corporate bonds and commercial paper; and Stock consists of new issues of new equity (stock market shares).

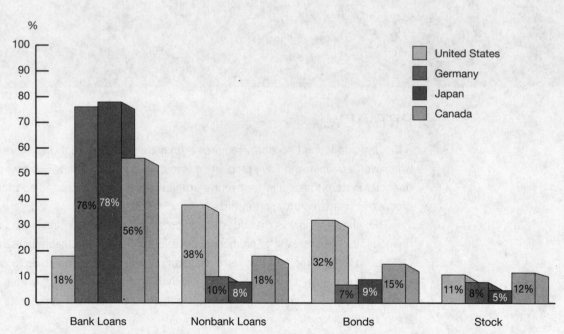

FIGURE 7.1 **Sources of External Funds for Nonfinancial Businesses: A Comparison of the United States with Germany, Japan, and Canada**

The Bank Loans category is made up primarily of loans from depository institutions; Nonbank Loans is composed primarily of loans by other financial intermediaries; the Bonds category includes marketable debt securities such as corporate bonds and commercial paper; and Stock consists of new issues of new equity (stock market shares).

Source: Andreas Hackethal and Reinhard H. Schmidt, "Financing Patterns: Measurement Concepts and Empirical Results," Johann Wolfgang Goethe-Universitat Working Paper No. 125, January 2004. The data are from 1970–2000 and are gross flows as percentages of the total, not including trade and other credit data, which are not available.

Now let's explore the eight facts.

1. ***Stocks are not the most important source of external financing for businesses.*** Because so much attention in the media is focused on the stock market, many people have the impression that stocks are the most important sources of financing corporations, especially in the Advanced Economies. However, as we can see from the bar chart in Figure 7.1, the stock market accounted for only a small fraction of the external financing of American businesses in the 1970–2000 period: 11%. Similarly small figures apply in the other countries presented in Figure 7.1 as well. Why is the stock market less important than other sources of financing even in the United States and other developed countries?

2. ***Issuing marketable debt and equity securities is not the primary way in which businesses finance their operations.*** Figure 7.1 shows that bonds are a far more important source of financing than stocks in the United States (32% versus 11%). However, stocks and bonds combined (43%), which make up the total share of marketable securities, still supply less than one-half of the external funds corporations need to finance their activities. The fact that issuing marketable securities is not the most important source of financing is true elsewhere in the world as well. Indeed, as we see in Figure 7.1, other countries have a much smaller share of external financing supplied by marketable securities than does the United States. Why don't businesses use marketable securities more extensively to finance their activities?

3. ***Indirect finance, which involves the activities of financial intermediaries, is many times more important than direct finance, in which businesses raise funds directly from lenders in financial markets.*** Direct finance involves the sale to households of marketable securities such as stocks and bonds. Much of these securities have been bought primarily by financial intermediaries such as insurance companies, pension funds, and mutual funds. In fact, direct finance is used in less than 10% of the external funding of American business. Because in most countries marketable securities are an even less important source of finance than in the United States, direct finance is also far less important than indirect finance in the rest of the world. Why are financial intermediaries and indirect finance so important in financial markets? In recent years, however, indirect finance has been declining in importance. Why is this happening?

4. ***Financial intermediaries, particularly banks, are the most important source of external funds used to finance businesses.*** As we can see in Figure 7.1, the primary source of external funds for businesses throughout the world comprises loans made by banks and other nonbank financial intermediaries such as insurance companies, pension funds, and finance companies (56% in the United States, but more than 70% in Germany, Japan, and Canada). In other industrialized countries, bank loans are the largest category of sources of external finance (more than 70% in Germany and Japan and more than 50% in Canada). Thus, the data suggest that banks in these countries have the most important role in financing business activities. In developing countries, banks play an even more important role in the financial system than they do in industrialized countries. What makes banks so important to the workings of the financial system? Although banks remain important, their share of external funds for businesses has been declining in recent years. What is driving this decline?

5. *The financial system is among the most heavily regulated sectors of the economy.* The financial system is heavily regulated in the United States and all other developed countries. Governments regulate financial markets primarily to promote the provision of information and to ensure the soundness (stability) of the financial system. Why are financial markets so extensively regulated throughout the world?

6. *Only large, well-established corporations have easy access to securities markets to finance their activities.* Individuals and smaller businesses that are not well established are less likely to raise funds by issuing marketable securities. Instead, they most often obtain their financing from banks. Why do only large, well-known corporations find it easier to raise funds in securities markets?

7. *Collateral is a prevalent feature of debt contracts for both households and businesses.* Collateral is property that is pledged to a lender to guarantee payment in the event that the borrower is unable to make debt payments. Collateralized debt (also known as **secured debt** to contrast it with **unsecured debt**, such as credit card debt, which is not collateralized) is the predominant form of household debt and is widely used in business borrowing as well. Why is collateral such an important feature of debt contracts?

8. *Debt contracts typically are extremely complicated legal documents that place substantial restrictions on the behavior of the borrower.* Many students think of a debt contract as a simple IOU that can be written on a single piece of paper. The reality of debt contracts is far different, however. In all countries, bond or loan contracts typically are long legal documents with provisions (called **restrictive covenants**) that restrict and specify certain activities that the borrower can engage in. Restrictive covenants are not just a feature of debt contracts for businesses; for example, personal automobile loan and home mortgage contracts have covenants that require the borrower to maintain sufficient insurance on the automobile or house purchased with the loan. Why are debt contracts so complex and restrictive?

As you may recall from Chapter 2, an important feature of financial markets is that they have substantial transaction and information costs. An economic analysis of how these costs affect financial markets provides us with explanations of the eight facts, which in turn enable a much deeper understanding of how our financial system works. In the next section, we examine the impact of transaction costs on the structure of our financial system. Then we turn to the effect of information costs on financial structure.

Transaction Costs

Transaction costs are a major problem in financial markets. An example will make this clear.

How Transaction Costs Influence Financial Structure

Say you have ₹5,000 you would like to invest, and you think about investing in the stock market. Because you have only ₹5,000, you can buy only a small number of shares. Even if you use online trading, your purchase is so small that the brokerage commission for buying the stock you picked will be a large percentage of the purchase price of the shares. If instead you decide to buy a bond, the problem is even worse because the smallest denomination for some bonds you might want to buy is as much as ₹10,000, and you do not have that much to invest. You are disappointed and realize that you will not be able to use financial markets to earn a return on your hard-earned savings. You can take some consolation, however, in the fact that you are not alone in being stymied by high transaction costs. This is a fact of life for many of us.

You also face another problem related to transaction costs. Because you have only a small amount of funds available, you can make only a restricted number of investments because a large number of small transactions would result in very high transaction costs. That is, you have to put all your eggs in one basket, and your inability to diversify will subject you to a lot of risk.

How Financial Intermediaries Reduce Transaction Costs

This example of the problems posed by transaction costs and the example outlined in Chapter 2 when legal costs kept you from making a loan to Manoj the Carpenter illustrate that small savers like you are frozen out of financial markets and are unable to benefit from them. Fortunately, financial intermediaries, an important part of the financial structure, have evolved to reduce transaction costs and allow small savers and borrowers to benefit from the existence of financial markets.

Economies of Scale One solution to the problem of high transaction costs is to bundle the funds of many investors together so that they can take advantage of *economies of scale*, the reduction in transaction costs per rupee of investment as the size (scale) of transactions increases. Bundling investors' funds together reduces transaction costs for the individual investors. Economies of scale exist because the total cost of carrying out a transaction in financial markets increases only a little as the size of the transaction grows. For example, the cost of arranging a purchase of 10,000 shares of stock is not much greater than the cost of arranging a purchase of 50 shares of stock.

The presence of economies of scale in financial markets helps explain why financial intermediaries developed and have become such an important part of our financial structure. The clearest example of a financial intermediary that arose because of economies of scale is a mutual fund. A *mutual fund* is a financial intermediary that sells shares to individuals and then invests the proceeds in bonds or stocks. Because it buys large blocks of stocks or bonds, a mutual fund can take advantage of lower transaction costs. These cost savings are then passed on to individual investors after the mutual fund has taken its cut in the form of management fees for administering their accounts. An additional benefit for individual investors is that a mutual fund is large enough to purchase a widely diversified portfolio of securities. The increased diversification for individual investors reduces their risk, making them better off.

Economies of scale are also important in lowering the costs of things such as computer technology that financial institutions need to accomplish their tasks. Once a large mutual fund has invested a lot of money in setting up a telecommunications system, for example, the system can be used for a huge number of transactions at a low cost per transaction.

Expertise Financial intermediaries are also better able to develop expertise to lower transaction costs. Their expertise in computer technology enables them to offer customers convenient services like being able to call a toll-free number for information on how well their investments are doing and to write checks on their accounts.

An important outcome of a financial intermediary's low transaction costs is the ability to provide its customers with *liquidity services*, services that make it easier for customers to conduct transactions. Money market mutual funds, for example, not only pay shareholders high interest rates but also allow them to write checks for convenient bill paying.

Asymmetric Information: Adverse Selection and Moral Hazard

The presence of transaction costs in financial markets explains in part why financial intermediaries and indirect finance play such an important role in financial markets (fact 3). To understand financial structure more fully, however, we turn to the role of information in financial markets.

Asymmetric information—a situation that arises when one party's insufficient knowledge about the other party involved in a transaction makes it impossible to make accurate decisions when conducting the transaction—is an important aspect of financial markets. For example, managers of a corporation know whether they are honest or have better information about how well their business is doing than the stockholders do. The presence of asymmetric information leads to adverse selection and moral hazard problems, which were introduced in Chapter 2.

Adverse selection is an asymmetric information problem that occurs *before* the transaction: Potential bad credit risks are the ones who most actively seek out loans. Thus, the parties who are the most likely to produce an undesirable outcome are the ones most likely to want to engage in the transaction. For example, big risk takers or outright crooks might be the most eager to take out a loan because they know that they are unlikely to pay it back. Because adverse selection increases the chances that a loan might be made to a bad credit risk, lenders might decide not to make any loans, even though good credit risks can be found in the marketplace.

Moral hazard arises *after* the transaction occurs: The lender runs the risk that the borrower will engage in activities that are undesirable from the lender's point of view because they make it less likely that the loan will be paid back. For example, once borrowers have obtained a loan, they may take on big risks (which have possible high returns but also run a greater risk of default) because they are playing with someone else's money. Because moral hazard lowers the probability that the loan will be repaid, lenders may decide that they would rather not make a loan.

The analysis of how asymmetric information problems affect economic behavior is called **agency theory.** We will apply this theory here to explain why financial structure takes the form it does, thereby explaining the facts outlined at the beginning of the chapter. In the next chapter, we will use the same theory to understand financial crisis.

The Lemons Problem: How Adverse Selection Influences Financial Structure

GO ONLINE

Access **http://www. nobelprize.org/nobel_prizes/ economic-sciences/ laureates/2001/** and find a complete discussion of the lemons problem on a site dedicated to Nobel Prize winners.

A particular aspect of the way the adverse selection problem interferes with the efficient functioning of a market was outlined in a famous article by Nobel Prize winner George Akerlof. It is called the "lemons problem" because it resembles the problem created by lemons in the used-car market.[1] Potential buyers of used cars are frequently unable to assess the quality of the car; that is, they can't tell whether a particular used car is one that will run well or a lemon that will continually give them grief. The price that a buyer pays must therefore reflect the *average* quality of the cars in the market, somewhere between the low value of a lemon and the high value of a good car.

The owner of a used car, by contrast, is more likely to know whether the car is a peach or a lemon. If the car is a lemon, the owner is more than happy to sell it at the price the buyer is willing to pay, which, being somewhere between the value of a lemon and a good car, is greater than the lemon's value. However, if the car is a peach, the owner knows that the car is undervalued at the price the buyer is willing to pay, and so the owner may not want to sell it. As a result of this adverse selection, few good used cars will come to the market. Because the average quality of a used car available in the market will be low and because few people want to buy a lemon, there will be few sales. The used-car market will function poorly, if at all.

Lemons in the Stock and Bond Markets

A similar lemons problem arises in securities markets—that is, the debt (bond) and equity (stock) markets. Suppose that our friend Raj the investor, a potential buyer of securities such as common stock, can't distinguish between good firms with high expected profits and low risk and bad firms with low expected profits and high risk. In this situation, Raj will be willing to pay only a price that reflects the *average* quality of firms issuing securities—a price that lies between the value of securities from bad firms and the value of those from good firms. If the owners or managers of a good firm have better information than Raj and *know* that they have a good firm, they know that their securities are undervalued and will not want to sell them to Raj at the price he is willing to pay. The only firms willing to sell Raj securities will be bad firms (because his price is higher than the securities are worth). Our friend Raj is not stupid; he does not want to hold securities in bad firms, and hence he will decide not to purchase securities in the market. In an outcome similar to that in the used-car market, this securities market will not work very well because few firms will sell securities in it to raise capital.

The analysis is similar if Raj considers purchasing a corporate debt instrument in the bond market rather than an equity share. Raj will buy a bond only if its interest rate is high enough to compensate him for the average default risk of the good

[1]George Akerlof, "The Market for 'Lemons': Quality, Uncertainty and the Market Mechanism," *Quarterly Journal of Economics* 84 (1970): 488–500. Two important papers that have applied the lemons problem analysis to financial markets are Stewart Myers and N. S. Majluf, "Corporate Financing and Investment Decisions When Firms Have Information That Investors Do Not Have," *Journal of Financial Economics* 13 (1984): 187–221; and Bruce Greenwald, Joseph E. Stiglitz, and Andrew Weiss, "Information Imperfections in the Capital Market and Macroeconomic Fluctuations," *American Economic Review* 74 (1984): 194–199.

and bad firms trying to sell the debt. The knowledgeable owners of a good firm realize that they will be paying a higher interest rate than they should, so they are unlikely to want to borrow in this market. Only the bad firms will be willing to borrow, and because investors like Raj are not eager to buy bonds issued by bad firms, they will probably not buy any bonds at all. Few bonds are likely to sell in this market, so it will not be a good source of financing.

The analysis we have just conducted explains fact 2—why marketable securities are not the primary source of financing for businesses in any country in the world. It also partly explains fact 1—why stocks are not the most important source of financing for businesses, even in the United States or other advanced economies. The presence of the lemons problem keeps securities markets such as the stock and bond markets from being effective in channeling funds from savers to borrowers.

Tools to Help Solve Adverse Selection Problems

In the absence of asymmetric information, the lemons problem goes away. If buyers know as much about the quality of used cars as sellers, so that all involved can tell a good car from a bad one, buyers will be willing to pay full value for good used cars. Because the owners of good used cars can now get a fair price, they will be willing to sell them in the market. The market will have many transactions and will do its intended job of channeling good cars to people who want them.

Similarly, if purchasers of securities can distinguish good firms from bad, they will pay the full value of securities issued by good firms, and good firms will sell their securities in the market. The securities market will then be able to move funds to the good firms that have the most productive investment opportunities.

Private Production and Sale of Information The solution to the adverse selection problem in financial markets is to eliminate asymmetric information by furnishing the people supplying funds with full details about the individuals or firms seeking to finance their investment activities. One way to get this material to saver-lenders is to have private companies collect and produce information that distinguishes good from bad firms and then sell it. In the United States, companies such as Standard & Poor's, Moody's, and Value Line gather information on firms' balance sheet positions and investment activities, publish these data, and sell them to subscribers (individuals, libraries, and financial intermediaries involved in purchasing securities). Similar services are provided in India by credit-rating agencies such as CRISIL, ICRA and CARE.

The system of private production and sale of information does not completely solve the adverse selection problem in securities markets, however, because of the **free-rider problem.** The free-rider problem occurs when people who do not pay for information take advantage of the information that other people have paid for. The free-rider problem suggests that the private sale of information will be only a partial solution to the lemons problem. To see why, suppose that you have just purchased information that tells you which firms are good and which are bad. You believe that this purchase is worthwhile because you can make up the cost of acquiring this information, and then some, by purchasing the securities of good firms that are undervalued. However, when our savvy (free-riding) investor Raj sees you buying certain securities, he buys right along with you, even though he has not paid for any information. If many other investors act as Raj does, the increased demand for the undervalued good securities will cause their low price to be bid up immediately to reflect the securities' true value. Because of all these free riders, you can no longer buy the securities for less than their true value. Now because you will not gain any profits from purchasing the information, you realize that you never should have paid for this information in the first place. If other investors come to the same realization, private firms and individuals may not be able to sell enough of this information to make it worth their while to gather and produce it. The weakened ability of private firms to profit from selling information will mean that less information is produced in the marketplace, so adverse selection (the lemons problem) will still interfere with the efficient functioning of securities markets.

Government Regulation to Increase Information The free-rider problem prevents the private market from producing enough information to eliminate all the asymmetric information that leads to adverse selection. Could financial markets benefit from government intervention? The government could, for instance, produce information to help investors distinguish good from bad firms and provide it to the public free of charge. This solution, however, would involve the government in releasing negative information about firms, a practice that might be politically difficult. A second possibility (and one followed by the United States and most governments throughout the world) is for the government to regulate securities markets in a way that encourages firms to reveal honest information about themselves so that investors can determine how good or bad the firms are. In the United States, the Securities and Exchange Commission (SEC) is the government agency that requires firms selling their securities to have independent **audits,** in which accounting firms certify that the firm is adhering to standard accounting principles and disclosing accurate information about sales, assets, and earnings. Similar regulations are found in other countries. In India, the Securities and Exchange Board of India (SEBI) has, as its objective, "protecting the interests of investors in securities and to promote the development of, and regulate the securities market, and for matters connected therewith and incidental thereto".[2] However, disclosure requirements do not always work well, as the collapse of Enron and accounting scandals at other corporations, such as WorldCom and Parmalat (an Italian company) suggest (see the Mini-Case box, "The Enron Implosion").

The asymmetric information problem of adverse selection in financial markets helps explain why financial markets are among the most heavily regulated sectors in the economy (fact 5). Government regulation to increase information for investors is needed to reduce the adverse selection problem, which interferes with the efficient functioning of securities (stock and bond) markets.

Although government regulation lessens the adverse selection problem, it does not eliminate it. Even when firms provide information to the public about their sales, assets, or earnings, they still have more information than investors: A lot more is involved in knowing the quality of a firm than statistics can provide. Furthermore, bad firms have an incentive to make themselves look like good firms because this would enable them to fetch a higher price for their securities. Bad firms will slant the information they are required to transmit to the public, thus making it harder for investors to sort out the good firms from the bad.

Financial Intermediation So far we have seen that private production of information and government regulation to encourage provision of information lessen, but do not eliminate, the adverse selection problem in financial markets. How, then, can the financial structure help promote the flow of funds to people with productive

[2]http://www.sebi.gov.in/sebiweb/stpages/about_sebi.jsp.

The Enron Implosion

Until 2001 Enron Corporation, a firm that specialized in trading in the energy market, appeared to be spectacularly successful. It had a quarter of the energy-trading market and was valued as high as $77 billion in August 2000 (just a little over a year before its collapse), making it the seventh-largest corporation in the United States at that time. However, toward the end of 2001, Enron came crashing down. In October 2001, Enron announced a third-quarter loss of $618 million and disclosed accounting "mistakes." The SEC then engaged in a formal investigation of Enron's financial dealings with partnerships led by its former finance chief. It became clear that Enron was engaged in a complex set of transactions by which it was keeping substantial amounts of debt and financial contracts off its balance sheet. These transactions enabled Enron to hide its financial difficulties.

Despite securing as much as $1.5 billion of new financing from J. P. Morgan Chase and Citigroup, the company was forced to declare bankruptcy in December 2001, up to that point the largest bankruptcy in U.S. history.

The Enron collapse illustrates that government regulation can lessen asymmetric information problems but cannot eliminate them. Managers have tremendous incentives to hide their companies' problems, making it hard for investors to know the true value of the firm.

The Enron bankruptcy not only increased concerns in financial markets about the quality of accounting information supplied by corporations but also led to hardship for many of the firm's former employees, who found that their pensions had become worthless. Outrage against the duplicity of executives at Enron was high, and several of them were sent to jail.

investment opportunities when asymmetric information exists? A clue is provided by the structure of the used-car market.

An important feature of the used-car market is that most used cars are not sold directly by one individual to another. An individual who considers buying a used car might pay for privately produced information by subscribing to a magazine like *Consumer Reports* to find out if a particular make of car has a good repair record. Nevertheless, reading *Consumer Reports* does not solve the adverse selection problem because even if a particular make of car has a good reputation, the specific car someone is trying to sell could be a lemon. The prospective buyer might also bring the used car to a mechanic for an inspection. But what if the prospective buyer doesn't know a mechanic who can be trusted or if the mechanic would charge a high fee to evaluate the car?

Because these roadblocks make it hard for individuals to acquire enough information about used cars, most used cars are not sold directly by one individual to another. Instead, they are sold by an intermediary, a used-car dealer who purchases used cars from individuals and resells them to other individuals. Used-car dealers produce information in the market by becoming experts in determining whether a car is a peach or a lemon. Once they know that a car is good, they can sell it with some form of a guarantee: either a guarantee that is explicit, such as a warranty, or an implicit guarantee, in which they stand by their reputation for honesty. People are more likely to purchase a used car because of a dealer's guarantee, and the dealer is able to make a profit on the production of information about automobile quality by being able to sell the used car at a higher price than the dealer paid for it. If dealers purchase and then resell cars on which they have produced information, they avoid the problem of other people free-riding on the information they produced.

Just as used-car dealers help solve adverse selection problems in the automobile market, financial intermediaries play a similar role in financial markets. A financial intermediary, such as a bank, becomes an expert in producing information about firms, so that it can sort out good credit risks from bad ones. Then it can acquire funds from depositors and lend them to the good firms. Because the bank is able to lend mostly to good firms, it is able to earn a higher return on its loans than the interest it has to pay to its depositors. The resulting profit that the bank earns gives it the incentive to engage in this information production activity.

An important element in the bank's ability to profit from the information it produces is that it avoids the free-rider problem by primarily making private loans rather than by purchasing securities that are traded in the open market. Because a private loan is not traded, other investors cannot watch what the bank is doing and bid up the loan's price to the point that the bank receives no compensation for the information it has produced. The bank's role as an intermediary that holds mostly nontraded loans is the key to its success in reducing asymmetric information in financial markets.

Our analysis of adverse selection indicates that financial intermediaries in general—and banks in particular, because they hold a large fraction of nontraded loans—should play a greater role in moving funds to corporations than securities markets do. Our analysis thus explains facts 3 and 4: why indirect finance is so much more important than direct finance and why banks are the most important source of external funds for financing businesses.

Another important fact that is explained by the analysis here is the greater importance of banks in the financial systems of developing countries. As we have seen, when the quality of information about firms is better, asymmetric information problems will be less severe, and it will be easier for firms to issue securities. Information about private firms is harder to collect in developing countries than in industrialized countries; therefore, the smaller role played by securities markets leaves a greater role for financial intermediaries such as banks. A corollary of this analysis is that as information about firms becomes easier to acquire, the role of banks should decline.

Our analysis of adverse selection also explains fact 6, which questions why large firms are more likely to obtain funds from securities markets, a direct route, rather than from banks and financial intermediaries, an indirect route. The better known a corporation is, the more information about its activities is available in the market-place. Thus, it is easier for investors to evaluate the quality of the corporation and determine whether it is a good firm or a bad one. Because investors have fewer worries about adverse selection with well-known corporations, they will be willing to invest directly in their securities. Our adverse selection analysis thus suggests that a pecking order for firms that can issue securities should be in place. The larger and more established a corporation is, the more likely it will be to issue securities to raise funds, a view that is known as the **pecking order hypothesis.** This hypothesis is supported in the data and is what fact 6 describes.

Collateral and Net Worth Adverse selection interferes with the functioning of financial markets only if a lender suffers a loss when a borrower is unable to make loan payments and thereby defaults. **Collateral,** property promised to the lender if the borrower defaults, reduces the consequences of adverse selection because it reduces the lender's losses in the event of a default. If a borrower defaults on a loan, the lender can sell the collateral and use the proceeds to make up for the losses on the loan. For example, if you fail to make your mortgage payments, the lender can take the title to your house, auction it off, and use the receipts to pay off the loan. Lenders are thus more willing to make loans secured by collateral, and borrowers are willing to supply collateral because the reduced risk for the lender makes it more likely they will get the loan in the first place and perhaps at a better loan rate. The presence of adverse selection in credit markets thus provides an explanation for why collateral is an important feature of debt contracts (fact 7).

Net worth (also called **equity capital**), the difference between a firm's assets (what it owns or is owed) and its liabilities (what it owes), can perform a similar role to that of collateral. If a firm has a high net worth, then even if it engages in investments that cause it to have negative profits and so defaults on its debt payments, the lender can take title to the firm's net worth, sell it off, and use the proceeds to recoup some of the losses from the loan. In addition, the more net worth a firm has in the first place, the less likely it is to default, because the firm has a cushion of assets that it can use to pay off its loans. Hence, when firms seeking credit have high net worth, the consequences of adverse selection are less important and lenders are more willing to make loans. This analysis lies behind the often-heard lament, "Only the people who don't need money can borrow it!"

Summary So far we have used the concept of adverse selection to explain seven of the eight facts about financial structure introduced earlier: The first four emphasize the importance of financial intermediaries and the relative unimportance of securities markets for the financing of corporations; the fifth, that financial markets are among the most heavily regulated sectors of the economy; the sixth, that only large, well-established corporations have access to securities markets; and the seventh, that collateral is an important feature of debt contracts. In the next section, we will see that the other asymmetric information concept of moral hazard provides additional reasons for the importance of financial intermediaries and the relative unimportance of securities markets for the financing of corporations, the prevalence of government regulation, and the importance of collateral in debt contracts. In addition, the concept of moral hazard can be used to explain our final fact (fact 8): why debt contracts are complicated legal documents that place substantial restrictions on the behavior of the borrower.

How Moral Hazard Affects the Choice Between Debt and Equity Contracts

Moral hazard is the asymmetric information problem that occurs after the financial transaction takes place, when the seller of a security may have incentives to hide information and engage in activities that are undesirable for the purchaser of the security. Moral hazard has important consequences for whether a firm finds it easier to raise funds with debt than with equity contracts.

Moral Hazard in Equity Contracts: The Principal–Agent Problem

Equity contracts, such as common stock, are claims to a share in the profits and assets of a business. Equity contracts are subject to a particular type of moral hazard called the **principal–agent problem.** When managers own only a small fraction of the firm they work for, the stockholders who own most of the firm's equity (called the *principals*) are not the same people as the managers of the firm, who are the *agents* of the owners. This separation of ownership and control involves moral hazard, in that the managers in control (the agents) may act in their own interest rather than in the interest of the stockholder-owners (the principals) because the managers have less incentive to maximize profits than the stockholder-owners do.

To understand the principal–agent problem more fully, suppose that your friend Gaurav asks you to become a silent partner in his ice cream store. The store requires an investment of ₹10,000 to set up and Gaurav has only ₹1,000. So you purchase an equity stake (stock shares) for ₹9,000, which entitles you to 90% of the ownership of the firm, while Gaurav owns only 10%. If Gaurav works hard to make tasty ice cream, keeps the store clean, smiles at all the customers, and hustles to wait on tables quickly, after all expenses (including Gaurav's salary), the store will have ₹50,000 in profits per year, of which Gaurav receives 10% (₹5,000) and you receive 90% (₹45,000).

But if Gaurav doesn't provide quick and friendly service to his customers, uses the ₹50,000 in income to buy artwork for his office, and even sneaks off to the beach while he should be at the store, the store will not earn any profit. Gaurav can earn the additional ₹5,000 (his 10% share of the profits) over his salary only if he works hard and forgoes unproductive investments (such as art for his office). Gaurav might decide that the extra ₹5,000 just isn't enough to make him expend the effort to be a good manager; he might decide that it would be worth his while only if he earned an extra ₹10,000. If Gaurav feels this way, he does not have enough incentive to be a good manager and will end up with a beautiful office, a good tan, and a store that doesn't show any profits. Because the store won't show any profits, Gaurav's decision not to act in your interest will cost you ₹45,000 (your 90% of the profits if he had chosen to be a good manager instead).

The moral hazard arising from the principal–agent problem might be even worse if Gaurav were not totally honest. Because his ice cream store is a cash business, Gaurav has the incentive to pocket ₹50,000 in cash and tell you that the profits were zero. He now gets a return of ₹50,000 and you get nothing.

Further indications that the principal–agent problem created by equity contracts can be severe are provided by past scandals in corporations such as Enron and Tyco International, in which managers were found to have diverted funds for their personal use. Besides pursuing personal benefits, managers might also pursue corporate strategies (such as the acquisition of other firms) that enhance their personal power but do not increase the corporation's profitability.

The principal–agent problem would not arise if the owners of a firm had complete information about what the managers were up to and could prevent wasteful expenditures or fraud. The principal–agent problem, which is an example of moral hazard, arises only because a manager, such as Gaurav, has more information about his activities than the stockholder does—that is, information is asymmetric. The principal–agent problem would not occur if Gaurav alone owned the store and ownership and control were not separated. If this were the case, Gaurav's hard work and avoidance of unproductive investments would yield him a profit (and extra income) of ₹50,000, an amount that would make it worth his while to be a good manager.

Tools to Help Solve the Principal–Agent Problem

Production of Information: Monitoring You have seen that the principal–agent problem arises because managers have more information about their activities and actual profits than stockholders do. One way for stockholders to reduce this moral hazard problem is for them to engage in a particular type of information production, the monitoring of the firm's activities: auditing the firm frequently and checking on what the management is doing. The problem is that the monitoring process can be expensive in terms of time and money, as reflected in the name economists give it, **costly state verification.** Costly state verification makes the equity contract less desirable, and it explains, in part, why equity is not a more important element in our financial structure.

As with adverse selection, the free-rider problem decreases the amount of information production undertaken to reduce the moral hazard (principal–agent) problem. In this example, the free-rider problem decreases monitoring. If you know that other stockholders are paying to monitor the activities of the company you hold shares in, you can take a free ride on their activities. Then you can use the money you save by not engaging in monitoring to vacation on a Caribbean island. If you can do this, though, so can other stockholders. Perhaps all the stockholders will go to the islands, and no one will spend any resources on monitoring the firm. The moral hazard problem for shares of common stock will then be severe, making it hard for firms to issue them to raise capital (providing an additional explanation for fact 1).

Government Regulation to Increase Information As with adverse selection, the government has an incentive to try to reduce the moral hazard problem created by asymmetric information, which provides another reason why the financial system is so heavily regulated (fact 5). Governments everywhere have laws to force firms to adhere to standard accounting principles that make profit verification easier. They also pass laws to impose stiff criminal penalties on people who commit the fraud of hiding and stealing profits. However, these measures can be only partly effective. Catching this kind of fraud is not easy; fraudulent managers have the incentive to make it very hard for government agencies to find or prove fraud.

Financial Intermediation Financial intermediaries have the ability to avoid the free-rider problem in the face of moral hazard, and this is another reason that indirect finance is so important (fact 3). One financial intermediary that helps reduce the moral hazard arising from the principal–agent problem is the **venture capital firm.** Venture capital firms pool the resources of their partners and use the funds to help budding entrepreneurs start new businesses. In exchange for the use of the venture capital, the firm receives an equity share in the new business. Because verification of earnings and profits is so important in eliminating moral hazard, venture capital firms usually insist on having several of their own people participate as members of the managing body of the firm, the board of directors, so that they can keep a close watch on the firm's activities. When a venture capital firm supplies start-up funds, the equity in the firm is not marketable to anyone *except* the venture capital firm. Thus, other investors are unable to take a free ride on the venture capital firm's verification activities. As a result of this arrangement, the venture capital firm is able to garner the full benefits of its verification activities and is given the appropriate incentives to reduce the moral hazard problem. Venture capital firms have been important in the development of the high-tech sector in the United States, which has resulted in job creation, economic growth, and increased international competitiveness.

Debt Contracts Moral hazard arises with an equity contract, which is a claim on profits in all situations, whether the firm is making or losing money. If a contract could be structured so that moral hazard would exist only in certain situations, the need to monitor managers would be reduced, and the contract would be more attractive than the equity contract. The debt contract has exactly these attributes because it is a contractual agreement by the borrower to pay the lender *fixed* rupee amounts at periodic intervals. When the firm has high profits, the lender receives the contractual payments and does not need to know the exact profits of the firm. If the managers are hiding profits or are pursuing activities that are personally beneficial but don't increase profitability, the lender doesn't care as long as these activities do not interfere with the ability of the firm to make its debt payments on time. Only when the firm cannot meet its debt payments, thereby being in a state of default, is there a need for the lender to verify the state of the firm's profits. Only in this situation do lenders involved in debt contracts need to act more like equity holders to get their fair share; now they must know how much income the firm has.

The less frequent need to monitor the firm, and thus the lower cost of state verification, helps explain why debt contracts are used more frequently than equity contracts to raise capital. The concept of moral hazard therefore helps explain fact 1, why stocks are not the most important source of financing for businesses.

How Moral Hazard Influences Financial Structure in Debt Markets

Even with the advantages just described, debt contracts are still subject to moral hazard. Because a debt contract requires the borrowers to pay out a fixed amount and lets them keep any profits above this amount, the borrowers have an incentive to take on investment projects that are riskier than the lenders would like.

For example, suppose that because you are concerned about the problem of verifying the profits of Gaurav's ice cream store, you decide not to become an equity partner. Instead, you lend Gaurav the ₹9,000 he needs to set up his business and have a debt contract that pays you an interest rate of 10%. As far as you are concerned, this is a surefire investment because demand for ice cream in your neighborhood is strong and steady. However, once you give Gaurav the funds, he might use them for purposes other than what you intended. Instead of opening up the ice cream store, Gaurav might use your ₹9,000 loan to invest in chemical research equipment because he thinks he has a 1-in-10 chance of inventing a diet ice cream that tastes every bit as good as the premium brands but has no fat or calories.

Obviously, this is a very risky investment, but if Gaurav is successful, he will become a multimillionaire. He has a strong incentive to undertake the riskier investment with your money because the gains to him would be so large if he succeeded. You would clearly be very unhappy if Gaurav used your loan for the riskier investment because if he were unsuccessful, which is highly likely, you would lose most, if not all, of the money you gave him. And if he were successful, you wouldn't share in his success—you would still get only a 10% return on the loan because the principal and interest payments are fixed. Because of the potential moral hazard (that Gaurav might use your money to finance a very risky venture), you would probably not make the loan to Gaurav, even though an ice cream store in the neighborhood is a good investment that would provide benefits for everyone.

Tools to Help Solve Moral Hazard in Debt Contracts

Net Worth and Collateral When borrowers have more at stake because their net worth (the difference between their assets and their liabilities) is high or the collateral they have pledged to the lender is valuable, the risk of moral hazard—

the temptation to act in a manner that lenders find objectionable—will be greatly reduced because the borrowers themselves have a lot to lose. Another way to say this is that if borrowers have more "skin in the game" because they have higher net worth or pledge collateral, they are likely to take less risk at the lender's expense. Let's return to Gaurav and his ice cream business. Suppose that the cost of setting up either the ice cream store or the research equipment is ₹100,000 instead of ₹10,000. So Gaurav needs to put ₹91,000 (instead of ₹1,000) of his own money into the business in addition to the ₹9,000 supplied by your loan. Now if Gaurav is unsuccessful in inventing the no-calorie nonfat ice cream, he has a lot to lose—the ₹91,000 of net worth (₹100,000 in assets minus the ₹9,000 loan from you). He will think twice about undertaking the riskier investment and is more likely to invest in the ice cream store, which is more of a sure thing. Hence, when Gaurav has more of his own money (net worth) in the business, and hence skin in the game, you are more likely to make him the loan. Similarly, if you have pledged your house as collateral, you are less likely to gamble away your earnings that month because you might not be able to make your mortgage payments and might lose your house.

One way of describing the solution that high net worth and collateral provides to the moral hazard problem is to say that it makes the debt contract **incentive compatible;** that is, it aligns the incentives of the borrower with those of the lender. The greater the borrower's net worth and collateral pledged, the greater the borrower's incentive to behave in the way that the lender expects and desires, the smaller the moral hazard problem in the debt contract, and the easier it is for the firm or household to borrow. Conversely, when the borrower's net worth and collateral are lower, the moral hazard problem is greater, and it is harder to borrow.

Monitoring and Enforcement of Restrictive Covenants As the example of Gaurav and his ice cream store shows, if you could make sure that Gaurav doesn't invest in anything riskier than the ice cream store, it would be worth your while to make him the loan. You can ensure that Gaurav uses your money for the purpose *you* want it to be used for by writing provisions (restrictive covenants) into the debt contract that restrict his firm's activities. By monitoring Gaurav's activities to see whether he is complying with the restrictive covenants and enforcing the covenants if he is not, you can make sure that he will not take on risks at your expense. Restrictive covenants are directed at reducing moral hazard either by ruling out undesirable behavior or by encouraging desirable behavior. There are four types of restrictive covenants that achieve this objective:

1. *Covenants to discourage undesirable behavior.* Covenants can be designed to lower moral hazard by keeping the borrower from engaging in the undesirable behavior of undertaking risky investment projects. Some covenants mandate that a loan can be used only to finance specific activities, such as the purchase of particular equipment or inventories. Others restrict the borrowing firm from engaging in certain risky business activities, such as purchasing other businesses.

2. *Covenants to encourage desirable behavior.* Restrictive covenants can encourage the borrower to engage in desirable activities that make it more likely that the loan will be paid off. One restrictive covenant of this type requires the breadwinner in a household to carry life insurance that pays off

the mortgage upon that person's death. Restrictive covenants of this type for businesses focus on encouraging the borrowing firm to keep its net worth high because higher borrower net worth reduces moral hazard and makes it less likely that the lender will suffer losses. These restrictive covenants typically specify that the firm must maintain minimum holdings of certain assets relative to the firm's size.

3. *Covenants to keep collateral valuable.* Because collateral is an important protection for the lender, restrictive covenants can encourage the borrower to keep the collateral in good condition and make sure that it stays in the possession of the borrower. This is the type of covenant ordinary people encounter most often. Automobile loan contracts, for example, require the car owner to maintain a minimum amount of collision and theft insurance and prevent the sale of the car unless the loan is paid off. Similarly, the recipient of a home mortgage must have adequate insurance on the home and must pay off the mortgage when the property is sold.

4. *Covenants to provide information.* Restrictive covenants also require a borrowing firm to provide information about its activities periodically in the form of quarterly accounting and income reports, thereby making it easier for the lender to monitor the firm and reduce moral hazard. This type of covenant may also stipulate that the lender has the right to audit and inspect the firm's books at any time.

We now see why debt contracts are often complicated legal documents with numerous restrictions on the borrower's behavior (fact 8): Debt contracts require complicated restrictive covenants to lower moral hazard.

Financial Intermediation Although restrictive covenants help reduce the moral hazard problem, they do not eliminate it. It is almost impossible to write covenants that rule out *every* risky activity. Furthermore, borrowers may be clever enough to find loopholes in restrictive covenants that make them ineffective.

Another problem with restrictive covenants is that they must be monitored and enforced. A restrictive covenant is meaningless if the borrower can violate it knowing that the lender won't check up or is unwilling to pay for legal recourse. Because monitoring and enforcement of restrictive covenants are costly, the free-rider problem arises in the debt securities (bond) market just as it does in the stock market. If you know that other bondholders are monitoring and enforcing the restrictive covenants, you can free-ride on their monitoring and enforcement. But other bondholders can do the same thing, so the likely outcome is that not enough resources are devoted to monitoring and enforcing the restrictive covenants. Moral hazard therefore continues to be a severe problem for marketable debt.

As we have seen before, financial intermediaries—particularly banks—have the ability to avoid the free-rider problem as long as they make primarily private loans. Private loans are not traded, so no one else can free-ride on the intermediary's monitoring and enforcement of the restrictive covenants. The intermediary making private loans thus receives the benefits of monitoring and enforcement and will work to shrink the moral hazard problem inherent in debt contracts. The concept of moral hazard has provided us with additional reasons why financial intermediaries play a more important role in channeling funds from savers to borrowers than marketable securities do, as described in facts 3 and 4.

TABLE 7.1   Asymmetric Information Problems and Tools to Solve Them SUMMARY

Asymmetric Information Problem	Tools to Solve It	Explains Fact Number
Adverse selection	Private production and sale of information	1, 2
	Government regulation to increase information	5
	Financial intermediation	3, 4, 6
	Collateral and net worth	7
Moral hazard in equity contracts (principal–agent problem)	Production of information: monitoring	1
	Government regulation to increase information	5
	Financial intermediation	3
	Debt contracts	1
Moral hazard in debt contracts	Collateral and net worth	6, 7
	Monitoring and enforcement of restrictive covenants	8
	Financial intermediation	3, 4

Note: List of facts:

1. Stocks are not the most important source of external financing.
2. Marketable securities are not the primary source of finance.
3. Indirect finance is more important than direct finance.
4. Banks are the most important source of external funds.
5. The financial system is heavily regulated.
6. Only large, well-established firms have access to securities markets.
7. Collateral is prevalent in debt contracts.
8. Debt contracts have numerous restrictive covenants.

Summary

The presence of asymmetric information in financial markets leads to adverse selection and moral hazard problems that interfere with the efficient functioning of those markets. Tools to help solve these problems involve the private production and sale of information, government regulation to increase information in financial markets, the importance of collateral and net worth to debt contracts, and the use of monitoring and restrictive covenants. A key finding from our analysis is that the existence of the free-rider problem for traded securities such as stocks and bonds indicates that financial intermediaries—particularly banks—should play a greater role than securities markets in financing the activities of businesses. Economic analysis of the consequences of adverse selection and moral hazard has helped explain the basic features of our financial system and has provided solutions to the eight facts about our financial structure outlined at the beginning of this chapter.

To help you keep track of all the tools that help solve asymmetric information problems, Table 7.1 summarizes the asymmetric information problems and tools that help solve them. In addition, it notes how these tools and asymmetric information problems explain the eight facts of financial structure described at the beginning of the chapter.

Financial Development and Economic Growth

Recent research has found that an important reason many developing countries experience very low rates of growth is that their financial systems are underdeveloped.[*] The economic analysis of financial structure helps explain how an underdeveloped financial system leads to a low state of economic development and economic growth.

The financial systems in developing countries face several difficulties that keep them from operating efficiently. As we have seen, two important tools used to help solve adverse selection and moral hazard problems in credit markets are collateral and restrictive covenants. In many developing countries, the system of property rights (the rule of law, constraints on government expropriation, absence of corruption) functions poorly, making it hard to use these two tools effectively. In these countries, bankruptcy procedures are often extremely slow and cumbersome. For example, in many countries, **creditors** (holders of debt) must first sue the defaulting debtor for payment, which can take several years; then, once a favorable judgment has been obtained, the creditor has to sue again to obtain title to the collateral. The process can take in excess of five years, and by the time the lender acquires the collateral, it may well have been neglected and thus have little value. In addition, governments often block lenders from foreclosing on borrowers in politically powerful sectors such as agriculture. Where the market is unable to use collateral effectively, the adverse selection problem will be worse because the lender will need even more information about the quality of the borrower so that it can screen out a good loan from a bad one. The result is that it will be harder for lenders to channel funds to borrowers with the most productive investment opportunities. There will be less productive investment, and hence a slower-growing economy. Similarly, a poorly developed or corrupt legal system may make it extremely difficult for lenders to enforce restrictive covenants. Thus, they may have a much more limited ability to reduce moral hazard on the part of borrowers and so will be less willing to lend. Again the outcome will be less productive investment and a lower growth rate for the economy. The importance of an effective legal system in promoting economic growth suggests that lawyers play a more positive role in the economy than we give them credit for.

Governments in developing countries often use their financial systems to direct credit to themselves or to favored sectors of the economy by setting interest rates at artificially low levels for certain types of loans, by creating development finance institutions to make specific types of loans, or by directing existing institutions to lend to certain entities. As we have seen, private institutions have an incentive to solve adverse selection and moral hazard problems and lend to borrowers with the most productive investment opportunities. Governments have less incentive to do so because they are not driven by the profit motive and thus their directed credit programs may not channel funds to sectors that will produce high growth for the economy. The outcome is again likely to result in less efficient investment and slower growth.

---

[*]See World Bank, *Finance for Growth: Policy Choices in a Volatile World* (World Bank and Oxford University Press, 2001) for a survey of the literature linking economic growth with financial development and a list of additional references.

In addition, banks in many developing countries are owned by their governments. Again, because of the absence of the profit motive, these **state-owned banks** have little incentive to allocate their capital to the most productive uses. Not surprisingly, the primary loan customer of these state-owned banks is often the government, which does not always use the funds wisely for productive investments to promote growth.

We have seen that government regulation can increase the amount of information in financial markets to make them work more efficiently. Many developing countries have an underdeveloped regulatory apparatus that retards the provision of adequate information to the marketplace. For example, these countries often have weak accounting standards, making it very hard to ascertain the quality of a borrower's balance sheet. As a result, asymmetric information problems are more severe, and the financial system is severely hampered in channeling funds to the most productive uses.

The institutional environment of a poor legal system, weak accounting standards, inadequate government regulation, and government intervention through directed credit programs and state ownership of banks all help explain why many countries stay poor while others, unhindered by these impediments, grow richer.

CASE

Is China a Counter-Example to the Importance of Financial Development?

Although China appears to be on its way to becoming an economic powerhouse, its financial development remains in the early stages. The country's legal system is weak so that financial contracts are difficult to enforce, while accounting standards are lax, so that high-quality information about creditors is hard to find. Regulation of the banking system is still in its formative stages, and the banking sector is dominated by large state-owned banks. Yet the Chinese economy has enjoyed one of the highest growth rates in the world over the past 20 years. How has China been able to grow so rapidly given its low level of financial development?

As noted above, China is in an early state of development, with a per capita income that is still less than $10,000, one-fifth of the per capita income in the United States. With an extremely high savings rate, averaging around 40% over the last two decades, the country has been able to rapidly build up its capital stock and shift a massive pool of underutilized labor from the subsistence-agriculture sector into higher-productivity activities that use capital. Even though available savings have not been allocated to their most productive uses, the huge increase in capital combined with the gains in productivity from moving labor out of low-productivity, subsistence agriculture have been enough to produce high growth.

As China gets richer, however, this strategy is unlikely to continue to work. The Soviet Union provides a graphic example. In the 1950s and 1960s, the Soviet Union shared many characteristics with modern-day China: high growth fueled by a high savings rate, a massive buildup of capital, and shifts of a large pool of underutilized labor from subsistence agriculture to manufacturing. During this high-growth phase, however, the Soviet Union was unable to develop the institutions needed to allocate capital efficiently. As a result, once the pool of subsistence laborers was used up, the Soviet Union's growth slowed dramatically and it was unable to keep up with the Western economies. Today no one considers the Soviet Union to have been an economic success story, and its inability to develop the institutions necessary to sustain financial development and growth was an important reason for the demise of this superpower.

To move into the next stage of development, China will need to allocate its capital more efficiently, which requires that it must improve its financial system. The Chinese leadership is well aware of this challenge: the government has announced that state-owned banks are being put on the path to privatization. In addition, the government is engaged in legal reform to make financial contracts more enforceable. New bankruptcy law is being developed so that lenders have the ability to take over the assets of firms that default on their loan contracts. Whether the Chinese government will succeed in developing a first-rate financial system, thereby enabling China to join the ranks of developed countries, is a big question mark.

Conflicts of Interest

Earlier in this chapter, we saw how financial institutions play an important role in the financial system. Specifically, their expertise in interpreting signals and collecting information from their customers gives them a cost advantage in the production of information. Furthermore, because they are collecting, producing, and distributing this information, financial institutions can use the information over and over again in as many ways as they would like, thereby realizing economies of scale. By providing multiple financial services to their customers, such as offering them bank loans or selling their bonds for them, they can also achieve **economies of scope;** that is, they can lower the cost of information production for each service by applying one information resource to many different services. A bank, for example, can evaluate how good a credit risk a corporation is when making a loan to the firm, which then helps the bank decide whether it would be easy to sell the bonds of this corporation to the public. Additionally, by providing multiple financial services to their customers, financial institutions develop broader and longer-term relationships with firms. These relationships both reduce the cost of producing information and increase economies of scope.

What Are Conflicts of Interest and Why Do We Care?

Although the presence of economies of scope may substantially benefit financial institutions, it also creates potential costs in terms of **conflicts of interest.** Conflicts of interest are a type of moral hazard problem that arise when a person or institution has multiple objectives (interests) and, as a result, has conflicts among those objectives. Conflicts of interest are especially likely to occur when a financial institution provides multiple services. The potentially competing interests of those services may lead an individual or firm to conceal information or disseminate misleading information. Here we use the analysis of asymmetric information problems to understand why conflicts of interest are important, why they arise, and what can be done about them.

We care about conflicts of interest because a substantial reduction in the quality of information in financial markets increases asymmetric information problems and prevents financial markets from channeling funds into the most productive investment opportunities. Consequently, the financial markets and the economy become less efficient.

Why Do Conflicts of Interest Arise?

Three types of financial service activities have led to prominent conflicts-of-interest problems in financial markets in recent years: underwriting and research in investment banks, auditing and consulting in accounting firms, and credit assessment and consulting in credit rating agencies. Why do combinations of these activities so often produce conflicts of interest?

Underwriting and Research in Investment Banking Investment banks perform two tasks: They *research* companies issuing securities, and they *underwrite* these securities by selling them to the public on behalf of the issuing corporations. Investment banks often combine these distinct financial services because information synergies are possible: That is, information produced for one task may also be useful in the other task. A conflict of interest arises between the brokerage and underwriting services because the banks are attempting to simultaneously serve two client groups—the security-issuing firms and the security-buying investors. These client groups have different information needs. Issuers benefit from optimistic research, whereas investors desire unbiased research. However, the same information will be produced for both groups to take advantages of economies of scope. When the potential revenues from underwriting greatly exceed the brokerage commissions from selling, the bank will have a strong incentive to alter the information provided to investors to favor the issuing firm's needs or else risk losing the firm's business to competing investment banks. For example, an internal Morgan Stanley memo excerpted in the *Wall Street Journal* on July 14, 1992, stated, "Our objective . . . is to adopt a policy, fully understood by the entire firm, including the Research Department, that we do not make negative or controversial comments about our clients as a matter of sound business practice."

Because of directives like this one, analysts in investment banks might distort their research to please issuers, and indeed this seems to have happened during the stock market tech boom of the 1990s. Such actions undermine the reliability of the information that investors use to make their financial decisions and, as a result, diminish the efficiency of securities markets.

Another common practice that exploits conflicts of interest is **spinning.** Spinning occurs when an investment bank allocates hot, but underpriced, **initial public offerings (IPOs)**—that is, shares of newly issued stock—to executives of other companies in return for their companies' future business with the investment banks. Because hot IPOs typically immediately rise in price after they are first purchased, spinning is a form of kickback meant to persuade executives to use that investment bank. When the executive's company plans to issue its own shares, he or she will be more likely to go to the investment bank that distributed the hot IPO shares, which is not necessarily the investment bank that would get the highest price for the company's securities. This practice may raise the cost of capital for the firm, thereby diminishing the efficiency of the capital market.

Auditing and Consulting in Accounting Firms Traditionally, an auditor checks the books of companies and monitors the quality of the information produced by firms to reduce the inevitable information asymmetry between the firm's managers and its shareholders. In auditing, threats to truthful reporting arise from several potential conflicts of interest. The conflict of interest that has received the most attention in the media occurs when an accounting firm provides its client with both auditing services and nonaudit consulting services such as advice on taxes, accounting, management information systems, and business strategy. Supplying clients with multiple services allows for economies of scale and scope but creates two potential sources of conflicts of interest. First, auditors may be willing to skew their judgments and opinions to win consulting business from these same clients. Second, auditors may be auditing information systems or tax and financial plans put in place by their nonaudit counterparts within the firm and therefore may be reluctant to criticize the systems or advice. Both types of conflicts may lead to biased audits, with the result that less reliable information is available in financial markets and investors find it difficult to allocate capital efficiently.

Another conflict of interest arises when an auditor provides an overly favorable audit to solicit or retain audit business. The unfortunate collapse of Arthur Andersen— once one of the five largest accounting firms in the United States—suggests that this may be the most dangerous conflict of interest.

Credit Assessment and Consulting in Credit Rating Agencies Investors use credit ratings (e.g., Aaa or Baa) that reflect the probability of default to determine the creditworthiness of particular debt securities. As a consequence, debt ratings play a major role in the pricing of debt securities and in the regulatory process. Conflicts of interest can arise when multiple users with divergent interests (at least in the short term) depend on the credit ratings. Investors and regulators are seeking a well-researched, impartial assessment of credit quality; the issuer needs a favorable rating. In the credit rating industry, the issuers of securities pay a rating firm such as Standard & Poor's or Moody's to have their securities rated. Because the issuers are the parties paying the credit rating agency, investors and regulators worry that the agency may bias its ratings upward to attract more business from the issuer.

Another kind of conflict of interest may arise when credit rating agencies also provide ancillary consulting services. Debt issuers often ask rating agencies to advise them on how to structure their debt issues, usually with the goal of securing a favorable rating. In this situation, the credit rating agencies would be auditing their own work and would experience a conflict of interest similar to the one found in accounting firms that provide both auditing and consulting services. Furthermore, credit rating agencies may deliver favorable ratings to garner new clients for the ancillary consulting business. The possible decline in the quality of credit assessments issued by rating agencies could increase asymmetric information in financial markets, thereby diminishing their ability to allocate credit. Such conflicts of interest came to the forefront because of the damaged reputations of the credit rating agencies during the financial crisis of 2007–2009 (see the Mini-Case box, "Credit Rating Agencies and the 2007–2009 Financial Crisis").

Credit Rating Agencies and the 2007–2009 Financial Crisis

The credit rating agencies have come under severe criticism for the role they played during the 2007–2009 financial crisis. Credit rating agencies advised clients on how to structure complex financial instruments that paid out cash flows from subprime mortgages. At the same time, they were rating these identical products, leading to the potential for severe conflicts of interest. Specifically, the large fees they earned from advising clients on how to structure products that they were rating meant they did not have sufficient incentives to make sure their ratings were accurate.

When housing prices began to fall and subprime mortgages began to default, it became crystal clear that the ratings agencies had done a terrible job of assessing the risk in the subprime products they had helped to structure. Many AAA-rated products had to be downgraded over and over again until they reached junk status. The resulting massive losses on these assets were one reason why so many financial institutions that were holding them got into trouble, with absolutely disastrous consequences for the economy, as discussed in the next chapter.

Criticisms of the credit rating agencies led the SEC to propose comprehensive reforms in 2008. The SEC concluded that the credit rating agencies' models for rating subprime products were not fully developed and that conflicts of interest may have played a role in producing inaccurate ratings. To address conflicts of interest, the SEC prohibited credit rating agencies from structuring the same products they rate, prohibited anyone who participates in determining a credit rating from negotiating the fee that the issuer pays for it, and prohibited gifts from bond issuers to those who rate them in any amount over $25. To make credit rating agencies more accountable, the SEC's new rules also required more disclosure of how the credit rating agencies determine ratings. For example, credit rating agencies were required to disclose historical ratings performance, including the dates of downgrades and upgrades, information on the underlying assets of a product that were used by the credit rating agencies to rate a product, and the kind of research they used to determine the rating. In addition, the SEC required the rating agencies to differentiate the ratings on structured products from those issued on bonds. The expectation is that these reforms will bring increased transparency to the ratings process and reduce conflicts of interest that played such a large role in the subprime debacle.

What Has Been Done to Remedy Conflicts of Interest?

Two major policy measures were implemented to deal with conflicts of interest: the Sarbanes-Oxley Act and the Global Legal Settlement.

Sarbanes-Oxley Act of 2002 The public outcry over the corporate and accounting scandals led in 2002 to the passage of the Public Accounting Return and Investor Protection Act, more commonly referred to as the Sarbanes-Oxley Act, after its two principal authors in Congress. This act increased supervisory oversight to monitor and prevent conflicts of interest:

- It established a Public Company Accounting Oversight Board (PCAOB), overseen by the SEC, to supervise accounting firms and ensure that audits are independent and controlled for quality.
- It increased the SEC's budget to supervise securities markets.

Sarbanes-Oxley also directly reduced conflicts of interest:

- It made it illegal for a registered public accounting firm to provide any nonaudit service to a client contemporaneously with an impermissible audit (as determined by the PCAOB).

Sarbanes-Oxley provided incentives for investment banks not to exploit conflicts of interest:

- It beefed up criminal charges for white-collar crime and obstruction of official investigations.

Sarbanes-Oxley also had measures to improve the quality of information in the financial markets:

- It required a corporation's chief executive officer (CEO) and chief financial officer (CFO), as well as its auditors, to certify that periodic financial statements and disclosures of the firm (especially regarding off-balance-sheet transactions) are accurate (Section 404).
- It required members of the audit committee (the subcommittee of the board of directors that oversees the company's audit) to be "independent"; that is, they cannot be managers in the company or receive any consulting or advisory fee from the company.

Global Legal Settlement of 2002 The second major policy measure arose out of a lawsuit brought by New York Attorney General Eliot Spitzer against the 10 largest investment banks (Bear Stearns, Credit Suisse First Boston, Deutsche Bank, Goldman Sachs, J. P. Morgan, Lehman Brothers, Merrill Lynch, Morgan Stanley, Salomon Smith Barney, and UBS Warburg). A global settlement was reached on December 20, 2002, with these investment banks by the SEC, the New York Attorney General, NASD, NASAA, NYSE, and state regulators. Like Sarbanes-Oxley, this settlement directly reduced conflicts of interest:

- It required investment banks to sever the links between research and securities underwriting.
- It banned spinning.

The Global Legal Settlement also provided incentives for investment banks not to exploit conflicts of interest:

- It imposed $1.4 billion of fines on the accused investment banks.

The global settlement had measures to improve the quality of information in financial markets:

- It required investment banks to make their analysts' recommendations public.
- Over a five-year period, investment banks were required to contract with at least three independent research firms that would provide research to their brokerage customers.

It is too early to evaluate the impact of the Sarbanes-Oxley Act and the Global Legal Settlement, but the most controversial elements were the separation of functions (research from underwriting, and auditing from nonaudit consulting). Although such a separation of functions may reduce conflicts of interest, it might also diminish economies of scope and thus potentially lead to a reduction of information in financial markets. In addition, there is a serious concern that implementation of these measures, particularly Sarbanes-Oxley, is too costly and is leading to a decline in U.S. capital markets (see the Mini-Case box "Has Sarbanes-Oxley Led to a Decline in U.S. Capital Markets?").

Has Sarbanes-Oxley Led to a Decline in U.S. Capital Markets?

There has been much debate in the United States in recent years regarding the impact of Sarbanes-Oxley, especially Section 404, on U.S. capital markets. Section 404 requires both management and company auditors to certify the accuracy of their financial statements. There is no question that Sarbanes-Oxley has led to increased costs for corporations, and this is especially true for smaller firms with revenues of less than $100 million, where the compliance costs have been estimated to exceed 1% of sales. These higher costs could result in smaller firms listing abroad and discourage IPOs in the United States, thereby shrinking U.S. capital markets relative to those abroad. However, improved accounting standards could work to encourage stock market listings and IPOs because better information could raise the valuation of common stocks.

Critics of Sarbanes-Oxley have cited it, as well as higher litigation and weaker shareholder rights,

as the cause of declining U.S. stock listings and IPOs, but other factors are likely at work. The European financial system experienced a major liberalization in the 1990s, along with the introduction of the euro, that helped make its financial markets more integrated and efficient. As a result, it became easier for European firms to list in their home countries. The fraction of European firms that list in their home countries has risen to over 90% currently from around 60% in 1995. As the importance of the United States in the world economy has diminished because of the growing importance of other economies, the U.S. capital markets have become less dominant over time. This process is even more evident in the corporate bond market. In 1995 corporate bond issues were double that of Europe, while issues of corporate bonds in Europe now exceed those in the United States.

Indian Companies and Internal Control Requirements

The Companies Act 2013 in India was a major step in enacting legislation around financial reporting controls with an objective of enhancing the robustness of the corporate governance structure in place within an organization. These mandate the board of directors, senior management and the auditors of the financial statements to assess and report on the adequacy and effectiveness of an organization's internal control over financial reporting.

In September 2015, the Institute of Chartered Accountants of India (ICAI) issued an updated "Guidance Note on Audit of Internal Financial Controls Over Financial Reporting" ("Guidance Note") that enhanced the requirements in The Companies Act by involving the external auditor in the compliance process in a substantive way.

Internal Financial Controls and Internal Controls Over Financial Reporting

Internal financial controls (IFC), as defined by the Companies Act refers to "the policies and procedures adopted by the company for ensuring the orderly and efficient conduct of its business, including adherence to [the] company's policies, the safeguarding of its assets, the prevention and detection of frauds and errors, the accuracy and completeness of the accounting records, and the timely preparation of reliable financial information." The Act further fixes the responsibility for issuing a Directors' Responsibility Statement (DRS) for listed companies on the company's board of directors. Such a DRS must assert, among other things, that the directors have established

IFC that are adequate and operating effectively. The requirement of the DRS effectively stipulates that the board is responsible for the overall control environment that ensures reliable financial reporting.

The ICAI Guidance Note involves external auditors of listed companies, unlisted public companies and private companies in the compliance process through the 'Internal controls over financial reporting' (ICFR). The note defines ICFR as "a process designed to provide reasonable assurance regarding the reliability of financial reporting and the preparation of financial statements for external purposes in accordance with generally accepted accounting principles. A company's internal financial control over financial reporting includes those policies and procedures that: pertain to the maintenance of records that, in reasonable detail, accurately and fairly reflect the transactions and dispositions of the assets of the company; provide reasonable assurance that transactions are recorded as necessary to permit preparation of financial statements in accordance with generally accepted accounting principles, and that receipts and expenditures of the company are being made only in accordance with authorizations of management and directors of the company; and provide reasonable assurance regarding prevention or timely detection of unauthorized acquisition, use, or disposition of the company's assets that could have a material effect on the financial statements."

The provisions of the ICFR are similar to the ones adopted by US regulators - Securities Exchange Commission (SEC) and the Public Company Accounting Oversight Board, in the Sarbanes-Oxley Act (Section 404). ICFR defines the scope of the audit by the statutory auditors in expressing an opinion on the effectiveness of internal control relating to the financial statements. As in the United States, this opinion encompasses both design effectiveness and operating effectiveness of ICFR.

Applicability of the Requirements

All Indian subsidiaries, associates and joint venture companies (on a standalone basis) of global multinationals registered under The Companies Act, 2013, irrespective of where the holding or group company is located, have to report with respect to IFC and ICFR. The DRS requirements became applicable to Indian listed companies with effect from the fiscal year ending on or after March 31, 2015. The auditor's report on the effectiveness of ICFR became effective from fiscal years ending on or after March 31, 2016. With respect to the remaining classes of companies beyond listed companies, the requirements relating to both the DRS and auditors' report became effective for fiscal years ending on or after March 31, 2016. Such reporting requirements are specific to Indian law and are in addition to reporting required in other countries, including compliance with Sarbanes-Oxley requirements in the United States where the global/group company is a SEC registrant.

Listed and unlisted public companies with a paid up share capital of ₹25 crores (250 million rupees, or US$3.7 million using exchange rate in 2015) came under the purview of the Act as also the Guidance Note. There is no such threshold for private companies.

Comparison with U.S. Sarbanes-Oxley Requirements

Such internal controls, as also requirements of external auditor reports on ICFR are part of the Sarbanes-Oxley Act of 2002 in the U.S. as well, and applicable to all SEC registrant companies.

The reporting requirement under Section 302 of Sarbanes-Oxley requiring an executive certification as to the "corporate responsibility for financial reports" is very similar to the Indian IFC reporting requirement by the board. The executive certification requires reporting on the effectiveness of disclosure controls and procedures. The "management assessment of internal controls" under Section 404 requires an annual internal control report by management and an attestation by statutory auditors on the effectiveness of ICFR is also very similar to the requirements of ICFR reporting under Indian law.

SUMMARY

1. There are eight basic facts about financial structure s across the world. The first four emphasize the importance of financial intermediaries and the relative unimportance of securities markets for the financing of corporations; the fifth recognizes that financial markets are among the most heavily regulated sectors of the economy; the sixth states that only large, well-established corporations have access to securities markets; the seventh indicates that collateral is an important feature of debt contracts; and the eighth presents debt contracts as complicated legal documents that place substantial restrictions on the behavior of the borrower.

2. Transaction costs freeze many small savers and borrowers out of direct involvement with financial markets. Financial intermediaries can take advantage of economies of scale and are better able to develop expertise to lower transaction costs, thus enabling their savers and borrowers to benefit from the existence of financial markets.

3. Asymmetric information results in two problems: adverse selection, which occurs before the transaction, and moral hazard, which occurs after the transaction. Adverse selection refers to the fact that bad credit risks are the ones most likely to seek loans, and moral hazard refers to the risk of the borrower's engaging in activities that are undesirable from the lender's point of view.

4. Adverse selection interferes with the efficient functioning of financial markets. Tools to help reduce the adverse selection problem include private production and sale of information, government regulation to increase information, financial intermediation, and collateral and net worth. The free-rider problem occurs when people who do not pay for information take advantage of information that other people have paid for. This problem explains why financial intermediaries, particularly banks, play a more important role in financing the activities of businesses than securities markets do.

5. Moral hazard in equity contracts is known as the principal–agent problem because managers (the agents) have less incentive to maximize profits than stockholders (the principals). The principal–agent problem explains why debt contracts are so much more prevalent in financial markets than equity contracts. Tools to help reduce the principal–agent problem include monitoring, government regulation to increase information, and financial intermediation.

6. Tools to reduce the moral hazard problem in debt contracts include collateral and net worth, monitoring and enforcement of restrictive covenants, and financial intermediaries.

7. Conflicts of interest arise when financial service providers or their employees are serving multiple interests and have incentives to misuse or conceal information needed for the effective functioning of financial markets. We care about conflicts of interest because they can substantially reduce the amount of reliable information in financial markets, thereby preventing them from channeling funds to parties with the most productive investment opportunities. Three types of financial service activities have had the greatest potential for conflicts of interest: underwriting and research in investment banking, auditing and consulting in accounting firms, and credit assessment and consulting in credit rating agencies. Two major policy measures have been implemented to deal with conflicts of interest in the US: the Sarbanes-Oxley Act of 2002 and the Global Legal Settlement of 2002, which arose from a lawsuit by the New York attorney general against the 10 largest investment banks.

8. In India, the Companies Act 2013 was a major step in enacting legislation around financial reporting controls with an objective of enhancing the robustness of the corporate governance structure in place within an organization. These mandate the board of directors, senior management and the auditors of the financial statements to assess and report on the adequacy and effectiveness of an organization's internal control over financial reporting.

KEY TERMS

QUESTIONS

1. How can economies of scale help explain the existence of financial intermediaries?

2. Describe two ways in which financial intermediaries help lower transaction costs in the economy.

3. Would moral hazard and adverse selection still arise in financial markets if information were not asymmetric? Explain.

4. How do standard accounting principles help financial markets work more efficiently?

5. Do you think the lemons problem would be more severe for stocks traded on the Bombay Stock Exchange or those traded over the counter? Explain.

6. Which firms are most likely to use bank financing than to issue bonds or stocks to finance their activities? Why?

7. How can the existence of asymmetric information provide a rationale for government regulation of financial markets?

8. Would you be more willing to lend to a friend if she put all of her life savings into her business than you would if she had not done so? Why?

9. Rich people often worry that others will seek to marry them only for their money. Is this a problem of adverse selection?

10. "The more collateral there is backing a loan, the less the lender has to worry about adverse selection."

Is this statement true, false, or uncertain? Explain your answer.

11. How does the free-rider problem aggravate adverse selection and moral hazard problems in financial markets?

12. Why can the provision of several types of financial services by one firm lead to a lower cost of information production?

13. How does the provision of several types of financial services by one firm lead to conflicts of interest?

14. How can conflicts of interest make financial service firms less efficient?

15. Describe two conflicts of interest that occur when underwriting and research are provided by a single investment firm.

16. How does spinning lead to a less efficient financial system?

17. Describe two conflicts of interest that occur in accounting firms.

18. Compare the provisions of the Indian Companies Act 2013 and the ICAI Guidance Note 2015 with the provisions of the U.S. Sarbanes Oxley Act 2002. Which of these provisions are beneficial?

QUANTITATIVE PROBLEMS

1. You are in the market for a used car. At a used car lot, you know that the blue book value for the cars you are looking at is between ₹2,00,000 and ₹2,40,000. If you believe the dealer knows *as much* about the car as you, how much are you willing to pay? Why? Assume that you only care about the expected value of the car you buy and that the car values are symmetrically distributed.

2. Now, you believe the dealer knows *more* about the cars than you. How much are you willing to pay? Why? How can this be resolved in a competitive market?

3. You wish to hire Ricky to manage your Kochi operations. The profits from the operations depend partially on how hard Ricky works, as follows.

	Probabilities	
	Profit = ₹1,00,000	Profit = ₹5,00,000
Lazy	60%	40%
Hard worker	20%	80%

If Ricky is lazy, he will surf the Internet all day, and he views this as a zero cost opportunity. However, Ricky would view working hard as a "personal cost" valued at ₹10,000. What fixed percentage of the profits should you offer Ricky? Assume Ricky only cares about his expected payment less any "personal cost."

4. You own a house worth ₹40,00,000 that is located on a river. If the river floods moderately, the house will be completely destroyed. This happens about once every 50 years. If you build a seawall, the river would have to flood heavily to destroy your house, which only happens about once every 200 years. What would be the annual premium for an insurance policy that offers full insurance? For a policy that only pays 75% of the home value, what are your expected costs with and without a seawall? Do the different policies provide an incentive to be safer (i.e., to build the seawall)?

WEB EXERCISES

Why Do Financial Institutions Exist?

1. In this chapter we discuss the lemons problem and its effect on the efficient functioning of a market. This theory was initially developed by George Akerlof. Go to **http://www.nobelprize.org/nobel_prizes/ economic-sciences/laureates/2001/**. This site reports that Akerlof, Spence, and Stiglitz were awarded the Nobel Prize in economics in 2001 for their work. Read this report down through the section on George Akerlof. Summarize his research ideas in one page.

2. This chapter discusses how an understanding of adverse selection and moral hazard can help us better understand financial crisis. The greatest financial crisis faced by the United States was the Great Depression from 1929 to 1933. Go to **www .amatecon.com/greatdepression.html**. This site contains a brief discussion of the factors that led to the Great Depression. Write a one-page summary explaining how adverse selection and moral hazard contributed to the Great Depression.

Why Do Financial Crisis Occur and Why Are They So Damaging to the Economy?

➤ PREVIEW

Financial crisis are major disruptions in financial markets characterized by sharp declines in asset prices and firm failures. Beginning in August of 2007, defaults in the mortgage market for subprime borrowers (borrowers with weak credit records) sent a shudder through the financial markets, leading to the worst U.S. financial crisis since the Great Depression. Alan Greenspan, former Chairman of the Fed, described the 2007–2009 financial crisis as a "once-in-a-century credit tsunami." Wall Street firms and commercial banks suffered losses amounting to hundreds of billions of dollars. Households and businesses found they had to pay higher rates on their borrowings—and it was much harder to get credit. World stock markets crashed, with U.S. shares falling by as much as half from their peak in October 2007. Many financial firms, including commercial banks, investment banks, and insurance companies, went belly up. A recession began in December 2007. By the fall of 2008, the economy was in a tailspin, with the recession, which ended in June of 2009, being the most severe since World War II.

Why did this financial crisis occur? Why have financial crisis been so prevalent throughout U.S. history, as well as in so many other countries, and what insights do they provide on the current crisis? Why are financial crisis almost always followed by severe contractions in economic activity? We will examine these questions in this chapter by developing a framework to understand the dynamics of financial crisis. Building on Chapter 7, we make use of the economic analysis of the effects of asymmetric information (adverse selection and moral hazard) on financial markets and the economy, to see why financial crisis occur and why they have such devastating effects on the economy. We will then apply the analysis to explain the course of events in a number of past financial crisis throughout the world, including the most recent global financial crisis.

What Is a Financial Crisis?

We established in Chapter 7 that a fully functioning financial system is critical to a robust economy. The financial system performs the essential function of channeling funds to individuals or businesses with productive investment opportunities. If capital goes to the wrong uses or does not flow at all, the economy will operate inefficiently or go into an economic downturn.

Agency Theory and the Definition of a Financial Crisis

Academic finance literature calls the analysis of how asymmetric information problems can generate adverse selection and moral hazard problems *agency theory*. Agency theory provides the basis for our definition of a financial crisis. Asymmetric information problems act as a barrier to financial markets channeling funds efficiently from savers to households and firms with productive investment opportunities and are often described by economists as **financial frictions.** When financial frictions increase, it is harder for lenders to ascertain the creditworthiness of borrowers. They need to charge a higher interest rate to protect themselves against the possibility that the borrower may not pay back the loan, which leads to a higher *credit spread*, the difference between the interest rate on loans to businesses and the interest rate on completely safe assets that are sure to be paid back.

A **financial crisis** occurs when information flows in financial markets experience a particularly large disruption, with the result that financial frictions and credit spreads increase sharply and financial markets stop functioning. Then economic activity will collapse.

Dynamics of Financial Crisis in Advanced Economies

As earth-shaking and headline-grabbing as the most recent financial crisis was, it was only one of a number of financial crisis that have hit industrialized countries like the United States over the years. These experiences have helped economists uncover insights into present-day economic turmoil.

Financial crisis in advanced economies have progressed in two and sometimes three stages. To understand how these crisis have unfolded, refer to Figure 8.1, which traces the stages and sequence of financial crisis in advanced economies.

Stage One: Initiation of Financial Crisis

Financial crisis can begin in several ways: credit and asset-price boom and busts or a general increase in uncertainty caused by failures of major financial institutions.

Credit Boom and Bust The seeds of a financial crisis are often sown when an economy introduces new types of loans or other financial products, known as **financial innovation,** or when countries engage in **financial liberalization,** the elimination of restrictions on financial markets and institutions. In the long run, financial liberalization promotes financial development and encourages a well-run

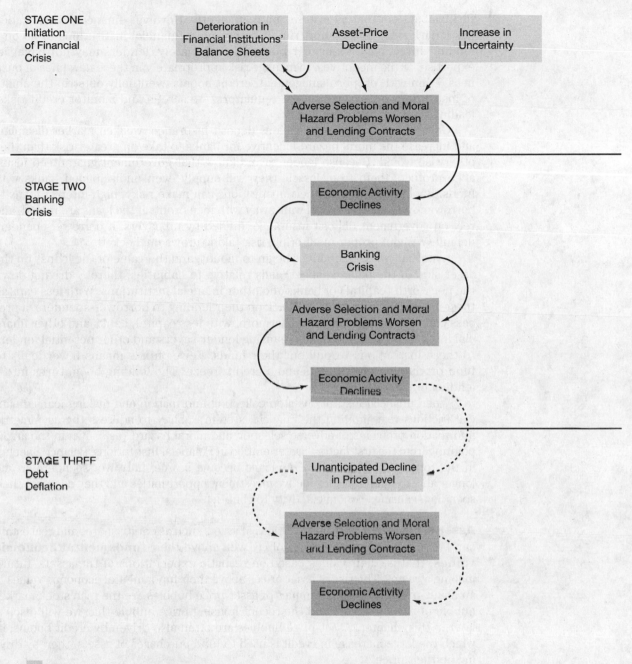

FIGURE 8.1 Sequence of Events in Financial Crisis in Advanced Economies

The solid arrows trace the sequence of events during a typical financial crisis; the dotted arrows show the additional set of events that occur if the crisis develops into a debt deflation. The sections separated by the dashed horizontal lines show the different stages of a financial crisis.

financial system that allocates capital efficiently. However, financial liberalization has a dark side: In the short run, it can prompt financial institutions to go on a lending spree, called a **credit boom.** Unfortunately, lenders may not have the expertise, or the incentives, to manage risk appropriately in these new lines of business. Even with proper management, credit booms eventually outstrip the ability of institutions—and government regulators—to screen and monitor credit risks, leading to overly risky lending.

Government safety nets, such as deposit insurance, weaken market discipline and increase the moral hazard incentive for banks to take on greater risk than they otherwise would. Because lender-savers know that government-guaranteed insurance protects them from losses, they will supply even undisciplined banks with funds. Banks and other financial institutions can make risky, high-interest loans to borrower-spenders. They will walk away with nice profits if the loans are repaid, and rely on government deposit insurance, funded by taxpayers, if borrower-spenders default. Without proper monitoring, risk-taking grows unchecked.

Eventually, losses on loans begin to mount, and the value of the loans (on the asset side of the balance sheet) falls relative to liabilities, thereby driving down the net worth (capital) of banks and other financial institutions. With less capital, these financial institutions cut back on their lending to borrower-spenders, a process called **deleveraging.** Furthermore, with less capital, banks and other financial institutions become riskier, causing lender-savers and other potential lenders to these institutions to pull out their funds. Fewer funds means fewer loans to fund productive investments and a credit freeze: The lending boom turns into a lending crash.

When financial institutions stop collecting information and making loans, financial frictions rise, limiting the financial system's ability to address the asymmetric information problems of adverse selection and moral hazard (as shown in the arrow pointing from the first factor, "Deterioration in Financial Institutions' Balance Sheets," in the top row of Figure 8.1). As loans become scarce, borrower-spenders are no longer able to fund their productive investment opportunities and they decrease their spending, causing economic activity to contract.

Asset-Price Boom and Bust   Prices of assets such as equity shares and real estate can be driven by investor psychology well above their **fundamental economic values,** that is, their values based on realistic expectations of the assets' future income streams. The rise of asset prices above their fundamental economic values is an **asset-price bubble.** Examples of asset-price bubbles are the tech stock market bubble of the late 1990s and the recent housing price bubble that we will discuss later in this chapter. Asset-price bubbles are often also driven by credit booms, in which the large increase in credit is used to fund purchases of assets, thereby driving up their price.

When the bubble bursts and asset prices realign with fundamental economic values, stock and real estate prices tumble, companies see their net worth (the difference between their assets and their liabilities) decline, and the value of collateral they can pledge drops. Now these companies have less at stake because they have less "skin in the game" and so they are more likely to make risky investments because they have less to lose, the problem of moral hazard. As a result, financial institutions tighten lending standards for borrower-spenders and lending contracts (as shown by the downward arrow pointing from the second factor, "Asset-Price Decline," in the top row of Figure 8.1).

The asset-price bust also causes a decline in the value of financial institutions' assets, thereby causing a decline in their net worth and hence a deterioration in their balance sheets (shown by the arrow from the second factor to the first factor in the top row of Figure 8.1), which causes them to deleverage, steepening the decline in economic activity.

Increase in Uncertainty U.S. financial crisis have usually begun in periods of high uncertainty, such as just after the start of a recession, a crash in the stock market, or the failure of a major financial institution. Crisis began after the failure of Ohio Life Insurance and Trust Company in 1857; Jay Cooke and Company in 1873; Grant and Ward in 1884; the Knickerbocker Trust Company in 1907; the Bank of the United States in 1930; and Bear Stearns, Lehman Brothers, and AIG in 2008. With information hard to come by in a period of high uncertainty, financial frictions increase, reducing lending and economic activity (as shown by the arrow pointing from the last factor, "Increase in Uncertainty," in the top row of Figure 8.1).

Stage Two: Banking Crisis

Deteriorating balance sheets and tougher business conditions lead some financial institutions into insolvency, when net worth becomes negative. Unable to pay off depositors or other creditors, some banks go out of business. If severe enough, these factors can lead to a **bank panic,** in which multiple banks fail simultaneously. The source of the contagion is asymmetric information. In a panic, depositors, fearing for the safety of their deposits (in the absence of or with limited amounts of deposit insurance) and not knowing the quality of banks' loan portfolios, withdraw their deposits to the point that the banks fail. Uncertainty about the health of the banking system in general can lead to runs on banks, both good and bad, which will force banks to sell off assets quickly to raise the necessary funds. These **fire sales** of assets may cause their prices to decline so much that the bank becomes insolvent, even if the resulting contagion can then lead to multiple bank failures and a full-fledged bank panic.

With fewer banks operating, information about the creditworthiness of borrower-spenders disappears. Increasingly severe adverse selection and moral hazard problems in financial markets deepen the financial crisis, causing declines in asset prices and the failure of firms throughout the economy who lack funds for productive investment opportunities. Figure 8.1 represents this progression in the stage two portion. Bank panics were a feature of all U.S. financial crisis during the nineteenth and twentieth centuries, occurring every twenty years or so until World War II—1819, 1837, 1857, 1873, 1884, 1893, 1907, and 1930–1933. (The 1933 establishment of federal deposit insurance, which protects depositors from losses, has prevented subsequent bank panics in the United States.)

Eventually, public and private authorities shut down insolvent firms and sell them off or liquidate them. Uncertainty in financial markets declines, the stock market recovers, and balance sheets improve. Financial frictions diminish and the financial crisis subsides. With the financial markets able to operate well again, the stage is set for an economic recovery.

Stage Three: Debt Deflation

If, however, the economic downturn leads to a sharp decline in the price level, the recovery process can be short-circuited. In stage three in Figure 8.1, **debt deflation** occurs when a substantial unanticipated decline in the price level sets in, leading to a further deterioration in firms' net worth because of the increased burden of indebtedness.

In economies with moderate inflation, which characterizes most advanced countries, many debt contracts with fixed interest rates are typically of fairly long maturity, ten years or more. Because debt payments are contractually fixed in nominal terms, an unanticipated decline in the price level raises the value of borrowing firms' liabilities in real terms (increases the burden of the debt) but does not raise the real value of borrowing firms' assets. The borrowing firm's net worth in real terms (the difference between assets and liabilities in real terms) thus declines.

To better understand how this decline in net worth occurs, consider what happens if a firm in 2015 has assets of INR 100 million (in 2015 rupees) and INR 90 million of long-term liabilities, so that it has INR 10 million in net worth (the difference between the value of assets and liabilities). If the price level falls by 10% in 2016, the real value of the liabilities would rise to INR 99 million in 2015 rupees, while the real value of the assets would remain unchanged at INR 100 million. The result would be that real net worth in 2015 rupees would fall from INR 10 million to INR 1 million (INR 100 million minus INR 99 million).

The substantial decline in real net worth of borrowers from a sharp drop in the price level causes an increase in adverse selection and moral hazard problems facing lenders. Lending and economic activity decline for a long time. The most significant financial crisis that displayed debt deflation was the Great Depression, the worst economic contraction in U.S. history.

CASE

The Mother of All Financial Crisis: The Great Depression

With our framework for understanding financial crisis in place, we are prepared to analyze how a financial crisis unfolded during the Great Depression and how it led to the worst economic downturn in U.S. history.

Stock Market Crash

In 1928 and 1929, prices doubled in the U.S. stock market. Federal Reserve officials viewed the stock market boom as excessive speculation. To curb it, they pursued a tightening of monetary policy to raise interest rates to limit the rise in stock prices. The Fed got more than it bargained for when the stock market crashed in October 1929, falling by 40% by the end of 1929, as shown in Figure 8.2.

Bank Panics

By the middle of 1930, stocks recovered almost half of their losses and credit market conditions stabilized. What might have been a normal recession turned into something far worse, however, when severe droughts in the Midwest led to a sharp decline in agricultural production, with the result that farmers could not pay back their bank loans. The resulting defaults on farm mortgages led to large loan losses on bank balance sheets in agricultural regions. The weakness of the economy and the banks in agricultural regions in particular prompted substantial withdrawals from banks, building to a full-fledged panic in November and December 1930, with the stock market falling sharply. For more than two years, the Fed sat idly by through one bank panic after another, the most severe spate of panics in U.S. history. After what would be the era's final panic in March 1933, President Franklin Delano Roosevelt

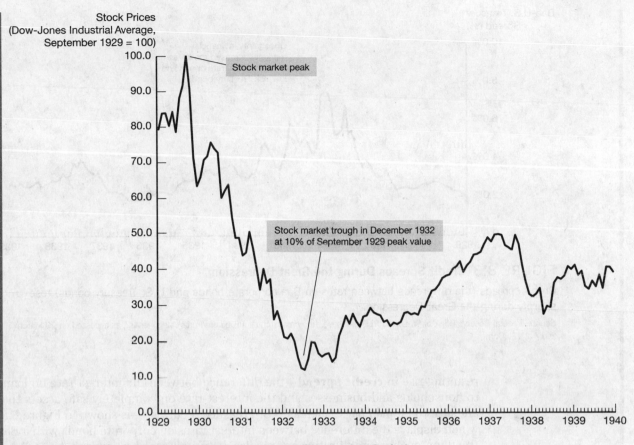

FIGURE 8.2 Stock Price Data During the Great Depression Period

Stock prices crashed in 1929, falling by 40% by the end of 1929, and then continued to fall to only 10% of their peak value by 1932.

Source: Dow-Jones Industrial Average (DJIA). Global Financial Data. www.globalfinancialdata.com/index_tabs.php?action=detailedinfo&ld=1165, as accessed on 20 March 2017 at 12pm.

declared a bank holiday, a temporary closing of all banks. "The only thing we have to fear is fear itself," Roosevelt told the nation. The damage was done, however, and more than one-third of U.S. commercial banks had failed.

Continuing Decline in Stock Prices

Stock prices kept falling. By mid-1932, stocks had declined to 10% of their value at the 1929 peak (as shown in Figure 8.2), and the increase in uncertainty from the unsettled business conditions created by the economic contraction worsened adverse selection and moral hazard problems in financial markets. With a greatly reduced number of financial intermediaries still in business, adverse selection and moral hazard problems intensified even further. Financial markets struggled to channel funds to borrower-spenders with productive investment opportunities. As our analysis predicts, the amount of outstanding commercial loans fell by half from 1929 to 1933, and investment spending collapsed, declining by 90% from its 1929 level.

A manifestation of the rise in financial frictions is that lenders began charging businesses much higher interest rates to protect themselves from credit losses. The

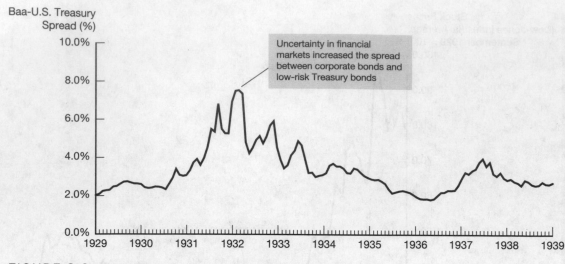

FIGURE 8.3 Credit Spreads During the Great Depression

Credit spreads (the difference between rates on Baa corporate bonds and U.S. Treasury bonds) rose sharply during the Great Depression.

Source: Federal Reserve Bank of St. Louis FRED database, http://research.stlouisfed.org/fred2/categories/22, as accessed on 20 March 2017 at 12.30pm.

resulting rise in **credit spread**—the difference between the interest rate on loans to households and businesses and the interest rate on completely safe assets that are sure to be paid back, such as U.S. Treasury securities—is shown in Figure 8.3, which displays the difference between interest rates on corporate bonds with a Baa (medium-quality) credit rating and similar-maturity Treasury bonds.

Debt Deflation

The ongoing deflation that started in 1930 eventually led to a 25% decline in the price level. This deflation short-circuited the normal recovery process that occurs in most recessions. The huge decline in prices triggered a debt deflation in which net worth fell because of the increased burden of indebtedness borne by firms. The decline in net worth and the resulting increase in adverse selection and moral hazard problems in the credit markets led to a prolonged economic contraction in which unemployment rose to 25% of the labor force. The financial crisis in the Great Depression was the worst ever experienced in the United States, and it explains why the economic contraction was also the most severe ever experienced by the nation.

International Dimensions

Although the Great Depression started in the United States, it was not just a U.S. phenomenon. Bank panics in the United States also spread to the rest of the world, and the contraction of the U.S. economy sharply decreased the demand for foreign goods. The worldwide depression caused great hardship, with millions upon millions of people out of work, and the resulting discontent led to the rise of fascism and World War II. The consequences of the Great Depression financial crisis were disastrous.

CASE

The Global Financial Crisis of 2007–2009

Most economists thought that financial crisis of the type experienced during the Great Depression were a thing of the past for advanced countries like the United States. Unfortunately, the financial crisis that engulfed the world in 2007–2009 proved them wrong.

Causes of the 2007–2009 Financial Crisis

We begin our look at the 2007–2009 financial crisis by examining three central factors: financial innovation in mortgage markets, agency problems in mortgage markets, and the role of asymmetric information in the credit-rating process.

Financial Innovation in the Mortgage Markets Before 2000, only the most credit-worthy (prime) borrowers could obtain residential mortgages. Advances in computer technology and new statistical techniques, known as data mining, however, led to enhanced, quantitative evaluation of the credit risk for a new class of risky residential mortgages. Households with credit records could now be assigned a numerical credit score, known as a FICO score (named after the Fair Isaac Corporation, which developed it), that would predict how likely they would be to default on their loan payments. In addition, by lowering transactions costs, computer technology enabled the bundling of smaller loans (like mortgages) into standard debt securities, a process known as **securitization.** These factors made it possible for banks to offer **subprime mortgages** to borrowers with less-than-stellar credit records.

The ability to cheaply quantify the default risk of the underlying high-risk mortgages and bundle them in standardized debt securities called **mortgage-backed securities** provided a new source of financing for these mortgages. Financial innovation didn't stop there. **Financial engineering,** the development of new, sophisticated financial instruments, led to **structured credit products** that pay out income streams from a collection of underlying assets, designed to have particular risk characteristics that appeal to investors with differing preferences. The most notorious of these products were **collateralized debt obligations (CDOs)** (discussed in the Mini-Case box, "Collateralized Debt Obligations (CDOs)").

Agency Problems in the Mortgage Markets The mortgage brokers that originated the loans often did not make a strong effort to evaluate whether the borrower could pay off the loan, since they would quickly sell (distribute) the loans to investors in the form of mortgage-backed securities. Indeed, in some cases mortgage brokers would even extend loans that they knew were beyond the capability of the borrower to pay back. This **originate-to-distribute** business model was exposed to **principal–agent (agency) problems** of the type discussed in Chapter 7, in which the mortgage brokers acted as agents for investors (the principals) but did not have the investors' best interests at heart. Once the mortgage broker earns his or her fee, why should the broker care if the borrower makes good on his or her payment? The more volume the broker originates, the more he or she makes.

> MINI-CASE

Collateralized Debt Obligations (CDOs)

The creation of a collateralized debt obligation involves a corporate entity called a *special purpose vehicle (SPV)* which buys a collection of assets such as corporate bonds and loans, commercial real estate bonds, and mortgage-backed securities. The SPV then separates the payment streams (cash flows) from these assets into a number of buckets that are referred to as tranches. The highest rated tranches, called super senior tranches, are the ones that are paid off first and so have the least risk. The super senior CDO is a bond that pays out these cash flows to investors, and because it has the least risk, it also has the lowest interest rate. The next bucket of cash flows, known as the senior tranche, is paid out next; the senior CDO has a little more risk and pays a higher interest rate. The next tranche of payment streams, the mezzanine tranche of the CDO, is paid out after the super senior and senior tranches and so it bears more risk and has an even higher interest rate. The lowest tranche of the CDO is the equity tranche; this is the first set of cash flows that are not paid out if the underlying assets go into

default and stop making payments. This tranche has the highest risk and is often not traded.

If all of this sounds complicated, it is. There were even CDO^2s and CDO^3s that sliced and diced risk even further, paying out the cash flows from CDOs to CDO^2s and from CDO^2s to CDO^3s. Although financial engineering has the potential benefit of creating products and services that match investors' risk appetites, it too has a dark side. Structured products like CDOs, CDO^2s, and CDO^3s can get so complicated that it can be hard to value cash flows of the underlying assets for a security or to determine who actually owns these assets. Indeed, at a speech given in October 2007, Ben Bernanke, the chairman of the Federal Reserve, joked that he "would like to know what those damn things are worth." In other words, the increased complexity of structured products can actually reduce the amount of information in financial markets, thereby worsening asymmetric information in the financial system and increasing the severity of adverse selection and moral hazard problems.

Not surprisingly, adverse selection became a major problem. Risk-loving investors lined up to obtain loans to acquire houses that would be very profitable if housing prices went up, knowing they could "walk away" if housing prices went down. The **principal–agent problem** also created incentives for mortgage brokers to encourage households to take on mortgages they could not afford or to commit fraud by falsifying information on a borrower's mortgage applications in order to qualify them for mortgages. Compounding this problem was lax regulation of originators, who were not required to disclose information to borrowers that would have helped them assess whether they could afford the loans.

The agency problems went even deeper. Commercial and investment banks, which were earning large fees by underwriting mortgage-backed securities and structured credit products like CDOs, also had weak incentives to make sure that the ultimate holders of the securities would be paid off. Large fees from writing financial insurance contracts called **credit default swaps,** which provide payments to holders of bonds if they default, also drove units of insurance companies like AIG to write hundreds of billions of dollars' worth of these risky contracts.

Asymmetric Information and Credit-Rating Services Credit-rating agencies, who rate the quality of debt securities in terms of the probability of default, were another contributor to asymmetric information in financial markets. The rating agencies advised clients on how to structure complex financial instruments, like CDOs, at the same time they were rating these identical products. The rating agencies were thus subject to conflicts of interest because the large fees they earned from advising clients on how to structure products they were rating meant that they did not have sufficient incentives to make sure their ratings were accurate. The result was wildly inflated ratings that enabled the sale of complex financial products that were far riskier than investors recognized.

Effects of the 2007–2009 Financial Crisis

Consumers and businesses alike suffered as a result of the 2007–2009 financial crisis. The impact of the crisis was most evident in five key areas: the U.S. residential housing market, financial institutions' balance sheets, the shadow banking system, global financial markets, and the headline-grabbing failures of major firms in the financial industry.

Residential Housing Prices: Boom and Bust   Aided by liquidity from huge cash inflows into the United States from countries like China and India, and low interest rates on residential mortgages, the subprime mortgage market took off after the recession ended in 2001. By 2007, it had become over a trillion-dollar market. The development of the subprime mortgage market was encouraged by politicians because it led to a "democratization of credit" and helped raise U.S. homeownership rates to the highest levels in history.[1] The asset-price boom in housing (see Figure 8.4), which took off after the 2000–2001 recession was over, also helped stimulate the growth of the subprime mortgage market. High housing prices meant that subprime borrowers could refinance their houses with even larger loans when their homes appreciated in value. With housing prices rising, subprime borrowers were also unlikely to default because they could always sell their house to pay off the loan, making investors happy because the securities backed by cash flows from subprime mortgages had high returns. The growth of the subprime mortgage market, in turn, increased the demand for houses and so fueled the boom in housing prices, resulting in a housing price bubble. (A highly controversial issue is whether the Federal Reserve was to blame for the housing price bubble, and this is discussed in the Inside the Fed box.)

As housing prices rose and profitability for mortgage originators and lenders was high, the underwriting standards for subprime mortgages fell to lower and lower standards. High-risk borrowers were able to obtain mortgages, and the amount of the mortgage relative to the value of the house, the loan-to-value ratio (LTV), rose. Borrowers were often able to get piggyback, second, and third mortgages on top of their original 80% loan-to-value mortgage, so that they had to put almost no money down. When asset prices rise too far out of line with fundamentals—in the case of housing, how much housing costs if purchased relative to the cost of renting it, or the cost of houses relative to households' median income—they must come down. Eventually, the housing price bubble burst. With housing prices falling after their peak in 2006 (see Figure 8.4), the rot in the financial system began to be revealed. The decline in housing prices led to many subprime borrowers finding that their

---

[1]For a discussion of the government's role in encouraging the boom which led to bust in the housing market, see Thomas Sowell, *The Housing Boom and Bust*, Revised Edition (New York, Basic Books, 2010).

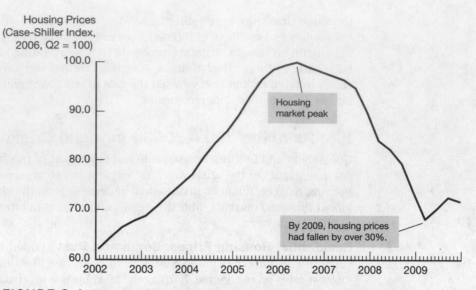

FIGURE 8.4 Housing Prices and the Financial Crisis of 2007–2009

Housing prices boomed from 2002 to 2006, fueling the market for subprime mortgages and forming an asset-price bubble. Housing prices began declining in 2006, falling by more than 30% subsequently, which led to defaults by subprime mortgage holders.

Source: Case-Shiller 20-City Home Price Index in Federal Reserve Bank of St. Louis, FRED Database. http://research. stlouisfed.org/fred2/, as accessed on 12 March 2017 at 2pm.

> INSIDE THE FED

Was the Fed to Blame for the Housing Price Bubble?

Some economists—most prominently, John Taylor of Stanford University—have argued that the low-rate interest policy of the Federal Reserve in the 2003–2006 period caused the housing price bubble.* During this period, the Federal Reserve relied on easing of monetary policy to set the federal funds rate well below the level that the Taylor rule, discussed in Chapter 16, suggested was appropriate. Taylor argues that the low federal funds rate led to low mortgage rates that stimulated housing demand and encouraged the issuance of subprime mortgages, both of which led to rising housing prices and a bubble.

In a speech given in January 2010, Federal Reserve Chairman Ben Bernanke countered this argument.** He concluded that monetary policy was not to blame for the housing price bubble. First, he said, it is not at all clear that the federal funds rate was below what the Taylor rule suggested would be appropriate. Rates seemed low only when current values, not forecasts, were used in the output and inflation calculations for the Taylor rule. Rather, the culprits were the proliferation of new mortgage products that lowered mortgage payments, a relaxation of lending standards that brought more buyers into the housing market, and capital inflows from countries such as China and India. Bernanke's speech was very controversial, and the debate over whether monetary policy was to blame for the housing price bubble continues to this day.

*John Taylor, "Housing and Monetary Policy," in Federal Reserve Bank of Kansas City, *Housing, Housing Finance and Monetary Policy* (Kansas City: Federal Reserve Bank of Kansas City, 2007), 463–476.

**Ben S. Bernanke, "Monetary Policy and the Housing Bubble," speech given at the annual meeting of the American Economic Association, Atlanta, Georgia, January 3, 2010, www.federalreserve.gov/newsevents/speech/bernanke20100103a.htm.

mortgages were "underwater"—that is, the value of the house fell below the amount of the mortgage. When this happened, struggling homeowners had tremendous incentives to walk away from their homes and just send the keys back to the lender. Defaults on mortgages shot up sharply, eventually leading to millions of mortgages in foreclosure.

Deterioration of Financial Institutions' Balance Sheets   The decline in U.S. housing prices led to rising defaults on mortgages. As a result, the value of mortgage-backed securities and CDOs collapsed, leaving banks and other financial institutions with a lower value of assets and thus a decline in net worth. With weakened balance sheets, these banks and other financial institutions began to deleverage, selling off assets and restricting the availability of credit to both households and businesses. With no one else able to step in to collect information and make loans, the reduction in bank lending meant that financial frictions increased in financial markets.

Run on the Shadow Banking System   The sharp decline in the value of mortgages and other financial assets triggered a run on the **shadow banking system,** composed of hedge funds, investment banks, and other nondepository financial firms, which are not as tightly regulated as banks. Funds from shadow banks flowed through the financial system and for many years supported the issuance of low interest-rate mortgages and auto loans.

These securities were funded primarily by **repurchase agreements (repos),** short-term borrowing that, in effect, uses assets like mortgage-backed securities as collateral. Rising concern about the quality of a financial institution's balance sheet led lenders to require larger amounts of collateral, known as **haircuts.** For example, if a borrower took out a $100 million loan in a repo agreement, it might have to post $105 million of mortgage-backed securities as collateral, and the haircut is then 5%.

With rising defaults on mortgages, the value of mortgage-backed securities fell, which then led to a rise in haircuts. At the start of the crisis, haircuts were close to zero, but they eventually rose to nearly 50%.[2] The result was that the same amount of collateral would allow financial institutions to borrow only half as much. Thus, to raise funds, financial institutions had to engage in fire sales and sell off their assets very rapidly. Because selling assets quickly requires lowering their price, the fire sales led to a further decline in financial institutions' asset values. This decline lowered the value of collateral further, raising haircuts and thereby forcing financial institutions to scramble even more for liquidity. The result was similar to the run on the banking system that occurred during the Great Depression, causing massive deleveraging that resulted in a restriction of lending and a decline in economic activity.

The decline in asset prices in the stock market (which fell by over 50% from October 2007 to March 2009, as shown in Figure 8.5) and the more than 30% drop in residential house prices (shown in Figure 8.4), along with the fire sales resulting from the run on the shadow banking system, weakened both firms' and households' balance sheets. This worsening of financial frictions manifested

---

[2]See Gary Gorton and Andrew Metrick, "Securitized Banking and the Run on Repo," *Journal of Financial Economics* 104 (2012): 425–451.

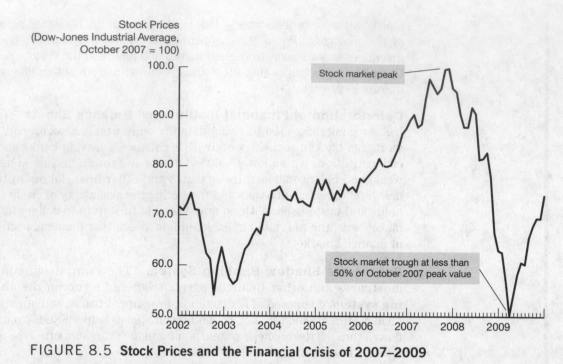

Stock Prices
(Dow-Jones Industrial Average,
October 2007 = 100)

Stock market peak

Stock market trough at less than
50% of October 2007 peak value

FIGURE 8.5 **Stock Prices and the Financial Crisis of 2007–2009**

Stock prices fell by 50% from October 2007 to March 2009.

Source: Dow-Jones Industrial Average (DJIA). Global Financial Data, www.globalfinancialdata.com/index_tabs.php?action= detailedinfo&id=1165, as accessed on 20 March 2017 at 12pm.

itself in widening credit spreads, causing higher costs of credit for households and businesses and tighter lending standards. The resulting decline in lending meant that both consumption expenditure and investment fell, causing the economy to contract.

Global Financial Markets   Although the problem originated in the United States, the wake-up call for the financial crisis came from Europe, a sign of how extensive the globalization of financial markets had become. After Fitch and Standard & Poor's announced ratings downgrades on mortgage-backed securities and CDOs totaling more than $10 billion, on August 7, 2007, a French investment house, BNP Paribas, suspended redemption of shares held in some of its money market funds, which had sustained large losses. The run on the shadow banking system began, only to become worse and worse over time. Despite huge injections of liquidity into the financial system by the European Central Bank and the Federal Reserve, banks began to horde cash and were unwilling to lend to each other. The drying up of credit led to the first major bank failure in the United Kingdom in over 100 years, when Northern Rock, which had relied on short-term borrowing in the repo market rather than deposits for its funding, collapsed in September 2007. A string of other European financial institutions then failed as well. Particularly hard hit were countries like Greece, Ireland, Portugal, Spain, and Italy, which led to a sovereign debt crisis, which is described in the Global box, "The European Sovereign Debt Crisis."

Failure of High-Profile Firms   The impact of the financial crisis on firm balance sheets forced major players in the financial markets to take drastic action. In March 2008 Bear Stearns, the fifth-largest investment bank in the United States, which had invested heavily in subprime-related securities, had a run on its repo funding and was forced to sell itself to J. P. Morgan for less than 5% of what it had been worth just a year earlier. To broker the deal, the Federal Reserve had to take over $30 billion of Bear Stearns's hard-to-value assets. In July Fannie Mae and Freddie Mac, the two privately owned government-sponsored enterprises that together insured over $5 trillion of mortgages or mortgage-backed assets, were propped up by the U.S. Treasury and the Federal Reserve after suffering substantial losses from their holdings of subprime securities. In early September 2008 they were then put into conservatorship (in effect run by the government).

> GLOBAL

The European Sovereign Debt Crisis

The global financial crisis in 2007–2009 led not only to a worldwide recession but also to a sovereign debt crisis that threatens to destabilize Europe. Up until 2007, all the countries that had adopted the euro found their interest rates converging to very low levels; but with the global financial crisis, several of these countries were hit very hard with the contraction in economic activity reducing tax revenues, while government bailouts of failed financial institutions required additional government outlays. The resulting surge in budget deficits then led to suspicions that the governments in these hard-hit countries would default on their debt. The result was a surge in interest rates that threatened to spiral out of control.*

Greece was the first domino to fall in Europe. With a weakening economy reducing tax revenue and increasing spending demands, the Greek government in September 2009 was projecting a budget deficit for the year of 6% and a debt-to-GDP ratio near 100%. However, when a new government was elected in October, it revealed that the budget situation was far worse than anyone had imagined because the previous government had provided misleading numbers both about the budget deficit, which was at least double the 6% number, and the amount of government debt, which was ten percentage points higher than previously reported. Despite

austerity measures to dramatically cut government spending and raise taxes, interest rates on Greek debt soared, eventually rising to nearly 40%, and the debt-to-GDP ratio climbed to 160% of GDP in 2012. Even with bailouts from other European countries and liquidity support from the European Central Bank, Greece was forced to write down the value of its debt held in private hands by more than half, and the country was subject to civil unrest, with massive strikes and the resignation of the prime minister.

The sovereign debt crisis spread from Greece to Ireland, Portugal, Spain, and Italy, with their governments forced to embrace austerity measures to shore up their public finances, while interest rates climbed to double-digit levels. Only with a speech in July 2012 by Mario Draghi, the president of the European Central Bank, in which he stated that the ECB was ready to do "whatever it takes" to save the euro, did the markets begin to calm down. Nonetheless, despite a sharp decline in interest rates in those countries, these countries experienced severe recessions, with unemployment rates rising to double-digit levels, with Spain's unemployment rate exceeding 25%. The stresses that the European sovereign debt crisis produced for the euro zone has raised doubts about the euro's survival, a topic we return to in Chapter 15.

*For a discussion of the dynamics of sovereign debt crisis and case studies of the European debt crisis, see David Greenlaw, James D. Hamilton, Frederic S. Mishkin, and Peter Hooper, "Crunch Time: Fiscal Crisis and the Role of Monetary Policy," *U.S. Monetary Policy Forum* (Chicago: Chicago Booth Initiative on Global Markets, 2013).

On Monday, September 15, 2008, after suffering losses in the subprime market, Lehman Brothers, the fourth-largest investment bank by asset size with over $600 billion in assets and 25,000 employees, filed for bankruptcy, making it the largest bankruptcy filing in U.S. history. The day before, Merrill Lynch, the third-largest investment bank, who had also suffered large losses on its holding of subprime securities, announced its sale to Bank of America for a price 60% below its value a year earlier. On Tuesday, September 16, AIG, an insurance giant with assets of over $1 trillion, suffered an extreme liquidity crisis when its credit rating was downgraded. It had written over $400 billion of insurance contracts (credit default swaps) that had to make payouts on possible losses from subprime mortgage securities. The Federal Reserve then stepped in with an $85 billion loan to keep AIG afloat (with total government loans later increased to $173 billion).

Height of the 2007–2009 Financial Crisis

The financial crisis reached its peak in September 2008 after the House of Representatives, fearing the wrath of constituents who were angry about bailing out Wall Street, voted down a $700 billion dollar bailout package proposed by the Bush administration. The Emergency Economic Stabilization Act finally passed nearly a week later. The stock market crash accelerated, with the week beginning October 6, 2008, showing the worst weekly decline in U.S. history. Credit spreads went through the roof over the next three weeks, with the spread between Baa corporate bonds (just above investment grade) and U.S. Treasury bonds going to over 5.5 percentage points (550 basis points), as illustrated by Figure 8.6.

The impaired financial markets and surging interest rates faced by borrower-spenders led to sharp declines in consumer spending and investment. Real GDP declined sharply, falling at a –1.3% annual rate in the third quarter of 2008 and then at a –5.4% and –6.4% annual rate in the next two quarters. The unemployment rate shot up, going over the 10% level in late 2009. The recession that started in December 2007 became the worst economic contraction in the United States since World War II and as a result is now referred to as the "Great Recession."

Starting in March 2009, a bull market in stocks got under way (see Figure 8.5), and credit spreads began to fall (Figure 8.6).[3] With the recovery in financial markets, the economy started to recover but, unfortunately, the pace of the recovery has been slow.

---

[3]The financial market recovery was aided by the U.S. Treasury's requirement announced in February 2009 that the nineteen largest banking institutions undergo what became known as the *bank stress tests* (the Supervisory Capital Assessment Program, or SCAP). The stress tests were a supervisory assessment, led by the Federal Reserve in cooperation with the Office of the Comptroller of the Currency and the FDIC, of the balance sheet position of these banks to ensure that they had sufficient capital to withstand bad macroeconomic outcomes. The Treasury announced the results in early May and they were well received by market participants, allowing these banks to raise substantial amounts of capital from private capital markets. The stress tests were a key factor that helped increase the amount of information in the marketplace, thereby reducing asymmetric information and adverse selection and moral hazard problems.

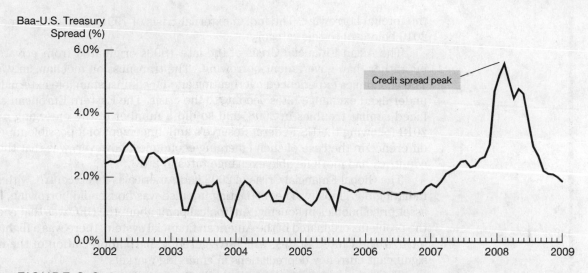

FIGURE 8.6 **Credit Spreads and the 2007–2009 Financial Crisis**

Credit spreads (the difference between rates on Baa corporate bonds and U.S. Treasury bonds) rose by more than 4 percentage points (400 basis points) during the crisis. Debate over the bailout package and the stock market crash caused credit spreads to peak in December 2008.

Source: Federal Reserve Bank of St. Louis FRED database, http://research.stlouisfed.org/fred2/, as accessed on 14 May 2016 at 3pm.

CASE

Financial Crisis: Past, Present and Future

Can we view the Global Financial Crisis as being the last of its kind? Will future crisis occur? Will they be different?

"The essence of the this-time-is-different syndrome is simple. It is rooted in the firmly held belief that financial crisis are things that happen to other people in other countries at other times; crisis do not happen to us, here and now. We are doing things better, we are smarter, we have learned from past mistakes. The old rules of valuation no longer apply. Unfortunately, a highly leveraged economy can unwittingly be sitting with its back at the edge of a financial cliff for many years before chance and circumstance provoke a crisis of confidence that pushes it off." (Reinhart and Rogoff, 2009, p.15)

The Indian Economic Survey 2015–16 (GOI, p. 8–9) has categorised external financial crisis originating since the 1980s into three basic forms: the Latin American, the Asian Financial Crisis (AFC), and the Global Financial Crisis (GFC) model.

The Latin American debt crisis of 1982 was one driven by government overspending financed by foreign borrowing of recycled petrodollars, while maintaining a fixed exchange rate. Such binge spending led to economic overheating, large current account deficits that eventually proved difficult to finance, and finally defaults on the foreign borrowing. The Indian external crisis of 1991, as also the Greek crisis of 2010 belonged to this category.

The Asian Financial Crisis of the late 1990s originated from private borrowing rather than government borrowing. The transmission mechanism was similar. The economies experienced overheating and faced unsustainable external positions under fixed exchange rates, leading to the crisis. The Eastern European economies faced similar troubles in 2008, and so did a number of the emerging markets in 2013 following the US Federal Reserve's announcement of a possible tapering. The difference in the case of such emerging economies, however, was that the affected countries had more flexible exchange rates in 2013.

The Global Financial Crisis of 2008 had America as its epicentre, with its effects radiating out globally. The instigating impulse was household borrowing, leading to asset price bubbles in housing. An ironical point about the GFC was that even though the problems originated in the American financial system, there was a flight of capital *toward* the United States, which triggered a sharp appreciation of the dollar and significant currency depreciations in emerging markets.

The Japanese crisis, though similar to the GFC in terms of the transmission mechanism, had corporate borrowing as the instigating impulse. Its financial impact, however, was limited since Japan was not a major international banking centre. Also, since the Japanese yen appreciated during the crisis, the Japanese crisis did not have a major impact on global exports, even though Japan was a major global trader.

China's situation in 2015–2016 was similar to the AFC case. Large capital outflows were triggered by fears of excessive corporate debt, together with slower growh and changing economic management. However, China's large foreign exchange reserves of $3 trillion and more made its situation different from that of Asian countries, which had limited foreign exchange reserves.

The Economic Survey comments that a major event triggering a crisis in China or another large emerging market would be very different from the three categories described above. It would have none of the built-in adjustment mechanism that was witnessed in the GFC in the form of appreciation of the crisis country's currency. The large currency depreciation in a systemically important country like China in such a scenario would spread outwards as a deflationary/competitiveness shock to the rest of the world, especially countries competing with it. In this sense, such crisis which are likely to occur in systematically important emerging markets are likely to resemble the Great Depression of the 1930s, leading to a collapse in global economic activity.

India: Lessons from the Financial Crisis

The Global Financial Crisis of 2008 challenged the predominant view at that time of the differential needs for both monetary and fiscal policy. In particular, it dispelled the notion that monetary policy should be used to stabilise the economy in the short-run, whereas fiscal policy should be used to address income distribution concerns and establish the foundations of long-run growth. It brought to the fore the need for better monetary-fiscal coordination.

The post-global financial crisis era also witnessed an addition to the objectives of monetary policy. Financial stability emerged as another important policy objective of monetary policy, besides growth and price stability.

TABLE 8.1 Anatomical Taxonomy of External Financial Crisis

Crisis Type	Originating Countries	Origin of Problem	Manifestation	Trigger	Exchange Rate Regime	Remarks
Latin American	Emerging Markets (Latin America 1982; India 1991); Small advanced country (Greece 2010 onwards)	Government borrowing	Current account deficit	Speculative attack and exchange rate collapse	Fixed rate	Greece was part of euro, so trigger was sharp rise in interest rates
Asian Financial Crisis	Emerging markets (East Asia 1997-9 Eastern Europe 2003; Fragile Five 2013); Small advanced country (Spain 2010)	Corporate borrowing	Asset price bubbles; high corporate leverage	"Sudden stop" of capital flows and exchange rate collapse	Fixed rate	Fragile Five had flexible exchange rates, Spain was part of euro
Japan	Systemically important	Corporate borrowing	Asset price bubbles; high corporate leverage	Asset price collapse	Floating rate	Yen appreciated after the crisis
The Global Financial Crisis	Systemically important (US 2008)	Bank and consumer borrowing	Asset price bubble in housing	Correction in asset prices	Flexible exchange rate	US dollar appreciated
The NEXT	Systemically important	Corporate borrowing	Rising debt, asset price bubbles	"Sudden stop" with potential for sharp exchange rate decline	Managed float	The crisis country's currency could depreciate substantially

Source: Government of India, Economic Survey 2015-16, February 2016, p. 9, http://indiabudget.nic.in/es2015-16/echapter-vol1.pdf, as accessed on 12 March 2017 at 9pm.

The specific policy lessons and challenges that were highlighted by the global financial crisis, especially in the context of India, included the following (RBI, 2012, 115–123):

- Macroeconomic stability is not a sufficient condition to guard against financial instability
- Financial stability, although a primary mandate for central banks, necessitates greater coordination with fiscal authorities
- Need to lay out a policy coordination framework
- Need to insulate financial sector from negative feedback from sovereign debt concerns
- Fiscal Consolidation needed for independent conduct of monetary policy
- Fiscal-monetary coordination not only at national level but also at international level
- Indian experience suggests that fiscal rules, though necessary, are not sufficient in optimising the outcomes of fiscal-monetary coordination
- Need for continuance of effective fiscal-monetary coordination and strengthening the Reserve Bank balance sheet in the light of various risks as witnessed during global financial crisis.
- Careful calibration towards reverting to fiscal consolidation and proper assessment of any likely institutional changes in public debt management constitute key imperatives for the outlook of fiscal-monetary debt management coordination in India.

References

Government of India, Economic Survey 2015–16, February 2016, http://indiabudget.nic.in/es2015–16/echapter-vol1.pdf

Carmen M. Reinhart and Kenneth S. Rogoff, This Time is Different, Eight Centuries of Financial Folly, Princeton: New Jersey, Princeton University Press, 2009.

Reserve Bank of India, Report on Currency and Finance 2009–12, Fiscal and Monetary Coordination, 2012, https://rbidocs.rbi.org.in/rdocs/Publications/PDFs/0RCF040313_F0912.pdf, as accessed on 3 January 2016 at 4pm.

SUMMARY

1. A financial crisis occurs when a particularly large disruption to information flows occurs in financial markets, with the result that financial frictions and credit spreads increase sharply, thereby rendering financial markets incapable of channeling funds to households and firms with productive investment opportunities, and causing a sharp contraction in economic activity.

2. Financial crisis can start in advanced countries like the United States in several possible ways: credit and asset-price booms and busts or a general increase in uncertainty when major financial institutions fail. The result is a substantial increase in adverse selection and moral hazard problems that lead to a contraction of lending and a decline in economic activity. The worsening business conditions and deterioration in bank balance sheets then trigger the second stage of the crisis, the simultaneous failure of many banking institutions, a banking crisis. The resulting decrease in the number of banks causes a loss of their information capital, leading to a further decline of lending and a spiraling down of the economy. In some instances, the resulting economic downturn leads to a sharp slide in prices, which increases the

real liabilities of firms and households and therefore lowers their net worth, leading to a debt deflation. The further decline in borrowers' net worth worsens adverse selection and moral hazard problems, so that lending, investment spending, and aggregate economic activity remain depressed for a long time.

3. The most significant financial crisis in U.S. history, that which led to the Great Depression, involved several stages: a stock market crash, bank panics,

worsening of asymmetric information problems, and finally a debt deflation.

4. The global financial crisis of 2007–2009 was triggered by mismanagement of financial innovations involving subprime residential mortgages and the bursting of a housing price bubble. The crisis spread globally, with substantial deterioration in banks' and other financial institutions' balance sheets, a run on the shadow banking system, and the failure of many high-profile firms.

KEY TERMS

asset-price bubble, p. 168
bank panic, p. 169
collateralized debt obligations (CDOs), p. 173
credit boom, p. 168
credit default swaps, p. 174
credit spreads, p. 172
debt deflation, p. 169
deleveraging, p. 168

financial crisis, p. 166
financial engineering, p. 173
financial frictions, p. 166
financial innovation, p. 166
financial liberalization, p. 166
fire sales, p. 169
fundamental economic values, p. 168
haircuts, p. 177
mortgage-backed securities, p. 173

originate-to-distribute model, p. 173
principal–agent problem, p. 173
repurchase agreements (repos), p. 177
securitization, p. 173
shadow banking system, p. 177
structured credit products, p. 173
subprime mortgages, p. 173

QUESTIONS

1. How does the concept of asymmetric information help to define a financial crisis?

2. How can a bursting of an asset-price bubble in the stock market help trigger a financial crisis?

3. How does an unanticipated decline in the price level cause a drop in lending?

4. How can a decline in real estate prices cause deleveraging and a decline in lending?

5. How does a deterioration in balance sheets of financial institutions cause a decline in economic activity?

6. How does a general increase in uncertainty as a result of a failure of a major financial institution lead to an increase in adverse selection and moral hazard problems?

7. What is a credit spread? Why do credit spreads rise during financial crisis?

8. What causes bank panics?

9. Why do bank panics worsen asymmetric information problems in credit markets?

10. How can financial liberalizations lead to financial crisis?

11. What role do weak financial regulation and supervision play in causing financial crisis?

12. Describe two similarities and two differences between the U.S. experiences during the Great Depression and those during the global financial crisis of 2007–2009.

13. What technological innovations led to the development of the subprime mortgage market?

14. Why is the originate-to-distribute business model subject to the principal–agent problem?

15. True, false, or uncertain: Financial engineering always leads to a more efficient financial system.

16. How did a decline in housing prices help trigger the subprime financial crisis starting in 2007?

17. What is the shadow banking system, and why was it an important part of the 2007–2009 financial crisis?

18. Why would haircuts on collateral increase sharply during a financial crisis? How would this lead to fire sales on assets?

19. Why are more resources not devoted to adequate, prudential supervision of the financial system to limit excessive risk taking, when it is clear that this supervision is needed to prevent financial crisis?

20. How did the global financial crisis promote a sovereign debt crisis in Europe?

21. How can a sovereign debt crisis make an economic contraction more likely?

22. What is likely to happen if the next financial crisis were to occur in a systemically important emerging country, such as China? Will it resemble the earlier crisis?

WEB EXERCISES

1. This chapter discusses how an understanding of adverse selection and moral hazard can help us better understand financial crisis. The greatest financial crisis faced by the United States was the Great Depression of 1929–1933. Go to **www.amatecon.com/ greatdepression.html**. This site contains a brief discussion of the factors that led to the Great Depression. Write a one-page summary explaining how adverse selection and moral hazard contributed to the Great Depression.

2. Go to the International Monetary Fund's Financial Crisis page at **www.imf.org/external/np/exr/key/ finstab.htm**. Report on the most recent three countries that the IMF has given emergency loans to in response to a financial crisis. According to the IMF, what caused the crisis in each country?

WEB REFERENCES

www.amatecon.com/gd/gdtimeline.html

A time line of the Great Depression.

www.imf.org

The International Monetary Fund is an organization of 185 countries that works on global policy coordination (both monetary and trade), stable and sustainable economic prosperity, and the reduction of poverty.

9

Central Banks and the Reserve Bank of India (RBI)

> PREVIEW

Among the most important players in financial markets throughout the world are central banks, the government authorities in charge of monetary policy. Central banks' actions affect interest rates, the amount of credit, and the money supply, all of which have direct impacts not only on financial markets but also on aggregate output and inflation. To understand the role that central banks play in financial markets and the overall economy, we need to understand how these organizations work. Who controls central banks and determines their actions? What motivates their behavior? Who holds the reins of power?

In this chapter we look at the institutional structure of major central banks and focus particularly on the Reserve Bank of India (RBI), the Indian central bank. We start by focusing on the elements of the RBI's institutional structure that determine where the true power within the Reserve Bank of India lies. By understanding who makes the decisions, we will have a better idea of how they are made. We then look at several other major central banks, particularly the European Central Bank, and see how they are organized. With this information, we will be better able to comprehend the actual conduct of monetary policy described in the following chapter.

Origin of the Reserve Bank of India

GO ONLINE

Access **https://www.rbi.org.in/Scripts/chronology.aspx** for information on the chronological milestones of the RBI.

The Reserve Bank of India is the central bank of the country. Central banks are a relatively recent innovation and most central banks, as we know them today, were established around the early twentieth century. The Reserve Bank of India was set up on the basis of the recommendations of the Royal Commission on Indian Currency and Finance, also known as the Hilton-Young Commission, and commenced its operations on April 1, 1935.

The statutory functioning of the RBI is under the Reserve Bank of India Act, 1934 (II of 1934), which also sets out the objectives of the Reserve Bank as '... *to regulate the issue of Bank notes and the keeping of reserves with a view to securing monetary stability in India and generally to operate the currency and credit system of the country to its advantage.*'

The Bank began its operations by taking over from the Government the functions so far being performed by the Controller of Currency and from the Imperial Bank of India, the management of Government accounts and public debt. The existing currency offices at Calcutta, Bombay, Madras, Rangoon, Karachi, Lahore and Cawnpore (Kanpur) became branches of the Issue Department. Offices of the Banking Department were established in Calcutta, Bombay, Madras, Delhi and Rangoon.

Burma (Myanmar) seceded from the Indian Union in 1937, however the Reserve Bank continued to act as the Central Bank for Burma till the Japanese occupation of Burma and later upto April 1947. After the partition of India, the Reserve Bank served as the central bank of Pakistan upto June 1948, when the State Bank of Pakistan commenced operations. The Bank, which was originally set up as a shareholder's bank, was nationalised in 1949.

The Reserve Bank of India since its very inception was seen as playing a special role in India's development, especially agriculture. When India commenced its plan endeavours, the Reserve Bank, in many ways, pioneered the concept and practise of using finance to catalyse development. The Bank was also instrumental in institutional development and helped set up institutions like the Deposit Insurance and Credit Guarantee Corporation of India (DICGC), the Unit Trust of India (UTI), the Industrial Development Bank of India (IDBI), the National Bank of Agriculture and Rural Development (NABARD), the Discount and Finance House of India (DFHI) etc. to build the financial infrastructure of the country.

With liberalisation, the Bank's focus has shifted back to core central banking functions like monetary policy, bank supervision and regulation, and overseeing the payments system and onto developing the financial markets.[1]

Structure of the Reserve Bank of India

The RBI comprises of a Central Board of Directors and Local Boards.

Central Board of Directors

A central board of directors governs the Reserve Bank's affairs. The Government of India, in keeping with the Reserve Bank of India Act, appoints the board. The Directors are appointed/nominated for a period of four years.

The Central Board consists of official and non-official Directors. The Official Directors are full time and include the Governor and not more than four Deputy Governors. Of the non-official Directors, 10 Directors are from various fields and one

---

[1]*Source*: https://www.rbi.org.in/Scripts/briefhistory.aspx, as accessed on 29 March 2017 at 11am.

government official is nominated by the Government. Four other Directors are nominated from the four respective local boards. The Central Board functions to provide general superintendence and direction of the Bank's affairs

Local Boards

There is one local board each for the four regions of the country in Mumbai, Kolkata, Chennai and New Delhi. Each board comprises of five members who are appointed by the Central Government for a term of four years

The functions of the local boards are to advise the Central Board on local matters and to represent territorial and economic interests of local cooperative and indigenous banks and to perform such other functions as delegated by the Central Board from time to time.

Offices of the RBI

It has 19 regional offices, most of them in state capitals and 9 sub-offices.

Training Establishments of the RBI

The RBI has five training establishments. Of these, two, namely, College of Agricultural Banking and Reserve Bank of India Staff College are part of the Reserve Bank, while others such as, National Institute for Bank Management (NIBM), Indira Gandhi Institute for Development Research (IGIDR), Institute for Development and Research in Banking Technology (IDRBT) are autonomous.

Subsidiaries of the RBI

Fully owned subsidiaries include the National Housing Bank (NHB), Deposit Insurance and Credit Guarantee Corporation of India (DICGC) and the Bharatiya Reserve Bank Note Mudran Private Limited (BRBNMPL).[2]

> INSIDE THE RBI

Functions of the Reserve Bank of India

The RBI has the following main functions:

Monetary Authority As monetary authority the RBI formulates, implements and monitors the monetary policy with the objective of maintaining price stability and ensuring adequate flow of credit to productive sectors.

Regulator and Supervisor of the Financial System In this role, the RBI prescribes broad parameters of banking operations within which the country's banking and financial system functions. The objective is to maintain public confidence in the system, protect depositors' interest and provide cost-effective banking services to the public.

Manager of Foreign Exchange The RBI manages the Foreign Exchange Management Act, 1999 with the objective of facilitating external trade and payment and promoting orderly development and maintenance of the foreign exchange market in India.

Issuer of Currency In this role, the RBI issues and exchanges or destroys currency and coins not fit for circulation. The objective is to give the public adequate quantity of supplies of currency notes and coins and in good quality.

Developmental Role The RBI performs a wide range of promotional functions to support national objectives.

Related Functions There are other related functions that the RBI performs:

- Banker to the government: It performs merchant banking function for the central and the state governments and also acts as their banker.
- Banker to banks: It maintains banking accounts of all scheduled banks.

Source: https://www.rbi.org.in/Scripts/AboutusDisplay.aspx, as accessed on 20 March 2017 at 11.30am

---

[2]*Source*: https://www.rbi.org.in/Scripts/AboutusDisplay.aspx, as accessed on 20 March 2017 at 11.30am.

GO ONLINE

Access **https://rbi.org.in/Scripts/BS_PressReleaseDisplay.aspx?prid=33817** to see the minutes of the meeting of the TAC on Monetary policy.

Technical Advisory Committee

In India, the Governor was in charge of all monetary policy decisions until August 2016. There was no formal committee structure like the Fed's Federal Open Market Committee (FOMC) or the Monetary Policy Committee (MPC) of the Bank of England. The Governor held structured consultations with the four Deputy Governors and they constituted an informal MPC, although a committee structure was not enjoined under the law or the rules. By its very nature, there was no voting in this committee and the final call was that of the Governor.

With a view to strengthening the consultative process in monetary policy, the Reserve Bank of India constituted a Technical Advisory Committee on Monetary Policy (TAC) for the first time in June, 2009. The RBI governor headed the TAC. The Vice Chairman of the TAC was the deputy governor in charge of monetary policy, with the other three deputy governors being members. Additionally, the committee also had five external members, two of whom were experts from the Central Board of the Bank while the other three were drawn from a wider pool. The Governor nominated the external members. The external members gave specific recommendations on policy options and these were minuted. The role of the TAC was mainly advisory. The Committee met at least once in a quarter.

The objective of the TAC on Monetary Policy was to periodically advise the Reserve Bank on the stance of monetary policy in the light of macroeconomic and monetary developments. The TAC was an outcome of the Reserve Bank's growing emphasis on strengthening the process of monetary policy formulation.

The terms of reference of the Committee were:

- to review macroeconomic and monetary developments, and
- to advise on the stance of monetary policy.

Since February 2011, the Reserve Bank had been placing the main points of discussions of the meetings of TAC on Monetary Policy in the public domain with a lag of roughly four weeks after the meeting.

The Monetary Policy Committee

The Expert Committee to Revise and Strengthen the Monetary Policy Framework 2014 (Chairman: Urjit Patel) had recommended the formation of a Monetary Policy Committee (MPC) which should be vested with the power of monetary policy decision-making. The MPC sought to replace the system where the RBI governor, with the aid and advice of his internal team and a technical advisory committee, had complete control over monetary policy decisions.

The Reserve Bank of India and Government of India signed the Monetary Policy Framework Agreement on 20 February 2015.

Subsequently, the government, in its Union Budget 2016–17, put forth a proposal to amend the Reserve Bank of India (RBI) Act, 1934 for giving a statutory backing to the aforementioned Monetary Policy Framework Agreement and for setting up a Monetary Policy Committee (MPC). Vide this amendment, it was written into the preamble of the RBI Act that the primary objective of the monetary policy is to maintain price stability, while keeping in mind the objective of growth. It also stated that to meet the challenge of an increasingly complex economy, the RBI would operate a Monetary Policy Framework. Thus the amendment provided a statutory and institutionalized basis for a Monetary Policy Framework (MPF) and the

MPC. This amendment to RBI Act was carried out through the Finance Bill, 2016 presented along with the Union Budget documents. A new chapter (Chapter IIIF, Section 45Z) was introduced in the RBI Act, through this Finance Bill, 2016, detailing the operation of MPC.

The Government decided to bring the provisions of the amended RBI Act regarding constitution of MPC into force on June 27, 2016, so that the statutory basis of MPC was made effective. Rules governing the procedure for Selection of Members of Monetary Policy Committee and Terms and Conditions of their appointment and factors constituting failure to meet the inflation target under the MPC Framework were also notified on June 27, 2016.

Constitution of the MPC

The MPC will comprise of six members. Of these, three members will be from the RBI, including the Governor who will be the ex-officio Chairperson, the Deputy Governor RBI, and one officer of the RBI. The other three members of the MPC will be appointed by the Central Government on the recommendations of a Search-cum-Selection Committee which will be headed by the Cabinet Secretary.

These three members of MPC will be experts in the field of economics or banking or finance or monetary policy and will be appointed for a period of four years and shall not be eligible for re-appointment. The meetings of the MPC shall be held at least four times a year and it shall publicise its decisions after each such meeting.[3]

Decision Making by the MPC

Each member of the MPC will have one vote with the outcome determined by majority voting, which has to be exercised without abstaining. To ensure transparency in the working of the MPC, minutes of the proceedings of the MPC was to be released with a lag of two weeks from the date of the meeting.

The Chairman, or in his absence, the Vice Chairman will exercise a casting vote in situations arising on account of unforeseen exigencies, necessitating the absence of a member for the MPC meeting in which voting is equally divided.

The decisions of the Monetary Policy Committee will be binding on the Reserve Bank. Each member of the Monetary Policy Committee must write a single statement stating the reasons for voting in favour of or against proposed resolutions.

The RBI will also place a bi-annual inflation report in the public domain, drawing on the experience gained with the publication of the document on Macroeconomic and Monetary Developments. The Inflation Report will essentially review the analysis presented to the MPC to inform its deliberations.

The MPC will be accountable for failure to establish and achieve the nominal anchor. Failure is defined as the inability to achieve the inflation target of 4 per cent (+/- 2 per cent) for three successive quarters. Such failure will require the MPC to issue a public statement, signed by each member, stating the reason(s) for failure, remedial actions proposed and the likely period of time over which inflation will return to the centre of the inflation target zone.[4]

GO ONLINE

Access the results of the Reserve Bank's periodic surveys that provide input to formulation of monetary policy made available through press releases at **https://www.rbi.org.in/Scripts/Publications.aspx?publication=Quarterly**. These are the Inflation Expectation Survey of households (IESH), Consumer Confidence survey (CCS), Industrial Outlook survey (IOS), Order book, Inventory and Capacity utilisation survey (OBICUS) and Survey of Professional Forecasters (SPF).

---

[3]*Source*: http://finmin.nic.in/press_room/2016/MPC_Press_notification27062016.pdf, as accessed on 20 March 2017 at 11.30am

[4]*Source*: https://www.rbi.org.in/Scripts/PublicationReportDetails.aspx?UrlPage=&ID=743; https://www.rbi.org.in/scripts/PublicationReportDetails.aspx?UrlPage=&ID=750, as accessed on 20 March 2017 at 11.30am

The Debate Over the MPC and Monetary Policy Decision Making in India

The Monetary Policy Committee, its scope and its constitution was the subject of much debate following the revised draft of the Indian Financial Code 2015. The debate pertained to the manner in which interest rates would be determined in the future and also on who should have the ultimate authority on the monetary policy stance. In the Indian context, a perceived tussle between the government and the RBI over interest rates formed the core of the debate, with the finance ministry often seen to pitch for lower rates to boost growth, while the central bank opted for a more careful policy keeping in mind a number of factors such as inflation. In response to the press reports and the debate on the Monetary Policy Committee, Dr. Raghuram Rajan, Governor RBI made the following observations on August 4, 2015:

"There has been a lot of commentary about the composition of the Monetary Policy Committee. Let me say at the outset that the Reserve Bank believes institutionalising the process of monetary policy formulation is vital, given that the Government has given the Reserve Bank a clear inflation objective.

We have already done a lot internally in the past to institutionalize the process, including having scheduled meetings with different constituencies before the policy decision, having serious discussions with internal staff based on incoming economic data and our models, and speaking with the Government to obtain its viewpoint. The final policy is usually a consensus arrived at by the Governor, the Deputy Governor in charge of monetary policy, and the Executive Director in charge of Monetary Policy, but ultimately the responsibility is that of the Governor's

Going forward, there are at least three virtues of taking the decision away from the Governor and giving it to a committee.

i. A committee can represent different viewpoints, and studies show that its decisions are typically better than an individual's.
ii. Spreading the responsibility for the decision can reduce the internal and external pressure that falls on an individual.
iii. A committee will ensure broad monetary policy continuity when any single member, including the Governor, changes.

We have been enthusiastic supporters of the idea of a committee. Since the Finance Minister's budget announcement that such a Monetary Policy Committee would be formed, we have been engaged in dialogue with the Government. From the Reserve Bank's side, we wanted that the structure should ensure continuity in policy as the market attempts to understand the voting patterns of different new MPC members.

I can reiterate the Finance Secretary's comment yesterday that the Government and the Reserve Bank have reached a broad consensus on what such a committee should look like and what the powers of the Governor might be. While the details have to be ironed out, there are no differences between the Government and the Reserve Bank in this matter".

Source: Transcript of Governor's Remarks at the Press Conference held after the Announcement of Third Bi-monthly Monetary Policy Statement, 2015-16, https://rbidocs.rbi.org.in/rdocs/Content/PDFs/POL533F4CE4E47C43E683EC81DCC30809EF.PDF; https://www.rbi.org.in/scripts/bs_viewcontent.aspx?Id=3045 as accessed on 20 March 2017 at 11.30am.

How Independent Is the RBI?

GO ONLINE
Access **https://rbidocs.rbi.org.in/rdocs/Speeches/PDFs/23663.pdf** to get an idea of the changing contours of central bank autonomy in India.

The RBI, like any other central bank performs the central banking functions of creation of money, or more broadly, monetary management, management of the government's public debt, regulation and supervision of banking entities, financing of developmental activities, and other associated functions.

For a central bank's independence, it is important to see how far it can exercise power to modulate the creation of money and the price of money, which impacts the value of money, both domestic and external. In particular, such independence boils

Research Documents of the RBI

The RBI comes out with its publications at timely intervals: annual, half-yearly, quarterly, monthly, fortnightly and weekly, which have an important role in the monetary policy process. While some of these publications are statutory in nature, there are some others, which aim at data dissemination. Among the statutory reports are the RBI's *Annual report* released every year in August. It is a report of the Central Board of Directors of the Reserve Bank to the Central Government of India and includes an assessment and prospects of the Indian economy, a review of the state of the economy, the working of the Reserve Bank during the year, the Reserve Bank's vision and agenda for the following year and the annual accounts of the Reserve Bank (July—June). The *Report on Trend and Progress of Banking in India* is another statutory publication produced by the central bank and presented annually. This document is a review of the policies for and performance of the financial sector for the preceding year. From December 2014, this publication is a part of the Financial Stability Report. The *Report on Currency and Finance* is presented by the staff of the central bank. Since 1998–99 the Report has focussed on a particular theme and presents a detailed economic analysis of the issues related to the theme.

Data oriented annual publications, which seek to improve data dissemination at various levels and for various entities include the following:

- **The Handbook of Statistics on the Indian Economy** It is a useful storehouse of statistical information which provides time-series data (annual/quarterly/monthly/fortnightly/daily) pertaining to a broad spectrum of economic variables, including data on national income, output, prices, money, banking, financial markets, public finance, trade and balance of payments.
- **State Finances: A Study of Budgets** This publication is a major source of disaggregated state-wise fiscal

data and provides an analytical discussion on the fiscal position of state governments.

- **Statistical Tables relating to Banks in India** This annual publication contains comprehensive time series data relating to the Scheduled Commercial Banks (SCBs) (excluding Regional Rural Banks). It covers balance sheet information as well as performance indicators of each SCB in India. The publication also includes disaggregated data on some important parameters bank-wise, bank group-wise and state-wise.
- **Basic Statistical Returns** The publication presents comprehensive data on number of offices, employees, deposits and credit of Scheduled Commercial Banks at a granular level.

The half-yearly publications include

- **The Monetary Policy Report** has all data/inputs that go into the formulation of monetary policy—the internal macroeconomic assessment and results of surveys—as also projections of growth and inflation over a short to medium term.
- **Financial Stability Report** focuses on reviewing the nature, magnitude, and implications of risks that have bearing on the macroeconomic environment, financial institutions, markets, and infrastructure. These reports also assess the resilience of the financial sector through stress tests.

Other publications include the Quarterly Statistics on Deposits and Credit of Scheduled Commercial Banks (Quarterly), RBI Bulletin, Monetary and Credit Information Review (Monthly), the Weekly Statistical Supplement to the RBI Bulletin (Weekly) and occasional research papers.

All these publications can either be purchased across the counter or subscribed. They are also available on the Reserve Bank's website (URL: http://www.rbi.org.in).

GO ONLINE

Access the database on the Indian economy at **http://dbie.rbi.org.in,** which hosts the public website called Database on the Indian Economy (DBIE). This is the most popular data communication channel for the Reserve Bank

down to the degrees of freedom the central bank has in deciding whether or not to fund the Government's expenditure out of created money.

The notion of central bank independence in terms of its power to decide on credit to the government is generally believed to have emerged only in the 20th century. However, even as early as 1806, Napoleon Bonaparte is reported to have commented on the Bank of France; "I want the bank to be in the hands of the Government, but not too much".

How RBI Governors Differ in Their Monetary Policy Stance

Every RBI Governor has a different style that affects policy decisions made by the RBI. There has been much discussion on the views of several Governors on Inflation Targeting. Inflation targeting, by its very nature, is an issue in central bank governance. The defining features of an inflation targeting central bank are a precise mandate, a single instrument (the policy interest rate) in its armoury, a single-minded devotion to achieving this target and a principal-agent relationship with the Government.

The Government of India and the RBI signed an agreement dated February 20, 2015 for following inflation targeting in India, called Flexible Inflation targeting (FIT). According to this agreement, the RBI would aim to bring inflation below 6 per cent by January 2016. The target for financial year 2016–17 and all subsequent years would be four (4) per cent with a band of +/– 2 per cent. A failure to meet the target would arise if the inflation was more than six (6) per cent for three consecutive quarters for the financial year 2015–16 and all subsequent years and less than two per cent for three consecutive quarters in 2016–17 and all subsequent years. If the Reserve Bank failed to meet the target, it shall set out in a report to the Central Government the reasons for its failure, remedial actions and estimated time period within which the target should be achieved pursuant to timely implementation of proposed remedial actions.

While FIT was recommended by the Expert Committee to Revise and Strengthen the Monetary Policy Framework 2014 (Chairman: Urjit Patel), and agreed upon by both the Government of India and the RBI under the Governorship of Dr. Raghuram Rajan, previous Governors held varying views on inflationary targeting.

Former central bank Governor Dr. Bimal Jalan (1997–2003), who was governor during the East Asian crisis in 1997–98, felt that inflation targeting should not be the sole objective of the central bank, especially in a developing country like India where the consumer price index has a strong weightage for food articles.

Another former Governor, Y.V. Reddy (2003–08), also expressed his discomfort at an inflation targeting central bank. "What is the purpose of inflation-targeting? Is it to say that the government is not responsible and the RBI is responsible?," he said at a conference organised by the Centre for Advanced Financial Research and Learning (CAFRAL) in January 2014.

Dr. Reddy further felt that monetary policy by itself had limited effectiveness in influencing inflation and that ideally it has to be joint responsibility (of the government and the RBI) and should be treated as a joint responsibility. He felt that there was a lot of pressure due to inflation targeting and RBI instead could have a self-imposed inflation target which could be reasonably flexible given the circumstances to peg the inflation.

Governor Dr. Duvvuri Subbarao, 22nd Governor of RBI (2008–13), was not in favour of FIT. According to him, inflation targeting in India was neither feasible nor advisable. He gave several reasons to justify his position. Firstly, in an emerging economy like India, it was not practical for the central bank to focus exclusively on inflation, oblivious to the larger development context. The Reserve Bank had to weigh the growth-inflation trade off in determining its monetary policy stance. Second, with the drivers of inflation in India often emanating from the supply side, especially on account of the relatively larger weight of food items in the consumption basket in India, these normally go beyond the pale of monetary policy. Thirdly, India lacked the necessary condition for successful inflation targeting, i.e., an efficient monetary transmission mechanism. Finally, the political economy argument of a divergence between the role of the government—promoting growth and employment versus that of a central bank, viz. lowering inflation, did not apply to the Indian case, because societal tolerance in India for inflation was low. Given the compulsions of democracy and the large section of the people living below the poverty line, any government in India always had to be sensitive to price stability, even if it meant sacrificing output in the short-term. Indeed, both the Government and the Reserve Bank had to factor in the short-term growth–inflation trade off in their policy calculations. (Source: **https://www.rbi.org.in/scripts/BS_SpeechesView.aspx?Id=563, as accessed on 20 March 2017 at 11.30am.**)

However, another former governor, Dr. C. Rangarajan (1992–97) disagreed with the views of these former governors. According to Rangarajan, the dominant objective of monetary policy was to control inflation and that was different from being an inflation targetter.

Based on: http://articles.economictimes.indiatimes.com/2014-01-15/news/46224711_1_inflation-targeting-yv-reddy-subbarao, as accessed on 20 March 2017 at 11.30am.

to disseminate large volume of macro-economic and financial sector data to researchers, market participants and various other stakeholders. Time series data is presented on this site subject area wise and periodicity wise. A major highlight of DBIE is time series data on aggregates in a flexible and reusable format. These tables can be downloaded and saved as excel files for further processing and analyses.

Central bank independence generally relates to three areas: personnel matters, financial aspects, and conduct of policy. Personnel independence refers to the extent to which the appointments, term of office, and dismissals of top central bank officials is restricted within itself, without any government intervention. It also includes the extent and nature of representation of the government in the governing body of the central bank. Financial independence relates to the extent to which the central bank's monetary policy is subordinated to the government's fiscal policy. It refers to the freedom of the central bank to decide the extent to which government expenditure is either directly or indirectly financed via central bank credits. Direct or automatic access of the executive branch in matters of central bank credits would imply lack of independence. Finally, policy independence is related to the flexibility given to the central bank in the formulation and execution of monetary policy.

Recent literature has stressed the difference between goal independence and instrument independence. Goal independence refers to the freedom to choose the policy priorities of stabilising output or prices at any given point of time, thus setting the goal of monetary policy. Instrument independence refers to the freedom to to choose the means to achieve the objective set by the government. In a survey of central banks (Fry. M, et al 1999)[5], 40 of the total 56 central banks across a broad range of economies defined independence predominantly in terms of instrument independence. Of the remaining 16 responses, many highlighted factors that had implications for the relationship between the Government and the central bank.

Current Status in India

GO ONLINE

Access **https://www.rbi.org. in/Scripts/BS_Speeches- View.aspx?Id=833** to read Governor Duvvuri Subbarao's speech his last public speech as the Governor of RBI to understand the difficult role played by the governor in the aftermath of the global financial crisis. Also read **http://www.businesstoday. in/management/leadership/ outgoing-rbi-governor- duvvuri-subbarao-profile- achievements/story/198306. html** to understand the management style of an RBI governor, who was considered controversial.

There has been an animated debate on the autonomy of RBI in recent times. In theory, the debate is essentially focused on the fiscal dominance of monetary policy. It is held that the pressure on the central bank (and its monetary policy) from the government is a natural outcome of a budget deficit bias in a democracy. The expansionary fiscal policy of the government is more often than not financed by easy money policy of the central bank. And the Indian experience is no exception. Under law, RBI does not have autonomy. The RBI Act says the government may give it directions after consulting the governor. In reality, the RBI functioned as an autonomous body and there had been no instance of the government exercising this power.

The much-prized autonomy of central banks has come under assault post the 2008 financial crisis with an influential view gaining ground that one of the principal causes of the crisis was the unbridled autonomy of central banks. The standard argument for central bank autonomy is that autonomy enhances the credibility of the central bank's inflation management credentials. Monetary policy typically acts with a lag, and price stability therefore has to be viewed in a medium-term perspective. Having autonomy, frees the central bank from the pressure of responding to short-term developments, deviating from its inflation target, and thereby, compromising its medium term inflation goals.

[5]Fry, M., D. Julius, L. Mahadeva, S. Roger and G. Sterne (1999), 'Monetary Policy Frameworks in a Global Context', Central Bank Governors' Symposium at the Bank of England, June.

It is important to note that new governance structures have emerged after the global crisis for overseeing systemic stability. These include the Financial Services Oversight Council (FSOC) in the US, the Financial Policy Committee (FPC) in the UK and the European Systemic Risk Board (ESRB) in the EU and the Financial Stability and Development Council (FSDC) in India. The precise institutional arrangements vary, but across all of them, central banks have a lead responsibility.

In the context of emergence of such new governance structures, it is instructive as well as interesting to quote former governor Dr. Subbarao: "With these new institutional arrangements for financial stability in place, the autonomy question has acquired an additional dimension. Note that central bank autonomy has worked because they could keep at arms length from the governments. But once a coordination mechanism is in place, these barriers may melt away. Also, even if that is what the book says, it may be difficult to straitjacket the discussion at the coordination forum to financial stability. As we have seen, there are no 'pure' financial stability issues; they are all inter-connected. A discussion on financial stability could very well lead to a discussion on monetary policy. What then of the autonomy of the central bank? This apprehension, as all of you will appreciate, is non-trivial".

Further, "......If we now add responsibility for sovereign debt sustainability to this already complex situation, the reason for apprehension about the threat to the autonomy of central banks becomes more obvious. Sovereign debt is a quintessentially political subject, and as we noted earlier, the very foundation of central bank autonomy is justified on the need to free monetary policy from fiscal dominance. By requiring central banks to be mindful of sovereign debt sustainability concerns as part of the 'new trilemma', is the hard won gain of freedom from fiscal compulsions being compromised? But look at it also from the opposite perspective. Given that investor trust in public debt is part of the foundation of a nation-state, is it realistic for a central bank to remain indifferent to sovereign debt sustainability?"

According to Dr. Subbarao, the tenets for central bank autonomy are the following:

1. The fundamental responsibility of central banks for price stability should not be compromised.
2. Central banks should have a lead, but not exclusive, responsibility, for financial stability.
3. The boundaries of central bank responsibility for sovereign debt sustainability should be clearly defined.
4. In the matter of ensuring financial stability, the government must normally leave the responsibility to the regulators, assuming an activist role only in times of crisis.

However, Dr. Subbarao admitted that central bank autonomy was difficult. At a panel discussion with other former central governors, organised by the Centre for Advanced Financial Research and Learning, promoted by the RBI, he admitted, "I want to say from my experience asserting monetary policy authority has been a challenge for RBI, it has been difficult. Asserting your authority and view, when there is difference of view, has been difficult."

In fact, Subbarao said that asserting monetary policy autonomy had been tough not only for the RBI but also for other central banks. "It's not just in India,

GO ONLINE

Access **http://www.cafral. org.in/sfControl/content/ DocumentFile/Autonomy_ of_the_central_bank.pdf** to read the transcripts of the interviews and views on central bank autonomy given by former governors Dr. Bimal Jalan, Dr. Y V Reddy and Dr. D Subbarao, Reserve Bank of India.

I have learnt from other governors that they face similar pressures," Subbarao said.[6]

Should the RBI Be Independent?

As we have seen, the Reserve Bank of India is probably the most independent government agency in India; this is also true for central banks in most other countries. Every few years, the question arises in Government whether the independence given to the RBI should be curtailed. Politicians who strongly oppose a particular RBI monetary policy often want to bring it under their supervision, to impose a policy more to their liking. Should the RBI be independent, or would we be better off with a central bank under the control of the Prime Minister or Government?

The Case for Independence

The strongest argument for an independent central bank rests on the view that subjecting it to more political pressures would impart an inflationary bias to monetary policy. In the view of many observers, politicians in a democratic society are short-sighted because they are driven by the need to win their next election. With this as the primary goal, they are unlikely to focus on long-run objectives, such as promoting a stable price level. Instead, they will seek short-run solutions to problems, such as high unemployment and high interest rates, even if the short run solutions have undesirable long-run consequences. For example, high money growth might lead initially to a drop in interest rates but might cause an increase later as inflation heats up. Would a Reserve Bank of India under the control of Government or the Prime Minister be more likely to pursue a policy of excessive money growth when interest rates are high, even though it would eventually lead to inflation and even higher interest rates in the future? The advocates of an independent Reserve Bank of India say yes. They believe that a politically insulated RBI is more likely to be concerned with long-run objectives and thus be a defender of a sound rupee and a stable price level.

A variation on the preceding argument is that the political process in India could lead to a **political business cycle,** in which just before an election, expansionary policies are pursued to lower unemployment and interest rates. After the election, the bad effects of these policies—high inflation and high interest rates—come home to roost, requiring contractionary policies that politicians hope the public will forget before the next election. There is some evidence that such a political business cycle exists in India, and a Reserve Bank of India under the control of Government or the Prime Minister might make the cycle even more pronounced.

Putting the RBI under the control of the Government (making it more subject to influence by the Prime Minister) is also considered dangerous because the RBI can be used to facilitate Government financing of large budget deficits by its purchases of Government bonds.[7] Government pressure on the RBI to "help out" might

---

[6]*Source*: http://www.moneycontrol.com/news/economy/inflationrbi-jalan-subbarao-reddy-defend-steps_1024396.html; http://www.freepressjournal.in/subbarao-says-asserting-rbis-autonomy-a-challenge/.

[7]The Fiscal Responsibility and Budget Management (FRBM) Act, 2003 prohibits RBI buying government securities (dated securities and treasury bills) in the primary market. RBI, however, buys these securities through open market operation, both outright and repo. One possible reason for this prohibition is consistent with the foregoing argument. RBI would find it harder to facilitate bond financing of larger budget deficits.

**GO
ONLINE**
Access RBI's communica-
tion with certain target
audiencesits objectives and
instruments at **https://rbi.org.
in/ Scripts/bs_viewcontent.
aspx?Id=1647.**

**GO
ONLINE**
Access **https://rbi.org.in/
Scripts/bs_viewcontent.
aspx?Id=1649** to get a detailed calendar of the information released by the RBI.

lead to more inflation in the economy. An independent RBI is better able to resist this pressure from the Government.

Another argument for central bank independence is that control of monetary policy is too important to leave to politicians, a group that has repeatedly demonstrated a lack of expertise at making hard decisions on issues of great economic importance, such as reducing the budget deficit or reforming the banking system. Another way to state this argument is in terms of the principal–agent problem discussed in Chapter 7. Both the Reserve Bank of India and politicians are agents of the public (the principals) and, as we have seen, both politicians and the RBI have incentives to act in their own interest rather than in the interest of the public. The argument supporting Reserve Bank of India independence is that the principal–agent problem is worse for politicians than for the RBI because politicians have fewer incentives to act in the public interest.

Indeed, some politicians may prefer to have an independent RBI, which can be used as a public "whipping boy" to take some of the heat off their backs. It is possible that a politician who in private opposes an inflationary monetary policy will be forced to support such a policy in public for fear of not being reelected. An independent RBI can pursue policies that are politically unpopular yet in the public interest.

The Case Against Independence

Proponents of a RBI under the control of the Prime Minister or Government argue that it is undemocratic to have monetary policy (which affects almost everyone in the economy) controlled by an elite group responsible to no one. The current lack of accountability of the Reserve Bank of India has serious consequences: If the RBI performs badly, no provision is in place for replacing members (as there is with politicians). True, the RBI needs to pursue long-run objectives, but elected officials of Government vote on long-run issues also (foreign policy, for example). If we push the argument further that policy is always performed better by elite groups like the RBI, we end up with such conclusions as the Joint Chiefs of Staff should determine military budgets or a Tax Council akin to the US Internal Revenue Service (IRS) should set tax policies with no oversight from the Prime Minister or Government. Would you advocate this degree of independence for the Joint Chiefs or the IRS?

The public holds the Prime Minister and Government responsible for the economic well-being of the country, yet they lack control over the central bank that may well be the most important factor in determining the health of the economy. In addition, to achieve a cohesive program that will promote economic stability, monetary policy must be coordinated with fiscal policy (management of government spending and taxation). Only by placing monetary policy under the control of the politicians who also control fiscal policy can these two policies be prevented from working at cross-purposes.

No consensus has yet been reached on whether central bank independence is a good thing, although public support for independence of the central bank seems to have been growing in both India and abroad. As you might expect, people who like the RBI's policies are more likely to support its independence, while those who dislike its policies advocate a less independent RBI.

INSIDE THE RBI

The RBI's Communication Policy

The long-term goals of the Reserve Bank's communication policy are intimately interlinked to its objectives. Faced with multiple tasks and a complex mandate, clear and structured communication is critical for effective functioning as well as enlarging the spheres of traditional policy instruments. The goal of communication policy thus would be to anchor inflation expectation by promoting credibility and understanding of monetary policy; and enabling private stakeholders to map the changing economic circumstances into anticipation of the broad policy direction with reasonable accuracy. In order to be realistic, the communication policy also highlights impediments to achieving stated objectives in a conditional sense. The role of communication policy, therefore, lies in articulating the hierarchy of objectives in a given context in a transparent manner, emphasising a consultative approach as well as autonomy in policy operations and harmony with other elements of macroeconomic policies. The principal goals of the Reserve Bank's communication strategy are:

- Transparency for strengthening accountability and credibility
- Clarity on the Reserve Bank's role and responsibilities with regard to its multiple objectives; managing inherent complementarities/ contradictions and transition
- Managing expectations and promoting two-way flow of information/ perceptions
- Dissemination of information, statistics, and research at various frequencies

The guiding principles of the Reserve Bank's communication policy in the context of its goals are transparency, comprehensiveness, relevance, and timeliness with a view to improving public understanding as a systematic process of continuous efforts. This communication policy is best described as principle-based rather than rule-based.

The overall approach to communication is driven by the principle of democratic accountability, enhancing the effectiveness of monetary policy by creating news and/or reducing noise. In this context, the Reserve Bank's communication policy recognises the complexity inherent in the Indian economy at this stage of its development. Communication, therefore, has to be carried out at different levels. Where projections on the future path of key macroeconomic variables are provided, they have to be set out in conditional forms and linked to incoming information with an assessment of the balance of risks. While policy and market preferences generally converge and communication is intended to improve the predictability of policy decisions, an element of surprise can often enhance the effectiveness of policy actions when the preferences are in opposing directions, albeit with concurrent or ex post communication of the rationale thereof.

The Reserve Bank of India communicates with various target groups ranging from other central banks, multilateral agencies and analysts to students and the general public. The Reserve Bank of India has established the practice of two-way communication. It closely monitors the media, which is first reference point for feedback. Any new regulation or a major change in the existing regulation is preceded by detailed consultations with stakeholders. The information is released through daily press releases, notifications and circulars, regular and occasional publications, reports of Committees and Working/ Study Groups and speeches of the Governor/Deputy Governors.

The Reserve Bank of India communicates with various types of audiences. In order to reach out to the common person, the Reserve Bank releases information in 11 regional languages spoken by a large section of the population, apart from in English and in Hindi.

Central Bank Independence and Macroeconomic Performance Throughout the World

We have seen that advocates of an independent central bank believe that macroeconomic performance will be improved by making the central bank more independent. Empirical evidence seems to support this conjecture: When central banks are ranked from least independent to most independent, inflation performance is found to be the best for countries with the most independent central banks. Although a more independent central bank appears to lead to a lower inflation rate, this is not achieved at the expense of poorer real economic performance. Countries with independent central banks are no more likely to have high unemployment or greater output fluctuations than countries with less independent central banks.

Structure and Independence of the Federal Reserve System (USA)

The Federal Reserve System was created in 1913 and includes the following entities: the Federal Reserve Banks, the Board of Governors of the Federal Reserve System, the Federal Open Market Committee, the Federal Advisory Council and around 2000 member commercial banks. Each of the 12 Federal Reserve Districts has one main Federal Reserve Bank. Of these, the three largest Federal Reserve banks (Chicago, San Francisco and New York) together hold more than 50 per cent of the assets of the Federal Reserve system.

A seven-member board of Governors heads the Fed and its headquarters is in Washington. Each governor is appointed by the President and approved by the senate. To ensure the autonomy of the Fed from political pressures, the governors can serve one non-renewable term for 14 years, plus part of another term, with one governor's term expiring every other January. The Chair of the Board of Governors (each of who comes from the different districts) is chosen from among the seven governors, and serves a four-year, renewable term. The Board of Governors is actively involved in decisions concerning the conduct of monetary policy.

The Federal Open Market Committee consists of the seven-member Board of Governors, the President of the Federal Reserve Bank of New York and the presidents of four other Federal Reserve Banks. The Chair of the Board of Governors presides as the Chair of the FOMC. All the presidents of the remaining seven district banks also attend the FOMC meetings, which are held about eight times a year, and participate in the discussions.

It is the FOMC which makes decisions about the conduct of open market operations and the setting of the policy interest rate, **the federal funds rate**, which is the interest rate on overnight loans from one bank to another. It is the focal point for policy making in the Federal Reserve System. Indeed, the FOMC is often referred to as the "Fed" in the press.

The FOMC does not set the discount rate or the reserve requirements; however, decisions in regard to these policy tools are effectively made there. The FOMC "advises" on the setting of the reserve requirements and the discount rates.

How Independent Is the Fed?

Stanley Fischer-a professor at MIT has defined two types of independence of central banks: **instrument independence,** the ability of the central bank to set monetary policy instruments, and **goal independence,** the ability of the central bank to set the goals of monetary policy. The Federal Reserve has both types of independence and is remarkably free of the political pressures that influence other government agencies. Not only are the members of the Board of Governors appointed for a 14-year term (and so cannot be ousted from office) but also the term is technically not renewable, eliminating some of the incentive for the governors to curry favor with the president and Congress.

Probably even more important to its independence from the whims of Congress is the Fed's independent and substantial source of revenue from its holdings of securities and, to a lesser extent, from its loans to banks. In 2015, for example, the Fed had net earnings after expenses of $100.2 billion[8]—not a bad living if you can find it! Because it returns the bulk of these earnings to the Treasury, it does not get rich from its activities, but this income gives the Fed an important advantage over other government agencies: It is not subject to the appropriations process usually controlled by Congress. Indeed, the General Accounting Office, the auditing agency of the federal government, cannot currently audit the monetary policy or foreign exchange market functions of the Federal Reserve. Because the power to control the purse strings is usually synonymous with the power of overall control, this feature of the Federal Reserve System contributes to its independence more than any other factor.

Yet the Federal Reserve is still subject to the influence of Congress because the legislation that structures it is written by Congress and is subject to change at any time. When legislators are upset with the Fed's conduct of monetary policy, they frequently threaten to weaken its independence. Threats like this are a powerful club to wield, and it certainly has some effect in keeping the Fed from straying too far from congressional wishes.

Congress has also passed legislation to make the Federal Reserve more accountable for its actions. Under the Humphrey-Hawkins Act of 1978 and later legislation, the Federal Reserve is required to issue a *Monetary Policy Report to the Congress* semiannually, with accompanying testimony by the Chair of the Board of Governors, to explain how the conduct of monetary policy is consistent with the objectives given by the Federal Reserve Act.

The president can also influence the Federal Reserve. First, because congressional legislation can affect the Fed directly or affect its ability to conduct monetary policy, the president can be a powerful ally through his influence on Congress. Second, although ostensibly a president might be able to appoint only one or two members to the Board of Governors during each presidential term, in actual practice the president appoints members far more often. One reason is that most governors do not serve out a full 14-year term. (Governors' salaries are substantially below what they can earn in the private sector or even at universities, thus providing an incentive for them to return to academia or take private sector jobs before their term expires.) In addition, the president is able to appoint a new Chair of the Board of Governors every four years, and a chair who is not reappointed is expected to resign from the board so that a new member can be appointed.

The power that the president enjoys through his appointments to the Board of Governors is limited, however. Because the term of the chair is not necessarily concurrent with that of the president, a president may have to deal with a chair of the Board of Governors appointed by a previous administration. Alan Greenspan, for example, was appointed chair in 1987 by President Ronald Reagan and was reappointed to another term by a Republican president, George H. W. Bush, in 1992.

---

[8]https://www.federalreserve.gov/newsevents/press/other/20160111a.htm.

When Bill Clinton, a Democrat, became president in 1993, Greenspan had several years left to his term. Clinton was put under tremendous pressure to reappoint Greenspan when his term expired and did so in 1996 and again in 2000, even though Greenspan is a Republican.[9] George W. Bush, a Republican, then reappointed Greenspan in 2004.

You can see that the Federal Reserve has extraordinary independence for a government agency. Nonetheless, the Fed is not free from political pressures. Indeed, to understand the Fed's behavior, we must recognize that public support for the actions of the Federal Reserve plays a very important role.[10]

Structure and Independence of the European Central Bank

GO ONLINE
Access **www.ecb.int** for details of the European Central Bank.

Until recently, the Federal Reserve had no rivals in terms of its importance in the central banking world. However, this situation changed in January 1999 with the start-up of the European Central Bank (ECB) and European System of Central Banks (ESCB), which now conducts monetary policy for countries that are members of the European Monetary Union. These countries, taken together, have a population that exceeds that in the United States and a GDP comparable to that of the United States. The Maastricht Treaty, which established the ECB and ESCB, patterned these institutions after the Federal Reserve in that central banks for each country (referred to as *National Central Banks*, or *NCBs*) have a similar role to that of the Federal Reserve banks. The European Central Bank, which is housed in Frankfurt, Germany, has an Executive Board that is similar in structure to the Board of Governors of the Federal Reserve; it is made up of the president, the vice president, and four other members, who are appointed to eight-year, nonrenewable terms. The Governing Council, which comprises the Executive Board and the presidents of the National Central Banks, is similar to the FOMC and makes the decisions on monetary policy. While the presidents of the National Central Banks are appointed by their countries' governments, the members of the Executive Board are appointed by a committee consisting of the heads of state of all the countries that are part of the European Monetary Union.

Differences Between the European System of Central Banks and the Federal Reserve System

In the popular press, the European System of Central Banks is usually referred to as the European Central Bank (ECB), even though it would be more accurate to refer to it as the *Eurosystem*, just as it would be more accurate to refer to the Federal Reserve System rather than the Fed. Although the structure of the Eurosystem is similar to that of the Federal Reserve System, some important differences distinguish

---

[9]Similarly, William McChesney Martin, Jr., the chair from 1951 to 1970, was appointed by President Truman (Dem.) but was reappointed by Presidents Eisenhower (Rep.), Kennedy (Dem.), Johnson (Dem.), and Nixon (Rep.). Also Paul Volcker, the chair from 1979 to 1987, was appointed by President Carter (Dem.) but was reappointed by President Reagan (Rep.). Ben Bernanke was appointed by President Bush (Rep.) but was reappointed by President Obama (Dem.).

[10]An inside view of how the Fed interacts with the public and the politicians can be found in Bob Woodward, *Maestro: Greenspan's Fed and the American Boom* (New York: Simon and Schuster, 2000) and David Wessel, *In Fed We Trust* (New York: Random House, 2009).

the two. First, the budgets of the Federal Reserve Banks are controlled by the Board of Governors, whereas the National Central Banks control their own budgets *and* the budget of the ECB in Frankfurt. The ECB in the Eurosystem therefore has less power than does the Board of Governors in the Federal Reserve System. Second, the monetary operations of the Eurosystem are conducted by the National Central Banks in each country, so monetary operations are not centralized as they are in the Federal Reserve System. Third, in contrast to the Federal Reserve, the ECB is not involved in supervision and regulation of financial institutions; these tasks are left to the individual countries in the European Monetary Union.

Governing Council

Just as there is a focus on meetings of the FOMC in the United States, there is a similar focus in Europe on meetings of the Governing Council, which meets monthly at the ECB in Frankfurt to make decisions on monetary policy. Currently, 17 countries are members of the European Monetary Union, and the head of each of the 17 National Central Banks has one vote in the Governing Council; each of the six Executive Board members also has one vote. In contrast to FOMC meetings, which staff from both the Board of Governors and individual Federal Reserve banks attend, only the 23 members of the Governing Council attend the meetings, with no staff present.

The Governing Council has decided that although its members have the legal right to vote, no formal vote will actually be taken; instead, the Council operates by consensus. One reason the Governing Council has decided not to take votes is because of worries that the casting of individual votes might lead the heads of National Central Banks to support a monetary policy that would be appropriate for their individual countries but not necessarily for the countries in the European Monetary Union as a whole. This problem is less severe for the Federal Reserve: Although Federal Reserve bank presidents do live in different regions of the country, all have the same nationality and are more likely to take a national view in monetary policy decisions rather than a regional view.

Just as the Federal Reserve releases the FOMC's decision on the setting of the policy interest rate (the federal funds rate) immediately after the meeting is over, the ECB does the same after the Governing Council meeting concludes (announcing the target for a similar short-term interest rate for interbank loans). Immediately after the decision is announced, the ECB also has a press conference in which the president and vice president of the ECB take questions from the news media. The large number of members in the Governing Council presents a particular dilemma. The current size of the Governing Council (23 voting members) is substantially larger than the FOMC (12 voting members). Many commentators have wondered whether the Governing Council is already too unwieldy—a situation that would get considerably worse as more countries join the European Monetary Union. To deal with this potential problem, the Governing Council has decided on a complex system of rotation, somewhat like that for the FOMC, in which National Central Banks from the larger countries will vote more often than National Central Banks from the smaller countries.

How Independent Is the ECB?

Although the Federal Reserve is a highly independent central bank, the Maastricht Treaty, which established the Eurosystem, has made the latter the most independent central bank in the world. Like the Board of Governors, the members of the Executive Board have long terms (eight years), while heads of National Central

Banks are required to have terms at least five years long. Like the Fed, the Eurosystem determines its own budget, and the governments of the member countries are not allowed to issue instructions to the ECB. These elements of the Maastricht Treaty make the ECB highly independent.

The Maastricht Treaty specifies that the overriding, long-term goal of the ECB is price stability, which means that the goal for the Eurosystem is more clearly specified than it is for the Federal Reserve System. However, the Maastricht Treaty did not specify exactly what "price stability" means. The Eurosystem has defined the quantitative goal for monetary policy to be an inflation rate slightly less than 2%. In one way, the ECB is substantially more goal-independent than the Federal Reserve System: The Eurosystem's charter cannot be changed by legislation; it can be changed only by revision of the Maastricht Treaty—a difficult process because *all* signatories to the treaty must agree to accept any proposed change.

Structure and Independence of Other Foreign Central Banks

Here we examine the structure and degree of independence of three other important foreign central banks: the Bank of Canada, the Bank of England, and the Bank of Japan.

Bank of Canada

GO ONLINE
Access **www.bank-banque-canada.ca/** and find details on the Bank of Canada.

Canada was late in establishing a central bank: The Bank of Canada was founded in 1934. Its directors are appointed by the government to three-year terms, and they appoint the governor, who has a seven-year term. A governing council, consisting of the four deputy governors and the governor, is the policy-making body comparable to the FOMC that makes decisions about monetary policy.

The Bank Act was amended in 1967 to give the ultimate responsibility for monetary policy to the government. So on paper, the Bank of Canada is not as instrument-independent as the Federal Reserve. In practice, however, the Bank of Canada does essentially control monetary policy. In the event of a disagreement between the bank and the government, the minister of finance can issue a directive that the bank must follow. However, because the directive must be in writing and specific and applicable for a specified period, it is unlikely that such a directive would be issued, and none has been to date. The goal for monetary policy, a target for inflation, is set jointly by the Bank of Canada and the government, so the Bank of Canada has less goal independence than the Fed.

Bank of England

GO ONLINE
Access **www.bankofengland.co.uk** for details on the Bank of England.

Founded in 1694, the Bank of England is the second oldest central bank (with the Riksban of Sweden, the oldest). The Bank Act of 1946 gave the government statutory authority over the Bank of England. The Court (equivalent to a board of directors) of the Bank of England is made up of the governor and two deputy governors, who are appointed for five-year terms, and 16 nonexecutive directors, who are appointed for three-year terms.

Until 1997, the Bank of England was the least independent of the central banks examined in this chapter because the decision to raise or lower interest rates resided not within the Bank of England but with the Chancellor of the Exchequer (the equivalent of the U.S. Secretary of the Treasury). All of this changed when Labour government came to power in May 1997. At this time, the Chancellor of the Exchequer, Gordon Brown, made a surprise announcement that the Bank of England would henceforth have the power to set interest rates. However, the Bank was not granted total instrument independence: The government can overrule the Bank and set rates "in extreme economic circumstances" and "for a limited period." Nonetheless, as in Canada, because overruling the Bank would be so public and is supposed to occur only in highly unusual circumstances and for a limited time, it is likely to be a rare occurrence.

Because the United Kingdom is not a member of the European Monetary Union, the Bank of England makes its monetary policy decisions independently from the European Central Bank. The decision to set interest rates resides in the Monetary Policy Committee, made up of the governor, two deputy governors, two members appointed by the governor after consultation with the chancellor (normally central bank officials), plus four outside economic experts appointed by the chancellor. (Surprisingly, two of the four outside experts initially appointed to this committee were not British citizens—one was Dutch and the other American—and some later appointments have also not been British, including the current Governor, Mark Carney, who is Canadian.) The inflation target for the Bank of England is set by the Chancellor of the Exchequer, so the Bank of England is also less goal-independent than the Fed.

Bank of Japan

The Bank of Japan (Nippon Ginko) was founded in 1882 during the Meiji Restoration. Monetary policy is determined by the Policy Board, which is composed of the governor; two vice-governors; and six outside members appointed by the cabinet and approved by the parliament, all of whom serve for five-year terms.

Until recently, the Bank of Japan was not formally independent of the government, with the ultimate power residing with the Ministry of Finance. However, the Bank of Japan Law, which took effect in April 1998 and was the first major change in the powers of the Bank of Japan in 55 years, changed this situation. In addition to stipulating that the objective of monetary policy is to attain price stability, the law granted greater instrument and goal independence to the Bank of Japan. Before this, the government had two voting members on the Policy Board, one from the Ministry of Finance and the other from the Economic Planning Agency. Now the government may send two representatives from these agencies to board meetings, but they no longer have voting rights, although they do have the ability to request delays in monetary policy decisions. In addition, the Ministry of Finance lost its authority to oversee many operations of the Bank of Japan, particularly the right to dismiss senior officials. However, the Ministry of Finance continues to have control over the part of the Bank's budget that is unrelated to monetary policy, and the recent episode in which the new Abe government put pressure on the Bank of Japan to adopt a 2% inflation target against the wishes of its current Governor, who then resigned, suggests that the Bank of Japan's independence is limited.

The Trend Toward Greater Independence

As our survey of the structure and independence of the major central banks indicates, in recent years we have been seeing a remarkable trend toward increasing independence. It used to be that the Federal Reserve was substantially more independent than almost all other central banks, with the exception of those in Germany and Switzerland. Now the later established European Central Bank is far more indepen-

GO ONLINE

Access **www.boj.or.jp/en/ index.htm** for details on the Bank of Japan.

dent than the Fed, and greater independence has been granted to central banks like the Bank of England and the Bank of Japan, putting them more on a par with the Fed, as well as to central banks in such diverse countries as New Zealand, Sweden, and the euro nations. Both theory and experience suggest that more independent central banks produce better monetary policy, thus providing an impetus for this trend.

SUMMARY

1. The Reserve Bank of India was set up on the basis of the recommendations of the Royal Commission on Indian Currency and Finance (also known as the Hilton-Young Commission), and commenced its operations on April 1, 1935.

2. The statutory functioning of the RBI is under the Reserve Bank of India Act, 1934 (II of 1934), which also sets out the objectives of the Reserve Bank as: '.. *to regulate the issue of Bank notes and the keeping of reserves with a view to securing monetary stability in India and generally to operate the currency and credit system of the country to its advantage.'*

3. The RBI comprises of a central board of Directors and local boards. The central board of directors, headed by the Governor, governs the Reserve Bank's affairs. The Government of India, in keeping with the Reserve Bank of India Act, appoints the board members. The Directors are appointed/nominated for a period of four years.

4. The RBI Governor, in consultation with the Technical Advisory Committee (TAC), used to take all monetary policy decisions in India until August 2016. The objective of the TAC on Monetary Policy was to periodically advise the Reserve Bank on the stance of monetary policy in the light of macroeconomic and monetary developments. The TAC was an outcome of the Reserve Bank's growing emphasis on strengthening the process of monetary policy formulation.

5. The Expert Committee to Revise and Strengthen the Monetary Policy Framework 2014 (Chairman: Urjit Patel) proposed the setting up of a Monetary Policy Committee which would be vested with the power of monetary policy decision-making. The MPC will be accountable for failure to establish and achieve the nominal anchor for inflation.

6. The government through an amendment to the RBI Act 1934 sought to provide a statutory and institutionalized basis for a Monetary Policy Framework (MPF) and the MPC. This amendment to RBI Act was carried out through the Finance Bill, 2016 presented along with the Union Budget documents 2015–16.

The provisions of the amended RBI Act regarding constitution of the MPC came into force from June 27, 2016. At the same time, the rules governing the procedure for Selection of Members of Monetary Policy Committee and Terms and Conditions of their Appointment and factors constituting failure to meet inflation target under the MPC Framework were also notified on June 27, 2016.

7. The MPC will consist of six members, with three members (including the Governor) from the RBI and the other three members being appointed by the Central Government.

8. The meetings of the MPC will be held at least four times a year. The MPC will be responsible for monetary policy decision making in India.

9. Decision making would be done by a majority vote, with the Governor having a casting vote in case of a tie.

10. The RBI has been largely autonomous in the past. However, in the recent years, some governors, particularly Duvvuri Subbarao have publicly expressed the difficulty in asserting monetary policy authority and view, when there have been differences in view with the government.

11. The case for an independent RBI rests on the view that curtailing the RBI's independence and subjecting it to more political pressures would impart an inflationary bias to monetary policy. An independent RBI can afford to take the long view and not respond to short-run problems that will result in expansionary monetary policy and a political business cycle. The case against an independent RBI holds that it is undemocratic to have monetary policy (so important to the public) controlled by an elite that is not accountable to the public. An independent RBI also makes the coordination of monetary and fiscal policy difficult.

12. The Federal Reserve System was created in 1913. The formal structure of the Federal Reserve System consists of 12 regional Federal Reserve banks, about 2,000 member commercial banks, the Board of Governors of the Federal Reserve System, the Federal Open Market Committee (FOMC), and the Federal Advisory Council.

13. The European System of Central Banks has a similar structure to the Federal Reserve System, with each member country having a National Central Bank, and an Executive Board of the European Central Bank being located in Frankfurt, Germany. The Governing Council, which is made up of the six members of the Executive Board (which includes the president of the European Central Bank) and the presidents of the National Central Banks, makes the decisions on monetary policy. The Eurosystem, which was established under the terms of the Maastricht Treaty, is even more independent than the Federal Reserve System because its charter cannot be changed by legislation. Indeed, it is the most independent central bank in the world.

14. There has been a remarkable trend toward increasing independence of central banks throughout the world. Greater independence has been granted to central banks such as the Bank of England and the Bank of Japan in recent years, as well as to other central banks in such diverse countries as New Zealand and Sweden. Both theory and experience suggest that more independent central banks produce better monetary policy.

KEY TERMS

Reserve Bank of India, p. 188
Governor of RBI, p. 194
Technical Advisory Committee, p. 190

Monetary Policy Committee, p. 190
Policy interest rate, p. 200

Goal independence, p. 200
Instrument Independence, p. 200
Political business cycle, p. 197

QUESTIONS AND PROBLEMS

1. Why was the Central Bank set up?

2. What explains the dual structure of the RBI, with one central board and four local boards?

3. What is the role of Technical Advisory Committee in monetary policy formulation?

4. What is the role of Monetary Policy Committee?

5. What is the term of Governor of the RBI? Is the appointment of the Governor subject to political pressures?

6. How independent is the RBI governor in monetary policy decisions, specifically in terms of goal independence and instrument independence?

7. How will the constitution of the Monetary Policy Committee affect RBI's autonomy?

8. Why might eliminating the RBI's independence lead to a more pronounced political business cycle?

9. What is the case for RBI's independence?

10. "The independence of the RBI has led to its being completely unaccountable for the larger national objective of growth." Critically analyse this statement.

11. How important is open, two-way communication of a central bank like the RBI? Are there any negatives of such communication?

12. What are the various target audiences that the RBI aims to reach out to through its communication policies? What are the objectives of each of these communication attempts?

13. Compare the structure and independence of the Federal Reserve System and the RBI.

14. Compare the structure and independence of the Federal Reserve System and the European System of Central Banks.

15. Which entities in the Federal Reserve System control the discount rate? Reserve Requirements? Open Market Operations?

WEB EXERCISES

The Structure of the Reserve Bank of India

1. Go to https://www.rbi.org.in/Scripts/AboutusDisplay.aspx. Based on the preamble of the Reserve Bank of India, which is the most important function of the RBI.

2. Go to RBI publications. Open annual publications at https://www.rbi.org.in/Scripts/Publications.aspx and go to the latest Macroeconomic and monetary developments. What is the macroeconomic outlook towards India? Is the economy weakening or strengthening?

3. Go to https://www.rbi.org.in/Scripts/bs_viewcontent.aspx?Id=1648 to understand RBI's communication policy. Can you as a layman, seek information and/or clarification from the RBI?

10

Conduct of Monetary Policy: Tools, Goals, Strategy, and Tactics

> PREVIEW

Understanding the conduct of monetary policy is important because it affects not only the money supply and interest rates but also the level of economic activity and hence our well-being. To explore this subject, we look first at the Reserve Bank of India's balance sheet and how the tools of monetary policy affect the money supply and interest rates. Then we examine in more detail how the RBI uses these tools and what goals the RBI and other countries' central banks establish for monetary policy. After examining strategies for conducting monetary policy, we can evaluate central banks' conduct of monetary policy in the past, with the hope that it will give us some clues to where monetary policy may head in the future.

The Reserve Bank of India's Balance Sheet

The conduct of monetary policy by the RBI involves actions that affect its balance sheet (holdings of assets and liabilities). The RBI's balance sheet largely reflects the activities carried out in pursuance of its currency issue functions, as also its monetary policy and reserve requirement objectives. Here we discuss the following simplified balance sheet:[1]

RBI's Balance Sheet	
Assets	Liabilities
Foreign currency assets	Currency in circulation
Rupee securities	
(including T-bills)	
Loans and advances	
Discount loans	Reserves

Liabilities

The two liabilities on the balance sheet, currency in circulation and reserves, are often referred to as the *monetary liabilities* of the RBI. They are an important part of the money supply story because increases in either or both will lead to an increase in the money supply (everything else being constant). The sum of the RBI's monetary liabilities (currency in circulation and reserves) and those of the Government of India (primarily coins) is called the **reserve money**. When discussing the reserve money, we will focus only on the monetary liabilities of the RBI because those of the Government of India account for less than 1% of the reserve money on an average.

GO
ONLINE
Access **https://www
.rbi.org.in/Scripts/
AnnualReportPublications
.aspx?Id=1154** to view the
trends in currency.

**GO
ONLINE**
Also access **https://www.
rbi.org.in/Scripts/Data_
ReserveMoney.aspx** to view
the RBI's data releases on
reserve money.

1. *Currency in circulation.*   The RBI issues currency notes of various denominations (₹5, 10, 20, 50, 100, 500, 2000) except the coins which are issued by the Ministry of Finance, Government of India. Currency in circulation is the amount of currency in the hands of the public (outside of banks)—an important component of the money supply. (Currency held by banks is also a liability of the RBI but is counted as part of reserves.)

   Rupee notes are IOUs from the RBI to the bearer and are also liabilities.

   People are more willing to accept IOUs from the RBI than from you or me because Reserve Bank notes are a recognized medium of exchange; that is, they are accepted as a means of payment and so function as money.

---

[1]A detailed discussion of the RBI's balance sheet can be found in the appendix to this chapter, which you can find on this book's Web site at www.pearsonhighered.com/mishkin_eakins. Also, find a detailed discussion of the various balance sheet items of the RBI.

GO ONLINE

Access **http://dbie. rbi.org.in/DBIE/dbie. rbi?site=publications** to view RBI's Liabilities and Assets on a weekly basis. (Access RBI's database on the Indian Economy, go to Time series publication and then Weekly Statistical Supplement. This contains RBI's historical balance sheet data from 2004 to the present). Now access **https:// www.rbi.org.in/Scripts/ AnnualReportMainDisplay. aspx** for the Annual reports of the RBI and view the analysis on the RBI's Balance sheet.

Unfortunately, neither you nor I, can convince people that our own IOUs are worth anything more than the paper on which they are written.[2]

2. *Reserves.* All banks have a current account at the RBI in which they hold deposits. **Reserves** consist of deposits at the RBI plus currency that is physically held by banks (called vault cash because it is stored in bank vaults or cash-in-hand.). Reserves are assets for the banks but liabilities for the RBI because the banks can demand payment on them at any time and the RBI is obliged to pay them. As you will see, an increase in reserves leads to an increase in the level of deposits and hence in the money supply.

Total reserves can be divided into two categories: reserves that the RBI requires banks to hold (**required reserves**), and any additional reserves the banks chooses to hold (**excess reserves**). For example, the RBI might fix that for every rupee of deposits at a bank, a certain fraction (say, 4%) must be held as reserves. This fraction (4%) is called the **cash reserve ratio (CRR)**. Any amount in excess of the CRR held by banks constitutes the excess reserves.

Assets

The two assets on the RBI's balance sheet are important for two reasons. First, changes in the asset items lead to changes in reserves and consequently to changes in the money supply. Second, these assets (investments in foreign currency assets and loans and advances to the government) earn higher interest rates than the liabilities (currency in circulation, which pays no interest, and reserves).

1. *Foreign currency assests*–foreign currency assets include investments in US Treasury Bonds, Bonds/Treasury Bills of other selected governments, deposits with foreign central banks, foreign commercial banks etc.
2. *Loans and advances*–the Reserve Bank gives loans and advances to the Central & State governments in the form of ways and means advances (WMAs)[3] with a maturity of 91 days.

Movements in the RBI's Balance Sheet

Cash Reserve Ratio (CRR)

Under Section 42(1) A of the RBI Act, the RBI prescribes the CRR for Scheduled Commercial Banks in India. There is no floor or ceiling to the CRR prescribed

---

[2]The currency item on the RBI's balance sheet refers only to currency in circulation, that is, the amount in the hands of the public. One rupee notes and rupee coins that have been printed and circulated by the Government of India are not automatically the liability of the RBI.

[3]The Reserve Bank makes advances to the central and state governments to tide over temporary mismatch in the cash flows. Such advances are termed as 'ways and means advances' (WMA), which are repayable in each case not later than three months from the date of making the advances in terms of Section 17 (5) of the RBI Act. To read more on WMAs, access https://rbi.org.in/scripts/BS_PressReleaseDisplay.aspx?prid=36535; https://www.rbi.org.in/scripts/BS_PressReleaseDisplay.aspx?prid=36110.

by the RBI. Currently, effective from the fortnight beginning February 09, 2013, the CRR is prescribed at 4% of a bank's total of Demand and Time Liabilities (DTL).[4]

The CRR is an important determinant of the movements in the balance sheet, the RBI's reserve money and hence money supply. To see how the CRR works as a monetary policy tool, let us use T-accounts to examine what happens when the RBI increases the CRR by say 1%, leading to an impounding of the reserves by ₹100 million.

When the CRR goes up, banks may sell securities worth ₹100 million to fulfill the higher CRR requirement. The banking system's T-accounts after this transaction is:

Banking System			
Assets		Liabilities	
Reserves	−100 m	Deposits	−100 m

The effect on the RBI's balance sheet is that it has gained ₹100 million of securities in its assets column, whereas reserves have increased by ₹100 million, as shown in its liabilities column:

RBI			
Assets		Liabilities	
Securities	+100 m	Reserves	+100 m

The result of the RBI's increase in the Cash Reserve Ratio (CRR) is an impounding of the reserves and a lower capacity of multiple credit creation by banks. Thus, imposition of higher CRR has a contractionary impact on money supply.

The reverse happens when the CRR is lowered.

Open Market Operations

OMOs are the market operations conducted by the Reserve Bank of India by way of sale/ purchase of government securities to/ from the market with an objective to

---

[4]Demand Liabilities of a bank are liabilities which are payable on demand. These include current deposits, demand liabilities portion of savings bank deposits, margins held against letters of credit/ guarantees, balances in overdue fixed deposits, cash certificates and cumulative/recurring deposits, outstanding Telegraphic Transfers (TTs), Mail Transfers (MTs), Demand Drafts (DDs), unclaimed deposits, credit balances in the cash credit account and deposits held as security for advances which are payable on demand. Time liabilities of a bank are those which are payable otherwise than on demand. These include fixed deposits, cash certificates, cumulative and recurring deposits, time liabilities portion of savings bank deposits, staff security deposits, margin held against letters of credit, if not payable on demand, deposits held as securities for advances which are not payable on demand and gold deposits.

adjust the rupee liquidity conditions in the market on a durable basis. When the RBI feels there is excess liquidity in the market, it resorts to sale of securities, thereby sucking out the rupee liquidity. Similarly, when the liquidity conditions are tight, the RBI will buy securities from the market, thereby releasing liquidity into the market.

To see how open market operations work, let's use T-accounts to examine what happens when the RBI conducts an open market purchase in which ₹100 million of approved government securities, as notified to the system by the RBI in advance, is bought from the banks.

When the RBI purchases ₹100 million approved government securities from the banks, it pays banks cash. The banks' reserves with the RBI go up by ₹100 million. The banks' T-account after this transaction is:

Banking System		
Assets		Liabilities
Securities	−₹100 m	
Reserves	+₹100 m	

The effect on the RBI's balance sheet is that it has gained ₹100 million of securities in its assets column, whereas reserves have increased by ₹100 million, as shown in its liabilities column:

RBI			
Assets		Liabilities	
Securities	+₹100 m	Reserves	+₹100 m

As you can see, the result of the RBI's open market purchase is an expansion of reserves and deposits in the banking system. Another way of seeing this is to recognize that open market purchases of approved government securities expands reserves because the central bank pays for these securities with reserves. Because the reserve money (monetary base) equals currency plus reserves, we have shown that an open market purchase increases the reserve money by an equal amount. Also, because deposits are an important component of the money supply, another result of the open market purchase is an increase in the money supply. This leads to the following important conclusion: *an open market purchase leads to an expansion of reserves and deposits in the banking system and hence to an expansion of the reserve money and the money supply.*

Similar reasoning indicates that when a central bank conducts an open market sale, the reverse happens. Thus, *an open market sale leads to a contraction of reserves and deposits in the banking system and hence to a decline in the reserve money and the money supply.*

The monetary authority in India, the RBI is vested with the responsibility of conducting monetary policy. Monetary policy refers to the use of instruments under the control of the central bank to regulate the availability, cost and use of money and credit.

GO ONLINE

Access **https://www.rbi.org.in/scripts/chro_bankrate.aspx** to view historical data on the Bank Rate, Cash Reserve Ratio and Statutory Liquidity Ratio (upto 2002).
Further, access **http://dbie.rbi.org.in/DBIE/dbie.rbi?site=statistics** to view the major monetary policy rates and reserve requirements—Bank Rate, LAF rate, CRR and SLR from 2001–2002 till the present.

Monetary Policy Tools

GO ONLINE
Access **https://rbi.org.in/home.aspx** to view all the current rates.

Several direct and indirect instruments are used in the implementation of monetary policy in India. These include:

- **Cash Reserve Ratio (CRR)**–the share of net demand and time liabilities (deposits), that banks must maintain as cash balance with the Reserve Bank.
- **Statutory Liquidity Ratio (SLR)**–the share of net demand and time liabilities (deposits), that banks must maintain in safe and liquid assets, such as, government securities, cash and gold. Changes in SLR often influence the availability of resources in the banking system for lending to the private sector.
- **Refinance facilities**–sector-specific refinance facilities aim at achieving sector specific objectives through provision of liquidity at a cost linked to the policy repo rate. The Reserve Bank has, however, been progressively de-emphasising sector specific policies as they interfere with the transmission mechanism.
- **Liquidity Adjustment Facility (LAF)**–consists of overnight and term repo/reverse repo auctions. Progressively, the Reserve Bank has increased the proportion of liquidity injected in the LAF through term-repos.
- **Term Repos**–since October 2013, the Reserve Bank has introduced term repos (of different tenors, such as, 7/14/28/56 days), to inject liquidity over a period that is longer than overnight. The aim of term repo is to help develop inter-bank money market, which in turn can set market based benchmarks for pricing of loans and deposits, and through that improve transmission of monetary policy.
- **Marginal Standing Facility (MSF)**–a facility under which scheduled commercial banks can borrow additional amount of overnight money from the Reserve Bank by dipping into their SLR portfolio up to a limit (currently 2% of their net demand and time liabilities deposits) at a penal rate of interest (currently 50 basis points above the repo rate). This provides a safety valve against unanticipated liquidity shocks to the banking system. MSF rate and reverse repo rate determine the corridor for the daily movement in short term money market interest rates.
- **Open Market Operations (OMOs)**–these include both, outright purchase/sale of government securities (for injection/absorption of liquidity).
- **Bank Rate**–it is the rate at which the Reserve Bank is ready to buy or rediscount bills of exchange or other commercial papers. This rate has been aligned to the MSF rate and, therefore, changes automatically as and when the MSF rate changes alongside policy repo rate changes.
- **Market Stabilisation Scheme (MSS)**–this instrument for monetary management was introduced in 2004. Surplus liquidity of a more enduring nature arising from large capital inflows is absorbed through sale of short-dated government securities and treasury bills. The mobilised cash is held in a separate government account with the Reserve Bank. The instrument thus has features of both, SLR and CRR.

CASE

Monetary Policy and Administrative Measures During the Crisis: Case of India

GO ONLINE

https://www.rbi.org.in/
Scripts/PublicationsView.
aspx?id=16679
https://www.rbi.org.in/
Scripts/PublicationsView.
aspx?id=16680

Historical information for inflation can be accessed from RBI websites. Till 2012, India measured inflation using the Wholesale Price Index (WPI). The Consumer Price Index Industrial Workers (CPI-IW) may be used as a proxy for inflation as well.

Developed countries distinguish between conventional and unconventional monetary policy tools. During normal times, the central banks of these countries use conventional monetary policy tools, including open market operations, discount policies and reserve requirements. Such conventional monetary policy tools expand the money supply and lower interest rates, and are enough to stabilize the economy during normal times. However, during periods when the economy experiences a full-blown financial crisis, such conventional tools do not work. Consequently, central banks of developed countries, especially in the aftermath of the global financial crisis of 2008, have resorted to non-interest rate tools, called nonconventional monetary policy tools. These nonconventional monetary policy tools in the US have taken three forms: (1) liquidity provision (2) asset purchases and (3) commitment to future monetary policy action.

Emerging market economies, including India, faced an enhanced uncertainty in the aftermath of the global financial crisis and the Euro zone debt crisis. Capital flows to EMEs became extremely volatile with excessive capital inflows to EMEs in search of better yields, followed by sudden stops and reversals. Many major EM currencies, including the Indian rupee, witnessed significant depreciation in the aftermath of the 'announcement effect', of the likely tapering of quantitative easing (QE), by the US Federal Reserve (Fed). The rupee depreciated sharply from 55.4 per US dollar on May 22, 2013 to a historic low of 68.85 per US dollar (by 119.4%) on August 28, 2013. (See Figure 10.1)

Indian financial markets tightened from May 22, 2013, following the statement by Fed Chairman Ben Bernanke, about the possible reduction in the bond purchases undertaken as part of quantitative easing (QE). The currencies of EMEs like India, with large current account deficits (CAD) and relatively weaker macroeconomic conditions were the worst affected. With long-term bond yields in the US and other advanced economies expected to increase following the tapering, foreign investors pulled their funds out of riskier emerging markets, which received large capital inflows in search of better yields in the past. The US recovery made the EME fixed income assets less attractive *vis-a-vis* the US, especially in the absence of large quantities of cheap money to invest in the event of QE tapering.

The RBI took a number of steps to contain forex volatility. Governor Subbarao announced a number of monetary policy measures on July 15, 2013. These measures primarily affected liquidity in the banking system, making it relatively scarce, thereby reducing demand for foreign currency. The measures included:

- Recalibrating the MSF rate with immediate effect to 300 basis points above the repo rate, i.e. the MSF rate was increased to 10.25% from the earlier 8.25%.
- Limiting overall allocation of funds under LAF to 1% of Net Demand and Time Liabilities (NDTL) of the banking system reckoned at ₹75,000 crore with effect from July 17, 2013
- Announcement to conduct open market sales of government securities of ₹12,000 crore on July 18, 2013.

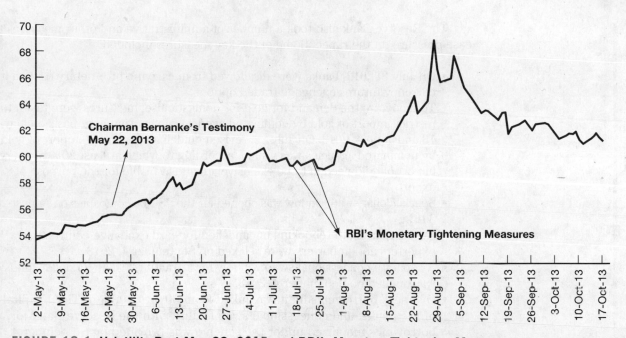

FIGURE 10.1 **Volatility-Post May 22, 2013 and RBI's Monetary Tightening Measures**

References: Prakash, A. (2012). Major Episodes of Volatility in the Indian Foreign Exchange Market in the Last Two Decades (1993–2013): Central Bank's Response. RBI Occasional Papers, Vol. 33, No. 1 & 2, pp. 162-199. https://rbidocs.rbi.org.in/rdocs/Content/PDFs/8MEVIF270614.pdf, as accessed on 24 March 2017 at 2pm.

These measures restrained volatility and stabilised the exchange rate. The RBI modified the liquidity tightening measures with effect from July 23, 2013, based on a review of these measures, and an assessment of the liquidity and on overall market conditions.

The RBI thus set the modified overall limit for access to LAF by each individual bank at 0.5% of its own NDTL outstanding as on the last Friday of the second preceding fortnight effective from July 24, 2013. Moreover, effective from the first day of the fortnight beginning from July 27, 2013, banks were required to maintain a minimum daily CRR balance of 99% of the average fortnightly requirement.

Markets recovered with the postponement of the tapering announced by the US Fed on September 18, 2013. Accordingly, with the return of stability in the forex market, in the mid-quarter review of Monetary Policy on September 19, 2013, the RBI announced a calibrated unwinding of exceptional measures in July 2013. The MSF rate was reduced by 75 bps to 9.5% and the requirement of maintenance of minimum daily CRR balance by the banks was reduced to 95% along with a 25 bps increase in repo rate to 7.5% MSF rate was reduced further by 50 bps to 9% on October 7, 2013 along with introduction of 7-day and 14-day term repo facility and liquidity injection to the tune of ₹99.74 billion through OMO purchase auction.

The monetary measures by the RBI were accompanied by net sales to the tune of USD 10.8 billion in the forex market during the period of May-August 2013 (around USD 6.0 billion in July 2013 and USD 2.5 billion in August 2013). The RBI also intervened in the forward market with RBI's outstanding net forward sales nearly doubling to USD 9.1 billion as at end-August 2013 from USD 4.7 billion in July 2013.

The Reserve Bank also took a number of administrative and other measures to ease pressure on the rupee. Some of the key measures included:

- On July 8, 2013, banks were disallowed from carrying proprietary trading in currency futures/exchange traded options.
- To moderate the demand for gold for domestic use, measures were taken to restrict import of gold by nominated agencies on consignment basis on May 13 and June 4, 2013. On July 22, revised guidelines regarding import of gold by nominated agencies was issued, according to which at least 20% of every import of gold needed to be exclusively made available for the purpose of export.
- Special dollar swap window was opened for the PSU oil companies on August 28, 2013.
- Norms relating to rebooking of cancelled forward exchange contracts for exporters and importers were relaxed on September 4, 2013.
- A separate concessional swap window for attracting FCNR(B) dollar funds was opened on September 4, 2013.
- Overseas borrowings limit was hiked from 50% to 100% of Tier I capital of the banks, and concessional swap facility with the Reserve Bank for borrowings mobilized under the scheme was provided on September 4, 2013.

The various measures taken by the RBI, both monetary as well as administrative, gave some stability to the rupee with the rupee exhibiting greater two-way movements and stabilizing around the level of 62–63 per US dollar in the second half of September 2013 and around 61–62 level during October 2013.

Consequently, when the commencement of tapering by the US Fed started from January 2014 and there were subsequent announcements about the increase in its pace, the stability of the rupee was not affected much, indicating that the markets had adjusted to QE tapering fears.

Source: https://rbi.org.in/Scripts/BS_PressReleaseDisplay.aspx?prid=29086; https://rbidocs.rbi.org.in/rdocs/Content/PDFs/8MEVIF270614.pdf, as accessed on 24 March 2017 at 2pm.

The Price Stability Goal and the Nominal Anchor

Over the past few decades, policy makers throughout the world have become increasingly aware of the social and economic costs of inflation and more concerned with maintaining a stable price level as a goal of economic policy. Indeed, **price stability,** which central bankers define as low and stable inflation, is increasingly viewed as the most important goal of monetary policy. Price stability is desirable because a rising price level (inflation) creates uncertainty in the economy, and that uncertainty might hamper economic growth. For example, when the overall level of prices is changing, the information conveyed by the prices of goods and services is harder to interpret, which complicates decision making for consumers, businesses, and government, thereby leading to a less efficient financial system.

Not only do public opinion surveys indicate that the public is hostile to inflation, but a growing body of evidence also suggests that inflation leads to lower economic growth.[5] The most extreme example of unstable prices is *hyperinflation*, such as Argentina, Brazil, and Russia have experienced in the recent past. Hyperinflation has proved to be very damaging to the workings of the economy.

Inflation also makes it difficult to plan for the future. For example, it is more difficult to decide how much to put aside to provide for a child's college education in an inflationary environment. Furthermore, inflation can strain a country's social fabric: conflict might erupt because each group in the society may compete with other groups to make sure that its income keeps up with the rising level of prices.

The Role of a Nominal Anchor

Because price stability is so crucial to the long-run health of an economy, a central element in successful monetary policy is the use of a **nominal anchor,** a nominal variable such as the inflation rate or the money supply, which ties down the price level to achieve price stability. A central bank can choose from among several nominal anchors, each of which has its pros and cons. Table 10.1 contains the various nominal anchors with their pros and cons.

TABLE 10.1   Nominal Anchors: Pros and Cons

Anchor	Advantages	Disadvantages
Monetary targeting	Some monetary aggregates can be quickly and easily controlled by the central bank. Monetary aggregates can be accurately measured (with short lags). Increases the transparency of monetary policy, thereby avoiding the time-inconsistency trap.	Depends on a well-defined and stable relationship between monetary aggregates and nominal income. With financial innovations, this stability often breaks down. Greater stress on making policy transparent (clear, simple and understandable) and on regular communication with the public may undermine credibility in the face deviations.
Nominal income targeting	It could be superior to monetary targeting, since it avoids the problem of velocity shocks and time inconsistency. Allows a country to maintain independent monetary policy.	Compels a central bank to announce a potential GDP growth number, over which it has limited control. Concept of nominal GDP is not clearly understood by the public, lowering transparency. Could engender time inconsistency if the central bank announces too low or too high a number, which subsequently is found to be different from the announced one.
Exchange rate targeting	The nominal anchor of the exchange rate fixes the inflation rate for internationally traded goods and thus, contributes directly to keeping inflation in check. If the exchange rate target is credible, it anchors inflation expectations to the inflation rate in the anchor country to whose currency it is pegged. Has the advantage of simplicity and clarity; well understood by the public.	The central bank has limited control over its monetary policy. The country becomes vulnerable to shocks emanating from the country to which its currency is pegged. Speculative attacks on the exchange rate might force the central bank to substantially raise its interest rates, with significant economic costs.

---

[5]For example, see Stanley Fischer, "The Role of Macroeconomic Factors in Growth," *Journal of Monetary Economics* 32 (1993): 485–512.

TABLE 10.1   Nominal Anchors: Pros and Cons (*continued.*)

Anchor	Advantages	Disadvantages
Inflation targeting	Preserves independence of monetary policy. Provides a nominal anchor for the path of price level. Clear and simple; hence, well-understood by the public. Transparency increases the potential for promoting low inflation expectations, which helps to produce a desirable inflation outcome.	Too much focus on inflation often at the cost of output stabilisation. Long and variable lags in monetary transmission means that a substantial amount of time must elapse before the success of monetary policy can be ascertained. Efficacy could be compromised if interest rates hit a zero lower bound. A rigid rule does not allow enough headroom (discretion) to respond flexibly to unforeseen contingencies.
Price level targeting	Lowers uncertainty about prices that would prevail in the near future. Allows economic agents to form forward-looking expectations, based on current price levels. Can prove effective when nominal interest rates hit the zero lower bound.	Poses communication challenges. Under this approach, the central bank, at a minimum, needs to specify both an intercept (level of target in the base period) and a slope (rate of increase in target price path over time), over and above a time period. No practical experience on the success or failure of its implementation across countries in modern times. The transition costs of moving to this practice (for countries already on inflation targeting) could be large and uncertain.
Just-Do-It Strategy	Constructive ambiguity in policy making often helps central bank achieve its long-term goal (price stability). Demonstrated success.	Non transparent; not clear to the public what the central bank intends to do (or, is doing). Strongly dependent on skills and preferences of individuals in charge of the central bank.

Source: https://rbidocs.rbi.org.in/rdocs/PublicationReport/Pdfs/14APPT270114.pdf.

Adherence to a nominal anchor that keeps the nominal variable within a narrow range promotes price stability by directly promoting low and stable inflation expectations. A more subtle reason for a nominal anchor's importance is that it can limit the **time-inconsistency problem,** in which monetary policy conducted on a discretionary, day-by-day basis leads to poor long-run outcomes.[6]

The Time-Inconsistency Problem

The time-inconsistency problem is something we deal with continually in everyday life. We often have a plan that we know will produce a good outcome in the long run, but when tomorrow comes, we just can't help ourselves and we renege on our plan

---

[6]The time-inconsistency problem was first outlined in papers by Nobel Prize winners Finn Kydland and Edward Prescott, "Rules Rather Than Discretion: The Inconsistency of Optimal Plans," *Journal of Political Economy* 85 (1977): 473–491; Guillermo Calvo, "On the Time Consistency of Optimal Policy in the Monetary Economy," *Econometrica* 46 (November 1978): 1411–1428; and Robert J. Barro and David Gordon, "A Positive Theory of Monetary Policy in a Natural Rate Model," *Journal of Political Economy* 91 (August 1983): 589–610.

because doing so has short-run gains. For example, we make a New Year's resolution to go on a diet, but soon thereafter we can't resist having one more bite of that rocky road ice cream—and then another bite, and then another bite—and the weight begins to pile back on. In other words, we find ourselves unable to *consistently* follow a good plan over *time*; the good plan is said to be *time-inconsistent* and will soon be abandoned.

Monetary policy makers also face the time-inconsistency problem. They are always tempted to pursue a discretionary monetary policy that is more expansionary than firms or people expect because such a policy would boost economic output (or lower unemployment) in the short run. The best policy, however, is *not* to pursue expansionary policy because decisions about wages and prices reflect workers' and firms' expectations about policy; when they see a central bank pursuing expansionary policy, workers and firms will raise their expectations about inflation, driving wages and prices up. The rise in wages and prices will lead to higher inflation but will not result in higher output on average.

A central bank will have better inflation performance in the long run if it does not try to surprise people with an unexpectedly expansionary policy but instead keeps inflation under control. However, even if a central bank recognizes that discretionary policy it will lead to a poor outcome (high inflation with no gains in output), it still may not be able to pursue the better policy of inflation control because politicians are likely to apply pressure on the central bank to try to boost output with overly expansionary monetary policy.

A clue as to how we should deal with the time-inconsistency problem comes from how-to books on parenting. Parents know that giving in to a child to keep him from acting up will produce a very spoiled child. Nevertheless, when a child throws a tantrum, many parents give him what he wants just to shut him up. Because parents don't stick to their "do not give in" plan, the child expects that he will get what he wants if he behaves badly, so he will throw tantrums over and over again. Parenting books suggest a solution to the time-inconsistency problem (although they don't call it that): Parents should set behavior rules for their children and stick to them.

A nominal anchor is like a behavior rule. Just as rules help to prevent the time-inconsistency problem in parenting by helping adults resist pursuing the discretionary policy of giving in, a nominal anchor can help prevent the time-inconsistency problem in monetary policy by providing an expected constraint on discretionary policy.

Other Goals of Monetary Policy

Although price stability is the primary goal of most central banks, five other goals are continually mentioned by central bank officials when they discuss the objectives of monetary policy: (1) high employment, (2) economic growth, (3) stability of financial markets, (4) interest-rate stability, and (5) stability in foreign exchange markets.

High Employment and Output Stability

High employment is a worthy goal for two main reasons: (1) the alternative situation—high unemployment—causes much human misery, and (2) when unemployment is high, the economy has both idle workers and idle resources (closed factories and unused equipment), resulting in a loss of output (lower GDP).

Although it is clear that high employment is desirable, how high should it be? At what point can we say that the economy is at full employment? At first, it might seem that full employment is the point at which no worker is out of a job—that is, when unemployment is zero. But this definition ignores the fact that some unemployment, called *frictional unemployment*, which involves searches by workers and firms to find suitable matchups, is beneficial to the economy. For example, a worker who decides to look for a better job might be unemployed for a while during the job search. Workers often decide to leave work temporarily to pursue other activities (raising a family, travel, returning to school), and when they decide to reenter the job market, it may take some time for them to find the right job.

Another reason that unemployment is not zero when the economy is at full employment is *structural unemployment*, a mismatch between job requirements and the skills or availability of local workers. Clearly, this kind of unemployment is undesirable. Nonetheless, it is something that monetary policy can do little about.

This goal for high employment is not an unemployment level of zero but a level above zero consistent with full employment at which the demand for labor equals the supply of labor. This level is called the **natural rate of unemployment.**

Although this definition sounds neat and authoritative, it leaves a troublesome question unanswered: what unemployment rate is consistent with full employment? In some cases, it is obvious that the unemployment rate is too high: the unemployment rate in excess of 20% during the Great Depression, for example, was clearly far too high. In the early 1960s, on the other hand, policy makers in the United States thought that a reasonable goal was 4%, a level that was probably too low because it led to accelerating inflation. Current estimates of the natural rate of unemployment in the United States place it between 4.5% and 6%, but even this estimate is subject to much uncertainty and disagreement. It is possible, for example, that appropriate government policy, such as the provision of better information about job vacancies or job training programs, might decrease the natural rate of unemployment.

The high employment goal can be thought of in another way. Because the level of unemployment is tied to the level of economic activity in the economy, a level of output is produced at the natural rate of unemployment, which naturally enough is referred to as the **natural rate of output** but is more often referred to as **potential output.**

Trying to achieve the goal of high employment thus means that central banks should try to move the level of output towards the natural rate of output. In other words, they should try to stabilize the level of output around its natural rate.

Economic Growth

The goal of steady economic growth is closely related to the high employment goal because businesses are more likely to invest in capital equipment to increase productivity and economic growth when unemployment is low. Conversely, if unemployment is high and factories are idle, it does not pay for a firm to invest in additional plants and equipment. Although the two goals are closely related, policies can be specifically aimed at promoting economic growth by directly encouraging firms to invest or by encouraging people to save, which provides more funds for firms to invest. In fact, this approach is the stated purpose of *supply-side economics* policies, which are intended to spur economic growth by providing tax incentives for businesses to invest in facilities and equipment and for taxpayers to save more. Active debate continues over what role monetary policy can play in boosting growth.

Stability of Financial Markets

Financial crisis can interfere with the ability of financial markets to channel funds to people with productive investment opportunities and lead to a sharp contraction in economic activity. The promotion of a more stable financial system in which financial crisis are avoided is thus an important goal for a central bank.

Interest-Rate Stability

Interest-rate stability is desirable because fluctuations in interest rates can create uncertainty in the economy and make it harder to plan for the future. Fluctuations in interest rates that affect consumers' willingness to buy houses, for example, make it more difficult for consumers to decide when to purchase a house and for construction firms to plan how many houses to build. A central bank may also want to reduce upward movements in interest rates for the reasons we discussed in Chapter 9. Upward movements in interest rates generate hostility toward central banks and lead to demands that their power be curtailed.

The stability of financial markets is also fostered by interest-rate stability because fluctuations in interest rates create great uncertainty for financial institutions. An increase in interest rates produces large capital losses on long-term bonds and mortgages, losses that can cause the failure of the financial institutions holding them.

Stability in Foreign Exchange Markets

With the increasing importance of international trade to the U.S. economy, the value of the rupee relative to other currencies has become a major consideration for the RBI. A fall in the value of the rupee makes Indian imports costlier and stimulates inflation in the economy. It also affects the volume of foreign exchange reserves held by the country. In addition, preventing large changes in the value of the rupee makes it easier for firms and individuals purchasing or selling goods abroad to plan ahead. Stabilizing extreme movements in the value of the rupee in foreign exchange markets is thus an important goal of monetary policy. In other countries, which are even more dependent on foreign trade, stability in foreign exchange markets takes on even greater importance.

Should Price Stability Be the Primary Goal of Monetary Policy?

In the long run, no inconsistency exists between the price stability goal and the other goals mentioned earlier. The natural rate of unemployment is not lowered by high inflation, so higher inflation cannot produce lower unemployment or more employment in the long run. In other words, there is no long-run trade-off between inflation and employment. In the long run, price stability promotes economic growth as well as financial and interest-rate stability. Although price stability is consistent with the other goals in the long run, in the short run price stability often conflicts with the goals of high employment and interest-rate stability. For example, when the economy is expanding and unemployment is falling, the economy may become overheated, leading to a rise in inflation. To pursue the price stability goal, a central bank would prevent this overheating by raising interest rates, an action that would initially lower employment and increase interest-rate instability. How should a central bank resolve this conflict among goals?

Hierarchical vs. Dual Mandates

Because price stability is crucial to the long-run health of the economy, many countries have decided that price stability should be the primary, long-run goal for central banks. For example, the Maastricht Treaty, which created the European Central Bank, states, "The primary objective of the European System of Central Banks [ESCB] shall be to maintain price stability. Without prejudice to the objective of price stability, the ESCB shall support the general economic policies in the Community," which include objectives such as "a high level of employment" and "sustainable and noninflationary growth." Mandates of this type, which put the goal of price stability first and then say that as long as it is achieved other goals can be pursued, are known as **hierarchical mandates.** They are the directives governing the behavior of central banks such as the Bank of England, the Bank of Canada, and the Reserve Bank of New Zealand, as well as for the European Central Bank.

In contrast, the legislation defining the mission of the Federal Reserve states, "The Board of Governors of the Federal Reserve System and the Federal Open Market Committee shall maintain long-run growth of the monetary and credit aggregates commensurate with the economy's long-run potential to increase production, so as to promote effectively the goals of maximum employment, stable prices, and moderate long-term interest rates." Because, as we learned in Chapter 4, long-term interest rates will be high if inflation is high, to achieve moderate long-term interest rates, inflation must be low. Thus, in practice, the Fed has a **dual mandate** to achieve two co-equal objectives: price stability and maximum employment.

CASE

Goals of Monetary Policy in India

The RBI's goals primarily includes price stability, while keeping in mind the objectives of growth. Following the recommendations of the Dr. Urjit Patel Committee Report, the Reserve Bank formally announced a "glide path" for disinflation in January 2014. This involved the objective of keeping CPI inflation below 8% by January 2015 and below 6% by January 2016. In February 2015, the agreement on the Monetary Policy Framework between the Government and the Reserve Bank of India defined the price stability objective explicitly in terms of the target for inflation as measured by the consumer price index-combined (CPI-C). The RBI set its target as (a) below 6% by January 2016, and (b) 4% [(+/−) 2%] for the financial year 2016–2017 and all subsequent years.

The RBI has viewed price stability as a necessary (if not sufficient), precondition to sustainable growth and financial stability.

As has been stated in the Report of the Expert Committee to Revise and Strengthen the Monetary Policy Framework, "Drawing from the lessons of the global financial crisis, there is a consensus gathering internationally that monetary policy should move away from its narrow focus on inflation towards a multiple target instrument approach without swerving from a commitment to price stability over the medium term. This emerging consensus, however, is reflected primarily in the form of institutionalising greater flexibility in the prevailing monetary policy frameworks rather than an explicit regime overhaul. The Committee recognizes the evolving global thinking on the subject. Yet, given the initial conditions facing India at the current juncture, bringing down inflation must be accorded primacy. Anchored inflation expectations will then provide the latitude to address other objectives without compromising on price stability".[7]

The RBI, however, has assigned differential relative emphasis to price stability and growth objectives in the conduct of its monetary policy depending on the evolving macroeconomic environment.

Financial stability is important for smooth transmission of monetary policy and, therefore, regulatory and financial market policies, including macro-prudential policies, are often announced along with monetary policy under Part B of monetary policy statements.

Price Stability as the Primary, Long-Run Goal of Monetary Policy

Because no inconsistency exists between achieving price stability in the long run and the natural rate of unemployment, these two types of mandates are not very different *if* maximum employment is defined as the natural rate of unemployment. In practice, however, a substantial difference between these two mandates could exist because the public and politicians may believe that a hierarchical mandate puts too much emphasis on inflation control and not enough on reducing business-cycle fluctuations.

Because low and stable inflation rates promote economic growth, central bankers have come to realize that price stability should be the primary, long-run goal of monetary policy. Nevertheless, because output fluctuations should also be a concern of monetary policy, the goal of price stability should be seen as primary only in the long run. Attempts are made to keep inflation at the same level in the short run no matter what would likely lead to an excessive fluctuation of output.

As long as price stability is a long-run but not short-run goal, central banks can focus on reducing output fluctuations by allowing inflation to deviate from the long run goal for short periods and, therefore, can operate under a dual mandate. However, if a dual mandate leads a central bank to pursue short-run expansionary policies that increase output and employment without worrying about the long-run consequences for inflation, the time-inconsistency problem may recur. Concerns that a dual mandate might lead to overly expansionary policy is a key reason why central bankers often favor hierarchical mandates in which the pursuit of price stability takes precedence. Hierarchical mandates can also be a problem if they lead to a central bank behaving as what the Governor of the Bank of England, Mervyn King, has referred to as an "inflation nutter"—that is, a central bank that focuses solely on inflation control, even in the short run, and so undertakes policies that lead to large output fluctuations. The choice of which type of mandate is better for a central bank ultimately depends on the subtleties of how it will work in practice. Either type of mandate is acceptable as long as it operates to make price stability the primary goal in the long run, but not the short run.

---

[7]https://rbi.org.in/Scripts/PublicationReportDetails.aspx?ID=743, as accessed on 24 March 2017 at 2pm.

In the following section, we examine the most prominent monetary policy strategy that monetary policy makers use today to achieve price stability: inflation targeting. This strategy features a strong nominal anchor and has price stability as the primary, long-run goal of monetary policy.

Inflation Targeting

The recognition that price stability should be the primary long-run goal of monetary policy and the value of having a nominal anchor to achieve this goal has led to a monetary policy strategy known as inflation targeting. **Inflation targeting** involves several elements: (1) public announcement of medium-term numerical targets for inflation; (2) an institutional commitment to price stability as the primary, long-run goal of monetary policy and a commitment to achieve the inflation goal; (3) an information-inclusive approach in which many variables are used in making decisions about monetary policy; (4) an increased transparency of the monetary policy strategy through communication with the public and the markets about the plans and objectives of monetary policy makers; and (5) an increased accountability of the central bank for attaining its inflation objectives. New Zealand was the first country to formally adopt inflation targeting in 1990, followed by Canada in 1991, the United Kingdom in 1992, Sweden and Finland in 1993, and Australia and Spain in 1994. Israel, Chile, and Brazil, among others, have also adopted a form of inflation targeting.[8] In fact, starting with Chile in 1991, the number of emerging market economies adopting inflation targeting as a monetary policy framework has outstripped that of advanced economies.

Table 10.2, "Inflation Targeting: The International Experience" outlines the inflation targeting experience of various advanced and emerging economies. Table 10.3 "Inflation Targets: The International Experience" and Table 10.4 "Time Horizon for Price Stability: The International Experience" further demonstrate the contours of inflation targeting and the price stability objective. Case box "Inflation targeting: the Indian experience" spells out the contours of India's Inflation targeting experience.

Advantages of Inflation Targeting

Inflation targeting has the key advantage that it is readily understood by the public and is thus highly transparent. Also because an explicit numerical inflation target increases the accountability of the central bank, inflation targeting has the potential to reduce the likelihood that the central bank will fall into the time-inconsistency trap of trying to expand output and employment in the short run by pursuing overly expansionary monetary policy. A key advantage of inflation targeting is that it can help focus the political debate on what a central bank can do in the long run, that is, control inflation, rather than what it cannot do, permanently increase economic growth and the number of jobs through expansionary monetary policy. Thus, inflation targeting has the potential to reduce political pressures on the central bank to pursue inflationary monetary policy and thereby to reduce the likelihood of the time-inconsistency problem.

---

[8]If you are interested in a more detailed discussion of experiences with inflation targeting in these and other countries, see Ben S. Bernanke, Thomas Laubach, Frederic S. Mishkin, and Adam S. Posen, *Inflation Targeting: Lessons from the International Experience* (Princeton: Princeton University Press, 1999).

TABLE 10.2   Inflation Targeting: The International Experience

Country	Since when	Previous / why inflation targeting	Who sets the Target /goal independence	Target indicator, time frame and style	Frequency of Meeting	Key policy rate / Operational target/ instrumental independence	Any other comments
Inflation Targeting Countries—Advanced Economies							
Austria	1993	None/Provide a new monetary anchor	Reserve Bank Board in agreement with Governor and the Minister of Finance (Treasurer)	Target range of 2–3% inflation on average over the economic cycle. Medium term	Normally meets 11 times each year, on the first Tuesday of each month (no meeting in January)	Target cash rate /Interbank cash rate	In determining monetary policy, the Bank has a duty to maintain price stability, full employment, and the economic prosperity and welfare of the Australian people.
Canada	1990–1991	None/Provide a new monetary anchor and bring down inflation	The inflation targets are agreed jointly by the Government of Canada and the Bank of Canada	A target rate for total CPI of 2% on a 12-month basis, with a 1–3% control range. The current target range extends to December 2016	In late 2000, the Bank of Canada adopted a system of eight pre-set dates per year on which it announces its key policy rate.	The Bank carries out monetary policy by influencing short-term interest rates. It does this by raising and lowering the target for the overnight rate.	The Bank also monitors a set of "core" inflation measures, including the CPIX, which strips out eight of the most volatile CPI components. These "core" measures allow the Bank to "look through" temporary changes in total CPI inflation and to focus on the underlying trend of inflation, which is a good indicator of where total CPI inflation is headed in the absence of policy action.
Japan	January 2013		The Act states, 'The Bank of Japan's autonomy regarding currency and monetary control shall be respected sufficiently.	Price stability target of 2% in terms of the year-on-year rate of change in the CPI at the earliest possible time, with a time horizon of about two years.	Monetary Policy Meetings (MPMs) are held once or twice a month, for one or two days. Disclosure via press releases, minutes of the meetings, press conference.	The Bank controls the amount of funds in the money market, mainly through money market operations.	The Bank supplies funds to financial institutions by, for example, extending loans to them, which are backed by collateral submitted to the Bank by these institutions. Such an operation is called a funds-supplying operation.

(continued.)

TABLE 10.2   **Inflation Targeting: The International Experience** (*continued.*)

New Zealand	1989–1990	None/Part of extensive reforms, dissatisfaction with earlier outcomes; provide a new nominal anchor	The Minister of Finance and the Governor of the Reserve Bank shall together have a separate agreement setting out specific targets for achieving and maintaining price stability. This is known as the Policy Targets Agreement (PTA).	The current agreement, signed in September 2012, calls for inflation to be kept within 1 to 3 percent a year, on average over the medium term, with a focus on keeping future average inflation near the 2 percent target midpoint. The Reserve Bank has published an interactive inflation calculator on its website.	Eight scheduled decision making meetings in a year.	Official cash rate (OCR)–the wholesale price of borrowed money.	The Reserve Bank publishes its Monetary Policy Statement (MPS) quarterly. Each Monetary Policy Statement must set out:1) how the Reserve Bank proposes to achieve its targets; 2) how it proposes to formulate and implement monetary policy during the next five years; and 3) how monetary policy has been implemented since the last Monetary Policy Statement.
Norway	2001	Exchange rate / gradual movement towards flexible exchange rate and stronger emphasis on price stability	The Government has set an inflation target for monetary policy.	The operational target of monetary policy shall be annual consumer price inflation of close to 2.5% over time.	The Executive Board sets the key rate at pre-announced times, normally six times a year.	Key policy rate, which is the interest rate on banks' deposits in Norges Bank.	The Norges Bank's focus is on price stability, financial stability and generating added value through investment management.
Sweden	Announced in January 1993, adopted in 1995	Exchange rate / Forced off a fixed exchange rate regime	The Executive Board of the Riksbank makes the monetary policy decisions without instruction from any other parties.	2% target in annual change in headline CPI	The Executive Board holds six scheduled monetary policy meetings a year.	Overnight repo rate / Overnight repo rate target	The Riksbank's function is to keep inflation close to the goal of 2%. If the credibility of this inflation target is not threatened, the Riksbank can make further contributions to reducing variations in areas such as production and employment–the 'real economy'.

South Korea	April 1998	Based on Bank of Korea Act, it sets the midterm inflation target to be applied for three years in consultation with the government.		The inflation target measure during the period from 2013 to 2015 is set at 2.5~3.5%, based on consumer price inflation (year-on-year).	The Base Rate, the BOK's policy rate, is set during the 'main meeting' of the Monetary Policy Committee that takes place once every month.	The Bank of Korea Base Rate is the reference policy rate.	In addition, the Bank of Korea also gives explanation to the general public as to the status of the medium term inflation target by monitoring it on an annual basis.
UK	October 1992	Exchange rate / Inflation targeting. Forced off a fixed exchange rate regime to maintain price stability/ Price stability is defined by the Government's inflation target of 2%.		The inflation target, of 2% is expressed in terms of an annual rate of inflation based on the Consumer Prices Index (CPI).	Monetary Policy Committee meets monthly for a two-day meeting. Decisions are made by a vote of the Committee on a one-person one-vote basis.	The 1998 Bank of England Act made the Bank independent to set interest rates. Bank rate is being used since 2009; asset purchase as an additional instrument.	In August 2013 the MPC provided some explicit guidance regarding the future conduct of monetary policy. The MPC intends at a minimum to maintain the present highly stimulative stance of monetary policy until economic slack has been substantially reduced, provided this does not entail material risks to price stability or financial stability.

Non-Inflation Targeting Countries—Advanced Economies

Euro Area		To maintain price stability is the primary objective of the Eurosystem and of the single monetary policy for which it is responsible. This is laid down in the Treaty on the Functioning of the European Union, Article 127 (1).	The Governing Council.	price stability is defined as 'a year-on-year increase in the Harmonised Index of Consumer Prices (HICP) for the euro area of below 2%. Price stability is to be maintained over the medium term'.	Twice a month, with first day discussing overall assessment of the economic situation and the risks to price stability based on a comprehensive economic and monetary analysis in the context of the ECB's (two-pillar) monetary policy strategy.	Minimum rate in main refinancing operation (MRO) and the interest rates on the marginal lending facility and the deposit facility.	The Euro system currently accepts a very broad range of debt instruments, issued both by public and private issuers.

(continued.)

TABLE 10.2 Inflation Targeting: The International Experience (continued.)

Switzerland		The Swiss National Bank (SNB) implements its monetary policy by fixing a target range for the three-month Swiss franc Libor.	Article 99 of the Federal Constitution entrusts the SNB, as an independent central bank, with the conduct of monetary policy in the interests of the country as a whole.	SNB equates price stability with a rise in the national consumer price index of less than 2% per annum in terms of total CPI.	Quarterly meetings (March, June, September and December) with press release and bulletin publication.	CHF 3-month Libor.	Medium-term inflation forecasts.
Singapore	Early 1980s	Centred on the management of the exchange rate.	The exchange rate policy band is periodically reviewed to ensure that it remains consistent with the underlying fundamentals of the economy.	The objective of Singapore's exchange rate policy has always been to promote sustained and non-inflationary growth for the Singapore economy.	Regular monetary policy announcements are scheduled in April and October.	The trade-weighted exchange rate is allowed to fluctuate within a policy band, and where necessary, Monetary Authority of Singapore (MAS) conducts direct interventions in the foreign exchange market to maintain the exchange rate within this band.	MAS' monetary policy is centred on the management of the exchange rate rather than targeting interest rate levels.
USA		No formal target/ The Committee judges that inflation at the rate of 2%, as measured by the annual change in the price index for personal consumption expenditures, is most consistent over the longer run.	Statutory Mandate from the Congress.	Maximum employment, stable prices, and moderate long-term interest rates.	FOMC meetings and press conference.	Decision by consensus/ Eight scheduled per year, with others as needed/ Meetings may last one or two days.	In the most recent projections, FOMC participants' estimates of the longer-run normal rate of unemployment had a central tendency of 5.2%–6%.

Inflation Targeting Countries—Emerging Market Economies

		Central bank/ Yes	Annual CPI (head-line) Point target: 3%/ +/–1 percentage point/ Around 2 years.	Monetary Policy Report/ 4 times a year.	Monetary Policy Interest Rate (Overnight interbank rate).
Chile	Sept 1999	High inflation due to expansionary policies, oil price hike during Gulf war, failure with exchange rate based stabilisation programme, instability of money demand and difficulty in monetary targeting, provide a new monetary anchor and gradual disinflation	Central bank/ Yes	Annual CPI (head-line) Point target: 3%/ +/–1 percentage point/ Around 2 years.	Monetary Policy Report/ 4 times a year.	Monetary Policy Interest Rate (Overnight interbank rate).
Brazil	June 1999	Due to concerns on fiscal front, collapse of currency under speculative attack and search for a nominal anchor within IMF programme.	National Monetary Council (both Govt and central bank Governor)/ Yes	Headline Broad National CPI/ 4.5% +/–2 percentage point Yearly target.	Inflation Report/ 4 times a year	An overnight interest rate (SELIC)
Hungary	June 2001	Increasing incompatibility of fixed exchange rate regime and disinflation; need to bring down inflation with future EU membership in mind	Central bank/ Yes	CPI/ 3% per annum/ Medium-term.	Quarterly Report on Inflation/ 4 times a year	Interest rate on 2-week central bank bond.

TABLE 10.2 Inflation Targeting: The International Experience (continued.)

Indonesia	July 2005	The relationship between monetary aggregates and nominal income becoming tenuous due to instability in income velocity of money following financial deregulation and less success with exchange rate as nominal anchor.	Government in consultation with central bank/ Yes.	CPI / 4.5% +/- 1 percentage point/ Mediumterm.	Monetary Policy Report/ 4 times a year.	BI Rate
Israel	Informally in 1992; full-fledged from June 1997	Lock in disinflation and define the slope of the exchange rate crawling peg.	Government. in consultation with central bank Governor/ Yes.	CPI / Target Range of 1–3%/ Within 2 years.	Inflation Report/ Twice a year.	Short-term interest rate (overnight transactions between central bank and banks).
Mexico	2001	Difficulty with monetary targeting, unreliability of relationship between monetary base and inflation, and lack of nominal anchor to guide inflation expectations.	The Board of Governors/ Yes.	CPI / Multiannual inflation target 3% +/- 1%/ Mediumterm.	Inflation Report/ 4 times a year.	Overnight inter-bank rate.
South Africa	Feb 2000	Following liberalisation and structural developments, changing relationship between output, prices and money growth, making monetary targeting less useful; need for greater transparency in policy.	Government in consultation with central bank/ Yes.	CPI / A Target range of 3–6% on a continuous basis.	Monetary Policy Review/ Twice a year.	Repo rate

Country	Date				Inflation Report / frequency	Reference Interest rate	
Peru	Jan 2002	Formalisation of earlier regime; greater transparency of policy.	Target is approved by the Board of Directors	CPI / 2% +/-1 percentage point/ At all times.	Inflation Report/ 4 times a year.	Reference Interest rate	
Phillipines	Jan 2002	Formalisation and simplification of earlier regime; greater transparency and focus on price stability.	Government in consultation with central bank-Yes.	CPI / 4 per cent +/- 1 percentage point for 2012, 2013 and 2014/ Mediumterm	Inflation Report/ 4 times a year	Key Policy interest rates for overnight repo/ reverse repo and term repo/ reverse repo and special deposit accounts	Target is announced 2 years in advance.
Poland	1998	Considered the most effective way to bring down inflation as a precondition for subsequent EU membership.	Monetary Policy Council/ Yes.	CPI / 2.5% +/- 1 percentage points/ Mediumterm	Inflation Report/ 3 times a year	Reference rate (the rate that determines the yield on the main OMOs).	
South Korea	April 1998	Unstable money demand following structural changes in financial markets, and with 1997 financial crisis; discontinuation of exchange rate.	Central Bank in consultation with the Govt./ Yes.	CPI / 3 % +/- 1 percentage point/ 3 years.	Monetary Policy Report/ Twice a year.	Bank of Korea Base rate.	
Thailand	May 2000	Inflation targeting considered more appropriate with floating exchange rate than money supply targeting after the financial crisis of 1997.	MPC in consultation with the Govt/ Yes.	3.0 % +/- 1.5 percentage points/ 8 quarters.	Inflation Report/ 4 times a year.	One day repo rate.	Target is set by MPC annually. The target decided in agreement with the Minister of Finance, which then requires approval by the Cabinet
Turkey	Jan 2006		MPC in consultation with the Govt	Annual CPI/ 5% +/-2 percentage points for 2012, 2013 and 2014/ Multi-year horizon 3 years.	Inflation Report/ 4 times a year.	One week repo auction rate.	Interest rate corridor and required reserve ratios also used as policy instruments.

Source: https://rbi.org.in/scripts/PublicationReportDetails.aspx?UrlPage=& ID=757, as accessed on 24 March 2017 at 2pm.

Table 10.3 Inflation Targets: The International Experience

Individual Countries Inflation Targets

Country	Target Measure	Target 2013	Target Type
Armenia	H CPI	4% ± 1.5 pp	P + T
Australia	H CPI	2%–3%	Range
Brazil	H CPI	4.5% ± 2 pp	P + T
Canada	H CPI	2% (mid-point of 1%-3%)	P + T
Chile	H CPI	3% ± 1 pp	P + T
Colombia	H CPI	2%–4%	Range
Czech Republic	H CPI	2% ± 1 pp	P + T
Ghana	H CPI	9% ± 2 pp	P + T
Guatemala	H CPI	4% ± 1 pp	P + T
Hungary	H CPI	3%	Point
Iceland	H CPI	2.5%	Point
Indonesia	H CPI	4.5% ± 1 pp	P + T
Israel	H CPI	1%–3%	Range
Mexico	H CPI	3% ± 1 pp	P + T
New Zealand	H CPI	1%–3%	Range
Norway	H CPI	2.5%	Point
Peru	H CPI	2% ± 1 pp	P + T
Phillippines	H CPI	4.0% ± 1 pp	P + T
Poland	H CPI	2.5% ± 1 pp	P + T
Romania	H CPI	2.5% ± 1 pp	P + T
Serbia	H CPI	4.0% ± 1.5 pp	P + T
South Africa	H CPI	3%–6%	Range
South Korea	H CPI	2.5% – 3.5%	Range
Sweden	H CPI	2%	Point
Thailand	Core Inflation	0.5% – 3.0%	Range
Turkey	H CPI	5.0% ± 2 pp	P + T
United Kingdom	H CPI	2%	Point

H CPI-Headline CPI; P+ T-Point with tolerance; PP–Percentage point
Source: Hammond G. (2012);"State of the art of inflation targeting", CCBS, Handbook–No.29, Bank of England and Website of Central Banks.

Non-Inflation Targeting Countries

Country	Target Measure	Desired level of Inflation
US	PCE	< 2 %
ECB	H CPI	Below but close to 2%
Malaysia	H CPI	2%–3%
Singapore	H CPI	3%–4%
Russia	H CPI	5%–6%
China	H CPI	3.50%

PCE: Personal Consumption Expenditure
Source: Website of Central Banks

GLOBAL

> GLOBAL

Table 10.4 Time Horizon for Price Stability: The International Experience

Time Horizon for Attending Price Stability

Inflation Targeting		Non-inflation Targeting	
Country	Time horizon	Country	Time horizon
Armenia	Medium term	US	Long-term
Australia	Medium term	ECB	Medium-term
Brazil	Yearly Target	Malaysia	Short-term
Canada	6–8 quarters; current target extends to Dec.2016	Singapore	Short-term
Chile	Around two years	Russia	Medium-term
Colombia	Medium term	China	Short-term
Czech Republic	Medium term, 12–18 months		
Ghana	18–24 months		
Guatemala	End of year		
Hungary	Medium term		
Iceland	On average		
Indonesia	Medium term		
Israel	Within two years		
Mexico	Medium term		
New Zealand	Medium term		
Norway	Medium term		
Peru	At all times		
Philippines	Medium term(from 2012 2014)		
Poland	Medium term		
Romania	Medium term target from 2013		
Serbia	Medium term		
South Africa	On a continuous basis		
South Korea	Three years		
Sweden	Normally two years		
Thailand	Eight quarters		
Turkey	Multi year(Three years)		
United Kingdom	At all times		

Source: Hammond G. (2012);"State of the art of inflation targeting", CCBS, Handbook–No.29, Bank of England and Website of Central Banks

Inflation Targeting: The Indian Experience

Since 2007, several high level committees in India highlighted that the RBI must consider switching over to inflation targeting.

In 2008–2012, India was faced with the unique challenge of experiencing one of the highest inflation rates among G-20 countries. This was accompanied by rising inflation expectations, which remained at elevated levels, creating macroeconomic vulnerabilities.

In the light of these unique circumstances, the Expert Committee to Review and Strengthen the Monetary Policy Framework in India (2014), popularly known as the Urjit Patel Committee, recommended that the foremost and dominant objective of monetary policy must be to anchor inflation expectations. A monetary policy framework with inflation as the nominal anchor would also be consistent with flexibility in exchange rate management.

The Committee made the following recommendations with regard to inflation targeting:

- Inflation should be the nominal anchor for the monetary policy framework. This nominal anchor should be set by the RBI as its predominant objective of monetary policy in its policy statements. The nominal anchor should be communicated without ambiguity, so as to ensure a monetary policy regime shift away from the current approach to one that is centered around the nominal anchor. Subject to the establishment and achievement of the nominal anchor, monetary policy conduct should be consistent with a sustainable growth trajectory and financial stability.
- The RBI should adopt the new CPI(Combined) as the measure of the nominal anchor for policy communication. The nominal anchor should be defined in terms of headline CPI inflation, which closely reflects the cost of living and influences inflation expectations relative to other available metrics.
- The nominal anchor or target should be set at 4% with a band of (+/–) 2% around it (a) in view of the vulnerability of the Indian economy to supply/external shocks and the relatively large weight of food in the CPI; and (b) the need to avoid a deflation bias in the conduct of monetary policy. This target should be set in the frame of a two-year horizon that is consistent with the need to balance the output costs of disinflation against the speed of entrenchment of credibility in policy commitment.
- The transition path to the target zone should be graduated to bringing down inflation from the level of 10% in 2014 to 8% over a period not exceeding the next 12 months and 6% over a period not exceeding the next 24 month period before formally adopting the recommended target of 4% inflation with a band of (+/–) 2%. The Committee also recommended that this transition path should be clearly communicated to the public.

Further, the Committee recognized the significance of second round effects on inflation and inflation expectations. It recommended, " Since food and fuel account for more than 57% of the CPI on which the direct influence of monetary policy is limited, the commitment to the nominal anchor would need to be demonstrated by timely monetary policy response to risks from second round effects and inflation expectations in response to shocks to food and fuel".

Finally, the Committee recommended that the Government too share in this goal of achieving price stability. "Consistent with the Fiscal Responsibility and Budget Management (Amendment) Rules, 2013, the Central Government needs to ensure that its fiscal deficit as a ratio to GDP is brought down to 3% by 2016–2017.

Administered setting of prices, wages and interest rates are significant impediments to monetary policy transmission and achievement of the price stability objective, requiring a commitment from the Government towards their elimination."

As per the agreement between the Government of India and the RBI in February 2015 (http://finmin.nic.in/reports/MPFAgreement28022015.pdf), the RBI would aim to bring inflation down to 6% by January 2016. The target for the financial year 2016– 2017 and all subsequent years shall be four percent with a band of (+/–) 2%.

As regards the Flexible Inflation Target, the agreement noted that, the RBI shall be said to have failed to meet the target if inflation turned out to be:

- more than 6% for three consecutive quarters for the financial year 2015–2016 and all subsequent years
- less than 2% for three consecutive quarters in 2016–2017 and all subsequent years.

The agreement also put down the actions in case of RBI's failure to meet the target. In such a case, the RBI would set out in a report to the Central Government:

- the reasons for its failure to achieve the target
- remedial actions proposed to be taken by the Reserve Bank and
- an estimate of the time period within which the target would be achieved through timely remedial actions.

Further, with a view to maintain price stability, while keeping in mind the objective of growth, the Reserve Bank of India Act, 1934 (RBI Act) was amended by the Finance Act, 2016 to provide for a statutory and institutionalised framework for a Monetary Policy Committee (MPC).

The Government of India decided to bring the provisions of amended RBI Act regarding constitution of MPC into force on June 27, 2016 so that statutory basis of MPC was made effective.

The Preamble in the RBI Act, as amended by the Finance Act, 2016, now provides that the primary objective of the monetary policy is to maintain price stability, while keeping in mind the objective of growth, and to meet the challenge of an increasingly complex economy. RBI would, accordingly, operate a Monetary Policy Framework. Thus, now there is a statutory basis for a Monetary Policy Framework and the MPC.

It was decided that out of the six Members of MPC, three Members would be from the Reserve Bank of India (RBI), including the Governor, RBI, who will be the ex-officio Chairperson, the Deputy Governor, RBI and one officer of RBI. The other three Members of MPC would be appointed by the Central Government, on the recommendations of a Search-cum- Selection Committee. These three Members of MPC would be experts in the field of economics or banking or finance or monetary policy and will be appointed for a period of 4 years and shall not be eligible for re-appointment. The meetings of the MPC would be held at least 4 times a year and the MPC would publicise its decisions after each such meeting.

Functions of the MPC

The MPC would be entrusted with the task of fixing the benchmark policy rate (repo rate) required to contain inflation within the specified target level. Under sub-section (1) of section 45ZA of the RBI Act, the Central Government, in consultation with the RBI, determines the inflation target in terms of the Consumer Price Index (CPI), once in every five years. This target would be notified in the Official Gazette.

Accordingly, the Central Government has notified in the Official Gazette 4 per cent Consumer Price Index (CPI) inflation as the target for the period from August 5, 2016 to March 31, 2021 with the upper tolerance limit of 6 per cent (i.e. 4% + 2%) and the lower tolerance limit of 2 per cent (i.e. 4% -2%).

The Central Government notified the following as factors that constitute failure to achieve the inflation target:

- the average inflation is more than the upper tolerance level of the inflation target for any three consecutive quarters; or
- the average inflation is less than the lower tolerance level for any three consecutive quarters. Where RBI fails to meet the inflation target, in terms of the provisions of RBI Act, it shall set out a report to the Central Government stating the reasons for failure to achieve the inflation target; remedial actions proposed to be taken by RBI; and an estimate of the time-period within which the inflation target shall be achieved pursuant to timely implementation of proposed remedial actions.

Source: https://rbidocs.rbi.org.in/rdocs/PublicationReport/Pdfs/3CHAP2T270114.pdf, as accessed on 24 March 2017 at 2pm; http://finmin.nic.in/press_room/2016/MonetaryPolicy05082016.pdf; http://www.finmin.nic.in/press_room/2016/MPC_Press_notification27062016.pdf.

The performance of inflation-targeting regimes has been quite good. Inflation-targeting countries seem to have significantly reduced both the rate of inflation and inflation expectations beyond what would likely have occurred in the absence of inflation targets. Furthermore, once down, inflation in these countries has stayed down; following disinflations, the inflation rate in targeting countries has not bounced back up during subsequent cyclical expansions of the economy.

Disadvantages of Inflation Targeting

Critics of inflation targeting cite four disadvantages of this monetary policy strategy: delayed signaling, too much rigidity, the potential for increased output fluctuations, and low economic growth. We look at each in turn and examine the validity of these criticisms.

Delayed Signaling Inflation is not easily controlled by the monetary authorities, and because of the long lags in the effects of monetary policy, inflation outcomes are revealed only after a substantial lag. Thus, an inflation target is unable to send immediate signals to both the public and markets about the stance of monetary policy.

Too Much Rigidity   Some economists have criticized inflation targeting because they believe it imposes a rigid rule on monetary policy makers and limits their ability to respond to unforeseen circumstances. However, useful policy strategies exist that are "rule-like," in that they involve forward-looking behavior that limits policy makers from systematically engaging in policies with undesirable long-run consequences. Such policies avoid the time-inconsistency problem and would best be described as "constrained discretion."

Indeed, inflation targeting can be described exactly in this way. Inflation targeting, as actually practiced, is far from rigid and is better described as "flexible inflation targeting." First, inflation targeting does not prescribe simple and mechanical instructions on how the central bank should conduct monetary policy. Rather, it requires the central bank to use all available information to determine which policy actions are appropriate to achieve the inflation target. Unlike simple policy rules, inflation targeting never requires the central bank to focus solely on one key variable. Second, inflation targeting as practiced contains a substantial degree of policy discretion. Inflation targets have been modified depending on economic circumstances, as we have seen. Moreover, central banks under inflation-targeting regimes have left themselves considerable scope to respond to output growth and fluctuations through several devices.

Potential for Increased Output Fluctuations   An important criticism of inflation targeting is that a sole focus on inflation may lead to monetary policy that is too tight when inflation is above target and thus may lead to larger output fluctuations. Inflation targeting does not, however, require a sole focus on inflation—in fact, experience has shown that inflation targeters display substantial concern about output fluctuations.

Inflation targeters have chosen inflation targets above zero (typically around 2%), and this reflects the concern of monetary policy makers that particularly low inflation can have substantial negative effects on real economic activity. Deflation (negative inflation in which the price level actually falls) is especially to be feared because of the possibility that it may promote financial instability and precipitate a severe economic contraction (Chapter 8). The deflation in Japan in recent years has been an important factor in the weakening of the Japanese financial system and economy. Targeting inflation rates of above zero makes periods of deflation less likely. This is one reason why economists, both within and outside of Japan, called for the Bank of Japan to adopt an inflation target at levels of 2%, which finally occurred in 2013.

Inflation targeting also does not ignore traditional stabilization goals. Central bankers in inflation-targeting countries continue to express their concern about fluctuations in output and employment, and the ability to accommodate short-run stabilization goals to some degree is built into all inflation-targeting regimes. All inflation-targeting countries have been willing to minimize output declines by gradually lowering medium-term inflation targets toward the long-run goal.

Low Economic Growth   Another common concern about inflation targeting is that it will lead to low growth in output and employment. Although inflation reduction has been associated with below-normal output during disinflationary phases in inflation-targeting regimes, once low inflation levels were achieved, output and employment returned to the levels at least as high as they had been before. A conservative conclusion is that once low inflation is achieved, inflation targeting is not harmful to the real economy. Given the strong economic growth after disinflation in many countries (such as New Zealand) that have adopted inflation targets, a case can be made that inflation targeting promotes real economic growth, in addition to controlling inflation.

Should Central Banks Respond to Asset-Price Bubbles? Lessons from the Global Financial Crisis

Over the centuries, economies have been periodically subject to *asset-price bubbles*, pronounced increases in asset prices that depart from fundamental values, which eventually burst resoundingly. The story of the 2007–2009 financial crisis, discussed in Chapter 8, indicates how costly these bubbles can be. The bursting of the asset-price bubble in the housing market brought down the financial system, leading to an economic downturn, a rise in unemployment, disrupted communities, and direct hardship for families forced to leave their homes after foreclosures.

The high cost of asset-price bubbles raises a key question for monetary policy strategy: what should central banks do about them? Should they use monetary policy to try to pop bubbles? Are there regulatory measures they can take to rein in asset-price bubbles? To answer these questions, we need to ask whether there are different bubbles that require different responses.

Because asset prices affect business and household spending and hence economic activity, monetary policy certainly needs to respond to asset prices in order to stabilize the economy. Hence, the issue of how monetary policy should respond to asset-price movements is not whether it should respond at all, but whether it should respond at a level higher than what is called for in terms of the objectives of stabilizing inflation and employment. Another way of defining the issue is whether monetary policy should try to pop, or slow, the growth of possibly developing asset-price bubbles to minimize damage to the economy when these bubbles burst. Alternatively, rather than responding directly to possible asset-price bubbles, should the monetary authorities respond to asset-price declines only after a bubble bursts, to stabilize both output and inflation? These opposing positions have been characterized as *leaning* against asset-price bubbles versus *cleaning up* after the bubble bursts, and so the debate over what to do about asset-price bubbles is often referred to as the "lean versus clean" debate.

Two Types of Asset-Price Bubbles

There are two types of asset-price bubbles: one that is driven by credit and a second that is driven purely by overly optimistic expectations (which former chairman of the Fed, Alan Greenspan, referred to as "irrational exuberance").

Credit-Driven Bubbles   When a credit boom begins, it can spill over into an asset-price bubble: easier credit can be used to purchase particular assets and thereby raise their prices. The rise in asset values, in turn, encourages further lending for these assets, either because it increases the value of collateral, making it easier to borrow, or because it raises the value of capital at financial institutions, which gives them more capacity to lend. The lending for these assets can then further increase the demand and hence raise their prices even more. This feedback loop—in which a credit boom drives up asset prices, which in turn fuels the credit boom, which drives asset prices even higher, and so on—can generate a bubble in which asset prices rise well above their fundamental values.

Credit-driven bubbles are particularly dangerous, as the recent global financial crisis has demonstrated. When asset prices come back down to Earth and the bubble bursts, the collapse in asset prices then leads to a reversal of the feedback loop in which loans go sour, lenders cut back on credit supply, the demand for assets declines further, and prices drop even more. These were exactly the dynamics in housing markets during the global financial crisis. Driven by a credit boom in subprime lending, housing prices rose way above fundamental values, but when housing prices crashed, credit shriveled up and housing prices plummeted.

The resulting losses on subprime loans and securities eroded the balance sheets of financial institutions, causing a decline in credit (deleveraging) and a sharp fall in business and household spending, and therefore in the economic activity. As we saw during the 2007–2009 financial crisis, the interaction between housing prices and the health of financial institutions following the collapse of the housing price bubble endangered the operation of the financial system as a whole and had dire consequences for the economy.

Bubbles Driven Solely by Irrational Exuberance   Bubbles that are driven solely by overly optimistic expectations, but which are not associated with a credit boom, pose much less risk to the financial system. For example, the bubble in technology stocks in the late 1990s described in Chapter 6 was not fueled by credit, and the bursting of the tech-stock bubble was not followed by a marked deterioration in financial institutions' balance sheets. The bursting of the tech-stock bubble thus did not have a very severe impact on the economy, and the recession that followed was quite mild. Bubbles driven solely by irrational exuberance are therefore far less dangerous than those driven by credit booms.

The Debate over Whether Central Banks Should Try to Pop Bubbles

Whether central banks should try to pop, or prick, bubbles was actively debated before the crisis, with Alan Greenspan arguing against, and his position held great sway in the central banking circles before the global financial crisis. However, the crisis has led to reevaluation of this viewpoint, and we look at the pros and cons of the argument below.

Cons: Why Central Banks Should Not Try to Pop Bubbles   Alan Greenspan's arguments that central banks should not take actions to prick bubbles became known as the "Greenspan doctrine." His position reflected five arguments.

1. Asset-price bubbles are nearly impossible to identify. If central banks or government officials knew that a bubble was in progress, why wouldn't market participants know as well? If so, it is unlikely that a bubble would develop because market participants would know that prices were getting out of line with fundamentals. Unless central bank or government officials are smarter than market participants, which is unlikely given the especially high wages that savvy market participants garner, they will be unable to identify when bubbles of this type are occurring.

2. Although some economic analysis suggests that raising interest rates can diminish the possibility of an increase in asset price, raising interest rates may be very ineffective in restraining the bubble because market participants expect such high rates of return from buying bubble-driven assets. Furthermore, raising interest rates has often been found to cause a bubble to burst more severely, thereby increasing the damage to the economy. Another way of saying this is that bubbles are departures from normal behavior, and it is unrealistic to expect that the usual tools of monetary policy will be effective in abnormal conditions.

3. Many different asset prices exist, and at any one time a bubble may be present in only a fraction of assets. Monetary policy actions are a very blunt instrument in such a case, as such actions would be likely to affect asset prices in general, rather than the specific assets that are experiencing a bubble.

4. Using monetary policy actions to prick bubbles can have harmful effects on the aggregate economy. If interest rates are raised significantly to curtail a bubble, the economy will slow, people will lose jobs, and inflation can fall below its desirable level. Indeed, as the first two arguments suggest, the rise in interest rates is necessary to prick a bubble which may be so high that it can only be done at great cost to the workers and the economy. This is not to say that monetary policy should not respond to asset prices per se. The level of asset prices does affect household and business spending and thus the evolution of the economy. Monetary policy should react to fluctuations in asset prices to the extent that they affect inflation and economic activity.

5. As long as monetary policy responds in a timely fashion, by easing monetary policy aggressively after an asset bubble bursts, the harmful effects of a bursting bubble could be kept at a manageable level. Indeed, the Greenspan Fed acted exactly in this way after the stock market crash of 1987, and the bursting of the tech bubble in the stock market in 2000. Aggressive easing after the stock market bubbles bursting in 1987 and 2000 was highly successful. The economy did not enter a recession after the stock market crash of 1987, whereas the recession was very mild after the tech bubble burst in 2000.

Pro: Why Central Banks Should Try to Pop Bubbles The recent crisis has clearly demonstrated that the bursting of credit-driven bubbles, in contrast to the Greenspan doctrine, can be not only extremely costly but also very hard to clean up after. The global financial crisis has therefore provided a much stronger case for trying to pop potential bubbles.

However, the distinction between the two types of bubbles, one of which (credit-driven) is much more costly than the other, suggests that the lean versus clean debate may have been miscast. Rather than leaning against potential asset-price bubbles, which would include both credit-driven and irrational exuberance-type bubbles, the case is much stronger for leaning against credit bubbles, which would involve leaning against credit-driven asset-price bubbles but not irrational exuberance asset-price bubbles. In addition, it is much easier to identify credit bubbles than asset-price bubbles. When asset-price bubbles are rising rapidly at the same time that credit is booming, the likelihood is greater that asset prices are deviating from fundamentals because laxer credit standards are driving asset prices upward. In this case, central bank or government officials have a greater likelihood of identifying that a bubble is in progress; this was indeed the case during the housing market bubble in the United States because these officials did have information that lenders had decreased lending standards and that credit extension in the mortgage markets was rising at an abnormally high rate.

The case for leaning against credit bubbles seems strong, but what policies will be most effective in restraining credit bubbles?

Macroprudential Policies   First, it is important to recognize that the key principle to consider in designing effective policies to lean against credit bubbles is to curb excessive risk taking. Only when this risk taking is excessive are credit bubbles likely to develop, and so it is natural to look at prudential regulatory measures to constrain credit bubbles. Regulatory policy to affect what is happening in credit markets in the aggregate is referred to as **macroprudential regulation,** and it does seem to be the right tool for reigning in credit-driven bubbles.

Financial regulation and supervision, either by central banks or by other government entities, with the usual elements of a well-functioning prudential regulatory and supervisory system, as described in Chapter 17, can prevent excessive risk taking that can trigger a credit boom, which in turn leads to an asset-price bubble. These elements include an adequate disclosure and capital requirements, prompt corrective action, close monitoring of financial institutions' risk management procedures, and close supervision to enforce compliance with regulations. More generally, regulation should focus on preventing leverage cycles. As the global financial crisis demonstrated, the rise in asset prices that accompanied the credit boom resulted in higher capital buffers at financial institutions, supporting further lending in the context of unchanging capital requirements, which led to higher asset prices, and so on; in the bust, the value of the capital dropped precipitously, leading to a cut in lending. Capital requirements that are countercyclical, that is, adjusted upward during a boom and downward during a bust, might help eliminate the pernicious feedback loops that promote credit-driven bubbles.

A rapid rise in asset prices accompanied by a credit boom provides a signal that market failures or poor financial regulation and supervision might be causing a bubble to form. Central banks and other government regulators could then consider implementing policies to rein in credit growth directly or implement measures to make sure credit standards are sufficiently high.

Monetary Policy   The fact that the low interest-rate policies of the Federal Reserve from 2002 to 2005, were followed by excessive risk taking suggests to many that overly easy monetary policy might promote financial instability, as was discussed in Chapter 8. Although it is far from clear that the Federal Reserve is primarily to blame for the housing bubble, research does suggest that low interest rates can encourage excessive risk taking in what has been called the "risk-taking channel of monetary policy." Low interest rates may increase the incentives for asset managers in financial institutions to search for yield and hence increase risk taking. Low interest rates may also increase the demand for assets, raising their prices and leading to increased valuation of collateral, which in turn encourages lenders to lend to riskier borrowers.

The risk-taking channel of monetary policy suggests that monetary policy should be used to lean against credit bubbles. However, many of the objections to using monetary policy to prick bubbles behind the Greenspan doctrine are still valid, so wouldn't it be better to use macroprudential supervision to constrain credit bubbles, leaving monetary policy to focus on price and output stability?

This argument would be quite strong if macroprudential policies were able to do the job. However, there are doubts on this score. Prudential supervision is subject to more political pressure than monetary policy because it affects the bottom line of financial institutions more directly. Thus they have greater incentives to lobby politicians to discourage macroprudential policies that would rein in credit bubbles, particularly during a credit bubble when they are making the most money. In addition, financial institutions are often very good at finding loopholes to avoid regulation, and so macroprudential supervision may not be very effective. The possibility that macroprudential policies may not be implemented sufficiently well to constrain credit bubbles suggests that monetary policy may have to be used instead.

An important lesson from the global financial crisis is that central banks and other regulators should not have a laissez-faire attitude and let credit-driven bubbles proceed without any reaction. How to do this well, however, is indeed a daunting task.

Tactics: Choosing the Policy Instrument

Now that we are familiar with strategies for monetary policy, let's look at how monetary policy is conducted day to day.

Monetary Policy Framework

GO ONLINE

Access **http://finmin. nic.in/reports/ MPFAgreement28022015. pdf** to view the latest Agreement on the Monetary Policy Framework between the Government of India and the RBI.

Achieving the monetary policy objectives requires articulation of a consistent monetary policy framework. This becomes necessary as central banks strive to achieve these objectives only indirectly through instruments which are under their direct control. For instance, under the monetary targeting framework, central banks, through the instruments under their direct control such as cash reserve ratio (CRR), tried to influence an intermediate target such as money supply which had a stable relationship with the final objectives of price and output. Monetary policy framework, however, has been a continuously evolving process contingent upon the level of development of financial markets and institutions, as also the degree of global integration. In India as in other countries, monetary policy framework has undergone significant transformation over time.

For effective implementation of monetary policy, the monetary policy framework needs a supporting operating procedure. An operating procedure is defined as day-to-day management of monetary conditions consistent with the overall stance of monetary policy. Generally, it involves: (i) defining an operational target, generally an interest rate; (ii) setting a policy rate which could influence the operational target; (iii) setting the width of corridor for short-term market interest rates; (iv) conducting liquidity operations to keep the operational target interest rate stable within the corridor; and (v) signalling of policy intentions.

Operating Framework of Monetary Policy[9]

The operating framework is all about implementation of monetary policy. It primarily involves three major aspects—choosing the operating target; choosing the intermediate target and choosing the policy instruments. The **operating target** pertains to the variable that monetary policy can directly control with its actions. The tool(s) with which the central bank seeks to impact the operating target is (are) the monetary policy instrument(s). The **intermediate target** is a variable which

---

[9]https://rbidocs.rbi.org.in/rdocs/PublicationReport/Pdfs/4CHAP3T270114.pdf, as accessed on 24 March 2017 at 2pm.

the central bank can hope to influence to a reasonable degree through the operating target and which displays a predictable and stable relationship with the **goal variable**(s). With growing instability in the relationship between the intermediate targets and the ultimate policy variables, intermediate targets have tended to be downgraded in monetary policy regimes of most central banks, although they are monitored as indicators/guides for their information content.

The key challenge for the liquidity desk in the central bank is to use a combination of **policy instruments**—standing facilities, open market operations (OMOs) and reserve requirements to achieve the operating target on a day to day basis, and thereby ensure the first leg of monetary policy transmission. Assessment of liquidity to arrive at the OMO volume (i.e., repo and outright are taken together) that can ensure achievement of the operating target is therefore critical, but remains a challenge for every central bank.

The current norm across central banks of advanced economies and emerging market economies is to have a short-term interest rate as the operating target, while using liquidity management instruments to modulate the liquidity conditions suitably so as to control the operating target. The Federal Funds Rate in the United States, the Bank Rate in the UK and the overnight repo rate in Sweden are some examples of operational targets of monetary policy. See Global Box "Monetary Policy Framework: The International Experience".

The key to the operating framework is **liquidity management.** Liquidity management (i) ensures controllability of the reserve target; (ii) ensures the first leg of monetary policy transmission by anchoring the short-term money market rates to the policy rate target; and (iii) prevents disruptions in payment and settlement, especially for liquidity deficit systems. In view of the market frictions that could arise from institution-specific and systemic funding liquidity problems and their interdependence, all central banks attempt to institutionalise a sound liquidity management framework. The specific institutional setup, however, varies to a great deal across countries—in terms of maturity and frequency of operations, counterparty arrangements, and eligible collateral (See Global Box "Standing Facilities, Main Liquidity Operations and Other Discretionary Operations of Some Major Central Banks"). Liquidity management frameworks typically involves maximum accommodation with ample discretionary provisions, particularly when short-term interest rates serve as the operating target.

Standing facilities (SFs) are transparent, available to banks and other counter parties without discretionary hurdles, and are generally considered as the safety valve of a liquidity management system. Virtually all central banks have a standing credit facility which extends funds to the deficit counterparty at a penal rate (e.g., marginal lending facility of the ECB, primary and secondary credit facilities of the Fed and the MSF of India). Eligible collaterals and tenure of borrowings, however, vary across countries. The standing deposit facility, though less in use, helps to define a floor rate in the inter-bank market, especially in liquidity surplus conditions. The main advantage of a SF is that it gives the central bank a window to intervene in both directions, when needed, to achieve the operating interest rate target, with volatility in inter-bank rates restricted to the corridor. Reducing the volatility in the inter-bank money market rate while achieving the interest rate target is both an objective and also a challenge for an efficient liquidity management.

In addition to SFs, **discretionary operations** of a central bank could be classified under two broad heads, viz., (a) the main refinance operations and (b) other discretionary operations. Under the main refinance operations, the most common instruments are OMOs, which are conducted on a pre-announced date by a central bank with voluntary participation from banks and primary dealers (PDs). Ideally, OMOs are used for both lending and borrowing, and include both outright purchase and repurchase agreements, depending upon the nature of liquidity requirements—structural or frictional. Some countries use both short term and long term repos (e.g., UK), and others use central bank bills (Switzerland), and stabilization bonds (Korea), to manage liquidity. Other discretionary operations to manage liquidity are mainly in response to unexpected short-term developments requiring non-standard, non-regular operations. Such operations include forex-swaps (Australia, Singapore), term deposits (Australia), compulsory deposits (Mexico), additional loans and deposits (Sweden) and funding for lending (UK).

Among the terms and conditions, eligibility of collateral is one of the most important aspects of liquidity management. All major central banks include public sector securities of their own country as eligible collateral. Since mid-2007, the eligibility frame has been widened in several countries to include financial entity debt (Japan, Mexico, Sweden and UK), covered bonds (Australia and UK), other asset backed securities (Australia, Canada, Mexico and UK), corporate debt and loans and other credit claims (Canada and UK) and cross-border collateral (Australia, Japan, Mexico and Singapore). With increased acceptance of diversified securities as collateral, countries have also adopted different policies relating to pricing, initial margins and haircuts.

As regards to the tenure of the liquidity facility, most central banks provide an overnight window, but country experiences show many instances of access to liquidity beyond overnight (for instance, the repo operation is up to one year in Australia and Japan, 65 days in the USA, one week in Korea, Switzerland and Sweden, and 25 days in Mexico). The frequency of such operations also varies considerably across countries, with short-term repos on a daily/weekly basis, but also with longer-term operations once in a month or as per the discretion of the central bank.

Liquidity versus Monetary Management In view of the legacy influence of monetary targeting, there is often the challenge of distinguishing between liquidity management and monetary management. The same set of instruments could be used for liquidity management under an interest rate targeting rule and for monetary management under a monetary or reserve targeting rule. Thus, every instrument of liquidity management is a monetary policy instrument as well, but in an interest rate based operating framework, it is through liquidity management that an operating target is attained. Other than explicit changes in the policy interest rate or interest rate target—which alone should convey the stance of monetary policy—all other instruments may have to be seen as primarily meant for liquidity management, but consistent with the stance of monetary policy. In India, however, at least in the past few years, changes in policy rates and reserve requirements have at times conveyed divergent signals, thereby becoming a source of market confusion, which needs to be avoided by ensuring consistency between interest rate actions and liquidity management.

Non-monetary Instruments While the use of monetary instruments in striving to achieve monetary policy objectives is quite pervasive, central banks have been employing non-monetary instruments as part of their overall policy toolkit and these instruments subserve monetary policy considerations eventually. These instruments are tailored to deal with various exigencies: surges in capital flows; credit allocation;

pro-cyclicality and interconnectedness; and the zero lower bound on the nominal interest rate, to note a few. Such non-monetary measures include:

- **Regulatory measures**—selective credit controls ranging from improving credit culture (establishing credit bureaus; credit registry; higher risk weights for sensitive sectors), supervisory measures (on-site and off-site inspection of banks) and moral persuasion.
- **Financial measures**—working their way through the foreign exchange market: liberalising/restricting capital flows; intervention in the foreign exchange market and sterilisation operations; reserve requirements on foreign currency instruments and variants of the Tobin tax.
- **Macroprudential measures**—these are designed to contain systemic risks.

Evolution of the Monetary Policy Framework in India

GO ONLINE

Access **https://www.rbi.org.in/scripts/PublicationReportDetails.aspx?ID=631#S6** to view the evolution of the operating procedure of monetary policy in India.

The monetary policy framework in India has evolved over time, alongwith changes in the concomitant operating procedures.

1947–1957—exchange rate anchor set by the proportional reserve system prescribed by the RBI Act wherein at least 40% of the total note issue was to be backed by gold bullion and sterling.

1957—moved to a minimum reserve system i.e. only ₹2 billion worth of foreign securities and billion needed to be maintained as a backing for currency issue, of which ₹1.15 billion had to be in gold:

- Use of credit aggregates as the nominal anchor for monetary policy.
- Changes in the bank rate and the cash reserve ratio (CRR) were the main instruments of monetary policy.
- Use of selective credit controls, credit authorisation and 'social control' measures to enhance the flow of credit to priority sectors.

1985—a new monetary policy framework was introduced based on monetary targeting with feedback, drawing on empirical evidence of a stable demand function for money.

- Broad money became the intermediate target while reserve money was one of the main operating instruments for achieving control on broad money growth

1998—move to a 'Multiple Indicator Approach', with a greater emphasis on rate channels for monetary policy formulation relative to quantity instruments.

- Under this approach, a number of quantity variables such as money, credit, output, trade, capital flows and fiscal position as well as rate variables such as rates of return in different markets, inflation rates and exchange rates were analyzed for drawing monetary policy perspectives.
- The multiple indicator approach was informed by forward looking indicators since the early 2000s, that were drawn from the RBI's surveys of industrial outlook, credit conditions, capacity utilization, professional forecasters, inflation expectations and consumer confidence.

- The assessment from these indicators and models were fed into the projection of growth and inflation.
- Simultaneously, the Reserve Bank also gave the projection for broad money (M3), which served as an important information variable, so as to make the resource balance in the economy consistent with the credit needs of the government and the private sector.
- The augmented multiple indicator approach is shown below in Figure 10.2:

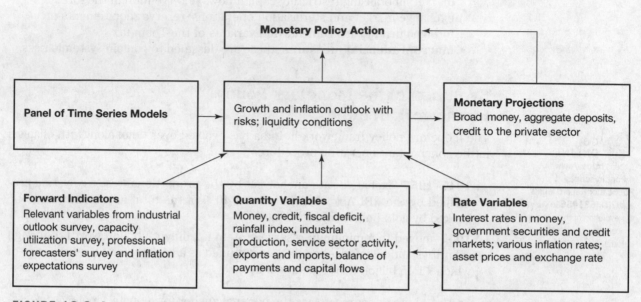

FIGURE 10.2 Augmented Multiple Indicator Approach

2011–on the recommendations of the Working Group on Operating Procedure of Monetary Policy (RBI, 2011),[10] a new framework was implemented having the following distinguishing features:

- the repo rate was the single policy rate;
- the operating target was the weighted average overnight call rate, which is aligned to the repo rate through: (i) a corridor around the repo rate of 100 basis points above the repo rate for the Marginal Standing Facility (MSF) and 100 basis points below the repo rate for the reverse repo rate[11], and (ii) full accommodation of liquidity management albeit with an indicative comfort zone of (+/–) 1% of net demand and time liabilities (NDTL) of the banking system; and
- transmission of changes in the repo rate through the weighted average call rate to the ultimate goals of monetary policy without any specific intermediate target.

---

[10]RBI (2011): "Working Group on Operating Procedure of Monetary Policy", Chairman: Deepak Mohanty, available on http://www.rbi.org.in.

[11]In the first bi-monthly monetary policy statement 2016–17, the RBI Governor announced a narrowing of the policy rate corridor from +/–100 basis points (bps) to +/–50 bps. Consequently the revised LAF framework is as seen in Figure 10.3.

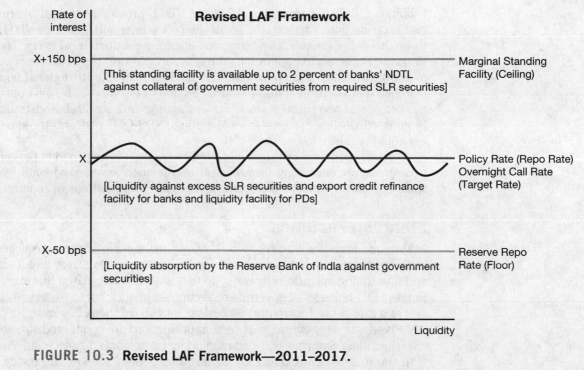

FIGURE 10.3 Revised LAF Framework—2011–2017.

Source: http://www.bis.org/review/r111202g.pdf, as accessed on 24 March 2017 at 2pm.

The Current Operating Framework For Monetary Policy In India

GO ONLINE

Access **https://www.rbi.org.in/scripts/PublicationsView.aspx?id=16823#C14** to view the Monetary Policy Reports brought out by the RBI on a half-yearly basis. View the section on Liquidity conditions to get insights into the RBI's liquidity management in response to the prevailing monetary and liquidity conditions, as also the transmission mechanism.

The Policy Rate The fixed overnight repurchase (repo) rate under the liquidity adjustment facility (LAF) is the single monetary policy rate.

The Operating Target of Monetary Policy The is the weighted average call money rate (WACR) is the operating target of monetary policy.

The Operating Procedure of Monetary Policy—once the policy rate is announced in the Bank's statements on monetary policy, the operating procedure aims at modulating liquidity conditions so as to achieve the operating target, i.e., to anchor the WACR around the policy rate. This is the first leg of monetary policy transmission to the financial system and the economy.

Liquidity Management

Pro-active liquidity management is the mechanism through which the operating target is achieved. The main features of the revised liquidity management framework announced on August 22, 2014 and implemented since September 5 are as follows: (i) assured access to central bank liquidity of 1% of banks' net demand and time liabilities (NDTL), comprising 0.25% of NDTL provided through overnight fixed rate repo auctions conducted daily at the policy rate, and 0.75% of NDTL provided through 14-day variable rate term repo auctions conducted on every Tuesday and Friday; (ii) fine-tuning operations through variable rate repo/reverse repo auctions of maturities ranging from overnight to 28 days to even out frictional liquidity mismatches that occur in spite of assured liquidity operations; and (iii) outright open market operations through auctions and anonymous screen-based trading on the Negotiated Dealing System-Order Matching (NDS-OM) platform to manage enduring liquidity mismatches.

Special operations are also conducted on holidays to help market participants tide over pressures emanating from one-off events such as tax payments, government spending, balance sheet adjustments and payment and settlement requirements.

Standing Facilities

A Marginal Standing Facility (MSF), allows market participants to access central bank liquidity at the end of the day (including Saturdays), over and above regular and fine-tuning operations by using up to 2% of their stipulated Statutory Liquidity Ratio (SLR) holdings of government securities, in addition to excess SLR as collateral at a rate set at (currently) 50 basis points above the policy rate.

Fixed rate daily overnight reverse repo auctions are conducted at the end of the day (including Saturdays), to allow market participants to place surplus liquidity with the Reserve Bank at a rate set at 50 basis points below the policy rate. The fixed rate daily overnight reverse repo operates as a de facto standing facility.

The MSF rate and the fixed overnight reverse repo rate define an informal corridor for limiting intra-day variations in the call rate.[12]

In the first bi-monthly monetary policy statement 2016–2017, the Governor announced that on the basis of an assessment of the current and evolving macroeconomic situation, it had been decided to:

- reduce the policy repo rate under the liquidity adjustment facility (LAF) by 25 basis points from 6.75–6.5%;
- reduce the minimum daily maintenance of the cash reserve ratio (CRR) from 95% of the requirement to 90% with effect from the fortnight beginning April 16, 2016, while keeping the CRR unchanged at 4% of net demand and time liabilities (NDTL);
- continue to provide liquidity as required but progressively lower the average ex ante liquidity deficit in the system from 1% of NDTL to a position closer to neutrality; and
- narrow the policy rate corridor from +/−100 basis points (bps) to +/− 50 bps by reducing the MSF rate by 75 basis points and increasing the reverse repo rate by 25 basis points, with a view to ensuring finer alignment of the weighted average call rate (WACR) with the repo rate;

Consequently, the reverse repo rate under the LAF was adjusted to 6%, and the marginal standing facility (MSF) rate to 7%. The Bank Rate which was aligned to the MSF rate also stood adjusted to 7%.

---

[12]*Source:* https://rbidocs.rbi.org.in/rdocs/Publications/PDFs/2015HYED1215458ES216FE667.pdf, as accessed on 24 March 2017 at 2pm.

Further, the following changes were announced in the Liquidity framework for monetary policy operations.

- smooth the supply of durable liquidity over the year using asset purchases and sales as needed;
- progressively lower the average ex ante liquidity deficit in the system to a position closer to neutrality;
- narrow the policy rate corridor from +/−100 bps to +/− 50 bps, with a view to ensuring finer alignment of the WACR with the repo rate;
- ease liquidity management for banks without abandoning liquidity discipline by reducing the minimum daily maintenance of CRR from 95% of the requirement to 90% with effect from the fortnight beginning April 16, 2016;
- allow substitution of securities in market repo transactions in order to facilitate development of the term money market; and
- consult with the Government on how to moderate the build-up of cash balances with the Reserve Bank.[13]

CASE

Liquidity Adjustment Facility (LAF)

The LAF, following international practice, as the operating procedure in India, was implemented in 2004. The LAF was operated through overnight fixed rate repo (central bank liquidity injection rate), and reverse repo (central bank liquidity absorption rate) to provide necessary guidance to market interest rate.

However, this procedure had two major drawbacks. First was the lack of a single policy rate. Consequently, the operating policy rate alternated between repo and reverse repo rates depending upon the prevailing liquidity condition. Second was the lack of a firm corridor which often led the implicit target rate ('call rate') breaching the upper and lower limits under liquidity stress conditions. Recognising these shortcomings, a new operating procedure was put in place in May 2011.

Revised LAF

The revised LAF retained the essential features of the earlier LAF framework with the following key modifications. First, the weighted average overnight call money rate was explicitly recognised as the operating target of monetary policy. Second, the repo rate was made as the only independent varying policy rate. Third, a new Marginal Standing Facility (MSF) was instituted under which scheduled commercial banks (SCBs) could borrow overnight at their discretion up to 1% (initially and currently 2%) of their respective net demand and time liabilities (NDTL) at 100 basis points above the repo rate. Fourth, the revised corridor was defined with a fixed width of 200 basis points. The repo rate was placed in the middle of the corridor, with the reverse repo rate 100 basis points below it and the MSF rate 100 basis points above it.

This operating framework is illustrated in Figure 10.3. The LAF corridor has been changed in April 2016 (see Section above).

---

[13]*Source:* https://www.rbi.org.in/scripts/BS_PressReleaseDisplay.aspx?prid=36654, as accessed on 24 March 2017 at 2pm

Who Decides the Monetary Policy in India?

Organisational Structure for Monetary Policy Decisions in the RBI

The responsibility, accountability and timing of decision-making relating to monetary policy remains with the Governor who is directly accountable to the Government of India. The RBI Act states that the Central Government shall appoint and remove the Governor and may give the RBI directions in the public interest.

Thus, in India, monetary policy decisions were made by the Governor alone. Indeed, quarterly policy statements were issued in the Governor's name. The process of monetary policy formulation in the RBI had, therefore, been traditionally internal.

Over time, the monetary policy formulation process became more consultative and participative with an external orientation. Following the introduction of quarterly policy reviews (April/May, July, October and January) in 2005, the RBI set up a Technical Advisory Committee on Monetary Policy (TACMP), with external experts in the areas of monetary economics, central banking, financial markets and public finance. The Committee was chaired by the Governor, with the Deputy Governor in charge of monetary policy as the vice-chairman and the other Deputy Governors of the RBI as internal members. The role of the TACMP has been purely advisory in nature.

In order to make monetary policy processes more transparent and predictable, the Expert Committee was asked to revise and strengthen the Monetary Policy Framework. In 2004, the Expert Committee also known as Urjit Patel Committee, felt that this consultative process of monetary policy making should be carried forward to its logical conclusion and be formalized into a decision-making process in preference over the purely advisory role of the TACMP.

As such, drawing on international experience, the evolving organizational structure in the context of the specifics of the Indian situation and the views of earlier committees, it recommended that monetary policy decision-making should be vested in a monetary policy committee (MPC).

In February 2016, the government of India announced the composition of the monetary policy committee (MPC), which would be mandated with the task of guiding interest rates in the economy. The proposed committee would have six members, with three appointed by the Reserve Bank of India (RBI) and the remaining nominated by an external selection committee. The RBI governor would have the casting vote in case of a tie.

Liquidity Management Framework and Operations in India

The liquidity management framework in India stands on two broad mutually reinforcing pillars of forward looking assessment.

Pillar-I is an assessment of the likely evolution of system-level liquidity demand based on near-term (four to six weeks) projections of autonomous drivers of liquidity. This forms the basis for taking decisions on use of discretionary liquidity absorbing/injecting measures to ensure that the liquidity conditions remain consistent with the goal of aligning money market rates to the policy repo rate.

TABLE 10.5 Current Liquidity Management Framework

Autonomous Drivers of Liquidity	Currency demand
	Bank reserves (required plus excess)
	Government's deposits with RBI
	Net forex market intervention
Liquidity Management	Net LAF (repo plus MSF plus reverse repo), Term Repos, OMOs, CRR, CMBs, MSS, Swaps, and Standing Refinance Windows

Pillar-II is an assessment of system-level liquidity over a relatively longer time horizon, focusing on the likely growth in broad money, bank credit and deposits, the corresponding order of base money expansion and this assessment is then juxtaposed with a breakdown into autonomous and discretionary drivers of liquidity derived under Pillar I.

Thus, Pillar II becomes the broader information set within which decisions relating to discretionary liquidity management measures are taken on the basis of Pillar I assessment.

Pillar-I

Liquidity management by the RBI primarily depends on near-term forecasts of the **autonomous drivers of liquidity**, particularly demand for currency (which reflects behavior of households), demand for excess reserves (which reflects behavior of the banking system), and the central government's balances with the RBI (which depends on cash flows of the Government). These form the core of Pillar-I.

Large fluctuations in the central government's balances with the RBI lead to corresponding automatic expansion/contraction in the RBI's balance sheet, which has a magnifying impact on the overall monetary conditions.

For the purpose of liquidity management, forex market intervention is also an autonomous driver of liquidity, but since there cannot be any near term forecasts for these interventions, they are considered on information as available – i.e., backward looking, impacting liquidity evolution on t+2 settlement basis (Table 10.5).

The extent of volatility seen in the major frictional drivers of liquidity has been large (Table 10.6), which poses the challenge of generating credible and precise

GO ONLINE
To understand the liquidity conditions and the operating procedure of monetary policy, access the half-yearly monetary policy report at https://rbi.org.in/Scripts/HalfYearlyPublications.aspx?head=Monetary%20Policy%20Report. The conditions for October 2016 are available at https://rbi.org.in/Scripts/PublicationsView.aspx?id=17385#4i2.

TABLE 10.6 Variations in Frictional Drivers of Liquidity since April 2012

(₹ crore)

Major Autonomous Determinants of Liquidity Conditions	Weekly Changes				Daily Changes			
	Positive		Negative		Positive		Negative	
	High	Low	High	Low	High	Low	High	Low
1 Govt. cash balances with the RBI	71,692	5	62,835	621	48,504	38	49,072	2
2 Currency Demand	25,160	80	15,282	90	N. A.			
3 SCB's balances with the RBI (changes in excess CRR)	55,916	57	90,182	571	48,090*	13	59,131	20

*Excluding the large change of ₹1,38,800 on July 16, 2013.
Source: https://rbi.org.in/scripts/PublicationReportDetails.aspx?UrlPage=&ID=747

short-term forecasts of liquidity demand in the system. Nevertheless, using a combination of forward looking information and a backward looking assessment of the time series evolution of the frictional determinants of liquidity, projections are generated on a regular basis to inform the RBI's decisions on discretionary liquidity management.

The RBI's discretionary liquidity management operations (primarily in the form of OMOs and changes in CRR, and also in terms of fixing limits for term repos and overnight repo amounts) is guided by the extent of LAF deficit that is 'reasonable' at any point of time, and the assessment of drivers of LAF deficit/surplus, i.e., whether frictional or structural.

Pillar-II

Broad money growth that is consistent with inflation and growth projections at the beginning of the year and reviewed from time to time in a state-contingent manner provides leads about the growth in base money that will be required in the system during the course of the year. After accounting for autonomous drivers of liquidity and borrowed reserves (i.e., access to LAF by banks), assessment of the amount of discretionary liquidity management operations becomes possible, given the desirable evolution of the base money path as also the extent of LAF deficit/surplus relative to a norm (communicated in the form of +/− 1% of NDTL). Rigid adherence to a base money rule is avoided due to uncertainties surrounding the relationship between monetary aggregates and the ultimate goal variables.

Transmission of Monetary Policy in India

Empirical evidence indicates that monetary transmission in India has been taking place through several channels. The broad consensus emerging from these studies is that monetary policy in India impacts output with a lag of about 2-3 quarters and WPI headline inflation with a lag of about 3-4 quarters and the impact persists for 8-12 quarters. Among the channels of transmission, the interest rate has been found to be the strongest.

Interest Rate Channel

Monetary policy interest rate movements have been found to share a co-integrating relationship with rates across different segments of financial markets. A bi-directional causality exists between call money rates and interest rates in other segments such as the government debt market, credit market or returns on equity market and the forex market. Medium to long term rates such as bank deposit and lending rates exhibit asymmetrical responses to policy rate changes under varied market conditions, responding faster with relatively larger responses in liquidity deficit conditions than in surplus conditions. Furthermore, lending rates for certain sectors such as housing and automobiles respond relatively faster to policy rate changes compared with other sectors.

Credit Channel

India is a bank-dominated economy, even though in recent years the role of equity and debt markets as sources of financing of economic activities has increased. The share of banks in domestic corporate borrowing has remained high. High-dependence on bank finance makes the bank lending and the balance sheet channels particularly important for monetary transmission. In terms of balance sheet effects, credit growth is seen to have an inverse relationship with movements in the policy rate.

Exchange Rate Channel

The exchange rate channel is found to be feeble in India with some evidence of weak exogeneity. While changes in policy interest rates may influence movements in exchange rates, the level of the exchange rate is not a policy goal, as the RBI does not target any level or band of the exchange rate. Exchange rate depreciation is a key source of risk to inflation as the estimated pass-through coefficients for India suggest.

Asset Price Channel

Empirical evidence for India indicates that asset prices, especially stock prices, react to interest rate changes, but the magnitude of the impact is small. Moreover, the wealth effect of increasing equity prices in the Indian case is found to be limited. With the increasing use of formal finance (from banks and non-banks) for acquisition of real estate, the asset price channel of transmission has improved. However, during periods of high inflation, there is a tendency for households to shift away from financial savings to other forms of savings such as gold and real estate that tend to provide a better hedge against inflation. To the extent that these acquisitions are funded from informal sources, they may respond less to contractionary monetary policy, thus weakening the asset price channel in India.

There are several impediments to the transmission of monetary policy such as sustained fiscal dominance, presence of a large informal sector and informal finance and financial and credit market frictions described below.

Impediments to Transmission of Monetary Policy

In India, financial sector reforms and progressive deregulation of the financial sector created pre-conditions for conducting monetary policy primarily through changes in the interest rate as the main policy instrument. The effectiveness of monetary policy, however, remains constrained by several country-specific factors that affect transmission of the policy impulses through the interest rate channel. Some of the major factors are briefly explained below.

1. Sustained Fiscal Dominance

Despite phasing out of the Reserve Bank's participation in primary issuances of Government securities (G-secs), fiscal dominance continues to impinge on monetary policy efficacy as open market operations are intermittently deployed to 'manage yields' in the face of large government borrowings. Data for the past decade show that whenever the net market borrowing of the government has increased, the ratio of incremental investment by banks in government securities has gone up, leading to lower share of non-food credit in bank finance, i.e., pointing to crowding out of the private sector (Figure 10.4 below).

i. Statutory Pre-emption through SLR Large government market borrowing has been supported by regulatory prescriptions under which most financial institutions in India, including banks, are statutorily required to invest a certain portion of their specified liabilities in government securities and/or maintain a statutory liquidity ratio (SLR). The SLR prescription provides a captive market for government securities and helps to artificially suppress the cost of borrowing for the Government, dampening the transmission of interest rate changes across the term structure. It is also observed that the Government often borrows at a negative real interest rate, especially in recent years. While banks generally invest in government securities above the statutory prescription since excess SLR securities serve as the only collateral for availing central bank resources under the LAF, a lower SLR prescription, ceteris paribus, is likely to decrease banks' investments in G-secs.

ii. Small Savings Schemes Besides market borrowings, the other main source of funding government deficits in India is small savings mobilised through, inter alia, post office deposits, saving certificates and the public provident fund, characterised by administered interest rates and tax concessions. The interest rates on small savings were earlier changed infrequently. Consequently, small savings in the past had acquired a competitive edge over bank deposits during the easing phase of monetary policy, as was evident during 2009–2010. The resultant substitution from bank deposits to small savings eroded the effectiveness of the monetary transmission mechanism, especially the bank lending channel.

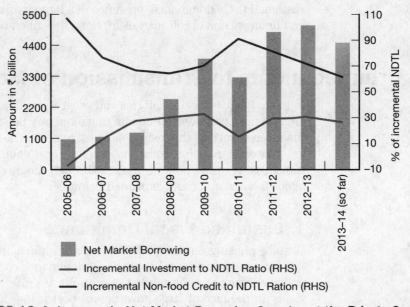

FIGURE 10.4 Increase in Net Market Borrowing Crowds out the Private Sector

Source: https://rbidocs.rbi.org.in/rdocs/PublicationReport/Pdfs/5CHAP4T270114.pdf, as accessed on 24 March 2017 at 2pm.

iii. Subventions The Government also influences the monetary policy transmission channel through its directives to banks. Keeping some economically and socially important objectives in mind, both the Central and State Governments offer interest rate subvention to certain sectors, including agriculture. There have also been non-interest subventions, such as the Agricultural Debt Waiver and Debt Relief Scheme in 2008.

iv. Taxation The tax advantage for the fixed maturity plans (FMPs) of the debt Mutual Funds of tenors of a year or more against fixed deposits of corresponding maturities also weakens the credit channel of monetary transmission. Similarly, to the extent the financial products of non-banks are not subjected to tax deduction at source, they have an advantage over bank deposits and weaken the transmission on the same grounds.

2. Large Informal Sector and Still Significant Presence of Informal Finance

Despite the growing reach of the formal banking and non-banking network, informal finance still caters to the financing requirements of the major part of India's population. The recourse to non-institutional sources is relatively high, both in rural and urban areas, particularly by lower income groups. Also, the cost of borrowing from informal/semi-formal sources is significantly higher than that of borrowing from banks (Table 10.7). High cost itself may be an impediment to transmission, particularly when incremental changes in the policy rate constitute only a small fraction of the overall funding costs. Thus, the significant presence of informal finance as well as its costs of intermediation can impede the impact of monetary policy on aggregate demand.

3. Financial and Credit Market Frictions, Bank Behaviour and Monetary Policy

There are certain facets of monetary policy that interface with credit and financial markets. In this context, market frictions and/or the endogenous response of the RBI to the demand for liquidity can weaken monetary transmission.

TABLE 10.7   Cost of Credit from Various Agencies in India

Lender Category	Interest Rate (% per annum)*
Self Help Groups (SHGs)	18–24
Microfinance Institutions (MFIs)	20–24
Informal credit providers	18–36
Banks (small borrowal accounts)	6–20

*Data pertains to 2006.
Source: Report on Currency and Finance, 2006–08, Reserve Bank of India. https://rbidocs.rbi.org.in/rdocs/PublicationReport/Pdfs/5CHAP4T270114.pdf, as accessed on 24 March 2017 at 2pm.

TABLE 10.8 **Asymmetry in Transmission in Different Phases of Monetary Policy Cycles (to Deposit and Lending Rates of Banks)**

Change (percentage points)				
	Tightening Phase (October 26, 2005 to October 19, 2008)	Easing Phase (October 20, 2008 to March 18, 2010)	Tightening Phase (March 19, 2010 to April 16, 2012)	Easing Phase (April 17, 2012 to July 15, 2013)
Repo Rate	3.00	−4.25.	3.75	−1.25
Modal Deposit Rate	2.38	−2.38	2.31	0.04
Modal Base Rate*	3.00	−2.00	2.75	−0.50
WALR	N.A.	N.A.	2.08	−0.49

*Base rate system was introduced from July 1, 2010. N. A. = Not Available.
Source: https://rbidocs.rbi.org.in/rdocs/PublicationReport/Pdfs/5CHAP4T270114.pdf, as accessed on 24 March 2017 at 2pm.

First, on the lending side, banks determine their interest rates with reference to the base rate. While banks are free to decide their base rates, they are required to take into consideration factors like cost of funds, adjustment for the negative in respect of CRR and SLR, overhead cost and a profit margin. The policy repo rate does not directly affect the determination of base rate of banks, except at the margin where wholesale funding is used. Even this role has greatly diminished, since wholesale funding (including borrowing from the Reserve Bank) constitute barely 10% of the total funds raised by banks (Table 10.8).

Secondly, with regard to deposits, while interest rates are re-priced when policy rates increase, this is only at the margin. A more complete transmission is impeded by the maturity pattern being largely concentrated in fixed tenor deposits. Moreover, the distribution of term deposits is tilted in favour of longer duration (i.e., one year and above) deposits. These fixed rate deposits, together with the pursuit of inflexible net interest margins by public sector banks, imparts rigidity to the entire interest rate structure.

Thirdly, the transmission of monetary policy to deposit and lending rates is sensitive to liquidity conditions prevailing at the time of a policy rate change and during the period thereafter. As shown in Table 10.9, cumulative increase of 175 bps in the repo rate in 2011–2012 was transmitted to both deposit and lending rates, albeit not nearly proportionately. In 2012–2013, however, the repo rate was cut by 100 bps, but despite the cut in CRR by 75 bps, deposit and lending rates did not soften much due to deficit and occasionally was tight in liquidity conditions. In 2013–2014, the cumulative increase in repo rate was 25 bps, but in the absence of any CRR cuts and because of the policy induced tightness in liquidity conditions, transmission to the modal deposit rate had been higher than the change in the policy rate. Empirical research for India corroborates the role of liquidity conditions in impacting the transmission—"monetary policy transmission is more effective during the liquidity deficit mode as compared to the surplus mode". Significant asymmetry is observed in the transmission of policy rate changes between the surplus and deficit liquidity conditions, suggesting that maintaining suitable liquidity environment is critical to yielding improved pass–through.

TABLE 10.9 Monetary Policy Transmission and Liquidity Conditions

Period	Change in Policy Rates (bps) Repo Rate	CRR	Average Liquidity Deficit* (₹ billion)	Modal Deposit Rate	Modal Base Rate	WALR
Q4 (2010–11)	50	–	–464	6.65	9.00	11.40
2011–12						
Q1	75	–	–378	7.08	9.50	11.45
Q2	75	–	–453	7.44	10.25	11.71
Q3	25	–	–916	7.46	10.50	12.24
Q4	–	–125	–1341	7.42	10.50	12.54
Change during the year	175	–125	–772	0.77	1.50	1.18
2012–13						
Q1	–50	–	–937	7.40	10.50	12.39
Q2	–	–25	–534	7.29	10.45	12.30
Q3	–	–25	–1046	7.33	10.25	12.18
Q4	–50	–25	–1101	7.31	10.20	12.18
Change during the year	–100	–75	–907	–0.11	–0.30	–0.40
2013–14						
Q1	–25	–	–847	7.26	10.20	12.11
Q2	25	–	–1007	7.46	10.25	12.21
Q3	25	–	–856	7.65	10.25	12.15#
Change up to Q3	25	–	–903	0.34	0.05	–0.03

*Include Repo, Reverse Repo, Term repo, MSF and ECR;
#Data relate to November;
'—' No change.
Source: https://rbi.org.in/scripts/PublicationReportDetails.aspx?UrlPage=&ID=748

Other Aspects of Monetary Policy Transmission

i. High Inflation and Financial Disintermediation High inflation in itself impedes transmission of monetary policy. This impact is exacerbated if interest rates on financial products do not adjust to inflation and yield negative returns. In India, gold and real estate compete with deposits, thereby constraining the degree of flexibility available to banks, particularly in lowering the deposit rates (given the fear of loss of deposits) in an easing phase of monetary policy. For four consecutive years between 2009–2010 and 2012–2013, average deposit rates remained below the CPI inflation for those years, whereas the annual return from gold and real estate exceeded CPI inflation most of the times, and by a significant margin as well.

ii. Endogenous Liquidity Under the Monetary Policy Framework Under the extant monetary policy framework, financing of large fiscal deficits through market borrowings has effectively resulted in the use of open market operations (OMO), primarily to smoothen G-sec yields rather than being employed as a pure monetary policy tool, contrary to cross-country practices which have increasingly favoured the separation of debt management operations from liquidity management.

In India, transmission has been impeded by: (a) not enforcing enough liquidity management discipline in the banking system; and (b) allowing excessive indirect monetisation of the fiscal deficit which also undermines the credibility of discretionary liquidity management operations. The LAF framework allows banks a complete freedom to access liquidity from the RBI at the repo rate, up to their excess SLR holdings. The cost of holding excess SLR gets reflected in the pricing of other assets.

As the government market's borrowing crowds out funds to the private sector, in turn placing pressure on liquidity, the central bank is often forced to accommodate the resultant liquidity shortages by providing additional liquidity through open market operations, especially via outright purchases of G-secs.

The net market borrowings of the central Government have increased 10-fold in the eight years till 2012–2013, even without counting for additional funding of ₹1.16 trillion through 364–day treasury bills during the terminal year. Even in 2010–2011, when monetary policy needed to be tightened aggressively and efforts were being made in that direction, large OMO purchases were affected. Reflecting these developments, OMO transactions have largely become one-sided in recent years and have turned into a dominant source of reserve money creation rather than a tool for managing liquidity mismatches. While some expansion of reserve money is consistent with the growth in broad money and nominal GDP is necessary (as set out under Pillar II), excessive monetary expansion at times results from indirect monetisation of the fiscal deficit through OMOs.

When the OMO cut-off yields in a given auction which are generally lower than the cut-off yield in the immediately following primary auction of G-secs, it creates opportunities for the banking system to profit from the RBI's liquidity management operations. In 2012–2013, in effect, 30% of the net borrowing requirement of the Government was supported through OMOs (Table 10.10).

Criteria for Choosing the Policy Instrument

Three criteria are applied when choosing a policy instrument: the instrument must be observable and measurable, it must be controllable by the central bank, and it must have a predictable effect on the goals.

Observability and Measurability   Quick observability and accurate measurement of a policy instrument is necessary because it will only be useful if it signals the policy stance rapidly. Reserve aggregates like nonborrowed reserves are straightforward to measure, but some lag still exists in reporting of other (e.g., M1, M2) reserve aggregates (a delay of two weeks). Short-term interest rates like the repo rate, by contrast, not only are easy to measure but also are observable immediately. Thus, it seems that interest rates are more observable and measurable than are reserves and, therefore, are a better policy instrument.

However, as we learned in Chapter 3, the interest rate that is easiest to measure and observe is the nominal interest rate. It is typically a poor measure of the real cost of borrowing, which indicates with more certainty what will happen to the real GDP. This real cost of borrowing is more accurately measured by the real interest rate—that is, the nominal interest rate adjusted for expected inflation ($i_r = i - \pi^e$). Unfortunately, real interest rates are extremely difficult to measure because we do not have a direct way to measure expected inflation. Given that both interest rates and aggregates have observability and measurability problems, it is not clear whether one should be preferred to the other as a policy instrument.

Controllability   A central bank must be able to exercise effective control over a variable if it is to function as a useful policy instrument. If the central bank cannot

TABLE 10.10 **Indirect Monetisation Eases Crowding-out Pressures but Affects Transmission of Changes in Repo Rate.**

Year	Net Market Borrowing (NMB) (₹ bn)	RBI Support through Direct Subscription and OMO* (₹ bn)	RBI Support as per cent of NMB	SCBs' Support to NMB (₹ bn)	SCBs' Support as % of NMB	Total Support from RBI and SCBs as % of NMB
1	2	3	4	5	6	7=4+6
2000–01	734	103	14	616	84	98
2001–02	908	–16	–2	711	78	77
2002–03	1041	–179	–17	1122	108	91
2003–04	889	–205	–23	1313	148	125
2004–05	509	–35	–7	642	126	119
2005–06	1062	–39	–4	–182	–17	–21
2006–07	1148	–51	–4	753	66	61
2007–08	1306	59	5	1826	140	144
2008–09	2470	945	38	1971	80	118
2009–10	3944	755	19	2226	56	76
2010–11	3264	672	21	1188	36	57
2011–12	4841	1342	28	2379	49	77
2012–13	5075	1545	30	2686	53	83

*Direct Subscription discontinued with effect from April 2006.
Courtesy: https://rbidocs.rbi.org.in/rdocs/PublicationReport/Pdfs/5CHAP4T270114.pdf, as accessed on 24 March 2017 at 2pm.

control the policy instrument, knowing that it is off track, it does little good because the central bank has no way of getting it back on track.

Because of shifts in and out of currency, even reserve aggregates such as non-borrowed reserves are not completely controllable. Conversely, the RBI can control short-term interest rates such as the policy repo rate very tightly. It might appear, therefore, that short-term interest rates would dominate reserve aggregates on the controllability criterion. However, a central bank cannot set short-term real interest rates because it does not have control over expectations of inflation. Once again, a clear-cut case cannot be made that short-term interest rates are preferable to reserve aggregates as a policy instrument, or vice versa.

Predictable Effect on Goals The most important characteristic of a policy instrument is that it must have a predictable effect on a goal. If a central bank can accurately and quickly measure the price of tea in China and can completely control its price, what good will that do? The central bank cannot use the price of tea in China to affect unemployment or the price level in its country. Because the ability to affect goals is so critical to the usefulness of any policy instrument, the tightness of the link from reserve or monetary aggregates to goals (output, employment, and inflation) or, alternatively, from interest rates to these goals, is a matter of much debate. In recent years, most central banks have concluded that the link between interest rates and goals such as inflation is tighter than the link between aggregates and inflation. For this reason, central banks throughout the world now generally use short-term interest rates as their policy instrument.

THE PRACTICING MANAGER

Using an RBI Watcher

As we have seen, the most important player in the determination of the Indian money supply and interest rates is the RBI. When the RBI wants to inject reserves into the system, it conducts open market purchases of approved government securities, which causes their prices to increase and their interest rates to fall, at least in the short term. If the RBI withdraws reserves from the system, it sells bonds, thereby depressing their price and raising their interest rates. From a long-run perspective, if the RBI pursues an expansionary monetary policy with high money growth, inflation will rise and interest rates will rise as well. Contractionary monetary policy is likely to lower inflation in the long run and lead to lower interest rates.

Knowing what actions the RBI might be taking can thus help financial institution managers predict the future course of interest rates with greater accuracy. Because, as we have seen, changes in interest rates have a major impact on a financial institution's profitability, the managers of these institutions are particularly interested in scrutinizing the RBI's behavior. To help in this task, managers hire so-called RBI watchers, experts on RBI behavior who may have worked in the RBI and so have an insider's view of RBI's operations.

Divining what the RBI is up to is by no means easy.

RBI watchers, with their specialized knowledge of the ins and outs of the RBI, scrutinize the public pronouncements of RBI officials to get a feel for where monetary policy is heading. They also carefully study the data on past RBI actions and current events in the bond markets to determine what the RBI is up to.

If an RBI watcher tells a financial institution manager that RBI concerns about inflation are high and the RBI will pursue a tight monetary policy and raise short-term interest rates in the near future, the manager may decide immediately to acquire funds at the currently low interest rates in order to keep the cost of funds from rising. If the financial institution trades foreign exchange, the rise in interest rates and the attempt by the RBI to keep inflation down might lead the manager to instruct traders to sell dollars in the foreign exchange market. As we will see in Chapter 14, these actions by the RBI would be likely to cause the value of the rupee to appreciate, so the sale of dollars by the financial institution should lead to substantial profits.

If, conversely, the RBI watcher thinks that the RBI is worried about a weak economy and will thus pursue an expansionary policy and lower interest rates, the financial institution manager will take very different actions. Now the manager might instruct loan officers to make as many loans as possible so as to lock in the higher interest rates that the financial institution can earn currently. Or the manager might buy bonds, anticipating that interest rates will fall and their prices will rise, giving the institution a nice profit. The more expansionary the policy is, it is also likely to lower the value of the rupee in the foreign exchange market, so the financial institution manager might tell foreign exchange traders to buy foreign currencies and buy dollars in order to make a profit when the rupee falls in the future.

An RBI watcher who is right is a very valuable commodity to a financial institution. Successful RBI watchers are actively sought out by financial institutions and often earn high salaries.

GO ONLINE

Access **https://www.rbi.org.in/home.aspx** and review what the RBI reports as its primary purposes and functions.

SUMMARY

1. The RBI's balance sheet comprises of assets and liabilities. The chief liabilities are currency in circulation and reserves. The chief assets are foreign currency assets, rupee securities and loans and advances.

2. Movements in the RBI's balance sheet occur either due to changes in the cash reserve ratios or due to open market operations (OMOs). An increase in the CRR impounds banks' reserves, leads to lesser loans and advances by the scheduled commercial banks, and hence lowers money supply, thereby having a contractionary impact. Similarly, an open market purchase by the RBI increases the monetary base and thereby has an expansionary impact.

3. The chief monetary tools used by the RBI are the cash reserve ratio (CRR), statutory liquidity ratio (SLR), refinance facilities, Liquidity adjustment facility (LAF), term repos, marginal standing facility (MSF), open market operations (OMOs), bank rate and the market stabilization scheme (MSS).

4. The RBI used several monetary and other administrative measures during the crisis following the Fed's announcement of the 'tapering' and the consequent depreciation of the rupee.

5. The six basic goals of monetary policy are price stability (the primary goal), high employment, economic growth, interest-rate stability, stability of financial markets, and stability in foreign exchange markets.

6. The goal of monetary policy in India is primarily price stability, while keeping in mind the objective of growth.

7. A nominal anchor is a key element in monetary policy strategy. It helps promote price stability by tying down inflation expectations and limiting the time-inconsistency problem, in which monetary policy makers conduct monetary policy in a discretionary way that might provide short-term benefits but produces poor long-run outcomes.

8. Inflation targeting has several advantages: (1) it enables monetary policy to focus on domestic considerations; (2) stability in the relationship between money and inflation is not critical to its success; (3) it is readily understood by the public and is highly transparent; (4) it increases accountability of the central bank; and (5) it appears to ameliorate the effects of inflationary shocks. It does have some disadvantages,

however: (1) inflation is not easily controlled by the monetary authorities, so that an inflation target is unable to send immediate signals to both the public and markets; (2) it might impose a rigid rule on policy makers, although this has not been the case in practice; and (3) a sole focus on inflation may lead to larger output fluctuations, although this has also not been the case in practice.

9. India follows flexible inflation targeting (FIT). As per the agreement between the Government of India and the RBI in February 2015, the RBI would bring down the inflation below 6% by January 2016, with the target for 2016–2017 and all subsequent years to be 4% with a band of $+/-2\%$.

10. Four lessons can be learned from the global financial crisis: (1) developments in the financial sector have a far greater impact on economic activity than was earlier realized; (2) the zero-lower-bound on interest rates can be a serious problem; (3) the cost of cleaning up after a financial crisis is very high; and (4) price and output stability do not ensure financial stability.

11. Achieving the monetary policy objectives requires articulation of a consistent monetary policy framework. For an effective implementation of monetary policy, the monetary policy framework needs a supporting operating procedure. The current operating framework of the monetary policy was implemented in September 2014, and was modified in the First bi-monthly report of the RBI in April 2016.

12. The monetary policy will be decided by a Monetary Policy Committee. In February 2016, the Government of India announced the composition of the monetary policy committee (MPC) which would be mandated with the task of guiding interest rates in the economy. The proposed committee would have six members, with three appointed by the Reserve Bank of India (RBI) and the remaining nominated by an external selection committee. The RBI governor would have the casting vote in case of a tie.

13. Because predicting the RBI's actions can help managers of financial institutions predict the course of interest rates, which has a major impact on financial institutions' profitability, such managers value the services of RBI watchers, who are experts on RBI behavior.

KEY TERMS

bubbles, p. 238
monetary policy tools, p. 213
deposit facility, p. 243
dual mandate, p. 222
excess reserves, p. 210
federal funds rate, p. 243
hierarchical mandate, p. 222
inflation targeting, p. 224
intermediate target, p. 242

macroprudential regulation, p. 241
monetary base, p. 212
natural rate of output, p. 220
natural rate of unemployment, p. 220
nominal anchor, p. 217
nonconventional monetary policy
    tools, p. 214
open market operations, p. 211
policy instrument, p. 243

potential output, p. 220
price stability, p. 216
primary dealers, p. 244
quantitative easing, p. 214
required reserves, p. 210
reserve money p. 209
reserve requirements, p. 212
reserves, p. 210
time-inconsistency problem, p. 218

QUESTIONS

1. "Unemployment is a bad thing, and the government should make every effort to eliminate it." Do you agree or disagree? Explain your answer.

2. Which goals of the RBI are frequently in conflict?

3. Which is of the following is an operating target, and explain why.

   a. Weighted average call rate

   b. Reserve money

   c. Money stock (M3)

4. What procedures can the RBI use to influence the three-month Treasury bill rate? Why does control of this interest rate imply that the RBI will lose control of the money supply?

5. If the RBI has an interest-rate target, why will an increase in the demand for reserves lead to a rise in the money supply?

6. "Interest rates can be measured more accurately and more quickly than the money supply. Hence an interest rate is preferred over the money supply as an intermediate target." Do you agree or disagree? Explain your answer.

7. Compare the monetary base to the money stock (M3) on the grounds of controllability and measurability. Which do you prefer as an intermediate target? Why?

9. Why is the composition of the RBI's balance sheet a potentially important aspect of monetary policy during a crisis?

9. What are the main advantage and the main disadvantage of an unconditional policy commitment?

10. What are the benefits of using a nominal anchor for the conduct of monetary policy?

11. Give an example of the time-inconsistency problem that you experience in your everyday life.

12. What incentives arise for a central bank to fall into the time-inconsistency trap of pursuing overly expansionary monetary policy?

13. What methods do an inflation-targeting central banks use to increase communication with the public and increase the transparency of monetary policy making?

14. Why might inflation targeting increase support for the independence of the central bank to conduct monetary policy?

15. "Because inflation targeting focuses on achieving the inflation target, it will lead to excessive output fluctuations." Is this statement true, false, or uncertain? Explain your answer.

16. "A central bank with a dual mandate will achieve lower unemployment in the long run than a central bank with a hierarchical mandate in which price stability takes precedence." Is this statement true, false, or uncertain?

17. If higher inflation is bad, then why might it be more advantageous to have a higher inflation target than a lower target closer to zero?

18. Why aren't most central banks more proactive at trying to use monetary policy to eliminate asset-price bubbles?

19. Why would it be better to *lean* against credit-driven bubbles and *clean* after other types of asset bubbles crash?

QUANTITATIVE PROBLEMS

1. Consider a bank policy to maintain 12% of deposits as reserves. The bank currently has ₹10 million in deposits and holds ₹400,000 in excess reserves. What is the required reserve on a new deposit of ₹50,000?

2. Estimates of unemployment for the upcoming year have been developed as follows:

Economy	Probability	Unemployment Rate (%)
Bust	0.15	20
Average	0.50	10
Good	0.20	5
Boom	0.15	1

What is the expected unemployment rate? The standard deviation?

3. The RBI wants to increase the supply of reserves, so it purchases 1 million dollars' worth of bonds from primary dealers. Show the effect of this open market operation using T-accounts.

4. Use T-accounts to show the effect of the RBI being paid back a ₹500,000 discount loan from a bank.

5. The short-term nominal interest rate is 5%, with an expected inflation of 2%. Economists forecast that next year's nominal rate will increase by 100 basis points, but inflation will fall to 1.5%. What is the expected change in real interest rates?

For Problems 6–8, recall from introductory macroeconomics that the money multiplier = 1/(required reserve ratio).

6. If the required reserve ratio is 10%, how much of a new ₹10,000 deposit can a bank lend? What is the potential impact on the money supply?

7. A bank currently holds ₹150,000 in excess reserves. If the current reserve requirement is 12.5%, how much could the money supply change? How could this happen?

8. The trading desk at the RBI sold ₹100,000,000 in T bills to the public. If the current reserve requirement is 8.0%, how much could the money supply change?

WEB EXERCISES

Conduct of Monetary Policy: Tools, Goals, Strategy, and Tactics

1. Go to **https//www.rbi.org.in**. What is the current policy repo rate? What is the current bank rate? Have short-term rates increased or declined since the end of 2005?

2. It is possible to access other central bank Web sites to learn about their structure. One example is the European Central bank. Go to **www.ecb.int**. On the ECB home page, find information about the ECB's strategy for monetary policy.

3. Many countries have central banks that are responsible for their nation's monetary policy. Go to **www.bis.org/cbanks.htm** and select one of the central banks (for example, Norway). Review that bank's Web site to determine its policies regarding application of monetary policy. How does this bank's policies compare to those of the U.S. central bank?

WEB APPENDICES

Please visit our Web site at **www.pearsonhighered.com/ mishkin_eakins** to read the Web appendix to Chapter 10: The RBI's Sheet and the Monetary Base.

CHAPTER

11

The Money Markets

> PREVIEW

If you were to review Apple's annual report for 2013, you would find that the company had over $11 billion in cash and equivalents. The firm also listed $18 billion in short-term securities. The firm chose to hold over $30 billion in highly liquid short-term assets in order to be ready to take advantage of investment opportunities and to avoid the risks associated with other types of investments. Apple will have much of these funds invested in the money markets. Recall that money market securities are short-term, low-risk, and very liquid. Because of the high degree of safety and liquidity these securities exhibit, they are close to being money, hence their name.

This chapter carefully reviews the money markets and the securities that are traded there. In addition, we discuss why the money markets are important to our financial system.

The Money Markets Defined

The term *money market* is actually a misnomer. Money—currency—is not traded in the money markets. Because the securities that do trade are short-term and highly liquid, they are close to being money. The money market is a key component of the financial system, as the monetary operations conducted by the central bank in its pursuit of monetary policy objectives critically hinges on it. Conceptually, it is a market for short-term funds which are deemed to be close substitutes of money, with maturity ranging from overnight to one year. The most important feature of the money market instrument is that they are liquid and can be turned in to money quickly at a low cost.

In terms of the above definition, money market performs three functions.

- It provides an equilibrating mechanism for demand and supply of short-term funds.
- It supports the borrowers and lenders of short-term funds to fulfill their borrowing and investment requirements at an efficient market clearing price.
- It provides an avenue for central bank intervention in influencing both quantum and cost of liquidity in the financial system, thereby transmitting monetary policy impulses to the real economy.

Money market transactions do not take place in any one particular location or building. Instead, traders usually arrange purchases and sales between participants over the phone and complete them electronically. Because of this characteristic, money market securities usually have an active *secondary market*. This means that after the security has been sold initially, it is relatively easy to find buyers who will purchase it in the future. An active secondary market makes money market securities very flexible instruments to use to fill short-term financial needs. For example, Microsoft's annual report states, "We consider all highly liquid interest-earning investments with a maturity of 3 months or less at date of purchase to be cash equivalents."

Another characteristic of the money markets is that they are **wholesale markets.** This means that most transactions are very large, usually in excess of ₹1 million. The size of these transactions prevents most individual investors from participating directly in the money markets. Instead, dealers and brokers, operating in the trading rooms of large banks and brokerage houses, bring customers together. These traders will buy or sell ₹50 or ₹100 million in mere seconds—certainly not a job for the faint of heart!

As you may recall from Chapter 2, flexibility and innovation are two important characteristics of any financial market, and the money markets are no exception. Despite the wholesale nature of the money market, innovative securities and trading methods have been developed to give small investors access to money market securities. We will discuss these securities and their characteristics later in the chapter.

Why Do We Need the Money Markets?

In a totally unregulated world, the money markets should not be needed. The banking industry exists primarily to provide short-term loans and to accept short-term deposits. Banks should have an efficient advantage in gathering information, an advantage that should eliminate the need for the money markets. Thanks to continuing relationships with customers, banks should be able to offer loans more cheaply than diversified markets, which must evaluate each borrower every time a new security is offered. Furthermore, short-term securities offered for sale in the money markets are neither liquid nor as safe as deposits placed in banks and thrifts. Given the advantages that banks have, why do the money markets exist at all?

The banking industry exists primarily to mediate the asymmetric information problem between saver-lenders and borrower-spenders, and banks can earn profits by capturing economies of scale while providing this service. However, the banking industry is subject to more regulations and governmental costs than the money markets. In situations where the asymmetric information problem is not severe, the money markets have a distinct cost advantage over banks in providing short-term funds.

Money Market Cost Advantages

Banks must put aside a portion of their deposits in the form of reserves that are held without interest at the Reserve Bank of India. Thus, a bank may not be able to invest 100% of every rupee it holds in deposits. This means that it must pay a lower interest rate to the depositor if the full deposit could be invested.

Interest-rate regulations were a second competitive obstacle for banks. The Indian financial system was subject to a system of administered interest rates until the 1990s. The process of financial deregulation began only in 1991. With less competition, regulators felt, banks were less likely to fail. The cost to consumers of the greater profits earned by banks because of the lack of free market competition was justified by the greater economic stability that a healthy banking system would provide.

One way the banking profits were assured was by regulations that set a ceiling on the rate of interest that banks could pay for funds. The financial liberalization in 1991 included interest rate deregulation, a phased reduction of the cash reserve ratio and statutory liquidity ratios, simplifying directed credit programs, development of money markets, etc. The system of administered interest rates was simplified, floor lending rates were fixed for large commercial borrowers while retaining fixed rates only for priority sector loans. Such a minimum lending rate too was eliminated in 1994. The deregulation of the Commercial paper (CP) markets and the markets for Certificates of Deposits (CDs) in 1992–1993, enabled companies to access credit at market rates lower than the minimum lending rate. Alongside the deregulation of interest rates, a number of new instruments such as the 14-day and 182-day treasury bills were introduced.

Such financial liberalization measures helped in the development of the money markets in India.[1] Central banks now operate on short-term policy rates, which under a regular term structure and a smooth market continuum would be able to influence long-term interest rates. In order to efficiently transmit monetary policy signals to long term rates, central banks foster development of the money market. The money market, thus, serves as the corner stone of a competitive and an efficient system of market-based intervention by the central bank. It stimulates an active secondary bond market by reducing the liquidity risk of bonds and other short term financial instruments and assists financial intermediaries in managing their liquidity risk. It also serves as the medium for government cash management.

Banks continue to provide valuable intermediation, as we will see in later chapters. In some situations, however, the cost structure of the banking industry makes

---

[1]https://www.rbi.org.in/scripts/PublicationReportDetails.aspx?ID=434; https://rbidocs.rbi.org.in/rdocs/Speeches/PDFs/SMMIED171212.pdf, as accessed on 24 March 2017 at 2pm.

it unable to compete effectively in the market for short-term funds against the less restricted money markets.

The Purpose of the Money Markets

The well-developed secondary market for money market instrument makes the money market an ideal place for a firm or financial institution to "warehouse" the surplus funds until they are needed. Similarly, the money markets provide a low-cost source of funds to firms, the government, and intermediaries that need a short-term infusion of funds.

The goal of most investors in the money market who are temporarily warehousing funds is not to earn particularly high returns on their funds. Rather, they use the money market as an interim investment that provides a higher return than holding cash or money in banks. They may feel that market conditions are not right to warrant the purchase of additional stock, or they may expect interest rates to rise and hence not want to purchase bonds. It is important to keep in mind that holding an idle surplus cash is expensive for an investor because cash balances earn no income for the owner. Idle cash represents an *opportunity cost* in terms of lost interest income. Recall from Chapter 4, that an asset's opportunity cost is the amount of interest sacrificed by not holding an alternative asset. The money markets provide a means to invest idle funds and to reduce this opportunity cost.

Investment advisers often hold some funds in the money market so that they will be able to act quickly to take advantage of investment opportunities they might identify. Most investment funds and financial intermediaries also hold money market securities to meet investment or deposit outflows.

The sellers of money market securities find that the money market provides a low-cost source of temporary funds. Table 11.1 shows the interest rates available on a variety of money market instruments sold by different firms and institutions.

Why do corporations and the Indian government sometimes need to get their hands on funds quickly? The primary reason is that cash inflows and outflows are rarely synchronized. Government tax revenues, for example, usually come only at

GO ONLINE

Go to the RBI website. Go into database on the Indian economy at **https://dbie. rbi.org.in/DBIE/dbic. rbi?site=home**. Access Money market on the left hand panel 'Indicators' to understand the daily money market operations. The Monthly RBI Bulletin under Time Series Publications gives details of CPs and CDs under 'Financial Markets'.

TABLE 11.1 Sample Money Market Rates, August 26, 2015

Instruments	Interest Rate (In %)
Call money (Overnight)	6.92 (Weighted average rate)
Collateralised borrowing and lending Rates (CBLO) (Overnight)	7.21 (Weighted average rate)
Market repo (Overnight)	7.24 (Weighted average rate)
Repo (Fixed overnight)	7.25
Reverse repo (Fixed)	6.25
Repo Variable (14 days)	7.30
Reverse repo variable (7 days)	7.24
Commercial paper	7.09–12.24 (August 15, 2015)
Certificate of deposits	6.65–7.36 (August 19, 2015)
Treasury bills (364 days)	7.54 (Cut off yield, yield to maturity)

Source: https://dbie.rbi.org.in/DBIE/dbie.rbi?site=publications.

certain times of the year, but expenses are incurred all year long. The government can borrow short-term funds that it will pay back when it receives tax revenues. Businesses also face problems caused by revenues and expenses occurring at different times. The money markets provide an efficient, low-cost way of solving these problems.

Who Participates in the Money Markets?

An obvious way to discuss the players in the money market would be to list those who borrow and those who lend. The problem with this approach is that most money market participants operate on both sides of the market. For example, any large bank will borrow aggressively in the money market by selling large commercial CDs. At the same time, it will lend short-term funds to businesses through its commercial lending departments. Nevertheless, we can identify the primary money market players—the Government of India (GoI), the Reserve Bank of India (RBI), primary dealers (PDs), scheduled commercial banks (SCBs), cooperative banks, private corporates, insurance companies, mutual funds, non-banking financial companies etc (summarized in Table 11.2).

Government of India

Government of India is a supplier (Borrower) of Treasury bills of varying maturities viz. 91, 182 and 364 days. The 91 and 182 days are essentially issued as a part of cash management, but the 364 day Treasury bills are issued as an instrument of financing fiscal deficit.

Reserve Bank of India

Reserve Bank of India conducts its monetary and liquidity management in the money market. As the debt manager of the government, it issues the calendar of Treasury bills and conducts the auction of Treasury bills.

TABLE 11.2   Money Market Participants

Participants	Role
Government of India	Sells Treasury bills of 91 days and 182 days as a part of cash management and 364 days treasury bills as a part of financing fiscal deficit
Reserve Bank of India	Injects/absorbs liquidity as a part of monetary policy operations
Primary dealers	Buy and sell government securities
Scheduled commercial banks	Buy and sell government securities and issue Certificates of Deposit
Cooperative banks	Buy and sell government securities
Private corporates	Buy and sell government securities and issue Commercial Paper (CP) for cash management
Insurance companies	Buy and sell government securities
Mutual funds	Buy and sell government securities
Non-banking finance companies	Buy and sell government securities

Primary Dealers

Primary dealers are financial institutions which hold a valid authorization from the RBI. PDs are permitted to buy and sell securities in the call money market.

Scheduled Commercial Banks

Scheduled bank means a bank (a banking company as defined in clause(c) of Section 5 of the Banking Regulation Act 1949) included in the Second Schedule of the Reserve Bank of India Act, 1934. They are permitted to buy and sell government securities in the money market.

Money Market Mutual Funds

Money Market Mutual Funds (MMMFs), were introduced in India in April 1991 to provide an additional short-term revenue to investors and to bring money market instruments within the reach of individuals. A detailed scheme of MMMFs was announced by the Reserve Bank in April 1992. The portfolio of MMMFs consists of short-term money market instruments. Investments in such funds provide an opportunity to investors to obtain yields close to short-term money market rates coupled with adequate liquidity. The Reserve Bank has made several modifications in the scheme to make it more flexible and attractive to banks and financial institutions. In October 1997, MMMFs were permitted to invest in rated corporate bonds and debentures with a residual maturity of up to one year, within the ceiling existing for CP's. The minimum lock in period was also reduced gradually to 15 days, making the scheme more attractive to investors

Additionally, private corporates, financial institutions, insurance companies and pension funds are also participants in the repo in corporate bonds, market repo and CBLO- both in overnight and term segments.[2]

Money Market Instruments

A variety of money market instruments are available to meet the diverse needs of market participants. One security will be perfect for one investor; a different security may be best for another. In this section, we gain a greater understanding of money market security characteristics and how money market participants use them to manage their cash.

Treasury Bills

Treasury bills or T-bills, which are money market instruments, are short-term debt instruments issued by the Government of India and are presently issued in three tenors, namely, 91-days, 182-days and 364-days. Treasury bills are zero coupon securities and pay no interest. They are issued at a discount and redeemed at the face value at maturity. For example, a 91-day Treasury bill of ₹100 (face value) may be issued at say ₹98.20, that is, at a discount of say, ₹1.80 and would be redeemed at the face value of ₹100. The return to the investors is the difference between the maturity value or the face value (that is ₹100) and the issue price. The Reserve Bank of India conducts auctions usually every Wednesday to issue T-bills. Payments

[2]*Source*: https://www.rbi.org.in/Scripts/PublicationsView.aspx?id=15762#10, as accessed on 24 March 2017 at 2pm.

for the T-bills purchased are made on the following Friday. The 91-day T-bills are auctioned on every Wednesday. The Treasury bills of 182 days and 364 days tenure are auctioned on alternate Wednesdays. T-bills of 364 days tenure are auctioned on the Wednesday preceding the reporting Friday while 182-days T-bills are auctioned on the Wednesday prior to non-reporting Fridays.

Details of Auctions of T-Bills in India

Type of T-Bill	Day of Auction	Day of Payment*
91-day	Wednesday	Following Friday
182-day	Wednesday of non-reporting week	Following Friday
364-day	Wednesday of reporting week	Following Friday

* If the day of payment falls on a holiday, the payment is made on the day after the holiday.

The Reserve Bank releases an annual calendar of T-bill issuances for a financial year in the last week of March of the previous financial year. The Reserve Bank of India announces the issue details of T-bills through a press release every week. Allottees at the auction are required to make payments by debit to their/custodian's current account.

CASE

Discounting the Price of Treasury Securities to Pay the Interest

Most money market securities do not pay interest. Instead, the investor pays less for the security than it will be worth when it matures, and the increase in price provides a return. This is called **discounting** and is common to short-term securities because they often mature before the issuer can mail out interest checks. (We discussed discounting in Chapter 3.)

Table 11.3 shows the results of a typical Treasury bill auction as reported on the RBI Web site. If we look at the first listing we see that the 91-day Treasury bill sold for ₹98.18 per ₹100. This means that a ₹1,000 bill was discounted to ₹981.8. The table also reports the discount rate percentage and the investment rate percentage. The discount rate percentage is computed as

$$i_{discount} = \frac{F - P}{F} \times \frac{360}{n} \tag{1}$$

where

$i_{discount}$ = annualized discount rate %
P = purchase price
F = face or maturity value
n = number of days until maturity

Notice a few features about this equation. First, the return is computed using the face amount in the denominator. You will actually pay less than the face amount, since this is sold as a discount instrument, so the return is underestimated. Second, a 360-day year (30×12) is used when annualizing the return. This also underestimates the return when compared to using a 365-day year.

TABLE 11.3   Recent Bill Auction Results

Security Term	Issue Date	Maturity Date	Discount Rate (per cent)	Investment Rate	Price per ₹100
91 days	8/21/2015	11/21/2015	7.2	7.4353	98.18
182 days	8/21/2015	2/22/2016	7.1208	7.4894	96.40
364 days	8/14/2015	8/13/2016	6.9131	7.536	93.01

The investment rate % is computed as

$$i_{investment} = \frac{F - P}{P} \times \frac{365}{n} \qquad (2)$$

The investment rate percentage is a more accurate representation of what an investor will earn since it uses the actual number of days per year and the true initial investment in its calculation. Note that when computing the investment rate percentage the Treasury uses the actual number of days in the following year. This means that there are 366 days in leap years.

EXAMPLE 11.1

Discount and Investment Rate Percent Calculations

You submit a non-competitive bid in August 2015 to purchase a 91-day Treasury bill, and you find that you are buying the bond for ₹98.18. What are the discount rate percentage and the investment rate percentage?

> Solution
Discount rate %

$$i_{discount} = \frac{₹100 - ₹98.18}{₹100} \times \frac{360}{91}$$

$$i_{discount} = 0.072 = 7.2$$

Investment rate %

$$i_{investment} = \frac{₹1000 - ₹981.8}{₹981.8} \times \frac{365}{91}$$

$$i_{investment} = 0.07435 = 7.4353$$

Risk   Treasury bills have virtually zero default risk because even if the government ran out of money, it could simply print more to redeem them when they mature. The risk of unexpected changes in inflation is also low because of the short term to maturity. The market for Treasury bills is extremely deep and liquid. A **deep market** is one with many different buyers and sellers. A **liquid market** is one in which securities can be bought and sold quickly and with low transaction costs. Investors in markets that are deep and liquid have little risk that they will not be able to sell their securities when they want to.

Treasury Bill Auctions

The RBI sells bills of varying maturities with a maximum tenor of upto 364 days on auction basis. The date and place of auction, and the exact tenor of bills are announced by the RBI from time to time.

The RBI notifies the nominal amounts[3] of bills to be sold to competitive bidders from time to time.

The RBI may make allocations at the auctions by means of either 'uniform price auction' or 'multiple price auction'. The method of auctions are announced by the RBI from time to time.

The Bills are issued at a discounted price.

In respect of competitive bids, the rate of discount and the corresponding issue price would be determined at each auction. In the case of uniform price auctions, competitive bids would be accepted at the minimum discounted price called cut-off price determined at the auction, irrespective of bid prices tendered. In the case of multiple price auction, competitive bids would be accepted upto the minimum discounted price called 'cut off' price determined at the auction, at bid prices tendered at the auction. Competitive bids at offer prices lower than the 'cut off' price are rejected in the case of both uniform and multiple price auctions (Illustrations in Box).

Allocation for 'non-competitive' bids are at the discretion of the RBI. These non-competitive bids are outside the notified amount. The allocation for 'non-competitive'

Illustration showing acceptance of Competitive bids on 'Uniform Price' and 'Multiple Price' Auction methods

Let us assume that RBI has notified an amount of ₹300 crore for competitive bidders in a Treasury bill auction and received the following bids.

Bidders	Bid Prices (In per cent)	Bid Amount (₹Crore)	Cumulative Bid Amount
A	98.5	90	90
B	98.4	60	150
C	98.35	80	230
D	98.3	70	300
E	98.2	85	385
F	98	30	415

Let us assume that the cut-off price fixed in the auction is ₹98.30 percent. Bids upto the cut-off price i.e. A, B, C & D will be accepted. E & F will be rejected. In the case of the 'Uniform Price' auction, each successful bidder will have to pay @ ₹98.30 irrespective of bid prices individually quoted. The total amount payable will be ₹98.30 x 300 = ₹294.90 crore; whereas in the case of Multiple Price Auction, each successful bidder will have to pay the bid price he had offered. The total amount payable will be (98.50 x 90) + (98.40 x 60) + (98.35 x 80) + (98.30 x 70) = ₹295.18 crore.

Source: http://finmin.nic.in/press_room/2016/Sale_ITBA19042016.pdf

---

[3]Nominal amount constitutes the face value of bonds/ bills that are being auctioned. In case of T-bills, the bidders quote discounted prices and bills are issued. The word 'nominal' is required as that will be the payable amount on the maturity date. "Notify" refers to the action of Government of India (GoI) giving the actual face value of T-Bills being auctioned.

bids is at the weighted average price arrived at on the basis of the competitive bids accepted at the auction.

The RBI has the full discretion to accept or reject any or all the bids either wholly or partially, as deemed fit by it, without assigning any reason.

The RBI may, if it considers appropriate to do so, participate in the auction as a 'non- competitor' and buy bills for part of or whole of the amount notified at the cut-off price[4] decided in the auction.

Eligibility for Investment

The investment in the Treasury Bills, through competitive route, may be made by any person resident in India, including firms, companies, corporate bodies, institutions and Trusts. Non-Resident Indians (NRIs, viz., Indian citizens and Persons of Indian origin), Foreign Institutional Investors (FIIs) registered with the Securities and Exchange Board of India (SEBI) and approved by Reserve Bank of India, and any other person not resident in India but specified by the Reserve Bank of India with the approval of the Government of India in this regard, are also eligible to invest in the Government Securities. However, investment by a person resident outside India or a Company which is incorporated outside India or any branch of such Company shall be subject to the provisions of the Foreign Exchange Management Act, 1999 and the Regulations framed there under, in addition to the other provisions of laws applicable to Government Securities.

A resident foreigner who is not an Indian citizen can invest if SEBI permits. The investment would be subject to FEMA.

Eligible entities could participate on 'non-competitive' basis in auctions for specified Bills as decided by the RBI from time to time. The State Governments, eligible provident funds in India, the Nepal Rashtra Bank and any Person or Institution, specified by the RBI, with the approval of Government, in this regard, can participate on non-competitive basis. Individuals can also participate on non competitive basis as retail investors. For retail investors, the allocation will be restricted to a maximum of 5 percentage of the aggregate nominal amount of the issue, within the notified amount as specified by the Government of India, or any other percentage determined by Reserve Bank of India.

(The allocation for individuals shall be within notified amount and for other eligible entities outside notified amount)[5].

---

[4]This is a legacy from 1998 and RBI was underwriting / subscribing to portion that market participants have not bid for. At that time, RBI was taking the T-Bills at the cut-off rate that emerges in auction. The situation has changed since enactment of FRBM and prohibition of RBI from subscribing to G-Sec/T-Bills in primary issuance (except under extraordinary circumstances). The possibility of RBI subscribing is now very remote and subject to FRBM Act. GOI can consider modifying the clause and changing it to weighted average price, but this is only theoretical. But one aspect that needs to be considered is that unlike other 'non- competitive bidders', RBI cannot buy T-bills outside notified amount. RBI would, in extreme cases, accept unsubscribed portion of notified amount, an allotment at cut-off price is more logical.

[5]In case of dated securities/ bonds, the non-competitive bidding allowed for individuals is within the notified amount. The same model is being used for T-bills for consistency sake. For State Governments/ Nepal Rashtra Bank; the transactions are huge and if they are allotted within the competitive portion of the notified amount, other bidders may not get allotment. Further, the transactions with States are cash neutral as the funds move from ITBs to ATBs. In case demand from individuals picks up, the position may be reviewed and retail individuals could be taken out of competitive portion and included in non-competitive portion with states.

Eligible Provident Funds are those non-government provident funds governed by the Provident Funds Act 1925 and Employees Provident Fund and Misc. Provisions Act, 1952 whose investment pattern is decided by the Government of India.

Tenders for purchase of Government of India Auction Treasury Bills:

Details of the procedure relating to auction for sale of the Bills are announced by the RBI from time to time.

Intending investors are required to submit their tender at the designated offices of the RBI, as notified by it, on the day of the auction, upto the close of banking hours for the issue of bills in the prescribed application form.

A competitive bidder is eligible to submit multiple tenders at different prices in separate forms.

Applications which do not contain necessary details such as the nominal value of the Bill and the price per ₹100/- at which the Bills are proposed to be purchased, are liable to be rejected without reference to the applicant.

The successful bidder/s then are required to deposit the requisite amount to the Bank by cash/ cheque/ DD/ e-banking/ Banker's Pay Order or by authorization to debit their current account at Reserve Bank of India.

The bidders are required to submit Cash/Cheque/DD/Banker's Pay Order[6], etc. in full while submitting their applications/ tenders.

Minimum Subscription

Bills are issued for a minimum amount of ₹10,000/- (Rupees Ten Thousand only) and in multiples of ₹10,000/- on competitive basis, as well as on non-competitive basis.

Form

The Bills are issued in the form of Promissory Note/ Credit to Subsidiary General Ledger (S.G.L.) Account.

The bills are transferable in terms of the Government Securities Act, 2006 and the Government Securities Regulations, 2007.

The Bills are repaid at par on the expiration of their tenor at the office of the RBI at which they are registered[7].

---

[6]The Government Securities Act allows physical bond issuance. There is presently no bar on individuals applying through physical application for competitive bids. The applications are accepted in RBI's Public Debt Offices and cheques etc. need to be enclosed. After the close of auction time, Public Debt Office (PDO) staff enter the details of physical applications in RBI's e-kuber system and RBI decides on allotment. In case of non-competitive bidding facility for individuals in dated securities auctions, individuals can submit bids only through Banks / Primary Dealers who will bid on behalf of individuals on RBI's e-kuber system. The Banks/primary dealers must ensure payment and RBI debits the concerned Bank / primary dealer. Operationally, this may not pose many hurdles—RBI has as yet not faced any instance of settlement failure in primary issuances.

[7]Almost (except for a miniscule percentage who can opt for physical certificate) all the T-bills are held in RBI's depository system in Mumbai. Hence, in general, the Core Banking Solution enables payment anywhere through ECS/ NEFT. Source: http://finmin.nic.in/press_room/2016/Sale_ITBA19042016.pdf.

**Copies of Tender documents used for purchase of Government
of India auction Treasury bills.**

FAX/TELEX

For: The Chief General Manager
        Public Accounts Department
        Reserve Bank of India

        _____

From:

        (Name) _____
        (Designation) _____
        (Address) _____
        _____

Dear Sir,

Tender for Government of India _____ @ day (Auction) Treasury Bills _____

I/We, the undersigned, hereby tender for purchase of _____ @ day Treasury Bills as set out
below at the auction to be held on _____.

     (i)   Nominal Value of _____ @ day ₹ _____
        Treasury Bills
     (ii) Form in which Treasury Bills are required Subsidiary General Ledger
         Account/Scrip

Undertaking

1.   On acceptance of my/our bid, I/we authorize Reserve Bank of India, Central
      Accounts Section, Nagpur, to debit our current account for value equivalent to
      the offer value of accepted bid. $

2.   On your acceptance of my/our bid, I/We, agree / undertake to immediately collect
      the letter of acceptance from your office. I/We undertake to deposit the requi-
      site amount at Reserve Bank of India, _____, on the day/time, as indicated
      therein/I/We authorize Reserve Bank of India, _____, to debit our Current
      Account for value equivalent to the offer value of accepted bid. $

I/We have read the Government notification no. _____ dated _____ and
hereby undertake to abide by them.

 (i) Signature: _____
    And office stamp of the bidder/s

 (ii) Designation: _____

@ indicate the appropriate number

(continued).

The Chief General Manager,
Public Accounts Department,
Reserve Bank of India

_____.

Dear Sir,

Tender for Government of India —— day @
Treasury Bills

I/We, the undersigned, hereby offer to purchase _____ day @ treasury bills as set out below at the auction to be held by you at your premises on _____.

   (i) Date of Auction   _____

   (ii) Name of Tenderer!!   _____

   (iii) Address   _____

   (iv) Telephone No.   _____

   (v) SGL Account No., PAD, (_____) @@ (for Treasury Bills)   _____

   (vi) Current Account NO. at DAD, (_____) @@   _____

   (vii) Nominal value of ____ day @ Treasury Bills   ₹ _____

   (viii) The price at which the bills are proposed to be purchased Per ₹ One hundred (nominal) #   ₹ _____

   (ix) Total purchase price of ____ day @ Treasury Bills #   ₹ _____
                                      (upto two decimals)

   (x) Form in which Treasury Bills are required credit to Subsidiary General Ledger Account / Scrip $

Undertaking

On your acceptance of my/our bid, I/We, agree/undertake to immediately collect the letter of acceptance from your office. I/We undertake to deposit the requisite amount at Reserve Bank of India, _____, on the day/time, as indicated therein / I/We authorize Reserve Bank of India, _____, to debit our Current Account for value equivalent to the offer value of accepted bid. $

I/We have read the Government notification no. _____ dated _____ and hereby undertake to abide by the requirements stated therein.

*(Ist) Signature: **(Ist) Signature:

   Designation: Designation:

(2nd) Signature: (2nd) Signature:

   Designation: Designation:

Office Stamp of the Bidder/s

@ Appropriation number to be filled in.
@@ Kindly mention the name of the office at which these accounts are maintained.
!! If the application is on behalf of a constituent, please indicate the name of the constituent.

Not to be filled in by non-competitive bidders.
$ Strike out whichever is not applicable.
* Those empowered to operate on the SGL Account with PAD.
** Those Authorized to operate on the Current Account with DAD, RBI.
(where applicable).

NOTES

(1) If the applicant's signature is by thumb mark, it should be witnessed by two persons. The full names, occupations and addresses of the witnesses should be appended to their signatures.

(2) If the application is made in the name of a registered body, the undernoted documents, if not already registered at the Public Debt Office, should be submitted to the Public Debt Office along with the investment amount:-

   (i) Certificate of Incorporation/Registration in original or a copy thereof certified as true by the issuing authority under his office seal.
   (ii) Certified copies of Memorandum and Articles of Association of the Rules and Regulations/Bye-laws of the company/body.
   (iii) Certified copy of resolution in favour of the person/s authorized to deal in Government Securities on behalf of the company/body together with his / their duly attested specimen signature (s).

Treasury Bill Interest Rates   Treasury bills are very close to being risk free. As expected for a risk-free security, the interest rate earned on Treasury bill securities is among the lowest in the economy. Investors in Treasury bills have found that in some years, their earnings did not even compensate them for changes in purchasing power due to inflation. Figure 11.1, shows the interest rate on Treasury bills and the inflation rate over the period 2000–2015. As discussed in Chapter 3, the *real rate* of interest has occasionally been less than zero. Several times since 2000 the inflation rate matched or exceeded the earnings on T-bills. Clearly, the T-bill is not an investment to be used for anything but temporary storage of excess funds because it may not even keep up with inflation.

Call Money

The call/notice money market forms an important segment of the Indian Money Market. Funds are transacted on an overnight basis in the call money market, and for a period of 2–14 days in the notice money market. Figure 11.2 depicts the volume and interest rates in the call money market over the period July 28, 2015 to September 1, 2015.

Since August 2005, the uncollateralised call money market in India is restricted to banks and Primary Dealers (PDs), subject to prudential limits. Banks/PDs/co-operative banks may, with the approval of their Boards, arrive at the prudential limits for borrowing/lending in call/notice money market in terms of the guidelines given. The limits so arrived at may be conveyed to the Clearing Corporation of India Ltd. (CCIL), for setting of limits in the Negotiated Dealing System-Call, i.e. NDS CALL System (a screen–based, negotiated, quote-driven system), under advice of the Financial Markets Regulation Department (FMRD) and Reserve Bank of India.

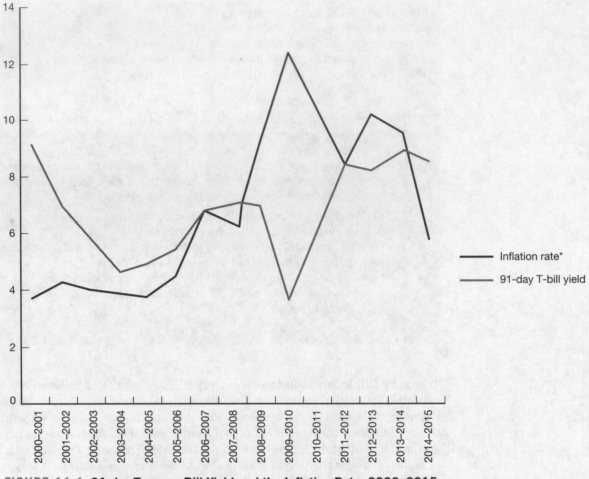

FIGURE 11.1 91-day Treasury Bill Yield and the Inflation Rate, 2000–2015

Courtesy: https://www.rbi.org.in/Scripts/AnnualReportPublications.aspx?Id=265, as accessed on 21 March 2017 at 10.30am.

The prudential limits of SCBs and PDs are indicated below:

Institutions	Borrowing	Lending
SCBs	On a fortnightly average basis, borrowing outstanding amount should not exceed 100% of capital funds (i.e., sum of Tier I and Tier II capital) of latest audited balance sheet. However, banks are allowed to borrow a maximum of 125% of their capital funds on any day, during a fortnight.	On a fortnightly average basis lending outstanding amount should not exceed 25% of their capital funds. However, banks are allowed to lend 50% of their capital funds any day during the fortnight.
PDs	PDs are allowed to borrow, on average in a reporting fortnight, up to 200% of their net owned funds (NOF) as at end-March of the previous financial year	PDs are allowed to lend in call/notice money market, on an average in a reporting fortnight, up to 25% of their NOF.

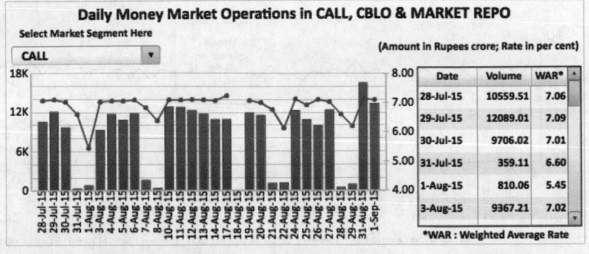

FIGURE 11.2 Volume and Interest Rates in the Call Money Market

Courtesy: http://dbie.rbi.org.in/DBIE/dbie.rbi?site=home, as accessed on 21 March 2017 at 10.30am.

Scheduled commercial banks (excluding RRBs), co-operative banks (other than Land Development Banks), and Primary Dealers (PDs), are permitted to participate in call/notice money market both as borrowers and lenders. Non-bank institutions (other than PDs), are not permitted in the call/notice money market. All dealings in call/notice/term money executed on the NDS-Call do not require separate reporting.

GO ONLINE
Access **https://www. rbi.org.in/Scripts/ BS_PressReleaseDisplay. aspx?prid=34857** to find detailed information on WACR.

Terms and Interest Rate of Call Money Call money is an overnight money market instrument, while the term segment is called Notice Money, with a tenor of 2 to 14 days.

Eligible participants are free to decide on interest rates in call/notice money market. The RBI releases the weighted average call rate (WACR) on a daily basis. For example, on August 29, 2015, WACR was 6.16 %.

Purpose of Call Money In India, the WACR is currently the operating target of monetary policy. Once the RBI announces the policy rate in its monetary policy statement, the operating procedure is aimed at modulating liquidity conditions so as to achieve the operating target i.e. to anchor the WACR around the policy rate.

Collateralized Borrowing and Lending Obligation (CBLO)

Collateralized Borrowing and Lending Obligation (CBLO), as the name implies is a fully collateralized and secured instrument for borrowing / lending money. CBLO is a money market instrument, which was introduced in 2003. This market was developed for the benefit of entities, which had either been phased out from the interbank call money market or had restricted access to the call money market. CBLO is

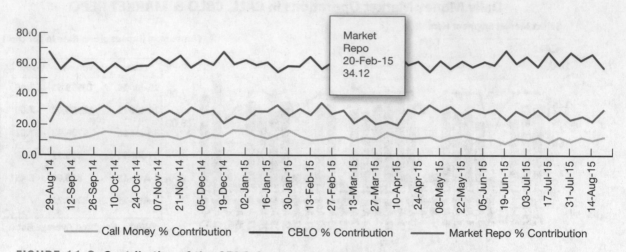

Movement in Call Money, CBLO and Market Repo Turnover

Market
Repo
20-Feb-15
34.12

Call Money % Contribution · CBLO % Contribution · Market Repo % Contribution

FIGURE 11.3 **Contribution of the CBLO Segment in the Overall Money Market**

Courtesy: http://dbie.rbi.org.in/DBIE/dbie.rbi?site=home, as accessed on 21 March 2017 at 10.30am.

a discounted instrument available through the Clearing Corporation of India Limited (CCIL). The maturity period ranges from one day to upto one year.

The collateralised market is now the predominant segment of the money market as seen in Figure 11.3. This has also provided an alternative avenue for banks to park their surplus funds beyond one day. Membership to the CBLO segment is generally extended to the repo eligible entities as per the RBI guidelines. Entities who have been granted CBLO membership are classified based on their NDS membership. CBLO members who are also NDS members are CBLO (NDS) members and other CBLO members are CBLO (Non NDS) members or associate members. Banks, financial institutions, insurance companies, mutual funds, primary dealers, NBFCs, provident/pension funds etc. are the participants in the CBLO market. The members are required to open an account for depositing securities, which are offered as collateral/margin for borrowing and lending. Eligible securities are central government securities including treasury bills.

CBLO has been conceived and developed by the Clearing Corporation of India Limited (CCIL), for facilitating deployment in a collateralized environment. The CBLO Dealing system is hosted and maintained by Clearcorp Dealing Systems (India) Ltd, a fully-owned subsidiary of CCIL. CCIL becomes a central counterparty to all CBLO trades and guarantees settlement of CBLO trades.

CBLO is an RBI approved money market instrument, which can be issued for a maximum tenure of one year. CBLO is a discounted instrument traded on yield time priority. CBLO instruments that are generally made available for trading are those with maturity of next seven business days and three month end dates. The balances are maintained in an electronic book entry. The access to CBLO dealing system for NDS members is made available through InfiNet and for-non NDS members through Internet. For members who maintain an RBI current account and are allowed to operate that current account for settlement of their secondary market transactions, funds settlement in the CBLO segment is achieved in the books of the RBI. In respect of other members, CBLO funds are settled in the books of the Settlement Bank.

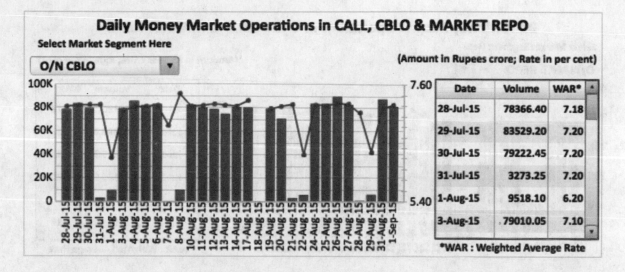

FIGURE 11.4 Volume and Interest Rates in the CBLO Market

Courtesy: http://dbie.rbi.org.in/DBIE/dbie.rbi?site=home, as accessed on 21 March 2017 at 10.30am.

Eligible securities are Central Government securities, including Treasury bills as specified by CCIL from time to time.[8] Figure 11.4 depicts the volume and interest rates on the CBLO markets over the period July 28, 2015 to September 1, 2015.

Repurchase Agreements

There are different players and instruments through which repurchase agreements are conducted. Market participants, as also the Indian central bank—the RBI—conduct repos of various types. These repos are conducted both overnight, as also in the term segment with a tenure of 2 to 14 days.

Market Repo   Repurchase agreements (repos) are recognized as a very useful money market instrument, which enable smooth adjustment of short-term liquidity among various categories of market participants such as banks, financial institutions, securities and investment firms. Unlike call/notice/term money transactions (which are non-collateralized), repos are fully collateralized by securities.

Market repos have several advantages over other collateralized instruments as well:

- While obtaining titles to securities in other collateralized lending instruments is a time-consuming and uncertain process, repos entail instantaneous legal transfer of ownership of the eligible securities.
- They help to promote greater integration between the money market and the government securities markets, thereby creating a more continuous yield curve.
- Repos are powerful and flexible money market instruments for modulating market liquidity. Since these are market-based instruments, they serve the purpose of an indirect instrument of monetary policy at the short-end of the yield curve.

---

[8]Source: https://www.ccilindia.com/CBLO/Pages/Introduction.aspx.

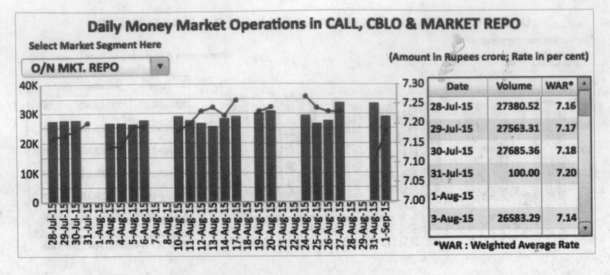

FIGURE 11.5 **Volume and Interest Rates in the Market Repo Market**

Courtesy: http://dbie.rbi.org.in/DBIE/dbie.rbi?site=home, as accessed on 21 March 2017 at 10.30am.

Since forward trading in securities was generally prohibited in India, repos were permitted under regulated conditions in terms of both, participants and instruments. Both banks and non-banks were allowed to participate in the market. All government securities and PSU bonds were eligible for repos till April 1988. Between April 1988 and mid June 1992, only inter-bank repos were allowed in all government securities. Double ready forward transactions[9] were part of the repos market throughout this period. Subsequent to the irregularities in securities transactions that surfaced in April 1992, repos were banned in all securities, except Treasury bills, while double-ready forward transactions were prohibited altogether. Repos were permitted only among banks and PDs. Reforms in this market have encompassed both institutions and instruments. Figure 11.5 depicts the volume and interest rates in the market repo market between July 28, 2015 and September 1, 2015.

Repo in Corporate bonds As part of the measures to develop the corporate bond market, repo transactions were permitted in corporate debt securities in 2010. In 2013, certain improvements were introduced. Listed corporate debt securities of original maturity of more than one year, which were rated 'AA' or above by the rating agencies, that were held in the security account of the repo seller in demat form, were deemed eligible for undertaking repo.

Commercial Papers (CPs), Certificates of Deposit (CDs) and Non-Convertible Debentures (NCDs) of less than one year of original maturity were also permitted as eligible security for undertaking repo in corporate debt. While listing requirements were not applicable for these money market instruments to be eligible as security for undertaking repo in corporate debt, rating requirements as specified by the RBI were applicable. These directions were referred to as the repo in

---

[9]A repo is also sometimes called a ready forward transaction as it is a means of funding by selling a security held on a spot (ready) basis and repurchasing the same on a forward basis. When an entity sells a security to another entity on repurchase agreement basis and simultaneously purchases some other security from the same entity on resell basis it is called a double-ready forward transaction.

TABLE 11.4   Liquidity Operations by the RBI

Liquidity Operations by RBI							
							(₹ Billion)
Date	Liquidity Adjustment Facility			MSF	Standing Liquidity Facilities	OMO (Outright)		Net Injection (+)/Absorption (-) (1+3+4+5+7-2-6)
	Repo	Reverse Repo	Term Repo			Sale	Purchase	
	1	2	3	4	5	6	7	8
3/18/2014	408.13	31.88	–	160.85	237.02	–	–	774.12
3/19/2014	409.03	24.02	100.04	119.87	2.11	–	–	607.03
3/20/2014	398.98	27.64	–	90.75	7.50	–	–	469.59
3/21/2014	373.84	29.63	400.09	176.30	–104.36	–	–	816.24

Corporate Debt Securities (Amendment) Directions, 2013 and were effective from January 8, 2013.[10]

Liquidity Adjustment Facility

Liquidity management refers to managing the appropriate level of liquidity and overall monetary conditions. For a central bank, the concept of liquidity management typically refers to the framework and set of instruments that the central bank follows in steering the amount of bank reserves in order to anchor the money market interest rates around the policy rate. Central bank liquidity management is important for its power to exercise influence and control over short-term interest rates and thereby affecting the entire interest rate term structure. This in turn, determines the effectiveness of monetary policy transmission. Central bank liquidity management has short-term effects on financial markets. However, the medium-term implications for the real sector and the inflation situation are particularly important.

Table 11. 4 contains information on daily injection/ absorption of liquidity by the RBI in the market through LAF (Liquidity Adjustment Facility like Repo, Term-Repo, Reverse Repo and MSF), Standing Liquidity Facilities and Open Market Operations (OMOs). OMO (outright) excludes RBI's agency operations. As per the standard practice, only data pertaining to one week (daily) needs to be published in this table.

As a part of the financial sector reforms in 1998 under the Committee on Banking Sector Reforms (Narasimham Committee II), Liquidity Adjustment Facility (LAF) was introduced under which the Reserve Bank would conduct auctions periodically, if not necessarily daily. The Reserve Bank could reset its repo and reverse repo rates, which would in a sense provide a reasonable corridor for the call money market. Figure 11.6 depicts the relationship between the weekly average call rate and the LAF corridor. At present, daily LAF operations are being conducted on an overnight basis, in addition to term repo auctions.

Repurchase Agreement (Repo) by RBI   Repo is a money market instrument combining elements of two different types of transactions *viz.*, lending-borrowing, and sale-purchase. The Repo transaction has two legs, which can be explained as follows – in the first leg, the seller sells securities and receives cash while the purchaser buys securities and parts with cash. In the second leg: the original holder repurchases

---

[10]https://www.rbi.org.in/scripts/NotificationUser.aspx?Id=7792&Mode=0, as accessed on 22 March 2017 at 4.30pm.

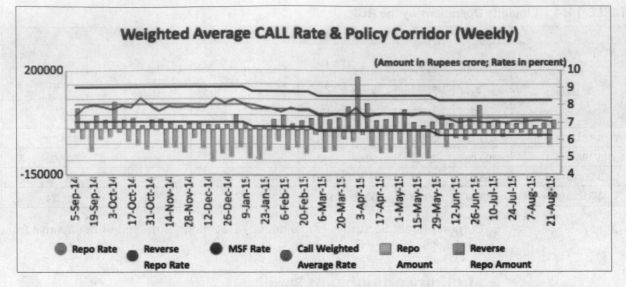

Weighted Average CALL Rate & Policy Corridor (Weekly)

(Amount in Rupees crore; Rates in percent)

Repo Rate • Reverse Repo Rate • MSF Rate • Call Weighted Average Rate • Repo Amount • Reverse Repo Amount

FIGURE 11.6 Weighted Average Call Rate and Liquidity Adjustment Facility (LAF)

Courtesy: http://dbie.rbi.org.in/DBIE/dbie.rbi?site=home, as accessed on 22 March 2017 at 4.30pm.

the securities by paying to the counterparty, the amount originally received by him plus the return on the money for the number of days for which the money was used by him, which was mutually agreed upon. Under Repo, the Reserve Bank of India injects funds to organisations (SCBs and Primary Dealers), which have both current account and SGL account with the Reserve Bank of India.

Reverse Repo by RBI   This is exactly the opposite of the Repo transaction and is used for absorption of liquidity. The Reverse Repo Rate at present is at 50 basis points below the repo rate. Reverse Repo facility is available to Primary Dealers also.

Marginal Standing Facility by RBI   In 2011, The Reserve Bank of India introduced Marginal Standing Facility (MSF), for banks and primary dealers to reduce the volatility in the inter-bank call money market. The interest rate was fixed at 100 bps above the repo rate, which is the rate at which banks borrow from the RBI for the short-term against the collateral of government securities. The rate may vary relatively to the repo rate as warranted by economic conditions. Currently, the MSF is 50 basis points above the repo rate.

Term Repos   Term repo is a new window for providing liquidity to the banking system. The RBI conducts term repo auctions of 7-day and 14-day tenure for a combined notified amount equivalent to 0.75% (at present), of net demand and time liabilities (NDTL) of the banking system. There are variable rate auctions conducted every Friday, since the beginning of October 11, 2013. Additional term repos of tenures ranging from 5-day to 28-day have also been auctioned on the basis of periodic assessment of liquidity conditions. The notified amount and tenure of the term repo auctions is announced prior to the dates of the auctions.[11] Figure 11.7 shows the volume and interest rates in the term money market for the period 28 July 2015 to September 1, 2015.

GO ONLINE
Access **https://rbi.org.in/scripts/NotificationUser.aspx?Id=8501&Mode=0** to understand the operational guidelines for the term repos under the LAF.

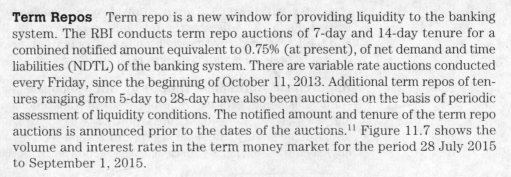

[11]*Source:* https://www.rbi.org.in/Scripts/PublicationsView.aspx?id=15762#10, as accessed on 25 March 2017 at 8pm.

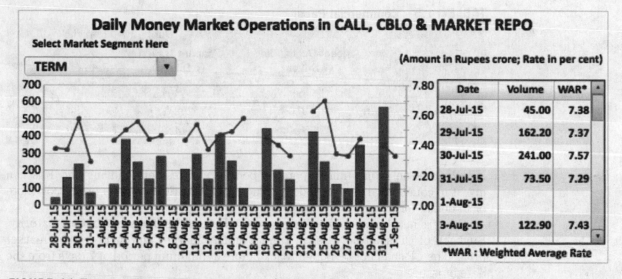

FIGURE 11.7 Volume and Interest Rates in the Term Money Market

Courtesy: http://dbie.rbi.org.in/DBIE/dbie.rbi?site=home, as accessed on 22 March 2017 at 4.30pm.

Commercial Paper

Commercial Paper (CP), is an unsecured money market instrument issued in the form of a promissory note. CP was introduced in India in January 1990 with a view to enable highly rated corporate borrowers to diversify their sources of short term borrowings and to provide an additional instrument to investors. Corporate, PDs and all-India financial institutions are permitted to issue commercial paper to enable them to meet their short term funding requirements for their operations.

A company would be eligible to issue CP provided that:

- The tangible net worth of the company, as per the latest audited balance sheet, is not less than ₹4 crore;
- The company has been sanctioned a working capital limit by banks or FIs; and
- The borrowal account of the company is classified as a standard asset by the financing bank/institution.

CPs are issued at a discount to face value as may be determined by the user. CPs are freely transferable; banks, financial institutions, insurance companies and others are able to invest their short-term surplus funds in a highly liquid instrument at attractive rates of return. The terms and conditions relating to issuing CPs such as eligibility, maturity periods and modes of issue have been gradually relaxed over the years by the Reserve Bank of India.

Table 11.5 contains the information on face value of outstanding amount of commercial paper, face value of the amount issued during the fortnight as well as the range of rate of interest. Rate of interest is the typical effective discount rate range per annum on issues during the fortnight.

Commercial paper is issued for 7 days to one year maturity in denomination of minimum ₹5 lakh and multiples of ₹5 lakh at a discount and redeemed at face value. Individuals, banking companies, other corporate bodies registered or

TABLE 11.5 **Commercial Paper**

| | Amount Outstanding (₹ Billion) | During the Fortnight | |
| | | Amount Issued (₹ Billion) | Rate of Interest % |
Fortnight Ended	**1**	**2**	**3**
2/28/2014	1,646.0	292.0	7.84–13.06
3/15/2014	1,653.4	414.2	7.96–14.18

incorporated in India, unincorporated bodies, non-resident Indians and FIIs can invest in commercial paper. Mode of issue is either in the form of a promissory note or in demat form.

Issuers may buyback the CP, issued by them to the investors, before maturity. Buyback of CP shall be through the secondary market and at prevailing market price. The CP shall not be bought back before a minimum period of 7 days from the date of issue.

Eligible participants/issuers need to obtain a credit rating for issuance of CP from any one of the Credit Rating Agencies (CRAs), registered with the Securities Exchange Board of India (SEBI). The minimum credit rating is 'A3' as per rating symbol and definition prescribed by SEBI. The issuers have to ensure at the time of issuance of the CP, that the rating so obtained is current and has not fallen due for review.[12]

Certificate of Deposits

A Certificate of Deposit (CD), is a negotiable money market instrument and is issued in dematerialised form or as a usance promissory note against funds deposited at a bank or other eligible financial institution for a specified time period. Guidelines for issue of CDs are presently governed by various directives / guidelines issued by the Reserve Bank of India (RBI), as amended from time to time.

CDs can be issued by, (i) scheduled commercial banks {excluding Regional Rural Banks and Local Area Banks}; and (ii) select All-India Financial Institutions (FIs) that have been permitted by RBI to raise short-term resources within the umbrella limit fixed by RBI.

Minimum amount of a CD should be ₹1 lakh, i.e., the minimum deposit that could be accepted from a single subscriber should not be less than ₹1 lakh, and in multiples of ₹1 lakh thereafter.

CDs can be issued to individuals, corporations, companies (including banks and PDs), trusts, funds, associations, etc. NRIs may also subscribe to CDs, but only on non-repatriable basis, which should be clearly stated on the certificate. Such CDs cannot be endorsed to another NRI in the secondary market.

CDs issued by banks should not have a maturity period of less than seven days and not more than one year from the date of issue. FIs can issue CDs for a period not less than one year and not exceeding three years from the date of issue.

CDs may be issued at a discount on face value. Banks / FIs are also allowed to issue CDs on floating rate basis, provided the methodology of compiling the floating rate is objective, transparent and market-based. The issuing bank / FI is free to determine the

---

[12]*Source*: https://www.rbi.org.in/Scripts/PublicationsView.aspx?id=15762#10, as accessed on 25 March 2017 at 8pm.

discount / coupon rate. The interest rate on floating rate CDs would have to be reset periodically in accordance with a pre-determined formula that indicates the spread over a transparent benchmark. The investor should be clearly informed of the same.

Banks have to maintain appropriate reserve requirements, i.e., cash reserve ratio (CRR) and statutory liquidity ratio (SLR), on the issue price of the CDs.

CDs in physical form are freely transferable by endorsement and delivery. CDs in demat form can be transferred as per the procedure applicable to other demat securities. There is no lock-in period for the CDs.[13]

Banker's Acceptances

A banker's acceptance is an order to pay a specified amount of money to the bearer on a given date. Banker's acceptances have been in use since the 12th century. However, they were not major money market securities until the volume of international trade ballooned in the 1960s. They are used to finance goods that have not yet been transferred from the seller to the buyer. For example, suppose that Kalpataru Construction Company wants to buy a bulldozer from Komatsu in Japan. Komatsu does not want to ship the bulldozer without being paid because Komatsu has never heard of Kalpataru and realizes that it would be difficult to collect if payment were not forthcoming. Similarly, Kalpataru is reluctant to send money to Japan before receiving the equipment. A bank can intervene in this standoff by issuing a banker's acceptance where the bank in essence substitutes its creditworthiness for that of the purchaser.

Because banker's acceptances are payable to the bearer, they can be bought and sold until they mature. They are sold on a discounted basis like commercial paper and T-bills. Dealers in this market match up firms that want to discount a banker's acceptance (sell it for immediate payment) with companies wishing to invest in banker's acceptances. Interest rates on banker's acceptances are low because the risk of default is very low.

Eurodollars

Many contracts around the world call for payment in U.S. dollars due to the dollar's stability. For this reason, many companies and governments choose to hold dollars. Prior to World War II, most of these deposits were held in New York's money center banks. However, as a result of the Cold War that followed, there was fear that deposits held on U.S. soil could be expropriated. Some large London banks responded to this opportunity by offering to hold dollar-denominated deposits in British banks. These deposits were dubbed Eurodollars (see the following Global box).

The Eurodollar market has continued to grow rapidly. The primary reason is that depositors receive a higher rate of return on a dollar deposited in the Eurodollar market than in the domestic market. At the same time, the borrower is able to receive a more favorable rate in the Eurodollar market than in the domestic market. This is because multinational banks are not subject to the same regulations restricting U.S. banks and because they are willing and able to accept narrower spreads between the interest paid on deposits and the interest earned on loans.

London Interbank Market   Some large London banks act as brokers in the Eurodollar market. Eurodollars are an alternative to federal funds. Banks from around the world buy and sell overnight funds in this market. The rate paid by banks

---

[13]*Source:* https://www.rbi.org.in/Scripts/BS_ViewMasCirculardetails.aspx?id=9882, as accessed on 25 March 2017 at 8pm.

buying funds is the **London interbank bid rate (LIBID).** Funds are offered for sale in this market at the **London interbank offer rate (LIBOR).** Because many banks participate in this market, it is extremely competitive. The spread between the bid and the offer rate seldom exceeds 0.125%. Eurodollar deposits are time deposits, which means that they cannot be withdrawn for a specified period of time. Although the most common time period is overnight, different maturities are available. Each maturity has a different rate.

The overnight LIBOR and the federal funds rate tend to be very close to each other. This is because they are near-perfect substitutes. Suppose that the federal funds rate exceeded the overnight LIBOR. Banks that need to borrow funds will borrow overnight Eurodollars, thus tending to raise rates, and banks with funds to lend will lend federal funds, thus tending to lower rates. The demand-and-supply pressure will cause a rapid adjustment that will drive the two rates together.

At one time, most short-term loans with adjustable interest rates were tied to the US Treasury bill rate. However, the market for Eurodollars is so broad and deep that it has recently become the standard rate against which others are compared. For example, the U.S. commercial paper market now quotes rates as a spread over LIBOR rather than over the US T-bill rate.

The Eurodollar market is not limited to London banks anymore. The primary brokers in this market maintain offices in all of the major financial centers worldwide.

Eurodollar Certificates of Deposit Because Eurodollars are time deposits with fixed maturities, they are to a certain extent illiquid. As usual, the financial markets created new types of securities to combat this problem. These new securities were transferable negotiable certificates of deposit (negotiable CDs). Because most Eurodollar deposits have a relatively short term to begin with, the market for Eurodollar negotiable CDs is relatively limited, comprising less than 10% of the amount of regular Eurodollar deposits. The market for the negotiable CDs is still thin.

Other Eurocurrencies The Eurodollar market is by far the largest short-term security market in the world. This is due to the international popularity of the U.S. dollar for trade. However, the market is not limited to dollars. It is possible to have an account denominated in Japanese yen held in a London or New York bank. Such an account would be termed a Euroyen account. Other Euro currencies are possible as well. Keep in mind that if market participants have a need for a particular security and are willing to pay for it, the financial markets stand ready and are willing to create it.

›GLOBAL

Ironic Birth of the Eurodollar Market

One of capitalism's great ironies is that the Eurodollar market, one of the most important financial markets used by capitalists, was fathered by the Soviet Union. In the early 1950s, during the height of the Cold War, the Soviets had accumulated a substantial amount of dollar balances held by banks in the United States. Because the Russians feared that the U.S. government might freeze these assets in the United States, they wanted to move the deposits to Europe, where they would be safe from expropriation. (This fear was not unjustified—consider the U.S. freeze on Iranian assets in 1979 and Iraqi assets in 1990.) However, they also wanted to keep the deposits in dollars so that they could be used in their international transactions. The solution was to transfer the deposits to European banks but to keep the deposits denominated in dollars. When the Soviets did this, the Eurodollar was born.

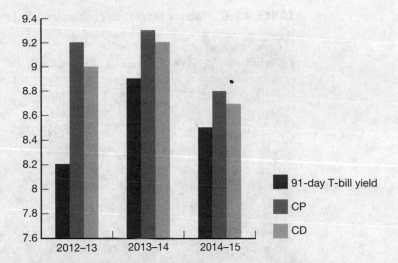

FIGURE 11.8 Interest Rates on T-Bills, Commercial Paper and Certificates of Deposits (2012–2015)

Courtesy: https://www.rbi.org.in/Scripts/AnnualReportPublications.aspx?Id=265, as accessed on 25 March 2017 at 8pm

Comparing Money Market Securities

Although money market securities share many characteristics, such as liquidity, safety, and short maturities, they all differ in some aspects.

Interest Rates

Figure 11.8 compares the interest rates on many of the money market instruments we have discussed. The most notable feature of this graph is that all of the money market instruments appear to move very closely together over time. This is because all have very low risk and a short term. They all have deep markets and so are priced competitively. In addition, because these instruments have so many of the same risk and term characteristics, they are close substitutes. Consequently, if one rate should temporarily depart from the others, market supply-and-demand forces would soon cause a correction.

Liquidity

As we discussed in Chapter 4, the *liquidity* of a security refers to how quickly, easily, and cheaply it can be converted into cash. Typically, the depth of the secondary market where the security can be resold determines its liquidity. For example, the secondary market for Treasury bills is extensive and well developed. As a result, Treasury bills can be converted into cash quickly and with little cost. By contrast, there is no well-developed secondary market for commercial paper. Most holders of commercial paper hold the securities until maturity. In the event that a commercial paper investor needed to sell the securities to raise cash, it is likely that brokers would charge relatively high fees.

In some ways, the depth of the secondary market is not as critical for money market securities as it is for long-term securities such as stocks and bonds. This is because money market securities are short-term to start with. Nevertheless, many

TABLE 11.6   Money Market Securities and Their Market

Money Market Securities	Issuer	Buyer	Usual Maturity	Secondary Market
Treasury bills	Government of India	Banks, PDs, insurance companies, pension funds, households, FPIs companies	91, 182, 364	Excellent
Call money	Banks and PDs	Banks and PDs	Overnight	None
Market repo	Government of India	Banks, PDs, insurance companies, pension funds, households, FPIS companies	Overnight and 2-14 days	None
Certificate of deposits	Banks	Companies	7 days to 1 year	Good
Commercial papers	Companies	Insurance companies, pension funds, households, FPIS	7 days to 1 year	Good

investors desire *liquidity intervention*: they seek an intermediary to provide liquidity where it did not previously exist. This is one function of money market mutual funds (discussed in Chapter 20).

Table 11.6 summarizes the types of money market securities and the depth of the secondary market in India.

SUMMARY

1. Money market securities are short-term instruments with an original maturity of less than one year. These securities in India include Treasury bills, commercial paper, Call money, repurchase agreements, Commercial Paper and negotiable certificates of deposit.

2. Money market securities are used to "warehouse" funds until needed. The returns earned on these investments are low due to their low risk and high liquidity.

3. Many participants in the money markets both buy and sell money market securities. The Government of India, commercial banks, businesses, and all benefit by having access to low-risk short-term investments.

4. Interest rates on all money market securities tend to follow one another closely over time. Treasury bill returns are the lowest because they are virtually devoid of default risk. Negotiable certificates of deposit are next to lowest because they are backed by the creditworthiness of large money center banks.

KEY TERMS

QUESTIONS

1. What characteristics define the money markets?

2. Is a Treasury bond issued 29 years ago with six months remaining before it matures a money market instrument?

3. Why do banks not eliminate the need for money markets?

4. Distinguish between a term security and a demand security.

5. Why does the Government of India use the money markets?

6. Why do businesses use the money markets?

7. Which of the money market securities is the most liquid and considered the most risk-free? Why?

8. Distinguish between competitive bidding and non-competitive bidding for Treasury securities.

9. Who are the participants in the call money market and what is the usual purpose of these funds?

10. Does the Reserve Bank of India directly set the call money interest rate? How does the RBI influence this rate?

11. Who issues commercial paper and for what purpose?

12. Who issues certificates of deposits and for what purpose?

QUANTITATIVE PROBLEMS

1. What would be your annualized discount rate percent and your annualized investment rate percent be on the purchase of a 182-day Treasury bill for ₹4,925 that pays ₹5,000 at maturity?

2. What are the annualized discount rate percent and your annualized investment rate percent be on a Treasury bill that you purchase for ₹9,940 that will mature in 91 days for ₹10,000?

3. If you want to earn an annualized discount rate of 3.5%, what is the most you can pay for a 91-day Treasury bill that pays ₹5,000 at maturity?

4. What is the annualized discount and investment rate percent on a Treasury bill that you purchase for ₹9,900 that will mature in 91 days for ₹10,000?

5. The price of 182-day commercial paper is ₹7,840. If the annualized investment rate is 4.093%, what will the paper pay at maturity be?

6. How much would you pay for a Treasury bill that matures in 182 days and pays ₹10,000 if you require a 1.8% discount rate?

7. The price of ₹8,000 face value commercial paper is ₹7,930. If the annualized discount rate is 4%, when will the paper mature? If the annualized investment rate is 4%, when will the paper mature?

8. How much would you pay for a Treasury bill that matures in one year and pays ₹10,000 if you require a 3% discount rate?

9. The annualized discount rate on a particular money market instrument is 3.75%. The face value is ₹200,000, and it matures in 51 days. What is its price? What would be the price if it had 71 days to maturity?

10. The annualized yield is 3% for 91-day commercial paper and 3.5% for 182-day commercial paper. What is the expected 91-day commercial paper rate, 91 days from now?

WEB EXERCISES

The Money Markets

1. Up-to-date interest rates are available from the Annual Report, Reserve Bank of India at **https://www.rbi.org.in/Scripts/AnnualReportPublications.aspx?Id=1159**.

   a. Call/notice money rate

   b. 91-day T-bill yield

   c. Commercial paper

   d. Certificates of deposit

Compare the rates for items a–c to those reported in Table 11.1. Have short-term rates generally increased or decreased?

2. The RBI conducts auctions of Treasury bills at regular intervals. Go to **https://rbidocs.rbi.org.in/rdocs/PressRelease/PDFs/IEPR277325D67282C73D477EB47DC6AD838BCC09.PDF** to locate the schedule of auctions. When is the next auction of 91-day, 182-day and 364-day treasury bills? How often are these securities auctioned?

REFERENCES

1. https://www.rbi.org.in/Scripts/BS_PressReleaseDisplay.aspx?prid=34833.
2. https://www.rbi.org.in/Scripts/BS_ViewMasCirculardetails.aspx?id=9882.
3. https://www.rbi.org.in/Scripts/BS_ViewMasCirculardetails.aspx?id=9881.
4. https://www.rbi.org.in/Scripts/BS_ViewMasCirculardetails.aspx?id=9858.
5. https://rbidocs.rbi.org.in/rdocs/Publications/PDFs/69298.pdf.
6. https://rbidocs.rbi.org.in/rdocs/Publications/PDFs/77574.pdf.
7. http://www.rbi.org.in/Scripts/financialmarketswatch.aspx.
8. https://www.rbi.org.in/Scripts/BS_PressReleaseDisplay.aspx?prid=34751.
9. https://www.rbi.org.in/Scripts/BS_PressReleaseDisplay.aspx?prid=34818.
10. https://www.rbi.org.in/scripts/FS_Speeches.aspx?fn=2752.

12

The Bond Market

> PREVIEW

The last chapter discussed the short-term securities that trade in a market which we call the money market. This chapter talks about the first of several securities that are traded in a market which we call the capital market. Capital markets are for securities with an original maturity that is greater than one year. These securities include bonds and stocks. We will devote an entire chapter to each major type of capital market security due to their importance to investors, businesses, and the economy. This chapter begins with a brief introduction on how the capital markets operate before launching into the study of bonds. In the next chapter we will study stocks and the stock market.

Purpose of the Capital Market

Firms that issue capital market securities and the investors who buy them have very different motivations than those who operate in the money markets. Firms and individuals use the money markets primarily to warehouse funds for short periods of time until a more important need or a more productive use for the funds arises. By contrast, firms and individuals use the capital markets for long-term investments.

Suppose that after a careful financial analysis, your firm determines that it needs a new plant to meet the increased demand for its products. This analysis will be made using interest rates that reflect the *current* long-term cost of funds to the firm. Now suppose that your firm chooses to finance this plant by issuing money market securities, such as commercial paper. As long as interest rates do not rise, all is well: When these short-term securities mature, they can be reissued at the same interest rate. However, if interest rates rise, the firm will still have to reissue, now at a higher rate. It may find that it does not have the cash flows or income to support the plant at this increased rate. If long-term securities, such as bonds or stock, had been used, the increased interest rates would not have been as critical. The primary reason that individuals and firms choose to borrow long-term is to reduce the risk that interest rates will rise before they pay off their debt. This reduction in risk comes at a cost, however. As you may recall from Chapter 5, most long-term interest rates are higher than short-term rates due to risk premiums. Despite the need to pay higher interest rates to borrow in the capital markets, these markets remain very active.

Capital Market Participants

The primary issuers of capital market securities are the Government of India and state governments and the private/public sector and treasury bills. The Government of India has long-term bonds and treasury bills to fund the national debt. State governments also issues long-term bonds called State Development Loans/Bonds. The Central government issues dated government securities with varying maturities, which are called government stocks. The State governments also issue dated securities with varying maturities, called State Development Loans (SDLs) or Bonds. Government never issues stock because they cannot sell ownership claims.

The public and private corporations issue both bonds and stocks. One of the most difficult decisions a firm faces can be whether it should finance its growth with debt or equity. The distribution of a firm's capital between debt and equity is called its capital structure. Corporations may enter the capital markets because they do not have sufficient capital to fund their investment opportunities. Alternatively, firms may choose to enter the capital markets because they want to preserve their capital to protect against unexpected needs. In either case, the availability of efficiently functioning capital markets is crucial to the continued health of the business sector. This was dramatically demonstrated during the 2008–2009 financial crisis. With the near collapse of the bond and stock markets, funds for business expansion dried up. This led to reduced business activity, high unemployment, and slow growth. Only after market confidence was restored did the recovery begin.

The largest purchasers of capital market securities are households. Frequently, individuals and households deposit funds in financial institutions that use the funds to purchase capital market instruments such as bonds or stock.

Capital Market Trading

Capital market trading occurs in either the *primary market* or the *secondary market*. The primary market is where new issues of stocks and bonds are introduced. Investment funds, corporations, and individual investors can all purchase securities offered in the primary market. You can think of a primary market transaction as one where the issuer of the security actually receives the proceeds of the sale. When firms sell securities for the very first time, the issue is an **initial public offering (IPO).** Subsequent sales of a firm's new stocks or bonds to the public are simply primary market transactions (as opposed to an initial one).

The capital markets have well-developed secondary markets. A secondary market is where the sale of previously issued securities takes place. Secondary markets are critical in capital markets because most investors plan to sell long-term bonds at some point. There are two types of exchanges in the secondary market for capital securities: *organized exchanges* and *over-the-counter exchanges*. Whereas most money market transactions originate over the phone, most capital market transactions, measured by volume, occur in organized exchanges. An organized exchange has a building where securities (including stocks, bonds, options, and futures) trade. Exchange rules govern trading to ensure the efficient and legal operation of the exchange, and the exchange's board constantly reviews these rules to ensure that they result in competitive trading.

⬆️ **GO ONLINE**

Find listed companies, member information, real-time market indices, and current stock quotes at **https://www.nseindia.com.**

Types of Bonds

Bonds are securities that represent a debt owed by the issuer to the investor. Bonds obligate the issuer to pay a specified amount at a given date, generally with periodic interest payments. The par, face, or maturity value of the bond is the amount that the issuer must pay at maturity. The **coupon rate** is the rate of interest that the issuer must pay, and this periodic interest payment is often called the coupon payment. This rate is usually fixed for the duration of the bond and does not fluctuate with market interest rates. If the repayment terms of a bond are not met, the holder of a bond has a claim on the assets of the issuer.

Long-term bonds traded in the capital market include long-term dated government securities and corporate bonds.

Treasury Bills and Dated Government Securities and Bonds

A bond is a debt instrument in which an investor loans money to an entity (typically corporate or governmental) which borrows the funds for a defined period of time at a variable or fixed interest rate. Bonds are used by companies, municipalities, states and sovereign governments to raise money and finance a variety of projects and activities. Owners of bonds are debt holders, or creditors, of the issuers.

A Government Security (G-Sec) is a tradable instrument issued by the Central Government or the State Governments. It acknowledges the Government's debt obligation. Such securities are short term (usually called treasury bills, with

TABLE 12.1   Government Securities

Type	Maturity
Treasury bill	Less than 1 year
Government security	2–30 years

original maturities of less than one year) or long term (usually called Government bonds or dated securities with original maturity of one year or more). In India, the Central Government issues both, treasury bills and bonds or dated securities while the State Governments issue only bonds or dated securities, which are called the State Development Loans (SDLs). G-Secs carry practically no risk of default and, hence, are called risk-free gilt-edged instruments.

Treasury bills or T-bills, which are money market instruments, are short-term debt instruments issued by the Government of India and are presently issued in three tenors, namely, 91 day, 182 day and 364 day. Treasury bills are zero coupon securities and pay no interest. They are issued at a discount and redeemed at the face value at maturity. For example, a 91-day Treasury bill of ₹100 (face value) may be issued at say ₹98.2, that is, at a discount of say, ₹1.8 and would be redeemed at the face value of ₹100. The return to the investors is the difference between the maturity value or the face value (that is ₹100) and the issue price (for calculation of yield on Treasury Bills).

Dated G-Secs are securities which carry a fixed or floating coupon (interest rate) which is paid on the face value, on half-yearly basis. Generally, the tenor of dated securities is between 5 years and 30 years. The Public Debt Office (PDO) of the Reserve Bank of India acts as the registry/depository of G-Secs and deals with the issue, interest payment and repayment of principal at maturity. Most of the dated securities are fixed coupon securities.

The Central and State governments issue dated securities (bonds) to finance the fiscal deficit and thus, national debt. The difference between a bill and a bond is that bills have an original maturity of less than one year, while bonds have an original maturity of two years and more. (Recall from Chapter 11 that Treasury *bills* mature in less than one year.) The Central Government currently issues bills with 91-, 182- and 365-day maturities. While the Central Government issues treasury bills, such bills are not issued by State Governments. Table 12.1 summarizes the maturity differences among Treasury securities.

Central government bills and bonds are free of default risk because the government can always print money to pay off the debt if necessary. This does *not* mean that these securities are risk-free. We will discuss interest-rate risk applied to bonds later in this chapter.

Treasury Bills and Bond Interest Rates

Government securities (both bonds and bills) have lower interest rates than corporate bonds because they have no default risk. Although investors in such securities have found themselves earning less than the rate of inflation in some years (see Figure 12.1), most of the time the interest rate on such securities is above that on money market securities because of interest-rate risk.

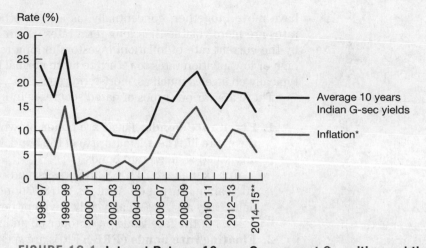

FIGURE 12.1 Interest Rate on 10-year Government Securities and the Inflation Rate (1996-1997 to 2014-2015)

Note: Inflation figures from 1996–1997 to 2006–2007 pertain to CPI-IW and have base 1982=100; inflation figures from 2007–2008 to 2011-2012 also pertain to CPI-IW and have base 2001=100; while figures from 2012-2013 pertain to the new CPI-C and have base 2010=100.

** Upto 21 Jan 2015

Sources: http://dhie.rbi.org.in/DBIE/dbie.rbi?site=statistics; https://www.rbl.org.in/scripts/AnnualPublications.aspx?head=Handbook%20of%20Statistics%20on%20Indian%20Economy, as accessed on 25 March 2017 at 8pm

Figure 12.2 plots the yield on 20-year Government securities against the yield on 91-day Treasury bills. Two things are noteworthy in this graph. First, in all the years, the rate of return on the short-term bill is below that on the 20-year government security. Second, while empirically in India, short-term and long-term yields

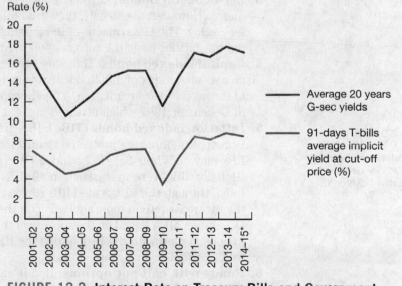

FIGURE 12.2 Interest Rate on Treasury Bills and Government Securities (2001–2002 to 2014–2015)

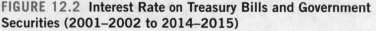

Source: http://dbie.rbi.org.in/DBIE/dbie.rbi?site=statistics, as accessed on 25 March 2017 at 8pm.

have moved together, conceptually, as also in other country settings, short-term rates are more volatile than long-term rates. Short-term rates are more influenced by the current rate of inflation. Investors in long-term securities expect extremely high or low inflation rates to return to more normal levels, so long-term rates do not typically change as much as short-term rates.

There are various types of dated securities in India. They include:

1. **Fixed rate bonds:** These are bonds on which the coupon rate is fixed for the entire life (i.e. till maturity) of the bond. Most Government bonds in India are issued as fixed rate bonds.

   For example, 8.24% GS2018 was issued on April 22, 2008 for a tenure of 10 years maturing on April 22, 2018. Coupon on this security will be paid half-yearly at 4.12% (half yearly payment being half of the annual coupon of 8.24%) of the face value on October 22 and April 22 of each year.

2. **Floating rate bonds (FRB):** FRBs are securities which do not have a fixed coupon rate. The coupon is reset at pre-announced intervals (say, every six months or one year) by adding a spread over a base rate. In the case of most floating rate bonds issued by the Government of India so far, the base rate is the weighted average cut-off yield of the last three 182-day Treasury Bill auctions preceding the coupon reset date and the spread is decided through the auction when the FRBs are first issued. FRBs were first issued in September 1995 in India.

   For example, a FRB was issued on July 2, 2002 for a tenure of 15 years, thus maturing on July 2, 2017. The base rate on the bond for the coupon payments was fixed at 6.50%, being the weighted average rate of implicit yield on 364-day Treasury bills during the preceding six auctions. In the bond auction, a cut-off spread (markup over the benchmark rate) of 34 basis points (0.34%) was decided. Hence the coupon for the first six months was fixed at 6.84%.

3. **Zero coupon bonds:** Zero coupon bonds are bonds with no coupon payments. However, like T-bills, they are issued at a discount and redeemed at face value. The Government of India issued such securities in the 1990s and did not further issue the zero coupon bond.

4. **Capital indexed bonds:** These are bonds, the principal of which is linked to an accepted index of inflation with a view to protecting the Principal amount of the investors from inflation. A 5-year capital indexed bond, was first issued in December 1997 which matured in 2002.

5. **Inflation indexed bonds (IIBs):** IIBs are bonds wherein both Coupon and Principal amounts are protected against inflation. The inflation index used in IIBs may be Whole Sale Price Index (WPI) or Consumer Price Index (CPI). Globally, IIBs were first issued in 1981 in UK. In India, the Government of India, through the RBI, issued IIBs (linked to WPI) in June 2013. Since then, they were issued on monthly basis (on the last Tuesday of each month) till December 2013. Based on the success of these IIBs, the Government of India, in consultation with the RBI, issued the IIBs (CPI based) exclusively for the retail customers in December 2013.

6. **Bonds with call/put options:** Bonds can also be issued with features of optionality wherein the issuer can have the option to buy-back (call option) or the investor can have the option to sell the bond (put option) to the issuer during the currency of the bond. It may be noted that such bonds

GO ONLINE

Access **https://www.rbi.org.in/ scripts/FAQView.aspx?Id=91** to view further details on IIBs in India may have put only or call only or both options. The first G-Sec with both call and put options viz. 6.72% GS2012 was issued on July 18, 2002 for a maturity of 10 years maturing on July 18, 2012. The optionality on the bond could be exercised after completion of five years tenure from the date of issuance on any coupon date falling thereafter. The Government has the right to buy-back the bond (call option) at par value (equal to the face value) while the investor has the right to sell the bond (put option) to the Government at par value on any of the half-yearly coupon dates starting from July 18, 2007.

7. **Special securities:** Under the market borrowing programme, the Government of India also issues, from time to time, special securities to entities like oil marketing companies, fertilizer companies, the Food Corporation of India, etc. (popularly called oil bonds, fertilizer bonds and food bonds respectively) as compensation to these companies in lieu of cash subsidies. These securities are usually long dated securities and carry marginally higher coupon (spread of about 20–25 bps) over the yield of the dated securities of comparable maturity. These securities are, however, not eligible as SLR securities but are eligible as collateral for market repo transactions. The beneficiary entities may divest these securities in the secondary market to banks, insurance companies/primary dealers, etc., for raising funds.

8. **STRIPS:** Separate Trading of Registered Interest and Principal of Securities, more commonly called STRIPS, are the securities created by way of separating the cash flows associated with a regular G-sec i.e. each semi-annual coupon payment and the final principal payment to be received from the issuer, into separate securities. They are essentially Zero Coupon Bonds (ZCBs). However, they are created out of existing securities only and unlike other securities, are not issued through auctions. Securities represent future cash flows (periodic interest and principal repayment) of an underlying coupon bearing bond. Being G-secs, STRIPS are eligible for SLR. In India, currently dated securities (other than FRBs, IIBs and special securities) having their coupon due on Jan 2 and Jul 2 are eligible for STRIPping. Guidelines for stripping and reconstitution of G-secs have already been issued (IDMD circular dated March 25, 2010). For example, when ₹100 of the 8.24% GS2018 is stripped, each cash flow of coupon (₹4.12 each half year) will become coupon STRIP and the principal payment (₹100 at maturity) will become a principal STRIP. These cash flows are traded separately as independent securities in the secondary market. STRIPS in G-Secs ensure availability of sovereign zero coupon bonds, which facilitate the development of a market determined zero coupon yield curve (ZCYC). STRIPS also provide institutional investors with an additional instrument for their asset liability management (ALM). Further, as STRIPS have zero reinvestment risk, being zero coupon bonds, they can be attractive to retail/non-institutional investors. The process of stripping/reconstitution of G-Secs is carried out at RBI, Public Debt Office (PDO) in the CBS package of RBI i.e. E-Kuber through any of the primary dealer at the option of the holder at any time from the date of issuance of a G-sec till its maturity. Physical securities are not eligible for stripping/reconstitution. Minimum amount of securities that needs to be submitted for stripping/reconstitution is ₹1 crore (face value) and in multiples thereof. They are currently tradable in both OTC market and in NDS-OM.

State Development Loans (SDLs)

State governments also raise loans from the market which are called SDLs. SDLs are dated securities issued through normal auction similar to the auctions conducted for dated securities issued by the Central Government. Interest is serviced at half-yearly intervals and the principal is repaid on the maturity date. Like dated securities issued by the Central Government, SDLs issued by the State governments also qualify for SLR. They are also eligible as collaterals for borrowing through market repo as well as borrowing by eligible entities from the RBI under the Liquidity Adjustment Facility (LAF).

Floatation of State Government Loans (State Development Loans)

In terms of Sec. 21A(1)(b) of the Reserve Bank of India Act, 1934, the RBI may, by agreement with any State Government undertake the management of the public debt of that State. Accordingly, the RBI has entered into agreements with 29 State governments and one Union Territory for management of their public debt. Under Article 293(3) of the Constitution of India (Under section 48A of Union territories Act, in case of Union Territory), a State Government has to obtain the permission of the Central Government for any borrowing as long as there is any outstanding loan that the State Government may have from the Centre.

Market borrowings are raised by the RBI on behalf of the State Governments to the extent of the allocations under the market borrowing programme as approved by the Ministry of Finance in consultation with the Planning Commission.

RBI in consultation with State Governments announces the indicative quantum of borrowing on a quarterly basis. All State Governments have issued general notifications which specify the terms and conditions for issue of State Government securities. Before every auction, respective state governments issue specific notifications indicating details of the securities being issued in the particular auction. RBI places a press release in its website and also issues advertisements in leading English and vernacular newspapers of the respective states.

Currently, SDL auctions are held on second and fourth Tuesdays of every month. As in case of Central G-secs, auction is held on the E-Kuber Platform. Here 10% of the notified amount is reserved for the retail investors under the non-competitive bidding.

Public Sector Bonds

In addition to the Central and State governments, central public sector enterprises (CPSEs) also issue bonds periodically. These include bonds issued by Indian Railways, Rural Electrification Corporation Ltd., National Highways Authority of India among others. These bonds carry fixed interest rates. The risk of default on such bonds is lower than corporate bonds. However, these bonds are not tradeable.

Corporate Bonds

When large corporations need to borrow funds for long periods of time, they may issue bonds. Most are also callable, meaning that the issuer may redeem the bonds after a specified date.

The **bond indenture** is a contract that states the lender's rights and privileges and the borrower's obligations. Any collateral offered as security to the bondholders is also described in the indenture.

The degree of risk varies widely among different bond issues because the risk of default depends on the company's health, which can be affected by a number of variables. The interest rate on corporate bonds varies with the level of risk, as we discussed in Chapter 5. Bonds with lower risk and a higher rating (AAA being the highest) have lower interest rates than more risky bonds (BBB). The spread between the differently rated bonds varies over time. A bond's interest rate also depends on its features and characteristics, which are described in the following sections.

Characteristics of Corporate Bonds

At one time bonds were sold with attached coupons that the owner of the bond clipped and mailed to the firm to receive interest payments. These were called *bearer bonds* because payments were made to whoever had physical possession of the bonds. Bearer bonds have now been largely replaced by **registered bonds,** which do not have coupons. Instead, the owner must register with the firm to receive interest payments. Despite the fact that bearer bonds with attached coupons have been phased out, the interest paid on bonds is still called the "coupon interest payment," and the interest rate on bonds is the coupon interest rate.

Restrictive Covenants A corporation's financial managers are hired, fired, and compensated at the direction of the board of directors, which represents the corporation's *stockholders*. This arrangement implies that the managers will be more interested in protecting stockholders than they are in protecting bondholders. You should recognize this as an example of the moral hazard problem introduced in Chapter 2 and discussed further in Chapter 7. Managers might not use the funds provided by the bonds as the bondholders might prefer. Since bondholders cannot look to managers for protection when the firm gets into trouble, they must include rules and restrictions on managers designed to protect the bondholders' interests. These are known as **restrictive covenants.** They usually limit the amount of dividends the firm can pay (so to conserve cash for interest payments to bondholders) and the ability of the firm to issue additional debt. Other financial policies, such as the firm's involvement in mergers, may also be restricted. Restrictive covenants are included in the bond indenture. Typically, the lower interest rates, the more restrictions are placed on management through these covenants because the bonds will be considered safer by investors.

Call Provisions Most corporate indentures include a **call provision,** which states that the issuer has the right to force the holder to sell the bond back. The call provision usually requires a waiting period between the time the bond is initially issued and the time when it can be called. The price bondholders are paid for the bond is usually set at the bond's par price or slightly higher (usually by one year's interest cost). For example, a 10% coupon rate ₹1,000 bond may have a call price of ₹1,100.

If interest rates fall, the price of the bond will rise. If rates fall enough, the price will rise above the call price, and the firm will call the bond. Because call provisions put a limit on the amount that bondholders can earn from the appreciation of a bond's price, investors do not like call provisions.

A second reason that issuers of bonds include call provisions is to make it possible for them to buy back their bonds according to the terms of the **sinking fund.** A sinking fund is a requirement in the bond indenture that the firm pay off a portion of the bond issued each year. This provision is attractive to bondholders because it reduces the probability of default when the issue matures. Because a sinking fund provision makes the issue more attractive, the firm can reduce the bond's interest rate.

A third reason that firms usually issue only callable bonds is that firms may have to retire a bond issue if the covenants of the issue restrict the firm from some activity that it feels is in the best interest of stockholders. Suppose that a firm needed to borrow additional funds to expand its storage facilities. If the firm's bonds carried a restriction against adding debt, the firm would have to retire its existing bonds before issuing new bonds or taking out a loan to build the new warehouse.

Finally, a firm may choose to call bonds if it wishes to alter its capital structure. A maturing firm with excess cash flow may wish to reduce its debt load if few attractive investment opportunities are available.

Because bondholders do not generally like call provisions, callable bonds must have a higher yield than comparable noncallable bonds. Despite the higher cost, firms still typically issue callable bonds because of the flexibility this feature provides the firm.

Conversion   Some bonds can be converted into shares of common stock. This feature permits bondholders to share in the firm's good fortunes if the stock price rises. Most convertible bonds will state that the bond can be converted into a certain number of common shares at the discretion of the bondholder. The conversion ratio will be such that the price of the stock must rise substantially before conversion is likely to occur.

Issuing convertible bonds is one way the firms can avoid sending a negative signal to the market. In the presence of asymmetric information between corporate insiders and investors, when a firm chooses to issue stock, the market usually interprets this action as indicating that the stock price is relatively high or that it is going to fall in the future. The market makes this interpretation because it believes that managers are most concerned with looking out for the interests of existing stockholders and will not issue stock when it is undervalued. If managers believe that the firm will perform well in the future, they can, instead, issue convertible bonds. If the managers are correct and the stock price rises, the bondholders will convert to stock at a relatively high price that managers believe is fair. Alternatively, bondholders have the option not to convert if managers turn out to be wrong about the company's future.

Bondholders like a conversion feature. It is very similar to buying just a bond but receiving both a bond and a stock option (stock options are discussed fully in Chapter 24). The price of the bond will reflect the value of this option and it so will be higher than the price of comparable nonconvertible bonds. The higher price received for the bond by the firm implies a lower interest rate.

Corporate bonds can be issued in two ways:

- **Public issue** In public issue, corporations issue bonds to the market as a whole. Institutions as well as retail investors can participate in this issue. The cost of borrowing is a little high in case of a public issue.

TABLE 12.2   Classification of Corporate Bonds in India

Issuer	Maturity	Coupon	Option	Redemption
Corporates	Short term	Zero coupon bond	Call option	Single redemption
Banks	Medium term	Fixed coupon	Put option	Multiple redemption/ Amortizing bond
PSUs	Long term	Floating coupon		
Local Bodies	Perpetual			

Source: https://www.nseindia.com/products/content/debt/corp_bonds/FAQ_corporate_bond.pdf

GO ONLINE

Access **http://www.sebi. gov.in/faq/pubissuefaq. pdf** to understand more about the different kinds of issues in India. The SEBI website at **http://www.sebi. gov.in/cms/sebi_data/at-tachdocs/1464953038053. html** also gives data on the private placement of corporate bonds. Further, the Economic Review section of the Annual Report of RBI at **https://www.rbi.org.in/scripts/ AnnualReportPublications. aspx?Id=1148** analyses the Private placements in India.

- **Private placement** In private placement in corporate, generally the bond issuance is with few institutions. In India, more than 90% of the corporate bonds are issued through private placement. It is the easiest and cheapest way of borrowing corporate bonds.[1]

Types of Corporate Bonds

Corporate Bonds can be broadly classified on the basis of Issuer, Maturity, Coupon, Option and Redemption. Table 12.2 shows the classification of corporate bonds in India.

Based on Issuer Issuers of corporate bonds can be broadly classified in to following classes:

- Bonds issued by local bodies
- Bonds issued by PSUs
- Bonds issued by financial institutions
- Bonds issued by banks
- Bonds issued by corporates

Based on Maturity Period

- Short-term maturity: Security with maturity period less than one year.
- Medium-term maturity: Security with maturity period between 1–5 years.
- Long-term maturity: Such securities have maturity period above five years
- Perpetual: Security with no maturity. Currently, in India banks issue perpetual bond.

Based on Coupon

- Fixed rate bonds have a coupon that remains constant throughout the life of the bond.
- Floating rate bonds: Coupon rates are reset periodically based on benchmark rate.
- Zero-coupon bonds: No coupons are paid. The bond is issued at a discount to its face value, at which it will be redeemed. There are no intermittent payments of interest.

---

[1]*Source*: https://www.nseindia.com/products/content/debt/corp_bonds/FAQ_corporate_bond.pdf, as accessed on 25 March 2017 at 8pm.

Based on Option

- Bond with call option: This feature gives a bond issuer the right, but not the obligation, to redeem his issue of bonds before the bond's maturity at a predetermined price and date.
- Bonds with put option: This feature gives bondholders the right but not the obligation to sell their bonds back to the issuer at a predetermined price and date. These bonds generally protect investors from interest rate risk.

Based on Redemption

- Bonds with single redemption: In this case the principal amount of bond is paid at the time of maturity only.
- Amortising bonds: A bond, in which payment made by the borrower over the life of the bond, includes both interest and principal.[2]

Bonds are rated by various companies according to their default risk. In India, CRISIL and ICRA rate corporate bonds. These companies study the issuer's financial characteristics and make a judgment about the issuer's possibility of default. A bond with a rating of AAA has the highest grade possible. Bonds with rating of C are defined as those with very high default risk (See Table 12.3).

In India, National Housing Bank (NHB), played a leading role in starting up Mortgage-backed securitisation and development of a secondary mortgage market in the country. NHB launched the pilot issues of Mortgage Backed Securities (MBS) in August 2000 in the Indian financial market, followed by other MBS issues cumulating to ₹862 crore.[3]

In April 2014, DLF launched India's first Commercial Mortgage Based Security (CMBS), by securitizing the lease rentals on two shopping malls in Vasant Kunj, Delhi. DLF would receive ₹800 cr. for a period of 7.5 years, where interest would be paid through rents received from tenants of the property.[4]

However, this market still continues to be underdeveloped.

CASE

India's corporate bond market puzzle

GO ONLINE

Access **https://www.rbi.org.in/scripts/AnnualReportPublications.aspx?Id=1148** and read the section on analysis of India's Corporate Bond Market. Look at the turnover in the market, as also the yield spread between corporate bonds and their corresponding G-secs and how these have varied over the years.

India has emerged as one of the fastest growing economies in the world. As the government emphasizes manufacturing and industrial growth to support such growth, the state of the languishing corporate bond market in India remains a challenge, as also a puzzle. Banks and equity markets remain the dominant sources of capital for business in India. In 2016, corporate bonds were a $287 billion (about ₹19 trillion) market- accounting for around 14% of gross domestic product (GDP), nowhere compared to bank assets (89% of GDP) and equity markets (80% of GDP). In its current state, the Indian corporate bond market is a market for highly rated, plain vanilla instruments, issued by financial firms and public sector enterprises. Also, issuance is fragmented and trading dries up within a few days of issuance.

---

[2]*Source*: https://www.nseindia.com/products/content/debt/corp_bonds/FAQ_corporate_bond.pdf, as accessed on 20 March 2017 at 12pm.

[3]*Source:* http://www.nhb.org.in/Financial/secur.php, as accessed on 25 March 2017 at 8pm.

[4]http://capitalmind.in/2014/04/indias-first-commercial-mortgage-based-security-cmbs-on-offer-by-dlf/, as accessed on 25 March 2017 at 8pm.

As banks tighten lending due to systemic stress, as also the increased capital requirements under Basel III, bond markets would need to assume a pivotal role in supporting the diverse financing requirements of the growing Indian economy, especially for the MSME sector and for infrastructure projects, with their higher risk, longer-term financing requirements.

Is a corporate bond market necessary or important?

Theoretically, all three stakeholder groups-corporations, the government and the investors should welcome such a market. As regarding the corporations, such a market will provide an important alternative source of funding for corporations without diluting corporate control. To the government, such a bond market represents a spur in corporate activity and thus economic growth. Finally, for investors dealing in pension funds and insurance companies, they provide a diversified set of instruments to invest in.

However, the reasons for the underdeveloped nature of the corporate bond market may be found in the significant amount of corporate debt held in the form of loans, especially by state-owned banks. The current Indian requirement of marking corporate bond holdings to market (but not corporate loans), makes corporate loans more attractive for banks than corporate bonds. Banks can show their balance sheets to be healthier than they actually are. The problem is not just of a demand from banks, but also that of supply from corporates themselves. Thus, large corporations with significant levels of unsustainable debt have no incentive to issue increased levels of debt, and indeed, have significant incentive to ensure the creation and perpetuation of information asymmetries that will inhibit liquidity in the market for their debt.

Finally, the government may also face a trade-off between enabling a vibrant corporate bond market resulting in significant losses to the banking sector, especially for nationalized banks, which are significantly exposed to bad corporate loans. There may also be more corporate failures if the full scale of the bad loans problem is revealed to the world. Governments may shy away from such solutions involving pains.

Thus, it appears that the development of a vibrant and robust corporate bond market requires fundamental reforms in financial markets, public finance and regulatory governance, something not easy to achieve.

References: http://www.livemint.com/Opinion/FlBq03pUT8MEDmcFXAp8pM/Indias-corporate-bond-market-puzzle.html; http://www.livemint.com/Opinion/64IOr9Q0A1GTu7AVGchIIqK/Why no corporate-bond-market.html, as accessed on 25 March 2017 at 8pm.

Financial Guarantees for Bonds

Financially weaker security issuers frequently purchase **financial guarantees** to lower the risk of their bonds. A financial guarantee ensures that the lender (bond purchaser) will be paid both principal and interest in the event the issuer defaults. Large, well-known insurance companies write what are actually insurance policies to back bond issues. With such a financial guarantee, bond buyers no longer have to be concerned with the financial health of the bond issuer. Instead, they are interested only in the strength of the insurer. Essentially, the credit rating of the insurer is substituted for the credit rating of the issuer. The resulting reduction in risk lowers the interest rate demanded by bond buyers. Of

TABLE 12.3 Debt Rating Descriptions in India

CRISIL	ICRA	Definition
AAA (Highest safety)	AAA	Instruments with this rating are considered to have the highest degree of safety regarding timely servicing of financial obligations. Such instruments carry lowest credit risk.
AA (High safety)	A	Instruments with this rating are considered to have a high degree of safety regarding timely servicing of financial obligations. Such instruments carry low credit risk.
A (Adequate safety)	AA	Instruments with this rating are considered to have an adequate degree of safety regarding timely servicing of financial obligations. Such instruments carry very low credit risk.
BBB (Moderate safety)	BBB	Instruments with this rating are considered to have moderate degree of safety regarding timely servicing of financial obligations. Such instruments carry moderate credit risk.
BB (Moderate risk)	BB	Instruments with this rating are considered to have moderate risk of default regarding timely servicing of financial obligations
B (High risk)	B	Instruments with this rating are considered to have high risk of default regarding timely servicing of financial obligations.
C (Very high risk)	C	Instruments with this rating are considered to have very high risk of default regarding timely servicing of financial obligations.
D (Default)		Instruments with this rating are in default or are expected to be in default soon.
NM		Instruments rated 'NM' have factors present in them, which render the outstanding rating meaningless. These include reorganisation or liquidation of the issuer, the obligation being under dispute in a court of law or before a statutory authority
(+) or (−)		Ratings from AA to C may be modified by the addition of a plus or minus sign to show relative standing within the major rating categories.

References: http://www.crisil.com/ratings/credit-rating-scale.html; http://www.icra.in/Content.aspx?cid=VEET9NEN9O4R1 FOD9G4HRLJKLJFKJWW4CY7OICKOFBC2GKL6OW, as accessed on 25 March 2017 at 8pm.

course, issuers must pay a fee to the insurance company for the guarantee. Financial guarantees make sense only when the cost of the insurance is less than the interest savings that result.

For example, in 1995, J.P. Morgan introduced a new way to insure bonds called the **credit default swap (CDS).** In its simplest form, a CDS provides insurance against default in the principle and interest payments of a credit instrument. Say you decided to buy a GE bond and wanted to insure yourself against any losses that

GO
ONLINE
Access **http://finmin.nic.in/
the_ministry/dept_eco_af-
fairs/budget/govern_guar-
antee_policy.pdf** to view teh
Government Guarantee Policy.

might occur should GE have problems. You could buy a CDS from a variety of sources that would provide this protection.

In India, financial guarantees of bonds issued by central and state governments are called 'contingent liabilities'. The Fiscal Responsibility and Budget Management Act (FRBM Act) 2003, mandates the Central Government to specify the annual target for assuming contingent liabilities which are in the form of guarantees. Accordingly, the FRBM Rules prescribe a cap of 0.5% of GDP in any financial year on the quantum of guarantees that the Central Government can assume in the particular financial year, beginning with the financial year 2004–05.

Similar provisions exist for state governments in their fiscal legislations as well.

Current Yield Calculation

Chapter 3 introduced interest rates and described the concept of yield to maturity. If you buy a bond and hold it until it matures, you will earn the yield to maturity. This represents the most accurate measure of the yield from holding a bond.

Current Yield

The **current yield** is an approximation of the yield to maturity on coupon bonds that is often reported because it is easily calculated. It is defined as the yearly coupon payment divided by the price of the security,

$$i_c = \frac{C}{P} \tag{1}$$

where
i_c = current yield
P = price of the coupon bond
C = yearly coupon payment

This formula is identical to the formula in Equation 5 of Chapter 3, which describes the calculation of the yield to maturity for a perpetuity. Hence for a perpetuity, the current yield is an exact measure of the yield to maturity. When a coupon bond has a long term to maturity (say, 20 years or more), it is very much like a perpetuity, which pays coupon payments forever. Thus, you would expect the current yield to be a rather close approximation of the yield to maturity for a long-term coupon bond, and you can safely use the current yield calculation instead of looking up the yield to maturity in a bond table. However, as the time to maturity of the coupon bond shortens (say, it becomes less than five years), it behaves less and less like a perpetuity and so the approximation afforded by the current yield becomes worse and worse.

We have also seen that when the bond price equals the par value of the bond, the yield to maturity is equal to the coupon rate (the coupon payment divided by the par value of the bond). Because the current yield equals the coupon payment divided by the bond price, the current yield is also equal to the coupon rate when the bond price is at par. This logic leads us to the conclusion that when the bond price is at par, the current yield equals the yield to maturity. This means that the nearer the bond price is to the bond's par value, the better the current yield will approximate the yield to maturity.

The current yield is negatively related to the price of the bond. In the case of our 10% coupon rate bond, when the price rises from ₹1,000 to ₹1,100, the current

EXAMPLE 12.1

Current Yield

What is the current yield for a bond that has a par value of ₹1,000 and a coupon interest rate of 10.95%? The current market price for the bond is ₹921.01.

> **Solution**
The current yield is 11.89%.

$$i_c = \frac{C}{P}$$

where

C = yearly payment = $0.1095 \times ₹1,000 = ₹109.50$

P = price of the bond = ₹921.01

Thus,

$$i_c = \frac{₹109.50}{₹921.01} = 0.1189 = 11.89\%$$

yield falls from 10% (= ₹100/₹1,000) to 9.09% (= ₹100/₹1,100). As Table 3.1 in Chapter 3 indicates, the yield to maturity is also negatively related to the price of the bond; when the price rises from ₹1,000 to ₹1,100, the yield to maturity falls from 10% to 8.48%. In this, we see an important fact: the current yield and the yield to maturity always move together; a rise in the current yield always signals that the yield to maturity has also risen.

The general characteristics of the current yield (the yearly coupon payment divided by the bond price) can be summarized as follows: the current yield better approximates the yield to maturity when the bond's price is nearer to the bond's par value and the maturity of the bond is longer. It becomes a worse approximation when the bond's price is further from the bond's par value and the bond's maturity is shorter. Regardless of whether the current yield is a good approximation of the yield to maturity, a change in the current yield *always* signals a change in the same direction of the yield to maturity.

Finding the Value of Coupon Bonds

Before we look specifically at how to price bonds, let us first look at the general theory behind computing the price of any business asset. Luckily, the value of all financial assets is found the same way. The current price is the present value of all future cash flows. Recall the discussion of present value from Chapter 3. If you have the present value of a future cash flow, you can exactly reproduce that future cash flow by investing the present value amount at the discount rate. For example, the present value of ₹100 that will be received in one year is ₹90.90 if the discount rate is 10%. An investor is completely indifferent between having the ₹90.90 today or having the ₹100 in one year. This is because the ₹90.90 can be invested at 10% to provide ₹100.00 in the future (₹90.90 × 1.10 = ₹100). This represents the essence of value. The current price must be such that the seller is indifferent between continuing to receive the cash flow stream provided by the asset and receiving the offer price.

One question we might ask is why prices fluctuate if everyone knows how value is established. It is because not everyone agrees about what the future cash flows are going to be. Let us summarize how to find the value of a security:

1. Identify the cash flows that result from owning the security.
2. Determine the discount rate required to compensate the investor for holding the security.
3. Find the present value of the cash flows estimated in step 1 using the discount rate determined in step 2.

The rest of this chapter focuses on how one important asset is valued: bonds. In the next chapter we discuss stock valuation.

Finding the Price of Semiannual Bonds

Recall that a bond usually pays interest semiannually in an amount equal to the coupon interest rate at times the face amount (or par value) of the bond. When the bond matures, the holder will also receive a lump sum payment equal to the face amount. Most corporate bonds have a face amount of ₹1,000. Basic bond terminology is reviewed in Table 12.4.

The issuing corporation will usually set the coupon rate close to the rate available on other similar outstanding bonds at the time the bond is offered for sale. Unless the bond has an adjustable rate, the coupon interest payment remains unchanged throughout the life of the bond.

The first step in finding the value of the bond is to identify the cash flow the holder of the bond will receive. The value of the bond is the present value of these cash flows. The cash flows consist of the interest payments and the final lump sum repayment.

TABLE 12.4   Bond Terminology

Coupon interest rate	The stated annual interest rate on the bond. It is usually fixed for the life of the bond.
Current yield	The coupon interest payment divided by the current market price of the bond.
Face amount	The maturity value of the bond. The holder of the bond will receive the face amount from the issuer when the bond matures. *Face amount* is synonymous with *par value*.
Indenture	The contract that accompanies a bond and specifies the terms of the loan agreement. It includes management restrictions, called covenants.
Market rate	The interest rate currently in effect in the market for securities of like risk and maturity. The market rate is used to value bonds.
Maturity	The number of years or periods until the bond matures and the holder is paid the face amount.
Par value	The same as *face amount*.
Yield to maturity	The yield an investor will earn if the bond is purchased at the current market price and held until maturity.

In the second step these cash flows are discounted back to the present using an interest rate that represents the yield available on other bonds of like risk and maturity.

The technique for computing the price of a simple bond with annual cash flow was discussed in detail in Chapter 3. Let us now look at a more realistic example. Most bonds pay interest semiannually. To adjust the cash flows for semiannual payments, divide the coupon payment by 2 since only half of the annual payment is paid each six months. Similarly, to find the interest rate effective during one-half of the year, the market interest rate must be divided by 2. The final adjustment is to double the number of periods because there will be two periods per year. Equation 2 shows how to compute the price of a semiannual bond:[5]

$$P_{semi} = \frac{C/2}{1+i} + \frac{C/2}{(1+i)^2} + \frac{C/2}{(1+i)^3} + \cdots + \frac{C/2}{(1+i)^{2n}} + \frac{F}{(1+i)^{2n}} \qquad (2)$$

where
P_{semi} = price of semiannual coupon bond
C = yearly coupon payment
F = face value of the bond
n = years to maturity date
$i = \frac{1}{2}$ annual market interest rate

Notice that the market price for the bond in Example 2 is below the ₹1,000 par value of the bond. When the bond sells for less than the par value, it is selling at a **discount.** When the market price exceeds the par value, the bond is selling at a **premium.**

What determines whether a bond will sell for a premium or a discount? Suppose that you are asked to invest in an old bond that has a coupon rate of 10% and ₹1,000 par. You would not be willing to pay ₹1,000 for this bond if new bonds with similar risk were available yielding 12%. The seller of the old bond would have to lower the price on the 10% bond to make it an attractive investment. In fact, the seller would have to lower the price until the yield earned by a buyer of the old bond equaled the yield on similar new bonds. This means that as interest rates in the market rise, the value of bonds with fixed interest rates falls. Similarly, as interest rates available in the market on new bonds fall, the value of old fixed-interest-rate bonds rises.

Investing in Bonds

Bonds represent one of the most popular long-term alternatives to investing in stocks. Bonds are a lower risk than stocks because they have a higher priority of payment. This means that when the firm is having difficulty meeting its obligations, bondholders get paid before stockholders. Additionally, should the firm have to liquidate, bondholders must be paid before stockholders.

---

[5]There is a theoretical argument for discounting the final cash flow using the full-year interest rate with the original number of periods. Derivative securities are sold, in which the principal and interest cash flows are separated and sold to different investors. The fact that one investor is receiving semiannual interest payments should not affect the value of the principal-only cash flow. However, virtually every text, calculator, and spreadsheet computes bond values by discounting the final cash flow using the same interest rate and number of periods as is used to compute the present value of the interest payments. To be consistent, we will use that method in this text.

EXAMPLE 12.2

Bond Valuation, Semiannual Payment Bond

Let us compute the price of a sample bond. Suppose the bonds have a 10% coupon rate, a ₹ 1,000 par value (maturity value), and mature in two years. Assume semiannual compounding and that market rates of interest are 12%.

> **Solution**

1. Begin by identifying the cash flows. Compute the coupon interest payment by multiplying 0.10 times ₹ 1,000 to get ₹ 100. Since the coupon payment is made during each six months, it will be one-half of ₹ 100, or ₹ 50. The final cash flow consists of repayment of the ₹ 1,000 face amount of the bond. This does not change because of semiannual payments.

2. We need to know what market rate of interest is appropriate to use for computing the present value of the bond. We are told that bonds being issued today with similar risk have coupon rates of 12%. Divide this amount by 2 to get the interest rate over six months. This provides an interest rate of 6%.

3. Find the present value of the cash flows. Note that with semiannual compounding the number of periods must be doubled. This means that we discount the bond payments for four periods.

Solution: Equation

$$P = \frac{₹100/2}{(1+.06)} + \frac{₹100/2}{(1+.06)^2} + \frac{₹100/2}{(1+.06)^3} + \frac{₹100/2}{(1+.06)^4} + \frac{₹1,000}{(1+.06)^4}$$

$$P = ₹47.17 + ₹44.50 + ₹41.98 + ₹39.60 + ₹792.10 = ₹965.35$$

Solution: Financial Calculator

$$N = 4$$
$$FV = ₹1,000$$
$$I = 6\%$$
$$PMT = ₹50$$

Compute PV = price of bond = ₹ 965.35.

Even healthy firms with sufficient cash flow to pay both bondholders and stockholders frequently have very volatile stock prices. This volatility scares many investors out of the stock market. Bonds are the most popular alternative. They offer relative security and dependable cash payments, making them ideal for retired investors and those who want to live off their investments.

Many investors think that bonds represent a very low risk investment since the cash flows are relatively certain. It is true that high-grade bonds seldom default; however, bond investors face fluctuations in price due to market interest-rate movements in the economy. As interest rates rise and fall, the value of bonds changes in the opposite direction. As discussed in Chapter 3, the possibility of suffering a loss because of interest-rate change is called **interest-rate risk.** The longer the time until the bond matures, the greater will be the change in price. This does not cause a loss to those investors who do not sell their bonds; however, many investors do not hold their bonds until maturity. If they attempt to sell their bonds after interest rates have risen, they will receive less than what they paid earlier. Interest-rate risk is an important consideration when deciding whether to invest in bonds.

SUMMARY

1. The capital markets exist to provide financing for long-term capital assets. Households, often through investments in pension and mutual funds, are net investors in the capital markets. Corporations and the Central and state governments are net users of these funds.

2. The three main capital market instruments are dated government securities (central and state government), public sector bonds and corporate bonds

3. Dated government securities account for a major share of the Indian capital market.

4. Corporate bonds can be classified on the basis of Issuer, maturity, coupon, option and redemption.

5. The value of any business asset is computed the same way, by computing the present value of the cash flows that will go to the holder of the asset. For example, a commercial building is valued by computing the present value of the net cash flow the owner will receive. We compute the value of bonds by finding the present value of the cash flows, which consist of periodic interest payments and a final principal payment.

6. The value of bonds fluctuates with current market prices. If a bond has an interest payment based on a 5% coupon rate, no investor will buy it at face value if new bonds are available for the same price with interest payments based on 8% coupon interest. To sell the bond, the holder will have to discount the price until the yield to the holder equals 8%. The longer the term of maturity, greater the amount of discounts are given.

KEY TERMS

bond indenture, p. 301
call provision, p. 301
coupon rate, p. 295
credit default swap (CDS), p. 306
current yield, p. 307
discount, p. 310

financial guarantees, p. 305
initial public offering, p. 295
interest-rate risk, p. 311
premium, p. 310
registered bonds, p. 301
restrictive covenants, p. 301

Separate Trading of Registered
    Interest and Principal Securities
    (STRIPS), p. 299
sinking fund, p. 302
zero-coupon securities, p. 303

QUESTIONS

1. Contrast investors' use of capital markets with their use of money markets.

2. What are the primary capital market securities, and who are the primary purchasers of these securities?

3. Distinguish between the primary market and the secondary market for securities.

4. A bond provides information about its par value, coupon interest rate, and maturity date. Define each of these.

5. The Government of India issues bills and dated securities. How do these two securities differ?

6. As interest rates in the market change over time, the market price of bonds rises and falls. The change in the value of bonds due to changes in interest rates is a risk incurred by bond investors. What is this risk called?

7. In addition to the government securities, some agencies of the government issue bonds. List three such agencies, and state what the funds raised by the bond issues are used for.

8. A call provision on a bond allows the issuer to redeem the bond at will. Investors do not like call provisions and so require higher interest on callable bonds. Why do issuers continue to issue callable bonds anyway?

9. What is a sinking fund? Do investors like bonds that contain this feature? Why?

10. What is the document called that lists the terms of a bond?

11. Describe the two ways whereby capital market securities pass from the issuer to the public.

QUANTITATIVE PROBLEMS

1. A bond makes an annual ₹80 interest payment (8% coupon). The bond has five years before it matures, at which time it will pay ₹1,000. Assuming a discount rate of 10%, what should be the price of the bond? (Review Chapters 3 and 12.)

2. A zero-coupon bond has a par value of ₹1,000 and matures in 20 years. Investors require a 10% annual return on these bonds. For what price should the bond sell? (Note: Zero-coupon bonds do not pay interest. Review Chapter 3.)

3. Consider the two bonds described below:

	Bond A	Bond B
Maturity (years)	15	20
Coupon rate (%) (paid semiannually)	10	6
Par value	₹1,000	₹1,000

a. If both bonds had a required return of 8%, what would the bonds' prices be?

b. Describe what it means if a bond sells at a discount, a premium, and at its face amount (par value). Are these two bonds selling at a discount, premium, or par?

c. If the required return on the two bonds rose to 10%, what would the bonds' prices be?

4. A two-year ₹1,000 par zero-coupon bond is currently priced at ₹819.00. A two-year ₹1,000 annuity is currently priced at ₹1,712.52. If you want to invest ₹50,000 in one of the two securities, which is a better buy? (Hint: Compute the yield of each security.)

5. Consider the following cash flows. All market interest rates are 12%.

Year	0	1	2	3	4
Cash Flow		160	170	180	230

a. What price would you pay for these cash flows? What total wealth do you expect after 2.5 years if you sell the rights to the remaining cash flows? Assume interest rates remain constant.

b. What is the duration of these cash flows?

c. Immediately after buying these cash flows, all market interest rates drop to 11%. What is the impact on your total wealth after 2.5 years?

6. M&E, Inc., has an outstanding convertible bond. The bond can be converted into 20 shares of common equity (currently trading at ₹52/share). The bond has five years of remaining maturity, a ₹1,000 par value, and a 6% annual coupon. M&E's straight debt is currently trading to yield 5%. What is the minimum price of the bond?

7. Assume the debt in the previous question is trading at ₹1,035. How can you earn a riskless profit from this situation (arbitrage)?

8. A 10-year, ₹1,000 par value bond with a 5% annual coupon is trading to yield 6%. What is the current yield?

9. A ₹1,000 par bond with an annual coupon has only one year until maturity. Its current yield is 6.713%, and its yield to maturity is 10%. What is the price of the bond?

10. A one-year discount bond with a face value of ₹1,000 was purchased for ₹900. What is the yield to maturity? What is the yield on a discount basis? (See Chapters 3 and 12.)

11. A seven-year, ₹1,000 par bond has an 8% annual coupon and is currently yielding 7.5%. The bond can be called in two years at a call price of ₹1,010. What is the bond yielding, assuming it will be called (known as the yield to call)?

12. A 20-year ₹1,000 par value bond has a 7% annual coupon. The bond is callable after the 10th year for a call premium of ₹1,025. If the bond is trading with a yield to call of 6.25%, what is the bond's yield to maturity?

13. A 10-year ₹1,000 par value bond has a 9% semiannual coupon and a nominal yield to maturity of 8.8%. What is the price of the bond?

14. Your company owns the following bonds:

Bond	Market Value	Duration
A	₹13 million	2
B	₹18 million	4
C	₹20 million	3

If general interest rates rise from 8% to 8.5%, what is the approximate change in the value of the portfolio? (Review Chapter 3.)

WEB EXERCISES

The Bond Market

1. Stocks tend to get more publicity than bonds, but many investors, especially those nearing or in retirement, find that bonds are more consistent with their risk preferences. Go to **http://finance.yahoo.com/** **calculator/index**. Under Retirement find the calculator "How should I allocate my assets?" After answering the questionnaire, discuss whether you agree with the recommended asset destination.

13

The Stock Market

> PREVIEW

In the last chapter we identified the capital markets as the place where long-term securities trade. We then examined the bond market and discussed how bond prices are established. In this chapter we continue our investigation of the capital markets by taking a close look at the stock market. The market for stocks is undoubtedly the one that receives the most attention and scrutiny. Great fortunes are made and lost as investors attempt to anticipate the market's ups and downs. India has a long history of stock market. However, it was only in the early 1990s, when stock market reforms were undertaken that the India stock market witnessed a metamorphic transformation in terms of liquidity, market capitalization, payments and settlements, players and stock exchange transactions. We have witnessed an unprecedented period of volatility over the last decade.

We begin by discussing the markets where stocks trade. We then examine the fundamental theories that underline the valuation of stocks. These theories are critical to an understanding of the forces that cause the value of stocks to rise and fall minute by minute and day by day. We will learn that determining a value for a common stock is very difficult and that it is this difficulty that leads to so much volatility in the stock markets.

Investing in Stocks

A share of stock in a firm represents ownership. A stockholder owns a percentage interest in a firm, consistent with the percentage of outstanding stock held.

Investors can earn a return from stock in one of two ways. Either the price of the stock rises over time or the firm pays the stockholder dividends. Frequently, investors earn a return from both sources. Stock is riskier than bonds because stockholders have a lower priority than bondholders when the firm is in trouble, dividends are less assured, and stock price increases are not guaranteed. Despite these risks, it is possible to make a great deal of money by investing in stock, whereas that is very unlikely by investing in bonds. Another distinction between stock and bonds is that stock does not mature.

Ownership of stock gives the stockholder certain rights regarding the firm. One is the right of a *residual claimant*: stockholders have a claim on all assets and income left over after all other claimants have been satisfied. If nothing is left over, they get nothing. As noted, however, it is possible to get rich as a stockholder if the firm does well.

Most stockholders have the *right to vote* for directors and on certain issues, such as amendments to the corporate charter and whether new shares should be issued.

A stock certificate does not list a maturity date, face value, or an interest rate, as indicated on bonds.

Common Stock vs. Preferred Stock

There are two types of stock, common and preferred. A share of common stock in a firm represents an ownership interest in that firm. **Common stockholders** vote, receive dividends, and hope that the price of their stock will rise. There are various classes of common stock, usually denoted type A, type B, and so on. Unfortunately, the type does not have any meaning that is standard across all companies. The differences among the types usually involve either the distribution of dividends or voting rights. It is important for an investor in stocks to know exactly what rights go along with the shares of stock being contemplated.

Preferred stock is a form of equity from a legal and tax standpoint. However, it differs from common stock in several important ways. First, because preferred stockholders receive a fixed dividend that never changes, a share of preferred stock is as much like a bond as it is like common stock. Second, because the dividend does not change, the price of preferred stock is relatively stable. Third, preferred stockholders do not usually vote unless the firm has failed to pay the promised dividend. Finally, preferred stockholders hold a claim on assets that has priority over the claims of common shareholders but after that of creditors such as bondholders.

Less than 25% of new equity issues are preferred stock, and only about 5% of all capital is raised using preferred stock. This may be because preferred dividends are not tax-deductible to the firm like bond interest payments. Consequently, issuing preferred stock usually costs the firm more than issuing debt, even though it shares many of the characteristics of a bond.

How Stocks Are Sold

Literally billions of shares of stock are sold each business day in India. The orderly flow of information, stock ownership, and funds through the stock markets is a critical feature of well-developed and efficient markets. This efficiency encourages investors to buy stocks and to provide equity capital to businesses with valuable growth opportunities. We traditionally discuss stocks as trading on either an organized exchange or over the counter. Recently, this distinction is blurring as electronic trading grows in both volume and influence.

Organized Securities Exchanges   Historically, the New York Stock Exchange (NYSE) has been known as one of the best organized exchanges. The NYSE first began trading in 1792, when 24 brokers began trading a few stocks on Wall Street. The NYSE is still the world's largest and most liquid equities exchange. The traditional definition of an organized exchange is that there is a specified location where buyers and sellers meet on a regular basis to trade securities using an open-outcry auction model. As more sophisticated technology has been adapted to securities trading, this model is becoming less frequently used.

There are also major organized stock exchanges around the world. The most active exchange in the world is the Nikkei in Tokyo. Other major exchanges include the London Stock Exchange in England, the DAX in Germany, and the Toronto Stock Exchange in Canada.

To have a stock listed for trading on one of the organized exchanges, a firm must file an application and meet certain criteria set by the exchange designed to enhance trading. For example, the NYSE encourages only the largest firms to list so that transaction volume will be high. There are several ways to meet the minimum listing requirements. Generally, the firm must have substantial earnings and market value (greater than $10 million per year and $100 million market value).

The two major stock exchanges in India are the Bombay Stock Exchange (BSE) and the National Stock Exchange (NSE).

The Bombay Stock Exchange (BSE)   Established in 1875, BSE (formerly known as Bombay Stock Exchange Ltd.), is Asia's first and the fastest stock exchange in the world with the speed of six micro seconds and one of India's leading exchange groups. Over the past 140 years, BSE has facilitated the growth of the Indian corporate sector by providing an efficient capital-raising platform. Popularly known as BSE, the bourse was established as "The Native Share & Stock Brokers' Association" in 1875. BSE is a corporatized and demutualised entity, with a broad shareholder-base which includes two leading global exchanges, Deutsche Bourse and Singapore Exchange as strategic partners. BSE provides an efficient and transparent market for trading in equity, debt instruments, derivatives, mutual funds. It also has a platform for trading in equities of small-and-medium enterprises (SME).

More than 5,500 companies are listed on BSE making it the world's no. 1 exchange in terms of listed members. The companies listed on BSE commanded a total market capitalization of USD 1.64 trillion as of September 2015. It is also one of the world's leading exchanges (5th largest in September 2015) for index options trading.[1]

BSE also provides a host of other services to capital market participants including risk management, clearing, settlement, market data services and education. It has a global reach with customers around the world and a nation-wide presence. BSE systems and processes are designed to safeguard market integrity, drive the growth of the Indian capital market and stimulate innovation and competition across all market segments. BSE is the first exchange in India and second in the world to

GO ONLINE

Find listed companies, member information, real-time market indices, and current stock quotes at **http://www.bseindia. com/markets/equity/ EQReports/MarketWatch. aspx?expandable=2.**

---

[1]*Source:* World Federation of Exchanges.

obtain an ISO 9001 : 2000 certification. It is also the first exchange in the country and second in the world to receive Information Security Management System Standard BS 7799-2-2002 certification for its online trading system (BOLT). It operates one of the most respected capital market educational institutes in the country (the BSE Institute Ltd.). BSE also provides depository services through its Central Depository Services Ltd. (CDSL) arm.

BSE's popular equity index—the S&P BSE SENSEX—is India's most widely tracked stock market benchmark index. It is traded internationally on the EUREX as well as leading exchanges of the BRICS nations (Brazil, Russia, China and South Africa).

BSE has won several awards and recognitions that acknowledge the work done and progress made. These include: The India Innovation Award for Big Data implementation; Best IT Implementation Award 2016 in the "Most Complex Project Category" by PCQuest; CIO Power List 2015; SKOCH; Achiever Award 2016 for SME enablement; the Golden Peacock Global CSR Award for its initiatives in corporate social responsibility; NASSCOM—CNBC-TV18's IT User Awards, 2010 in financial services category, among others. Its recent milestones include the launching of BRICSMART indices derivatives, BSE-SME Exchange platform, S&P BSE GREENEX to promote investments in Green India.[2]

National Stock Exchange   The National Stock Exchange (NSE) is India's leading stock exchange covering various cities and towns across the country. NSE was set up by leading institutions to provide a modern, fully automated screen-based trading system with national reach. The exchange has brought about unparalleled transparency, speed and efficiency, safety and market integrity. It has set up facilities that serve as a model for the securities industry in terms of systems, practices and procedures.

NSE has played a catalytic role in reforming the Indian securities market in terms of microstructure, market practices and trading volumes. The market today uses state-of-art information technology to provide an efficient and transparent trading, clearing and settlement mechanism, and has witnessed several innovations in products and services viz. demutualisation of stock exchange governance, screen based trading, compression of settlement cycles, dematerialisation and electronic transfer of securities, securities lending and borrowing, professionalisation of trading members, fine-tuned risk management systems, emergence of clearing corporations to assume counterparty risks, market of debt and derivative instruments and intensive use of information technology.[3]

Over-the-Counter Markets   If Microsoft's stock is not traded on any of the organized stock exchanges, where does it sell its stock? Securities not listed on one of the exchanges trade in the over-the-counter (OTC) market. This market is not organized in the sense of having a building where trading takes place. Instead, trading occurs over sophisticated telecommunications networks. One such network is called the **National Association of Securities Dealers Automated Quotation System (NASDAQ).** This system, introduced in 1971, provides current bid and ask prices on about 3,000 actively traded securities. Dealers "make a market" in these stocks by buying for inventory when investors want to sell and selling from inventory when

---

[2]http://www.bseindia.com/#about; http://www.bseindia.com/static/about/introduction.aspx?expandable=0, as accessed on 25 March 2017 at 8pm.

[3]https://www.nseindia.com/global/content/about_us/about_us.htm, as accessed on 25 March 2017 at 8pm.

investors want to buy. These dealers provide small stocks with the liquidity that is essential to their acceptance in the market. Total volume on the NASDAQ is usually slightly lower than on the NYSE; however, NASDAQ volume has been growing and occasionally exceeds NYSE volume.

In India, the Over-the-Counter Exchange of India (OTCEI) is an electronic stock exchange that is comprised of small- and medium-sized firms looking to gain access to the capital markets. Like electronic exchanges in the U.S. such as the NASDAQ, there is no central place of exchange and all trading is done through electronic networks.

The first electronic OTC stock exchange in India was established in 1990 to provide investors and companies with an additional way to trade and issue securities. This was the first exchange in India to introduce market makers, which are firms that hold shares in companies and facilitate the trading of securities by buying and selling from other participants.

Organized vs. Over-the-Counter Trading   There is a significant difference between how organized and OTC exchanges operate. Organized exchanges are characterized as auction markets that use floor traders who specialize in particular stocks. These specialists oversee and facilitate trading in a group of stocks. Floor traders, representing various brokerage firms with buy and sell orders, meet at the trading post on the exchange and learn about current bid and ask prices. These quotes are called out loud. In about 90% of trades, the specialist matches buyers with sellers. In the other 10%, the specialists may intervene by taking ownership of the stock themselves or by selling stock from inventory. It is the specialist's duty to maintain an orderly market in the stock even if that means buying stock in a declining market.

About one of four orders on the New York Stock Exchange is filled by floor traders personally approaching the specialist on the exchange. The other three-quarters of trades are executed by the SuperDOT system (Super Designated Order Turnaround system). The SuperDOT is an electronic order routing system that transmits orders directly to the specialist who trades in a stock. This allows for much faster communication of trades than is possible using floor traders. SuperDOT is for trades under 100,000 shares and gives priority to trades of under 2,100 shares. About 75% of orders to buy or sell on the NYSE are executed using this system.

Whereas organized exchanges have specialists who facilitate trading, over-the-counter markets have market makers. Rather than trade stocks in an auction format, they trade on an electronic network where the bid and ask prices are set by the market makers. There are usually multiple market makers for any particular stock. They each enter their bid and ask quotes. Once this is done, they are obligated to buy or sell at least 1,000 securities at that price. Once a trade has been executed, they may enter a new bid and ask quote. Market makers are important to the economy in that they assure there is continuous liquidity for every stock, even those with little transaction volume. Market makers are compensated by the spread between the **bid price** (the price they pay for stocks) and **ask price** (the price they sell the stocks for). They also receive commissions on trades.

Although NASDAQ, the NYSE, the BSE, the NSE and the other exchanges are heavily regulated, they are still public for-profit businesses. They have shareholders, directors, and officers who are interested in market share and generating profits. This means that the NYSE is vigorously competing with NASDAQ for the high-volume stocks that generate the big fees. For example, the NYSE has been trying to entice Microsoft to leave the NASDAQ and list with them for many years.

Electronic Communications Networks (ECNs) In the United States, ECNs have been challenging both NASDAQ and the organized exchanges for business in recent years. An ECN is an electronic network that brings together major brokerages and traders so that they can trade among themselves and bypass the middleman. ECNs have a number of advantages that have led to their rapid growth.

- *Transparency:* All unfilled orders are available for review by ECN traders. This provides valuable information about supply and demand that traders can use to set their strategy. Although some exchanges make this information available, it is not always as current or complete as what the ECN provides.
- *Cost reduction:* Because the middleman and the commission are cut out of the deal, transaction costs can be lower for trades executed over an ECN. The spread is usually reduced and sometimes eliminated.
- *Faster execution:* Since ECNs are fully automated, trades are matched and confirmed faster than can be done when there is human involvement. For many traders this is not of great significance, but for those trying to trade on small price fluctuations, this is critical.
- *After-hours trading:* Prior to the advent of ECNs only institutional traders had access to trading securities after the exchanges had closed for the day. Many news reports and information become available after the major exchanges have closed, and small investors were locked out of trading on this data. Since ECNs never close, trading can continue around the clock.

Along with the advantages of ECNs there are disadvantages. The primary one is that they work well only for stocks with substantial volume. Since ECNs require there to be a seller to match against each buyer and vice versa, thinly traded stocks may go long intervals without trading. One of the largest ECNs is Instinet. It is mainly for institutional traders. Instinet also owns Island, which is for active individual trades.

The major exchanges are fighting the ECNs by expanding their own automatic trading systems. For example, the NYSE recently announced changes to its own Direct+ order routing system and merged with Archipelago to give it an established place in this market. Although the NYSE still dominates the American stock market in terms of share and dollar volume, its live auction format may not survive technological challenges for many more years.

Exchange Traded Funds Exchange traded funds (ETFs) have become the latest market innovation to capture investor interest. They were first introduced in 1990 and by 2010 nearly 1,000 separate ETFs were being traded. In their simplest form, ETFs are formed when a basket of securities is purchased and a stock is created based on this basket that is traded on an exchange. The makeup and structure are continuing to evolve, but ETFs share the following features:

1. They are listed and traded as individual stocks on a stock exchange.
2. They are indexed rather than actively managed.
3. Their value is based on the underlying net asset value of the stocks held in the index basket. The exact content of the basket is public so that intraday arbitrage keeps the ETF price close to the implied value.

In essence, ETFs trade like stocks and therefore offer a degree of flexibility unavailable with traditional mutual funds. Specifically, investors can trade ETFs throughout the trading day as in stocks. In comparison, in a traditional mutual fund, investors can purchase units only at the fund's NAV, which is published at the end of each trading day. In fact, investors cannot purchase ETFs at the closing NAV. This difference gives rise to an important advantage of ETFs over traditional funds: ETFs are immediately tradable and consequently, the risk of price differential between the time of investment and time of trade is substantially less in the case of ETFs.

ETFs are cheaper than traditional mutual funds and index funds in terms of fees. However, while investing in an ETF, an investor pays a commission to the broker. The tracking error of ETFs is generally lower than traditional index funds due to the "in-kind" creation/redemption facility and the low expense ratio. This "in-kind" creation/redemption facility ensures that long-term investors do not suffer at the cost of short-term investor activity.

ETFs can be bought/sold through trading terminals anywhere across the country. Table 13.1 presents a comparative view ETFs vis-à-vis other funds.

ETF features some of the more exotic names found in finance, including Vipers, Diamonds, Spiders, and Qubes. These names are derived from the index that is tracked or the name of the issuing firm. For example, Diamonds are indexed to the Dow Jones Industrial Average, Spiders track the S&P 500, and Qubes follow the NASDAQ (ticker symbol QQQQ). Vipers are Vanguard's ETFs. The list of available indexes that can be tracked by purchasing ETFs is rapidly expanding to include virtually every sector, commodity, and investment style (value, growth, capitalization, etc.). Their popularity is likely to increase as more investors learn about how they can be effectively used as a low-cost way to help diversify a portfolio.

In India, the ETF is a basket of stocks that reflects the composition of an Index, like S&P CNX Nifty or BSE Sensex. The ETFs trading value is based on the net asset value of the underlying stocks that it represents. Think of it as a mutual fund that you can buy and sell in real-time at a price that changes throughout the day.

GO ONLINE

Access **http://www.money-control.com/mf/etf/** to view the various ETF schemes in India and their latest performance. Also access **http://www.moneycontrol.com/mf/etf/faq/display_faq.php** to view some FAQs on ETFs.

TABLE 13.1 ETF vs. Open Ended vs. Close Ended Funds

Parameter	Open Ended Fund	Close Ended Fund	Exchange Traded Fund
Fund Size	Flexible	Fixed	Flexible
Nav	Daily	Daily	Real Time
Liquidity Provider	Fund itself	Stock Market	Stock Market/Fund itself
Sale Price	At NAV, plus load, if any	Significant premium/discount to NAV	Very close to actual NAV of the scheme
Availability	Fund itself	Through exchange where listed	Through exchange where listed/fund itself
Portfolio Disclosure	Monthly	Monthly	Daily/Real time
Uses	Equitising cash	-	Equitising cash, arbitrage, hedging
Intra Day Trading	Not possible	Expensive	Possible at low cost

Source: https://www.nseindia.com/products/content/equities/etfs/comparison_etfs.htm

Computing the Price of Common Stock

One basic principle of finance is that the value of any investment is found by computing the value today of all cash flows the investment will generate over its life. For example, a commercial building will sell for a price that reflects the net cash flows (rents–expenses) it is projected to have over its useful life. Similarly, we value common stock as the value in today's dollars of all future cash flows. The cash flows a stockholder may earn from stock are dividends, the sales price, or both.

To develop the theory of stock valuation, we begin with the simplest possible scenario. This assumes that you buy the stock, hold it for one period to get a dividend, then sell the stock. We call this the *one-period valuation model*.

The One-Period Valuation Model

GO ONLINE

Access **http://stockcharts.com/freecharts/historical** for detailed stock quotes, charts, and historical stock data.

Suppose that you have some extra money to invest for one year. After a year you will need to sell your investment to pay tuition. After going through *Money Control*, you decide that you want to buy Infosys' stock. You call your broker and find that Infosys is currently selling for ₹ 50 per share and pays ₹ 0.16 per year in dividends. The analyst on *Money Control* predicts that the stock will be selling for ₹ 60 in one year. Should you buy this stock?

To answer this question you need to determine whether the current price accurately reflects the analyst's forecast. To value the stock today, you need to find the present discounted value of the expected cash flows (future payments) using the formula in Equation 1 of Chapter 3 in which the discount factor used to discount the cash flows is the required return on investments in equity. The cash flows consist of one dividend payment plus a final sales price, which, when discounted back to the present, leads to the following equation that computes the current price of the stock.

$$P_0 = \frac{Div_1}{(1 + k_e)} + \frac{P_1}{(1 + k_e)} \tag{1}$$

where P_0 = the current price of the stock. The zero subscript refers to time period zero, or the present.

Div_1 = the dividend paid at the end of year 1.

k_e = the required return on investments in equity.

P_1 = the price at the end of the first period. This is the assumed sales price of the stock.

EXAMPLE 13.1

Stock Valuation: One-Period Model

Find the value of the Infosys stock given the figures reported above. You will need to know the required return on equity to find the present value of the cash flows. Since a stock is more risky than a bond, you will require a higher return than that offered in the bond market. Assume that after careful consideration you decide that you would be satisfied to earn 12% on the investment.

> Solution

Putting the numbers into Equation 1 yields the following:

$$P_0 = \frac{.16}{1 + 0.12} + \frac{₹60}{1 + 0.12} = ₹.14 + ₹53.57 = ₹53.71$$

Based on your analysis, you find that the stock is worth ₹53.71. Since the stock is currently available for ₹50 per share, you would choose to buy it. Why is the stock selling for less than ₹53.71? It may be because other investors place a different risk on the cash flows or estimate the cash flows to be less than you do.

The Generalized Dividend Valuation Model

The one-period *dividend* valuation model can be extended to any number of periods. The concept remains the same. The value of stock is the present value of all future cash flows. The only cash flows that an investor will receive are dividends and a final sales price when the stock is ultimately sold. The generalized formula for stock can be written as in Equation 2.

$$P_0 = \frac{D_1}{(1 + k_e)^1} + \frac{D_2}{(1 + k_e)^2} + \cdots + \frac{D_n}{(1 + k_e)^n} + \frac{P_n}{(1 + k_e)^n} \tag{2}$$

If you were to attempt to use Equation 2 to find the value of a share of stock, you would soon realize that you must first estimate the value the stock will have at some point in the future before you can estimate its value today. In other words, you must find P_n in order to find P_0. However, if P_n is far in the future, it will not affect P_0. For example, the present value of a share of stock that sells for ₹50, seventy-five years from now using a 12% discount rate is just one paise [₹50/(1.12^{75}) = ₹0.01]. This means that the current value of a share of stock can be found as simply the present value of the future dividend stream. The **generalized dividend model** is rewritten in Equation 3 without the final sales price.

$$P_0 = \sum_{t=1}^{\infty} \frac{D_t}{(1 + k_e)^t} \tag{3}$$

Consider the implications of Equation 3 for a moment. The generalized dividend model says that the price of stock is determined only by the present value of the dividends and that nothing else matters. Many stocks do not pay dividends, so how is it that these stocks have value? *Buyers of the stock expect that the firm will pay dividends someday.* Most of the time a firm institutes dividends as soon as it has completed the rapid growth phase of its life cycle. The stock price increases as the time approaches for the dividend stream to begin.

The generalized dividend valuation model requires that we compute the present value of an infinite stream of dividends, a process that could be difficult, to say the least. Therefore, simplified models have been developed to make the calculations easier. One such model is the **Gordon growth model,** which assumes constant dividend growth.

The Gordon Growth Model

Many firms strive to increase their dividends at a constant rate each year. Equation 4 rewrites Equation 3 to reflect this constant growth in dividends.

$$P_0 = \frac{D_0 \times (1 + g)^1}{(1 + k_e)^1} + \frac{D_0 \times (1 + g)^2}{(1 + k_e)^2} + \cdots + \frac{D_0 \times (1 + g)^\infty}{(1 + k_e)^\infty} \tag{4}$$

where
D_0 = the most recent dividend paid.
g = the expected constant growth rate in dividends.
k_e = the required return on an investment in equity.

Equation 4 has been simplified using algebra to obtain Equation 5.[4]

$$P_0 = \frac{D_0 \times (1 + g)}{(k_e - g)} = \frac{D_1}{(k_e - g)} \tag{5}$$

This model is useful for finding the value of stock, given a few assumptions:

1. *Dividends are assumed to continue growing at a constant rate forever.* Actually, as long as they are expected to grow at a constant rate for an extended period of time (even if not forever), the model should yield reasonable results. This is because errors about distant cash flows become small when discounted to the present.
2. *The growth rate is assumed to be less than the required return on equity,* k_e. Myron Gordon, in his development of the model, demonstrated that this is a reasonable assumption. In theory, if the growth rate were faster than the rate demanded by holders of the firm's equity, in the long run the firm would grow impossibly large.

EXAMPLE 13.2

Stock Valuation: Gordon Growth Model

Find the current market price of Coca-Cola stock assuming dividends grow at a constant rate of 10.95%, $D_0 = ₹1.00$, and the required return is 13%.

Solution

$$P_0 = \frac{D_0 \times (1 + g)}{k_e - g}$$

$$P_0 = \frac{₹1.00 \times (1.1095)}{.13 - .1095}$$

$$P_0 = \frac{₹1.1095}{0.0205} = ₹54.12$$

Coca-Cola stock should sell for ₹54.12 if the assumptions regarding the constant growth rate and required return are correct.

---

[4]To generate Equation 5 from Equation 4, first multiply both sides of Equation 4 by $(1 + k_e)/(1 + g)$ and subtract Equation 4 from the result. This yields

$$\frac{P_0 \times (1 + k_e)}{(1 + g)} - P_0 = D_0 - \frac{D_0 \times (1 + g)^\infty}{(1 + k_e)^\infty}$$

Assuming that ke is greater than g, the term on the far right will approach zero and can be dropped. Thus, after factoring P_0 out of the left side,

$$P_0 \times \left[\frac{1 + k_e}{1 + g} - 1\right] = D_0$$

Next, simplify by combining terms to

$$P_0 \times \frac{(1 + k_e) - (1 + g)}{(1 + g)} = D_0$$

$$P_0 = \frac{D_0 \times (1 + g)}{k_e - g} = \frac{D_1}{k_e - g}$$

Price Earnings Valuation Method

Theoretically, the best method of stock valuation is the dividend valuation approach. Sometimes, however, it is difficult to apply. If a firm is not paying dividends or has a very erratic growth rate, the results may not be satisfactory. Other approaches to stock valuation are sometimes applied. Among the more popular is the price/earnings multiple.

The **price earnings ratio (PE)** is a widely watched measure of how much the market is willing to pay for ₹1 of earnings from a firm. A high PE has two interpretations.

1. A higher-than-average PE may mean that the market expects earnings to rise in the future. This would return the PE to a more normal level.
2. A high PE may alternatively indicate that the market feels the firm's earnings are very low risk and is therefore willing to pay a premium for them.

The PE ratio can be used to estimate the value of a firm's stock. Note that algebraically the product of the PE ratio times expected earnings is the firm's stock price.

$$\frac{P}{E} \times E = P \tag{6}$$

Firms in the same industry are expected to have similar PE ratios in the long run. The value of a firm's stock can be found by multiplying the average industry PE times the expected earnings per share.

EXAMPLE 13.3

Stock Valuation: PE Ratio Approach

The average industry PE ratio for restaurants similar to Hard Rock Cafe, a pub restaurant chain, is 23. What is the current price of Hard Rock Cafe if earnings per share are projected to be ₹1.13?

> Solution
Using Equation 6 and the data given we find:

$$P_0 = P/E \times E$$
$$P_0 = 23 \times ₹1.13 = ₹26$$

The PE ratio approach is especially useful for valuing privately held firms and firms that do not pay dividends. The weakness of the PE approach to valuation is that by using an industry average PE ratio, firm-specific factors that might contribute to a long-term PE ratio above or below the average are ignored in the analysis. A skilled analyst will adjust the PE ratio up or down to reflect unique characteristics of a firm when estimating its stock price.

How the Market Sets Security Prices

Suppose you go to an auto auction. The cars are available for inspection before the auction begins, and you find a little Chevrolet Spark that you like. You test-drive it in the parking lot and notice that it makes a few strange noises, but you decide that you would still like the car. You decide ₹5,00,000 would be a fair price that would allow you to pay some repair bills should the noises turn out to be serious. You see that the auction is ready to begin, so you go in and wait for the Chevrolet Spark to enter.

Suppose there is another buyer who also spots the Chevrolet. He test-drives the car and recognizes that the noises are simply the result of worn brake pads that he can fix himself at a nominal cost. He decides that the car is worth ₹7,00,000. He also goes in and waits for the Chevrolet to enter.

Who will buy the car and for how much? Suppose only the two of you are interested in the Chevrolet. You begin the bidding at ₹4,00,000. He ups your bid to ₹4,50,000. You bid your top price of ₹5,00,000. He counters with ₹5,10,000. The price is now higher than you are willing to pay, so you stop bidding. The car is sold to the more informed buyer for ₹5,10,000.

This simple example raises a number of points. First, the price is set by the buyer willing to pay the highest price. The price is not necessarily the highest price the asset could fetch, but it is incrementally greater than what any other buyer is willing to pay.

Second, the market price will be set by the buyer who can take the best advantage of the asset. The buyer who purchased the car knew that he could fix the noise easily and cheaply. Because of this, he was willing to pay more for the car than you were. The same concept holds for other assets. For example, a piece of property or a building will sell to the buyer who can put the asset to the most productive use. Consider why one company often pays a substantial premium over current market prices to acquire ownership of another (target) company. The acquiring firm may believe that it can put the target firm's assets to work better than they currently are and that this justifies the premium price.

Finally, the example shows the role played by information in asset pricing. Superior information about an asset can increase its value by reducing its risk. When you consider buying a stock, there are many unknown possibilities about the future cash flows. The buyer who has the best information about these cash flows will discount them at a lower interest rate than will a buyer who is very uncertain.

Now let us apply these ideas to stock valuation. Suppose that you are considering the purchase of stock expected to pay dividends of ₹2 next year ($D_1 = ₹2$). The firm is expected to grow at 3% indefinitely. You are quite *uncertain* about both the constancy of the dividend stream and the accuracy of the estimated growth rate. To compensate yourself for this risk, you require a return of 15%.

Now suppose Anshuman, another investor, has spoken with industry insiders and feels more confident about the projected cash flows. Anshuman only requires a 12% return because his perceived risk is lower than yours. Varun, on the other hand, is dating the CEO of the company. He knows with near certainty what the future of the firm actually is. He thinks that both the estimated growth rate and the estimated cash flows are lower than what they will *actually* be in the future. Because he sees almost no risk in this investment, he only requires a 7% return.

What are the values each investor will give to the stock? Applying the Gordon growth model yields the following stock prices.

Investor	Discount Rate	Stock Price
You	15%	₹16.67
Anshuman	12%	₹22.22
Varun	7%	₹50.00

You are willing to pay ₹16.67 for the stock. Anshuman would pay up to ₹22.22, and Varun would pay ₹50. The investor with the lowest perceived risk is willing to pay the most for the stock. If there were no other traders, the market price would be just above ₹22.22. If you already held the stock, you would sell it to Varun.

The point of this section is that the players in the market, bidding against each other, establish the market price. When new information is released about a firm, expectations change, and with them, prices change. New information can cause changes in expectations about the level of future dividends or the risk of those dividends. Since market participants are constantly receiving new information and constantly revising their expectations, it is reasonable that stock prices are constantly changing as well.

Errors in Valuation

In this chapter, we learned about several asset valuation models. An interesting exercise is to apply these models to real firms. Students who do this find that computed stock prices do not match market prices much of the time. Students often question whether the models are wrong or incomplete or whether they are simply being used incorrectly. There are many opportunities for errors in applying the models. These include problems estimating growth, estimating risk, and forecasting dividends.

Problems with Estimating Growth

The constant growth model requires the analyst to estimate the constant rate of growth the firm will experience. You may estimate future growth by computing the historical growth rate in dividends, sales, or net profits. This approach fails to consider any changes in the firm or economy that may affect the growth rate. Robert Haugen, a professor of finance at the University of California, writes in his book, *The New Finance*, that competition will prevent high-growth firms from being able to maintain their historical growth rate. He demonstrates that, despite this, the stock prices of historically high-growth firms tend to reflect a continuation of the high growth rate. The result is that investors in these firms receive lower returns than they would by investing in mature firms. This just points out that even the experts have trouble estimating future growth rates. Table 13.2 shows the stock price for a firm with a 15% required return, a ₹2 dividend, and a range of different growth rates. The stock price varies from ₹14.43 at 1% growth to ₹228 at 14% growth rate. Estimating growth at 13% instead of 12% results in a ₹38.33 price difference.

TABLE 13.2   Stock Prices for a Security with $D_0 = ₹2.00$, $k_e = 15\%$, and Constant Growth Rates as Listed

Growth (%)	Price (₹)
1	14.43
3	17.17
5	21.00
10	44.00
11	55.50
12	74.67
13	113.00
14	228.00

Problems with Estimating Risk

The dividend valuation model requires the analyst to estimate the required return for the firm's equity. Table 13.3 shows how the price of a share of stock offering a $2 dividend and a 5% growth rate changes with different estimates of the required return. Clearly, stock price is highly dependent on the required return, despite our uncertainty regarding how it is found.

Problems with Forecasting Dividends

Even if we are able to accurately estimate a firm's growth rate and its required return, we are still faced with the problem of determining how much of the firm's earnings will be paid as dividends. Clearly, many factors can influence the dividend payout ratio. These will include the firm's future growth opportunities and management's concern over future cash flows.

Putting all of these concerns together, we see that stock analysts are seldom very certain that their stock price projections are accurate. This is why stock prices fluctuate so widely on news reports. For example, information that the economy is slowing can cause analysts to revise their growth expectations. When this happens across a broad spectrum of stocks, major market indexes can change.

TABLE 13.3   Stock Prices for a Security with $D_0 = ₹2.00$, $g = 5\%$, and Required Returns as Listed

Required Return (%)	Price (₹)
10	42.00
11	35.00
12	30.00
13	26.25
14	23.33
15	21.00

Does all this mean that you should not invest in the market? No, it only means that short-term fluctuations in stock prices are expected and are natural. Over the long term, the stock price will adjust to reflect the true earnings of the firm. If high-quality firms are chosen for your portfolio, they should provide fair returns over time.

CASE

The 2007–2009 Financial Crisis and the Stock Market

The subprime financial crisis that started in August 2007 led to one of the worst bear markets in the last 50 years. Our analysis of stock price valuation, again using the Gordon growth model, can help us understand how this event affected stock prices.

The subprime financial crisis had a major negative impact on the economy leading to a downward revision of the growth prospects for U.S. companies, thus lowering the dividend growth rate (g) in the Gordon model. The resulting increase in the denominator in Equation 5 would lead to a decline in P_0 and hence a decline in stock prices.

Increased uncertainty for the U.S. economy and the widening credit spreads resulting from the subprime crisis would also raise the required return on investment in equity. A higher ke also leads to an increase in the denominator in Equation 5, a decline in P_0, and a general fall in stock prices.

In the early stages of the financial crisis, the decline in growth prospects and credit spreads were moderate and so, as the Gordon model predicts, the stock market decline was also moderate. However, when the crisis entered a particularly virulent stage, credit spreads shot through the roof, the economy tanked, and as the Gordon model predicts, the stock market crashed. Between 6 January 2009, and 6 March 2009, the Dow Jones Industrial Average fell from 9,015 to 6,547. Between October 2007 (high of 14,066) and March 2009, the market lost 53% of its value. Within a year the index was back over 10,000.

The global stock market crash was widespread as the stock prices in almost all countries around the world witnessed substantial correction, notwithstanding the differences across countries in terms of fundamentals and the extent of impact of the financial crisis on the real economies. Many EMEs became part of the global asset price bubble, as the turmoil in the advanced countries became widespread. The Indian domestic equity market remained generally weak during 2008–2009 and witnessed high degrees of volatility in stock prices. The BSE Sensex fell to a low of 8160 on 9 March 2009 witnessing a decline of 60.9% from the peak of 8 January 2008. The corresponding decline in market capitalisation was 63%. During 2008–2009, the BSE Sensex and S&P CNX Nifty decreased by 37.9% and 36.2%, respectively. The slide in the stock prices during 2008–2009 reflected the response to a series of negative news.

The market capitalisation of BSE contracted sharply by 39.9% by end-March 2009, reflecting fall in stock prices and significantly lower listing of new securities. The price-earning (P/E) ratio of BSE Sensex also declined significantly. Volatility in the stock markets increased sharply during 2008–2009 with a significant drop in the turnover—both in cash and derivatives segments.

TABLE 13.4   Indian Equity Markets During the Financial Crisis: Key Indicators

Indicator	BSE			NSE		
	2006–07	2007–08	2008–09	2006–07	2007–08	2008–09
1	2	3	4	5	6	7
1. BSE SENSEX/SP CNX Nifty						
(i) Average	12,277	16,569	12,366	3,572	4,897	3,731
(ii) End of the year	13,072	15,644	9,709	3,822	4,735	3,021
2. Coefficient of variation (%)	11.1	13.7	24.2	10.4	14.4	23.2
3. Price-Earning ratio@	20.3	20.1	13.7	18.4	20.6	14.3
4. Price-Book value ratio@	5.1	5.2	2.7	4.9	5.1	2.5
5. Yield (per cent per annum)@	1.3	1.1	1.8	1.3	1.1	1.9
6. Listed companies (number)	4,821	4,887	4,929	1,228	1,381	1,432
7. Cash segment turnover (Rupees crore)	9,56,185	15,78,858	11,00,074	19,45,285	35,51,038	27,52,023
8. Derivative segment turnover (Rupees crore)	59,007	2,42,308	12,268	73,56,242	1,30,90,478	1,10,10,482
9. Market capitalisation (Rupees crore)#	35,45,041	51,38,015	30,86,076	33,67,350	48,58,122	28,96,194
10. Market capitalisation to GDP ratio (%)	85.5	108.8	58.0	81.6	102.9	54.4

@: Based on 30 scrips included in the BSE Sensex and are as at end–March.
#: As at end–March.
Source: Bombay Stock Exchange Limited (BSE) and National Stock Exchange of India Limited (NSE).

The losses suffered in the domestic stock market during 2008–2009 were spread across stocks in all sectors. Consumer durables, metal, capital goods and banking sector indices suffered higher losses than the average BSE Sensex during 2008–2009, while information technology, auto, oil and gas, public sector units, healthcare and fast moving consumer goods sectoral indices posted relatively lower losses. The higher losses encountered by the former group of sectors of BSE Sensex perhaps revealed the greater sensitivity of these sectors to economic slowdown and the impact of the global financial crisis. The BSE mid-cap and BSE small-cap recorded higher losses during 2008–2009, which could be partly because of the greater impact of credit squeeze on these categories of companies and also the greater impact of export slowdown on small and medium sized companies.

As a part of the global deleveraging process and general increase in risk aversion towards EMEs, the foreign institutional investors (FIIs) withdrew large amount of their investments from the Indian market. According to the data released by the SEBI, FIIs made swift reversals from large net purchases in the Indian equity market during 2007–2008 to large net sales during 2008–2009. Investments by mutual funds in equities also declined during 2008–2009, whereas their investments in debt increased, reflecting the lesser risk involved in government debt.[5] Table 13.4 depicts the key indicators in Indian equity markets during the global financial crisis.

---

[5]RBI Annual Report, 2009. https://www.rbi.org.in/scripts/AnnualReportPublications.aspx?Id=896, as accessed on 8 February 2017 at 3pm.

The September 11 Terrorist Attack, the Enron Scandal, and the Stock Market

In 2001, two big shocks hit the stock market: the September 11 terrorist attack and the Enron scandal. Our analysis of stock price evaluation, again using the Gordon growth model, can help us understand how these events affected stock prices.

The September 11 terrorist attack raised the possibility that terrorism against the United States would paralyze the country. These fears led to a downward revision of the growth prospects for U.S. companies, thus lowering the dividend growth rate, g, in the Gordon model. The resulting rise in the denominator in Equation 5 should lead to a decline in P_0 and hence a decline in stock prices.

Increased uncertainty for the U.S. economy would also raise the required return on investment in equity. A higher k_e also leads to a rise in the denominator in Equation 5, a decline in P_0, and a general fall in stock prices. As the Gordon model predicts, the stock market fell by over 10% immediately after September 11.

Subsequently, the U.S. successes against the Taliban in Afghanistan and the absence of further terrorist attacks reduced market fears and uncertainty, causing g to recover and k_e to fall. The denominator in Equation 5 then fell, leading to a recovery in P_0 and the stock market in October and November. However, by the beginning of 2002, the Enron scandal and disclosures that many companies had overstated their earnings caused many investors to doubt the formerly rosy forecast of earnings and dividend growth for corporations. The resulting revision of g downward, and the rise in k_e because of increased uncertainty about the quality of accounting information, should have led to a rise in the denominator in the Gordon Equation 5, thereby lowering P_0 for many companies and hence the overall stock market. As predicted by our analysis, this is exactly what happened. The stock market recovery was aborted and it entered a downward slide.

Stock Market Indexes

A stock market index is used to monitor the behavior of a group of stocks. By reviewing the average behavior of a group of stocks, investors are able to gain some insight as to how a broad group of stocks may have performed. Various stock market indexes are reported to give investors an indication of the performance of different groups of stocks. The most commonly quoted index is the Dow Jones Industrial Average (DJIA), which is based on the performance of the stocks of 30 large companies. The following Mini-Case box provides more background on this famous index. Table 13.5 lists the 30 stocks that currently made up the index.

In India, the S&P BSE SENSEX, first compiled in 1986, was calculated on a Market Capitalization-Weighted methodology of 30 component stocks representing large, well-established and financially sound companies across key sectors. The base year of S&P BSE SENSEX was taken as 1978–1979. S&P BSE SENSEX today is widely reported in both domestic and international markets through print as well

TABLE 13.5 The Thirty Companies That Make Up the Dow Jones Industrial Average

Company	Stock Symbol
3 M	MMM
American Express	AXP
Apple	AAPL
Boeing	BA
Caterpillar	CAT
Chevron	CVX
Cisco	CSCO
Coca Cola	KO
Disney	DIS
E I du Pont de Nemours and Co	DD
Exxon Mobil	XOM
General Electric	GE
Goldman Sachs	GS
Home Depot	HD
IBM	IBM
Intel	INTC
Johnson & Johnson	JNJ
J P Morgan Chase	JPM
McDonald's	MCD
Merck	MRK
Microsoft	MSFT
Nike	NKE
Pfizer	PFE
Procter & Gamble	PG
Travelers Companies Inc.	TRV
United Technologies	UTX
United Health	UNH
Verizon	VZ
Visa	V
WalMart	WMT

Source: http://money.cnn.com/data/dow30/

as electronic media. It is scientifically designed and is based on globally accepted construction and review methodology. Since 1 September 2003, S&P BSE SENSEX is being calculated on a free-float market capitalization methodology. The "free-float market capitalization-weighted" methodology is a widely followed index construction methodology on which majority of global equity indices are based on; all major index providers like MSCI, FTSE, STOXX, and Dow Jones use the free-float methodology. Table 13.6 lists the 30 stocks that make up the BSE Sensex.

TABLE 13.6 The Thirty Companies That Make up the BSE Sensex

Company	Scrip Code
Adani Ports and Special Economic Zone	532921
Asian Paints	500820
Axis Bank Ltd	532215
Bajaj Auto Ltd	532977
Bharti Airtel Ltd	532454
Cipla Ltd/India	500087
Coal India Ltd	533278
Dr Reddy's Laboratories Ltd	500124
Gail India Ltd	532155
HDFC Bank Ltd	500180
Hero MotoCorp Ltd	500182
Hindustan Unilever Ltd	500696
Housing Development Finance Corp	500010
ICICI Bank Ltd	532174
Infosys Ltd	500209
ITC Ltd	500875
Larsen & Toubro Ltd	500510
Lupin Ltd	500257
Mahindra & Mahindra Ltd	500520
Maruti Suzuki India Ltd	532500
NTPC Ltd	532555
Oil & Natural Gas Corp Ltd	500312
Power Grid Corp of India Ltd	532898
Reliance Industries Ltd	500325
State Bank of India	500112
Sun Pharmaceutical Industries Ltd	524715
Tata Consultancy Services Ltd	532540
Tata Motors Ltd	500570
Tata Steel Ltd	500470
Wipro Ltd	507685

Source: http://www.bseindia.com/sensexview/IndicesWatch_Weight.aspx?iname=BSE30&index_Code=16, as accessed on 8 February 2017 at 3pm.

One can identify the booms and busts of the Indian equity market through S&P BSE SENSEX. As the oldest index in the country, it provides the time series data over a fairly long period of time, starting from 1979 onwards. Figure 13.1 plots the BSE Sensex from 2007 onwards. Figure 13.2 plots the Nifty for the same period.

Other indexes, such as Standard & Poor's 500 Index, the NASDAQ composite, and the NYSE composite, may be more useful for following the performance of different groups of stocks.

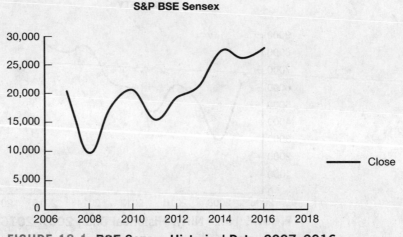

FIGURE 13.1 **BSE Sensex Historical Data, 2007–2016**

Source: http://www.bseindia.com/indices/IndexArchiveData.aspx, as accessed on 8 February 2017 at 3pm.
The prices indicated here are the closing prices.

> ## MINI-CASE

History of the Dow Jones Industrial Average

The Dow Jones Industrial Average (DJIA) is an index composed of 30 "blue chip" industrial firms. On 26 May 1896, Charles H. Dow added up the prices of 12 of the best-known stocks and created an average by dividing the number of stocks. In 1916, eight more stocks were added, and in 1928, the 30 stock average made its debut.

Today the editors of the *Wall Street Journal* select the firms that make up the DJIA. They take a broad view of the type of firm that is considered "industrial": in essence, it is almost any company that is not in the transportation or utility business (because there are also Dow Jones averages for those kinds of stocks). In choosing a new company for DJIA, they look among sub-stantial industrial companies with a history of successful growth and wide interest among investors. The components of the DJIA are changed periodically. For example, in 2009, General Motors and Citigroup were replaced with The Travelers Companies and Cisco Systems. In 2012, United Health Group replaced Kraft Foods.

Most market watchers agree that the DJIA is not the best indicator of the market's overall day-to-day performance. Indeed, it varies substantially from broader-based stock indexes in the short run. It con-tinues to be followed so closely, primarily because it is the oldest index and was the first to be quoted by other publications. But it tracks the performance of the market reasonably well over the long run.

Buying Foreign Stocks

> **GO ONLINE**
> Access a wealth of information about the current DJIA and its history at
> **www.djindexes.com.**

In Chapter 4, we learned that diversification of a portfolio reduces risk. In recent years, investors have come to realize that some risk can also be eliminated by diver-sifying across different countries. When one country is suffering from a recession, others may be booming. If inflationary concerns in the United States cause stock prices to drop, falling inflation in Japan may cause Japanese stocks to rise.

The problem with buying foreign stocks is that most foreign companies are not listed on any of the U.S. stock exchanges, so the purchase of shares is difficult. Intermediaries have found a way to solve this problem by selling **American deposi-tory receipts (ADRs).** A U.S. bank buys the shares of a foreign company and places

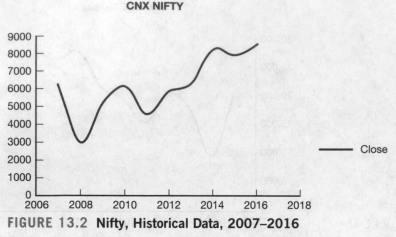

FIGURE 13.2   Nifty, Historical Data, 2007–2016

Courtesy: http://www.moneycontrol.com/stocks/hist_index_result.php?indian_indices=9, as
accessed on 8 February 2017 at 3pm.
The prices indicated here are the closing prices.

them in its vault. The bank then issues receipts against these shares, and these
receipts can be traded domestically, usually on the NASDAQ. Trade in ADRs is conducted entirely in U.S. dollars, and the bank converts stock dividends into U.S. currency. One advantage of the ADR is that it allows foreign firms to trade in the United
States without the firms having to meet the disclosure rules required by the SEC.

Foreign stock trading has been growing rapidly. Interest is particularly keen in
the stocks of firms in emerging economies such as Mexico, Brazil, and South Korea.

As the worldwide recession of 2008 demonstrated, while volatility peculiar to
one country can be reduced by diversification, the degree of economic interconnec-
tivity among nations means that some risk always remains.

Regulation of the Stock Market

Properly functioning capital markets are a hallmark of an economically advanced
economy. For an economy to flourish, firms must be able to raise funds to take
advantage of growth opportunities as they become available. Firms raise funds in
the capital markets, and for these to function properly investors must be able to
trust the information that is released about the firms that are using them. Markets
can collapse in the absence of this trust. The most notable example of this in the
United States was the Great Depression. During the 1920s, about $50 billion in new
securities were offered for sale. By 1932, half had become worthless. The public's
confidence in the capital markets justifiably plummeted, and lawmakers agreed that
for the economy to recover, public faith had to be restored. Following a series of
investigative hearings, Congress passed the Securities Act of 1933, and shortly after
the Securities Act of 1934. The main purpose of these laws was to,

(i) require firms to tell public the truth about their businesses and
(ii) require brokers, dealers, and exchanges to treat investors fairly.

The US Congress established the Securities and Exchange Commission (SEC) to
enforce these laws. In India, such a regulatory role with regard to the capital markets
is vested with the Securities and Exchange Board of India (SEBI).

Securities and Exchange Board of India (SEBI)

GO ONLINE

Access **http://www.sebi. gov.in/sebiweb/stpages/ about_sebi.jsp** to know more about the SEBI. Also, go on line to view regulations of SEBI at **http://www.sebi.gov.in/ sebiweb/home/list/1/3/0/0/ Regulations**.

The Securities and Exchange Board of India was established on 12 April 1992 in accordance with the provisions of the Securities and Exchange Board of India Act, 1992.

The Preamble of the Securities and Exchange Board of India describes the basic functions of the Securities and Exchange Board of India as,

"...to protect the interests of investors in securities and to promote the development of, and to regulate the securities market and for matters connected therewith or incidental thereto".

SUMMARY

1. There are both organized and over-the-counter exchanges. Organized exchanges are distinguished by a physical building where trading takes place. The over-the-counter market operates primarily over phone lines and computer links. Typically, larger firms trade on organized exchanges and smaller firms trade in the over-the-counter market, though there are many exceptions to this rule. In recent years, ECNs have begun to capture a significant portion of business traditionally belonging to the stock exchanges. These electronic networks are likely to become increasingly significant players in the future.

2. Stocks are valued as the present value of the dividends. Unfortunately, we do not know precisely what these dividends will be. This introduces a great deal of error to the valuation process. The Gordon growth model is a simplified method of computing stock value that depends on the assumption that the dividends are growing at a constant rate forever. Given our uncertainty regarding future dividends, this assumption is often the best we can do.

3. An alternative method for estimating a stock price is to multiply the firm's earnings per share times the industry price earnings ratio. This ratio can be adjusted up or down to reflect specific characteristics of the firm.

4. The interaction among traders in the market is what actually sets prices on a day-to-day basis. The trader that values the security the most, either because of less uncertainty about the cash flows or because of greater estimated cash flows, will be willing to pay the most. As new information is released, investors will revise their estimates of the true value of the security and will either buy or sell it depending upon how the market price compares to their estimated valuation. Because small changes in estimated growth rates or required return result in large changes in price, it is not surprising that the markets are often volatile.

KEY TERMS

American depository receipts (ADRs), p. 333
ask price, p. 318
bid price, p. 318

common stockholder, p. 315
generalized dividend model, p. 322
Gordon growth model, p. 322

BSE, p. 316
preferred stock, p. 315
price earnings ratio (PE), p. 324

QUESTIONS

1. What basic principle of finance can be applied to the valuation of any investment asset?

2. Identify the cash flows available to an investor in stock. How reliably can these cash flows be estimated? Compare the problem of estimating stock cash flows to estimating bond cash flows. Which security would you predict to be more volatile?

3. Discuss the features that differentiate organized exchanges from the over-the-counter market.

4. What is the National Association of Securities Dealers Automated Quotation System (NASDAQ)?

5. What is the BSE?

6. What distinguishes stocks from bonds?

7. Review the list of firms now included in the Dow Jones Industrial Average listed in Table 13.5. How many firms appear to be technology related? Discuss what this means in terms of the risk of the index.

8. Review the list of the firms included in the BSE Sensex in Table 13.6. What is the composition of these firms? Which sectors do these firms belong to? What does this mean in terms of the risk of the index?

QUANTITATIVE PROBLEMS

eBay, Inc., went public in September of 1998. The following information on shares outstanding was listed in the final prospectus filed with the SEC.[6]

In the IPO, eBay issued 3,500,000 new shares. The initial price to the public was $18.00 per share. The final first-day closing price was $44.88.

1. If the investment bankers retained $1.26 per share as fees, what were the net proceeds to eBay? What was the market capitalization of the new shares of eBay?

2. Two common statistics in IPOs are *underpricing* and *money left on the table*. Underpricing is defined as percentage change between the offering price and the first day closing price. Money left on the table is the difference between the first day closing price and the offering price, multiplied by the number of shares offered. Calculate the underpricing and money left on the table for eBay. What does this suggest about the efficiency of the IPO process?

3. The shares of NTPC Ltd., are expected to generate the following possible returns over the next 12 months:

Return (%)	Probability
−5	.10
5	.25
10	.30
15	.25
25	.10

If the stock is currently trading at ₹25 per share, what is the expected price in one year? Assume that the stock pays no dividends.

4. Suppose SoftPeople, Inc., is selling at ₹19.00 and currently pays an annual dividend of ₹0.65 per share. Analysts project that the stock will be priced around ₹23.00 in one year. What is the expected return?

5. Suppose ICICI Bank Ltd., is trading at ₹27.29 per share. It pays an annual dividend of ₹0.32 per share, and analysts have set a one-year target price around ₹33.30 per share. What is the expected return of this stock?

6. LaserAce is selling at ₹22.00 per share. The most recent annual dividend paid was ₹0.80. Using the Gordon growth model, if the market requires a return of 11%, what is the expected dividend growth rate for LaserAce?

7. Huskie Motors just paid an annual dividend of ₹1.00 per share. Management has promised shareholders to increase dividends at a constant rate of 5%. If the required return is 12%, what is the current price per share?

8. Suppose ITC Ltd., is trading at ₹27.29 per share. It pays an annual dividend of ₹0.32 per share, which is double last year's dividend of ₹0.16 per share. If this trend is expected to continue, what is the required return on ITC?

9. Gordon & Co.'s stock has just paid its annual dividend of ₹1.10 per share. Analysts believe that Gordon will maintain its historic dividend growth rate of 3%. If the required return is 8%, what is the expected price of the stock next year?

10. Macro Systems just paid an annual dividend of ₹0.32 per share. Its dividend is expected to double for the next four years (D_1 through D_4), after which it will grow at a more modest pace of 1% per year. If the required return is 13%, what is the current price?

11. Nat-T-Cat Industries just went public. As a growing firm, it is not expected to pay a dividend for the first five years. After that, investors expect Nat-T-Cat to pay an annual dividend of ₹1.00 per share (i.e., D_6 = 1.00), with no growth. If the required return is 10%, what is the current stock price?

12. Analysts are projecting that CB Railways will have earnings per share of ₹3.90. If the average industry PE ratio is about 25, what is the current price of CB Railways?

---

[6]This information is summarized from http://www.sec.gov/Archives/edgar/data/1065088/0001012870-98-002475.txt.

13. Suppose Microsoft, Inc., reports earnings per share of around ₹0.75. If Microsoft is in an industry with a PE ratio ranging from 30 to 40, what is a reasonable price range for Microsoft?

14. Consider the following security information for four securities making up an index:

Security	Price Time = 0	Price Time = 1	Shares Outstanding (millions)
1	8	13	20
2	22	25	50
3	35	30	120
4	50	55	75

What is the change in the value of the index from Time = 0 to Time = 1 if the index is calculated using a value-weighted arithmetic mean?

15. An index had an average (geometric) mean return over 20 years of 3.8861%. If the beginning index value was 100, what was the final index value after 20 years?

16. Compute the price of a share of stock that pays a ₹1 per year dividend and that you expect to be able to sell in one year for ₹20, assuming you require a 15% return.

17. The projected earnings per share for Risky Ventures, Inc., is ₹3.50. The average PE ratio for the industry composed of Risky Ventures' closest competitors is 21. After careful analysis, you decide that Risky Ventures is a little more risky than average, so you decide a PE ratio of 23 better reflects the market's perception of the firm. Estimate the current price of the firm's stock.

WEB EXERCISES

The Stock Market

1. Visit the BSE and NSE sites. Review the S&P BSE Sensex and CNX Nifty. Which index appears most volatile? In which index would you have rather invested in 2005 if the investment had been allowed to compound until now?

2. There are a number of indexes that track the performance of the stock market. It is interesting to review how well they track along with each other. Go to **http://bloomberg.com**. Click the "Charts" tab at the top of the screen. Alternatively, choose to display the DJIA, S&P 500, NASDAQ, and Russell 2000. Set the time frame to five years. Click "Get Chart."

a. Which index has been most volatile over the last five years?

b. Which index has posted the greatest gains over the last five years?

c. Now adjust the time frame to intraday. Which index has performed the best today? Which has been most volatile?

3. Visit **https://www.rbi.org.in/scripts/ AnnualReportPublications.aspx?Id=896**. Look at the BSE sectoral stock indices in the aftermath of the global financial crisis (Table 2.68). Do you find that all sectors shared in the losses equally? What could be the possible reasons for these trends?

14

The Foreign Exchange Market

> PREVIEW

The foreign exchange market in India has evolved over time in line with shifts in India's exchange rate policies, from a par value system to a basket-peg and further to a managed float exchange rate system. A par value system followed between 1947–1991 meant that the forex market was almost defunct. The market was highly regulated, with restrictions on external transactions, barriers to entry, low liquidity and high transaction costs. The period since 1992 witnessed wide ranging reform measures aimed at widening and deepening the foreign exchange market and liberalisation of exchange control regimes.

The price of one currency in terms of another is called the **exchange rate.** As you can see in Figure 14.1, exchange rates are highly volatile. The exchange rate affects the economy and our daily lives, because when the Indian rupee becomes more valuable relative to foreign currencies, foreign goods become cheaper for Indians and Indian goods become more expensive for foreigners. When the Indian rupee falls in value, foreign goods become more expensive for Indians and Indian goods become cheaper for foreigners.

We begin our study of international finance by examining the **foreign exchange market,** the financial market where exchange rates are determined.

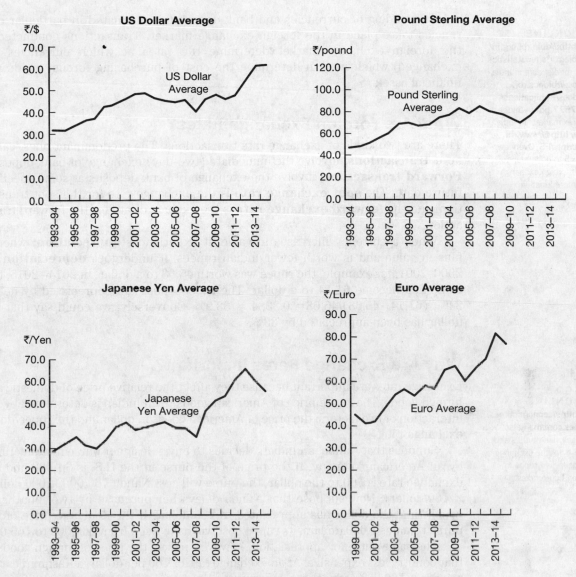

FIGURE 14.1 Exchange Rates, 1993–1994 to 2014–2015.

Exchange rates are highly volatile. Note that exchange rates are quoted as ₹/currency, so that a rise in these plots indicates a strengthening of the currency (weakening of the rupee).

Source: Reserve Bank of India, http://dbie.rbi.org.in/DBIE/dbie.rbi?site=statistics, as accessed on 8 February 2017 at 3pm.

Foreign Exchange Market

Most countries of the world have their own currencies: The United States has its dollar; the European Monetary Union, its euro; Brazil, its real; and China, its yuan. Trade between countries involves the mutual exchange of different currencies (or, more usually, bank deposits denominated in different currencies). When an Indian firm buys foreign goods, services, or financial assets, for example, Indian rupees (typically, bank deposits denominated in rupees) must be exchanged for foreign currency (bank deposits denominated in the foreign currency).

GO ONLINE

Access **http://dbie.rbi.org.in/ DBIE/dbie.rbi?site=statistics** for forex market data in India and **https://rbidocs.rbi. org.in/rdocs/Publications/ PDFs/77577.pdf** to understand forex markets in India. Also view **https://www.rbi. org.in/scripts/FS_Overview. aspx?fn=5** to understand the RBI's foreign exchange management function..

The trading of currencies and bank deposits denominated in particular currencies takes place in the foreign exchange market. Transactions conducted in the foreign exchange market determine the rates at which currencies are exchanged, which in turn determine the cost of purchasing foreign goods and financial assets.

What Are Foreign Exchange Rates?

There are two kinds of exchange rate transactions. The predominant ones, called **spot transactions,** involve the immediate (two-day) exchange of bank deposits. **Forward transactions** involve the exchange of bank deposits at some specified future date. The **spot exchange rate** is the exchange rate for the spot transaction, and the **forward exchange rate** is the exchange rate for the forward transaction.

When a currency increases in value, it experiences **appreciation;** when it falls in value and is worth fewer Indian rupees, it undergoes **depreciation.** In 2000–2001, for example, the rupee was worth 45.68 to a dollar. In 2014– 2015, this value had become 61.14 to a dollar. The rupee, thus, had depreciated by nearly 34%: $(61.14-45.68)/45.68= 0.3384 = 33.9\%$. Conversely, we could say that the dollar has been appreciated by 33%.

Why Are Exchange Rates Important?

Exchange rates are important because they affect the relative price of domestic and foreign goods. The rupee price of American goods to an Indian is determined by the interaction of two factors: the price of American goods in dollar and the rupee/dollar exchange rate.

Suppose that Nanda, an Indian, decides to buy a designer purse manufactured by an American company. If the price of the purse in the U.S. is $ 1,000 and the exchange rate is ₹60 to the dollar, the purse will cost Nanda ₹60,000 (1000 dollars × ₹60/dollar). Now suppose that Nanda delays her purchase by two months, at which time the dollar has appreciated to ₹65/dollar. If the domestic price of the purse remains 1,000 dollars, its rupee cost will have risen from ₹60,000 to ₹65,000.

The same currency appreciation, however, makes the price of foreign goods in that country less expensive. At an exchange rate of ₹60 per dollar, a Kashmiri carpet priced at ₹60,000 costs Peter, the rugs and carpet dealer in Boston, $1000; if the exchange rate increases to ₹65 per dollar, the carpet will cost only $923.07.

A depreciation of the dollar lowers the cost of American goods in India but raises the cost of Indian goods in the United States. If the dollar drops in value to ₹ 40 per dollar, Nanda's purse will cost her only ₹40,000 instead of ₹60,000, and the Kashmiri rug will cost Peter $1500 rather than $1000.

Such reasoning leads to the following conclusion: ***When a country's currency appreciates (rises in value relative to other currencies), the country's goods abroad become more expensive and foreign goods in that country become cheaper (holding domestic prices constant in the two countries). Conversely, when a country's currency depreciates, its goods abroad become cheaper and foreign goods in that country become more expensive.***

Depreciation of a currency makes it easier for domestic manufacturers to sell their goods abroad and makes foreign goods less competitive in domestic markets.

GO ONLINE

Access **http://economictimes. indiatimes.com/markets/ forex** to get market rates and time charts for the exchange rate of the Indian rupee to major world currencies.

How Is Foreign Exchange Traded?

You cannot go to a centralized location to watch exchange rates being determined; currencies are not traded on exchanges such as the New York Stock Exchange. Instead, the foreign exchange market is organized as an over-the-counter market in which several hundred dealers (mostly banks) stand ready to buy and sell deposits denominated in foreign currencies. Because these dealers are in constant telephone and computer contact, the market is very competitive; in effect, it functions no differently from a centralized market.

An important point to note is that although banks, companies, and governments talk about buying and selling currencies in foreign exchange markets, they do not take a fistful of dollar bills and sell them for British pound notes. Rather, most trades involve the buying and selling of bank deposits denominated in different currencies. So when we say that a bank is buying dollars in the foreign exchange market, what we actually mean is that the bank is buying *deposits denominated in dollars*. The volume in this market is colossal, exceeding $4 trillion per day.

Trades in the foreign exchange market consist of transactions in excess of $1 million. The market that determines the exchange rates in "Following the Financial News" box given below is not where one would buy foreign currency for a trip abroad. Instead, we buy foreign currency in the retail market from dealers such as American Express or from banks. Because retail prices are higher than wholesale, when we buy foreign exchange, we obtain fewer units of foreign currency per dollar —that is, we pay a higher price for foreign currency—than the exchange rates quoted in the newspaper indicates.

Exchange Rates in the Long Run

Like the price of any good or asset in a free market, exchange rates are determined by the interaction of supply and demand. To simplify our analysis of exchange rates in a free market, we divide it into two parts. First, we examine how exchange rates are determined in the long run; then we use our knowledge of the long-run determinants of the exchange rate to help us understand how they are determined in the short run.

> FOLLOWING THE FINANCIAL NEWS

Foreign Exchange Rates

Foreign exchange rates are published daily in newspapers and Internet sites such as www.finance.yahoo.com. Exchange rates for a currency such as the euro are quoted in two ways: U.S. dollars per unit of domestic currency or domestic currency per U.S. dollar. For example, on 7 June, 2013, the euro exchange rate was quoted as $1.3218 per euro and 0.7565 euro per dollar. Americans generally would regard the exchange rate with the euro as $1.32 per euro, while Europeans think of it as 0.76 euro per dollar.

Exchange rates are quoted for the spot transaction (the spot exchange rate) and for forward transactions (the forward exchange rates) that will take place one month, three months, and six months in the future.

Law of One Price

The starting point for understanding how exchange rates are determined is a simple idea called the **law of one price:** if two countries produce an identical good, and transportation costs and trade barriers are very low, the price of the good should be the same throughout the world no matter which country produces it. Suppose that American steel costs $100 per ton and identical Japanese steel costs 10,000 yen per ton. For the law of one price to hold, the exchange rate between the yen and the dollar must be 100 yen per dollar ($0.01 per yen), so that one ton of American steel sells for 10,000 yen in Japan (the price of Japanese steel) and one ton of Japanese steel sells for $100 in the United States (the price of U.S. steel). If the exchange rate were 200 yen to the dollar, Japanese steel would sell for $50 per ton in the United States or half the price of American steel, and American steel would sell for 20,000 yen per ton in Japan, twice the price of Japanese steel. Because American steel would be more expensive than Japanese steel in both countries and is identical to Japanese steel, the demand for American steel would go to zero. Given a fixed dollar price for American steel, the resulting excess supply of American steel will be eliminated only if the exchange rate falls to 100 yen per dollar, making the price of American steel and Japanese steel the same in both countries.

EXAMPLE 14.1

Law of One Price

Recently, the yen price of Japanese steel has increased by 10% (to 11,000 yen) relative to the dollar price of American steel (unchanged at $100). By what amount must the dollar increase or decrease in value for the law of one price to hold true?

> Solution

For the law of one price to hold, the exchange rate must rise to 110 yen per dollar, which is a 10% appreciation of the dollar.

The exchange rate rises to 110 yen so that the price of Japanese steel in dollars remains unchanged at $100 (11,000 per dollar). In other words, the 10% depreciation of the yen (10% appreciation of the dollar) just offsets the 10% increase in the yen price of the Japanese steel.

Theory of Purchasing Power Parity

GO ONLINE

Access the purchasing power parities home page at **http:// www.oecd.org/std/prices-ppp/** and find details about the PPP program overview, statistics, research, publications, and OECD meetings on PPP.

One of the most prominent theories of how exchange rates are determined is the **theory of purchasing power parity (PPP).** It states that exchange rates between any two currencies will adjust to reflect changes in the price levels of the two countries. The theory of PPP is simply an application of the law of one price to national price levels.

As example 14.1 illustrates, if the law of one price holds, a 10% rise in the yen price of Japanese steel results in a 10% appreciation of the dollar. Applying the law of one price to the price levels in the two countries produces the theory of purchasing power parity, which maintains that if the Japanese price level rises 10% relative to the U.S. price level, the dollar will appreciate by 10%. As our U.S./Japanese example illustrates, *the theory of PPP suggests that if one country's price level rises relative to another's, its currency should depreciate (the other country's currency should appreciate).*

Another way of thinking about purchasing power parity is through a concept called the **real exchange rate,** the rate at which domestic goods can be exchanged for foreign goods. In effect, it is the price of domestic goods relative to the price of foreign goods denominated in the domestic currency. For example, if a basket of goods in New Delhi costs ₹50, while the cost of the same basket of goods in New York is $75, because it costs 7,500 rupees while the exchange rate is at 100 rupees per dollar, then the real exchange rate is 0.66 (= ₹50/$75). The real exchange rate is below 1.0, indicating that it is cheaper to buy the basket of goods in India than in the United States. The real exchange rate indicates whether a currency is relatively cheap or not.

Another way of describing the theory of PPP is to say that it predicts that the real exchange rate is always equal to 1.0, so that the purchasing power of the rupee is the same as that of other currencies such as the yen, the dollar or the euro.

As you can see in Figure 14.2, this prediction of the theory of PPP is borne out in the long run. From 1991–2007, the Indian price levels rose relative to the U.S. price level, and as the theory of PPP predicts, the rupee depreciated against the dollar, though by 63%, an amount smaller than the 96% increase predicted by PPP.

Yet, as the same figure indicates, PPP theory often has little predictive power in the short run. Between 2002–2005, for example, the Indian price level rose by about 3% relative to that of the United States. At the same time, instead of depreciating, as the PPP theory predicts, the rupee actually appreciated by about 8% against the dollar. So even though PPP theory provides some guidance to the long-run movement of exchange rates, it is not perfect and in the short run is a particularly poor predictor. What explains PPP theory's failure to predict well?

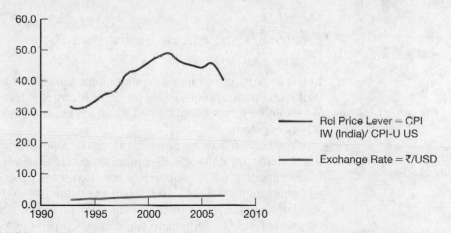

FIGURE 14.2 Purchasing Power Parity, India/United States, 1993–2007 (Index: 1982 = 100)

The PPP theory is analyzed using data from 1993–2007. The start year corresponds to the period of liberalization in India when the exchange rates were allowed to be determined by the market forces. From 2008 onwards, differential base years make U.S. and Indian price level data incomparable. Thus, from 2008 onwards, while the U.S. CPI is tracked with base 1982–84 = 100, the base for Indian CPI-IW changes to 2001 = 100. However, as can be seen, as the relative price levels in India increase, the Indian rupee depreciates vis-à-vis the dollar.

References: CPI-U data source: http://www.bls.gov/cpi/cpid1605.pdf; CPI-IW data for India, http://dbie.rbi.org.in/DBIE/dbie.rbi?site=publications; Exchange rate data, http://dbie.rbi.org.in/DBIE/dbie.rbi?site=statistics, as accessed on 8 February 2017 at 3pm.

Why the Theory of Purchasing Power Parity Cannot Fully Explain Exchange Rates

The PPP conclusion that exchange rates are determined solely by changes in relative price levels rests on the assumption that all goods are identical in both countries and that transportation costs and trade barriers are very low. When this assumption is true, the law of one price states that the relative prices of all these goods (that is, the relative price level between the two countries) will determine the exchange rate. The assumption that goods are identical may not be too unreasonable for say, American and Indian steel, but is it a reasonable assumption for American and Indian cars? Is a Maruti the equivalent of a Chevrolet or a Ford?

Because Marutis and Chevys or Fords are obviously not identical, their prices do not have to be equal. Marutis can be cheaper relative to Chevys and both Americans and Indians will still purchase Marutis. Because the law of one price does not hold for all goods, a rise in the price of Marutis relative to Chevys will not necessarily mean that the rupee must depreciate by the amount of the relative price increase of Marutis over Chevys.

Furthermore, PPP theory does not take into account that many goods and services (whose prices are included in a measure of a country's price level) are not traded across borders. Housing, land, and services such as restaurant meals, haircuts, and golf lessons are not traded goods. So even though the prices of these items might rise and lead to a higher price level relative to another country's, the exchange rate would experience little effect.

Factors That Affect Exchange Rates in the Long Run

In the long run, four major factors affect the exchange rate: relative price levels, tariffs and quotas, preferences for domestic versus foreign goods, and productivity. We examine how each of these factors affects the exchange rate while holding the others constant.

The basic reasoning proceeds along the following lines: Anything that increases the demand for domestically produced goods that are traded relatively to foreign traded goods tends to appreciate the domestic currency because domestic goods will continue to sell well even when the value of the domestic currency is higher. Similarly, anything that increases the demand for foreign goods relatively to domestic goods tends to depreciate the domestic currency because domestic goods will continue to sell well only if the value of the domestic currency is lower. In other words, *if a factor increases the demand for domestic goods relative to foreign goods, the domestic currency will appreciate; if a factor decreases the relative demand for domestic goods, the domestic currency will depreciate.*

Relative Price Levels In line with PPP theory, when prices of Indian goods rise (holding prices of foreign goods constant), the demand for Indian goods falls and the rupee tends to depreciate so that Indian goods can still sell well. By contrast, if prices of American goods rise so that the relative prices of Indian goods fall, the demand for Indian goods increases, and the rupee tends to appreciate because Indian goods will continue to sell well even with a higher value of the domestic currency. *In the long run, a rise in a country's price level (relative to the foreign price level) causes its currency to depreciate, and a fall in the country's relative price level causes its currency to appreciate.*

Trade Barriers Barriers to free trade such as **tariffs** (taxes on imported goods) and **quotas** (restrictions on the quantity of foreign goods that can be imported) can affect the exchange rate. Suppose that India increases its tariff or puts a lower quota on American steel. These increases in trade barriers increase the demand for Indian steel, and the rupee tends to appreciate because Indian steel will still sell well even with a higher value of the rupee. *Increasing trade barriers causes a country's currency to appreciate in the long run.*

Preferences for Domestic Versus Foreign Goods If the Americans develop an appetite for Indian goods—say, for Basmati rice and Bollywood movies— the increased demand for Indian goods (exports) tends to appreciate the rupee because the Indian goods will continue to sell well even at a higher value for the rupee. Likewise, if Indians decide that they prefer American cars to Indian cars, the increased demand for American goods (imports) tends to depreciate the rupee. *Increased demand for a country's exports causes its currency to appreciate in the long run; conversely, increased demand for imports causes the domestic currency to depreciate.*

Productivity When productivity in a country rises, it tends to rise in domestic sectors that produce traded goods rather than nontraded goods. Higher productivity, therefore, is associated with a decline in the price of domestically produced traded goods relative to foreign traded goods. As a result, the demand for traded domestic goods rises, and the domestic currency tends to appreciate. If, however, a country's productivity lags behind that of other countries, its traded goods become relatively more expensive, and the currency tends to depreciate. *In the long run, as a country becomes more productive relative to other countries, its currency appreciates.*[1]

Our long-run theory of exchange rate behavior is summarized in Table 14.1. We use the convention that the exchange rate E is quoted so that an appreciation of the currency corresponds to a rise in the exchange rate. In the case of India, this means that we are quoting the exchange rate as units of foreign currency per rupee (say dollar per rupee).[2]

---

[1]A country might be so small that a change in productivity or the preferences for domestic or foreign goods would have no effect on prices of these goods relative to foreign goods. In this case, changes in productivity or changes in preferences for domestic or foreign goods affect the country's income but will not necessarily affect the value of the currency. In our analysis, we are assuming that these factors can affect relative prices and consequently the exchange rate.

[2]Exchange rates can be quoted either as units of foreign currency per domestic currency or as units of domestic currency per foreign currency. In professional writing, many economists quote exchange rates as units of domestic currency per foreign currency so that an appreciation of the domestic currency is portrayed as a fall in the exchange rate. In India, we follow this convention i.e. the exchange rate is quoted as ₹per dollar, so that a movement in the exchange rate from ₹60/$ to ₹68/$ indicates a depreciation, and vice-versa. The opposite convention is used in the text here because it is more intuitive to think of an appreciation of the domestic currency as a rise in the exchange rate.

TABLE 14.1   **Summary Factors That Affect Exchange Rates**
SUMMARY   **in the Long Run**

Factor	Change in Factor	Response of the Exchange Rate, E^*
Domestic price level[†]	↑	↓
Trade barriers[†]	↑	↑
Import demand	↑	↓
Export demand	↑	↑
Productivity[†]	↑	↑

*Units of foreign currency per rupee: ↑ indicates domestic currency appreciation; ↓, depreciation.
[†]Relative to other countries.

Note: Only increases (↑) in the factors are shown; the effects of decreases in the variables on the exchange rate are the opposite of those indicated in the "Response" column.

Exchange Rates in the Short Run: A Supply and Demand Analysis

GO ONLINE
Access **https://www.rbi. org.in/scripts/Publications-View.aspx?id=16589** and study how the Reserve Bank reports current and historical exchange rates for many countries.

We have developed a theory of the long-run behavior of exchange rates. However, because factors driving long-run changes in exchange rates move slowly over time, if we are to understand why exchange rates exhibit such large changes (sometimes several percent) from day to day, we must develop a supply-and-demand analysis of how current exchange rates (spot exchange rates) are determined in the short run.

The key to understanding the short-run behavior of exchange rates is to recognize that an exchange rate is the price of domestic assets (bank deposits, bonds, equities, etc., denominated in the domestic currency) in terms of foreign assets (similar assets denominated in the foreign currency). Because the exchange rate is the price of one asset in terms of another, the natural way to investigate the short-run determination of exchange rates is to use an asset market approach that relies heavily on the theory of portfolio choice developed in Chapter 4 in which we outlined the determinants of asset demand. As you will see, however, the long-run determinants of the exchange rate we have just outlined, also play an important part in the short-run asset market approach.

In the past, supply-and-demand approaches to exchange rate determination emphasized the role of import and export demand. The more modern asset market approach used here emphasizes the stocks of assets rather than the flows of exports and imports over short periods because export and import transactions are small as compared to the amount of domestic and foreign assets at any given time. Thus, over short periods, decisions to hold domestic or foreign assets have a much greater role in exchange rate determination than the demand for exports and imports.

Supply Curve for Domestic Assets

We start by discussing the supply curve. In this analysis we treat India as the home country, so domestic assets are denominated in rupees. For simplicity, we use dollars to stand for any foreign country's currency, so foreign assets are denominated in dollars.

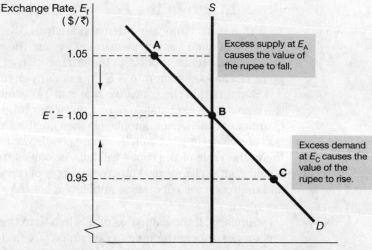

FIGURE 14.3 Equilibrium in the Foreign Exchange Market

Equilibrium in the foreign exchange market occurs at point B, the intersection of the demand curve D and the supply curve S. The equilibrium exchange rate is $E^* = 1$ dollar per rupee.

The quantity of rupee assets supplied is primarily the quantity of bank deposits, bonds, and equities in India, and for all practical purposes we can take this amount as fixed with respect to the exchange rate. The quantity supplied at any exchange rate does not change, so the supply curve, S, is vertical, as shown in Figure 14.3.

Demand Curve for Domestic Assets

The demand curve traces out the quantity demanded at each current exchange rate by holding everything else constant, particularly the expected future value of the exchange rate. We write the current exchange rate (the spot exchange rate) as E_t, and the expected exchange rate for the next period as E_{t+1}^e. As the theory of portfolio choice suggests, the most important determinant of the quantity of domestic (rupee) assets demanded is the relative expected return of domestic assets. Let's see what happens as the current exchange rate E_t falls.

Suppose we start at point A in Figure 14.3 where the current exchange rate is at 1.05 dollars per rupee. With the future expected value of the exchange rate held constant at E_{t+1}^e, a lower value of the exchange rate—say at $E^* = 1$ dollar per rupee—implies that the rupee is more likely to rise in value, that is, appreciate. The greater the expected rise (appreciation) of the rupee, the higher the relative expected return on rupee (domestic) assets. The theory of portfolio choice then tells us that because rupee assets are now more desirable to hold, the quantity of rupee assets demanded will rise, as is shown by point B in Figure 14.3. If the current exchange rate is even lower at 0.95 dollars per rupee, there is an even higher expected appreciation of the rupee, a higher expected return, and therefore an even greater quantity of rupee assets demanded. This effect is shown in point C in Figure 14.3. The resulting demand curve, D, which connects these points, is downward-sloping, indicating that at lower current values of the rupee (everything else being equal), the quantity demanded of rupee assets is higher.

Equilibrium in the Foreign Exchange Market

As in the usual supply-and-demand analysis, the market is in equilibrium when the quantity of rupee assets demanded equals the quantity supplied. In Figure 14.3, equilibrium occurs at point B, the intersection of the demand and supply curves. At point B, the exchange rate is $E^* = 1$ dollar per rupee.

Suppose that the exchange rate is at 1.05 dollars per rupee, which is higher than the equilibrium exchange rate of 1 dollar per rupee. As we can see in Figure 14.3, the quantity of rupee assets supplied is then greater than the quantity demanded, a condition of excess supply. Given that more people want to sell rupee assets than want to buy them, the value of the rupee will fall. As long as the exchange rate remains above the equilibrium exchange rate, an excess supply of rupee assets will continue to be available, and the rupee will fall in value until it reaches the equilibrium exchange rate of 1 dollar per rupee.

Similarly, if the exchange rate is less than the equilibrium exchange rate at 0.95 dollars per rupee, the quantity of rupee assets demanded will exceed the quantity supplied, a condition of excess demand. Given that more people want to buy rupee assets than want to sell them, the value of the rupee will rise until the excess demand disappears and the value of the rupee is again at the equilibrium exchange rate of 1 dollar per rupee.

Explaining Changes in Exchange Rates

The supply-and-demand analysis of the foreign exchange market can explain how and why exchange rates change. We have simplified this analysis by assuming the amount of rupee assets is fixed and the supply curve is vertical at a given quantity and does not shift. Under this assumption, we need to look at only those factors that shift the demand curve for rupee assets to explain how exchange rates change over time.

Shifts in the Demand for Domestic Assets

As we have seen, the quantity of domestic (rupee) assets demand depends on the expected return of rupee assets. To see how the demand curve shifts, we need to ask how the quantity demands change, holding the current exchange rate, E_t, constant, when other factors change over time.

For insight into which direction the demand curve shifts, suppose you are an investor who is considering putting funds into domestic (rupee) assets. When a factor changes, decide whether at a given level of the current exchange rate, holding all other variables constant, you would earn a higher or lower expected return on rupee assets versus foreign assets. This decision tells you whether you want to hold more or fewer rupee assets and thus whether the quantity demand increases or decreases at each level of the exchange rate. Knowing the direction of the change in the quantity demand at each exchange rate indicates which way the demand curve shifts. In other words, if the relative expected return of rupee assets rises holding the current exchange rate constant, the demand curve shifts to the right. If the relative expected return falls, the demand curve shifts to the left.

Domestic Interest Rate, i^D Suppose that rupee assets pay an interest rate of i^D. When the domestic interest rate on rupee assets, i^D, rises, holding the current exchange rate E_t and everything else constant, the return on rupee assets increases

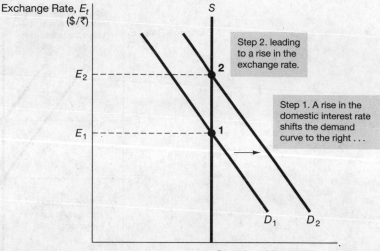

FIGURE 14.4 Response to an Increase in the Domestic Interest Rate, i^D

When the domestic interest rate i^D increases, the relative expected return on domestic (rupee) assets increases and the demand curve shifts to the right. The equilibrium exchange rate rises from E_1 to E_2.

relative to foreign assets, so people will want to hold more rupee assets. The quantity of rupee assets demanded increases at every value of the exchange rate, as shown by the rightward shift of the demand curve from D_1 to D_2 in Figure 14.4. The new equilibrium is reached at point 2, the intersection of D_2 and S, and the equilibrium exchange rate rises from E_1 to E_2. ***An increase in the domestic interest rate i^D shifts the demand curve for domestic assets, D, to the right and causes the domestic currency to appreciate ($E\uparrow$).***

Conversely, if i^D falls, the relative expected return on rupee assets falls, the demand curve shifts to the left, and the exchange rate falls. ***A decrease in the domestic interest rate i^D shifts the demand curve for domestic assets, D, to the left and causes the domestic currency to depreciate ($E\downarrow$).***

Foreign Interest Rate, i^F Suppose that the foreign asset pays an interest rate of i^F. When the foreign interest rate i^F rises, holding the current exchange rate and everything else constant, the return on foreign assets rises relatively to rupee assets. Thus the relative expected return on rupee assets falls. Now people want to hold fewer rupee assets, and the quantity demanded decreases at every value of the exchange rate. This scenario is shown by the leftward shift of the demand curve from D_1 to D_2 in Figure 14.5. The new equilibrium is reached at point 2, when the value of the rupee has fallen. Conversely, a decrease in i^F raises the relative expected return on rupee assets, shifts the demand curve to the right, and raises the exchange rate. To summarize, ***an increase in the foreign interest rate i^F shifts the demand curve D to the left and causes the domestic currency to depreciate; a fall in the foreign interest rate i^F shifts the demand curve D to the right and causes the domestic currency to appreciate.***

Changes in the Expected Future Exchange Rate, E^e_{t+1} Expectations about the future value of the exchange rate plays an important role in shifting the current

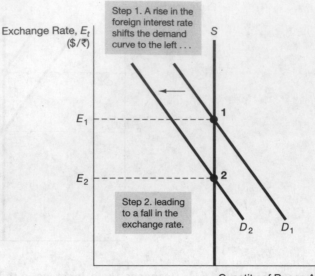

Exchange Rate, E_t ($\$/\mathbb{\bar{R}}$)

Step 1. A rise in the foreign interest rate shifts the demand curve to the left . . .

S

E_1

1

E_2

2

Step 2. leading to a fall in the exchange rate.

D_2 D_1

Quantity of Rupee Assets

FIGURE 14.5 Response to an Increase in the Foreign Interest Rate, i^F

When the foreign interest rate i^F increases, the relative expected return on domestic (rupee) assets falls and the demand curve shifts to the left. The equilibrium exchange rate falls from E_1 to E_2.

demand curve because the demand for domestic assets, like that for any durable good, depends on the future resale price. Any factor that causes the expected future exchange rate, E^e_{t+1}, to rise increases the expected appreciation of the rupee. The result is a higher relative expected return on rupee assets, which increases the demand for rupee assets at every exchange rate, thereby shifting the demand curve to the right from D_1 to D_2 in Figure 14.6. The equilibrium exchange rate rises to point 2 at the intersection of the D_2 and S curves. ***A rise in the expected future exchange rate, E^e_{t+1}, shifts the demand curve to the right and causes an appreciation of the domestic currency. Using the same reasoning, a fall in the expected future exchange rate, E^e_{t+1}, shifts the demand curve to the left and causes a depreciation of the currency.***

Earlier we discussed the determinants of the exchange rate in the long run: the relative price level, relative tariffs and quotas, import and export demand, and relative productivity (refer to Table 14.1). These four factors influence the expected future exchange rate. The theory of purchasing power parity suggests that if a higher Indian price level relative to the foreign price level is expected to persist, the rupee will depreciate in the long run. A higher expected relative Indian price level should thus have a tendency to lower E^e_{t+1}, lower the relative expected return on rupee assets, shift the demand curve to the left, and then lower the current exchange rate.

Similarly, the other long-run determinants of the exchange rate can influence the relative expected return on rupee assets and the current exchange rates. Briefly, the following changes, all of which increase the demand for domestic goods relative to foreign goods, will raise E^e_{t+1}: (1) expectations of a fall in the Indian price level relative to the foreign price level, (2) expectations of higher Indian trade barriers

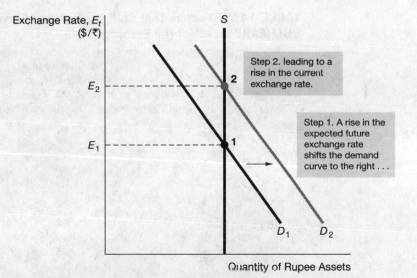

FIGURE 14.6 Response to an Increase in the Expected Future Exchange Rate, E^e_{t+1}

When the expected future exchange rate increases, the relative expected return on domestic (rupee) assets rises and the demand curve shifts to the right. The equilibrium exchange rate rises from E_1 to E_2.

relative to foreign trade barriers, (3) expectations of lower Indian import demand, (4) expectations of higher foreign demand for Indian exports, and (5) expectations of higher Indian productivity relative to foreign productivity. By increasing E^e_{t+1}, all of these changes increase the relative expected return on rupee assets, shift the demand curve to the right, and cause an appreciation of the domestic currency, the rupee.

Recap: Factors That Change the Exchange Rate

Summary Table 14.2 outlines all the factors that shift the demand curve for domestic assets and thereby cause the exchange rate to change. Shifts in the demand curve occur when one factor changes, holding everything else constant, including the current exchange rate. Again, the theory of portfolio choice tells us that changes in the relative expected return on rupee assets are the source of shifts in the demand curve.

Let's review what happens when each of the seven factors in Table 14.2 changes. Remember that to understand which direction the demand curve shifts, consider what happens to the relative expected return on rupee assets when the factor changes. If the relative expected return rises, holding the current exchange rate constant, the demand curve shifts to the right. If the relative expected return falls, the demand curve shifts to the left.

1. When the interest rates on domestic assets, i^D, rise, the expected return on rupee assets rises at each exchange rate and so the quantity demanded increases. The demand curve therefore shifts to the right, and the equilibrium exchange rate rises, as is shown in the first row of Table 14.2.

2. When the foreign interest rate i^F rises, the return on foreign assets rises, so the relative expected return on rupee assets falls. The quantity demanded of rupee assets then falls, the demand curve shifts to the left, and the exchange rate declines, as in the second row of Table 14.2.

TABLE 14.2
SUMMARY
Factors That Shift the Demand Curve for Domestic Assets and Affect the Exchange Rate

Factor	Change in Factor	Change in Quantity Demanded of Domestic Assets at Each Exchange Rate	Response of Exchange Rate, E_t	
Domestic interest rate, i^D	↑	↑	↑	
Foreign interest rate, i^F	↑	↓	↓	
Expected domestic price level*	↑	↓	↓	
Expected trade barriers*	↑	↑	↑	
Expected import demand	↑	↓	↓	
Expected export demand	↑	↑	↑	
Expected productivity*	↑	↑	↑	

*Relative to other countries.

Note: Only increases (↑) in the factors are shown; the effects of decreases in the variables on the exchange rate are the opposite of those indicated in the "Response" column. The exchange rate in this analysis is expressed as $/₹.

3. When the expected price level is higher, our analysis of the long-run deter-minants of the exchange rate indicates that the value of the rupee will fall in the future. The expected return on rupee assets thus falls, the quantity demanded declines, the demand curve shifts to the left, and the exchange rate falls, as in the third row of Table 14.2.

4. With higher expected trade barriers, the value of the rupee is higher in the long run and the expected return on rupee assets is higher. The quantity demanded of rupee assets thus rises, the demand curve shifts to the right, and the exchange rate rises, as in the fourth row of Table 14.2.

5. When expected import demand rises, we expect the exchange rate to depre-ciate in the long run, so the expected return on rupee assets falls. The quan-tity demanded of rupee assets at each value of the current exchange rate therefore falls, the demand curve shifts to the left, and the exchange rate declines, as in the fifth row of Table 14.2.

6. When expected export demand rises, the opposite occurs because the exchange rate is expected to appreciate in the long run. The expected return on rupee assets rises, the demand curve shifts to the right, and the exchange rate rises, as in the sixth row of Table 14.2.

7. With higher expected domestic productivity, the exchange rate is expected to appreciate in the long run, so the expected return on domestic assets rises. The quantity demanded at each exchange rate therefore rises, the demand curve shifts to the right, and the exchange rate rises, as in the seventh row of Table 14.2.

CASE

Effect of Changes in Interest Rates on the Equilibrium Exchange Rate

Our analysis has revealed the factors that affect the value of the equilibrium exchange rate. Now we use this analysis to take a close look at the response of the exchange rate to changes in interest rates.

Changes in domestic interest rates i^D are often cited as a major factor affecting exchange rates. For example, we see headlines in the financial press like this one: "Rupee Recovers as Interest Rates Edge Upward." But is the view presented in this headline always correct?

Not necessarily, because to analyze the effects of interest rate changes, we must carefully distinguish the sources of the changes. The Fisher equation (Chapter 3) states that a nominal interest rate such as i^D equals the *real* interest rate plus expected inflation: $i = i_r + \pi^e$. The Fisher equation thus indicates that the interest rate i^D can change for two reasons: either the real interest rate i_r changes or the expected inflation rate π^e changes. The effect on the exchange rate is quite different, depending on which of these two factors is the source of the change in the nominal interest rate.

Suppose that the domestic real interest rate increases so that the nominal interest rate i^D rises while expected inflation remains unchanged. In this case, it is reasonable to assume that the expected future exchange rate is unchanged because expected inflation is unchanged. In this case, the increase in i^D increases the relative expected return on rupee assets, raises the quantity of rupee assets demanded at each level of the exchange rate, and shifts the demand curve to the right. We end up with the situation depicted in Figure 14.4, which analyzes an increase in i^D, holding everything else constant. Our model of the foreign exchange market produces the following result: ***When domestic real interest rates rise, the domestic currency appreciates.***

When the nominal interest rate rises because of an increase in expected inflation, we get a different result from the one shown in Figure 14.4. The rise in expected domestic inflation leads to a decline in the expected appreciation of the rupee, which is typically thought to be larger than the increase in the domestic interest rate i^D.* As a result, at any given exchange rate, the relative expected return on domestic (rupee) assets falls, the demand curve shifts to the left, and the exchange rate falls from E_1 to E_2, as shown in Figure 14.7. Our analysis leads to this conclusion: ***When domestic interest rates rise due to an expected increase in inflation, the domestic currency depreciates.***

Because this conclusion is completely different from the one reached when the rise in the domestic interest rate is associated with a higher real interest rate, we must always distinguish between *real* and *nominal* measures when analyzing the effects of interest rates on exchange rates.

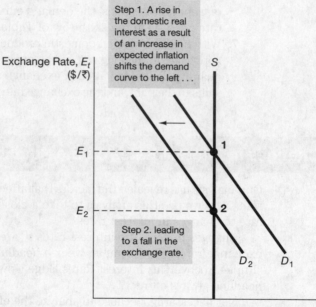

FIGURE 14.7 Effect of a Rise in the Domestic Interest Rate as a Result of an Increase in Expected Inflation

Because a rise in domestic expected inflation leads to a decline in expected rupee appreciation that is larger than the increase in the domestic interest rate, the relative expected return on domestic (rupee) assets falls. The demand curve shifts to the left, and the equilibrium exchange rate falls from E_1 to E_2.

*This conclusion is standard in asset market models of exchange rate determination; see Rudiger Dornbusch, "Expectations and Exchange Rate Dynamics," *Journal of Political Economy* 84 (1976): 1061–1076. It is also consistent with empirical evidence that suggests that nominal interest rates do not rise one-for-one with increases in expected inflation. See Frederic S. Mishkin, "The Real Interest Rate: An Empirical Investigation," *Carnegie-Rochester Conference Series on Public Policy* 15 (1981): 151–200; and Lawrence Summers, "The Nonadjustment of Nominal Interest Rates: A Study of the Fisher Effect," in *Macroeconomics, Prices and Quantities,* ed. James Tobin (Washington, DC: Brookings Institution, 1983), pp. 201–240.

CASE

India's Exchange Rate Policy

GO ONLINE

Access **https://www.rbi.org. in/scripts/BS_ViewBulletin. aspx?Id=7129** to understand REER. Further, access **https://rbi.org.in/ scripts/BS_ViewBulletin. aspx?Id=16164#C6** to view Governor, Dr. Raghuram Rajan's speech and his analysis of India's exchange rate.

India's exchange rate policy has evolved in tandem with the domestic as well as international developments. The period after independence was marked by a fixed exchange rate regime, which was in line with the Bretton Woods system prevalent then. The Indian rupee was pegged to the Pound Sterling on account of historic links with Britain. After the breakdown of Bretton Woods System in the early seventies, most of the countries moved towards a system of flexible/managed exchange rates. With the decline in the share of Britain in India's trade, increased diversification of India's international transactions together with the weaknesses of pegging to a single currency, the Indian rupee was de-linked from the Pound Sterling in September 1975.

The exchange rate subsequently came to be determined with reference to the daily exchange rate movements of an undisclosed basket of currencies of India's major trading partners. As the basket-linked management of the exchange rate of the rupee did not capture the market dynamics and the developments in the exchange rates of competing countries fully, the rupee's external value was allowed to be determined by market forces in a phased manner following the balance of payment difficulties in the nineties.

A significant two-step downward adjustment in the exchange rate of the rupee was made in 1991. In March 1992, Liberalised Exchange Rate Management System (LERMS) involving the dual exchange rate was instituted. A unified single market-determined exchange rate system, based on the demand for and supply of foreign exchange replaced the LERMS effective on 1 March 1993.

The Reserve Bank's exchange rate policy focusses on ensuring orderly conditions in the foreign exchange market. For the purpose, it closely monitors the developments in the financial markets at home and abroad. When necessary, it intervenes in the market by buying or selling foreign currencies. The market operations are undertaken either directly or through public sector banks.

In addition to the traditional instruments like forward and swap contracts, the Reserve Bank has facilitated increased availability of derivative instruments in the foreign exchange market. It has allowed trading in rupee-foreign currency swaps, foreign currency-rupee options, cross-currency options, interest rate swaps and currency swaps, forward rate agreements and currency futures.

The volatility in exchange rate is with reference to the Nominal Exchange rate. However, another way to study volatility is through Real Effective Exchange Rate (REER).

Source: https://www.rbi.org.in/scripts/FS_Overview.aspx?fn=5, as accessed on 8 February 2017 at 3pm.

CASE

Why Are Exchange Rates So Volatile?

☁ **GO ONLINE**

Access **https://rbidocs.rbi. org.in/rdocs/Publications/ PDFs/77577**.pdf and read Section V to understand the behaviour of the foreign exchange market in the 1993–2003 period.

The high volatility of foreign exchange rates surprises many people. Around forty years ago, economists generally believed that allowing exchange rates to be determined in the free market would not lead to large fluctuations in their values. Recent experience however appears to be in contrast to this. There have been episodes of exchange rate volatility in India since 1993.

The second major episode of exchange rate volatility was witnessed during the global financial crisis. Thus, the movement in the average exchange rate (₹/$) witnessed a depreciation of 12.4% in 2008–2009, as against an appreciation of 1.5%, 2.2% and 12.5% respectively in 2005–2006, 2006–2007 and 2007–2008.

In 2013, the rupee came under severe pressure after the signalling of tapering of quantitative easing by the U.S. Federal in May 2013, reaching an all-time low of ₹68.36 (RBI reference rate) against the dollar as on 28 August 2013. The rupee began its recovery thereafter responding to the measures taken by the Reserve Bank and the government and a contraction in Current Account Deficit (CAD). It moved in a range of ₹60.1 to ₹63.0 during Q4 of 2013–2014 and appreciated further in Q1 of 2014–2015.

The asset market approach to exchange rate determination that we have outlined in here gives a straightforward explanation of volatile exchange rates. Because expected appreciation of the domestic currency affects the expected return on foreign deposits, expectations about the price level, inflation, trade barriers, productivity, import demand, export demand, and the money supply play important roles in determining the exchange rate. When expectations about any of these variables change, as they often do, our model indicates that the expected return on foreign deposits, and therefore on the exchange rate, will be immediately affected. Because expectations on all these variables change with just about every bit of news that appears, it is not surprising that the exchange rate is volatile.

Because earlier models of exchange rate behavior focused on goods markets rather than asset markets, they did not emphasize changing expectations as a source of exchange rate movements, and so these earlier models could not predict substantial fluctuations in exchange rates. The failure of earlier models to explain volatility is one reason why they are no longer so popular. The more modern approach developed here emphasizes that the foreign exchange market is like any other asset market in which expectations of the future matter. The foreign exchange market, like other asset markets such as the stock market, displays substantial price volatility, and foreign exchange rates are notoriously hard to forecast.

References: https://www.rbi.org.in/Scripts/AnnualReportPublications.aspx?Id=1120; https://www.rbi.org.in/Scripts/PublicationsView.aspx?id=12303, as accessed on 8 February 2017 at 3pm.

The Rupee and Interest Rates

The trends of exchange rates and interest rates in India over the period 2004–2005 to 2013– 2014, provides insights into the direction of exchange rate movements. As can be seen from Figure 14.8, which plots measures of real and nominal interest rates and the value of the rupee in terms of dollars (both in real and nominal terms), there is, by and large, a co-movement between interest rates and exchange rates.

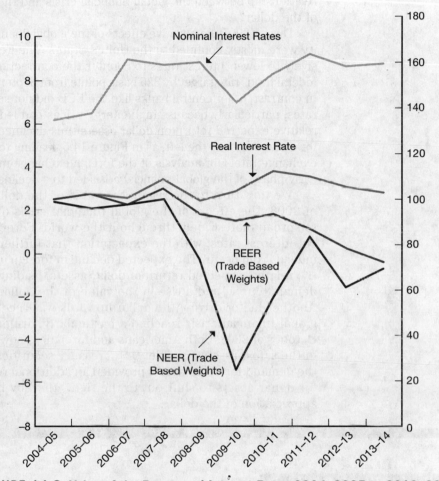

FIGURE 14.8 Value of the Rupee and Interest Rates 2004–2005 to 2013–2014.
The Indices of the Real Effective Exchange rate (REER) and the Nominal Effective Exchange Rate (NEER) of the Indian rupee pertain to the 36-currency bilateral weights and are computed as annual averages for the financial year. They have the base 2004–2005=100. Nominal interest rates are measured with reference to Weighted Average Deposit rates and refer to data from five major banks. Real interest rates are computed using the formula: Real Interest rate = Nominal Interest rate-inflation rate.

Source: http://dbie.rbi.org.in/DBIE/dbie.rbi?site=publications; http://dbie.rbi.org.in/DBIE/dbie.rbi?site=statistics, as accessed on 8 February 2017 at 3pm.

CASE

The Global Financial Crisis and the Dollar

With the start of the global financial crisis in August 2007, the dollar began an accelerated decline in value, falling by 9% against the euro until mid-July of 2008, and 6% against a wider basket of currencies. After hitting an all-time low against the euro on July 11, the dollar suddenly shot upward, by over 20% against the euro by the end of October and 15% against a wider basket of currencies. What is the relationship between the global financial crisis and these large swings in the value of the dollar?

During 2007 the negative effects of the global financial crisis on economic activity were mostly confined to the United States. The Federal Reserve acted aggressively to lower interest rates to counter the contractionary effects, decreasing the federal funds rate target by 325 basis points from September of 2007 to April of 2008. In contrast, other central banks like the ECB did not see the need to lower interest rates, particularly because high energy prices had led to a surge in inflation. The relative expected return on dollar assets thus declined, shifting the demand curve for dollar assets to the left, as in Figure 14.5, leading to a decline in the equilibrium exchange rate. Our analysis of the foreign exchange market thus explains why the early phase of the global financial crisis led to a decline in the value of the dollar.

We now turn to the rise in the value of the dollar. Starting in the summer of 2008, the effects of the global financial crisis on economic activity began to spread more widely throughout the world. Foreign central banks started to cut interest rates, with the expectation that further rate cuts would follow, as indeed it did occur. The expected decline in foreign interest rates then increased the relative expected return of dollar assets, leading to a rightward shift in the demand curve, and a rise in the value of the dollar, as shown in Figure 14.4. Another factor driving the dollar upwards was the "flight to quality" when the global financial crisis reached a particularly virulent stage in September and October of 2008. Both Americans and foreigners now wanted to put their money in the safest assets possible: U.S. Treasury securities. The resulting increase in the demand for dollar assets provided an additional reason for the demand curve for dollar assets to shift out to the right, thereby helping to produce a sharp appreciation of the dollar.

THE PRACTICING MANAGER

Profiting from Foreign Exchange Forecasts

Managers of financial institutions care a great deal about what foreign exchange rates will be in the future because these rates affect the value of assets on their balance sheet that are denominated in foreign currencies. In addition, financial institutions often engage in trading foreign exchange, both for their own account and for their customers. Forecasts of foreign exchange rates can thus have a big impact on the profits that financial institutions make on their foreign exchange trading operations.

Managers of financial institutions obtain foreign exchange forecasts either by hiring their own staff economists to generate them or by purchasing forecasts from other financial institutions or economic forecasting firms. In predicting the exchange rate movements, forecasters look at the factors mentioned in this chapter. For example, if they expect domestic real interest rates to rise, they will predict, in line with our analysis, that the domestic currency will appreciate; conversely, if they expect domestic inflation to increase, they will predict that the domestic currency will depreciate.

Managers of financial institutions, particularly those engaged in international banking, rely on foreign exchange forecasts to make decisions about which assets denominated in foreign currencies they should hold. For example, if a financial institution manager has a reliable forecast that the euro will appreciate in the future but the yen will depreciate, the manager will want to sell off assets denominated in yen and instead purchase assets denominated in euros. Alternatively, the manager might instruct loan officers to make more loans denominated in euros and fewer loans denominated in yen. Likewise, if the yen is forecast to appreciate and the euro to depreciate, the manager would want to switch out of euro-denominated assets into yen-denominated assets and would want to make more loans in yen and fewer in euros.

If the financial institution has a foreign exchange trading operation, a forecast of an appreciation of the yen means that the financial institution manager should tell foreign exchange traders to buy yen. If the forecast turns out to be correct, the higher value of the yen means that the trader can sell the yen in the future and pocket a tidy profit. If the euro is forecasted to depreciate, the trader can sell euros and buy them back in the future at a lower price if the forecast turns out to be correct, and again the financial institution will make a profit.

Accurate foreign exchange rate forecasts can thus help a financial institution manager generate substantial profits for the institution. Unfortunately, exchange rate forecasters are no more or less accurate than other economic forecasters, and they often make large errors. Reports on foreign exchange rate forecasts and how well forecasters are doing appear from time to time in the *Wall Street Journal* and in the trade magazine, *Euromoney*.

SUMMARY

1. Foreign exchange rates (the price of one country's currency in terms of another's) are important because they affect the price of domestically produced goods sold abroad and the cost of foreign goods bought domestically.

2. The theory of purchasing power parity suggests that long-run changes in the exchange rate between the currencies of two countries are determined by changes in the relative price levels in the two countries. Other factors that affect exchange rates in the long run are tariffs and quotas, import demand, export demand, and productivity.

3. In the short run, exchange rates are determined by changes in the relative expected return on domestic

assets, which cause the demand curve to shift. Any factor that changes the relative expected return on domestic assets will lead to changes in the exchange rate. Such factors include changes in the interest rates on domestic and foreign assets as well as changes in any of the factors that affect the long-run exchange rate and hence the expected future exchange rate.

4. Forecasts of foreign exchange rates are very valuable to managers of financial institutions because these rates influence decisions about the type of assets denominated in foreign currencies that the institutions should hold and what kinds of trades should be made by their traders in the foreign exchange market.

KEY TERMS

appreciation, p. 340
depreciation, p. 340
exchange rate, p. 338
foreign exchange market, p. 338
forward exchange rate, p. 340

forward transactions, p. 340
law of one price, p. 342
quotas, p. 345
real exchange rate, p. 343
spot exchange rate, p. 340

spot transactions, p. 340
tariffs, p. 345
theory of purchasing power parity
    (PPP), p. 342

QUESTIONS

1. When the euro appreciates, are you more likely to drink California or French wine?

2. "A country is always worse off when its currency is weak (falls in value)." Is this statement true, false, or uncertain? Explain your answer.

3. When the Indian rupee depreciates, what happens to exports and imports in India?

4. If the American price level rises by 5% relative to the price level in India, what does the theory of purchasing power parity predict will happen to the value of the U.S. dollar in terms of rupees?

5. If the demand for a country's exports falls at the same time that tariffs on imports are raised, will the country's currency tend to appreciate or depreciate in the long run?

6. In the mid- to late 1970s, the yen appreciated relative to the dollar even though Japan's inflation rate was higher than America's. How can this be explained by an improvement in the productivity of Japanese industry relative to American industry?

Predicting the Future

Answer the remaining questions by drawing the appropriate exchange market diagrams.

7. The Prime Minister of India announces that he will reduce inflation with a new anti-inflation program. If the public believes him, predict what will happen to the exchange rate for the Indian rupee.

8. If the British central bank prints money to reduce unemployment, what will happen to the value of the pound in the short run and the long run?

9. If the Indian government unexpectedly announces that it will be imposing higher tariffs on foreign goods one year from now, what will happen to the value of the Indian rupee today?

10. If nominal interest rates in America rise but real interest rates fall, predict what will happen to the U.S. exchange rate.

11. If American auto companies make a breakthrough in automobile technology and are able to produce a car that gets 60 miles to the gallon, what will happen to the U.S. exchange rate?

12. If Mexicans go on a spending spree and buy twice as much French perfume, Japanese TVs, English sweaters, Swiss watches, and Italian wine, what will happen to the value of the Mexican peso?

13. If expected inflation drops in Europe so that interest rates fall there, predict what will happen to the exchange rate for the U.S. dollar.

14. If the European central bank decides to contract the money supply to fight inflation, what will happen to the value of the U.S. dollar?

15. If there is a massive strike in France that blocks roads and entrance to ports, making it harder to buy French goods, what will happen to the value of the euro?

QUANTITATIVE PROBLEMS

1. A German sports car is selling for 70,000 euros. What is the dollar price in the United States for the German car if the exchange rate is 0.90 euros per dollar?

2. An investor in England purchased a 91-day T-bill for $987.65. At that time, the exchange rate was $1.75 per pound. At maturity, the exchange rate was $1.83 per pound. What was the investor's holding period return in pounds?

3. An investor in Canada purchased 100 shares of IBM on January 1 at $93.00 per share. IBM paid an annual dividend of $0.72 on December 31. The stock was sold that day as well for $100.25. The exchange rate was $0.68 per Canadian dollar on January 1 and $0.71 per Canadian dollar on December 31. What is the investor's total return in Canadian dollars?

4. The current exchange rate is 0.75 euro per dollar, but you believe the dollar will decline to 0.67 euro

per dollar. If a euro-denominated bond is yielding 2%, what return do you expect in U.S. dollars?

5. The six-month forward rate between the British pound and the U.S. dollar is $1.75 per pound. If six-month interest rates are 3% in the United States and 150 basis points higher in England, what is the current exchange rate?

6. If the Canadian dollar to U.S. dollar exchange rate is 1.28 and the British pound to U.S. dollar exchange rate is 0.62, what must the Canadian dollar to British pound exchange rate be?

7. The New Zealand dollar to U.S. dollar exchange rate is 1.36, and the British pound to U.S. dollar exchange rate is 0.62. If you find that the British pound to New Zealand dollar were trading at 0.49, what would you do to earn a riskless profit?

8. In 1999 the euro was trading at $0.90 per euro. If the euro is now trading at $1.16 per euro, what is the percentage change in the euro's value? Is this an appreciation or depreciation?

9. The Brazilian real is trading at 0.375 real per U.S. dollar. What is the U.S. dollar per real exchange rate?

10. The Mexican peso is trading at 10 pesos per dollar. If the expected U.S. inflation rate is 2% while the expected Mexican inflation rate is 23% over the next year, what is the expected exchange rate in one year?

11. The current exchange rate between the United States and Britain is $1.825 per pound. The six-month for

ward rate between the British pound and the U.S. dollar is $1.79 per pound. What is the percentage difference between current six-month U.S. and British interest rates?

12. The current exchange rate between the Japanese yen and the U.S. dollar is 120 yen per dollar. If the dollar is expected to depreciate by 10% relative to the yen, what is the new expected exchange rate?

13. If the price level recently increased by 20% in England while falling by 5% in the United States, how much must the exchange rate change if PPP holds? Assume that the current exchange rate is 0.55 pounds per dollar.

14. A one-year CD in Europe is currently paying 5%, and the exchange rate is currently 0.99 euros per dollar. If you believe the exchange rate will be 1.04 euros per dollar one year from now, what is the expected return in terms of dollars?

15. Short-term interest rates are 2% in Japan and 4% in the United States. The current exchange rate is 120 yen per dollar. What is the expected forward exchange rate?

16. Short-term interest rates are 2% in Japan and 4% in the United States. The current exchange rate is 120 yen per dollar. If you can enter into a forward exchange rate of 115 yen per dollar, how can you arbitrage the situation?

17. The interest rate in the United States is 4%, and the euro is trading at 1 euro per dollar. The euro is expected to depreciate to 1.1 euros per dollar. Calculate the interest rate in Germany.

WEB EXERCISES

The Foreign Exchange Market

1. The Federal Reserve maintains a Web site that lists the exchange rates between the U.S. dollar and many other currencies. Go to **http://www.newyorkfed .org/markets/foreignex.html**. Go to the historical data from 2000 and later and find the euro.

   a. What has the percentage change in the euro–dollar exchange rate been between the euro's introduction and now?

   b. What has been the annual percentage change in the euro–dollar exchange rate for each year since the euro's introduction?

2. International travelers and business people frequently need to accurately convert from one currency to another. It is often easy to find the rate needed to convert the U.S. dollar into another currency. It can be more difficult to find exchange rates between two non-U.S. currencies. Go to **www.oanda.com/convert/ classic**. This site lets you convert from any currency into any other currency. How many Lithuanian litas can you currently buy with one Chilean peso?

3. Go online and understand the episodes of volatility of the rupee-dollar exchange rate in India. Understand the policy measures undertaken by the authorities to curb such volatility and the effectiveness of such measures.

The International Financial System

> PREVIEW

Thanks to the growing interdependence between the Indian economy and the economies of the rest of the world, the international financial system now plays a more prominent role in economic events in India. In this chapter, we see how fixed and managed exchange rate systems work and how they can provide substantial profit opportunities for financial institutions. We also look at the controversies over the capital controls and the role International Monetary Fund should play in the international financial system.

Intervention in the Foreign Exchange Market

In Chapter 14 we analyzed the foreign exchange market as if it were a completely free market that responds to all market pressures. Like many other markets, however, the foreign exchange market is not free of government intervention; central banks regularly engage in international financial transactions called **foreign exchange interventions** to influence exchange rates. In our current international environment, exchange rates fluctuate from day to day, but central banks attempt to influence their countries' exchange rates by buying and selling currencies. We can use the exchange rate analysis we developed in Chapter 14 to explain the effect of central bank intervention on the foreign exchange market.

Foreign Exchange Intervention and the Money Supply

The first step in understanding how central bank intervention in the foreign exchange market affects exchange rates is to see the effect on the monetary base from a central bank sale in the foreign exchange market of some of its holdings of assets denominated in a foreign currency (called **international reserves**). Suppose that the RBI decides to sell ₹1 billion of its foreign assets in exchange for ₹1 billion of Indian rupees. In the US, such a transaction is conducted at the foreign exchange desk at the Federal Reserve Bank of New York—see the Inside the Fed box.) The RBI's purchase of rupees has two effects. First, it reduces the RBI's holding of international reserves by ₹1 billion. Second, because the RBI's purchase of currency removes it from the hands of the public, currency in circulation falls by ₹1 billion. We can see this in the following T-account for the RBI:

Reserve Bank of India			
Assets		**Liabilities**	
Foreign assets (international reserves)	−₹1 billion	Currency in circulation	−₹1 billion

Because the monetary base is made up of currency in circulation plus reserves, this decline in currency implies that the monetary base has fallen by ₹1 billion.

If instead of paying for the foreign assets sold by the RBI with currency, the persons buying the foreign assets pay for them with checks written on accounts at domestic banks, then the RBI deducts the ₹1 billion from the reserve deposits it holds for these banks. The result is that deposits with the RBI (reserves) decline by ₹1 billion, as shown in the following T-account:

Reserve Bank of India			
Assets		**Liabilities**	
Foreign assets (international reserves)	−₹1 billion	Deposits with the RBI (reserves)	−₹1 billion

In this case, the outcome of the RBI sale of foreign assets and the purchase of rupee deposits is at ₹1 billion decline in reserves and, as before, a ₹1 billion decline in the monetary base because reserves are also a component of the monetary base.

We now see that the outcome for the monetary base is exactly the same when a central bank sells foreign assets to purchase domestic bank deposits or domestic currency. This is why when we say that a central bank has purchased its domestic currency, we do not have to distinguish whether it actually purchased currency or bank deposits denominated in the domestic currency. We have thus reached an important conclusion: *A central bank's purchase of domestic currency and corresponding sale of foreign assets in the foreign exchange market leads to an equal decline in its international reserves and the monetary base.*

We could have reached the same conclusion by a more direct route. A central bank's sale of a foreign asset is no different from an open market sale of a government bond. We learned in our exploration of monetary policy that an open market sale leads to an equal decline in the monetary base; therefore, a sale of foreign assets also leads to an equal decline in the monetary base. By similar reasoning, a central bank purchase of foreign assets paid for by selling domestic currency, like an open market purchase, leads to an equal rise in the monetary base. Thus, we reach the following conclusion: *A central bank's sale of domestic currency to purchase foreign assets in the foreign exchange market results in an equal rise in its international reserves and the monetary base.*

INSIDE THE FED

A Day at the Federal Reserve Bank of New York's Foreign Exchange Desk

Although the U.S. Treasury is primarily responsible for foreign exchange policy, decisions to intervene in the foreign exchange market are made jointly by the U.S. Treasury and the Federal Reserve's FOMC (Federal Open Market Committee). The actual conduct of foreign exchange intervention is the responsibility of the foreign exchange desk at the Federal Reserve Bank of New York, which is right next to the open market desk.

The manager of foreign exchange operations at the New York Federal Reserve supervises the traders and analysts who follow developments in the foreign exchange market. Every morning at 7:30, a trader on staff who has arrived at the New York Federal Reserve in the predawn hours speaks on the telephone with counterparts at the U.S. Treasury and provides an update on overnight activity in overseas financial and foreign exchange markets. Later in the morning, at 9:30, the manager and his or her staff hold a conference call with senior staff at the Board of Governors of the Federal Reserve in Washington. In the afternoon, at 2:30, they have a second conference call, which is a joint briefing of officials at the board and the Treasury. Although by statute the Treasury has the lead role in setting foreign exchange policy, it strives to reach a consensus among all three parties—the Treasury, the Board of Governors, and the Federal Reserve Bank of New York. If they decide that a foreign exchange intervention is necessary that day—an unusual occurrence, as a year may go by without a U.S. foreign exchange intervention—the manager instructs his traders to carry out the agreed-on purchase or sale of foreign currencies. Because funds for exchange rate intervention are held separately by the Treasury (in its Exchange Stabilization Fund) and the Federal Reserve, the manager and his or her staff are not trading the funds of the Federal Reserve Bank of New York; rather, they act as an agent for the Treasury and the FOMC in conducting these transactions.

As part of their duties, before every FOMC meeting, the staff helps prepare a lengthy document full of data for the FOMC members, other Reserve bank presidents, and Treasury officials. It describes developments in the domestic and foreign markets over the previous five or six weeks, a task that keeps them especially busy right before the FOMC meeting.

The intervention we have just described, in which a central bank allows the purchase or sale of domestic currency to have an effect on the monetary base, is called an **unsterilized foreign exchange intervention.** But what if the central bank does not want the purchase or sale of domestic currency to affect the monetary base? All it has to do is counter the effect of the foreign exchange intervention by conducting an offsetting open market operation in the government bond market. For example, in the case of a ₹1 billion purchase of rupees by the RBI and a corresponding ₹1 billion sale of foreign assets, which, as we have seen, would decrease the monetary base by ₹1 billion, the RBI can conduct an open market purchase of ₹1 billion of government bonds, which would increase the monetary base by ₹1 billion. The resulting T-account for the foreign exchange intervention and the offsetting open market operation leaves the monetary base unchanged:

Reserve Bank of India			
Assets		Liabilities	
Foreign assets (international reserves)	−₹1 billion	Monetary base	0
Government bonds	+₹1 billion		

A foreign exchange intervention with an offsetting open market operation that leaves the monetary base unchanged is called a **sterilized foreign exchange intervention.**

Now that we understand that there are two types of foreign exchange interventions—unsterilized and sterilized—let's look at how each affects the exchange rate.

Unsterilized Intervention

Intuition might lead you to suspect that if a central bank wants to raise the value of the domestic currency, it should buy its currency in the foreign exchange market and sell foreign assets. Indeed, this intuition is correct for the case of an unsterilized intervention.

Recall that in an unsterilized intervention, if the RBI decides to buy rupees and therefore sells foreign assets in exchange for rupee assets, this works just like an open market sale of bonds to decrease the monetary base. Hence the purchase of rupees leads to a decrease in the money supply, which raises the domestic interest rate, and we find ourselves analyzing a similar situation to that described in Figure 14.4 in Chapter 14, which is reproduced here as Figure 15.1.[1] The decrease in the money supply causes the interest rate on rupee assets to rise and so increases the relative expected return on rupee assets. The demand curve shifts to the right from D_1 to D_2, and the exchange rate rises to E_2.

---

[1]An unsterilized intervention, in which the RBI buys rupees, decreases the amount of rupee assets slightly because it leads to a decrease in the monetary base while leaving the amount of government bonds in the hands of the public unchanged. The curve depicting the supply of rupee assets would thus shift to the left slightly, which also works toward raising the exchange rate, yielding the same conclusion derived from Figure 15.1. Because the resulting fall in the monetary base would be only a minuscule fraction of the total amount of dollar assets outstanding, the supply curve would shift by an imperceptible amount. This is why Figure 15.1 is drawn with the supply curve unchanged.

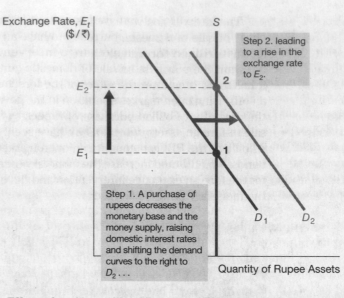

Exchange Rate, E_t ($/₹)

Step 2. leading to a rise in the exchange rate to E_2.

E_2

2

E_1

1

Step 1. A purchase of rupees decreases the monetary base and the money supply, raising domestic interest rates and shifting the demand curves to the right to D_2 . . .

D_1 D_2

Quantity of Rupee Assets

FIGURE 15.1 Effect of an Unsterilized Purchase of Rupees and Sale of Foreign Assets
A purchase of rupees and the consequent open market sale of foreign assets decreases the monetary base and the money supply. The resulting fall in the money supply leads to a rise in domestic interest rates that raises the relative expected return on rupee assets. The demand curve shifts to the right, from D_1 to D_2, and the equilibrium exchange rate rises from E_1 to E_2.

Our analysis leads us to the following conclusion about unsterilized interventions in the foreign exchange market: ***An unsterilized intervention in which domestic currency is bought and foreign assets are sold leads to a fall in international reserves, a fall in the money supply, and an appreciation of the domestic currency.***

The reverse result is found for an unsterilized intervention in which domestic currency is sold and foreign assets are purchased. The sale of domestic currency and purchase of foreign assets (increasing international reserves) works like an open market purchase to increase the monetary base and the money supply. The increase in the money supply lowers the interest rate on rupee assets. The resulting decrease in the relative expected return on rupee assets means that people will buy fewer rupee assets, so the demand curve shifts to the left and the exchange rate falls. ***An unsterilized intervention in which domestic currency is sold and foreign assets are purchased leads to a rise in international reserves, a rise in the money supply, and a depreciation of the domestic currency.***

Sterilized Intervention

The key point to remember about a sterilized intervention is that the central bank engages in offsetting open market operations, so that there is no impact on the monetary base and the money supply. In the context of the model of exchange rate determination we have developed here, it is straightforward to show that a sterilized intervention has almost *no effect* on the exchange rate. A sterilized intervention leaves the money supply unchanged and thus has no direct way of affecting interest rates.[2] Because the relative expected return on rupee assets is unaffected, the demand curve would remain at D_1 in Figure 15.1, and the exchange rate would remain unchanged at E_1.

At first it might seem puzzling that a central bank purchase or sale of domestic currency that is sterilized does not lead to a change in the exchange rate. A central bank purchase of domestic currency cannot raise the exchange rate because with no effect on the domestic money supply or interest rates, any resulting rise in the exchange rate would mean that an excess supply of rupee assets would arise. With more people willing to sell rupee assets than to buy them, the exchange rate would have to fall back to its initial equilibrium level, where the demand and supply curves intersect.

Balance of Payments

Because international financial transactions such as foreign exchange interventions have considerable effects on monetary policy, it is worth knowing how these transactions are measured. The **balance of payments** is a bookkeeping system for recording all receipts and payments that have a direct bearing on the movement of funds between a nation (private sector and government) and foreign countries. Here we examine the key items in the balance of payments that you often hear about in the media.[3]

The **current account** shows international transactions that involve currently produced goods and services. The difference between merchandise exports and imports, the net receipts from trade, is called the **trade balance.** When merchandise imports are greater than exports, we have a trade deficit; if exports are greater than imports, we have a trade surplus.

Additional items included in the current account are the net receipts (cash flows received from abroad minus cash flows sent abroad) from three categories: primary income, service transactions, and secondary income (unilateral transfers) (gifts, pensions, and foreign aid).

GO ONLINE

Access **https://rbi.org.in/#.** This Web site contains exchange rates, balance of payments, and trade data.

---

[2]A sterilized intervention changes the amount of foreign securities relative to domestic securities in the hands of the public, called a *portfolio balance effect*. Through this effect, the central bank might be able to affect the interest differential between domestic and foreign assets, which in turn affects the relative expected return of domestic assets. Empirical evidence has not revealed this portfolio balance effect to be significant. However, a sterilized intervention *could* indicate what central banks want to happen to the future exchange rate and so might provide a signal about the course of future monetary policy. In this way a sterilized intervention could lead to shifts in the demand curve for domestic assets and ultimately affect the exchange rate. However, the future change in monetary policy—not the sterilized intervention—is the source of the exchange rate effect. For a further discussion of the signaling and portfolio balance effects and the possible differential effects of sterilized versus unsterilized intervention, see Paul Krugman and Maurice Obstfeld, *International Economics*, 9th ed. (Boston: Addison-Wesley, 2012).

[3]A more detailed discussion of the balance of payments account can be found in an appendix that is on the book's Web site at www.pearson.highered.com/mishkin_eakins.

Another important item in the balance of payments is the **capital and financial account,** the net receipts from financial transactions (e.g., purchases of stocks and bonds, bank loans). The change in reserves, which represents the official transactions balance, is part of the financial account. A negative sign (−) attached to this item in the BoP indicates an accretion to the RBI's reserves and a positive (+) sign indicates a depletion of the RBI's foreign exchange reserves. When economists refer to a surplus or deficit in the balance of payments, they actually mean a surplus or deficit in the official reserve transactions balance. The item 'Errors & Omissions' in the Balance of Payments is the balancing item and is equal to the negative of the sum of the current account and capital and financial account.

CASE

India's Balance of Payments

Key Features of India's BoP in Q2 of 2016–17

India's current account deficit (CAD) at US$ 3.4 billion (0.6 per cent of GDP) in Q2 of 2016–17 was lower than US$ 8.5 billion (1.7 per cent of GDP) in Q2 of 2015–16 but higher than US$ 0.3 billion (0.1 per cent of GDP) in the preceding quarter.

- The contraction in the CAD on a year-on-year (y-o-y) basis was primarily on account of a lower trade deficit (US$ 25.6 billion) brought about by a larger decline in merchandise imports relative to exports.
- Net services receipts moderated on y-o-y basis, primarily owing to the fall in earnings from software, financial services and charges for intellectual property rights.
- Private transfer receipts, mainly representing remittances by Indians employed overseas, amounted to US$ 15.2 billion, having declined by 10.7 per cent from their level a year ago.
- In the financial account, net inflows of both foreign direct investment and portfolio investment were significantly higher in Q2 on a y-o-y basis.
- Non-resident Indian (NRI) deposits declined to US$ 2.1 billion in Q2 of 2016–17 from US$ 4.2 billion in Q2 of 2015–16.
- Net loans availed by banks witnessed a net repayment of US$ 9.0 billion in Q2 of 2016–17 as against net borrowing of US$ 3.1 billion in Q2 of 2015–16.
- In Q2 of 2016–17, foreign exchange reserves (on BoP basis) increased by US$ 8.5 billion as against a decline of US$ 0.9 billion in Q2 of last year .

BoP during April-September 2016 (H1 of 2016–17)

- On a cumulative basis, the CAD narrowed to 0.3 per cent of GDP in H1 of 2016–17 from 1.5 per cent in H1 of 2015–16 on the back of the contraction in the trade deficit.
- India's trade deficit narrowed to US$ 49.5 billion in H1 of 2016–17 from US$ 71.3 billion in H1 of 2015–16.
- Net invisible receipts were lower, mainly due to moderation in software exports and private transfers and higher outgo on account of primary income (profit, interest and dividends).
- Net FDI inflows during H1 of 2016–17 rose by more than 28.8 per cent over the level during the corresponding period of the previous year.

- Portfolio investment recorded a net inflow of US$ 8.2 billion during H1 as against a net outflow of US$ 3.5 billion a year ago.
- In H1 of 2016–17, there was an accretion of US$ 15.5 billion to foreign exchange reserves.

Major Items of India's Balance of Payments

(US$ Billion)

	July-September 2016 P			July-September 2015			April-September 2016–17 P			April-September 2015–16		
	Credit	Debit	Net	Credit	Debit	Net	Credit	Debit	Net	Credit	Debit	Net
A. Current Account	127.4	130.9	–3.4	127.3	135.8	–8.5	252.6	256.4	–3.7	254.2	268.8	–14.7
1. Goods	67.4	93.1	–25.6	67.6	104.7	–37.2	134.0	183.5	–49.5	135.6	206.9	–71.3
Of which:												
POL	7.8	20.5	12.7	8.6	23.5	–14.9	14.8	39.5	–24.7	17.0	48.3	–31.3
2. Services	40.5	24.3	16.3	38.7	20.9	17.8	80.1	48.0	32.0	77.0	41.4	35.6
3. Primary Income	4.2	12.2	–7.9	3.9	9.4	5.5	8.0	22.1	–14.1	7.2	18.6	–11.3
4. Secondary Income	15.2	1.4	13.9	17.1	0.8	16.3	30.5	2.7	27.9	34.3	1.9	32.4
B. Capital Account and Financial Account	139.5	135.3	4.2	127.5	118.5	9.0	268.6	264.3	4.3	268.5	252.4	16.2
Of which:												
Change in Reserve (Increase (–)/ Decrease (+))	0.0	8.5	–8.5	0.9	0.0	0.9	0.0	15.5	–15.5	0.9	11.4	–10.6
C. Errors & Omissions (–) (A+B)		0.7	–0.7		0.4	–0.4		0.6	–0.6		1.5	–1.5

P: Preliminary; PR: Partially Revised
Note: Total of subcomponents may not tally with aggregate due to rounding off.

The current account balance tells us whether India (private sector and government combined) is increasing or decreasing its claims on foreign wealth. A surplus indicates that India is increasing its claims on foreign wealth and thus is increasing its holdings of foreign assets (both good things for Indians); a deficit indicates that India is reducing its holdings of foreign assets and foreign countries are increasing their claims on India.[4] The large Indian current account deficit in the past few years, which had reached USD 87,843 million in 2012–13, has raised serious concerns that these large deficits may have negative consequences for the Indian economy (see the box, "Why the Large Current Account Deficit Worries Economists").

---

[4]The current account balance can also be viewed as showing the amount by which total saving exceeds private sector and government investment in India. Total Indian saving equals the increase in total wealth held by the Indian private sector and government. Total investment equals the increase in the Indian capital stock (wealth physically in India). The difference between them is the increase in India's claims on foreign wealth.

Why the Large Current Account Deficit Worries Economists

The large current account deficits in recent years—in 2012–13, it was USD 87,843 million, 4.8% of GDP—worries economists for several reasons. First, it indicates that at current exchange rate values, foreigners' demand for India's exports is far less than Indians' demand for imports. As we saw in the previous chapter, low demand for India's exports and high Indian demand for imports may lead to a future decline in the value of the Indian rupee.

Second, the current account deficit means that foreigners' claims on India's assets are growing, and these claims will have to be paid back at some point. Indians are mortgaging their future to foreigners; when the bill comes due, Indians will be poorer. Furthermore, if Indians have a greater preference for rupee assets than foreigners do, the movement of Indian wealth to foreigners could decrease the demand for rupee assets over time, also causing the rupee to depreciate.

The hope is that the eventual decline in the rupee resulting from the large Indian current account deficits will be a gradual one, occurring over a period of several years. If the decline is precipitous, however, it could disrupt financial markets and hurt the Indian economy.

Exchange Rate Regimes in the International Financial System

Exchange rate regimes in the international financial system are classified into two basic types: fixed and floating. In a **fixed exchange rate regime,** the value of a currency is pegged relative to the value of one other currency (called the **anchor currency**) so that the exchange rate is fixed in terms of the anchor currency. In a **floating exchange rate regime,** the value of a currency is allowed to fluctuate against all other currencies. When countries intervene in foreign exchange markets in an attempt to influence their exchange rates by buying and selling foreign assets, the regime is referred to as a **managed float regime** (or a **dirty float**).

Fixed Exchange Rate Regimes

After World War II, the victors set up a fixed exchange rate system that became known as the **Bretton Woods system,** after the New Hampshire town in which the agreement was negotiated in 1944. The Bretton Woods system remained in effect until 1971.

The Bretton Woods agreement created the **International Monetary Fund (IMF),** headquartered in Washington, D.C., which had 30 original member countries in 1945 and currently has over 185. The IMF was given the task of promoting the growth of world trade by setting rules for the maintenance of fixed exchange rates and by making loans to countries that were experiencing balance-of-payments difficulties. As part of its role of monitoring the compliance of member countries with its rules, the IMF also took on the job of collecting and standardizing international economic data.

The Bretton Woods agreement also set up the International Bank for Reconstruction and Development, commonly referred to as the **World Bank.** Headquartered in Washington, D.C., it provides long-term loans to help developing countries build dams, roads, and other physical capital that would contribute to their economic development. The funds for these loans are obtained primarily by issuing World Bank bonds, which are sold in the capital markets of the developed countries. In addition, the General Agreement on Tariffs and Trade (GATT), headquartered in Geneva, Switzerland, was set up to monitor rules for the conduct of trade between countries (tariffs and quotas). The GATT has since evolved into the **World Trade Organization (WTO).**

Because the United States emerged from World War II as the world's largest economic power, with over half of the world's manufacturing capacity and the greater part of the world's gold, the Bretton Woods system of fixed exchange rates was based on the convertibility of U.S. dollars into gold (for foreign governments and central banks only) at $35 per ounce. The fixed exchange rates were to be maintained by intervention in the foreign exchange market by central banks in countries besides the United States that bought and sold dollar assets, which they held as international reserves. The U.S. dollar, which was used by other countries to denominate the assets that they held as international reserves, was called the **reserve currency.** Thus, an important feature of the Bretton Woods system was the establishment of the United States as the reserve currency country. Even after the breakup of the Bretton Woods system, the U.S. dollar has kept its position as the reserve currency in which most international financial transactions are conducted. The fixed exchange rate, which was a feature of the Bretton Woods system, was finally abandoned in 1973. From 1979 to 1990, however, the European Union instituted among its members its own fixed exchange rate system, the European Monetary System (EMS). In the *exchange rate mechanism (ERM)* in this system, the exchange rate between any pair of currencies of the participating countries was not supposed to fluctuate outside narrow limits, called the "snake." In practice, all of the countries in the EMS pegged their currencies to the German mark.

How a Fixed Exchange Rate Regime Works

Figure 15.2 shows how a fixed exchange rate regime works in practice by using the supply-and-demand analysis of the foreign exchange market we learned in the previous chapter. Panel (a) describes a situation in which the domestic currency is fixed relative to an anchor currency at E_{par}, while the demand curve has shifted left to D_1, perhaps because foreign interest rates have risen, thereby lowering the relative expected return of domestic assets. At E_{par} the exchange rate is now *overvalued*: the demand curve D_1 intersects the supply curve at exchange rate E_1, which is lower than the fixed (par) value of the exchange rate E_{par}. To keep the exchange rate at E_{par}, the central bank must intervene in the foreign exchange market to purchase domestic currency by selling foreign assets. This action, like an open market sale, means that both the monetary base and the money supply decline, driving up the interest rate on domestic assets, i_D.[5] This increase in the domestic interest rate raises the relative expected return on domestic assets, shifting the demand curve to the right. The central bank will continue purchasing domestic currency until the demand curve reaches D_2 and the equilibrium exchange rate is at E_{par} at point 2 in panel (a).

[5]Because the exchange rate will continue to be fixed at E_{par}, the expected future exchange rate remains unchanged and so does not need to be addressed in the analysis.

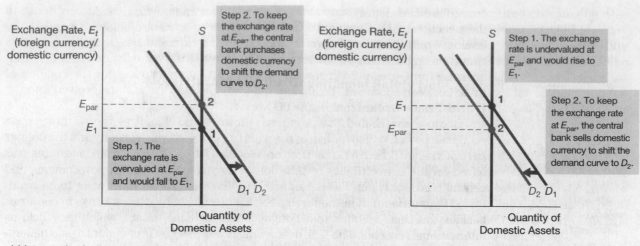

(a) Intervention in the case of an overvalued exchange rate   (b) Intervention in the case of an undervalued exchange rate

FIGURE 15.2 **Intervention in the Foreign Exchange Market Under a Fixed Exchange Rate Regime**
In panel (a), the exchange rate at E_{par} is overvalued. To keep the exchange rate at E_{par} (point 2), the central bank must purchase domestic currency to shift the demand curve to D_2. In panel (b), the exchange rate at E_{par} is undervalued, so the central bank must sell domestic currency to shift the demand curve to D_2 and keep the exchange rate at E_{par} (point 2).

We have thus come to the conclusion that **when the domestic currency is overvalued, the central bank must purchase domestic currency to keep the exchange rate fixed, but as a result it loses international reserves.**

Panel (b) in Figure 15.2 describes the situation in which the demand curve has shifted to the right to D_1 because the relative expected return on domestic assets has risen and hence the exchange rate is undervalued: the initial demand curve D_1 intersects the supply curve at exchange rate E_1, which is above E_{par}. In this situation, the central bank must sell domestic currency and purchase foreign assets. This action works like an open market purchase to increase the money supply and lower the interest rate on domestic assets i^D. The central bank keeps selling domestic currency and lowering i^D until the demand curve shifts all the way to D_2, where the equilibrium exchange rate is at E_{par}—point 2 in panel (b). Our analysis thus leads us to the following result: **When the domestic currency is undervalued, the central bank must sell domestic currency to keep the exchange rate fixed, but as a result, it gains international reserves.**

Devaluation and Revaluation   As we have seen, if a country's currency is overvalued, its central bank's attempts to keep the currency from depreciating will result in a loss of international reserves. If the country's central bank eventually runs out of international reserves, it cannot keep its currency from depreciating, and a **devaluation** must occur, in which the par exchange rate is reset at a lower level.

If, by contrast, a country's currency is undervalued, its central bank's intervention to keep the currency from appreciating leads to a gain of international reserves. As we will see shortly, the central bank might not want to acquire these international reserves, and so it might want to reset the par value of its exchange rate at a higher level (a **revaluation**).

Perfect Capital Mobility If perfect capital mobility exists—that is, if there are no barriers to domestic residents purchasing foreign assets or foreigners purchasing domestic assets—then a sterilized exchange rate intervention cannot keep the exchange rate at E_{par} because, as we saw earlier, the relative expected return of domestic assets is unaffected. For example, if the exchange rate is overvalued, a sterilized purchase of domestic currency will leave the relative expected return and the demand curve unchanged—so pressure for a depreciation of the domestic currency is not removed. If the central bank keeps purchasing its domestic currency but continues to sterilize, it will just keep losing international reserves until it finally runs out of them and is forced to let the value of the currency seek a lower level.

The Policy Trilemma

One important implication of the foregoing analysis is that a country that ties its exchange rate to an anchor currency of a larger country loses control of its monetary policy. If the larger country pursues a more contractionary monetary policy and decreases its money supply, this would lead to lower expected inflation in the larger country, thus causing an appreciation of the larger country's currency and a depreciation of the smaller country's currency. The smaller country, having locked in its exchange rate to the anchor currency, will now find its currency overvalued and will therefore have to sell the anchor currency and buy its own to keep its currency from depreciating. The result of this foreign exchange intervention will then be a decline in the smaller country's international reserves, a contraction of its monetary base, and thus a decline in its money supply. Sterilization of this foreign exchange intervention is not an option because this would just lead to a continuing loss of international reserves until the smaller country was forced to devalue its currency. The smaller country no longer controls its monetary policy because movements in its money supply are completely determined by movements in the larger country's money supply.

Our analysis therefore indicates that a country (or a currency union like the Eurozone) can't pursue the following three policies at the same time: (i) free capital mobility, (ii) a fixed exchange rate, and (iii) an independent monetary policy. Economists call this result the **policy trilemma** (or, more graphically, the **impossible trinity**). Figure 15.3 illustrates the policy trilemma. A country can choose only two of the three options, which are denoted by each side of the triangle. In option 1, a country (or monetary union) chooses to have capital mobility and an independent monetary policy but not a fixed exchange rate. The Eurozone and the United States have made this choice. Hong Kong and Belize have chosen option 2, in which there is free capital mobility and the exchange rate is fixed, so the country does not have an independent monetary policy. China, has chosen option 3, in which it has a fixed exchange rate and pursue an independent monetary policy but do not have free capital mobility because it has **capital controls,** restrictions on the free movement of capital across the borders.

The policy trilemma thus leaves countries with a difficult choice. Do they accept exchange rate volatility (option 1), give up on independent monetary policy (option 2), or restrict capital flows (option 3)?

India and the Policy Trilemma

The best way to understand the challenge of monetary policy formulation in a globalizing world is through the 'impossible trinity' trilemma. This trilemma asserts that a country cannot simultaneously maintain all three policy goals of free capital flows, a fixed exchange rate and an independent monetary policy.

Given the 'impossible trinity' trilemma, countries have made different choices. The most common choice, typical across advanced economies, is to give up on a fixed exchange rate so as to run an open economy with an independent monetary policy. On the other hand, economies that adopt a hard peg give up on the independence of monetary policy. Examples include the currency boards set up by Hong Kong and, for a time, Argentina.

In contrast to advanced economies which opt for corner solutions, emerging economies here typically opted for middle solutions, giving up on some flexibility on each of the variables to maximize overall macroeconomic advantage.

As India integrates with the global economy, the main challenge it faces is managing the trade-offs presented by the Impossible Trinity or the Open Economy Trilemma. In the past two decades, India has used capital controls along with active intervention in the foreign exchange market to maintain exchange rate stability to manage the policy trilemma.

India's Approach to the Impossible Trinity

In India too, we have opted for a middle solution to the 'impossible trinity' whose contours are the following: (i) We let our exchange rate be largely market determined, but intervene in the market to smooth excess volatility and/or to prevent disruptions to macroeconomic stability; (ii) Our capital account is only partly open; while foreigners enjoy mostly unfettered access to our equity markets, access to debt markets is restricted; there are limits to the quantum of funds resident corporates and individuals can take out for investment abroad, but the limits are quite liberal; and (iii) Because of the liberalization on the exchange rate and capital account fronts, some monetary policy independence is forefeited. What the middle solution also implies is that we have to guard on all the three fronts with the relative emphasis across the three pillars shifting according to our macroeconomic situation.

Foreign Exchange Management and Capital Controls For a long time, foreign exchange in India was treated as a controlled commodity because of its limited availability. The early stages of foreign exchange management in the country focussed on control of foreign exchange by regulating the demand due to its limited supply. Exchange control was introduced in India under the Defence of India Rules on September 3, 1939 on a temporary basis. The statutory power for exchange control was provided by the Foreign Exchange Regulation Act (FERA) of 1947, which was subsequently replaced by a more comprehensive Foreign Exchange Regulation Act, 1973. This Act empowered the Reserve Bank, and in certain cases the Central Government, to control and regulate dealings in foreign exchange payments outside India, export and import of currency notes and bullion, transfer of securities between residents and non-residents, acquisition of foreign securities, and acquisition of immovable property in and outside India, among other transactions.

Extensive relaxations in the rules governing foreign exchange were initiated, prompted by the liberalisation measures introduced since 1991 and the Act was amended as a new Foreign Exchange Regulation (Amendment) Act 1993. Significant developments in the external sector, such as, substantial increase in foreign exchange reserves, growth in foreign trade, rationalisation of tariffs, current account convertibility, liberalisation of Indian investments abroad, increased access to external commercial borrowings by Indian corporates and participation of foreign institutional investors in Indian stock market, resulted in a changed environment. Keeping in view the changed environment, the Foreign Exchange Management Act (FEMA) was enacted in 1999 to replace FERA. FEMA became effective from June 1, 2000.

The Reserve Bank issues licences to banks and other institutions to act as Authorised Dealers in the foreign exchange market. In keeping with the move towards liberalisation, the Reserve Bank has undertaken substantial elimination of licensing, quantitative restrictions and other regulatory and discretionary controls.

Apart from easing restrictions on foreign exchange transactions in terms of processes and procedure, the Reserve Bank has also provided the exchange facility for liberalised travel abroad for purposes, such as, conducting business, attending international conferences, undertaking technical study tours, setting up joint ventures abroad, negotiating foreign collaboration, pursuing higher studies and training, and also for medical treatment. Moreover, the Reserve Bank has permitted residents to hold liberal amount of foreign currency. Residents can now also open foreign currency accounts in India and credit specified foreign exchange receipts into it.

Foreign Investments Foreign investment comes into India in various forms. Following the reforms path, the Reserve Bank has liberalised the provisions relating to such investments. The Reserve Bank has permitted foreign investment in almost all sectors, with a few exceptions. In many sectors, no prior approval from the Government or the Reserve Bank is required for non-residents investing in India. Foreign institutional investors are allowed to invest in all equity securities traded in the primary and secondary markets. Foreign institutional investors have also been permitted to invest in Government of India treasury bills and dated securities, corporate debt instruments and mutual funds. The NRIs have the flexibility of investing under the options of repatriation and non-repatriation.Similarly, Indian entities can also make investment in an overseas joint venture or in a wholly-owned subsidiary abroad upto a certain limit.

External Commercial Borrowings Indian companies are allowed to raise external commercial borrowings including commercial bank loans, buyers' credit, suppliers' credit, and securitised instruments. Foreign Currency Convertible Bonds (FCCBs) and Foreign Currency Exchangeable Bonds (FCEBs) are also governed by the ECB guidelines.

Liberalised Remittance Scheme As a step towards further simplification and liberalisation of the foreign exchange facilities available to the residents, the Reserve Bank has permitted resident individuals to freely remit abroad up to liberal amount per financial year for any permissible purposes.

Currency Futures Exchange-traded currency futures are permitted in India. The National Stock Exchange, the Bombay Stock Exchange and the MCX-Stock

Exchange are currently offering such trading facilities. As the product is exchange traded, the Reserve Bank and the Securities and Exchange Board of India are regulating the conduct of currency futures trading facility jointly.

Exchange Rate Policy   India's exchange rate policy has evolved in tandem with the domestic as well as international developments. The period after independence was marked by a fixed exchange rate regime, which was in line with the Bretton Woods system prevalent then. The Indian Rupee was pegged to the Pound Sterling on account of historic links with Britain. After the breakdown of Bretton Woods System in the early seventies, most of the countries moved towards a system of flexible/managed exchange rates. With the decline in the share of Britain in India's trade, increased diversification of India's international transactions together with the weaknesses of pegging to a single currency, the Indian Rupee was de-linked from the Pound Sterling in September 1975.

The exchange rate subsequently came to be determined with reference to the daily exchange rate movements of an undisclosed basket of currencies of India's major trading partners. As the basket-linked management of the exchange rate of the Rupee did not capture the market dynamics and the developments in the exchange rates of competing countries fully, the Rupee's external value was allowed to be determined by market forces in a phased manner following the balance of payment difficulties in the nineties.

A significant two-step downward adjustment in the exchange rate of the Rupee was made in 1991. In March 1992, Liberalised Exchange Rate Management System (LERMS) involving the dual exchange rate was instituted. A unified single market-determined exchange rate system based on the demand for and supply of foreign exchange replaced the LERMS effective March 1, 1993.

The Reserve Bank's exchange rate policy focuses on ensuring orderly conditions in the foreign exchange market. For the purpose, it closely monitors the developments in the financial markets at home and abroad. When necessary, it intervenes in the market by buying or selling foreign currencies. The market operations are undertaken either directly or through public sector banks.

In addition to the traditional instruments like forward and swap contracts, the Reserve Bank has facilitated increased availability of derivative instruments in the foreign exchange market. It has allowed trading in Rupee-foreign currency swaps, foreign currency-Rupee options, cross-currency options, interest rate swaps and currency swaps, forward rate agreements and currency futures.

Source: https://www.rbi.org.in/scripts/FS_Overview.aspx?fn=5; https://www.rbi.org.in/scripts/FS_Speeches.aspx?fn=2759#

Monetary Unions

A variant of a fixed exchange rate regime is a **monetary union** (or **currency union**) in which a group of countries decide to adopt a common currency, thereby fixing their exchange rates vis à vis each other. One of the early examples of a monetary union occurred when the thirteen colonies formed the United States in 1787 and gave up their individual currencies for the U.S. dollar. The most recent monetary union is the European Monetary Union (EMU), in which eleven initial countries adopted a new currency, the euro, in January of 1999.

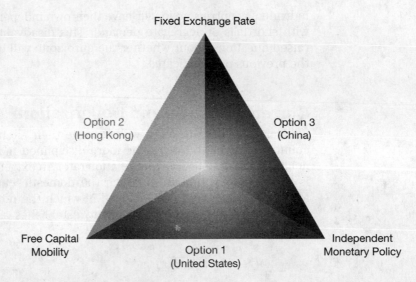

FIGURE 15.3 **The Policy Trilemma**

A country (or monetary union) cannot pursue the following three policies at the same time: (1) free capital mobility, (2) a fixed exchange rate, and (3) an independent monetary policy. Instead, it must choose two of the three policies on each side of the triangle.

The key economic advantage of a monetary union is that it makes trade across borders easier because goods and services in all the member countries are now priced in the same currency. However, as we have seen above, as with any fixed exchange rate regime and free capital mobility, a currency union means that

Will the Euro Survive?

The global financial crisis of 2007–2009 led to economic contraction throughout Europe, with the countries in the southern part of the euro zone hit especially hard. Unemployment in the hard hit countries climbed much faster than in in the northern countries, especially Germany. Furthermore, with the contraction in their economies, many of the southern countries began to experience large government budget deficits and sovereign debt crisis, in which investors pulled back from purchasing these countries' bonds, sending interest rates to extremely high levels. The resulting collapse of the southern countries' economies meant that they could benefit from much easier monetary policy to stimulate economic activity, but this option was unavailable because the European Central Bank had to conduct monetary policy for the euro zone as a whole, which was not suffering as badly as the southern countries.

The straightjacket of the euro has resulted in a weakening of support for the euro in the southern countries and there is an increasing talk of exiting the euro. Support for the euro has also weakened in the stronger, northern countries because they have been called on to provide bailouts to the weaker member countries. With the prospect that the stronger countries might want to exit in order to limit their transfer of funds to the weaker countries, and the weaker countries to exit so they can boost their economies by more expansionary monetary policy and depreciation of their currency if they abandon the euro, there are doubts the European Monetary Union can survive. However, the euro is seen as an important step to the creation of a more united and powerful Europe and this political consideration has created strong forces to retain the monetary union.

individual countries no longer have their own independent monetary policy to deal with shortfalls of aggregate demand. This disadvantage of a currency union has raised questions about whether the euro zone will break up, as the Mini-Case on the previous page indicates.

Currency Boards and Dollarization

Smaller countries are often willing to tie their exchange rate to that of a larger country in order to inherit the more disciplined monetary policy of their bigger neighbor, thus ensuring a low inflation rate. An extreme example of such a strategy is the **currency board,** in which the domestic currency is backed 100% by a foreign currency (say dollars), and in which the note-issuing authority, whether the central bank or the government, establishes a fixed exchange rate to this

---

> GLOBAL

Argentina's Currency Board

Argentina has had a long history of monetary instability, with inflation rates fluctuating dramatically and sometimes surging to beyond 1,000% per year. To end this cycle of inflationary surges, Argentina decided to adopt a currency board in April 1991. The Argentine currency board worked as follows: Under Argentina's convertibility law, the peso/dollar exchange rate was fixed at one to one, and a member of the public could go to the Argentine central bank and exchange a peso for a dollar, or vice versa, at any time.

The early years of Argentina's currency board looked stunningly successful. Inflation, which had been running at an 800% annual rate in 1990, fell to less than 5% by the end of 1994, and economic growth was rapid, averaging almost 8% per year from 1991 to 1994. In the aftermath of the Mexican peso crisis, however, concern about the health of the Argentine economy resulted in the public pulling money out of the banks (deposits fell by 18%) and exchanging pesos for dollars, thus causing a contraction of the Argentine money supply. The result was a sharp drop in Argentine economic activity, with real GDP shrinking by more than 5% in 1995 and the unemployment rate jumping above 15%. Only in 1996 did the economy begin to recover.

Because the central bank of Argentina had no control over monetary policy under the currency board system, it was relatively helpless to counteract the contractionary monetary policy stemming

from the public's behavior. Furthermore, because the currency board did not allow the central bank to create pesos and lend them to the banks, it had very little capability to act as a lender of last resort. With help from international agencies, such as the IMF, the World Bank, and the Inter-American Development Bank, which lent Argentina more than $5 billion in 1995 to help shore up its banking system, the currency board survived.

However, in 1998 Argentina entered another recession, which was both severe and very long lasting. By the end of 2001, unemployment reached nearly 20%, a level comparable to that experienced in the United States during the Great Depression of the 1930s. The result was civil unrest and the fall of the elected government, as well as a major banking crisis and a default on nearly $150 billion of government debt. Because the Central Bank of Argentina had no control over monetary policy under the currency board system, it was unable to use monetary policy to expand the economy and get out of its recession, nor could it act as a lender of last resort to prop up its banks. In January 2002, the currency board finally collapsed and the peso depreciated by more than 70%. The result was the full-scale financial crisis (described in Chapter 8), with inflation shooting up and an extremely severe depression. Clearly, the Argentine public is not as enamored of its currency board as it once was.

foreign currency and stands ready to exchange domestic currency for the foreign currency at this rate whenever the public requests it. Currency boards have been established in countries such as Hong Kong (1983), Argentina (1991), Estonia (1992), Lithuania (1994), Bulgaria (1997), and Bosnia (1998). (Argentina's currency board, which operated from 1991 to 2002, is one of the most interesting and is described in the Global box, "Argentina's Currency Board.") An even more extreme strategy is **dollarization,** in which a country abandons its currency altogether and adopts that of another country, typically the U.S. dollar (see the Global box, "Dollarization").

Speculative Attacks

A serious shortcoming of fixed exchange rate systems such as the Bretton Woods system or the European Monetary System is that they can lead to foreign exchange crisis involving a **speculative attack** on a currency—massive sales of a weak currency or purchases of a strong currency that cause a sharp change in the exchange rate. In the following case, we use our model of exchange rate determination to understand how the September 1992 exchange rate crisis that rocked the European Monetary System came about.

Managed Float

Although most exchange rates are currently allowed to change daily in response to market forces, many central banks have not been willing to give up their option of intervening in the foreign exchange market. Preventing large changes in exchange rates makes it easier for firms and individuals purchasing or selling goods abroad to plan into

Dollarization

Dollarization, which involves the adoption of another country's currency, usually the U.S. dollar (but other sound currencies like the euro and the yen are also possibilities), is a more extreme version of a fixed exchange rate than is a currency board. A currency board can be abandoned, allowing a change in the value of the currency, but a change of value is impossible with dollarization: A dollar bill is always worth one dollar whether it is held in the United States or outside of it. Panama has been dollarized since the inception of the country in the early twentieth century, while El Salvador and Ecuador have recently adopted dollarization.

Dollarization, like a currency board, prevents a central bank from creating inflation. Another key advantage is that it completely avoids the possibility of a speculative attack on the domestic currency (because there is none) that is still a danger even under a currency board arrangement. However, like a currency board, dollarization does not allow a country to pursue its own monetary policy or have a lender of last resort. Dollarization has one additional disadvantage not characteristic of a currency board: Because a country adopting dollarization no longer has its own currency, it loses the revenue that a government receives by issuing money, which is called *seigniorage*. Because governments (or their central banks) do not have to pay interest on their currency, they earn revenue (seigniorage) by using this currency to purchase income-earning assets such as bonds. In the case of the Federal Reserve in the United States, this revenue is usually in excess of $20 billion dollars per year. If an emerging-market country dollarizes and gives up its currency, it needs to make up this loss of revenue somewhere, which is not always easy for a poor country.

The Foreign Exchange Crisis of September 1992

In the aftermath of German reunification in October 1990, the German central bank, the Bundesbank, faced rising inflationary pressures, with inflation having accelerated from below 3% in 1990 to near 5% by 1992. To get monetary growth under control and to dampen inflation, the Bundesbank raised German interest rates to near double-digit levels. Figure 15.4 shows the consequences of these actions by the Bundesbank in the foreign exchange market for British pounds. Note that in the diagram, the pound is the domestic currency and the German mark (deutsche mark, DM, Germany's currency before the advent of the euro in 1999) is the foreign currency.

The increase in German interest rates i^F lowered the relative expected return of British pound assets and shifted the demand curve to D_2 in Figure 15.4. The intersection of the supply and demand curves at point 2 was now below the lower exchange rate limit at that time (2.778 marks per pound, denoted E_{par}). To increase the value of the pound relative to the mark and to restore the mark/pound exchange rate to within the exchange rate mechanism limits, one of two things had to happen. The Bank of England would have to pursue a contractionary monetary policy, thereby raising British interest rates sufficiently to shift the demand curve back to D_1 so that the equilibrium would remain at point 1, where the exchange rate would remain at E_{par}. Alternatively, the Bundesbank would have to pursue an expansionary monetary

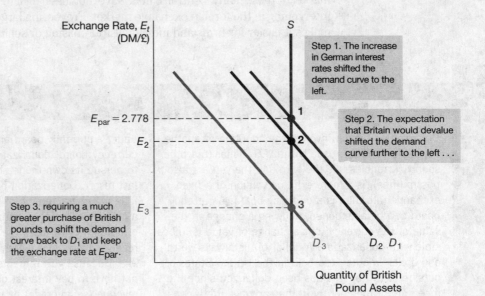

FIGURE 15.4 Foreign Exchange Market for British Pounds in 1992

The realization by speculators that the United Kingdom would soon devalue the pound decreased the relative expected return on British pound assets, resulting in a leftward shift of the demand curve from D_2 to D_3. The result was the need for a much greater purchase of pounds by the British central bank to raise the interest rate so that the demand curve would shift back to D_1 and keep the exchange rate E_{par} at 2.778 German marks per pound.

policy, thereby lowering German interest rates. Lower German interest rates would raise the relative expected return on British assets and shift the demand curve back to D_1 so that the exchange rate would be at E_{par}.

The catch was that the Bundesbank, whose primary goal was fighting inflation, was unwilling to pursue an expansionary monetary policy, and the British, who were facing their worst recession in the postwar period, were unwilling to pursue a contractionary monetary policy to prop up the pound. This impasse became clear when in response to great pressure from other members of the EMS, the Bundesbank was willing to lower its lending rates by only a token amount on September 16 after a speculative attack was mounted on the currencies of the Scandinavian countries. So at some point in the very near future, the value of the pound would have to decline to point 2. Speculators now knew that depreciation of the pound was imminent. As a result, the relative expected return of the pound immediately fell sharply, shifting the demand curve left to D_3 in Figure 15.4.

As a result of the large leftward shift of the demand curve, a huge excess supply of pound assets now existed at the par exchange rate E_{par}, which caused a massive sell-off of pounds (and purchases of marks) by speculators on September 16. The need for the British central bank to intervene to raise the value of the pound now became much greater and required a huge rise in British interest rates. After a major intervention effort on the part of the Bank of England, which included a rise in its lending rate from 10% to 15%, which still wasn't enough, the British were finally forced to give up on that day: They pulled out of the ERM indefinitely and allowed the pound to depreciate by 10% against the mark.

Speculative attacks on other currencies forced devaluation of the Spanish peseta by 5% and the Italian lira by 15%. To defend its currency, the Swedish central bank was forced to raise its daily lending rate to the astronomical level of 500%! By the time the crisis was over, the British, French, Italian, Spanish, and Swedish central banks had intervened to the tune of $100 billion; the Bundesbank alone had laid out $50 billion for foreign exchange intervention. Because foreign exchange crisis lead to large changes in central banks' holdings of international reserves and thus significantly affect the official reserve asset items in the balance of payments, these crisis are also referred to as **balance-of-payments crisis.**

The attempt to prop up the European Monetary System was not cheap for these central banks. It is estimated that they lost $4 to $6 billion as a result of exchange rate intervention during the crisis.

THE PRACTICING MANAGER

Profiting from a Foreign Exchange Crisis

Large banks and other financial institutions often conduct foreign exchange trading operations that generate substantial profits for their parent institution. When a foreign exchange crisis like the one that occurred in September 1992 comes along, foreign exchange traders and speculators are presented with a golden opportunity. The foregoing analysis of this crisis helps explain why.

As we saw in Figure 15.4, the high German interest rates resulted in a situation in which the British pound was overvalued, in that the equilibrium exchange rate in the absence of intervention by the British and German central banks was below the lower exchange rate limit of 2.778 German marks per British pound. Once foreign exchange traders realized that the central banks would not be willing to intervene sufficiently or alter their policies to keep the value of the pound above the 2.778-mark-per-pound lower limit, the traders were presented with a, "heads I win, tails you lose" bet. They knew that there was only one direction in which the exchange rate could go—down—and so they were almost sure to make money by buying marks and selling pounds. Our analysis of Figure 15.4 reflects this state of affairs; another way of looking at this one-sided bet is to recognize that it implies that the expected return on mark-denominated deposits increased sharply, shifting the demand curve far to the left to D_3 in Figure 15.4.

Savvy foreign exchange traders, who read the writing on the wall early in September 1992, sold pounds and bought marks. When the pound depreciated 10% against the mark after September 16, they made huge profits because the marks they had bought could now be sold at a price 10% higher. Foreign exchange traders at Citibank are reported to have made $200 million in the week of the September 1992 exchange rate crisis—not bad for a week's work! But these profits pale in comparison to those made by George Soros, an investment fund manager whose funds are reported to have run up profits of $1 billion during the crisis. (However, Soros gave some of these profits back in 1994 when he acknowledged that he had suffered a $600 million loss from trades on the yen.) Clearly, foreign exchange trading can be a highly profitable enterprise for financial institutions, particularly during foreign exchange rate crisis.

CASE

How Did China Accumulate over $3 Trillion of International Reserves?

By the end of 2013, China had accumulated more than $2 trillion of international reserves, and its international reserves are expected to keep growing in the near future. How did the Chinese get their hands on this vast amount of foreign assets? After all, China is not yet a rich country.

The answer is that China pegged its exchange rate to the U.S. dollar at a fixed rate of 8.28 yuan (also called renminbi), to the dollar in 1994. Because of China's rapidly growing productivity and an inflation rate that is lower than that in the United States, the long-run value of the yuan has increased, leading to a higher relative expected return for yuan assets and a rightward shift of the demand for yuan assets. As a result, the Chinese found themselves in the situation depicted in panel (b) of Figure 15.2, in which the yuan is undervalued. To keep the yuan from appreciating above E_{par} to E_1 in the figure, the Chinese central bank has been engaging in massive purchases of U.S. dollar assets. Today the Chinese government is one of the largest holders of U.S. government bonds in the world.

The pegging of the yuan to the U.S. dollar has created several problems for Chinese authorities. First, the Chinese now own a lot of U.S. assets, particularly U.S. Treasury securities, which have very low returns. Second, the undervaluation of the yuan has meant that Chinese goods are so cheap abroad that many countries have threatened to erect trade barriers against these goods if the Chinese government does not allow an upward revaluation of the yuan. Third, the Chinese purchase of dollar assets has resulted in a substantial increase in the Chinese monetary base and money supply, which has the potential to produce high inflation in the future. Because the Chinese authorities have created substantial roadblocks to capital mobility, they have been able to sterilize most of their exchange rate interventions while maintaining the exchange rate peg. Nevertheless, they still worry about inflationary pressures. In July 2005, China finally made its peg somewhat more flexible by letting the value of the yuan rise 2.1%. This was done in order to tame economic instability. China fixed its exchange rate in 1995 at slightly more than 8 yuan to the United States dollar and maintained that peg until July 2005, when it made a move toward a liberalization of its currency policy by introducing a narrow trading band. The central bank also indicated that it would no longer fix the yuan to the U.S. dollar but would instead maintain its value relative to a basket of currencies. Why have the Chinese authorities maintained this exchange rate peg for so long despite the problems? One answer is that they want to keep their export sector humming by keeping the prices of their export goods low. A second answer might be that they want to accumulate a large amount of international reserves as a "war chest" that could be sold to buy yuan in the event of a speculative attack against the yuan at some future date. Over the past decade, the government has gradually allowed the trading band to widen, starting at +/-0.3% and finally reaching +/-2% by March 2014.

In August 2015, China took a step further by allowing its currency to devalue outside of the previous trading band. In its policy move, the government said it would consider the previous day's trading in the establishment of the currency rate, effectively considering the influence of the market.

In a statement in August 2015, China's government said that "henceforth the mid-point of an expanded 2% band within which the currency can move on any single day would be based on the previous day's closing value." It also said the currency rate would be determined by "demand and supply conditions in the foreign exchange markets and the movement of major currencies." With this change, the country was seen moving its policy from a rigid band and toward a floating currency rate.

References: https://www.fxcm.com/insights/how-does-china-control-exchange-rates/; http://www.theaustralian.com.au/business/business-spectator/why-china-changed-its-exchange-rate-policy/news-story/41a76a098ec0e7e5cad1ea19da14c5f1

the future. Furthermore, countries with surpluses in their balance of payments frequently do not want to see their currencies appreciate because it makes their goods more expensive abroad and foreign goods cheaper in their country. Because an appreciation might hurt sales for domestic businesses and increase unemployment, surplus countries have often sold their currency in the foreign exchange market and acquired international reserves.

Countries with balance-of-payments deficits do not want to see their currency lose value because it makes foreign goods more expensive for domestic consumers and can stimulate inflation. To keep the value of the domestic currency high, deficit countries have often bought their own currency in the foreign exchange market and given up international reserves.

The current international financial system is a hybrid of a fixed and a flexible exchange rate system. Rates fluctuate in response to market forces but are not determined solely by them. Furthermore, many countries continue to keep the value of their currency fixed against other currencies.

Capital Controls

Because capital flows were an important element in the currency crisis in Mexico and East Asia, politicians and some economists have advocated that emerging market countries avoid financial instability by restricting capital mobility. Are capital controls a good idea?

Controls on Capital Outflows

Capital outflows can promote financial instability in emerging market countries because when domestic residents and foreigners pull their capital out of a country, the resulting capital outflow forces a country to devalue its currency. This risk is why some politicians in emerging market countries have recently found capital controls particularly attractive. For example, Prime Minister Mahathir of Malaysia instituted capital controls in 1998 to restrict outflows in the aftermath of the East Asian crisis.

Although these controls sound like a good idea, they suffer from several disadvantages. First, empirical evidence indicates that controls on capital outflows are seldom effective during a crisis because the private sector finds ingenious ways to evade them and has little difficulty moving funds out of the country. Second, the evidence suggests that capital flight may even increase after controls are put into place because confidence in the government is weakened. Third, controls on capital outflows often lead to corruption, as government officials get bribed to look the other way when domestic residents are trying to move funds abroad. Fourth, controls on capital outflows may lull governments into thinking they do not have to take the steps to reform their financial systems to deal with the crisis, with the result that opportunities to improve the functioning of the economy are lost.

Controls on Capital Inflows

Although most economists find the arguments against controls on capital outflows persuasive, controls on capital inflows receive more support. Supporters reason that if speculative capital cannot come in, then it cannot go out suddenly and create a crisis. Our analysis of the financial crisis in East Asia in Chapter 8, provides support for this view by suggesting that capital inflows can lead to a lending boom and excessive risk taking on the part of banks, which then helps trigger a financial crisis.

However, controls on capital inflows have the undesirable feature that they may block those funds from entering a country that would be used for productive investment opportunities. Although such controls may limit the fuel supplied to lending booms through capital flows, over time they produce substantial distortions and misallocation of resources as households and businesses try to get around them. Indeed, as with controls on capital outflows, controls on capital inflows can lead to corruption. Serious doubts arise over whether capital controls can be effective in today's environment, in which trade is open and where many financial instruments make it easier to get around these controls.

On the other hand, a strong case can be made for improving bank regulation and supervision so that capital inflows are less likely to produce a lending boom and encourage excessive risk taking by banking institutions. For example, restricting banks in how fast their borrowing can grow might substantially limit capital inflows. Supervisory controls that focus on the sources, rather than the symptoms, of financial fragility can enhance the efficiency of the financial system rather than hamper it.

The Role of the IMF

The International Monetary Fund was originally set up under the Bretton Woods system to help countries deal with balance-of-payments problems and stay with the fixed exchange rates by lending to deficit countries. When the Bretton Woods system of fixed exchange rates collapsed in 1971, the IMF took on new roles.

Although the IMF no longer attempts to encourage fixed exchange rates, its role as an international lender has become more important recently. This role first came to the fore in the 1980s during the Third World debt crisis, in which the IMF assisted developing countries in repaying their loans. The financial crisis in Mexico in 1994–1995 and in East Asia in 1997–1998 led to huge loans by the IMF to these and other affected countries to help them recover from their financial crisis and to prevent the spread of these crisis to other countries. Then starting in 2010, the IMF made large loans to Greece, Ireland, and Portugal to help them avoid a default on their government debt. This role, in which the IMF acts like an international lender of last resort to cope with financial instability, is indeed highly controversial.

Should the IMF Be an International Lender of Last Resort?

As we saw in Chapter 8, in large industrialized countries when a financial crisis occurs and the financial system threatens to seize up, domestic central banks can address matters with a lender-of-last-resort operation to limit the degree of instability in the banking system. In emerging market countries, however, where the credibility of the central bank as an inflation fighter may be in doubt and debt contracts are typically short-term and denominated in foreign currencies, a lender-of-last-resort operation becomes a double-edged sword—as likely to exacerbate the financial crisis as to alleviate it. For example, when the U.S. Federal Reserve engaged in a lender-of-last-resort operation during the global financial crisis, there was almost no sentiment in the markets that substantially a higher inflation would result. However, for a central bank with less inflation-fighting credibility than the Fed, central bank lending to the financial system in the wake of a financial crisis—even under the lender-of-last-resort rhetoric—may well arouse fears of inflation spiraling out of control, causing an even greater currency depreciation and still greater deterioration of balance sheets. The resulting increase in moral hazard and adverse selection problems in financial markets would only worsen the financial crisis.

Central banks in emerging market countries therefore have only a very limited ability to successfully engage in a lender-of-last-resort operation. However, liquidity provided by an international lender of last resort does not have these undesirable consequences, and in helping to stabilize the value of the domestic currency, it strengthens domestic balance sheets. Moreover, an international lender of last resort may be able to prevent contagion, the situation in which a successful speculative attack on one emerging market currency leads to attacks on other emerging market currencies, spreading financial and economic disruption as it goes. Because a lender of last resort for emerging market countries is needed at times, and because it cannot be provided domestically, a strong rationale exists for an international institution to fill this role. Indeed, since Mexico's financial crisis in 1994, the International Monetary Fund and other international agencies have stepped into the lender-of-last-resort role and provided emergency lending to countries threatened by financial instability.

However, support from an international lender as a last resort brings risks of its own, especially the risk of the perception that it is standing ready to bail out irresponsible financial institutions may lead to excessive risk taking of the sort that makes financial crisis more likely. In the Mexican and East Asian crisis, governments in the crisis countries used IMF support to protect depositors and other creditors of banking institutions from losses. This safety net creates a well-known moral hazard problem because the depositors and other creditors have less incentive to monitor these banking institutions and withdraw their deposits if the institutions are taking on too much risk. The result is that these institutions are encouraged to take on excessive risks.

An international lender of last resort must find ways to limit this moral hazard problem, or it can actually make the situation worse. The international lender of last resort can make it clear that it will extend liquidity only to governments that put the proper measures in place to prevent excessive risk taking. In addition, it can reduce the incentives for risk taking by restricting the ability of governments to bail out stockholders and large uninsured creditors of domestic financial institutions. Some critics of the IMF believe that the IMF has not put enough pressure on the governments to which it lends to contain the moral hazard problem.

One problem that arises for international organizations like the IMF engaged in lender-of-last-resort operations is that they know if they don't come to the rescue, the country will suffer extreme hardship and possible political instability. Politicians in the crisis country may exploit these concerns and engage in a game of chicken with the international lender of last resort: they resist necessary reforms, hoping that the IMF will cave in. Elements of this game were present in the Mexican crisis of 1994 and were also a particularly important feature of the negotiations between the IMF and Indonesia during the Asian crisis.

How Should the IMF Operate?

The IMF would produce better outcomes if it made clear that it will not play this game. Just as giving in to ill-behaved children may be the easy way out in the short run but supports a pattern of poor behavior in the long run, some critics worry that the IMF may not be tough enough when confronted by short-run humanitarian concerns. For example, these critics have been particularly critical of the IMF's lending to the Russian government, which resisted adopting appropriate reforms to stabilize its financial system.

The IMF has also been criticized for imposing so-called austerity programs that focus on tight macroeconomic policies rather than on microeconomic policies to fix the crisis-causing problems in the financial sector. Such programs are likely to increase resistance to IMF recommendations, particularly in emerging market countries. Austerity programs allow politicians in these countries to label institutions such as the IMF as being antigrowth, rhetoric that helps them mobilize the public against the IMF and avoid doing what they really need to do to reform the financial system in their country. IMF programs focused instead on reforms of the financial sector which would increase the likelihood that the IMF will be seen as a helping hand in the creation of a more efficient financial system.

An important historical feature of successful lender-of-last-resort operations is that the faster the lending is done, the lower the amount that actually has to be lent. An excellent example involving the Federal Reserve occurred in the aftermath of the stock market crash on October 19, 1987. At the end of that day, to service their customers' accounts, securities firms needed to borrow several billion dollars to maintain orderly trading. However, given the unprecedented developments, banks were nervous about extending further loans to these firms. Upon learning this, the Federal Reserve engaged in an immediate lender-of-last-resort operation, making it clear that it would provide liquidity to banks making loans to the securities industry. What is striking about this episode is that the extremely quick intervention of the Fed not only resulted in a negligible impact of the stock market crash on the economy but also meant that the amount of liquidity that the Fed needed to supply to the economy was not very large.

The ability of the Fed to engage in a lender-of-last-resort operation within a day of a substantial shock to the financial system stands in sharp contrast to the amount of time it has taken the IMF to supply liquidity during the recent crisis. Because IMF lending facilities were originally designed to provide funds after a country was experiencing a balance-of-payment crisis and because the conditions for the loan have to be negotiated, it takes several months before the IMF can make funds available. By this time, the crisis can get much worse—and much larger sums of funds are then needed to cope with the crisis, often stretching the resources of the IMF. One reason central banks can lend so much more quickly than the IMF is that they have set up procedures in advance to provide loans, with the terms and conditions for this lending agreed upon beforehand. The need for quick provision of liquidity, to keep the loan amount manageable, argues for similar credit facilities at the international lender of last resort, so that funds can be provided quickly as long as the borrower meets conditions such as properly supervising its banks or keeping budget deficits low. The debate on whether the world will be better off with the IMF operating as an international lender of last resort is currently a hot one. Much attention is being focused on making the IMF more effective in performing this role, and a redesign of the IMF is at the center of proposals for a new international financial architecture to help reduce international financial instability.

SUMMARY

1. An unsterilized central bank intervention in which the domestic currency is sold to purchase foreign assets leads to a gain in international reserves, an increase in the money supply, and a depreciation of the domestic currency. Available evidence suggests, however, that sterilized central bank interventions have little long-term effect on the exchange rate.

2. The balance of payments is a bookkeeping system for recording all payments between a country and foreign countries that have a direct bearing on the

movement of funds between them. The official reserve transactions balance is the sum of the current account balance plus the items in the capital account. It indicates the amount of international reserves that must be moved between countries to finance international transactions.

3. After World War II, the Bretton Woods system and the IMF were established to promote a fixed exchange rate system in which the U.S. dollar, the reserve currency, was convertible into gold. The Bretton Woods system collapsed in 1971. We now

have an international financial system that has elements of a managed float and a fixed exchange rate system. Some exchange rates fluctuate from day to day, although central banks intervene in the foreign exchange market, while other exchange rates are fixed.

4. Controls on capital outflows receive support because they may prevent domestic residents and foreigners from pulling capital out of a country during a crisis and make devaluation less likely. Controls on capital inflows make sense under the theory that if speculative capital cannot flow in, then it cannot go out suddenly and create a crisis. However, capital controls suffer from several disadvantages: They are seldom effective, they lead to corruption, and they may allow governments to avoid taking the steps needed

to reform their financial systems to deal with the crisis.

5. The IMF has recently taken on the role of an international lender of last resort. Because central banks in emerging market countries are unlikely to be able to perform a lender-of-last-resort operation successfully, an international lender of last resort like the IMF is needed to prevent financial instability. However, the IMF's role as an international lender of last resort creates a serious moral hazard problem that can encourage excessive risk taking and make a financial crisis more likely, but refusing to lend may be politically hard to do. In addition, it needs to be able to provide liquidity quickly during a crisis to keep manageable the amount of funds lent.

KEY TERMS

anchor currency, p. 370
balance of payments, p. 367
balance-of-payments crisis, p. 381
Bretton Woods system, p. 370
capital and financial account, p. 368
capital controls, p. 373
currency board, p. 378
currency union, p. 376
current account, p. 367
devaluation, p. 372
dollarization, p. 379

fixed exchange rate regime, p. 370
floating exchange rate regime, p. 370
foreign exchange interventions, p. 363
impossible trinity, p. 373
International Monetary Fund
 (IMF), p. 370
international reserves, p. 363
managed float regime
 (dirty float), p. 370
monetary union, p. 376
policy trilemma, p. 373

reserve currency, p. 371
revaluation, p. 373
speculative attack, p. 379
sterilized foreign exchange
 intervention, p. 365
trade balance, p. 367
unsterilized foreign exchange
 intervention, p. 365
World Bank, p. 370
World Trade Organization
 (WTO), p. 371

QUESTIONS

1. If the Federal Reserve buys dollars in the foreign exchange market but conducts an offsetting open market operation to sterilize the intervention, what will be the effect on international reserves, the money supply, and the exchange rate?

2. If the Federal Reserve buys dollars in the foreign exchange market but does not sterilize the intervention, what will be the effect on international reserves, the money supply, and the exchange rate?

3. For each of the following, identify in which part of the balance-of-payments account it appears (current

account, capital and financial account, or net change in international reserves) and whether it is a receipt or a payment:

a. A British subject's purchase of a share of Johnson & Johnson stock

b. An American's purchase of an airline ticket from Air France

c. The Swiss government's purchase of U.S. Treasury bills

d. A Japanese's purchase of California oranges

e. $50 million of foreign aid to Honduras

f. A loan by an American bank to Mexico

g. An American bank's borrowing of Eurodollars

h. India forgiving the debt owed to it by Nepal

4. Why does a balance-of-payments deficit for the United States have a different effect on its international reserves than a balance-of-payments deficit for the Netherlands?

5. Under fixed exchange rates, if Britain becomes more productively relative to the United States, what foreign exchange intervention is necessary to maintain the fixed exchange rate between dollars and pounds? Which country undertakes this intervention?

6. What is the exchange rate between dollars and Swiss francs if one dollar is convertible into 1/20 ounce of gold and one Swiss franc is convertible into 1/40 ounce of gold?

7. If a country's par exchange rate was undervalued during the Bretton Woods fixed exchange rate regime, what kind of intervention would that country's central bank be forced to undertake, and what effect would it have on its international reserves and the money supply?

8. How can a large balance-of-payments surplus contribute to the country's inflation rate?

9. "If a country wants to keep its exchange rate from changing, it must give up some control over its money supply." Is this statement true, false, or uncertain? Explain your answer.

10. Why can balance-of-payments deficits force some countries to implement a contractionary monetary policy?

11. "Balance-of-payments deficits always cause a country to lose international reserves." Is this statement true, false, or uncertain? Explain your answer.

12. How can the persistence of U.S. balance-of-payments deficits stimulate world inflation?

13. Why did the exchange rate peg lead to difficulties for the countries in the ERM when German reunification occurred?

14. Why is it that in a pure flexible exchange rate system, the foreign exchange market has no direct effects on the monetary base and the money supply? Does this mean that the foreign exchange market has no effect on monetary policy?

15. "The abandonment of fixed exchange rates after 1973 has meant that countries have pursued more independent monetary policies." Is this statement true, false, or uncertain? Explain your answer.

16. Are controls on capital outflows a good idea? Why or why not?

17. Discuss the pros and cons of controls on capital inflows.

18. Why might central banks in emerging-market countries find that engaging in a lender-of-last-resort operation might be counterproductive? Does this provide a rationale for having an international lender of last resort like the IMF?

19. Has the IMF done a good job in performing the role of the international lender of last resort?

20. What steps should an international lender of last resort take to limit moral hazard?

QUANTITATIVE PROBLEMS

1. The RBI purchases $1,000,000 of foreign assets for equivalent rupees based on the rupee-dollar exchange rate (say ₹65 to a dollar). Show the effect of this open market operation using T-accounts.

2. Again, the RBI purchases $1,000,000 of foreign assets. However, to raise the funds, the trading desk sells an equivalent amount of rupees in government securities. Show the effect of this open market operation using T-accounts.

3. If the interest rate is 4% on euro deposits and 2% on dollar deposits, while the euro is trading at $1.30 per euro, what does the market expect the exchange rate to be one year from now?

4. If the dollar begins trading at $1.30 per euro, with the same interest rates given in Problem 3, and the ECB raises interest rates so that the rate on euro deposits rises by 1 percentage point, what will happen to the exchange rate (assuming that the expected future exchange rate is unchanged)?

5. If the balance in the current account increases by $2 billion while the capital account is off $3.5 billion, what is the effect on governmental international reserves?

WEB EXERCISES

The International Financial System

1. The International Monetary Fund stands ready to help nations facing monetary crisis. Go to **www.imf.org**.

Click on the tab labeled "About the IMF." What is the stated purpose of the IMF? How many nations participate, and when was it established?

WEB APPENDICES

Please visit our Web site at
www.pearsonhighered.com/mishkin_eakins to read
the Web appendix to Chapter 15:

- **Appendix:** The Balance of Payments Account

16

Banking and the Management of Financial Institutions

> PREVIEW

Because banking plays such a major role in channeling funds to borrowers with productive investment opportunities, this financial activity is important in ensuring that the financial system and the economy run smoothly and efficiently. They provide loans to businesses, help us finance our college educations or the purchase of a new car or home, and provide us with services such as checking and savings accounts.

In this chapter, we examine how banking is conducted to earn the highest profits possible: how and why banks make loans, how they acquire funds and manage their assets and liabilities (debts), and how they earn income. Although we focus on commercial banking because this is the most important financial intermediary activity, many of the same principles are applicable to other types of financial intermediation.

The Bank Balance Sheet

To understand how banking works, we start by looking at the bank **balance sheet,** a list of the bank's assets and liabilities. As the name implies, this list balances; that is, it has the characteristic that

$$\text{total assets} = \text{total liabilities} + \text{capital}$$

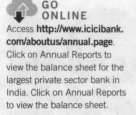

GO ONLINE

Access **http://www.icicibank. com/aboutus/annual.page**. Click on Annual Reports to view the balance sheet for the largest private sector bank in India. Click on Annual Reports to view the balance sheet.

A bank's balance sheet is also a list of its *sources* of bank funds (liabilities) and *uses* to which the funds are put (assets). Banks obtain funds by borrowing and by issuing other liabilities such as deposits. They then use these funds to acquire assets such as securities and loans. Banks make profits by charging an interest rate on their asset holdings of securities and loans that is higher than the interest and other expenses on their liabilities. The consolidated balance sheet of all scheduled commercial banks in India in the year (end March) 2013–14 appears in Table 16.1.

Liabilities

A bank acquires funds by issuing (selling) liabilities, such as deposits, which are the *sources of funds* the bank uses. The funds obtained from issuing liabilities are used to purchase income-earning assets.

GO ONLINE

Access **https://dbie.rbi.org.in/ DBIE/dbie.rbi?site=statistics** to view the latest figures for the consolidated balance sheet of scheduled commercial banks in India.

Deposits—it includes all demand deposits (from banks and others), savings bank deposits and term deposits (from banks and others).

Demand deposits include all bank deposits repayable on demand, and also all demand deposits of the non-bank sectors. Credit balances in overdrafts, cash credit accounts deposits payable at call, overdue deposits, inoperative current accounts, matured time deposits and cash certificates, etc. are to be included under this category.

TABLE 16.1   Consolidated Balance Sheet of Scheduled Commercial Banks in India (Excluding Regional Rural Banks) Year (end-March) 2013–14

Assets (Rupees Billion)	Percentage of total assets/liabilities	Liabilities (Rupees Billion)
Cash and Balances with RBI	4717.29	4.30
Capital	760.67	0.69
Balances with Banks and Money at Call and Short Notice	4063.04	3.71
Reserves and Surplus	7298.32	6.66
Investments	28828.53	0.26
Deposits	85331.38	77.83
Loans and Advances	67352.32	61.43
Borrowings	11008.19	10.04
Fixed Assets	756.10	0.69
Other Liabilities and Provisions	5236.19	4.78
Other Assets	3917.47	3.57
Total Liabilities/Assets	109634.75	100.00

Source: http://dbie.rbi.org.in/DBIE/dbie.rbi?site=statistics, as accessed on 12 February 2017 at 5pm.

Savings bank deposits (including inoperative savings bank accounts) are an important component of the liability component 'deposits'.

Finally, term deposits, which includes all types of banks deposits repayable after a specified term, also form a part of deposits. It also includes all types of deposits of the non-bank sector repayable after a specified term. Fixed deposits, cumulative and recurring deposits, cash certificates, annuity deposits, deposits mobilised under various schemes, ordinary staff deposits, foreign currency non-resident deposits accounts, etc. are to be included under this category.

As Table 16.1 demonstrates, deposits are the most important 'liability' component in India. They accounted for about 77% of the liabilities of all scheduled commercial banks in the year ending March 2013–14.

Borrowings   Banks also obtain funds by borrowing from the Reserve Bank of India, and from other commercial banks (including cooperative banks). These constitute borrowings from within India. Borrowings from the RBI are called **repo loans**. Banks also borrow reserves overnight in the call money market from other commercial banks and financial institutions. Banks borrow funds overnight to have enough deposits at the RBI to meet the amount required by the RBI under the Cash Reserve Ratio requirement. Other sources of borrowings include borrowings/refinance and rediscount from Industrial Development Bank of India, Export-Import Bank of India, National Bank for Agricultural and Rural Development and other institutions, agencies (including liability against participation certificates, if any). Borrowings from outside India include borrowings and rediscounts of Indian branches abroad as well as borrowings of foreign branches. Borrowings have become a more important source of bank funds over time: In 1990–91 they made up about 8% of bank liabilities; currently, they are 10% of bank liabilities.

Bank Capital   The final category on the liability side of the balance sheet is bank capital, the bank's net worth, which equals the difference between total assets and liabilities (0.69% of bank assets in Table 16.1). Bank capital is raised by selling new equity (stock) or from retained earnings. Bank capital is a cushion against a drop in the value of its assets, which could force the bank into insolvency (having liabilities in excess of assets, meaning that the bank can be forced into liquidation).

Assets

A bank uses the funds that it has acquired by issuing liabilities to purchase income-earning assets. Bank assets are thus naturally referred to as *uses of funds*, and the interest payments earned on them are what enables the banks to make profits.

Reserves   All banks hold some of the funds they acquire as deposits in an account at the RBI. **Reserves** are these deposits plus currency that is physically held by banks (called **vault cash** because it is stored in bank vaults overnight). Although reserves currently do not pay interest, banks hold them for two reasons. First, some reserves, called **required reserves,** are held because of **reserve requirements,** the regulation that for every rupee of net demand and time deposits at a bank, a certain fraction (10%, for example) must be kept as reserves. This fraction (10% in the example) is called the **required reserve ratio.** Banks hold additional reserves, called **excess reserves,** because they are the most liquid of all bank assets and a bank can use them to meet its obligations when funds are withdrawn, either directly by a depositor or indirectly when a check is written on an account.

Cash and Balances with the Reserve Bank of India This includes cash in hand, including foreign currency notes and also of foreign branches in the case of banks having such branches. It also includes the balance maintained with the Reserve Bank of India in the current account.

Balances with Banks and Money at Call and at Short Notice Such balances held by scheduled commercial banks are categorised into two: within India and outside India.

Such balances within India include balances held with the Reserve Bank of India other than in current accounts, if any. It includes all balances with banks in India (including co-operative banks). Balances in current accounts and deposit accounts should be shown separately. This category also includes deposits repayable within 15 days or less than 15 days' notice lent in the inter-bank call money market.

Such balances outside India include balances held by foreign branches and balances held by Indian branches of the banks outside India. Balances held with foreign branches by other branches of the bank should not be shown under this head but should be included in inter branch accounts. The amounts held in 'current accounts' and 'deposit accounts' are shown separately.

Investments A bank's holdings of securities are typically an important income-earning assets. However, such securities comprised only 0.26% of the overall assets of all scheduled commercial banks in the year-ending March 2013–14. Scheduled commercial banks' investments are classified into two categories—investments in India and investments outside India. The former category includes Central and State Government securities and Government treasury bills. This category also includes securities other than Government securities, which according to the Statutes are treated as approved securities. Investments in India also include investments in shares of companies and corporations not included in 'approved securities'.

Further, the category also includes investments in debentures and bonds of companies not included in 'approved securities'. Also included are investments in subsidiaries/associate companies. A company is considered as an associate company for the purpose of this classification if more than 25% of the share capital of that company is held by the bank. Other investments including residual investments, if any, like gold are also included. Investments outside India include investments in foreign government securities, including securities issued by local authorities, as also other residual investments.

Loans Banks make their profits primarily by issuing loans. In Table 16.1, some 61% of bank assets are in the form of loans, and in recent years they have generally produced more than half of bank revenues. A loan is a liability for the individual or corporation receiving it, but an asset for a bank, because it provides income to the bank. Loans are typically less liquid than other assets because they cannot be turned into cash until the loan matures. If the bank makes a one-year loan, for example, it cannot receive back the funds until the loan comes due in one year. Loans also have a higher probability of default than other assets. Because of the lack of liquidity and higher default risk, the bank earns its highest return on loans.

In India, such loans and advances include all outstandings—both in India as well as outside—less provisions are made, which are classified under three heads:

1. Bills purchased and discounted
2. Cash credits, overdrafts and loans repayable on demand, and
3. Term loans

Both secured and unsecured advances will be included under these heads.

Another basis for classification of such advances is secured and unsecured. Secured advances, including advances within and outside India, include advances secured by tangible assets. This category also includes advances in India and outside India covered by guarantees of Indian and foreign governments and Indian and foreign banks.

Unsecured advances are all the remaining advances which are not covered for or are unsecured.

Fixed Assets it includes premises, wholly or partly owned by the banking company, other fixed assets (including furniture and fixtures) and capital work-in progress or premises-under-construction.

Other Assets—this category includes:

1. Inter-office adjustments (net)
2. Interest accrued
3. Tax paid in advance/tax deducted at source
4. Stationery and stamps, and
5. Others

The physical capital (bank buildings, computers, and other equipment) owned by the banks is included in this category.

Basic Banking

Before proceeding to a more detailed study of how a bank manages its assets and liabilities to make the highest profit, you should understand the basic operation of a bank.

In general terms, banks make profits by selling liabilities with one set of characteristics (a particular combination of liquidity, risk, size, and return) and using the proceeds to buy assets with a different set of characteristics. This process is often referred to as an *asset transformation*. For example, a savings deposit held by one person can provide the funds that enables the bank to make a mortgage loan to another person. The bank has, in effect, transformed the savings deposit (an asset held by the depositor) into a mortgage loan (an asset held by the bank). Another way this process of asset transformation is described is to say that the bank "borrows short and lends long", because it makes long-term loans and funds them by issuing short-dated deposits.

The process of transforming assets and providing a set of services (check clearing, record keeping, credit analysis, and so forth) is like any other production process in a firm. If the bank produces desirable services at low cost and earns substantial income on its assets, it earns profits; if not, the bank suffers losses.

Let's say that Reena Gupta has heard that the First National Bank provides excellent service, so she opens a checking account with a ₹100 note. She now has a ₹100 checkable deposit at the bank, which shows up as a ₹100 liability on the bank's balance sheet. The bank now puts her ₹100 bill into its vault so that the bank's assets rise by the ₹100 increase in vault cash. The T-account for the bank looks like this:

First National Bank		
Assets		Liabilities
Vault cash	+₹100	Checkable deposits	+₹100

Because vault cash is also part of the bank's reserves, we can rewrite the T-account as follows:

Assets		Liabilities
Reserves	+₹100	Checkable deposits	+₹100

Note that Reena Gupta's opening of a checking account leads to *an increase in the bank's reserves which is equal to the increase in checkable deposits.*

If Reena had opened her account with a ₹100 check written on an account at another bank, say, the Second National Bank, we would get the same result. The initial effect on the T-account of the First National Bank is as follows:

Assets		Liabilities
Cash items in process of collection	+₹100	Checkable deposits	+₹100

Checkable deposits increase by ₹100 as before, but now the First National Bank is owed ₹100 by the Second National Bank. This asset for the First National Bank is entered in the T-account as ₹100 of cash items in process of collection because the First National Bank will now try to collect the funds that it is owed. It could go directly to the Second National Bank and ask for payment of the funds, but if the two banks are in separate states, that would be a time-consuming and costly process. Instead, the First National Bank deposits the check in its account at the RBI, and the RBI collects the funds from the Second National Bank. The result is that the RBI transfers ₹100 of reserves from the Second National Bank to the First National Bank, and the final balance sheet positions of the two banks are as follows:

First National Bank				Second National Bank			
Assets		Liabilities		Assets		Liabilities	
Reserves	+₹100	Checkable deposits	+₹100	Reserves	−₹100	Checkable deposits	−₹100

The process initiated by Reena Gupta can be summarized as follows: When a check written on an account at one bank is deposited in another, the bank receiving the deposit gains reserves equal to the amount of the check, while the bank on which the check is written sees its reserves fall by the same amount. Therefore, *when a bank receives additional deposits, it gains an equal amount of reserves; when it loses deposits, it loses an equal amount of reserves.*

Now that you understand how banks gain and lose reserves, we can examine how a bank rearranges its balance sheet to make a profit when it experiences a change in its deposits. Let's return to the situation when the First National Bank has just received the extra ₹100 of checkable deposits. As you know, the bank is obliged to keep a certain fraction of its checkable deposits as required reserves. If the fraction (the required reserve ratio) is 10%, the First National Bank's required reserves have increased by ₹10, and we can rewrite its T-account as follows.

First National Bank			
Assets		Liabilities	
Required reserves	+₹10	Checkable deposits	+₹100
Excess reserves	+₹90		

Let's see how well the bank is doing as a result of the additional checkable deposits. Servicing the extra ₹100 of checkable deposits is costly because the bank must keep records, pay tellers, pay for check clearing, and so forth. The bank is taking a loss! The situation is even worse if the bank makes interest payments on the deposits, as with savings accounts. If it is to make a profit, the bank must put to productive use all or part of the ₹90 of excess reserves it has available. One way to do this is to invest in securities. The other is to make loans; as we have seen, loans account for approximately 61% of the total value of bank assets (uses of funds). Because lenders are subject to the asymmetric information problems of adverse selection and moral hazard(discussed in Chapter 7), banks take steps to reduce the incidence and severity of these problems. Bank loan officers evaluate potential borrowers using what are called the "five Cs": character, capacity (ability to repay), collateral, conditions (in the local and national economies), and capital (net worth) before they agree to lend. (Chapter 19 provides a more detailed discussion of the methods banks use to reduce the risk involved in lending.)

Let us assume that the bank chooses not to hold any excess reserves but to make loans instead. The T-account then looks like this:

First National Bank			
Assets		Liabilities	
Required reserves	+₹10	Checkable deposits	+₹100
Loans	+₹90		

The bank is now making a profit because it holds short-term liabilities such as checkable deposits and uses the proceeds to buy longer-term assets such as loans with higher interest rates. As mentioned earlier, this process of asset transformation is frequently described by saying that banks are in the business of "borrowing short and lending long." For example, if the loans have an interest rate of 10% per year, the bank earns ₹9 in income from its loans over the year. If the ₹100 of checkable deposits is in a savings account with a 5% interest rate and it costs another ₹3 per year to service the account, the cost per year of these deposits is ₹8. The bank's profit on the new deposits is then ₹1 per year.

General Principles of Bank Management

Now that you have some idea of how a bank operates, let's look at how a bank manages its assets and liabilities to earn the highest possible profit. The bank manager has four primary concerns. The first is to make sure that the bank has enough ready cash to pay its depositors when there are **deposit outflows**—that is, when deposits are lost because depositors make withdrawals and demand payment. To keep enough cash on hand, the bank must engage in **liquidity management,** the acquisition of sufficiently liquid assets to meet the bank's obligations to depositors. Second, the bank manager must pursue an acceptably low level of risk by acquiring assets that have a low rate of default and by diversifying asset holdings (**asset management**). The third concern is to acquire funds at low cost (**liability management**). Finally, the manager must decide the amount of capital the bank should maintain and then acquire the needed capital (**capital adequacy management**).

To understand bank and other financial institution management fully, we must go beyond the general principles of bank asset and liability management described next and look in more detail at how a financial institution manages its assets. Chapter 19 provides an in-depth discussion of how a financial institution manages **credit risk,** the risk arising because borrowers may default, and how it manages **interest-rate risk,** the riskiness of earnings and returns on bank assets that results from interest-rate changes.

Liquidity Management and the Role of Reserves

Let us see how a typical bank, the First National Bank, can deal with deposit outflows that occur when its depositors withdraw cash from checking or savings accounts or write checks that are deposited in other banks. In the example that follows, we assume that the bank has ample excess reserves and that all deposits have the same required reserve ratio of 10% (the bank is required to keep 10% of its net demand and time liabilities (NDTL) as reserves). Suppose that the First National Bank's initial balance sheet is as follows:

Assets		Liabilities	
Reserves	₹20 million	Deposits	₹100 million
Loans	₹80 million	Bank capital	₹ 10 million
Securities	₹10 million		

The bank's required reserves are 10% of ₹100 million, or ₹10 million. Given that it holds ₹20 million of reserves, the First National Bank has excess reserves of ₹10 million. If a deposit outflow of ₹10 million occurs, the bank's balance sheet is as follows:

Assets		Liabilities	
Reserves	₹10 million	Deposits	₹90 million
Loans	₹80 million	Bank capital	₹10 million
Securities	₹10 million		

The bank loses ₹10 million of deposits *and* ₹10 million of reserves, but because its required reserves are now 10% of only ₹90 million (₹9 million), its reserves still exceed this amount by ₹1 million. In short, *if a bank has ample excess reserves, a deposit outflow does not necessitate changes in other parts of its balance sheet.*

The situation is quite different when a bank holds insufficient excess reserves. Let's assume that instead of initially holding ₹10 million in excess reserves, the First National Bank makes additional loans of ₹10 million, so that it holds no excess reserves. Its initial balance sheet would then be as follows:

Assets		Liabilities	
Reserves	₹10 million	Deposits	₹100 million
Loans	₹90 million	Bank capital	₹ 10 million
Securities	₹10 million		

When it suffers the ₹10 million deposit outflow, its balance sheet becomes:

Assets		Liabilities	
Reserves	₹ 0	Deposits	₹90 million
Loans	₹90 million	Bank capital	₹10 million
Securities	₹10 million		

After ₹10 million has been withdrawn from deposits and hence reserves, the bank has a problem: It has a reserve requirement of 10% of ₹90 million, or ₹9 million, but it has no reserves! To eliminate this shortfall, the bank has four basic options. One is to acquire reserves to meet a deposit outflow by borrowing them from other banks in the call money market or by borrowing from corporations.[1] If the First National Bank acquires the ₹9 million shortfall in reserves by borrowing it from other banks or corporations, its balance sheet would then be as follows:

Assets		Liabilities	
Reserves	₹ 9 million	Deposits	₹90 million
Loans	₹90 million	Borrowings from other banks or corporations	₹ 9 million
Securities	₹10 million	Bank capital	₹10 million

The cost of this activity is the interest rate on these borrowings, such as the Call Money Rate.

A second alternative is for the bank to sell some of its securities to help cover the deposit outflow. For example, it might sell ₹9 million of its securities and deposit the proceeds with the RBI, resulting in the following balance sheet:

Assets		Liabilities	
Reserves	₹ 9 million	Deposits	₹90 million
Loans	₹90 million	Bank capital	₹10 million
Securities	₹ 1 million		

The bank incurs some brokerage and other transaction costs when it sells these securities. The government securities that are classified as secondary reserves are very liquid, so the transaction costs of selling them are quite modest. However, the other securities the bank holds are less liquid, and the transaction cost can be appreciably higher.

---

[1]One way the First National Bank can borrow from other banks and corporations is by selling negotiable certificates of deposit. This method for obtaining funds is discussed in the section on liability management.

A third way that the bank can meet a deposit outflow is to acquire reserves by borrowing from the RBI. In our example, the First National Bank could leave its security and loan holdings the same and borrow ₹9 million in discount loans from the RBI at the prevailing repo rate. Its balance sheet would then be as follows:

Assets		Liabilities	
Reserves	₹ 9 million	Deposits	₹90 million
Loans	₹90 million	Borrowings from the RBI	₹ 9 million
Securities	₹10 million	Bank capital	₹10 million

The cost associated with discount loans is the interest rate that must be paid to the RBI (called the **repo rate**).

Finally, a bank can acquire the ₹9 million of reserves to meet the deposit outflow by reducing its loans by this amount and depositing the ₹9 million it then receives with the RBI, thereby increasing its reserves by ₹9 million. This transaction changes the balance sheet as follows:

Assets		Liabilities	
Reserves	₹ 9 million	Deposits	₹90 million
Loans	₹81 million	Bank capital	₹10 million
Securities	₹10 million		

The First National Bank is once again in good shape because its ₹9 million of reserves satisfies the reserve requirement.

However, this process of reducing its loans is the bank's costliest way of acquiring reserves when a deposit outflow occurs. If the First National Bank has numerous short-term loans renewed at fairly short intervals, it can reduce its total amount of loans outstanding fairly quickly by *calling in* loans—that is, by not renewing some loans when they come due. Unfortunately for the bank, this is likely to antagonize the customers whose loans are not being renewed because they have not done anything to deserve such treatment. Indeed, they are likely to take their business elsewhere in the future, a very costly consequence for the bank.

A second method for reducing its loans is for the bank to sell them off to other banks. Again, this is very costly because other banks do not personally know the customers who have taken out the loans and so may not be willing to buy the loans at their full value. (This is just the lemons adverse selection problem described in Chapter 7.)

The foregoing discussion explains why banks hold excess reserves even though loans or securities earn a higher return. When a deposit outflow occurs, holding excess reserves allows the bank to escape the costs of (1) borrowing from other banks or corporations, (2) selling securities, (3) borrowing from the RBI, or (4) calling in or selling off loans. *Excess reserves are insurance against the costs associated with deposit outflows. The higher the costs associated with deposit outflows, the more excess reserves banks will want to hold.*

Just as you and I would be willing to pay an insurance company to insure us against a casualty loss such as the theft of a car, a bank is willing to pay the cost of holding excess reserves (the opportunity cost, that is, the earnings forgone by not holding income-earning assets such as loans or securities) to insure against losses due to deposit outflows. Because excess reserves, like insurance, have a cost, banks also take other steps to protect themselves; for example, they might shift their holdings of assets to more liquid securities (secondary reserves).

Asset Management

Now that you understand why a bank has a need for liquidity, we can examine the basic strategy a bank pursues in managing its assets. To maximize its profits, a bank must simultaneously seek the highest returns possible on loans and securities, reduce risk, and make adequate provisions for liquidity by holding liquid assets. Banks try to accomplish these three goals in four basic ways.

First, banks try to find borrowers who will pay high interest rates and are unlikely to default on their loans. They seek out loan business by advertising their borrowing rates and by approaching corporations directly to solicit loans. It is up to the bank's loan officer to decide if potential borrowers are good credit risks who will make interest and principal payments on time (i.e., engage in screening to reduce the adverse selection problem). Typically, banks are conservative in their loan policies; the default rate is usually less than 1%. It is important, however, that banks not be so conservative that they miss out on attractive lending opportunities that earn high interest rates.

Second, banks try to purchase securities with high returns and low risk. Third, in managing their assets, banks must attempt to lower the risk by diversifying. They accomplish this by purchasing many different types of assets and approving many types of loans to a number of customers. Banks that have not sufficiently sought the benefits of diversification often come to regret it later. For example, in the US, banks that had overspecialized in making loans to energy companies, real estate developers, or farmers suffered huge losses in the 1980s with the slump in energy, property, and farm prices. Indeed, many of these banks went broke because they had "put too many eggs in one basket."

Finally, the bank must manage the liquidity of its assets so that it can satisfy its reserve requirements without bearing huge costs. This means that it will hold liquid securities even if they earn a somewhat lower return than other assets. The bank must decide, for example, how much in excess reserves must be held to avoid costs from a deposit outflow. In addition, it will want to hold government securities as secondary reserves so that even if a deposit outflow forces some costs on the bank, these will not be terribly high. Again, it is not wise for a bank to be too conservative. If it avoids all costs associated with deposit outflows by holding only excess reserves, the bank suffers losses because reserves earn no interest, while the bank's liabilities are costly to maintain. The bank must balance its desire for liquidity against the increased earnings that can be obtained from less liquid assets such as loans.

Liability Management

Before the 1980s, liability management was a staid affair: For the most part, banks took their liabilities as fixed and spent their time trying to achieve an optimal mix of assets. There were two main reasons for the emphasis on asset management. First, more than 70% of the sources of bank funds were obtained through checkable (demand) deposits that by law were regulated by the RBI. Thus, banks could not actively compete with one another for these deposits by paying differential interest rates on them. Second, because the markets for making overnight loans between banks were not well developed, banks rarely borrowed from other banks to meet their reserve needs.

A notable feature in the case of scheduled commercial banks in India over the period 1990–91 to 2013–14 has been the increase in the proportion of liabilities in the form of deposits and borrowings from 71% to 77% and from 8% to 10% respectively, as also a simultaneous decline in the proportion of bank capital.[2]

Because of the increased importance of liability management, most banks now manage both sides of the balance sheet together in an *asset–liability management (ALM) committee*.

Capital Adequacy Management

Banks have to make decisions about the amount of capital they need to hold for three reasons. First, bank capital helps prevent *bank failure*, a situation in which the bank cannot satisfy its obligations to pay its depositors and other creditors and so goes out of business. Second, the amount of capital affects returns for the owners (equity holders) of the bank. Third, a minimum amount of bank capital (bank capital requirements) is required by regulatory authorities.

How Bank Capital Helps Prevent Bank Failure Let's consider two banks with identical balance sheets, except that High Capital Bank has a ratio of capital to assets of 10% while Low Capital Bank has a ratio of 4%.

High Capital Bank				Low Capital Bank			
Assets		Liabilities		Assets		Liabilities	
Reserves	₹10 million	Deposits	₹90 million	Reserves	₹10 million	Deposits	₹96 million
Loans	₹90 million	Bank capital	₹10 million	Loans	₹90 million	Bank capital	₹ 4 million

Suppose that both banks got caught up in the euphoria of the real estate market, only to find that ₹5 million of their real estate loans became worthless later. When these bad loans are written off (valued at zero), the total value of assets declines by ₹5 million. As a consequence, bank capital, which equals total assets minus liabilities, also declines by ₹5 million. The balance sheets of the two banks now look like this:

High Capital Bank				Low Capital Bank			
Assets		Liabilities		Assets		Liabilities	
Reserves	₹10 million	Deposits	₹90 million	Reserves	₹10 million	Deposits	₹96 million
Loans	₹85 million	Bank capital	₹ 5 million	Loans	₹85 million	Bank capital	–₹ 1 million

---

[2]http://dbie.rbi.org.in/DBIE/dbie.rbi?site=statistics, as accessed on 13 March 2017 at 2pm.

High Capital Bank takes the ₹5 million loss in stride because its initial cushion of ₹10 million in capital means that it still has a positive net worth (bank capital) of ₹5 million after the loss. Low Capital Bank, however, is in big trouble. The value of its assets has fallen below its liabilities, and its net worth is now −₹1 million. Because the bank has a negative net worth, it is insolvent: It does not have sufficient assets to pay off all holders of its liabilities. When a bank becomes insolvent, government regulators close the bank, its assets are sold off, and its managers are fired. Because the owners of Low Capital Bank will find their investment wiped out, they would clearly have preferred the bank to have had a large enough cushion of bank capital to absorb the losses, as was the case for High Capital Bank. We therefore see an important rationale for a bank to maintain a sufficient level of capital: *A bank maintains bank capital to lessen the chance that it will become insolvent.*

How the Amount of Bank Capital Affects Returns to Equity Holders   Because owners of a bank must know whether their bank is being managed well, they need good measures of bank profitability. A basic measure of bank profitability is the **return on assets (ROA),** the net profit after taxes per dollar of assets:

$$\text{ROA} = \frac{\text{net profit after taxes}}{\text{assets}}$$

The return on assets provides information on how efficiently a bank is being run because it indicates how much profit is generated on average by each rupee of assets.

However, what the bank's owners (equity holders) care about most is how much the bank is earning on their equity investment. This information is provided by the other basic measure of bank profitability, the **return on equity (ROE),** the net profit after taxes per rupee of equity (bank) capital:

$$\text{ROE} = \frac{\text{net profit after taxes}}{\text{equity capital}}$$

There is a direct relationship between the return on assets (which measures how efficiently the bank is run) and the return on equity (which measures how well the owners are doing on their investment). This relationship is determined by the **equity multiplier (EM),** the amount of assets per rupee of equity capital:

$$\text{EM} = \frac{\text{assets}}{\text{equity capital}}$$

To see this, we note that

$$\frac{\text{net profit after taxes}}{\text{equity capital}} = \frac{\text{net profit after taxes}}{\text{assets}} \times \frac{\text{assets}}{\text{equity capital}}$$

which, using our definitions, yields

$$\text{ROE} = \text{ROA} \times \text{EM} \tag{1}$$

The formula in Equation 1 tells us what happens to the return on equity when a bank holds a smaller amount of capital (equity) for a given amount of assets. As we have seen, High Capital Bank initially has ₹100 million of assets and ₹10 million of equity, which gives it an equity multiplier of 10 (₹100 million/₹10 million). Low Capital Bank, by contrast, has only ₹4 million of equity, so its equity multiplier is higher, equaling 25 (₹100 million/₹4 million). Suppose that these banks have been equally well run so that they both have the same return on assets, 1%. The return on equity for High Capital Bank equals $1\% \times 10 = 10\%$, whereas the return on equity for Low Capital Bank equals $1\% \times 25 = 25\%$. The equity holders in Low Capital Bank are clearly a lot happier than the equity holders in High Capital Bank because they are earning more than twice as high a return. We now see why owners of a bank may not want it to hold too much capital. *Given the return on assets, the lower the bank capital, the higher the return for the owners of the bank.*

Trade-off Between Safety and Returns to Equity Holders   We now see that bank capital has both benefits and costs. Bank capital benefits the owners of a bank in that it makes their investment safer by reducing the likelihood of bankruptcy. But bank capital is costly because the higher it is, the lower will be the return on equity for a given return on assets. In determining the amount of bank capital, managers must decide how much of the increased safety that comes with higher capital (the benefit) they are willing to trade off against the lower return on equity that comes with higher capital (the cost).

In more uncertain times, when the possibility of large losses on loans increases, bank managers might want to hold more capital to protect the equity holders. Conversely, if they have confidence that loan losses won't occur, they might want to reduce the amount of bank capital, have a higher equity multiplier, and thereby increase the return on equity.

Bank Capital Requirements   Banks also hold capital because they are required to do so by regulatory authorities. Because of the high costs of holding capital for the reasons just described, bank managers often want to hold less bank capital relative to assets than is required by the regulatory authorities. In this case, the amount of bank capital is determined by the bank capital requirements. We discuss the details of bank capital requirements and their important role in bank regulation in Chapter 17.

THE PRACTICING MANAGER

Strategies for Managing Bank Capital

Mona, the manager of the First National Bank, has to make decisions about the appropriate amount of bank capital. Looking at the balance sheet of the bank, which like High Capital Bank has a ratio of bank capital to assets of 10% (₹10 million of capital and ₹100 million of assets), Mona is concerned that the large amount of bank capital is causing the return on equity to be too low. She concludes that the bank has a capital surplus and should increase the equity multiplier to increase the return on equity.

To lower the amount of capital relative to assets and raise the equity multiplier, she can do any of three things: (1) She can reduce the amount of bank capital by buying back some of the bank's stock. (2) She can reduce the bank's capital by paying out higher dividends to its stockholders, thereby reducing the bank's retained earnings. (3) She can keep bank capital constant but increase the bank's assets by acquiring new funds—say, by issuing CDs—and then seeking out loan business or purchasing more securities with these new funds. Because the manager thinks that it would enhance her position with the stockholders, she decides to pursue the second alternative and raise the dividend on the First National Bank stock.

Now suppose that the First National Bank is in a situation similar to that of Low Capital Bank and has a ratio of bank capital to assets of 4%. The bank manager now might worry that the bank is short on capital relative to assets because it does not have a sufficient cushion to prevent bank failure. To raise the amount of capital relative to assets, she now has the following three choices: (1) She can raise capital for the bank by having it issue equity (common stock). (2) She can raise capital by reducing the bank's dividends to shareholders, thereby increasing retained earnings that it can put into its capital account. (3) She can keep capital at the same level but reduce the bank's assets by making fewer loans or by selling off securities and then using the proceeds to reduce its liabilities. Suppose that raising bank capital is not easy to do at the current time because capital markets are tight or because shareholders will protest if their dividends are cut. Then Mona might have to choose the third alternative and decide to shrink the size of the bank.

In past years, many banks have experienced capital shortfalls and had to restrict asset growth, as Mona might have to do if the First National Bank were short of capital. The important consequences of this for the credit markets are illustrated in the case that follows.

CASE

How a Capital Crunch Caused a Credit Crunch During the Global Financial Crisis

The dramatic slowdown in the growth of credit in the wake of the financial crisis starting in 2007 triggered a "credit crunch" in which credit was hard to get. As a result, the performance of the economy in 2008 and 2009 was very poor. What caused the credit crunch?

Our analysis of how a bank manages its capital indicates that the 2008–2009 credit crunch was caused, at least in part, by the capital crunch, in which shortfalls of bank capital led to slower credit growth.

As we discussed in Chapter 8, there was a major boom and bust in the housing market that led to huge losses for banks from their holdings of securities backed by residential mortgages. In addition, banks had to take back onto their balance sheets many of the structured investment vehicles (SIVs) they had sponsored. The losses that reduced bank capital, along with the need for more capital to support the assets coming back onto their balance sheets, led to capital shortfalls: Banks had to either raise new capital or restrict asset growth by cutting back on lending. Banks did raise some capital but with the growing weakness of the economy, raising new capital was extremely difficult, so banks also chose to tighten their lending standards and reduce lending. Both of these helped produce a weak economy in 2008 and 2009.

Off-Balance-Sheet Activities

Although asset and liability management has traditionally been the major concern of banks, in the more competitive environment of recent years, banks have been aggressively seeking out profits by engaging in off-balance-sheet activities.[3] **Off-balance-sheet activities** involve trading financial instruments and generating income from fees and loan sales, activities that affect bank profits but do not appear on bank balance sheets. Indeed, off-balance-sheet activities have been growing in importance for banks.

Loan Sales

One type of off-balance-sheet activity that has grown in importance in recent years involves income generated by loan sales. A **loan sale,** also called a *secondary loan participation*, involves a contract that sells all or part of the cash stream from a specific loan and thereby removes the loan from the bank's balance sheet. Banks earn profits by selling loans for an amount slightly greater than that of the original loan. Because the high interest rate on these loans makes them attractive, institutions are willing to buy them, even though the higher price means that they earn a slightly lower interest rate than the original interest rate on the loan, usually on the order of 0.15 percentage point.

Generation of Fee Income

Another type of off-balance-sheet activity involves the generation of income from fees that banks receive for providing specialized services to their customers, such as making foreign exchange trades on a customer's behalf, servicing a mortgage-backed security by collecting interest and principal payments and then paying them out, guaranteeing debt securities such as banker's acceptances (by which the bank promises to make interest and principal payments if the party issuing the security cannot), and providing backup lines of credit. There are several types of backup lines of credit. The most important is the **loan commitment,** under which for a fee the bank agrees to provide a loan at the customer's request, up to a given rupee amount, over a specified period of time. Credit lines are also now available to bank depositors with "overdraft privileges"—these bank customers can write checks in excess of their deposit balances and, in effect, write themselves a loan. Other lines of credit for which banks get fees include standby letters of credit to back up issues of commercial paper and other securities and credit lines (called *note issuance facilities*, NIFs, and *revolving underwriting facilities*, RUFs) for underwriting Euronotes, which are medium-term Eurobonds.

Off-balance-sheet activities involving guarantees of securities and backup credit lines increase the risk a bank faces. Even though a guaranteed security does not appear on a bank balance sheet, it still exposes the bank to default risk: If the issuer of the security defaults, the bank is left holding the bag and must pay off the security's owner. Backup credit lines also expose the bank to risk because the bank may be forced to provide loans when it does not have sufficient liquidity or when the borrower is a very poor credit risk.

---

[3]Other financial intermediaries, such as insurance companies, pension funds, and finance companies, also make private loans, and the credit risk management principles we outline here apply to them as well.

Trading Activities and Risk Management Techniques

As we will see in Chapter 20, banks' attempts to manage interest-rate risk have led them to trading in financial futures, options for debt instruments, and interest-rate swaps. Banks engaged in international banking also conduct transactions in the foreign exchange market. All transactions in these markets are off-balance-sheet activities because they do not have a direct effect on the bank's balance sheet. Although bank trading in these markets is often directed towards reducing risk or facilitating other bank business, banks may also try to outguess the markets and engage in speculation. This speculation can be a very risky business and indeed has led to bank insolvencies, the most dramatic being the failure of Barings, a British bank, in 1995.

Trading activities, although often highly profitable, are dangerous because they make it easy for financial institutions and their employees to make huge bets quickly. A particular problem for management of trading activities is that the principal–agent problem, discussed in Chapter 7, is especially severe. Given the ability to place large bets, a trader (the agent), whether she trades in bond markets, in foreign exchange markets, or in financial derivatives, has an incentive to take on excessive risks: If her trading strategy leads to large profits, she is likely to receive a high salary and bonuses, but if she takes large losses, the financial institution (the principal) will have to cover them. As the Barings Bank failure in 1995 so forcefully demonstrated, a trader subject to the principal–agent problem can take an institution that is quite healthy and drive it into insolvency very rapidly (see the Conflicts of Interest box).

To reduce the principal–agent problem, managers of financial institutions must set up internal controls to prevent debacles like the one at Barings. Such controls include the complete separation of the people in charge of trading activities from those in charge of the bookkeeping for trades. In addition, managers must set limits on the total amount of traders' transactions and on the institution's risk exposure. Managers must also scrutinize risk assessment procedures using the latest computer technology. One such method involves the value-at-risk approach. In this approach, the institution develops a statistical model with which it can calculate the maximum loss that its portfolio is likely to sustain over a given time interval, dubbed the value at risk, or VAR. For example, a bank might estimate that the maximum loss it would be likely to sustain over one day with a probability of 1 in 100 is ₹1 million; the ₹1 million figure is the bank's calculated value at risk. Another approach is called "stress testing." In this approach, a manager asks models what would happen if a doomsday scenario occurs; that is, she looks at the losses the institution would sustain if an unusual combination of bad events occurred. With the value-at-risk approach and stress testing, a financial institution can assess its risk exposure and take steps to reduce it.

The Bank for International Settlements is developing additional bank capital requirements based on value-at-risk calculations for a bank's trading activities.

GO ONLINE

Access **https://rbidocs.rbi.org.in/rdocs/notification/PDFs/32085.pdf** which provides a guidance note on market risk management for financial institutions.

> CONFLICTS OF INTEREST

Barings, Daiwa, Sumitomo, Société Générale, and J.P. Morgan Chase: Rogue Traders and the Principal–Agent Problem

The demise of Barings, a venerable British bank more than a century old, is a sad morality tale of how the principal–agent problem operating through a rogue trader can take a financial institution that has a healthy balance sheet one month and turn it into an insolvent tragedy the next.

In July 1992 Nick Leeson, Barings' new head clerk at its Singapore branch, began to speculate on the Nikkei, the Japanese version of the Dow Jones stock index. By late 1992, Leeson had suffered losses of $3 million, which he hid from his superiors by stashing the losses in a secret account. He even fooled his superiors into thinking he was generating large profits, thanks to a failure of internal controls at his firm, which allowed him to execute trades on the Singapore exchange *and* oversee the bookkeeping of those trades. (As anyone who runs a cash business, such as a bar, knows, there is always a lower likelihood of fraud if more than one person handles the cash. Similarly, for trading operations, you never mix management of the back room with management of the front room; this principle was grossly violated by Barings' management.)

Things didn't get better for Leeson, who by late 1994 had losses exceeding $250 million. In January and February 1995, he bet the bank. On January 17, 1995, the day of the earthquake in Kobe, Japan, he lost $75 million, and by the end of the week had lost more than $150 million. When the stock market declined on February 23, leaving him with a further loss of $250 million, he called it quits and fled Singapore. Three days later, he turned himself in at the Frankfurt airport. By the end of his wild ride, Leeson's losses, $1.3 billion in all, ate up Barings' capital and caused the bank to fail. Leeson was subsequently convicted and sent to jail in Singapore for his activities. He was released in 1999 and apologized for his actions.

Our asymmetric information analysis of the principal–agent problem explains Leeson's behavior and the danger of Barings' management lapse. Letting Leeson control both his own trades and the back room increased asymmetric information because it reduced the principal's (Barings') knowledge about Leeson's trading activities.

This lapse increased the moral hazard incentive for him to take risks at the bank's expense, as he was now less likely to be caught. Furthermore, once he had experienced large losses, he had even greater incentives to take on even higher risk because if his bets worked out, he could reverse his losses and keep in good standing with the company, whereas if his bets soured, he had little to lose because he was out of a job anyway. Indeed, the bigger his losses, the more he had to gain by bigger bets, which explains the escalation of the amount of his trades as his losses mounted. If Barings' managers had understood the principal–agent problem, they would have been more vigilant at finding out what Leeson was up to, and the bank might still be here today.

Unfortunately, Nick Leeson is no longer a rarity in the rogue traders' billionaire club, those who have lost more than $1 billion. Over 11 years, Toshihide Iguchi, an officer in the New York branch of Daiwa Bank, also had control of both the bond trading operation and the back room, and he racked up $1.1 billion in losses over the period. In July 1995 Iguchi disclosed his losses to his superiors, but the management of the bank did not disclose them to its regulators. The result was that Daiwa was slapped with a $340 million fine and the bank was thrown out of the country by U.S. bank regulators.

Yasuo Hamanaka is another member of the billionaire club. In July 1996 he topped Leeson's and Iguchi's record, losing $2.6 billion for his employer, the Sumitomo Corporation, one of Japan's top trading companies. J. Jerome Kerviel's loss for his bank, Société Générale, in January 2008 set the all-time record for a rogue trader: his unauthorized trades cost the bank $7.2 billion. Even the highly successful J.P. Morgan Chase bank experienced in 2012 over a $2 billion trading loss by Bruno Iksill, who was colorfully nicknamed "the London Whale."

The moral of these stories is that management of firms engaged in trading activities must reduce the principal–agent problem by closely monitoring their traders' activities, or the rogues' gallery will continue to grow.

Measuring Bank Performance

To understand how well a bank is doing, we need to start by looking at a bank's income statement, the description of the sources of income and expenses that affect the bank's profitability.

Bank's Income Statement

The end-of-year 2012 income statement for all scheduled commercial banks in India appears in Table 16.2.

Operating Income It is the income that comes from a bank's ongoing operations. Most of a bank's operating income is generated by interest on its assets, particularly loans. As we see in Table 16.2, in 2012–13 interest income represented 88.6% of commercial banks' operating income in India. Interest income fluctuates with the level of interest rates, and so its percentage of operating income is highest when interest rates are at peak levels.

Noninterest income, which made up 11.3% of operating income in 2012–13, is generated partly by service charges on deposit accounts, but the bulk of it comes from the off-balance-sheet activities mentioned earlier, which generates fees or trading profits for the bank. The importance of these off-balance-sheet activities to bank profits has been growing in recent years.

TABLE 16.2   Trends in Income and Expenditure of Scheduled Commercial Banks

Amount in ₹ billion

| Item | 2011–12 | | 2012–13 | |
	Amount	Percentage Variation	Amount	Percentage Variation
1	2	3	4	5
1. Income	7,416	29.8	8,614	16.2
a. Interest income	6,553	33.4	7,636	16.5
b. Other income	863	8.1	978	13.3
2. Expenditure	6,600	31.8	7,702	16.7
a. Interest expended	4,304	44	5,138	19.4
b. Operating expenses	1,376	11.7	1,566	13.8
of which: Wage Bill	780	7.3	873	11.9
c. Provisions and contingencies	920	16.8	998	8.5
3. Operating profit	1,737	16.5	1,910	10
4. Net profit	817	16.1	912	11.6
5. Net interest income (NII) (1a-2a)	2,249	16.9	2,498	11.1
6. Net interest margin (NII as percentage of average assets)	2.9		2.8	

Source: https://www.rbi.org.in/scripts/PublicationsView.aspx?id=15440#t7, as accessed on 13 March 2017 at 2pm.

Operating Expenses They are the expenses incurred in conducting the bank's ongoing operations. An important component of a bank's operating expenses is the interest payments that it must make on its liabilities, particularly on its deposits. Just as interest income varies with the level of interest rates, so do interest expenses. Interest expenses as a percentage of total operating expenses were about 67% in 2012–13 for scheduled commercial banks in India. Noninterest expenses include the costs of running a banking business: Salaries for tellers and officers, rent, maintenance and utilities for bank buildings, purchases of equipment such as desks and vaults, and servicing costs of equipment such as computers. These expenses accounted for about 20% of the overall expenses of scheduled commercial banks in India in 2013–14.

The final item listed under operating expenses is provisions for loan losses. When a bank has a bad debt or anticipates that a loan might become a bad debt, it can write up the loss as a current expense in its income statement under the "provision for loan losses" heading. Provisions for loan losses are directly related to loan loss reserves. When a bank wants to increase its loan loss reserves account by, say, ₹1 million, it does this by adding ₹1 million to its provisions for loan losses. Loan loss reserves rise when this is done because by increasing expenses when losses have not yet occurred, earnings are being set aside to deal with the losses in the future.

Provisions for loan losses have been a major element in fluctuating bank profits in recent years. The 1980s brought the third-world debt crisis; a sharp decline in energy prices in 1986, which caused substantial losses on loans to energy producers; and a collapse in the real estate market. As a result, provisions for loan losses in US commercial banks were particularly high in the late 1980s, reaching a peak of 13% of operating expenses in 1987. After that, losses on loans began to subside, but they rose sharply during the 2007–2009 financial crisis. In 2009 provisions for loan losses reached a new peak of 32.7% of operating expenses.

Income Subtracting the operating expenses from the operating income yields net operating income or net operating profits. Net operating income is closely watched by bank managers, bank shareholders, and bank regulators because it indicates how well the bank is doing on an ongoing basis.

Two items, gains (or losses) on securities sold by banks and net extraordinary items, which are events or transactions that are both unusual and infrequent are added to the net operating income figure to get the net income before taxes. Net income before taxes is more commonly referred to as profits before taxes. Subtracting the income taxes then results in net income. Net income, more commonly referred to as profits after taxes, is the figure that directly tells us how well the bank is doing because it is the amount that the bank can keep as retained earnings or pay out to stockholders as dividends. In 2012–13, the scheduled commercial banks in India had net income (or net profits) of ₹912 billion.

Measures of Bank Performance

Although net income gives us an idea of how well a bank is doing, it suffers from one major drawback: It does not adjust for the bank's size, thus making it hard to compare how well one bank is doing relative to another. A basic measure of bank profitability that corrects for the size of the bank is the return on assets (ROA), mentioned earlier, which divides the net income of the bank by the amount of its assets. ROA is a useful measure of how well a bank manager is doing on the job because it indicates how well a bank's assets are being used to generate profits.

In 2012–13, the Return on assets (RoA), the most commonly used indicator of profitability, showed a reduction by about 5 basis points compared to the previous year. This reduction was discernible in the case of public sector banks in general, and nationalised banks in particular. The ROA of all SCBs put together was 1.03 in 2012–13.

New private sector banks and foreign banks reported an increase in RoA in 2012–13 as against nationalised banks and the State Bank of India (SBI) Group. The growth of profits of new private sector/foreign banks did not show a sharp fall in 2012–13, as was the case with nationalised banks and SBI Group. Although the interest income of new private/foreign banks posted a lower growth during the year, they could manage to maintain their profits growth through a reduction in the growth of their operating expenses, particularly wage bill.

Although ROA provides useful information about bank profitability, we have already seen that it is not what the bank's owners (equity holders) care about most. They are more concerned about how much the bank is earning on their equity investment, an amount that is measured by the return on equity (ROE), the net income per dollar of equity capital. The Return on Equity for all SCBs in India experienced contraction to 13.84% in 2012–13.

Another commonly watched measure of bank performance is called the **net interest margin (NIM),** the difference between interest income and interest expenses as a percentage of total assets:

$$\text{NIM} = \frac{\text{interest income} - \text{interest expenses}}{\text{assets}}$$

As we have seen, one of a bank's primary intermediation functions is to issue liabilities and use the proceeds to purchase income-earning assets. If a bank manager has done a good job of asset and liability management such that the bank earns substantial income on its assets and has low costs on its liabilities, profits will be high. How well a bank manages its assets and liabilities is affected by the spread between the interest earned on the bank's assets and the interest costs on its liabilities. This spread is exactly what the net interest margin measures. If the bank is able to raise funds with liabilities that have low interest costs and is able to acquire assets with high interest income, the net interest margin will be high, and the bank is likely to be highly profitable. If the interest cost of its liabilities rises relative to the interest earned on its assets, the net interest margin will fall, and bank profitability will suffer.

Table 16.3 provides the return on Assets and Return on Equity for the Scheduled Commercial Banks in India for the years 2011–12 and 2012–13 according to the various bank groups, viz. Public sector banks, Private sector Banks and Foreign Banks. While the performance of public sector banks, especially nationalised banks has deteriorated, that of private sector banks, as also foreign banks had improved over the period concerned. In the Indian context, Net Interest Margin for SCBs in India declined marginally from 2.9% in 2011–12 to 2.8% in 2012–13.

Recent Trends in Bank Performance Measures

Both interest earnings and interest expended recorded a lower growth during 2014–15 as compared to the previous year. Interest earnings reflected the impact of slower credit growth. However, decline in interest income was marginally higher

TABLE 16.3   Return on Assets and Return on Equity of SCBs–Bank Group-wise

S. No.	Bank Group/Year	ROA		ROE	
		2011–12	2012–13	2011–12	2012–13
1	Public sector banks	0.88	0.78	15.33	13.24
	1.1 Nationalised banks*	0.88	0.44	15.05	12.34
	1.2 SBI group	0.89	0.88	16	15.29
2	Private sector banks	1.53	1.63	15.25	16.46
	2.1 Old private sector banks	1.2	1.26	15.18	16.22
	2.2 New private sector banks	1.63	1.74	15.27	16.51
3	Foreign banks	1.76	1.94	10.79	11.52
	All SCBs	1.08	1.03	14.6	13.84

Notes:
Return on Assets = Net profit/Average total assets.
Return on Equity = Net profit/Average total equity.
*Nationalised banks include IDBI Bank Ltd.
Source: https://www.rbi.org.In/scripts/PublicationsView.aspx?id=15440, as accessed on 13 March 2017 at 2pm.

than interest expended. As a result, net interest income grew less than the previous year despite an improvement in the operating expenses (through reduction in the growth of wage bill). Also, the pace of increase in provisions and contingencies due to delinquent loans declined sharply. This led to an increase in net profits at the aggregate level by 10.1 per cent during 2014–15 as against a decline in net profits during the previous year (Figure 16.1).

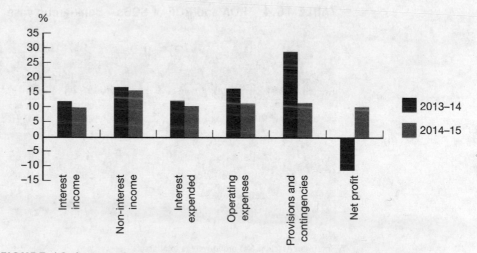

FIGURE 16.1 Growth of Select Items of Income and Expenditure

Source: Annual accounts of banks and staff calculations. RBI, Trends and Progress of Banking in India, 2014–15, https://www.rbi.org.in/scripts/PublicationsView.aspx?id=16718#C8, as accessed on 13 March 2017 at 2pm.

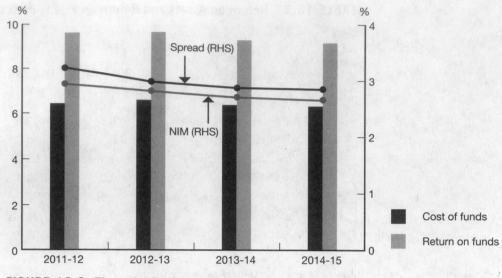

FIGURE 16.2 Financial Performance of SCBs

Source: Annual accounts of banks and staff calculations. RBI, Trends and Progress of Banking in India, 2014–15, https://www.rbi.org.in/scripts/PublicationsView.aspx?id=16718#C8, as accessed on 13 March 2017 at 2pm.

Following the trend in the recent past, both net interest margin (NIM) and spread (difference between return and cost of funds) witnessed marginal decline (Figure 16.2).

During 2014–15, return on assets (RoA) remained at the same level as previous year, however, return on equity (RoE) dipped marginally (Table 16.4). At the bank-group level, the RoA of PSBs declined though that of PVBs and FBs showed an improvement.

TABLE 16.4   ROA and ROE of SCBs—Bank-group wise

(per cent)

Sr. No.	Bank group	Return on Assets		Return on Equity	
		2013–14	2014–15	2013–14	2014–15
1	Public sector banks	0.50	0.46	8.47	7.76
	1.1 Nationalised banks*	0.45	0.37	7.76	6.44
	1.2 State Bank group	0.63	0.66	10.03	10.56
2	Private sector banks	1.65	1.68	16.22	15.74
3	Foreign banks	1.54	1.87	9.03	10.24
4	All SCBs	0.81	0.81	10.68	10.42

Notes:

Return on Assets = Net profit/Average total assets.

Return on Equity = Net profit/Average total equity.

*Nationalised banks include IDBI Bank Ltd.

Source: Annual accounts of banks and RBI staff calculations.

SUMMARY

1. The balance sheet of commercial banks can be thought of as a list of the sources and uses of bank funds. The bank's liabilities are its sources of funds, which include checkable deposits, time deposits, discount loans from the Fed, borrowings from other banks and corporations, and bank capital. The bank's assets are its uses of funds, which include reserves, cash items in process of collection, deposits at other banks, securities, loans, and other assets (mostly physical capital).

2. Banks make profits through the process of asset transformation: They borrow short (accept deposits) and lend long (make loans). When a bank takes in additional deposits, it gains an equal amount of reserves; when it pays out deposits, it loses an equal amount of reserves.

3. Although more liquid assets tend to earn lower returns, banks still desire to hold them. Specifically, banks hold excess reserves because they provide insurance against the costs of a deposit outflow. Banks manage their assets to maximize profits by seeking the highest returns possible on loans and securities while at the same time trying to lower risk and making adequate provisions for liquidity. Although liability management was once a staid

affair, large (money center) banks now actively seek out sources of funds by issuing liabilities such as negotiable CDs or by actively borrowing from other banks and corporations. Banks manage the amount of capital they hold to prevent bank failure and to meet bank capital requirements set by the regulatory authorities. However, they do not want to hold too much capital because by so doing they will lower the returns to equity holders.

4. Off-balance-sheet activities consist of trading financial instruments and generating income from fees and loan sales, all of which affect bank profits but are not visible on bank balance sheets. Because these off-balance-sheet activities expose banks to increased risk, bank management must pay particular attention to risk assessment procedures and internal controls to restrict employees from taking on too much risk.

5. A bank's net operating income equals operating income minus operating expenses. Adding gains (or losses) on securities and net extraordinary items to net operating income and then subtracting taxes yields net income (profits after taxes). Additional measures of bank performance include the return on assets (ROA), the return on equity (ROE), and the net interest margin (NIM).

KEY TERMS

asset management, p. 398
balance sheet, p. 392
capital adequacy
   management, p. 398
credit risk, p. 398
deposit outflows, p. 398
equity multiplier (EM), p. 404
excess reserves, p. 393
interest-rate risk, p. 398

liability management, p. 398
liquidity management, p. 398
loan commitment, p. 407
loan sale, p. 407
net interest margin (NIM), p. 412
off-balance-sheet activities, p. 407
operating expenses, p. 411
operating income, p. 410
repo loans, p. 393

repo rate, p. 401
required reserve ratio, p. 393
required reserves, p. 393
reserve requirements, p. 393
reserves, p. 393
return on assets (ROA), p. 404
return on equity (ROE), p. 404
secondary reserves, p. 402
vault cash, p. 393

QUESTIONS

1. Rank the following bank assets from most to least liquid:
   a. Commercial loans
   b. Securities
   c. Reserves
   d. Physical capital

2. If the president of a bank told you that the bank was so well run that it has never had to call in loans, sell securities, or borrow as a result of a deposit outflow, would you be willing to buy stock in that bank? Why or why not?

3. If the bank you own has no excess reserves and a sound customer comes in asking for a loan, should you automatically turn the customer down, explaining that you don't have any excess reserves to loan out? Why or why not? What options are available for you to provide the funds your customer needs?

4. Why has the development of overnight loan markets made it more likely that banks will hold fewer excess reserves?

5. If you are a banker and expect interest rates to rise in the future, would you want to make short-term or long-term loans?

6. "Bank managers should always seek the highest return possible on their assets." Is this statement true, false, or uncertain? Explain your answer.

7. "Banking has become a more dynamic industry because of more active liability management." Is this statement true, false, or uncertain? Explain your answer.

8. Why has noninterest income been growing as a source of bank operating income?

9. Why do equity holders care more about ROE than about ROA?

10. What does the net interest margin measure, and why is it important to bank managers?

11. If a bank doubles the amount of its capital and ROA stays constant, what will happen to ROE?

12. If a bank finds that its ROE is too low because it has too much bank capital, what can it do to raise its ROE?

13. What are the benefits and costs for a bank when it decides to increase the amount of its bank capital?

14. If a bank is falling short of meeting its capital requirements by ₹1 million, what three things can it do to rectify the situation?

QUANTITATIVE PROBLEMS

1. The balance sheet of TriBank starts with an allowance for loan losses of ₹1.33 million. During the year, TriBank charges off worthless loans of ₹0.84 million, recovers ₹0.22 million on loans previously charged off, and charges current income for a ₹1.48 million provision for loan losses. Calculate the end-of-year allowance for loan losses.

2. X-Bank reported an ROE of 15% and an ROA of 1%. How well capitalized is this bank?

3. Wiggley S&L issues a standard 30-year fixed-rate mortgage at 7.8% for ₹150,000. Thirty-six months later, mortgage rates jump to 13%. If the S&L sells the mortgage, how much of a loss is incurred?

4. For the upcoming week, Nobel National Bank plans to issue ₹25 million in mortgages and purchase ₹100 million in 31-day T-bills. New deposits of ₹35 million are expected, and other sources will generate ₹15 million in cash. What is Nobel's estimate of funds needed?

5. A bank estimates that demand deposits are, on average, ₹100 million with a standard deviation of ₹5 million. The bank wants to maintain a minimum of 8% of deposits in reserves at all times. What is the highest expected level of deposits during the month? What reserves do they need to maintain? Use a 99% confidence level.

The remaining questions relate to the first month's operations of NewBank.

6. NewBank started its first day of operations with ₹6 million in capital. ₹100 million in checkable deposits is received. The bank issues a ₹25 million commercial loan and another ₹25 million in mortgages, with the following terms:
   - Mortgages: 100 standard 30-year fixed-rate mortgages with a nominal annual rate of 5.25% each for ₹250,000
   - Commercial loan: 3-year loan, simple interest paid monthly at 0.75% per month

   If required reserves are 8%, what do the bank balance sheets look like? Ignore any loan loss reserves.

7. NewBank decides to invest ₹45 million in 30-day T-bills. The T-bills are currently trading at ₹4,986.70 (including commissions) for a ₹5,000 face value instrument. How many do they purchase? What does the balance sheet look like?

8. On the third day of operations, deposits fall by ₹5 million. What does the balance sheet look like? Are there any problems?

9. To meet any shortfall in the previous question, NewBank will borrow the cash in the market for repo loans. Management decides to borrow the needed funds for the remainder of the month (now 29 days). The required yield on a discount basis is 2.9%. What does the balance sheet look like after this transaction?

10. The end of the month finally arrives for NewBank, and it receives all the required payments from its mortgages, commercial loans, and T-bills. How much cash was received? How are these transactions recorded?

11. NewBank also pays off its repo funds borrowed. How much cash is owed? How is this recorded?

12. What does the month-end balance sheet for NewBank look like? Calculate this before any income tax consideration.

13. Calculate NewBank's ROA and NIM for its first month. Assume that net interest equals earnings before taxes, and that NewBank is in the 34% tax bracket.

14. Calculate NewBank's ROE and final balance sheet, including its tax liabilities.

15. If NewBank were required to establish a loan loss reserve at 0.25% of the loan value for commercial loans, how would this be recorded? Recalculate NewBank's ROE and final balance sheet, including its tax liabilities.

16. If NewBank's target ROE is 4.5%, how much net fee income must it generate to meet this target?

17. After making payments for three years, one of the mortgage borrowers defaults on the mortgage. NewBank immediately takes possession of the house and sells it at auction for ₹175,000. Legal fees amount to ₹25,000. If no loan loss reserve was established for the mortgage loans, how is this event recorded?

WEB EXERCISES

Banking and the Management of Financial Institutions

1. Table 16.1 reports the balance sheet of all commercial banks based on aggregate data found in the RBI database. Compare this table to the balance sheet reported by ICICI in its latest annual report, which can be found at **http://www.icicibank.com/managed-assets/docs/investor/annual-reports/2015/ICICI-Bank-Annual-report-FY2015.pdf**. Does ICICI have more or less of its portfolio in loans than the average bank? Which type of loan is most common?

2. Go to statistical tables relating to Banks in India. https://www.rbi.org.in/Scripts/AnnualPublications.aspx?head=Statistical+Tables+Relating+to+Banks+in+India.

This gives you data pertaining to SCBs in India.

Go to Table 3 at http://dbie.rbi.org.in/OpenDocument/opendoc/openDocument.jsp to look at the earnings and expenses of different banks in India for the latest year 2015.

a. What is happening to banks' earnings and expenses across different groups—SBI and its associates, nationalised banks, private sector banks and foreign banks.

b. How does such performance compare to the average of all SCBs in India?

c. How many institutions are currently being reported?

17

Financial Regulation

> PREVIEW

As we have seen the in previous chapters, the financial system is amongst the most heavily regulated sectors of the economy, and banks are amongst the most heavily regulated of financial institutions. In this chapter, we develop a framework to see why regulation of the financial system takes the form it does.

Unfortunately, the regulatory process may not always work very well, as was evident by the recent global and other financial crisis, not only in the United States but in many countries throughout the world. Here we also use our analysis of financial regulation to explain the worldwide crisis in banking and to consider how the regulatory system can be reformed to prevent future disasters.

Asymmetric Information and Financial Regulation

GO ONLINE

Access **https://rbidocs.rbi.org. in/rdocs/Publications/PDFs/ BANKI15122014.pdf**
to view the law pertaining to the regulation of banking in India—the Banking Regulation Act, 1949.

In earlier chapters, we have seen how asymmetric information—the fact that different parties in a financial contract do not have the same information—leads to adverse selection and moral hazard problems that have an important impact on our financial system. The concepts of asymmetric information, adverse selection, and moral hazard are especially useful in understanding why government has chosen the form of financial regulation we see in India and in other countries. There are ten basic categories of financial regulation: The government safety net, restrictions on asset holdings, capital requirements, prompt corrective action, chartering and examination, assessment of risk management, disclosure requirements, consumer protection, restrictions on competition, and macroprudential supervision.

Government Safety Net

As we saw in Chapter 7, financial intermediaries, like banks, are particularly well suited to solving adverse selection and moral hazard problems because they make private loans that help avoid the free-rider problem. However, this solution to the free-rider problem creates another asymmetric information problem because depositors lack information about the quality of these private loans. This asymmetric information problem leads to several reasons why the financial system might not function well.

Bank Panics and the Need for Deposit Insurance   Before the Deposit Insurance Corporation (DIC) (the precursor to the Deposit Insurance and Credit Guarantee Corporation which came into existence in 1978), started its operations in 1962, a **bank failure** (in which a bank is unable to meet its obligations to pay its depositors and other creditors and so must go out of business) meant that depositors would have to wait to get their deposit funds until the bank was liquidated (until its assets had been turned into cash); at that time, they would be paid only a fraction of the value of their deposits. Unable to learn if bank managers were taking on too much risk or were outright crooks, depositors would be reluctant to put money in the bank, thus making banking institutions less viable. Second, depositors' lack of information about the quality of bank assets can lead to bank panics, which, as we saw in Chapter 8, can have serious harmful consequences for the economy.

To understand the concept, consider the following situation. Deposit insurance does not exist, and an adverse shock hits the economy. As a result of the shock, 5% of banks have such large losses on loans that they become insolvent (have a negative net worth and so are bankrupt). Because of asymmetric information, depositors are unable to tell whether their bank is a good bank or one of the 5% that are insolvent. Depositors at bad *and* good banks recognize that they may not get back 100 paise on the rupee for their deposits and will want to withdraw them. Indeed, because banks operate on a "sequential service constraint" (a first-come, first-served basis), depositors have a very strong incentive to show up at the bank first because if they are last in line, the bank may run out of funds and they will get nothing. Uncertainty about the health of the banking system in general can lead to runs on banks both good and bad, and the failure of one bank can hasten the failure of others (referred to as the *contagion effect*). If nothing is done to restore the public's confidence, a bank panic can ensue.

Indeed, bank panics were a fact even in developed countries like the US in the nineteenth and early twentieth centuries, with major ones occurring every 20 years or so in 1819, 1837, 1857, 1873, 1884, 1893, 1907, and 1930–1933. Bank failures were a serious problem even during the boom years of the 1920s, when the number of bank failures averaged around 600 per year.

In India, the concept of insuring deposits kept with banks received attention for the first time in 1948 after the banking crisis in Bengal. The question came up for reconsideration in the year 1949, but it was decided to hold it in abeyance till the Reserve Bank of India ensured adequate arrangements for inspection of banks. Subsequently, in 1950, the Rural Banking Enquiry Committee also supported the concept. Serious thought to the concept was, however, given by the Reserve Bank of India and the Central Government after the crash of the Palai Central Bank Ltd, and the Laxmi Bank Ltd in 1960. The Deposit Insurance Corporation (DIC) Bill was introduced in the Parliament on August 21, 1961. After it was passed by the Parliament, the Bill got the assent of the President on December 7, 1961 and the Deposit Insurance Act, 1961 came into force on January 1, 1962.

A government safety net for depositors can short-circuit runs on banks and bank panics, and by providing protection for the depositor, it can overcome reluctance to put funds in the banking system. One form of the safety net is deposit insurance, a guarantee such as that provided by the DICGC in India in which depositors are paid off in full on the first ₹ 1 lakh they have deposited in a bank if the bank fails. With fully insured deposits, depositors don't need to run to the bank to make withdrawals—even if they are worried about the bank's health—because their deposits will be worth 100 paise on the rupee no matter what.

The DICGC insures deposits made with all commercial banks including branches of foreign banks functioning in India, local area banks and regional rural banks. The DICGC also covers all state, central and primary Cooperative Banks, except those from the State of Meghalaya and the Union Territories of Chandigarh, Lakshadweep and Dadra and Nagar Haveli . It does not cover the primary cooperative societies.

The DICGC insures all deposits such as savings, fixed, current, recurring, etc. except the following types of deposits:

- Deposits of foreign governments
- Deposits of central/state governments
- Inter-bank deposits
- Deposits of the State Land Development Banks with the State co-operative bank
- Any amount due on account of and deposit received outside India
- Any amount, which has been specifically exempted by the corporation with the previous approval of Reserve Bank of India.

Each depositor in a bank is insured upto a maximum of ₹ 1,00,000 for both principal and interest amount held by them in the same right and same capacity as on the date of liquidation/cancellation of bank's licence or the date on which the scheme of amalgamation/merger/reconstruction comes into force.

With effect from April 26, 2007, there are revised norms pertaining to deposits held in joint accounts. Thus, if more than one deposit accounts (Savings, Current, Recurring or Fixed deposit) are jointly held by individuals in one or more branch of a bank, say three individuals A, B & C hold more than one joint deposit accounts in which their names appear in the same order, then all these accounts are considered

GO ONLINE

Access **https://rbidocs.rbi.org.in/rdocs/Publications/PDFs/86727.pdf** for information on the evolution of banking in India and the history of bank failures beginning 1913.

as held in the same capacity and in the same right. Accordingly, balances held in all these accounts will be aggregated for the purpose of determining the insured amount within the limit of ₹1,00,000.

However, if individuals open more than one joint accounts in which their names are not in the same order for example, A, B and C; C, B and A; C, A and B; A, C and B; or group of persons are different say A, B and C and A, B and D etc. then, the deposits held in these joint accounts are considered as held in the different capacity and different right. Accordingly, insurance cover will be available separately upto rupees one lakh to every such joint account where the names appearing in different order or names are different.

The deposit insurance premium is borne entirely by the insured bank. The scheme itself is compulsory for all banks and no bank can withdraw from it.

The DICGC enters into the picture to pay depositors in two cases:

One, if a bank goes into liquidation, the DICGC is liable to pay to each depositor through the liquidator, the amount of his deposit upto rupees one lakh within two months from the date of receipt of claim list from the liquidator. In this case, the liquidator prepares depositor wise claim list and sends it to the DICGC for scrutiny and payment. The DICGC pays the money to the liquidator who is liable to pay to the depositors.

Secondly, in case a bank is reconstructed or amalgamated/merged with another bank, the DICGC pays the bank concerned, the difference between the full amount of deposit or the limit of insurance cover in force at the time, whichever is less and the amount received by him under the reconstruction / amalgamation scheme within two months from the date of receipt of claim list from the transferee bank/Chief Executive Officer of the insured bank/transferee bank as the case may be. In the case of amalgamation/merger of banks, the amount due to each depositor is paid to the transferee bank.[1]

In recent years, government deposit insurance has been growing in popularity and has spread to many countries throughout the world. Whether this trend is desirable is discussed in the Global box, "The Spread of Government Deposit Insurance Throughout the World: Is This a Good Thing?"

Other Forms of the Government Safety Net   Deposit insurance is not the only form of government safety net. In other countries, governments have often stood ready to provide support to domestic banks facing runs even in the absence of explicit deposit insurance. Furthermore, banks are not the only financial intermediaries that can pose a systemic threat to the financial system, as our discussion of financial crisis in Chapter 8 has illustrated. When financial institutions are very large or highly interconnected with other financial institutions or markets, their failure has the potential to bring down the entire financial system. Indeed, as we saw in Chapter 8, this is exactly what happened with Bear Stearns and Lehman Brothers, two investment banks, and AIG, an insurance company, during the recent financial crisis in 2008.

One way though which the governments provide support is through lending from the central bank to troubled institutions, as the Federal Reserve–the Central Bank of the US did during the global financial crisis. This form of support is often referred to as the "lender of last resort" role of the central bank. In other cases,

---

[1] *Source:* http://www.dicgc.org.in/English/FD_A-GuideToDepositInsurance.html, as accessed on 17 March 2017 at 4pm.

funds are provided directly to troubled institutions, as was done by the U.S. Treasury and by other governments in 2008 during a particularly virulent phase of the 2007–2009 financial crisis. Governments can also take over (nationalize) troubled institutions and guarantee that all creditors will be repaid their loans in full.

Moral Hazard and the Government Safety Net Although a government safety net can help protect depositors and other creditors and prevent, or ameliorate, financial crisis, it is a mixed blessing. The most serious drawback of the government safety net stems from moral hazard, the incentives of one party to a transaction to engage in activities detrimental to the other party. Moral hazard is an important concern in insurance arrangements in general because the existence of insurance provides increased incentives for taking risks that might result in an insurance payoff. For example, some drivers with automobile collision insurance that has a low deductible might be more likely to drive recklessly because if they get into an accident, the insurance company pays most of the costs for damage and repairs.

Moral hazard is a prominent concern in government arrangements to provide a safety net. With a safety net, depositors and creditors know they will not suffer losses if a financial institution fails, so they do not impose the discipline of the marketplace on these institutions by withdrawing funds when they suspect that the financial institution is taking on too much risk. Consequently, financial institutions with a government safety net have an incentive to take on greater risks than they otherwise would, with taxpayers paying the bill if the bank subsequently goes belly up. Financial institutions have been given the following bet: "Heads I win, tails the taxpayer loses."

GLOBAL

The Spread of Government Deposit Insurance Throughout the World: Is This a Good Thing?

For the first 30 years after federal deposit insurance was established in the United States, only six countries emulated the United States and adopted deposit insurance. However, this began to change in the late 1960s, with the trend accelerating in the 1990s, when the number of countries adopting deposit insurance topped 70. Government deposit insurance has taken off throughout the world because of growing concern about the health of banking systems, particularly after the increasing number of banking crisis in recent years (documented at the end of this chapter). Has this spread of deposit insurance been a good thing? Has it helped improve the performance of the financial system and prevent banking crisis?

The answer seems to be *no* under many circumstances. Research at the World Bank has found that, on average, the adoption of explicit government deposit insurance is associated with less banking

sector stability and a higher incidence of banking crisis.* Furthermore, on average, it seems to retard financial development. However, the negative effects of deposit insurance appear only in countries with weak institutional environments: an absence of rule of law, ineffective regulation and supervision of the financial sector, and high corruption. This situation is exactly what might be expected because, as we will see later in this chapter, a strong institutional environment is needed to limit the moral hazard incentives for banks to engage in the excessively risky behavior encouraged by deposit insurance. The problem is that developing a strong institutional environment may be very difficult to achieve in many emerging market countries. We are left with the following conclusion: Adoption of deposit insurance may be exactly the wrong medicine for promoting stability and efficiency of banking systems in emerging market countries.

*See World Bank, *Finance for Growth: Policy Choices in a Volatile World* (Oxford: World Bank and Oxford University Press, 2001).

Adverse Selection and the Government Safety Net   A further problem with a government safety net like deposit insurance arises because of adverse selection, the fact that the people who are most likely to produce the adverse outcome insured against (bank failure) are those who most want to take advantage of the insurance. For example, bad drivers are more likely to take out automobile collision insurance with a low deductible than the good drivers. Because depositors and creditors protected by a government safety net have little reason to impose discipline on financial institutions, risk-loving entrepreneurs might find the financial industry a particularly attractive one to enter—they know that they will be able to engage in highly risky activities. Even worse, because protected depositors and creditors have so little reason to monitor the financial institution's activities, without government intervention, outright crooks might also find finance for an attractive industry for their activities because it is easy for them to get away with fraud and embezzlement.

Too Big to Fail   The moral hazard created by a government safety net and the desire to prevent financial institution failures have presented financial regulators with a particular quandary, the **too-big-to-fail problem,** in which regulators are reluctant to close down large financial institutions and impose losses on to its depositors and creditors because doing so might precipitate a financial crisis. The too-big-to-fail problem arose when Continental Illinois, one of the 10 largest banks in the United States, became insolvent in May 1984. Not only did the Federal Deposit Insurance Corporation (FDIC) of the US guarantee depositors up to the $100,000 limit (the maximum at the time), but it also guaranteed accounts exceeding $100,000 and even prevented losses for Continental Illinois bondholders. Shortly thereafter, the Comptroller of the Currency (the regulator of national banks) testified to Congress that 11 of the largest banks would receive a similar treatment to that of Continental Illinois. Although the comptroller did not use the term "too big to fail" (it was actually used by Congressman Stewart McKinney in those hearings), this term is now applied to a policy in which the government provides guarantees of repayment of large uninsured creditors of the largest banks, so that no depositor or creditor suffers a loss, even when they are not automatically entitled to this guarantee. The too-big-to-fail policy was extended to big banks that were not even among the 11 largest. (Note that "too big to fail" is a somewhat misleading term because when a financial institution is closed or merged into another financial institution, the managers are usually fired and the stockholders in the financial institution lose their investment.)

One problem with the too-big-to-fail policy is that it increases the moral hazard incentives for big banks. If the FDIC were willing to close a bank using the payoff method, paying depositors only up to the current $250,000 insurance limit, large depositors with more than $250,000 would suffer losses if the bank failed. Thus they would have an incentive to monitor the bank by examining the bank's activities closely and pulling their money out, if the bank was taking on too much risk. To prevent such a loss of deposits, the bank would be more likely to engage in less risky activities. However, once large depositors know that a bank is too big to fail, they have no incentive to monitor the bank and pull out their deposits when it takes on too much risk: No matter what the bank does, large depositors will not suffer losses. The result of the too-big-to-fail policy is that big financial institutions might take on even greater risks, thereby making bank failures more likely. Similarly, the too-big-to-fail policy increases the moral hazard incentives for nonbank financial institutions that are extended a government safety net. Knowing that the financial institution will get bailed out, creditors have little incentive to monitor the institution and pull their money out when the institution is taking on excessive risk. As a result, large or interconnected financial institutions will be more likely to engage in highly risky activities, making it more likely that a financial crisis will occur.

Indeed, financial institutions that were considered to be too big to fail—including Bear Stearns, Lehman Brothers, and AIG—did take on excessive risk in the run up to the global financial crisis and their subsequent collapse helped trigger the worst financial crisis since the Great Depression.

Restrictions on Asset Holdings

As we have seen, the moral hazard associated with a government safety net encourages too much risk taking on the part of financial institutions. Bank regulations that restrict asset holdings are directed at minimizing this moral hazard, which can cost the taxpayers dearly.

Even in the absence of a government safety net, financial institutions still have the incentive to take on too much risk. Risky assets may provide the financial institution with higher earnings when they pay off, but if they do not pay off and the institution fails, depositors and creditors are left holding the bag. If depositors and creditors were able to monitor the bank easily by acquiring information on its risk-taking activities, they would immediately withdraw their funds if the institution was taking on too much risk. To prevent such a loss of funds, the institution would be more likely to reduce its risk-taking activities. Unfortunately, acquiring information on an institution's activities to learn how much risk it is taking can be a difficult task. Hence most depositors and many creditors are incapable of imposing discipline that might prevent financial institutions from engaging in risky activities. A strong rationale for government regulation to reduce risk taking on the part of financial institutions therefore existed even before the establishment of government safety nets like deposit insurance.

Because banks are most prone to panics, they are subjected to strict regulations to restrict their holding of risky assets such as common stocks. Bank regulations also promote diversification, which reduces risk by limiting the rupee amount of loans in particular categories or to individual borrowers.

Capital Requirements

Government-imposed capital requirements are another way of minimizing moral hazard at financial institutions. When a financial institution is forced to hold a large amount of equity capital, the institution has more to lose if it fails and is thus more likely to pursue less risky activities. In addition, as was illustrated in Chapter 16, capital functions as a cushion when bad shocks occur, making it less likely that the financial institution will fail, thereby directly adding to the safety and soundness of financial institutions.

Capital requirements for banks and investment banks take two forms. The first type is based on the **leverage ratio,** the amount of capital divided by the bank's total assets.

In the wake of the Continental Illinois and savings and loans bailouts, regulators in the United States and the rest of the world became increasingly worried about banks' holdings of risky assets and about the increase in banks' **off-balance-sheet activities,** activities that involve trading financial instruments and generating income from fees, which do not appear on bank balance sheets but nevertheless expose

GO ONLINE

Access **https://rbidocs.rbi.org.in/rdocs/notification/PDFs/64MLC010714FL.PDF** to view RBI's restrictions on loans and advances by scheduled commercial banks in India. These restrictions regulate banks' holdings of risky assets.

banks to risk. An agreement among banking officials from industrialized nations set up the **Basel Committee on Banking Supervision** (because it meets under the auspices of the Bank for International Settlements in Basel, Switzerland), which has implemented the **Basel Accord,** which deals with a second type of capital requirements, risk-based capital requirements. The initial Basel Accord, requires that banks hold as capital at least 8% of their risk-weighted assets. The accord was adopted by more than 100 countries, including India. Assets and off-balance-sheet activities were allocated into various categories, each with a different weight to reflect the degree of credit risk.

In the Indian context, the RBI vide its Master Circular dated July 1, 2008[2] provided prudential guidelines on Capital Adequacy and Market Discipline. The capital charge for credit risks was specified for various categories of assets and off-balance sheet activities. These included claims on domestic sovereigns; on foreign sovereigns; on public sector entities; claims on the Bank for International Settlements (BIS), the International Monetary Fund (IMF) and Multilateral Development Banks (MDBs); claims on Banks; on Primary Dealers; on corporates; claims included in the regulatory retail portfolios; claims secured by residential property; claims secured by commercial real estate; non-performing assets; other assets; off-balance sheet items and securitisation exposures. Similarly the guidelines also specified the capital charges for market risks and operational risks.

Over time, limitations of the Basel Accord became apparent because the regulatory measure of bank risk as stipulated by the risk weights differed substantially from the actual risk the bank faced. This resulted in **regulatory arbitrage,** a practice in which banks keep on their books assets that have the same risk-based capital requirement but are relatively risky, such as a loan to a company with a very low credit rating, while taking off their books low-risk assets, such as a loan to a company with a very high credit rating. The Basel Accord thus led to an increase in risk taking, the opposite of its intent. To address these limitations, the Basel Committee on Bank Supervision came up with a new capital accord, referred to as Basel 2, but in the aftermath of the global financial crisis, it developed an even newer accord, which the media has dubbed "Basel 3." These accords are described in the Global box, "Where Is the Basel Accord Heading After the Global Financial Crisis?" The Indian Basel III framework for bank risk-based capital requirements came into force in April 2013. It applied to all scheduled commercial banking institutions, including the public sector banks. The framework was updated periodically to include amendments and the last version was published in July 2014.

The RBI had applied a minimum Capital to Risk-weighted Assets ratio (CRAR) requirement of 9% on banks in India, which was higher than the 8% minimum ratio required under the Basel Framework.

Prompt Corrective Action

If the amount of a financial institution's capital falls to low levels, two serious problems result. First, the bank is more likely to fail because it has a smaller capital cushion if it suffers loan losses or other asset write-downs. Second, with less capital, a financial institution has less "skin in the game" and is therefore more likely to take on excessive risks. In other words, the moral hazard problem becomes more severe,

GO ONLINE
Access **https://rbidocs. rbi.org.in/rdocs/content/ pdfs/85BL010715FC.pdf** to view the prudential guidelines on capital adequacy and market discipline under the New Capital Adequacy Framework. Section 5 outlines the capital charge for credit risk.

GO ONLINE
Access **http://www.bis.org/ bcbs/publ/d320.pdf** to view the Regulatory Consistency Assessment Programme (RCAP) assessment of Basel III risk-based capital regulations in India.

---

[2]*Source:* https://rbi.org.in/scripts/BS_ViewMasCirculardetails.aspx?id=4353#5.13, as accessed on 17 March 2017 at 4pm.

making it more likely that the institution will fail and the taxpayer will be left holding the bag. To prevent this, in countries like the US, Acts such as the Federal Deposit Insurance Corporation Improvement Act of 1991 provided for prompt corrective actions by the FDIC when a bank got into trouble.

Thus, banks in the United States are now classified into five groups based on bank capital. Group 1, classified as "well capitalized," comprises banks that significantly exceed minimum capital requirements and are allowed privileges such as the ability to do some securities underwriting. Banks in group 2, classified as "adequately capitalized," meet minimum capital requirements and are not subject to corrective actions but are not allowed the privileges of the well-capitalized banks. Banks in group 3, "undercapitalized," fail to meet capital requirements. Banks in groups 4 and 5 are "significantly undercapitalized" and "critically undercapitalized," respectively, and are not allowed to pay interest on their deposits at rates that are higher than average. In addition, for group 3 banks, the FDIC is required to take prompt corrective actions such as requiring them to submit a capital restoration plan, restrict their asset growth, and seek regulatory approval to open new branches or develop new lines of business. Banks that are so undercapitalized as to have equity capital that amounts to less than 2% of assets fall into group 5, and the FDIC must take steps to close them down.

The Reserve Bank of India PCA Framework for Commercial Banks

The Reserve Bank of India has specified certain regulatory trigger points, as a part of prompt corrective action (PCA) Framework, in terms of three parameters, i.e. capital to risk weighted assets ratio (CRAR), net non-performing assets (NPA) and Return on Assets (RoA), for initiation of certain structured and discretionary actions in respect of banks hitting such trigger points. The PCA framework is applicable only to commercial banks and not extended to co-operative banks, non-banking financial companies (NBFCs) and Microfinance Institutions (MFIs).

The trigger points along with structured and discretionary actions that could be taken by the Reserve Bank are described below.

1. CRAR

(i) If the CRAR is less than 9%, but equal or more than 6% then banks have to submit capital restoration plan; restrictions on Risk Weighted Assets (RWA) expansion, entering into new lines of business, accessing/renewing costly deposits and CDs, and making dividend payments; order recapitalisation; restrictions on borrowing from inter-bank market, reduction of stake in subsidiaries, reducing its exposure to sensitive sectors like capital market, real estate or investment in non-SLR securities, etc.

(ii) If the CRAR is less than 6%, but equal or more than 3% then in addition to actions in hitting the first trigger point, RBI could take steps to bring in new management/ board, appoint consultants for business/organizational restructuring, take steps to change ownership, and also take steps to merge the bank if it fails to submit recapitalization plan.

(iii) If the CRAR is less than 3% then in addition to actions in hitting the first and second trigger points, more close monitoring will be done; steps to merge/ amalgamate/liquidate the bank or impose moratorium on the bank if its CRAR does not improve beyond 3% within one year or within such extended period as agreed to.

2. Net NPAs

(i) If the Net NPAs are over 10% but less than 15%, a special drive to reduce NPAs and contain generation of fresh NPAs will be introduced; review loan policy and take steps to strengthen credit appraisal skills, follow-up of advances and suit-filed/decreed debts, put in place proper credit-risk management policies; reduce loan concentration; restrictions in entering new lines of business, making dividend payments and increasing its stake in subsidiaries.

(ii) If the Net NPAs are 15% and above, then in addition to actions on hitting the above trigger point, bank's Board is called for discussion on corrective plan of action.

3. Suppose the ROA is less than 0.25% then there will be restrictions on accessing/ renewing costly deposits and CDs, entering into new lines of business, bank's borrowings from inter-bank market, making dividend payments and expanding its staff; steps to increase fee-based income; contain administrative expenses; special drive to reduce NPAs and contain generation of fresh NPAs; and restrictions on incurring any capital expenditure other than for technological upgradation and for some emergency situations.[3]

Financial Supervision

Overseeing the person who operates financial institutions and how they are operated, is referred to as **financial supervision** or **prudential supervision,** which is an important method for reducing adverse selection and moral hazard in the financial industry.

The legal and institutional framework for bank supervision in India is provided under the Banking Regulation Act, 1949. Until 1994, the different departments in Reserve Bank of India were exercising supervision over banks, non-banking financial companies and financial institutions. To keep a close watch on financial markets and avoid recurrence of crisis in the financial system, the Board for Financial Supervision was set up under the aegis of the Reserve Bank under Reserve Bank of India (Board for Financial Supervision) Regulations, 1994 with the objective of paying undivided attention to the supervision of the institutions in the financial sector.

In India, the Department of Banking Supervision of the RBI exercises the supervisory role relating to commercial banks in the following forms:

a. Preparing of independent inspection programmes for different institutions.

b. Undertaking scheduled and special on-site inspections, off-site surveillance, ensuring follow-up and compliance.

c. Determining the criteria for the appointment of statutory auditors and special auditors and assessing audit performance and disclosure standards.

d. Dealing with financial sector frauds.

e. Exercising supervisory intervention in the implementation of regulations which includes—recommendation for removal of managerial and other persons, suspension of business, amalgamation, merger/winding up, issuance of directives and imposition of penalties.

In addition, the Department of Non-Banking Supervision (DNBS) has the role of focused regulatory and supervisory attention towards the Non-bank Financial Corporations (NBFCs) segment.

---

[3] *Source:* https://www.rbi.org.in/scripts/PublicationReportDetails.aspx?UrlPage=&ID=780, as accessed on 17 March 2017 at 4pm.

>GLOBAL

Where Is the Basel Accord Heading After the Global Financial Crisis?

Starting in June 1999, the Basel Committee on Banking Supervision released several proposals to reform the original 1988 Basel Accord. These efforts culminated in what bank supervisors refer to as Basel 2, which is based on three pillars.

1. Pillar 1 links capital requirements for large, internationally active banks more closely to actual risk of three types: market risk, credit risk, and operational risk. It does so by specifying many more categories of assets with different risk weights in its standardized approach. Alternatively, it allows sophisticated (typically the largest) banks to pursue an internal ratings-based approach that permits banks to use their own models of credit risk.

2. Pillar 2 focuses on strengthening the supervisory process, particularly in assessing the quality of risk management in banking institutions and evaluating whether these institutions have adequate procedures to determine how much capital they need.

3. Pillar 3 focuses on improving market discipline through increased disclosure of details about a bank's credit exposures, its amount of reserves and capital, the officials who control the bank, and the effectiveness of its internal rating system.

Although Basel 2 made strides toward limiting excessive risk taking by internationally active banking institutions, it greatly increased the complexity of the accord. The document describing the original Basel Accord was 26 pages, whereas the final draft of Basel 2 exceeded 500 pages. The original timetable called for the completion of the final round of consultation by the end of 2001, with the new rules taking effect by 2004. However, criticism from banks, trade associations, and national regulators led to several postponements. The final draft was not published until June 2004, and Basel 2 began to be implemented at the start of 2008 by European banks, but full implementation in the United States did not occur until 2009. Only a dozen or so of the largest U.S. banks are subject to Basel 2: All others are allowed to use a simplified version of the standards it imposes.

The global financial crisis, however, revealed many limitations of the new accord. First, Basel 2 did not require banks to have sufficient capital to survive the financial disruption during this period. Second, risk weights in the standardized approach are heavily reliant on credit ratings, which proved to be so unreliable in the run-up to the financial crisis. Third, Basel 2 is very procyclical. That is, it demands that banks hold less capital when times are good but more when times are bad, thereby exacerbating credit cycles. Because the probability of default and expected losses for different classes of assets rises during bad times, Basel 2 may require more capital at exactly the time when capital is most short. This has been a particularly serious concern in the aftermath of the 2007–2009 financial crisis. As a result of this crisis, banks' capital balances eroded, leading to a cutback on lending that was a big drag on the economy. Basel 2 has made this cutback in lending even worse, doing yet more harm to the economy. Fourth, Basel 2 did not focus sufficiently on the dangers of a possible drying up of liquidity, which brought financial institutions down during the financial crisis.

As a result of these limitations, in 2010 the Basel Committee developed a new accord, Basel 3. It beefs up capital standards by not only raising them substantially but also improving the quality of the capital, making them less procyclical by raising capital requirements in good times and lowering them in bad, making new rules on the use of credit ratings, and requiring financial institutions to have more stable funding so that they are better able to withstand liquidity shocks. Measures to achieve these objectives are highly controversial because of concerns that tightening up capital standards might cause banks to restrict their lending, which would make it harder for economies throughout the world to recover from the recent deep recession. Basel 3 is being implemented slowly over time, with the target for full implementation extending out to the end of 2019. Whether Basel 3 will be fully in place by that date and be successful in restraining risk taking is highly uncertain.

The major instrument of supervision of the financial sector in India is inspection. The inspection process focuses mainly on aspects crucial to the bank's financial soundness with a recent shift in focus towards risk management. Areas relating to internal control, credit management, overseas branch operations, profitability, compliance with prudential regulations, developmental aspects, proper valuation of asset/liability portfolio investment portfolio, and the bank's role in social lending are covered in the course of the inspection. The DBS undertakes statutory inspections of banks on the basis of an annual programme, which is co-terminus with the financial year for public sector banks. After the inspection report is released to the bank, followed by a 'supervisory letter' based on the inspection findings to the bank, the concerns of the inspections are discussed with the CEO of the bank and a Monitorable Action Plan is given to the bank for rectification of those deficiencies. The Department submits a memorandum covering supervisory concerns brought out by the inspection to the Board for Financial Supervision (BFS). Specific corrective directions of the BFS are conveyed to the banks concerned for immediate compliance. The Memoranda submitted by the departments for supervisory scrutiny and consideration of BFS generally covers matters relating to supervisory strategy and operational supervision of individual banks, financial institutions and non-banking financial companies as also industry-wide issues and sectoral performance reviews.[4]

Regular on-site examinations, which allow regulators to monitor whether the institution is complying with capital requirements and restrictions on asset holdings, also function to limit moral hazard. Bank examiners give banks a *CAMELS rating*. The acronym is based on the six areas assessed: capital adequacy, asset quality, management, earnings, liquidity, and sensitivity to market risk. With this information about a bank's activities, regulators can enforce regulations by taking such formal actions as *cease and desist orders* to alter the bank's behavior or even close a bank if its CAMELS rating is sufficiently low. Actions taken to reduce moral hazard by restricting banks from taking on too much risk help reduce the adverse selection problem further because with less opportunity for risk taking, risk-loving entrepreneurs will be less likely to be attracted to the banking industry. Note that the methods regulators use to cope with adverse selection and moral hazard have their counterparts in private financial markets.

Assessment of Risk Management

Traditionally, on-site examinations have focused primarily on assessment of the quality of a financial institution's balance sheet at a point in time and whether it complies with capital requirements and restrictions on asset holdings. Although the traditional focus is important for reducing excessive risk taking by financial institutions, it is no longer thought to be adequate in today's world, in which financial innovation has produced new markets and instruments that make it easy for financial institutions and their employees to make huge bets easily and quickly. In this new financial environment, a financial institution that is healthy at a particular point in time can be driven into insolvency extremely rapidly from trading losses, as forcefully demonstrated by the failure of Barings in 1995 (discussed in Chapter 16). Thus an examination that focuses only on a financial institution's

---

[4]*Source:* https://www.rbi.org.in/SCRIPTs/PublicationsView.aspx?id=2545, as accessed on 17 March 2017 at 4pm.

position at a point in time may not be effective in indicating whether it will, in fact, be taking on excessive risk in the near future.

This change in the environment for financial institutions has resulted in a major shift in thinking about the prudential supervisory process throughout the world. Bank examiners, for example, are now placing far greater emphasis on evaluating the soundness of a bank's management processes with regard to controlling the risk.

In India, the various Financial Stability Reports (FSRs) recognised the challenges posed by technology enabled innovations like 'virtual currency schemes' and 'peer-to-peer lending' to the established framework of institutions and market mechanisms.

The RBI has stressed on the need to identify and mitigate 'operational risks'. The latter are defined as the "risk of loss resulting from inadequate or failed processes, people and systems or from external events. This definition includes legal risk, but excludes strategic and reputational risk".[5]

The RBI further clarifies that many of the emerging risks like technology risks, cyber risks, risk of frauds, risks related to people and governance, business and control processes, legal risks etc. are covered under the ambit of operational risks which pervade every aspect of the functioning of a financial institution. It further states that the identification, measurement and management of operational risks remain among the biggest challenges for financial institutions and regulatory authorities.

Operational risks tend to amplify system-wide risks and have the potential to manifest themselves in catastrophic events, given the increased size, interconnectedness and complexity of financial institutions. Thus, the RBI recommends that the approach to operational risk issues and their systemic significance needs to go beyond the challenges of measuring capital charge for operational risk.

Particularly important is the implementation of **stress testing,** which calculates losses under dire scenarios, and **value-at-risk (VaR) calculations,** which measures the size of the loss on a trading portfolio that might happen 1% of the time—say, over a two-week period. In addition to these guidelines, bank examiners will continue to consider interest-rate risk in deciding the bank's capital requirements.

In India, the RBI had provided a set of guidelines on stress testing to the commercial banks. (This was issued vide circular DBOD.No.BP.BC. 101/21.04.103/2006-07 dated June 26, 2007). Banks were required to operationalise their formal stress testing framework in accordance with these guidelines from March 31, 2008. It was expected that the stress testing framework being set up would help banks in building a sound and forward looking risk management framework.

The depth and duration of the recent global financial crisis led many banks and supervisory authorities across the world to question whether the existing stress testing practices were sufficient and robust to cope with rapidly changing circumstances. In particular, the crisis was far more severe in many respects than was assumed by banks for their stress testing and consequently the weaknesses in stress testing practices impaired their resilience. Against this backdrop, the Basel Committee on Banking Supervision (BCBS) issued the Principles for Sound Stress Testing Practices and Supervision in May 2009.

In tune with these principles, the RBI updated the extant guidelines on stress testing in 2013.[6]

GO ONLINE

Access **https://rbidocs.rbi. org.in/rdocs/PublicationReport/Pdfs/07C3EDD1BD5E D04B4207A1782587D3 F63BF9.PDF** to view RBI's Financial Stability Report December 2015.

---

[5]*Source:* https://rbidocs.rbi.org.in/rdocs/PublicationReport/Pdfs/07C3EDD1BD5ED04B4207A1782587D3 F63BF9.PDF, as accessed on 17 March 2017 at 4pm.

[6]https://www.rbi.org.in/Scripts/NotificationUser.aspx?Id=8605&Mode=0 for the updated guidelines on stress testing, as accessed on 17 March 2017 at 4pm.

GO ONLINE

Access See **https://www.rbi.org.in/Scripts/NotificationUser.aspx?Id=8605&Mode=0** for the updated guidelines on stress testing.

The updated guidelines provided the overall objectives, governance, design and implementation of stress testing programmes.

All banks are required to carry out the stress tests involving shocks prescribed in the updated guidelines at a minimum. It was felt that while a bank should assess its resilience to withstand shocks of all levels of severity indicated therein, the bank should be able to survive, at least the baseline shocks.

Further, the RBI, in its communication to banks made it clear that it expected the degree of sophistication adopted by banks in their stress testing programmes to be commensurate with the nature, scope, scale and the degree of complexity in the bank's business operations and the risks associated with those operations. Banks were expected to adopt these guidelines on stress testing from April 1, 2014.

In addition to these guidelines, bank examiners will continue to consider interest-rate risk in deciding the bank's capital requirements.

Disclosure Requirements

The free-rider problem described in Chapter 7 indicates that individual depositors and creditors will not have enough incentive to produce private information about the quality of a financial institution's assets. To ensure that better information is available in the marketplace, regulators can require that financial institutions adhere to certain standard accounting principles and disclose a wide range of information that helps the market assess the quality of an institution's portfolio and the amount of its exposure to risk. More public information about the risks incurred by financial institutions and the quality of their portfolios can better enable stockholders, creditors, and depositors to evaluate and monitor financial institutions and so act as a deterrent to excessive risk taking.

Disclosure requirements are a key element of financial regulation. Basel 2 puts a particular emphasis on disclosure requirements with one of its three pillars focusing on increasing market discipline by mandating increased disclosure by banking institutions of their credit exposure, amount of reserves, and capital.

In India, such disclosure requirements were mandatory under Section 35A of the Banking Regulation Act, 1949.

Recognising the need for the users of the financial statements of a bank for information about its financial position and performance in making economic decisions, the RBI released additional instructions pertaining to bank disclosures on financial statements vide its circular dated July 1, 2015.[7]

The following instructions were laid out for all scheduled commercial banks (excluding Regional Rural Banks):

- A summary of 'Significant Accounting Policies' and 'Notes to Accounts' should be shown under Schedule 17 and Schedule 18 respectively, to maintain uniformity.
- **Minimum Disclosures** At a minimum, the items listed in the circular should be disclosed in the 'Notes to Accounts'. Banks are also encouraged to make more comprehensive disclosures than the minimum required under the circular if they become significant and aid in the understanding of the financial position and performance of the bank. The disclosures

---

[7] https://www.rbi.org.in/Scripts/BS_ViewMasCirculardetails.aspx?id=9906#C5, as accessed on 17 March 2017 at 4pm.

GO
ONLINE

Access **https://www.
rbi.org.in/Scripts/BS_
ViewMasCirculardetails.
aspx?id=9906#C5** to
view the RBI's disclosure
requirements for banks.

listed are intended only to supplement, and not to replace, other disclosure requirements under relevant legislation or accounting and financial reporting standards. Where relevant, a bank should comply with such other disclosure requirements as applicable.

- **Summary of Significant Accounting Policies**   Banks should disclose the accounting policies regarding key areas of operations at one place (under Schedule 17) along with 'Notes to Accounts' in their financial statements. A suggestive list includes–Basis of Accounting, Transactions involving Foreign Exchange, Investments—Classification, Valuation, etc., Advances and Provisions thereon, Fixed Assets and Depreciation, Revenue Recognition, Employee Benefits, Provision for Taxation, Net Profit, etc.

- **Disclosure Requirements**   In order to encourage market discipline, Reserve Bank of India, over the years has developed a set of disclosure requirements, which allows the market participants to assess key pieces of information on capital adequacy, risk exposures, risk assessment processes and key business parameters, to provide a consistent and understandable disclosure framework that enhances comparability. Banks are also required to comply with the Accounting Standard 1 (AS 1) on Disclosure of Accounting Policies issued by the Institute of Chartered Accountants of India (ICAI). The enhanced disclosures have been achieved through revision of Balance Sheet and Profit & Loss Account of banks and enlarging the scope of disclosures to be made in 'Notes to Accounts'. In addition to the 16 detailed prescribed schedules to the balance sheet, banks are required to furnish other information pertaining to capital, investments, derivatives, asset quality, business ratios, asset-liability management etc. in 'Notes to Accounts'.

Particularly controversial in the wake of the global financial crisis is the move to so-called **mark-to-market accounting,** also called **fair-value accounting,** in which assets are valued in the balance sheet at what they could sell for in the market (see the Mini-Case box, "Mark-to-Market Accounting and the Global Financial Crisis").

Consumer Protection

The existence of asymmetric information also suggests that consumers may not have enough information to protect themselves fully.

The Financial Sector Legislative Reforms Commission (FSLRC) in India in its report in 2013 commenting on the issue of consumer protection in the context of the financial sector had stated:

"A prime motivation of all financial regulation is to protect consumers. The relationship between financial firms and their customers is one where, many times, the outcomes may harm customers. These problems are not sporadic or accidental; but are often rooted in basic problems of information and incentives and will not be alleviated through financial literacy campaigns. The central purpose of financial regulation is to intervene in the relationship between financial firms and their customers, and address market failures. This requires a comprehensive consumer protection framework that covers both the problem of prevention (interventions that induce financial firms towards fair play) and cure (addressing consumer grievances)".

Mark-to-Market Accounting and the Global Financial Crisis

The controversy over mark-to-market accounting has made accounting a hot topic. Mark-to-market accounting was made a standard practice in the U.S. accounting industry in 1993. The rationale behind mark-to-market accounting is that market prices provide the best basis for estimating the true value of assets, and hence capital, in the firm. Before mark-to-market accounting, firms relied on the traditional historical-cost (book value) basis in which the value of an asset was set at its initial purchase price. The problem with historical-cost accounting is that fluctuations in the value of assets and liabilities because of changes in interest rates or default are not reflected in the calculation of the firm's equity capital. Yet changes in the market value of assets and liabilities—and hence changes in the market value of equity capital—are what indicates if a firm is in good shape, or alternatively, if it is getting into trouble and may therefore be more susceptible to moral hazard.

Mark-to-market accounting, however, is subject to a major flaw. At times markets stop working, as occurred during the global financial crisis. The price of an asset sold at a time of financial distress does not reflect its fundamental value. That is, the fire-sale liquidation value of an asset can at times be well below the present value of its expected future cash flows. Many people, particularly bankers, have criticized mark-to-market accounting during the recent financial crisis episode, claiming that it has been an important factor driving the crisis. They claim that the seizing up of financial markets has led to market prices being well below fundamental values. Mark-to-market accounting requires that the financial firms' assets be marked down in value. This markdown creates a shortfall in capital that leads to a cutback in lending, which causes a further deterioration in asset prices, which in turn causes a further cutback in lending. The resulting adverse feedback loop can then make the financial crisis even worse. Although the criticisms of mark-to-market accounting have some validity, some of the criticism by bankers is self-serving. The criticism was made only when asset values were falling, when mark-to-market accounting was painting a bleaker picture of banks' balance sheets, as opposed to when asset prices were booming, when it made banks' balance sheets look very good.

The criticisms of mark-to-market accounting led to a congressional focus on mark-to-market accounting that resulted in a provision in the Emergency Economic Stabilization Act of 2008 that required the SEC, in consultation with the Federal Reserve and the U.S. Treasury, to submit a study of mark-to-market accounting applicable to financial institutions. Who knew that accounting could get even politicians worked up!

Protection of depositor interest was one of the mandates of the RBI, and was contained in the Banking Regulation Act 1949 as well.

However, with the rapid increase in the nature and scope of financial services, customer protection has gone beyond merely protecting depositor interest. The RBI realised that with financial inclusion and the extension of banking services to underserved sections of the population whose financial literacy is low, combined with the growing complexity of financial products and the use of technology, the risks of mis-selling were high. Reinforcing financial consumer protection also strengthens the benefits of financial inclusion and financial education policies to economic growth, besides contributing to strengthening financial stability.

Taking these factors into account, both the Reserve Bank and the Government of India have been concerned with financial consumer protection. The RBI has articulated its core purpose, values and vision as its commitment to the nation to include regulating markets and institutions under its ambit to ensure financial system stability and consumer protection. Similarly, the FSLRC constituted by the Ministry of Finance, Government of India in its 2013 report also highlighted consumer protection in its report.

The FSLRC's work in the field of consumer protection marks a watershed compared with traditional approaches in Indian financial law. From placing the onus on the consumer—in the form of the tradition of caveat emptor, the 'buyers beware' concept, the FSLRC's Draft Indian Financial Code places a significant burden of consumer protection upon financial firms.

The draft Code first establishes certain basic rights for all financial consumers. In addition, the Code defines what is an unsophisticated consumer, and an additional set of protections are defined for these consumers. The proposed basic protections are:

a. Financial service providers must act with professional diligence.
b. Protection against unfair contract terms.
c. Protection against unfair conduct.
d. Protection of personal information.
e. Requirement of fair disclosure.
f. Redress of complaints by financial service providers.

In addition, unsophisticated consumers will have three additional protections:

a. The right to receive suitable advice.
b. Protection from conflicts of interest of advisors.
c. Access to the redress agency for redress of grievances.

The regulator will be given an enumerated set of powers through which it must implement these protections. Alongside these objectives and powers, the regulator will also be given a set of principles that guide the use of the powers.

Financial consumer protection sets clear rules of conduct for financial firms regarding their retail customers. It aims to ensure that consumers: (1) receive information to allow them to make informed decisions, (2) are not subject to unfair or deceptive practices, and (3) have access to recourse mechanisms to resolve disputes. Complementary financial literacy initiatives are aimed at giving consumers the knowledge and skills to understand the risks and rewards of using financial products and services—and their legal rights and obligations in using them. Clear rules of conduct for financial institutions, combined with programs of financial education for consumers, will increase consumer trust in financial markets and will support the development of these markets.[8]

As a structured measure towards protection of bank customers and setting standards of customer service, a Charter of Customer Rights as broad, over-arching principles for protecting bank customers was formulated by the Reserve Bank in 2014–15. The Indian Banks' Association (IBA) and Banking Codes and Standards Board of India (BCSBI) have since jointly formulated a model customer rights policy/ code based on the Charter of Customer Rights. Banks were advised to formulate board approved customer rights policies by July 31, 2015 incorporating the Charter of Customer Rights, and periodically review its implementation internally.

---

[8] *Source:* Gandhi, R. (2015), "Financial Consumer (Depositor) Protection: Reflections on some Lingering questions", https://rbidocs.rbi.org.in/rdocs/Speeches/PDFs/CPSP092954730FD81F419CBEE1E1C206F1B47B.PDF, as accessed on 17 March 2017 at 4pm.

Charter of Customer Rights

The Charter of Customer Rights released on December 3, 2014, enshrines broad, over-arching principles for protection of bank customers and enunciates five basic rights for bank customers as:

1. **Right to Fair Treatment:** Both the customer and the financial services provider have a right to be treated with courtesy. The customer should not be unfairly discriminated against on grounds such as gender, age, religion, caste and physical ability when offering and delivering financial products.

2. **Right to Transparency, Fair and Honest Dealing:** The financial services provider should make every effort to ensure that the contracts or agreements it frames are transparent, easily understood and well communicated to the common person. The product's price, associated risks, customer's responsibilities and the terms and conditions that govern its use over the product's life-cycle, should be clearly disclosed. The customer should not be subjected to unfair business or marketing practices, coercive contractual terms or misleading representations. Over the course of their relationship, the financial services provider cannot threaten the customer with physical harm, exert undue influence or engage in blatant harassment.

3. **Right to Suitability:** The products offered should be appropriate to the needs of the customer and based on an assessment of the customer's financial circumstances and understanding.

4. **Right to Privacy:** Customers' personal information should be kept confidential unless they have offered specific consent to the financial services provider or such information is required to be provided under the law or it is provided for a mandated business purpose (for example, to credit information companies). The customer should be informed upfront about likely mandated business purposes. Customers have the right to protection from all kinds of communications, electronic or otherwise, which infringe upon their privacy.

5. **Right to Grievance Redress and Compensation:** The customer has a right to hold the financial services provider accountable for the products offered and to have a clear and easy way to have any valid grievances redressed. The provider should also facilitate the redress of grievances stemming from the sale of third party products. The financial services provider must communicate its compensation policy for mistakes, lapses in conduct, as well as non-performance or delays in performance, whether caused by the provider or otherwise. The policy must lay out the rights and duties of the customer when such events occur.

These rights aim to protect the customer against unfair discrimination, unfair business or marketing practices, coercive contractual terms or misleading representations and aims to promote appropriate need-based warranted financial products with a better understanding of the various risks and charges involved therein.[9]

---

[9]*Source:* RBI, Annual Report, August 2015, https://rbidocs.rbi.org.in/rdocs/AnnualReport/PDFs/06P25F E529C3320E45CAA10E8B9B27D312FB.PDF, as accessed on 17 March 2017 at 4pm.

The global financial crisis has illustrated the need for greater consumer protection because so many borrowers took out loans with terms they did not understand and that were well beyond their means to repay. The result was millions of foreclosures, with many households losing their homes. Because weak consumer protection regulation played a prominent role in this crisis, demands to strengthen this regulation have been increasing, as is discussed in the Mini-Case box, "The Global Financial Crisis and Consumer Protection Regulation."

Restrictions on Competition

Increased competition can also increase moral hazard incentives for financial institutions to take on more risk. Declining profitability as a result of increased competition could tip the incentives of financial institutions toward assuming greater risk in an effort to maintain former profit levels. Thus governments in many countries have instituted regulations to protect financial institutions from competition. Thus, for instance, in the US, these regulations have taken two forms in the past. First were restrictions on branching, which are described in Chapter 18, which reduced competition between banks, but these were eliminated in 1994. The second form involved preventing nonbank institutions from competing with banks by engaging in banking business, as embodied in the Glass-Steagall Act, which was repealed in 1999.

Although restrictions on competition propped up the health of banks, they also had serious disadvantages: They led to higher charges to consumers and decreased the efficiency of banking institutions, which did not have to compete as vigorously. Thus, although the existence of asymmetric information provided a rationale for anti-competitive regulations, it did not mean that they would be beneficial. Indeed, in recent years, the impulse of governments in industrialized countries to restrict competition has been waning. Electronic banking has raised a new set of concerns for regulators to deal with. See the E-Finance box for a discussion of this challenge.

Macroprudential Versus Microprudential Supervision

Before the global financial crisis, the regulatory authorities engaged in **microprudential supervision,** which focuses on the safety and soundness of *individual* financial institutions. Microprudential supervision looks at each institution separately and assesses the riskiness of its activities and whether it complies with disclosure requirements. Most importantly, it checks whether that institution satisfies capital *ratios* and, if not, either it engages in prompt corrective action to force the institution to raise its capital ratios or the supervisor closes it down, along the lines we have discussed.

Discussion of the global financial crisis in Chapter 8 reveals that a focus on microprudential supervision is not enough to prevent financial crisis. The run on the shadow banking system illustrates how the problems of one financial institution can harm other financial institutions that are otherwise healthy. When the troubled financial institution is forced to engage in fire sales and sell off assets to meet target capital ratios or haircut requirements, this leads to a decline in asset values. This decline in asset values then causes other institutions to engage in fire sales, leading to a rapid deleveraging process and a systemic crisis. In situations like this, even institutions that would normally be healthy and have high capital ratios may find themselves in trouble.

The Global Financial Crisis and Consumer Protection Regulation

Because of the principal–agent problem inherent in the originate-to-distribute model for subprime mortgages discussed in Chapter 8, incentives were weak for mortgage originators, typically mortgage brokers who were virtually unregulated, to ensure that subprime borrowers had an ability to pay back their loans. After all, mortgage brokers keep their large fees from mortgage originations even if sometime down the road the borrowers default on their loans and lose their houses. With these incentives, mortgage brokers weakened their underwriting standards, leading to subprime mortgage products such as "no-doc loans," more pejoratively referred to as "liar loans," in which borrowers did not have to produce documentation about their assets or income. A particularly infamous variant of the no-doc loan was dubbed the NINJA loan because it was issued to borrowers with No Income, No Job, and No Assets. Mortgage brokers also had incentives to put households into very complicated mortgage products that borrowers could not understand and which they couldn't afford to pay. In some cases, mortgage brokers even engaged in fraud by falsifying information on borrowers' mortgage applications in order to qualify them for mortgage loans.

Lax consumer protection regulation was an important factor in producing the global financial crisis. Mortgage originators were not required to disclose information to borrowers that would have helped them understand complicated mortgage products and whether they could afford to repay them. Outrage over the surge of foreclosures has been an important stimulus for new regulation to provide better information to mortgage borrowers and to ban the so-called

unfair and deceptive practices. Under Regulation Z of the Truth in Lending Act, in July of 2008, the Federal Reserve issued a final rule for subprime mortgage loans with the following four elements: (1) a ban on lenders making loans without regard to borrowers' ability to repay the loan from income and assets other than the home's value, (2) a ban on no-doc loans, (3) a ban on prepayment penalties (i.e., a penalty for paying back the loan early) if the interest payment can change in the first four years of the loan, and (4) a requirement that lenders establish an escrow account for property taxes and homeowner's insurance to be paid on a monthly basis. In addition, the rule stipulated the following new regulations for all mortgage loans, not just subprime mortgages: (1) a prohibition on mortgage brokers coercing a real estate appraiser to misstate a home's value, (2) a prohibition on putting one late fee on top of another and a requirement to credit consumers' loan payments as of the date of receipt, (3) a requirement for lenders to provide a good-faith estimate of the loan costs within three days after a household applies for a loan, and (4) a ban on a number of misleading advertising practices, including representing that a rate or payment is "fixed" when the payment can be changed.

Because the view was held that more needed to be done, the Obama administration and the Congress have stepped in by creating a new consumer protection agency as part of the financial reform legislation of 2010. The mandate of this agency is to further strengthen consumer protection regulation on subprime mortgages and other financial products.

The global financial crisis has therefore made it clear that there is a need for **macroprudential supervision,** which focuses on the safety and soundness of the financial system *in the aggregate*. Rather than focus on the safety and soundness of individual institutions, macroprudential supervision seeks to mitigate systemwide fire sales and deleveraging by assessing the overall capacity of the financial system to avoid them. In addition, because many institutions that were well capitalized faced liquidity shortages and found that their access to short-term funding was cut off, macroprudential supervision focuses not only on capital adequacy as a whole but also on whether the financial system has sufficient liquidity.

Macroprudential policies can take several forms. The run-up to the global financial crisis included a so-called **leverage cycle,** in which there was a feedback loop from a boom in issuing credit, which led to higher asset prices, which resulted in higher capital buffers at financial institutions, which supported further lending in the context of unchanging capital requirements, which then raised asset prices further, and so on; in the bust, the value of the capital dropped precipitously, leading to a cut in lending. To short-circuit this leverage cycle, macroprudential policies would make capital requirements countercyclical; that is, they would be adjusted upward during a boom and downward during a bust. In addition, during the upward swing in the leverage cycle, macroprudential policies might involve forcing financial institutions to tighten credit standards or even direct limits on the growth of credit. In the downward swing, macroprudential supervision might be needed to force the banking system as a whole to raise an aggregate amount of new capital so that banks would not curtail lending in order to reduce the level of their assets and raise capital ratios. To ensure that financial institutions have enough liquidity, macroprudential policies could require that financial institutions have a sufficiently low *net stable funding ratio* (NSFR), which is the percentage of the institution's short-term funding in relation to total funding. Macroprudential policies of the type discussed here are being considered as part of the Basel 3 framework but have not yet been completely worked out.

In India, the RBI has been using a macroprudential framework to achieve its objective of financial stability—an objective that the RBI adopted as an additional objective in 2004, in addition to its primary objective of growth and price stability. This is despite the fact that the RBI has not really christened these policies as macroprudential policies as is the case with other Asian countries. Operationally, while pursuing multiple objectives, the RBI has used multiple indicators, including growth in credit and money, to track the macroeconomic conditions. India being a bank-dominated economy, bank credit has been a key monetary policy transmission channel, and the RBI has used aggregate bank credit growth as an important variable in the conduct of monetary and countercyclical policies.

Macro-prudential Framework in India

GO ONLINE
Access **https://rbi. org.in/scripts/BS_ ViewMasCirculardetails. aspx?id=9908** to view the master circular on prudential norms on income recognition, asset classification and provisioning pertaining to advances.

With the banking system occupying critical centre stage in the Indian economy, as also the challenges faced in application of countercyclical policies to the Non Banking Financial Companies (NBFCs), RBI's countercyclical policies have been concentrated on banks. These policies have aimed at increasing the resilience of the banking system. The instruments used have been time varying risk weights and provisioning norms on standard assets for certain specific sectors wherein excessive credit growth, in conjunction with sharp rise in asset prices, has caused apprehension of potential build-up of systemic risk and asset bubbles. In the process, the policies have "leaned" against the wind and have had the desired effect of moderating the credit boom in the specified sectors both through signaling effect and affecting the cost of credit. Evidence, though limited, suggests that the leaning against the wind has been more effective in dampening the lending exuberance in the boom phase than in the downturn in ensuring a stable credit supply.

The RBI has initiated several measures to reduce the inter-connectedness among banks on the one hand and between banks and NBFCs on the other, and has placed limits on common exposures to address the cross-sectional dimension of systemic risk.[10]

---

[10]*Source:* Sinha, A. (2011). "Macroprudential Policies: Indian Experience", https://rbi.org.in/scripts/BS_SpeechesView.aspx?Id=576, as accessed on 17 March 2017 at 4pm.

Three salient macroprudential measures have characterized the process of financial reforms in India:

One, the tightening of capital adequacy norms for banks—the capital-to risk-weighted assct ratio (CRAR) for banks was raised to 8% in 1996 and further to 9% in 2000.

Second, in 2000, the Reserve Bank of India (RBI) introduced a provisioning of a minimum of 0.25% on standard loans. During the crisis, these provisions were initially raised to 0.4% and thereafter to a peak of 2% in January 2007 before being subsequently lowered.

Finally, the RBI has rationalized the norms for recognizing a loan as non-performing in line with international best practices since 1993. Accordingly, the time period for classifying a loan as "sub-standard" was gradually reduced from the initial 12 months to 3 months (90 days) by 2004. Concomitantly, the period for classifying a loan as "doubtful" was also lowered, from 24 months at the beginning of reforms to 12 months by 2005.

Summary

Asymmetric information analysis explains what types of financial regulations are needed to reduce moral hazard and adverse selection problems in the financial system. However, understanding the theory behind regulation does not mean that

> E-FINANCE

Electronic Banking: New Challenges for Bank Regulation

The advent of electronic banking has raised new concerns for banking regulation, specifically about security and privacy. Worries about the security of electronic banking and e-money are an important barrier to their increased use. With electronic banking, you might worry that criminals can access your bank account and steal your money by moving your balances to someone else's account. Private solutions to deal with this problem have arisen with the development of a more secure encryption technologies to prevent this kind of fraud. However, because bank customers are not knowledgeable about computer security issues, there is a role for the government in regulating electronic banking to make sure that encryption procedures are adequate. Similar encryption issues apply to e-money, so requirements that banks make it difficult for criminals to engage in digital counterfeiting make sense. To meet these challenges, bank examiners in the United States assess how a bank deals with the special security issues raised by electronic banking and also oversee third-party providers of electronic banking platforms. Also, because consumers want to know that electronic banking transactions are executed correctly, bank examiners assess the technical skills of banks in setting up electronic banking services and the bank's capabilities for dealing with problems. Another security issue of concern to bank customers is the validity of digital signatures. The Electronic Signatures in Global and National Commerce Act of 2000 makes electronic signatures as legally binding as written signatures in most circumstances.

Electronic banking also raises serious privacy concerns. Because electronic transactions can be stored on databases, banks are able to collect a huge amount of information about their customers—their assets, creditworthiness, purchases, and so on—that can be sold to other financial institutions and businesses. This potential invasion of our privacy rightfully makes us very nervous. To protect customers' privacy, the Gramm-Leach-Bliley Act of 1999 has limited the distribution of these data, but it does not go as far as the European Data Protection Directive, which prohibits the transfer of information about online transactions. How to protect consumers' privacy in our electronic age is one of the great challenges faced by our society, so privacy regulations for electronic banking are likely to evolve over time.

regulation and supervision of the financial system are easy in practice. Getting regulators and supervisors to do their jobs properly is difficult for several reasons. First, as we will see in the discussion of financial innovation in Chapter 18, in their search for profits, financial institutions have strong incentives to avoid existing regulations by loophole mining. Thus regulation applies to a moving target: Regulators are continually playing cat-and-mouse with financial institutions—financial institutions think up clever ways to avoid regulations, which then lead regulators to modify their regulation activities. Regulators continually face new challenges in a dynamically changing financial system—and unless they can respond rapidly to change, they may not be able to keep financial institutions from taking on excessive risk. This problem can be exacerbated if regulators and supervisors do not have the resources or expertise to keep up with clever people in financial institutions seeking to circumvent the existing regulations.

Financial regulation and supervision are difficult for two other reasons. In the regulation and supervision game, the devil is in the details. Subtle differences in the details may have unintended consequences; unless regulators get the regulation and supervision just right, they may be unable to prevent excessive risk taking. In

›GLOBAL

International Financial Regulation

Because asymmetric information problems in the banking industry are a fact of life throughout the world, financial regulation exists in other countries similar to that in India. Financial institutions are regulated and supervised by government regulators, just as they are in India. Disclosure requirements for financial institutions and corporations issuing securities are similar in other countries. Deposit insurance is also a feature of the regulatory systems in most other countries, although its coverage may be often small. We have also seen that capital requirements are in the process of being standardized across countries in compliance with agreements like the Basel Accord.

Particular problems in financial regulation occur when financial institutions operate in many countries and thus can readily shift their business from one country to another. Financial regulators closely examine the domestic operations of financial institutions in their country, but they often do not have the knowledge or ability to keep a close watch on operations in other countries, either by domestic institutions' foreign affiliates or by foreign institutions with domestic branches. In addition, when a financial institution operates in many countries, it is not always clear which national regulatory authority should have primary responsibility for keeping the institution from engaging in overly risky activities.

The difficulties inherent in international financial regulation was highlighted by the collapse of the Bank of Credit and Commerce International (BCCI). BCCI, which was operating in more than 70 countries, including the United States and the United Kingdom, was supervised by Luxembourg, a tiny country unlikely to be up to the task. When massive fraud was discovered, the Bank of England closed BCCI down, but not before depositors and stockholders were exposed to huge losses. Cooperation among regulators in different countries and standardization of regulatory requirements provide potential solutions to the problems of international financial regulation. The world has been moving in this direction through agreements like the Basel Accord and oversight procedures announced by the Basel Committee in July 1992, which requires a bank's worldwide operations to be under the scrutiny of a single home-country regulator with enhanced powers to acquire information on the bank's activities. The Basel Committee also ruled that regulators in other countries can restrict the operations of a foreign bank if they believe it lacks effective oversight. Whether agreements of this type will solve the problem of international financial regulation in the future is an open question.

GO ONLINE

Access **http:// financialservices.gov.in/ banking/banking_actrules. asp?pageid=2** to view the entire list and details of laws pertaining to financial services administered in India.

TABLE 17.1   Major Financial Legislations in India

RBI Act, 1934

Established and incorporated the Reserve Bank of India.

Banking Regulation Act, 1949

An Act to restrict the liability of banking companies in connection with certain transactions by legal practitioners.

The Deposit Insurance and Credit Guarantee Corporation Act, 1961

An Act to provide for the establishment of a corporation for the purpose of insurance of deposits [and guaranteeing of credit facilities] and for other matters connected therewith or incidental thereto.

The Banking Companies (Acquisition and Transfer of Undertakings) Act, 1970

Provided for the first round of nationalization of banks in India. Through this, the Government of India nationalised the 14 largest commercial banks, accounting for 85 percent of bank deposits in the country.

The Banking Companies (Acquisition and Transfer of Undertakings) Act, 1980

Provided for the second round of bank nationalization in India. The government acquired six more banks.

The Securitization and Reconstruction of Financial Assets and Enforcement of Security Interest (SARFAESI) Act, 2002

An Act to regulate securitisation and reconstruction of financial assets and enforcement of security interest and for matters connected therewith or incidental thereto.

Source: http://financialservices.gov.in/banking/banking_actrules.asp?pageid=2, as accessed on 17 March 2017 at 4pm.

addition, regulated firms may lobby politicians to lean on regulators and supervisors to go easy on them. For all these reasons, there is no guarantee that regulators and supervisors will be successful in promoting a healthy financial system. These same problems bedevil financial regulators in other countries besides the United States, as the Global box, "International Financial Regulation," indicates. Indeed, as we will see, financial regulation and supervision have not always worked well, leading to banking crisis in the United States and throughout the world.

Because so many laws regulating the financial system have been passed in the United States, it is hard to keep track of them all. As a study aid, Table 17.1 lists the major financial legislation in India since the beginning of the 20th century and its key provisions.

Banking Crisis Throughout the World in Recent Years

The United States is one of the countries which suffered banking crisis even before the global financial crisis of 2007–2009. Indeed, as Figure 17.1 and Table 17.2 illustrate, banking crisis have struck a large number of countries throughout the world since the 1980s, and many of them have been substantially worse than the ones the United States experienced.

FIGURE 17.1 Banking Crisis Throughout the World Since 1970

Banking crisis have been very common throughout the world.

Courtesy: Luc Laeven and Fabian Valencia, "Systemic Banking Crisis Database: An Update," IMF Working Paper No. WP/12/163 (June 2012).

"Déjà Vu All Over Again"

GO ONLINE

Access **https://rbidocs.rbi. org.in/rdocs/Content/PDFs/ FR122013DRS.pdf** to view RBI's draft framework for dealing with Domestic Systematically Important Banks (D-SIBs).

In banking crisis in different countries, history keeps repeating itself. The parallels between the banking crisis episodes in all these countries are remarkably similar, creating a feeling of déjà vu. They all started with financial liberalization or innovation, with weak bank regulatory systems and a government safety net. Although financial liberalization is generally a good thing because it promotes competition and can make a financial system more efficient, it can lead to an increase in moral hazard, with more risk taking on the part of banks if regulation and supervision are lax; the result can then be banking crisis.[11]

However, the banking crisis episodes listed in Table 17.2 do differ as in that deposit insurance has not played an important role in many of the countries experiencing banking crisis. For example, the size of the Japanese equivalent of the FDIC, the Deposit Insurance Corporation, was so tiny relative to the FDIC that it did not play a prominent role in the banking system and exhausted its resources almost immediately with the first bank failures. This example indicates that deposit insurance is not to blame for some of these banking crisis. However, what is common to

---

[11]A second Web appendix to this chapter, which can be found on this book's Web site www.pearsonhighered. com/mishkin_eakins, discusses in detail many of the episodes of banking crisis listed in Table 17.2.

TABLE 17.2 The Cost of Rescuing Banks in a Number of Countries

Country	Date	Fiscal Cost as Percentage of GDP
Indonesia	1997–2001	57
Argentina	1980–1982	55
Iceland	2008	44
Jamaica	1996–1998	44
Thailand	1997–2000	44
Chile	1981–1985	43
Ireland	2008–	41*
Macedonia	1993–1995	32
Turkey	2000–2001	32
South Korea	1997–1998	31
Israel	1977	30
Ecuador	1998–2002	22
Mexico	1994–1996	19
China	1998	18
Malaysia	1997–1999	16
Philippines	1997–2001	13
Brazil	1994–1998	13
Finland	1991–1995	13
Argentina	2001–2003	10
Jordan	1989–1991	10
Hungary	1991–1995	10
Czech Republic	1996–2000	7
Sweden	1991–1995	4
United States	1988	4
Norway	1991–1993	
Luxembourg	2008–	8*
Netherlands	2008–	13*
Belgium	2008–	6*
United Kingdom	2008	8*
United States	2007	4
Germany	2008–	1*

Source: Luc Laeven and Fabian Valencia, "Systemic Banking Crisis Database: An Update," IMF Working Paper No. WP/12/163 (June 2012).

Note: An * indicates that the fiscal cost has been estimated only up to 2012.

all the countries discussed here is the existence of a government safety net, in which the government stands ready to bail out banks whether deposit insurance is an important feature of the regulatory environment or not. It is the existence of a government safety net, and not deposit insurance per se, that increases moral hazard incentives for excessive risk taking on the part of banks.

The Dodd-Frank Wall Street Reform and Consumer Protection Act of 2010 in the US

Dodd-Frank

In the US, the global financial crisis raised calls for a new regulatory structure to make a repeat of the crisis less likely. The result was The Dodd-Frank bill, which was passed in July 2010 after more than a year of discussion. It is the most comprehensive financial reform legislation since the Great Depression. It addresses five categories of regulation, which are discussed next.

Consumer Protection—this legislation creates a new Consumer Financial Protection Bureau that is funded and housed within the Federal Reserve, although it is a completely independent agency. It has the authority to examine and enforce regulations for all businesses engaged in issuing residential mortgage products that have more than $10 billion in assets, as well as for issuers of other financial products marketed to poor people. It requires lenders to make sure there is an ability to repay residential mortgages by requiring verification of income, credit history, and job status. It also bans payments to brokers for pushing borrowers into higher-priced loans. It allows states to impose stricter consumer protection laws on national banks and gives state attorneys-general power to enforce certain rules issued by the new bureau. It also permanently increases the level of federal deposit insurance to $250,000.

Resolution Authority—although before this legislation the FDIC had the ability to seize failing banks and wind them down, the government did not have such a resolution authority over the largest financial institutions—those structured as holding companies. Indeed, the U.S. Treasury and the Federal Reserve argued that one reason they were unable to rescue Lehman Brothers and instead had to let it go into bankruptcy was that they did not have the legal means to take Lehman over and break it up. The Dodd-Frank bill now provides the U.S. government with this authority for financial firms that are deemed **systemic,** that is, firms who pose a risk to the overall financial system because their failure would cause widespread damage. It also gives regulators the right to levy fees on financial institutions with more than $50 billion in assets to recoup any losses.

Systemic Risk Regulation—the bill creates a Financial Stability Oversight Council, chaired by the Treasury secretary, which would monitor markets for asset-price bubbles and the buildup of systemic risk. In addition, it would designate which financial firms are systemically important and so would receive the official designation of **systemically important financial institutions (SIFIs).** These firms would be subjected to additional regulation by the Federal Reserve, which would include higher capital standards and stricter liquidity requirements, as well as requirements that they draw up a "living will," that is, a plan for orderly liquidation if the firm gets into financial difficulties.

Volcker Rule—banks would be limited in the extent of their **proprietary trading,** that is, trading with their own money, and would be allowed to own only a small percentage of hedge and private equity funds. These provisions are named after Paul Volcker, a former Chairman of the Board of Governors of the Federal Reserve, who argued that banks should not be allowed to take large trading risks when they receive the benefits of federal deposit insurance.

Derivatives—financial instruments whose payoffs are linked to (i.e., derived from) previously issued securities are known as **financial derivatives.** As is discussed in Chapter 8, derivatives such as credit default ended up being "weapons of mass destruction" that helped lead to a financial meltdown when AIG had to be rescued after making overly extensive use of them. To prevent this from happening again, the Dodd-Frank bill requires many standardized derivative products to be traded on exchanges and cleared through clearing houses to reduce the risk of losses if one counterparty in the derivative transaction goes bankrupt. More customized derivative products would be subjected to higher capital requirements. Banks would be banned from some of their derivatives dealing operations such as those involving riskier swaps. In addition, the bill imposes capital and margin requirements on firms dealing in derivatives and forces them to disclose more information about their activities.

SUMMARY

1. The concepts of asymmetric information, adverse selection, and moral hazard help explain the ten types of financial regulation that we see in most countries: the government safety net, restrictions on financial institutions' asset holdings, capital requirements, prompt corrective action, chartering and examination, assessment of risk management, disclosure requirements, consumer protection, restrictions on competition, and macroprudential supervision.

2. The parallels between the banking crisis episodes that have occurred in countries throughout the world are striking, indicating that similar forces are at work.

3. The Dodd-Frank Act of 2010 in the US is the most comprehensive financial reform legislation since the Great Depression. It has provisions in five areas: (1) consumer protection, (2) resolution authority, (3) systemic risk regulation, (4) Volcker rule, and (5) derivatives.

KEY TERMS

bank failure, p. 419
Basel Accord, p. 425
Basel Committee on Banking Supervision, p. 425
fair-value accounting, p. 432
financial derivatives, p. 444
financial supervision (prudential supervision), p. 427

leverage cycle, p. 437
leverage ratio, p. 424
macroprudential supervision, p. 437
mark-to-market accounting, p. 432
microprudential supervision, p. 436
off-balance-sheet activities, p. 424
proprietary trading, p. 444
regulatory arbitrage, p. 425

stress testing, p. 430
systemic, p. 444
systemically important financial institutions (SIFIs), p. 444
value-at-risk (VaR) calculations, p. 430

QUESTIONS

1. Give one example each of moral hazard and adverse selection in private insurance arrangements.

2. If casualty insurance companies provided fire insurance without restrictions, what kind of adverse selection and moral hazard problems might result?

3. What bank regulation is designed to reduce adverse selection problems for deposit insurance? Will it always work?

4. What bank regulations are designed to reduce moral hazard problems created by deposit insurance? Will they eliminate the moral hazard problem?

5. What are the costs and benefits of a too-big-to-fail policy?

6. What special problem do off-balance-sheet activities present to bank regulators, and what have they done about it?

7. Why does imposing bank capital requirements on banks help limit risk taking?

8. What forms does bank supervision take, and how do they promote a safe and sound banking system?

9. Why has the trend in bank supervision moved away from a focus on capital requirements to a focus on risk management?

10. How do disclosure requirements help limit excessive risk taking by banks?

11. Do you think that eliminating or limiting the amount of deposit insurance would be a good idea? Explain your answer.

12. Do you think that removing the impediments to a nationwide banking system will be beneficial to the economy? Explain.

13. How could higher deposit insurance premiums for banks with riskier assets benefit the economy?

14. How could market-value accounting for bank capital requirements (discussed in the first Web appendix to this chapter) benefit the economy? How difficult would it be to implement?

QUANTITATIVE PROBLEMS

1. Consider a bank with the following balance sheet:

Assets		Liabilities	
Required reserves	₹8 million	Checkable deposits	₹100 million
Excess reserves	₹3 million	Bank capital	₹6 million
T-bills	₹45 million		
Commercial loans	₹50 million		

Calculate the bank's risk-weighted assets.

2. Consider a bank with the following balance sheet:

Assets		Liabilities	
Required reserves	₹8 million	Checkable deposits	₹100 million
Excess reserves	₹3 million	Bank capital	₹6 million
T-bills	₹45 million		
Mortgages	₹40 million		
Commercial loans	₹10 million		

The bank commits to a loan agreement for ₹10 million to a commercial customer. Calculate the bank's capital ratio before and after the agreement. Calculate the bank's risk-weighted assets before and after the agreement.

Problems 3 through 8 relate to a sequence of transactions at Oldhat Financial.

3. Oldhat Financial started its first day of operations with ₹9 million in capital. ₹130 million in checkable deposits are received. The bank issues a ₹25 million commercial loan and another ₹50 million in mortgages, with the following terms:

- Mortgages: 200 standard 30-year, fixed-rate with a nominal annual rate of 5.25% each for ₹250,000.
- Commercial loan: Three-year loan, simple interest paid monthly at 0.75% per month.

  a. If required reserves are 8%, what does the bank balance sheet look like? Ignore any loan loss reserves.

  b. How well-capitalized is the bank?

4. Calculate the risk-weighted assets and risk-weighted capital ratio after Oldhat's first day.

5. The next day, terrible news hits the mortgage markets, and mortgage rates jump to 13%. What is the market value of Oldhat's mortgages? What is Oldhat's "market value" capital ratio?

6. Oldhat decides to invest the ₹77 million in excess reserves in commercial loans. What will be the impact on its capital ratio? Its risk-weighted capital ratio?

7. The bad news about the mortgages is featured in the local newspaper, causing a minor bank run. ₹6 million in deposits is withdrawn. Examine the bank's condition after this occurs.

8. Oldhat borrows ₹5.5 million in the overnight call money market to meet its resources requirement. What is the new balance sheet for Oldhat? How well-capitalized is the bank?

WEB EXERCISES

Banking Regulation

1. Go to **http://financialservices.gov.in/banking/banking_actrules.asp?pageid=2**. This site reports on the most significant pieces of legislation affecting banks since 1881. Summarize the most recently enacted bank regulation listed on this site.

WEB APPENDICES

Please visit our Web site at **www.pearsonhighered.com/mishkin_eakins** to read the Web appendices to Chapter 17:

- **Appendix 1:** Banking Crisis Throughout the World

18

Banking Industry: Structure and Competition

> PREVIFW

The operations of individual banks (how they acquire, use, and manage funds to make a profit) are roughly similar throughout the world. In all countries, banks are financial intermediaries in the business of earning profits.

In this chapter we try to examine the historical trends in the commercial banking industry in India and its overall structure.

We start by examining the historical development of the banking system. We then go on to look at the commercial industry in detail. In addition to looking at our domestic banking system, we also examine the forces behind the growth in international banking. Finally, we examine how financial innovation has increased the competitive environment for the banking industry and is causing fundamental changes in it.

Historical Development of the Banking System

Globally, the story of banking has much in common, as it evolved with the moneylenders accepting deposits and issuing receipts in their place. According to the Central Banking Enquiry Committee (1931), money lending activity in India could be traced back to the Vedic period, i.e., 2000–1400 BC. The existence of professional banking in India could be traced to 500 BC. Kautilya's Arthashastra, dating back to 400 BC contained references to creditors, lenders and lending rates. Banking was fairly varied and catered to the credit needs of the trade, commerce, agriculture and as well as individuals in the economy. Mr. W. E. Preston, member, Royal Commission on Indian Currency and Finance set up in 1926, observed "....it may be accepted that a system of banking that was eminently suited to India's then requirements was in force in that country many centuries before the science of banking became an accomplished fact in England." An extensive network of Indian banking houses existed in the country connecting all cities/towns that were of commercial importance. They had their own inland bills of exchange or hundis, which were the major forms of transactions between Indian bankers and their trans-regional connections. Banking practices in India were vastly different from the European counterparts. The dishonoring of hundis was a rare occurrence. Most banking worked on mutual trust, confidence and without securities and facilities that were considered essential by British bankers. Northcote Cooke observed "....the fact that Europeans are not the originators of banking in this country does not strike us with surprise."

The first bank of a joint stock variety was Bank of Bombay, a Bombay-based bank established in 1720. This was followed by Bank of Hindustan in Calcutta, which was established in 1770 by an agency house. The first 'Presidency bank' was the Bank of Bengal established in Calcutta on June 2, 1806 with a capital of ₹50 lakh. The Government subscribed to 20% of its shares capital and shared the privilege of appointing directors with voting rights. The bank had the task of discounting the Treasury bills to provide accommodation to the Government. The bank was given powers to issue notes in 1823. The Bank of Bombay was the second Presidency bank set up in 1840 with a capital of ₹52 lakh, and the Bank of Madras was the third Presidency bank established in July 1843 with a capital of ₹30 lakh. They were known as Presidency banks as they were set up in the three presidencies that were the units of administrative jurisdiction in the country for the East India Company. The Presidency banks were governed by Royal Charters. The Presidency banks issued currency notes until the enactment of the Paper Currency Act, 1861, when this right to issue currency notes by the Presidency banks was abolished and that function was entrusted to the Government.

The first Indian-owned bank was the Allahabad Bank set up in Allahabad in 1865, the second, Punjab National Bank was set up in 1895 in Lahore, and the third, Bank of India was set up in 1906 in Mumbai. All these banks were founded under private ownership.

In fact, the pre-independence period was largely characterised by the existence of private banks organised as joint stock companies. Most banks were small and had private shareholding of the closely held variety. They were largely localised and many of them failed. They came under the purview of the Reserve Bank that was established as a central bank for the country in 1935. But the provisions of the Reserve Bank of India Act, 1934 and the Companies Act, 1913, limited the process of regulation and supervision. The indigenous bankers and moneylenders had

GO ONLINE
Access **https://www.rbi.org. in/Scripts/PublicationsView. aspx?id=10487** to learn more about the evolution of banking in India.

remained mainly isolated from the institutional part of the system. The outrageous network was still rampant and exploitative. Co-operative credit was the only hope for credit but the movement was successful only in a few regions.

The early years of independence (1947–1967) posed several challenges with an underdeveloped economy presenting the classic case of market failure in the rural sector, where information asymmetry limited the foray of banks. Further, the non-availability of adequate assets made it difficult for people to approach banks. With the transfer of undertaking of Imperial Bank of India to State Bank of India (SBI) and its subsequent massive expansion in the under-banked and unbanked centres, institutional credit spread into regions which were un-banked before. Proactive measures like credit guarantee and deposit insurance promoted the spread of credit and savings habits to the rural areas. There were, however, problems of connected lending as many of the banks were under the control of business houses.

The year 1948 was one of the worst years for the relatively larger banks as 45 institutions (out of more than 637 banks) with paid-up capital averaging about ₹4 lakh were closed down. They failed as they had over-reached themselves by opening more branches than they could sustain on the strength of their resources and by making large loans against property or inadequate security. Some of these, however, had prudential issues as they were functioning with very low capital base. Repeated bank failures caused great hardships to the savers.

The problem of bank failure in some measure was addressed by the Banking Companies Act, 1949 (later renamed as the Banking Regulation Act), but only to a limited extent. The Banking Companies Act of 1949 conferred on the Reserve Bank the extensive powers for banking supervision as the central banking authority of the country.

The period 1967–1991 was characterised by major developments, viz., social control on banks in 1967 and nationalisation of 14 banks in 1969 and six more in 1980. The nationalisation of banks was an attempt to use the scarce resources of the banking system for the purpose of planned development. The task of maintaining a large number of small accounts was not profitable for the banks, as a result of which they had limited lending in the rural sector. The problem of lopsided distribution of banks and the lack of explicit articulation of the need to channel credit to certain priority sectors was sought to be achieved first by social control on banks and then by the nationalisation of banks in 1969 and 1980. The Lead Bank Scheme provided the blue-print for further bank branch expansion. The course of evolution of the banking sector in India since 1969 has been dominated by the nationalisation of banks. This period was characterised by rapid branch expansion that helped to draw the channels of monetary transmission far and wide across the country. The share of unorganised credit fell sharply and the economy seemed to come out of the low level of equilibrium trap. However, the stipulations that made this possible and helped spread institutional credit and nurture the financial system, also led to distortions in the process. The administered interest rates and the burden of directed lending constrained the banking sector significantly. There was very little operational flexibility for the commercial banks. Profitability occupied a back seat. Banks also suffered from poor governance. The financial sector became the 'Achilles heel' of the economy (Rangarajan, 1998). Fortunately, for the Indian economy, quick action was taken to address these issues.

The period beginning from the early 1990s witnessed the transformation of the banking sector as a result of financial sector reforms that were introduced as a part of structural reforms initiated in 1991. The reform process in the financial sector

GO ONLINE
Access **https://rbidocs.rbi. org.in/rdocs/Publications/ PDFs/BANKI15122014.pdf** to learn more about the Banking Regulation Act 1949.

was undertaken with the prime objective of having a strong and resilient banking system. The progress that was achieved in the areas of strengthening the regulatory and supervisory norms ushered in greater accountability and market discipline amongst the participants. The Reserve Bank made sustained efforts towards adoption of international benchmarks in a gradual manner, as appropriate to the Indian conditions, in various areas such as prudential norms, risk management, supervision, corporate governance and transparency and disclosures. The reform process helped in taking the management of the banking sector to the level, where the RBI ceased to micro-manage commercial banks and focused largely on the macro goals. The focus on deregulation and liberalisation coupled with enhanced responsibilities for banks made the banking sector resilient and capable of facing several newer global challenges.[1]

Regulatory Agency

GO ONLINE
Access **https://www.rbi.org.in/Scripts/AnnualPublications.aspx?head=Statistical%20Tables%20Relating%20to%20Banks%20in%20India#** to learn about the detailed indicators pertaining to banks in India.

The Reserve Bank of India was conferred the extensive powers for banking supervision as the central bank of the country under the Banking Companies Act of 1949.

The Banking Regulation Act was aimed at protecting depositors' interests, orderly development and conduct of banking operations and fostering of the overall health of the banking system and financial stability.

91 commercial banks, 5 All India Financial Institutions. 4 Credit Information Companies, 56 Regional Rural Banks and 4 Local Area Banks were covered under this Regulation.

Regulatory functions have evolved with the development of the Indian banking system and adoption of prudential norms based on international best practices.

The tools used for regulation are statutory, prudential regulation, other regulatory guidelines and moral persuasion through speeches of the Governor, Deputy Governors and periodic meetings, seminars, etc.

The Focal points for providing framework for regulation include:

- Issuance of 'licences' for opening of banks
- 'Authorisations' for opening of branches by banks in India
- Governing foreign banks entry and expansion and approval of Indian banks to operate overseas
- Policy formulation, review and implementation on Prudential Norms, Basel – II and III frameworks, validation of quantitative models on Credit, Market and Operational Risks, Stress testing
- International Financial Reporting Standards (IFRS), Securitisation, Resolution mechanism, etc.
- Monitoring maintenance of SLR and CRR by banks
- Approving appointments of chief executive officers (private sector and foreign banks) and their compensation packages
- Overseeing the amalgamation, reconstruction and liquidation of banking companies
- Policy issues relating to customer service
- Anti-Money Laundering and Combating Financing of Terrorism and issuing of instructions regarding KYC
- Regulation of financial institutions

---

[1]*Source:* https://www.rbi.org.in/Scripts/PublicationsView.aspx?id=10487, as accessed on 17 March 2017 at 4pm.

Financial Innovation and the Growth of the Shadow Banking System

Although banking institutions are still the most important financial institutions in any economy including that of India, in recent years the traditional banking business of making loans that are funded by deposits has been in decline. Some of this business has been replaced by the **shadow banking system,** in which bank lending has been replaced by lending via the securities market.

To understand how the banking industry has evolved over time, we must first understand the process of financial innovation, which has transformed the entire financial system. Like other industries, the financial industry is in business to earn profits by selling its products. If a soap company perceives that a need exists in the marketplace for a laundry detergent with fabric softener, it develops a product to fit the need. Similarly, to maximize their profits, financial institutions develop new products to satisfy their own needs as well as those of their customers; in other words, innovation—which can be extremely beneficial to the economy— is driven by the desire to get (or stay) rich. This view of the innovation process leads to the following simple analysis: *A change in the financial environment will stimulate a search by financial institutions for innovations that are likely to be profitable.*

Starting in the 1960s, individuals and financial institutions operating in financial markets globally, especially in the United States and other advanced economies, were confronted with drastic changes in the economic environment: Inflation and interest rates climbed sharply and became harder to predict, a situation that changed demand conditions in financial markets. The rapid advance in computer technology changed supply conditions. In addition, financial regulations became more burdensome. Financial institutions found that many of the old ways of doing business were no longer profitable; the financial services and products they had been offering to the public were not selling. Many financial intermediaries found that they were no longer able to acquire funds with their traditional financial instruments, and without these funds they would soon be out of business. To survive in the new economic environment, financial institutions had to research and develop new products and services that would meet customer needs and prove profitable, a process referred to as **financial engineering.** In their case, necessity was the mother of innovation.

Our discussion of why financial innovation occurs suggests that there are three basic types of financial innovation: responses to changes in demand conditions, responses to changes in supply conditions, and avoidance of regulations. These three motivations often interact to produce particular financial innovations. Now that we have a framework for understanding why financial institutions produce innovations, let's look at examples of how financial institutions in their search for profits have produced financial innovations of the three basic types.

Responses to Changes in Demand Conditions: Interest Rate Volatility

The most significant change in the economic environment that altered the demand for financial products in recent years in the U.S. was the dramatic increase in the volatility of interest rates. In the 1950s, the interest rate on three-month U.S. Treasury bills fluctuated between 1.0% and 3.5%; in the 1970s, it fluctuated between 4.0% and 11.5%; in the 1980s, it ranged from 5% to more than 15%. Large fluctuations in interest rates lead to substantial capital gains or losses and greater uncertainty about returns on investments. Recall, that the risk that is related to the uncertainty about interest-rate movements and returns is called *interest-rate risk*, and high volatility of interest rates, such as those in the 1970s and 1980s, leads to a higher level of interest-rate risk.

We would expect the increase in interest-rate risk to increase the demand for financial products and services that could reduce that risk. This change in the economic environment would thus stimulate a search for profitable innovations by financial institutions that meet this new demand and would spur the creation of new financial instruments that help lower interest-rate risk. Two examples of financial innovations that appeared in the 1970s in the U.S. confirm this prediction: the development of adjustable-rate mortgages and financial derivatives.

Adjustable-Rate Mortgages   Like other investors, financial institutions find that lending is more attractive if interest-rate risk is lower. They would not want to make a mortgage loan at a 10% interest rate and two months later find that they could obtain 12% in interest on the same mortgage. To reduce interest-rate risk, in 1975 savings and loans in California began to issue adjustable-rate mortgages, that is, mortgage loans on which the interest rate changes when a market interest rate (usually the Treasury bill rate) changes. Initially, an adjustable-rate mortgage might have a 5% interest rate. In six months, this interest rate might increase or decrease by the amount of the increase or decrease in, say, the six-month Treasury bill rate, and the mortgage payment would change. Because adjustable-rate mortgages allow mortgage-issuing institutions to earn higher interest rates on mortgages when rates rise, profits remain high during these periods.

This attractive feature of adjustable-rate mortgages has encouraged mortgage-issuing institutions to issue adjustable-rate mortgages with lower initial interest rates than on conventional fixed-rate mortgages, making them popular with many households. However, because the mortgage payment on a variable-rate mortgage can increase, many households continue to prefer fixed-rate mortgages. Hence, both types of mortgages are widespread in the United States.

Financial Derivatives   Given the greater demand for the reduction of interest-rate risk, commodity exchanges such as the Chicago Board of Trade recognized that if they could develop a product that would help investors and financial institutions to protect themselves from, or **hedge,** interest-rate risk, then they could make profits by selling this new instrument. **Futures contracts,** in which the seller agrees to provide a certain standardized commodity to the buyer on a specific future date at an agreed-on price, had been around for a long time. Officials at the Chicago Board of Trade realized that if they created futures contracts in financial instruments, which are called *financial derivatives* because their payoffs are linked to (i.e., derived from) previously issued securities, they could be used to hedge risk. Thus, in 1975 financial derivatives were born.

Responses to Changes in Supply Conditions: Information Technology

The most important source of the changes in supply conditions that stimulate financial innovation has been the improvement in computer and telecommunications technology. This technology, called *information technology*, has had two effects.

First, it has lowered the cost of processing financial transactions, making it profitable for financial institutions to create new financial products and services for the public. Second, it has made it easier for investors to acquire information, thereby making it easier for firms to issue securities. The rapid developments in information technology have resulted in many new financial products and services that we examine here.

Bank Credit and Debit Cards   Credit cards have been around since well before World War II. Many individual stores in the U.S. (Sears, Macy's, Goldwater's) institutionalized charge accounts by providing customers with credit cards that allowed them to make purchases at these stores without cash. Nationwide credit cards were not established until after World War II, when Diners Club in the U.S. developed one to be used in restaurants all over the country (and abroad). Similar credit card programs were started by American Express and Carte Blanche, but because of the high cost of operating these programs, cards were issued only to selected persons and businesses that could afford expensive purchases.

A firm issuing credit cards earns income from loans it makes to credit card holders and from payments made by stores on credit card purchases (a percentage of the purchase price, say, 5%). A credit card program's costs arise from loan defaults, stolen cards, and the expense involved in processing credit card transactions.

Seeing the success of Diners Club, American Express, and Carte Blanche, bankers wanted to share in the profitable credit card business. Several commercial banks attempted to expand the credit card business to a wider market in the 1950s, but the cost per transaction of running these programs was so high that their early attempts failed.

In the late 1960s, improved computer technology, which lowered the transaction costs for providing credit card services, made it more likely that bank credit card programs would be profitable. The banks tried to enter this business again, and this time their efforts led to the creation of two successful bank credit card programs: BankAmericard (originally started by the Bank of America but now an independent organization called Visa) and MasterCharge (now MasterCard, run by the Interbank Card Association). These programs have become phenomenally successful; around 500 million of their cards are in use. Indeed, bank credit cards have been so profitable that nonfinancial institutions such as Sears (which launched the Discover card), General Motors, and AT&T have also entered the credit card business. Consumers have benefited because credit cards are more widely accepted than checks to pay for purchases (particularly abroad), and they allow consumers to take out loans more easily.

The success of bank credit cards led these institutions to come up with a new financial innovation, *debit cards*. Debit cards often look just like credit cards and can be used to make purchases in an identical fashion. However, in contrast to credit cards, which extend the purchaser a loan that does not have to be paid off immediately, a debit card purchase is immediately deducted from the card holder's bank account. Debit cards depend even more on low costs of processing transactions because their profits are generated entirely from the fees paid by merchants on debit card purchases at their stores. Debit cards have grown extremely popular in recent years.

Electronic Banking   The wonders of modern computer technology have also enabled banks to lower the cost of bank transactions by having the customer interact with an electronic banking (e-banking) facility rather than with a human being. One important form of an e-banking facility is the **automated teller machine (ATM),** an electronic machine that allows customers to get cash, make deposits, transfer

GO ONLINE

Access **https://www.rbi.org. in/scripts/ATMView.aspx** to see the bank-wise ATM and card statistics in July 2016.

funds from one account to another, and check balances. The ATM has the advantage that it does not have to be paid overtime and never sleeps, thus being available for use 24 hours a day. Not only does this result in cheaper transactions for the bank, but it also provides more convenience for the customer. Because of their low cost, ATMs can be put at locations other than a bank or its branches, further increasing customer convenience. The low cost of ATMs has meant that they have sprung up everywhere and now number more than 200,000 in India alone in 2016. In July 2016, the number of on-site and off-site ATMs in India were 201,861. Furthermore, it is now as easy to get foreign currency from an ATM when you are traveling in Europe as it is to get cash from your local bank.

With the drop in the cost of telecommunications, banks have developed another financial innovation, *home banking*. It is now cost-effective for banks to set up an electronic banking facility in which the bank's customer is linked up with the bank's computer to carry out transactions by using either a telephone or a personal computer. Now the bank's customers can conduct many of their bank transactions without ever leaving the comfort of home. The advantage for the customer is the convenience of home banking, while banks find that the cost of transactions is substantially less than having the customer come to the bank. The success of ATMs and home banking has led to another innovation, the **automated banking machine (ABM),** which combines in one location an ATM, an Internet connection to the bank's Web site, and a telephone link to customer service.

With the decline in the price of personal computers and their increasing presence in the home, we have seen a further innovation in the home banking area, the appearance of a new type of banking institution, the **virtual bank,** a bank that has no physical location but rather exists only in cyberspace. In 1995 Security First Network Bank, based in Atlanta but now owned by Royal Bank of Canada, became the first virtual bank, offering an array of banking services on the Internet—accepting checking account and savings deposits, selling certificates of deposits, issuing ATM cards, providing bill-paying facilities, and so on. The virtual bank thus takes home banking one step further, enabling the customer to have a full set of banking services at home 24 hours a day. In 1996, Bank of America and Wells Fargo, entered the virtual banking market, to be followed by many others, with Bank of America now being the largest Internet bank in the United States. Will virtual banking be the predominant form of banking in the future (see the E-Finance box, "Will 'Clicks' Dominate 'Bricks' in the Banking Industry?").

Electronic Payment The development of inexpensive computers and the spread of the Internet now make it very cheap for banks to allow their customers to make bill payments electronically. Whereas in the past you had to pay your bills by mailing a check, now banks provide a Web site in which you just log on, make a few clicks, and your payment is transmitted electronically. You not only save the cost of the stamp, but paying bills now becomes (almost) a pleasure, requiring little effort. Electronic payment systems provided by banks now even allow you to avoid the step of having to log on to pay the bill. Instead, recurring bills can be automatically deducted from your bank account without your having to do a thing. Providing these services increases profitability for banks in two ways. First, payment of a bill electronically means that banks don't need people to process what would have otherwise been a paper transaction. Second, the extra convenience for you, the customer, means that you are more likely to open an account with the bank. Electronic payment is thus becoming far more common.

> E-FINANCE

Will "Clicks" Dominate "Bricks" in the Banking Industry?

With the advent of virtual banks ("clicks") and the convenience they provide, a key question is whether they will become the primary form in which banks do their business, eliminating the need for physical bank branches ("bricks") as the main delivery mechanism for banking services. Indeed, will stand-alone Internet banks be the wave of the future?

The answer seems to be no. Internet-only banks such as Wingspan (owned by Bank One), First-e (Dublin-based), and Egg (a British Internet-only bank owned by Prudential) have had disappointing revenue growth and profits. The result is that pure online banking has not been the success that proponents had hoped for. Why has Internet banking been a disappointment?

Internet banking has several strikes against it. First, bank depositors want to know that their savings are secure, and so are reluctant to put their money into new institutions without a long track record. Second, customers worry about the security of their online

transactions and whether their transactions will truly be kept private. Traditional banks are viewed as being more secure and trustworthy in terms of releasing private information. Third, customers may prefer services provided by physical branches. For example, banking customers prefer purchasing long-term savings products face-to-face. Fourth, Internet banking has run into technical problems—server crashes, slow connections over phone lines, mistakes in conducting transactions—that will probably diminish over time as technology improves.

The wave of the future thus does not appear to be pure Internet banks. Instead it looks as though "clicks and bricks" will be the predominant form of banking, in which online banking is used to complement the services provided by traditional banks. Nonetheless, the delivery of banking services is undergoing massive changes, with more and more banking services delivered over the Internet and the number of physical bank branches likely to decline in the future.

E-Money Electronic payments technology can not only substitute for checks but can, in the form of **electronic money** (or **e-money**), money that exists only in electronic form, substitute for cash as well. The first form of e-money is a stored-value card. The simplest form of a stored-value card is purchased for a preset rupee amount that the consumer spends down. The more sophisticated stored-value card is known as a **smart card.** It contains its own computer chip so that it can be loaded with digital cash from the owner's bank account whenever needed. Smart cards can be loaded either from ATM machines, personal computers with a smart card reader, or from specially equipped telephones.

A second form of electronic money is often referred to as **e-cash,** and it is used on the Internet to purchase goods or services. A consumer gets e-cash by setting up an account with a bank that has links to the Internet and then has the e-cash transferred to her PC. When she wants to buy something with e-cash, she surfs to a store on the Web, clicks the "buy" option for a particular item, whereupon the e-cash is automatically transferred from her computer to the merchant's computer. The merchant can then have the funds transferred from the consumer's bank account to his before the goods are shipped.

Given the convenience of e-money, you might think that we would move quickly to the cashless society in which all payments were made electronically. However, this hasn't happened, as discussed in the E-Finance box "Are We Headed for a Cashless Society?"

Junk Bonds Before the advent of computers and advanced telecommunications, it was difficult to acquire information about the financial situation of firms that might want to sell securities. Because of the difficulty in screening out bad from good credit risks, the only firms that were able to sell bonds were very well-established corporations that had high credit ratings.[2] Before the 1980s, then, only corporations that could issue bonds with ratings of Baa or above could raise funds by selling newly issued bonds. Some firms that had fallen on bad times, known as *fallen angels*, had previously issued long-term corporate bonds which had ratings that had now fallen below Baa, bonds that were pejoratively dubbed "junk bonds."

With the improvement in information technology in the 1970s, it became easier for investors to acquire financial information about corporations, making it easier to screen out bad from good credit risks. With easier screening, investors were more willing to buy long-term debt securities from less well-known corporations with lower credit ratings. With this change in supply conditions, we would expect that some smart individual would pioneer the concept of selling new public issues of junk bonds, not for fallen angels but for companies that had not yet achieved investment-grade status. This is exactly what Michael Milken of Drexel Burnham Lambert, an investment banking firm, started to do in 1977. Junk bonds became an important factor in the corporate bond market, with the amount outstandingly exceeding $200 billion by the late 1980s. Although there was a sharp slowdown in activity in the junk bond market after Milken was indicted for securities law violations in 1989, it heated up again in the 1990s and 2000s.

> E-FINANCE

Are We Headed for a Cashless Society?

Predictions of a cashless society have been around for decades, but they have not come to fruition. For example, *Business Week* predicted in 1975 that electronic means of payment "would soon revolutionize the very concept of money itself," only to reverse itself several years later. Pilot projects in recent years with smart cards to convert consumers to the use of e-money have not been a success. Mondex, one of the widely touted, early stored-value cards that was launched in Great Britain in 1995, is only used on a few British university campuses. In Germany and Belgium, millions of people carry bank cards with computer chips embedded in them that enable them to make use of e-money, but very few use them. Why has the movement to a cashless society been so slow in coming?

Although e-money might be more convenient and may be more efficient than a payments system based on paper, several factors work against the disappearance of the paper system. First, it is very expensive to set up the computer, card reader, and telecommunications networks necessary to make electronic money the dominant form of payment. Second, electronic means of payment raise security and privacy concerns. We often hear media reports that an unauthorized hacker has been able to access a computer database and to alter information stored there. Because this is not an uncommon occurrence, unscrupulous persons might be able to access bank accounts in electronic payments systems and steal funds by moving them from someone else's accounts into their own. The prevention of this type of fraud is no easy task, and a whole new field of computer science has developed to cope with security issues. A further concern is that the use of electronic means of payment leaves an electronic trail that contains a large amount of personal data on buying habits. There are worries that government, employers, and marketers might be able to access these data, thereby encroaching on our privacy.

The conclusion from this discussion is that although the use of e-money will surely increase in the future, to paraphrase Mark Twain, "The reports of cash's death are greatly exaggerated."

---

[2]The discussion of adverse selection problems in Chapter 7 provides a more detailed analysis of why only well-established firms with high credit ratings were able to sell securities.

Commercial Paper Market   *Commercial paper* is a short-term debt security issued by large banks and corporations. These are unsecured money market intruments issued in the form of a promissory note. In India, CPs were introduced in 1990 with a view to enabling highly rated corporate borrowers to diversify their sources of short-term borrowings and to provide an additional instrument to investors. Subsequently, primary dealers and all-India financial institutions were also permitted to issue CP to enable them to meet their short-term funding requirements for their operations.

A corporate would be eligible to issue CP provided:

- The tangible net worth of the company, as per the latest audited balance sheet, is not less than ₹4 crore.
- The company has been sanctioned a working capital limit by bank(s) or all-India financial institution(s).
- The borrowal account of the company is classified as a standard asset by the financing bank(s)or institution(s).

For issuance of CP, all eligible participants have to obtain the credit rating either from Credit Rating Information Services of India Ltd. (CRISIL) or the Investment Information and Credit Rating Agency of India Ltd. (ICRA) or the Credit Analysis and Research Ltd. (CARE) or the FITCH Ratings India Pvt. Ltd. or such other credit rating agency (CRA) as may be specified by the Reserve Bank of India from time to time for the purpose.

The minimum credit rating has to be be A-2 [as per rating symbol and definition prescribed by SEBI].

The issuers have to ensure at the time of issuance of CP that the rating so obtained is current and has not fallen due for review.

CP can be issued for maturities between a minimum of seven days and a maximum of up to one year from the date of issue. However, the maturity date of the CP should not go beyond the date up to which the credit rating of the issuer is valid. The aggregate amount of CP from an issuer shall be within the limit as approved by its Board of Directors or the quantum indicated by the Credit Rating Agency for the specified rating, whichever is lower.

As regards to FIs, they can issue CP within the overall umbrella limit prescribed in the Master Circular on Resource Raising Norms for FIs, issued by Department of Banking Operations and Development (DBOD, RBI) and updated from time-to-time. CP can be issued in denominations of ₹5 lakh or multiples thereof.

Individuals, banking companies, other corporate bodies (registered or incorporated in India) and unincorporated bodies, NRIs and FIIs etc. can invest in CPs. However, investment by FIIs would be within the limits set for them by SEBI from time-to-time.[3]

Securitization   An important example of a financial innovation arising from improvements in both transaction and information technology is securitization, one of the most important financial innovations in the past two decades, and one which played an especially prominent role in the development of the subprime mortgage market in the mid-2000s. **Securitization** is the process of transforming

---

[3]*Source:* https://rbi.org.in/scripts/FAQView.aspx?Id=25, as accessed on 17 March 2017 at 4pm.

otherwise illiquid financial assets (such as residential mortgages, auto loans, and credit card receivables), which have typically been the bread and butter of banking institutions, into marketable capital market securities. Improvements in the ability to acquire information have made it easier to sell marketable capital market securities. In addition, with low transaction costs because of improvements in computer technology, financial institutions find that they can cheaply bundle together a portfolio of loans (such as mortgages) with varying small denominations, collect the interest and principal payments on the mortgages in the bundle, and then "pass them through" (pay them out) to third parties. By dividing the portfolio of loans into standardized amounts, the financial institution can then sell the claims to these interest and principal payments to third parties as securities. The standardized amounts of these securitized loans makes them liquid securities, and the fact that they are made up of a bundle of loans helps diversify risk, making them desirable. The financial institution selling the securitized loans makes a profit by servicing the loans (collecting the interest and principal payments and paying them out) and charging a fee to the third party for this service.

Avoidance of Existing Regulations

The process of financial innovation we have discussed so far is much like innovation in other areas of the economy: It occurs in response to changes in demand and supply conditions. However, because the financial industry is more heavily regulated than other industries, government regulation is a much greater spur to innovation in this industry. Government regulation leads to financial innovation by creating incentives for firms to skirt regulations that restrict their ability to earn profits. Edward Kane, an economist at Boston College, describes this process of avoiding regulations as "loophole mining." The economic analysis of innovation suggests that when the economic environment changes such that regulatory constraints are so burdensome that large profits can be made by avoiding them, loophole mining and innovation are more likely to occur.

CASE

Loophole Mining and Financial Innovations

The U.S. case can be studied as an important case where financial innovations were prompted by the desire to avoid existing regulations. Because banking is one of the most heavily regulated industries in America, loophole mining is especially likely to occur. The rise in inflation and interest rates in the U.S. from the late 1960s to 1980 made the regulatory constraints imposed on this industry even more burdensome, leading to financial innovation.

Two sets of regulations have seriously restricted the ability of banks to make profits: reserve requirements that force banks to keep a certain fraction of their deposits as reserves (vault cash and deposits in the Federal Reserve System) and restrictions on the interest rates that can be paid on deposits. For the following reasons, these regulations have been major forces behind financial innovation.

1. *Reserve requirements.* The key to understanding why reserve requirements led to financial innovation is to recognize that they act, in effect, as a tax on deposits. Because up until 2008 the Fed did not pay interest on reserves, the

opportunity cost of holding them was the interest that a bank could otherwise earn by lending the reserves out. For each dollar of deposits, reserve requirements therefore imposed a cost on the bank equal to the interest rate, i, that could be earned if the reserves could be lent out times the fraction of deposits required as reserves, r. The cost of $i \times r$ imposed on the bank is just like a tax on bank deposits of $i \times r$ per dollar of deposits.

It is a great tradition to avoid taxes if possible, and banks also play this game. Just as taxpayers look for loopholes to lower their tax bills, banks seek to increase their profits by mining loopholes and by producing financial innovations that allow them to escape the tax on deposits imposed by reserve requirements.

2. *Restrictions on interest paid on deposits.* Until 1980, legislation prohibited banks in most states from paying interest on checking account deposits, and through Regulation Q, the Fed set maximum limits on the interest rate that could be paid on time deposits. To this day, banks are not allowed to pay interest on corporate checking accounts. The desire to avoid these **deposit rate ceilings** also led to financial innovations.

If market interest rates rose above the maximum rates that banks paid on time deposits under Regulation Q, depositors withdrew funds from banks to put them into higher-yielding securities. This loss of deposits from the banking system restricted the amount of funds that banks could lend (called **disintermediation**) and thus limited bank profits. Banks had an incentive to get around deposit rate ceilings because by so doing, they could acquire more funds to make loans and earn higher profits.

We can now look at how the desire to avoid restrictions on interest payments and the tax effect of reserve requirements led to two important financial innovations.

Money Market Mutual Funds   Money market mutual funds issue shares that are redeemable at a fixed price (usually $1) by writing checks. For example, if you buy 5,000 shares for $5,000, the money market fund uses these funds to invest in short-term money market securities (Treasury bills, certificates of deposit, commercial paper) that provide you with interest payments. In addition, you are able to write checks up to the $5,000 held as shares in the money market fund. Although money market fund shares effectively function as checking account deposits that earn interest, they are not legally deposits and so are not subject to reserve requirements or prohibitions on interest payments. For this reason, they can pay higher interest rates than deposits at banks.

The first money market mutual fund was created by two Wall Street mavericks, Bruce Bent and Henry Brown, in 1970. However, the low market interest rates from 1970 to 1977 (which were just slightly above Regulation Q ceilings of 5.25% to 5.5%) kept them from being particularly advantageous relative to bank deposits. In early 1978 the situation changed rapidly as inflation rose and market interest rates began to climb over 10%, well above the 5.5% maximum interest rates payable on savings accounts and time deposits under Regulation Q. In 1977 money market mutual funds had assets of less than $4 billion; in 1978 their assets climbed to close to $10 billion; in 1979, to more than $40 billion; and in 1982, to $230 billion. Currently, their assets are around $2.6 trillion. To say the least, money market mutual funds have been a successful financial innovation, which is exactly what we would have predicted to occur in the late 1970s and early 1980s when interest rates soared beyond Regulation Q ceilings.

In a supreme irony, risky investments by a money market mutual fund founded by Bruce Bent almost brought down the money market mutual fund industry during the global financial crisis in 2008 (see the Mini-Case box, "Bruce Bent and the Money Market Mutual Fund Panic of 2008").

Sweep Accounts   Another innovation that enables banks to avoid the "tax" from reserve requirements is the **sweep account.** In this arrangement, any balances above a certain amount in a corporation's checking account at the end of a business day are "swept out" of the account and invested in overnight securities that pay interest. Because the "swept out" funds are no longer classified as checkable deposits, they are not subject to reserve requirements and thus are not "taxed." They also have the advantage that they allow banks in effect to pay interest on these checking accounts, which otherwise is not allowed under existing regulations. Because sweep accounts have become so popular, they have lowered the amount of required reserves to the degree that most banking institutions do not find reserve requirements binding: In other words, they voluntarily hold more reserves than they are required to.

The financial innovations of sweep accounts and money market mutual funds are particularly interesting because they were stimulated not only by the desire to avoid a costly regulation but also by a change in supply conditions—in this case, information technology. Without low-cost computers to inexpensively process the additional transactions required by these accounts, these innovations would not have been profitable and therefore would not have been developed. Technological factors often combine with other incentives, such as the desire to get around a regulation, to produce innovation.

MINI-CASE

Bruce Bent and the Money Market Mutual Fund Panic of 2008

Bruce Bent, one of the originators of money market mutual funds, almost brought down the industry during the global financial crisis in the fall of 2008. Mr. Bent told his shareholders in a letter written in July 2008 that the fund was managed on a basis of "unwavering discipline focused on protecting your principal." He also wrote the Securities and Exchange Commission in September 2007, "When I first created the money market fund back in 1970, it was designed with the tenets of safety and liquidity." He added that these principles had "fallen by the wayside as portfolio managers chased the highest yield and compromised the integrity of the money fund." Alas, Bent did not follow his own advice, and his fund, the Reserve Primary Fund, bought risky assets so that its yield was higher than the industry average.

When Lehman Brothers went into bankruptcy on September 15, 2008, the Reserve Primary Fund, with assets over $60 billion, was caught holding the bag on $785 million of Lehman's debt, which then had to be marked down to zero. The resulting losses meant that on September 16, Bent's fund could no longer afford to redeem its shares at the par value of $1, a situation known as "breaking the buck." Bent's shareholders began to pull their money out of the fund, causing it to lose 90% of its assets.

The fear that this could happen to other money market mutual funds led to a classic panic in which shareholders began to withdraw their funds at an alarming rate. The whole money market mutual fund industry looked as though it could come crashing down. To prevent this, the Federal Reserve and the U.S. Treasury rode to the rescue on September 19. The Fed set up a facility, to make loans to purchase commercial paper from money market mutual funds so they could meet the demands for redemptions from their investors. The Treasury then put in a temporary guarantee for all money market mutual fund redemptions and the panic subsided.

THE PRACTICING MANAGER

Profiting from a New Financial Product: A Case Study of Treasury Strips

We have seen that the advent of high-speed computers, which lowered the cost of processing financial transactions, led to such financial innovations as bank credit and debit cards. Because there is money to be made from financial innovation, it is important for managers of financial institutions to understand the thinking that goes into producing new, highly profitable financial products that take advantage of computer technology. To illustrate how financial institution managers can figure out ways to increase profits through financial innovation, we look at Treasury strips, a financial instrument first developed in 1982 by Salomon Brothers and Merrill Lynch. (Indeed, this innovation was so successful that the U.S. Treasury copied it when they issued STRIPS in 1985).

One problem for investors in long-term coupon bonds, even when investors have a long holding period, is that there is some uncertainty in their returns arising from what is called *reinvestment risk*. Even if an investor holding a long-term coupon bond has a holding period of 10 years, the return on the bond is not certain. The problem is that coupon payments are made before the bond matures in 10 years, and these coupon payments must be reinvested. Because the interest rates at which the coupon payments will be reinvested fluctuate, the eventual return on the bond fluctuates as well. In contrast, long-term zero-coupon bonds have no reinvestment risk because they make no cash payments before the bond matures. The return on a zero-coupon bond if it is held to maturity is known at the time of purchase. The absence of reinvestment risk is an attractive feature of zero-coupon bonds, and as a result, investors are willing to accept a slightly lower interest rate on them than on coupon bonds, which do bear some reinvestment risk.

The fact that zero-coupon bonds have lower interest rates, along with the ability to use computers to create so-called hybrid securities, which are securities derived from other underlying securities, gave employees of Salomon Brothers and Merrill Lynch a brilliant idea for making profits. They could use computers to separate ("strip") a long-term Treasury coupon bond into a set of zero-coupon bonds. For example, a $1 million 10-year Treasury bond might be stripped into ten $100,000 zero-coupon bonds, which, naturally enough, are called *Treasury strips*. The lower interest rates on the more desirable Treasury strip zero-coupon bonds would mean that the value of these bonds would exceed the price of the underlying long-term Treasury bond, allowing Salomon Brothers and Merrill Lynch to make a profit by purchasing the long-term Treasury bond, separating it into Treasury strips, and selling them off as zero-coupon bonds.

To see in more detail how their thinking worked, let's look more closely at a $1 million 10-year Treasury bond with a coupon rate of 10% whose yield to maturity is also 10%, so it is selling at par. The cash payments for this bond are listed in the second column of Table 18.1. To make things simple, let's assume that the yield curve is absolutely flat so that the interest rate used to discount all the future cash payments is the same. Because zero-coupon bonds, which have no reinvestment risk, are more desirable than the 10-year Treasury coupon bond, the interest rate on the zero-coupon bonds is 9.75%, a little lower than the 10% interest rate on the coupon bond.

How would Fran, a smart and sophisticated financial institution manager, figure out if she could make a profit from creating and selling the Treasury strips? Her first step is to figure out what the zero-coupon Treasury strips would sell for. She would find this easy to do if she had read the chapter in this text on "What Do Interest Rates Mean": she would use the present value equation from that chapter

$$PV = \frac{CF}{(1 + i)^n} \tag{1}$$

and she would figure out that each of the Treasury strip zero-coupon bonds would sell for its present discounted value:

$$\frac{\text{Cash payment in year } n}{(1 + 0.09752)^n}$$

The results of this calculation for each year are listed in column (4) of Table 18.1. When Fran adds up the values of the collection of the Treasury strip zero-coupon bonds, she gets a figure of $1,015,528, which is greater than the $1 million purchase price of the Treasury bond. As long as it costs less than $15,528 to collect the payments from the Treasury and then pass them through to the owners of the zero-coupon strips, which is likely to be the case since computer technology makes the cost of conducting these financial transactions low, the zero-coupon strips will be profitable for her financial institution. Fran would thus recommend that her firm go ahead and market the new financial product. Because the financial institution can now generate much higher profits by selling substantial numbers of Treasury strips, it would amply reward Fran with a spanking new red BMW and a $100,000 bonus!

TABLE 18.1 Market Value of Treasury Strip Zero-Coupon Bonds Derived from a $1 Million 10-Year Treasury Bond with a 10% Coupon Rate and Selling at Par

(1) Year	(2) Cash Payment ($)	(3) Interest Rate on Zero-Coupon Bond (%)	(4) Present Discounted Value of Zero-Coupon Bond ($)
1	100,000	9.75	91,116
2	100,000	9.75	83,022
3	100,000	9.75	75,646
4	100,000	9.75	68,926
5	100,000	9.75	62,802
6	100,000	9.75	57,223
7	100,000	9.75	52,140
8	100,000	9.75	47,508
9	100,000	9.75	43,287
10	100,000	9.75	39,442
10	1,000,000	9.75	394,416
Total			$1,015,528

Shadow Banking in India

GO ONLINE

Access **http://www.bis.org/review/r130204g.pdf** to understand the issues and challenges associated with shadow banking.

The term "shadow banking system" was first used in 2007, and gained popularity during the global financial crisis, as it highlighted the bank-like functions performed by entities outside the regular banking system. The more comprehensive definition, as adopted by the Financial Stability Board (FSB), i.e., "credit intermediation involving entities and activities (fully or partially) outside the regular banking system" has been globally accepted. This definition has two important components. First, non bank financial entities or entities outside the banking system that engage in the "bank like" activities of maturity transformation, undertaking credit risk transfer and using direct or indirect financial leverage. Second, activities such as securitization, securities lending and repo transactions that act as important sources of funding for non-bank entities. Thus, shadow banks comprise entities which conduct financial intermediation directly, such as finance companies or NBFCs, and entities which provide finance to such entities, such as mutual funds. Globally, shadow banking entities could be covered under the broad heads of (i) money market funds, (ii) credit investment funds, hedge funds, etc, (iii) finance companies accepting deposits or deposit like funding, (iv) securities brokers dependent on wholesale funding, (v) credit insurers, financial guarantee providers and (vi) securitisation vehicles. Such non-bank intermediation, when appropriately conducted, provides a valuable alternative to bank funding and supports real economic activity. But experience from the crisis demonstrates the capacity of some non-bank entities and transactions to operate on a significantly large scale, in ways that create bank-like risks to financial stability (longer-term credit extension based on short-term funding and leverage). Such risk creation may take place at an entity level but it can also form part of a complex chain of transactions, in which leverage and maturity transformation occurs in stages, creating multiple forms of feedback into the regulated banking system. Like banks, a leveraged and maturity-transforming shadow banking system can also be vulnerable to "runs" and generate contagion, thereby amplifying systemic risk. Shadow banking can also heighten procyclicality by accelerating credit supply and asset price increases during upswings and exacerbating fall in asset prices during downswings.

Traditionally, regulation of banks has assumed greater importance than that of their non-banking counterparts. However, when non-bank financial entities, which are subject to no regulation or light touch regulation, undertake bank-like functions, large risks are created which could potentially be destabilizing for the entire system. The global financial crisis demonstrated many ways in which shadow banking can have an impact on the global financial system, both directly and through its interconnectedness with the regular banking system, prompting the move to overhaul the regulation of shadow banking system.

Notwithstanding the data constraints in actual evaluation of its size, the shadow banking sector in India is still small in size compared to its counterparts in advanced economies. In 2011, assets of Other Financial Institutions in India were $375 billion vis-a-vis bank assets of $1,518 billion and GDP of $1,766 billion. The assets of the shadow banking system accounted for 21% of GDP as compared to bank assets which were 86% of GDP. Apart from the fact that the sector is not significant in terms of size, the activities carried out by these entities are also limited.[4]

---

[4]*Source:* http://www.bis.org/review/r130204g.pdf, as accessed on 17 March 2017 at 4pm.

CASE

India's Non Banking Financial Companies (NBFC) Sector

India has financial institutions which are not banks but which accept deposits and extend credit like banks. These are called Non-Banking Financial Companies (NBFCs) in India. NBFCs in India, not just includes the finance companies that the general public is largely familiar with; the term also entails wider group of companies that are engaged in investment business, insurance, chit fund, nidhi, merchant banking, stock broking, alternative investments, etc., as their principal business. However, not all these are under the regulatory purview of the RBI.

- There were 12,029 NBFCs in India as on March 31, 2014, of which deposit taking NBFCs were 241 and non-deposit taking NBFCs with asset size of ₹100 crore and above were 465, non-deposit taking NBFCs with asset size between ₹50 crore and ₹100 crore were 314 and those with asset size less than ₹50 crore were 11,009. The sector today has a total asset size of just around 14% of that of scheduled commercial banks (other than RRBs).

- Being financial intermediaries, NBFCs are engaged in the activity of bringing the saving and the investing community together. In this role they are perceived to be playing a complimentary role to banks rather than competitors, as majority population in the country does not yet have access to mainstream financial products and services including a bank account. NBFCs especially NBFC-MFIs (Micro Finance Institutions) and asset finance companies thus have a complimentary role in the financial inclusion agenda of the country.

- Further, some of the big NBFCs, namely, infrastructure finance companies or those in factoring business, give fillip to the growth and development of the important sectors, like infrastructure. NBFCs have carved niche business areas for themselves within the financial sector space and are popular for providing customised products like second hand vehicle financing, mostly at the doorstep of the customer. In short, NBFCs bring the much needed diversity to the financial sector thereby diversifying the risks, increasing liquidity in the markets thereby promoting financial stability and bringing efficiency to the financial sector.

- In the wake of failure of several banks in the late 1950s and early 1960s in India, large number of ordinary depositors lost their money. At this time, the Reserve Bank noted that there were deposit taking activities undertaken by non-banking companies. Though they were not systemically as important as the banks, the RBI initiated regulating them, as they had the potential to cause pain to their depositors. These institutions have thus been under the regulatory oversight of the Reserve Bank of India since 1963. Since then regulation has generally kept pace with the dynamism displayed by the sector. Later in 1996, in the wake of the failure of a big NBFC, the RBI tightened the regulatory structure over the NBFCs, with rigorous registration requirements, enhanced reporting and supervision. The RBI also decided that no additional NBFC will be permitted to raise deposits from the public. Further, in 1999 capital requirement for fresh registration was enhanced from ₹25 lakh to ₹200 lakh. Later when the NBFCs sourced their funding heavily from the banking system, it raised systemic risk issues. At the same time, their growing size and interconnectedness also raised concerns on financial stability. Sensing this, the Reserve Bank brought asset side prudential regulations onto the NBFCs. The RBI's endeavour has been to streamline NBFC regulation, address the risks posed by them to financial stability, address depositors' and customers' interests, address regulatory arbitrage and help the sector grow in a healthy and efficient manner.

- Some of the regulatory measures include identifying systemically important non-deposit taking NBFCs as those with asset size of ₹100 crore and above in the year 2006 and bringing them under stricter prudential norms (CRAR and exposure norms), issuing guidelines on fair practices code, aligning the guidelines on restructuring and securitisation with that of banks, permitting systemically important non-deposit taking non-banking financial companies (NBFCs-ND-SI) to issue perpetual debt instruments etc. In November 2014, the entire regulatory framework was reviewed with a view to transitioning, over time, to an activity based regulation of NBFCs. As a first step in this direction, certain changes to the regulatory framework are sought to be made to (i) address risks wherever they existed, (ii) address regulatory gaps and arbitrage arising from differential regulations, both within the sector as well as vis-a-vis other financial institutions, (iii) harmonise and simplify regulations to facilitate a smoother compliance culture among NBFCs, and (iv) strengthen governance standards. Threshold for systemic significance has been redefined as ₹500 crore from the extant ₹100 crore in assets. Systemically important NBFCs along with deposit taking NBFCs would be subject to inter alia, higher minimum Tier 1 capital, higher corporate governance standards and also stricter asset classification norms.

- The challenge for the NBFC sector is to grow in a prudential manner while not stopping altogether on financial innovations. The key lies in having in place adequate risk management systems and procedures before entering into risky areas. It is the constant endeavour of the RBI to enable prudential growth of the sector, keeping in view the multiple objectives of financial stability, consumer and depositor protection, and need for more players in the financial market, addressing regulatory arbitrage concerns while not forgetting the uniqueness of the NBFC sector.

Source: https://www.rbi.org.in/scripts/FS_Overview.aspx?fn=14.

Structure of the Commercial Banking and Branch Authorization in India

GO ONLINE
Access https://www.rbi.org.in/commonman/English/scripts/banksinindia.aspx#FB to learn about banks in India.

There are 97 Scheduled Commercial Banks in India. Of these, 19 are nationalised banks, 25 private Indian banks, 46 private foreign banks, one other public sector bank (IDBI) and State Bank of India and its five subsidiaries. The banking sector in the country, even in 2015, remained predominantly in the public sector, with the Public Sector Banks (PSBs) accounting for 72.1% of total banking sector assets, notwithstanding a gradual decline in their share in recent years.

GO ONLINE

Access **https://rbidocs.rbi.org.in/rdocs/Publications/PDFs/APB30091213F.pdf** to understand the profile of banks in India.

The Government of India continued to have more than the stipulated 51% shareholding in all the public sector banks in 2015, despite decline in the stake in some of them in recent years. The maximum foreign shareholding in the case of PSBs was around 17% as at end-March 2015 (20% is the regulatory maximum prescribed by the RBI). In case of the private sector banks, the maximum non-resident shareholding was 73.4% (74% is regulatory maximum prescribed by the RBI).

However, despite substantive share in total assets, the PSBs accounted for only 42.1% in total profits during 2014–2015, with the Private Sector Banks (PVBs) surpassing the PSBs in the share of total banking sector profits.

The opening of new branches and shifting of existing branches of banks is governed by the provisions of Section 23 of the Banking Regulation Act, 1949. In terms of these provisions, banks cannot, without the prior approval of the RBI, open a new place of business in India or abroad or change, otherwise than within the same city, town or village, the location of the existing place of business. Section 23 (2) of the Banking Regulation Act lays down that before granting any permission under this section, the RBI may require to be satisfied, by an inspection under Section 35 or otherwise, as to the financial condition and history of the banking company, the general character of its management, the adequacy of its capital structure and earning prospects and that public interest will be served by the opening or, as the case may be, change of location of the existing place of business. Commercial banks (other than RRBs) including Local Area Banks should approach the Department of Banking Operations & Development, Reserve Bank of India, Central Office (DBOD, CO) in this regard.

The policy for authorisation of branches in India is summarized in the following paragraphs.

Definition   For the purpose of branch authorisation policy, a "branch" would include a full-fledged branch, including a specialised branch, a satellite or mobile office, an extension counter, an off site ATM (Automated Teller Machine), administrative office, controlling office, service branch (back office or processing centre) and credit card centre. A call centre will not be treated as a branch. A call centre is one, where only accounts or product information is provided to the customer through tele-banking facility and no banking transaction is undertaken through such centres. Also, no direct interface with clients/customers is permitted at call centres.

Branch Authorization Policy   With the objective of liberalising and rationalising authorisation of branches, a framework for a branch authorisation policy, which would be consistent with the medium term corporate strategy of banks and public interest, has been put in place. In addition to the requirement relating to the financial condition and history of the banking company, the general character of its management, and the adequacy of its capital structure and earning prospects, the branch authorisation policy framework would possess the following elements:

As regards the public interest dimensions of the policy framework, the following aspects would be kept in view while processing branch authorisation requests:

- The RBI, while considering applications for opening branches, will give weightage to the nature and scope of banking facilities provided by banks to common persons, particularly in underbanked areas (districts), actual credit flow to the priority sector, pricing of products and overall efforts for promoting financial inclusion, including introduction of appropriate new products and the enhanced use of technology for delivery of banking services.

- Such an assessment will include the policy of the bank on minimum balance requirements and whether depositors have access to minimum banking or "no frills" banking services, commitment to basic banking activity, viz. acceptance of deposits and provision of credit and quality of customer service as evidenced by the number of complaints received and the redressal mechanism in place in the bank for the purpose.
- The need to induce enhanced competition in the banking sector at various locations.
- The RBI would also seek regulatory comfort in matters relating to branch authorization. Thus, it would look at whether the bank's activities are in compliance with the spirit (and not just in letter) and the underlying principles of the regulations.; the activities of the banking group and the nature of relationship of the bank with its subsidiaries, affiliates and associates.; and finally, at the quality of corporate governance, proper risk management systems and internal control mechanisms.

As regards to the procedural aspects, the existing system of granting authorisations for opening individual branches from time to time has been replaced by a system of giving aggregated approvals, on an annual basis. The medium term framework and the specific proposals would cover the opening, closing, shifting, merger and conversion of all categories of branches.

Domestic scheduled commercial banks (other than RRBs) are permitted to open branches, administrative offices, central processing centres (CPCs) and service branches in tier 2 to tier 6 centres (with population up to 99,999 as per Census 2001) and in rural, semi-urban and urban centres in North Eastern States and Sikkim, and to open mobile branches in tier 3 to tier 6 centres (with population up to 49,999 as per Census 2001) and in rural, semi-urban and urban centres in North Eastern States and Sikkim without permission from RBI in each case, subject to reporting.

With a view to further increasing operational flexibility of banks, domestic scheduled commercial banks (other than RRBs) are permitted to open offices exclusively performing administrative and controlling functions (Regional Offices/Zonal Offices) in Tier 1 Centres without the need to obtain prior permission in each case, subject to reporting.

Opening of branches/central processing centres (CPCs)/service branches by domestic scheduled commercial banks (other than RRBs) in tier 1 centres (centres with population of 1,00,000 and above as per 2001 Census) will continue to require prior permission of the Reserve Bank of India, except in the case of North Eastern States and Sikkim, where the general permission would cover tier 1 centres also.

Domestic scheduled commercial banks, while preparing their Annual Branch Expansion Plan (ABEP), should allocate at least 25% of the total number of branches proposed to be opened during a year in unbanked rural (tier 5 and tier 6) centres. An unbanked rural centre would mean a rural (tier 5 and tier 6) centre that does not have a brick and mortar structure of any scheduled commercial bank for customer based banking transactions.

In view of the requirement for opening at least 25% of the branches under ABEP in unbanked rural centres, it would now not be mandatory to open at least one third of the total number of branches proposed to be opened in tier 2 to tier 6 centres in underbanked districts of underbanked states. However, as there is a continuing need for opening more branches in underbanked districts of underbanked

States for ensuring more uniform spatial distribution, banks would be provided incentive for opening such branches. Accordingly, for each branch proposed to be opened in tier 2 to tier 6 centres of underbanked districts of underbanked States, (excluding such of the rural branches proposed to be opened in unbanked rural centres that may be located in the underbanked districts of underbanked States in compliance with the legal requirement), authorisation will be given for opening of a branch in a tier 1 centre. This will be in addition to the authorisation given for branches in tier 1 centres based on the considerations stated above.

Credit will be given for the branches opened in unbanked rural centres in excess of the required 25% of the ABEP for the year which will be carried forward for achieving the criteria in the subsequent ABEP/year of the financial inclusion plan.

Setting Up of Offsite/Mobile ATMs

Domestic scheduled commercial banks are permitted to install offsite/mobile ATMs at centres/places identified by them, without permission from the RBI. This would, however, be subject to any direction which the RBI may issue, including for closure/shifting of any such Off-site/ Mobile ATMs, wherever so considered necessary by the Reserve Bank.

Domestic Scheduled Commercial Banks are permitted to set up offsite ATMs at centres/places identified by them including Special Economic Zones (SEZs), without the requirement of prior permission from RBI subject to the terms and conditions stipulated in Annexure 12 of the Master Circular on Branch Authorization. These ATMs installed in SEZs should deal in Indian rupee only.

Foreign Banks and Branch Authorization

The general permission granted to domestic scheduled commercial banks as explained above will not be applicable to foreign banks.

TABLE 18.2   Population Group-Wise Number of Branches of Scheduled Commercial Banks in India: 1969–2016

Year	Rural	Semi-Urban	Urban	Metropolitan	Total
2016	50,554	35,959	24,363	21,958	132,834
2015	48,247	34,113	23,115	20,824	126,299
2014	44,843	31,835	21,584	19,554	117,816
2013	39,368	28,798	19,971	18,342	106,479
2012	36,093	26,068	18,920	17,493	98,574
2011	33,460	23,318	17,681	16,447	90,906
2010	31,971	21,013	16,748	15,432	85,164
2009	30,943	19,282	15,356	14,288	79,869
2008	30,293	17,960	14,343	13,325	75,921
2007	29,771	16,716	13,103	12,349	71,939

(Continued...)

TABLE 18.2 Population Group-Wise Number of Branches of Scheduled Commercial Banks in India: 1969–2016 (Number) *(Continued...)*

Year	Rural	Semi-Urban	Urban	Metropolitan	Total
2006	29,649	15,943	12,258	11,728	69,578
2005	32,082	15,403	11,500	9,370	68,355
2004	32,121	15,091	11,000	8,976	67,188
2003	32,303	14,859	10,693	8,680	66,535
2002	32,380	14,747	10,477	8,586	66,190
2001	32,562	14,597	10,293	8,467	65,919
2000	32,734	14,407	10,052	8,219	65,412
1999	32,857	14,168	9,898	8,016	64,939
1998	32,878	13,980	9,597	7,763	64,218
1997	32,915	13,766	9,340	7,529	63,550
1996	32,995	13,561	9,086	7,384	63,026
1995	33,004	13,341	8,868	7,154	62,367
1994	35,329	11,890	8,745	5,839	61,803
1993	35,389	11,465	8,562	5,753	61,169
1992	35,269	11,356	8,279	5,666	60,570
1991	35,206	11,344	8,046	5,624	60,220
1990	34,791	11,324	8,042	5,595	59,752
1989	33,014	11,166	7,524	5,995	57,699
1988	31,114	11,132	7,322	5,842	55,410
1987	30,209	10,637	7,218	5,795	53,859
1986	29,703	10,585	7,209	5,790	53,287
1985	30,185	9,816	6,578	4,806	51,385
1984	25,380	9,326	6,116	4,510	45,332
1983	22,686	9,081	5,917	4,395	42,079
1982	20,401	8,809	5,693	4,274	39,177
1981	17,656	8,471	5,454	4,126	35,707
1980	15,105	8,122	5,178	4,014	32,419
1979	13,337	7,889	5,037	3,939	30,202
1978	11,806	7,628	4,843	3,739	28,016
1977	9,537	7,248	4,542	3,475	24,802
1976	7,690	6,421	3,998	3,111	21,220
1975	6,807	5,598	3,489	2,836	18,730
1974	6,166	5,116	3,091	2,563	16,936
1973	5,561	4,751	2,764	2,286	15,362
1972	4,817	4,401	2,504	1,900	13,622
1971	4,280	4,040	1,949	1,744	12,013
1970	3,063	3,718	1,744	1,606	10,131
1969	1,833	3,342	1,584	1,503	8,262

TABLE 18.3 ATM and Card Statistics for July 2016 in India

Sr. No.	Bank Name	ATMs On-site (1)	ATMs Off-site (2)	POS On-line (3)	POS Off-line (4)	Credit Cards — No. of outstanding cards as at the end of the month (5)	Credit Cards — No. of Transactions (Actuals) ATM (6)	POS (7)	Credit Cards — Amount of transactions (₹ Millions) ATM (8)	POS (9)	Debit Cards — No. of outstanding cards as at the end of the month (10)	Debit Cards — No. of Transactions (Actuals) ATM (11)	POS (12)	Debit Cards — Amount of transactions (₹ Millions) ATM (13)	POS (14)
1	Allahabad Bank	807	410	10	0	0	0	0	0.00	0	9302086	5545099	529431	15971.59	674.27
2	American Express	0	0	15603	0	874724	4103	4459312	28.61	32066.57	0	0	0	0	0
3	Andhra Bank	2940	791	2360	0	153312	13589	232756	63.60	543.80	19254763	15597070	1298355	48947.50	1295.50
4	Axis Bank Ltd	3037	9972	269443	0	2677047	98300	5913088	252.04	19736.00	16655284	25484831	9045422	122915.34	13506.04
5	Bandhan Bank	239	0	0	0				0.00	0	8138449	2800332	218872	4168.70	178.20
6	Bank of America	0	0	0	0	6724	104	23500	0.75	130.61	0	0	0	0	0
7	Bank of Baroda	6320	4135	35307	0	120176	7349	253373	26.87	579.61	35510473	16383371	3427918	67016.74	3217.55
8	Bank of India	3436	4371	5561	304	143316	19945	151210	111.98	387.06	38472119	26310165	3539048	58315.94	3410.44
9	Bank of Maharashtra	1281	587	0	0				0.00	0.00	5851718	5962580	491851	21092.90	854.32
10	Barclays Bank Plc	0	0	0	0				0.00	0	3470	277	158	1.98	0.55
11	Canara Bank	5289	4498	4974	0	200890	39976	328445	196.43	801.46	33414614	19205244	3427148	76972.44	4265.92
12	Catholic Syrian Bank Ltd	188	58	0	0				0.00	0	810815	402495	30544	1246.31	81.02
13	Central Bank of India	3509	1803	1339	0	108152	4335	140197	21.41	307.17	20662104	10179718	1223679	39599.44	1557.05
14	Citi Bank	58	500	24364	0	2404885	52867	12025637	314.90	31679.05	1598706	3073495	3252889	11905.76	6378.86
15	City Union Bank	668	673	3732	0	433	95	1613	0.20	2	1547193	1950884	434207	8165.70	484.26
16	Corporation Bank	2247	847	101813	0	82236	2142	104565	11.11	257.04	10116268	6226302	1421158	23831.08	1758.78
17	Dbs Bank	5	25	0	0				0.00	0	157400	31273	50932	110.98	76.61
18	Dena Bank	1272	199	0	0				0.00	0	6221883	2501608	324186	9182.37	327.77
19	Deutsche Bank Ltd	13	18	0	0				0.00	0	98677	173290	128782	820.28	252.82
20	Development Credit Bank	166	288	792	0	5123	781	9210	3.73	18.63	341747	537072	135438	1896.01	202.09
21	Dhanalakshmi Bank Ltd	190	183	719	0	7042	32	13589	0.13	29.85	609109	440740	54345	1746.92	116.46
22	Federal Bank Ltd	1096	466	9087	0				0.00	0	5022074	4839055	1144459	23740.02	1738.41
23	Firstrand	1	6	0	0				0.00	0	57670	22876	2401	124.85	4.52
24	Hdfc Bank Ltd	5622	6398	284777	0	7814027	179127	25196487	1041.80	73510.07	24121066	37645690	20112655	181954.41	27907.79
25	Hongkong and Shanghai BKG Corpn	68	51	14130	0	446041	4115	1083805	29.58	3339.85	440558	410942	404464	1967.03	797.86
26	ICICI Bank Ltd	4827	9359	202056	0	3876656	27126	10706103	105.67	26571.66	33989826	36035298	19338502	174040.37	27866.46
27	Idbi Ltd	1748	1622	17732	0	10402	278	32439	1.40	73.40	9475839	8984780	2199235	37781.70	2609.60
28	Idfc Bank Ltd	15	1	0	0				0.00	0	41999	54289	21035	172.80	27.60
29	Indian Bank	2287	701	1052	0	75950	4305	123676	17.20	262.40	15461004	21128238	1995862	42078.50	2050.80
30	Indian Overseas Bank	2718	976	3699	0	42364	1318	32642	4.78	78.34	14459458	21241901	701255	37988.90	1503.14

Sr.	Bank	ATM on site (1)	ATM off site (2)	POS online (3)	POS offline (4)	Credit cards issued (5)	Credit txn ATM (6)	Credit txn POS (7)	Value credit ATM (8)	Value credit POS (9)	Debit cards issued (10)	Debit txn ATM (11)	Debit txn POS (12)	Value debit ATM (13)	Value debit POS (14)
31	Indusind Bank Ltd	788	1116	1432	0	475314	8503	1174239	46.07	6842.02	2821667	2136712	789864	9100.75	1074.11
32	Jammu and Kashmir Bank	607	425	5751	0	47920	3833	67795	14.14	165.02	3330888	3282232	45985	16371.50	147.48
33	Karnataka Bank Ltd	518	781	3342	0	0	0	0	0.00	0	3283869	3415719	642227	12508.80	813.40
34	Karur Vysya Bank Ltd	743	935	10647	0	0	0	0	0.00	0	4004235	5038724	927181	21933.10	1004.90
35	Kotak Mahindra Bank Ltd	934	1102	0	0	823046	15927	1774830	70.79	4245.37	3915102	5459131	2494538	21197.58	3593.43
36	Oriental Bank of Commerce	2265	326	2737	0	0	0	0	0.00	0	9335097	5122417	399188	20809.70	727.87
37	Punjab and Sind Bank	1100	259	0	0	0	0	0	0.00	0	2359672	1191467	102446	3611.64	154.00
38	Punjab National Bank	5168	4545	22105	0	200226	7044	246137	30.08	498.53	46342213	23038140	4732150	101351.07	5050.27
39	Ratnakar Bank Limited	148	224	3105	0	131227	4232	485478	27.25	2074.98	485502	330264	103726	1226.88	141.84
40	Royal Bank of Scotland N V	12	5	0	0	0	0	0	0.00	0	92901	135981	61712	610.26	108.36
41	South Indian Bank	765	532	3343	0	1023678	4800	3121099	22.53	7973.80	3260078	2626595	540213	9654.70	838.70
42	Standard Chartered Bank Ltd	102	138	0	0	0	0	0	0.00	0	773776	1760619	1259795	5957.94	1866.05
43	State Bank of Bikaner and Jaipur	1186	784	2855	0	0	0	0	0.00	0	12454969	10450234	832907	24641.23	770.66
44	State Bank of Hyderabad	1818	562	6244	0	0	0	0	0.00	0	13195495	19761619	1548028	43810.08	2052.91
45	State Bank of India	20419	29496	310744	0	3862254	88246	11429744	408.40	29553.30	202702641	316701872	32500690	656769.12	39541.56
46	State Bank of Mysore	1055	330	4957	0	0	0	0	0.00	0	0	7523816	608689	13847.74	941.54
47	State Bank of Patiala	1174	342	5474	0	0	0	0	0.00	0	7290866	5408913	530834	13402.77	665.59
48	State Bank of Travancore	1135	595	3560	0	0	0	0	0.00	0	11732034	15927164	1149698	39547.63	1826.96
49	Syndicate Bank	3332	377	2336	0	60644	2479	98287	16.42	172.83	12228868	10654384	632234	29364.13	889.30
50	Tamilnad Mercantile Bank Ltd	427	607	2097	0	7772	0	10666	3.00	27.44	971905	3384368	76753	13440.94	181.10
51	The Laxmi Vilas Bank Ltd	530	594	2779	0	0	0	0	0.00	0	1070252	762595	61633	2802.10	125.36
52	Uco Bank	2072	568	0	0	0	0	0	0.00	0	9015764	5202186	1074881	19311.80	1054.60
53	Union Bank of India	4374	2519	29798	0	151333	2493	107900	11.40	468.84	17533461	17269852	1091026	53594.79	1477.23
54	United Bank of India	921	1128	0	0	0	0	0	0.00	0	8210566	5021188	556137	19371.40	666.73
55	Vijaya Bank	1120	272	1463	0	46957	8740	96791	48.87	292.54	4790889	4539980	508706	14133.40	856.06
56	Yes Bank Ltd	528	1079	9318	0	3125	70	7221	0.30	25	1243373	2868367	844406	9523.12	1204.55
	Grand Total	103282	98579	1443595	504	25548794	606314	79440734	2922.41	243414.15	697222455	752133454	129069978	2191650.70	170919.23

1. Number of ATM deployed on site by the bank.
2. Number of ATM deployed off site by the bank.
3. Number of Point of sale (POS) deployed online by the bank
4. Number of POS deployed offline by the bank
5. Total number of credit cards issued outstanding (after adjusting the number of cards withdrawn/cancelled).
6. Total number of financial transactions done by the credit card issued by the bank at ATMs
7. Total number of financial transactions done by the credit card issued by the bank at POS terminals
8. Total value of financial transactions done by the credit card issued by the bank at ATMs
9. Total value of financial transactions done by the credit card issued by the bank at POS terminals.
10. Total number of debit cards issued outstanding (after adjusting the number of cards withdrawn/cancelled).
11. Total number of financial transactions done by the debit card issued by the bank at ATMs
12. Total number of financial transactions done by the debit card issued by the bank at POS terminals
13. Total value of financial transactions done by the debit card issued by the bank at ATMs
14. Total value of financial transactions done by the debit card issued by the bank at POS terminals.

The Branch Authorisation Policy would be applicable to foreign banks, subject to the following :

i. Foreign banks are required to bring an assigned capital of $25 million upfront at the time of opening the first branch in India.

ii. Existing foreign banks having only one branch would have to comply with the above requirement before their request for opening of second branch is considered.

iii. Foreign banks will be required to submit their branch expansion plan on an annual basis.

iv. In addition to the parameters laid down for Indian banks, the following parameters would also be considered:

    a. Foreign bank and its groups track record of compliance and functioning in the global markets would be considered. Reports from home country supervisors will be sought, wherever necessary.

    b. Weightage would be given to even distribution of home countries of foreign banks having presence in India.

    c. The treatment extended to Indian banks in the home country of the applicant foreign bank would be considered.

    d. Due consideration would be given to the bilateral and diplomatic relations between India and the home country.

    e. The branch expansion of foreign banks would be considered keeping in view India's commitments at World Trade Organisation (WTO). ATMs would not be included in the number of branches for such computation.

Accordingly, foreign banks should submit their ABEP to the RBI.[5]

GO ONLINE

Access **https://rbi.org.in/scripts/BS_SpeechesView.aspx?Id=828** to read former governor, RBI, Duvvuri Subba Rao's speech, "Banking Structure in India: Looking Ahead by Looking Back".

Banking Structure In India: The Way Forward

The Reserve Bank of India in its discussion paper on 'Banking Structure in India—The Way Forward' on August 27, 2013 identified certain building blocks for the reorientation of the banking structure with a view to address various issues such as enhancing competition, financing higher growth, providing specialised services and furthering financial inclusion. It also emphasised the need to address the concerns arising out of such changes with a view to manage the trade-off for ensuring financial stability. The overall thrust of the reorientation was to impart dynamism and flexibility to the evolving banking structure, while ensuring that the structure remained resilient and promoted financial stability.

The structure of the banking industry in India was studied from the following perspectives:

- **Small banks vs. large banks:** Small local banks play an important role in the supply of credit to small enterprises and agriculture and banking services in unbanked and under-banked regions in the country. While permitting large number of small banks, however, the issues relating to their size, numbers, capital requirements, exposure norms, regulatory prescriptions, corporate governance and resolution need to be suitably addressed.

---

[5]*Source:* RBI's Master Circular for Branch Authorization, July 1, 2013, https://www.rbi.org.in/scripts/BS_ViewMasCirculardetails.aspx?id=8136#24, as accessed on 17 March 2017 at 4pm.

GO ONLINE

Access **https://www.rbi.org.in/scripts/BS_SpeechesView.aspx?Id=999** to understand the issues pertaining to Bank consolidation in India.

- **Universal banking:** Universal banking model remains the dominant and preferred model in most of the post crisis world, given the failure of many investment banks during the crisis. Under the universal banking model, the Financial Holding Company (FHC) structure has distinct advantages and may be a preferred model. Additionally, in a changing economic environment, there is a need for niche banking and differentiated licensing could be a desirable step in this direction, particularly for infrastructure financing, wholesale banking and retail banking. There is also a need to promote investment banks/investment banking activities.

- **Continuous authorisation:** There is a case for reviewing the current 'Stop and Go' licensing policy and consider adopting a 'continuous authorisation' policy, as continuous authorisation keeps the competitive pressure on the existing banks and also does not strain the banking system as the 'block' licensing may do. However, it is important that the entry norms should be stringent so as to encourage entry by only well-qualified entities in order to improve the quality of the banking system and promote competition.

- **Conversion of UCBs into commercial banks:** There is a case of exploring the possibilities of converting some Urban Cooperative Banks (UCBs) into commercial banks or small banks as these banks, freed from dual control and with more avenues to raise capital, could extend banking services in the regions characterised by poor banking outreach.

- **Consolidation:** The issue of consolidation in the banking sector has assumed significance, considering the need for a few Indian banks to cater to global needs by becoming global players and the growing corporate and infrastructure funding needs. Taking into account the pros and cons of consolidation, it has to be borne in mind that while consolidation of commercial banks with established synergies and on the basis of voluntary initiatives is welcome, it cannot be imposed on banks. A measured approach is to be made both on consolidation and global presence even if attaining global size is not imminent.

- **Presence of foreign banks in India:** The significance and need for foreign banks' participation in India arises primarily to increase competition, promote efficiency of the local banking system and also to bring in sophisticated financial services and risk management methodologies which can be adopted by the domestic banks. Post crisis, domestic incorporation of foreign banks through the subsidiarisation route has acquired importance.

- **Indian banks' presence overseas:** Given the highly competitive environment overseas coupled with enhanced regulation, the way forward for the Indian banks could be, apart from representative office and branch form of presence overseas, local incorporation by large banks either individually or in joint venture mode with other banks or with overseas banks. This will enable the large Indian banks to engage in a much wider range of activities and have greater potential for growth. Eventually, this may facilitate banks increasing their global reach.

- **Government ownership:** An optimal ownership mix in the banking sector is required to promote a balance between efficiency, equity and financial stability. Going forward, there is a better pay-off in enabling PSBs to improve their performance while promoting private sector banks. As regards the reduction in fiscal burden on account of recapitalisation of the Public Sector Banks (PSBs), Government may consider options from menu of choices available such as issue of non-voting equity shares or differential voting equity shares, adopting FHC structure or diluting stake in PSBs.

- **Deposit insurance and resolution:** The existence of an effective resolution regime is essential for any type of banking structure India may pursue. The FSB key attributes could be the guiding principles for setting up a resolution framework in India.
- **Indicative reorientation of the banking structure:** The reoriented banking structure would comprise four tiers. The first tier may consist of three or four large Indian banks with domestic and international presence along with branches of foreign banks in India. The second tier is likely to comprise several mid-sized banking institutions including niche banks with economy-wide presence. The third tier may encompass old private sector banks, regional rural banks, and multi state urban cooperative banks. The fourth tier may embrace many small privately owned local banks and cooperative banks.

Building on the Discussion Paper and after carefully examining the views/comments received on the draft guidelines from banks, non-banking financial institutions, industrial houses, other institutions and the public at large, as also, using the learning from the recent licensing process, such as, the experience of licensing two universal banks in 2014 and granting in-principle approvals for small finance banks and payments banks, the RBI worked out the framework for granting licences to universal banks on a continuous basis in August 2016.

Consequently, the Reserve Bank of India, on August 1, 2016 released on its website, "Guidelines for 'on tap' Licensing of Universal Banks in the Private Sector".

Some of the key aspects of the Guidelines include: (i) resident individuals and professionals having 10 years of experience in banking and finance at a senior level are also eligible to promote universal banks; (ii) large industrial houses are excluded as eligible entities but are permitted to invest in the banks up to 10%; (iii) Non-Operative Financial Holding Company (NOFHC) has been made non-mandatory in case of promoters being individuals or standalone promoting/converting entities who/which do not have other group entities; (iv) Not less than 51% of the total paid-up equity capital of the NOFHC shall be owned by the promoter/promoter group, instead being wholly owned by the promoter group; and (v) Existing specialised activities have been permitted to be continued from a separate entity proposed to be held under the NOFHC subject to prior approval from the Reserve Bank and subject to it being ensured that similar activities are not conducted through the bank as well.[6]

Separation of Banking and Other Financial Services Industries: Banking Regulation Throughout the World

Not many other countries in the aftermath of the Great Depression followed the lead of the United States in separating the banking and other financial services industries. In fact, in the past this separation was the most prominent difference between banking regulation in the United States and in other countries. Around the world, there are three basic frameworks for the banking and securities industries.

---

[6]*Source:* https://rbi.org.in/scripts/BS_PressReleaseDisplay.aspx?prid=29405; https://www.rbi.org.in/scripts/BS_PressReleaseDisplay.aspx?prid=37658, as accessed on 17 March 2017 at 4pm.

The first framework is *universal banking*, which exists in Germany, the Netherlands, and Switzerland. It provides no separation at all between the banking and securities industries. In a universal banking system, commercial banks provide a full range of banking, securities, real estate, and insurance services, all within a single legal entity. Banks are allowed to own sizable equity shares in commercial firms, and often they do.

The *British-style universal banking system*, the second framework, is found in the United Kingdom and countries with close ties to it, such as Canada and Australia, and now the United States. The British-style universal bank engages in securities underwriting, but it differs from the German-style universal bank in three ways: Separate legal subsidiaries are more common, bank equity holdings of commercial firms are less common, and combinations of banking and insurance firms are less common.

The third framework features some legal separation of the banking and other financial services industries, as in Japan. A major difference between the U.S. and Japanese banking systems is that Japanese banks are allowed to hold substantial equity stakes in commercial firms, whereas American banks cannot. Although the banking and securities industries are legally separated in Japan, commercial banks are increasingly being allowed to engage in securities activities and, like U.S. banks, are becoming more like British-style universal banks.

International Banking

GO ONLINE
Access **https://www.rbi.org in/scripts/AnnualPublications.aspx?head=Branch%20Banking%20Statistics** to see the distribution of Indian bank branches overseas.

In 2002, only eight nationalised banks and one private sector bank: Bharat Overseas Bank operated 94 branches in foreign countries. Currently, 11 nationalised banks, one other public sector bank (IDBI) and three private sector banks (ICICI, Axis Bank and HDFC Bank) operate about 183 branches across 30 countries.[7]

While international liabilities of banks in India stood at $173,212 million at end December 2015, international claims of banks in India stood at $76,047 million. The shares of international liabilities and claims of banks in India in total international liabilities and claims of all reporting countries (world) banks stood at around 0.7% and 0.3% at end December 2015.[8] As can be seen from Figure 18.1, the international liabilities of banks in India recorded a gradual deceleration during the last four quarters. On the other hand, annual growth in international claims showed a steady increase since June 2015.

International liabilities of Indian banks comprises non-resident external (NRE) deposits, Foreign Currency Non Resident (Bank) (FCNR (B)) deposits, foreign currency borrowings, Bonds, American Depository Receipts/ Global Depository Receipts (ADRs/GDRs), equities of banks and other liabilities. Other liabilities include Resident Foreign Currency (RFC) accounts deposits, Exchange Earner Foreign Currency (EEFC) accounts deposits, other foreign currency deposits (including inter-bank foreign currency deposits), vostro balances and balances in exchange houses and in term deposits, non-resident ordinary (NRO) rupee accounts, embassy accounts, Foreign Institutional Investor (FII) accounts, escrow accounts deposits, floating rate notes

---

[7]https://www.rbi.org.in/scripts/PublicationsView.aspx?id=5051; https://rbidocs.rbi.org.in/rdocs/Content/pdfs/71206.pdf, as accessed on 17 March 2017 at 4pm.
[8]https://www.rbi.org.in/scripts/BS_ViewBulletin.aspx?Id=16337, as accessed on 17 March 2017 at 4pm.

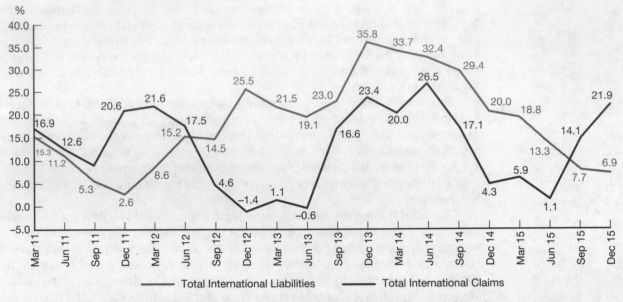

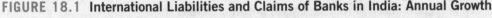

FIGURE 18.1 International Liabilities and Claims of Banks in India: Annual Growth

Source: https://www.rbi.org.in/scripts/BS_ViewBulletin.aspx?Id=16337,as accessed on 17 March 2017 at 4pm.

(FRN), other own issues of international debt securities and capital/ remittable profits of foreign banks in India and other unclassified international liabilities. (Figure 18.2). As can be seen, after a sharp jump in December 2013 in the share of FCNR(B) deposits due to the special concessional dollar swap window announced (in August 2013) by the RBI, the share declined slightly and remained steady in 2015. Also, share of outstanding non-resident external (NRE) rupee deposits remained almost at the same level during 2015. Share of foreign currency borrowings of banks in total international liabilities increased to 14.7% at end December 2015 from 11.6% a year ago.

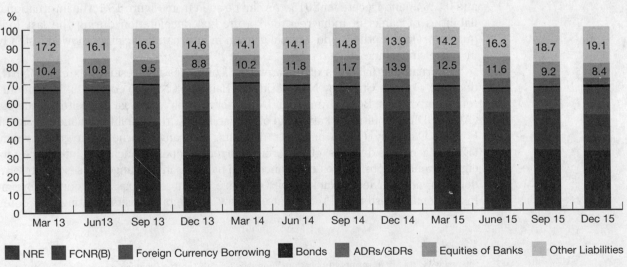

FIGURE 18.2 Components of International Liabilities of Indian Banks

Source: https://www.rbi.org.in/scripts/BS_ViewBulletin.aspx?Id=16337, as accessed on 17 March 2017 at 4pm.

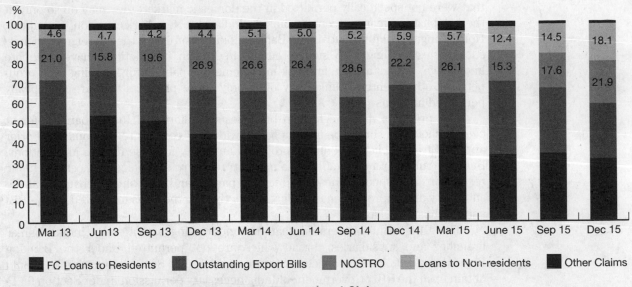

FIGURE 18.3 Components of Indian Banks' International Claims

Source: https://www.rhi.org.in/scripts/BS_ViewBulletin.aspx?Id–16337, as accessed on 17 March 2017 at 4pm.

International claims of Indian banks, on the other hand, comprised of foreign currency loans to residents, outstanding export bills, nostro, loans to non-residents and other claims, including Forign Currency/Telegraphic Transfers (TTs) in hands, investments in equity abroad, capital supplied to and receivable profits from foreign branches of Indian banks and other unclassified international claims (Figure 18.3). As can be seen, the share of 'Loans to Non-Residents' in international claims expanded at end December 2015 compared to that in a year ago, while the share of 'Foreign Currency Loans to Residents' in international claims recorded sharp deceleration during the year 2015 and stood at 30.7% in December 2015 as compared to 47.1% a year ago (Figure 18.3).

Structure of Indian Banking Overseas

Indian banks have most of their foreign branches in the United Kingdom (30), followed by Hong Kong (19), Singapore (17) and UAE (15). The largest volume of assets is held by branches in London because it is a major international financial center and the central location for the Eurodollar market. Parts of the Caribbean (especially the Bahamas and the Cayman Islands) have become important as tax havens, with minimal taxation and few restrictive regulations. In actuality, the bank branches in the Bahamas and the Cayman Islands are "shell operations" because they function primarily as bookkeeping centers and do not provide normal banking services.

In 2008, the RBI restricted the operations of foreign branches/foreign subsidiaries of the Indian banks which proposed to handle structured financial products by making it mandatory for these banks to obtain prior approval of the RBI for the purpose.

In May 2014, based on a review, the RBI decided that if foreign branches/subsidiaries of Indian banks proposed to offer structured financial and derivative products that were not specifically permitted in the domestic market, they may do so only at the established financial centers outside India like New York, London, Singapore, Hong Kong, Frankfurt, Dubai, etc. Banks should ensure that their foreign branches/ subsidiaries, dealing with such products in foreign jurisdictions, have adequate knowledge, understanding, and risk management capability for handling such products. At other centers, banks may offer only those products that are specifically permitted in India.

The products that the foreign branches/subsidiaries of Indian banks offer at overseas location should be in compliance with host country regulations, with prior approval from their Board and appropriate authority in these foreign jurisdictions. Banks should continue to adhere to more stringent rules among the host and home regulations in respect of these products. In particular, banks should ensure that the suitability and appropriateness policy is strictly adhered to as mandated by the RBI and the host regulators.

The RBI further reiterated that for undertaking activities by Indian banks' branches and subsidiaries abroad which are not permitted under the Banking Regulations Act, 1949 / respective Statute of the Public Sector Banks, banks should obtain from the RBI / Government of India necessary permission under Section 6 (1) (m) or 19 (1) (c) of the Banking Regulations Act, 1949, as the case may be, for undertaking such activities.[9]

Foreign Banks in India

The growth in international trade has not only encouraged Indian banks to open offices overseas, but it has also encouraged foreign banks to establish offices in India. As of December 31, 2015, 46 foreign banks, with a total of 325 bank branches operated in India.[10]

A roadmap for foreign banks in India, announced in 2005, allowed foreign banks wishing to establish their presence in India for the first time to either (i) choose to operate through branch presence or (ii) set up 100% wholly owned subsidiary (WOS). However, following the one-mode presence criterion, no foreign bank chose to set up 100% owned subsidiary.

In the aftermath of the crisis and building on the lessons from the crisis, the RBI issued a Discussion Paper in January 2011 on the mode of presence of foreign banks in India. Taking into account the feedback received on the Discussion Paper and factoring in the lessons from the crisis which favored a subsidiary mode of presence from a financial stability perspective, the framework for setting up of WOS by foreign banks in India was finalised.

Key Features of the Framework

- Banks with complex structures, banks which do not provide adequate disclosure in their home jurisdiction, banks which are not widely held, banks from jurisdictions having legislation giving a preferential claim to depositors of home country in a winding up proceedings, etc., would be mandated for entry into India only in the WOS mode.

---

[9]Reference: https://www.rbi.org.in/scripts/NotificationUser.aspx?Id=8874&Mode=0; https://rbi.org.in/scripts/NotificationUser.aspx?Mode=0&Id=4676, as accessed on 17 March 2017 at 4pm.
[10]https://www.rbi.org.in/commonman/upload/english/content/pdfs/71207.pdf, as accessed on 17 March 2017 at 4pm.

- Foreign banks in whose case the above conditions do not apply can opt for a branch or WOS form of presence.
- A foreign bank opting for branch form of presence shall convert into a WOS as and when the above conditions become applicable to it or it becomes systemically important on account of its balance sheet size in India.
- Foreign banks which commenced banking business in India before August 2010 shall have the option to continue their banking business through the branch mode. However, they will be incentivised to convert into WOS because of the attractiveness of the near national treatment afforded to WOS.
- To prevent domination by foreign banks, restrictions would be placed on further entry of new WOSs of foreign banks/ capital infusion, when the capital and reserves of the WOSs and foreign bank branches in India exceed 20% of the capital and reserves of the banking system.
- The initial minimum paid-up voting equity capital for a WOS shall be ₹5 billion for new entrants. Existing branches of foreign banks desiring to convert into WOS shall have a minimum net worth of ₹5 billion.
- The parent of the WOS would be required to issue a letter of comfort to the RBI for meeting the liabilities of the WOS.
- Corporate governance: (i) no less than two-third of the directors should be non-executive directors; (ii) a minimum of one-third of the directors should be independent of the management of the subsidiary in India, its parent or associates; (iii) no less than 50% of the directors should be Indian nationals/NRIs/PIOs subject to the condition that not less than one-third of the directors are Indian nationals resident in India.
- The branch expansion guidelines as applicable to domestic scheduled commercial banks would generally be applicable to WOSs of foreign banks except that they will require prior approval of RBI for opening branches at certain locations that are sensitive from the perspective of national security.
- Priority sector lending requirement would be 40% for WOS like domestic scheduled commercial banks with adequate transition period for existing foreign bank branches converting into WOS.
- On arm's length basis, WOS would be permitted to use parental guarantee/ credit rating only for the purpose of providing custodial services and for their international operations. However, WOS should not provide counter guarantee to its parent for such support.
- Wholly Owned subsidiaries may, at their option, dilute their stake to 74% or less in accordance with the existing FDI policy. In the event of dilution, they will have to list themselves.

The issue of permitting WOS to enter into M&A transactions with any private sector bank in India subject to the overall investment limit of 74% would be considered after a review is made with regard to the extent of penetration of foreign investment in Indian banks and functioning of foreign banks (branch mode and WOS).[11]

---

[11]*Source*: https://www.rbi.org.in/scripts/BS_PressReleaseDisplay.aspx?prid=29922. For details of this notification, see; https://www.rbi.org.in/Scripts/bs_viewcontent.aspx?Id=2758, as accessed on 17 March 2017 at 4pm.

SUMMARY

1. As in the rest of the world, banking in India evolved out of moneylending. The latter can be traced back to the Vedic period i.e., 2000–1400 BC. The existence of professional banking in India could be traced to 500 BC.. The Bank of Bengal, the Bank of Bombay and the Bank of Madras were the three Presidency Banks- i.e. banks in the three presidencies that were the units of administrative jurisdiction in the country for the East India Company- that were set up in 1806, 1840 and 1843 respectively. The Presidency banks issued currency notes until the enactment of the Paper Currency Act, 1861, when this right to issue currency notes by the Presidency banks was abolished and that function was entrusted to the Government. The earliest banks in India – the Allahabad Bank, the Punjab National Bank and the Bank of India- were set up under private ownership.

2. The period 1967–1991 was characterised by major developments, viz., social control on banks in 1967 and nationalisation of 14 banks in 1969 and six more in 1980. The period beginning from the early 1990s witnessed the transformation of the banking sector as a result of financial sector reforms that were introduced as a part of structural reforms initiated in 1991.

3. A change in the economic environment will stimulate financial institutions to search for financial innovations.

   Changes in demand conditions, especially an increase in interest-rate risk; changes in supply conditions, especially improvements in information technology; and the desire to avoid costly regulations have been major driving forces behind financial innovation. Financial innovation has caused banks to suffer declines in cost advantages in acquiring funds and in income advantages on their assets. The resulting squeeze has hurt profitability in banks' traditional lines of business and has led to a decline in traditional banking.

4. Shadow banks comprise entities which conduct financial intermediation directly, such as finance companies or NBFCs, and entities which provide finance to such entities, such as mutual funds. The size of the shadow banking sector in India is small and its activities are limited. The RBI has been trying to bring the Non Bank Financial Companies, especially the Systemically Important (SI) NBFCs under the purview of its regulatory measures.

5. The structure of commercial banking and branch authorization in India lies under the purview of the RBI. The opening of new branches and shifting of existing branches of banks, for banks including foreign banks is governed by the provisions of Section 23 of the Banking Regulation Act, 1949.

6. The Reserve Bank of India in its discussion paper on 'Banking Structure in India— The Way Forward' on August 27, 2013 identified certain building blocks for the reorientation of the banking structure with a view to address various issues such as enhancing competition, financing higher growth, providing specialised services and furthering financial inclusion. It also emphasised the need to address the concerns arising out of such changes with a view to manage the trade-off for ensuring financial stability. The overall thrust of the reorientation was to impart dynamism and flexibility to the evolving banking structure, while ensuring that the structure remained resilient and promoted financial stability.

7. With the rapid growth of world trade since 1960, international banking has grown dramatically. The growth in international trade has not only encouraged Indian banks to open offices overseas, but it has also encouraged foreign banks to establish offices in India.

KEY TERMS

automated banking machine (ABM), p. 454
automated teller machine (ATM), p. 453
branches, p. 466
deposit rate ceilings, p. 459

disintermediation, p. 459
e-cash, p. 455
electronic money (e-money), p. 455
financial engineering, p. 451
futures contracts, p. 452

hedge, p. 452
securitization, p. 457
shadow banking system, p. 451
smart card, p. 455
sweep account, p. 460
virtual bank, p. 454

QUESTIONS

1. Why was the United States one of the last of the major industrialized countries to have a central bank?

2. Which regulatory agency has the primary responsibility for supervising the following categories of commercial banks?
   a. National banks
   b. Bank holding companies
   c. Non-Federal-Reserve-member state banks
   d. Federal-Reserve-member state banks

3. "The commercial banking industry in Canada is less competitive than the commercial banking industry in the United States because in Canada only a few large banks dominate the industry, while in the United States there are around 6,000 commercial banks." Is this statement true, false, or uncertain? Explain your answer.

4. Why did new technology make it harder to enforce limitations on bank branching?

5. Why has there been such a dramatic increase in bank holding companies?

6. What incentives have regulatory agencies created to encourage international banking? Why have they done this?

7. How could the approval of international banking facilities (IBFs) by the Fed in 1981 have reduced employment in the banking industry in Europe?

8. If the bank at which you keep your checking account is owned by Saudi Arabians, should you worry that your deposits are less safe than if the bank were owned by Americans?

9. If reserve requirements were eliminated in the future, as some economists advocate, what effects would this have on the size of money market mutual funds?

10. Why have banks been losing cost advantages in acquiring funds in recent years?

11. "If inflation had not risen in the 1960s and 1970s, the banking industry might be healthier today." Is this statement true, false, or uncertain? Explain your answer.

12. Why have banks been losing income advantages on their assets in recent years?

13. "The invention of the computer is the major factor behind the decline of the banking industry." Is this statement true, false, or uncertain? Explain your answer.

WEB EXERCISES

Commercial Banking Industry: Structure and Competition

1. Go to RBI's Database on Indian Economy and see 'Profile of Banks' at **https://dbie.rbi.org.in/DBIE/dbie.rbi?site=publications#!4**. The website gives you data both bank group wise (public sector banks, foreign banks etc.), and also bank wise. On the basis of this data, what are the largest bank groups operating in India based on criteria such as, number of offices, employees, capital and reserves and surplus, advances, deposits, return on advances adjusted to cost of funds, return on assets and net NPA ratios. What would be your comments on the health of the Indian banking sector based on this analysis?

2. What are the ten largest banks operating in India

3. Go to the Database on Indian Economy and look at the Data on International banking Statistics of India **https://dbie.rbi.org.in/DBIE/dbie.rbi?site=publications#!4 IBS:** Statement 01 contains the International Claims/ Liabilities of Indian banks classified according to the type of instrument. Compare the total international liabilities and total international asset positions of India. What can you deduce about India's net international liability position? What are main instruments in terms of which India's international liabilities and assets are held?

CHAPTER

19

Risk Management in Financial Institutions

> PREVIEW

Managing financial institutions has never been an easy task, but in recent years it has become even more difficult because of greater uncertainty in the economic environment. Interest rates have become much more volatile, resulting in substantial fluctuations in profits and in the value of assets and liabilities held by financial institutions. Furthermore, as we have seen in Chapter 5, defaults on loans and other debt instruments have also climbed dramatically, leading to large losses at financial institutions. In light of these developments, it is not surprising that financial institution managers have become more concerned about managing the risk their institutions face as a result of greater interest-rate fluctuations and defaults by borrowers.

In this chapter we examine how managers of financial institutions cope with credit risk, the risk arising because borrowers may default on their obligations, and with interest-rate risk, the risk arising from fluctuations in interest rates. We will look at the tools these managers use to measure risk and the strategies they employ to reduce it.

Managing Credit Risk

GO ONLINE

Access the home page of CIBIL at **https://www.cibil. com**, India's leading credit information company, with one of the largest collection of consumer information.

A major part of the business of financial institutions, such as banks, insurance companies, pension funds, and finance companies, is making loans. For these institutions to earn high profits, they must make successful loans that are paid back in full (and so have low credit risk). The concepts of adverse selection and moral hazard (discussed in Chapters 2 and 7) provide a framework for understanding the principles that financial institution managers must follow to minimize credit risk and make successful loans.

Adverse selection in loan markets occurs because bad credit risks (those most likely to default on their loans) are the ones who usually line up for loans; in other words, those who are most likely to produce an *adverse* outcome are the most likely to be *selected*. Borrowers with very risky investment projects have much to gain if their projects are successful, so they are the most eager to obtain loans. Clearly, however, they are the least desirable borrowers because of the greater possibility that they will be unable to pay back their loans.

Moral hazard exists in loan markets because borrowers may have incentives to engage in activities that are undesirable from the lender's point of view. In such situations, it is more likely that the lender will be subjected to the *hazard* of default. Once borrowers have obtained a loan, they are more likely to invest in high-risk investment projects—projects that pay high returns to the borrowers if successful. The high risk, however, makes it less likely that they will be able to pay the loan back.

To be profitable, financial institutions must overcome the adverse selection and moral hazard problems that make loan defaults more likely. The attempts of financial institutions to solve these problems help explain a number of principles for managing credit risk: screening and monitoring, establishment of long-term customer relationships, loan commitments, collateral, compensating balance requirements, and credit rationing.

Screening and Monitoring

Asymmetric information is present in loan markets because lenders have less information about the investment opportunities and activities of borrowers than borrowers do. This situation leads to two information-producing activities by financial institutions—screening and monitoring.

Screening Adverse selection in loan markets requires that lenders screen out the bad credit risks from the good ones so loans are profitable to them. To accomplish effective screening, lenders must collect reliable information from prospective borrowers. Effective screening and information collection together form an important principle of credit risk management.

When you apply for a consumer loan (such as a car loan or a mortgage to purchase a house), the first thing you are asked to do is fill out forms that elicit a great deal of information about your personal finances. You are asked about your salary, your bank accounts and other assets (such as cars, insurance policies, and furnishings), and your outstanding loans; your record of loan, credit card, and charge account repayments; and the number of years you've worked and who your employers have been. You also are asked personal questions such as your age, marital status, and number of children. The lender uses this information to evaluate how good a credit risk you are by calculating your "credit score," a statistical measure derived from your answers that predicts whether you are likely to have trouble making your loan payments. Deciding on how good a risk you are cannot be entirely scientific, so the lender must also use judgment. The loan officer, whose job is to decide whether you should be given the loan, might call your employer or talk to some of the personal references you supplied. The officer might even make a judgment based on your demeanor or your appearance.

The process of screening and collecting information is similar when a financial institution makes a business loan. It collects information about the company's profits and losses (income) and about its assets and liabilities. The lender also has to evaluate the likely future success of the business. So, in addition to obtaining information on such items as sales figures, a loan officer might ask questions about the company's future plans, the purpose of the loan, and the competition in the industry. The officer may even visit the company to obtain a firsthand look at its operations. The bottom line is that, whether for personal or business loans, financial institutions need to be nosy.

Specialization in Lending   One puzzling feature of lending by financial institutions is that they often specialize in lending to local firms or to firms in particular industries, such as energy. In one sense, this behavior seems surprising because it means that the financial institution is not diversifying its portfolio of loans and thus is exposing itself to more risk. But from another perspective, such specialization makes perfect sense. The adverse selection problem requires that the financial institution screen out bad credit risks. It is easier for the financial institution to collect information about local firms and determine their creditworthiness than to collect comparable information on firms that are far away. Similarly, by concentrating its lending on firms in specific industries, the financial institution becomes more knowledgeable about these industries and is therefore better able to predict which firms will make timely payments on their debt.

Monitoring and Enforcement of Restrictive Covenants   Once a loan has been made, the borrower has an incentive to engage in risky activities that make it less likely for the loan to be paid off. To reduce this moral hazard, financial institutions must adhere to the principle for managing credit risk that a lender should write provisions (restrictive covenants) into loan contracts restricting borrowers from engaging in risky activities. By monitoring borrowers' activities to see whether they are complying with the restrictive covenants and by enforcing the covenants if they are not, lenders can make sure that borrowers are not taking on risks at the lenders' expense. The need for financial institutions to engage in screening and monitoring explains why they spend so much money on auditing and information-collecting activities.

Long-Term Customer Relationships

An additional way for financial institution managers to obtain information about their borrowers is through long-term customer relationships, another important principle of credit risk management.

If a prospective borrower has had a checking or savings account or other loans with a financial institution over a long time, a loan officer can look at past activity on the accounts and learn quite a bit about the borrower. The balances in the checking and savings accounts tell the loan officer how liquid the potential borrower is and at what time of year the borrower has a strong need for cash. A review of the checks the borrower has written reveals the borrower's suppliers. If the borrower has borrowed previously from the financial institution, the institution has a record of the loan payments. Thus, long-term customer relationships reduce the costs of information collection and make it easier to screen out bad credit risks.

The need for monitoring by lenders adds to the importance of long-term customer relationships. If the borrower has borrowed from the financial institution before, the institution has already established procedures for monitoring that customer. Therefore, the costs of monitoring long-term customers are lower than those for new customers.

Long-term relationships benefit the customers as well as the financial institution. A firm with a previous relationship will find it easier to obtain a loan at a low interest rate because the financial institution has an easier time determining if the prospective borrower is a good credit risk and incurs fewer costs in monitoring the borrower.

A long-term customer relationship has another advantage for the financial institution. No financial institution manager can think of every contingency when the institution writes a restrictive covenant into a loan contract; there will always be risky borrower activities that are not ruled out. However, what if a borrower wants to preserve a long-term relationship with the financial institution because it will be easier to get future loans at low interest rates? The borrower then has the incentive to avoid risky activities that would upset the financial institution, even if restrictions on these risky activities are not specified in the loan contract. Indeed, if the financial institution manager doesn't like what a borrower is doing even when the borrower isn't violating any restrictive covenants, the manager has some power to discourage the borrower from such activity: She can threaten not to let the borrower have new loans in the future. Long-term customer relationships therefore enable financial institutions to deal with even unanticipated moral hazard contingencies.

Loan Commitments

Banks have a special vehicle for institutionalizing a long-term customer relationship called a **loan commitment.** A loan commitment is a bank's commitment (for a specified future period of time) to provide a firm with loans up to a given amount at an interest rate that is tied to some market interest rate. The majority of commercial and industrial loans from banks are made under the loan commitment arrangement. The advantage for the firm is that it has a source of credit when it needs it. The advantage for the bank is that the loan commitment promotes a long-term relationship, which in turn facilitates information collection. In addition, provisions in the loan commitment agreement require that the firm continually supply the bank with information about the firm's income, asset and liability position, business activities, and so on. A loan commitment arrangement is a powerful method for reducing the bank's costs for screening and information collection.

Collateral

Collateral requirements for loans are important credit risk management tools. Loans with these collateral requirements are often referred to as **secured loans.** Collateral, which is property promised to the lender as compensation if the borrower defaults, lessens the consequences of adverse selection because it reduces the lender's losses in the case of a loan default. It also reduces moral hazard because the borrower has more to lose from a loan default. If a borrower defaults on a loan, the lender can sell the collateral and use the proceeds to make up for its losses on the loan. Collateral requirements thus offer important protection for financial institutions making loans, and that is why they are extremely common in loans made by financial institutions.

Compensating Balances

One particular form of collateral required when a bank makes commercial loans is called **compensating balances:** A firm receiving a loan must keep a required minimum amount of funds in a checking account at the bank. For example, a business getting a ₹10 million loan may be required to keep compensating balances of at least ₹1 million in its checking account at the bank. This ₹1 million in compensating balances can then be taken by the bank to make up some of the losses on the loan if the borrower defaults.

Besides serving as collateral, compensating balances help increase the likelihood that a loan will be paid off. They do this by helping the bank monitor the borrower and consequently reduce moral hazard. Specifically, by requiring the borrower to use a checking account at the bank, the bank can observe the firm's check payment practices, which may yield a great deal of information about the borrower's financial condition. For example, a sustained drop in the borrower's checking account balance may signal that the borrower is having financial trouble, or account activity may suggest that the borrower is engaging in risky activities; perhaps a change in suppliers means that the borrower is pursuing new lines of business. Any significant change in the borrower's payment procedures is a signal to the bank that it should make inquiries. Compensating balances therefore make it easier for banks to monitor borrowers more effectively and are another important credit risk management tool.

Credit Rationing

Another way in which financial institutions deal with adverse selection and moral hazard is through **credit rationing:** refusing to make loans even though borrowers are willing to pay the stated interest rate or even a higher rate. Credit rationing takes two forms. The first occurs when a lender refuses to make a loan *of any amount* to a borrower, even if the borrower is willing to pay a higher interest rate. The second occurs when a lender is willing to make a loan but restricts the size of the loan to less than the borrower would like.

At first, you might be puzzled by the first type of credit rationing. After all, even if the potential borrower is a credit risk, why doesn't the lender just extend the loan but at a higher interest rate? The answer is that adverse selection prevents this solution. Individuals and firms with the riskiest investment projects are exactly those that are willing to pay the highest interest rates. If a borrower took on a high-risk investment and succeeded, the borrower would become extremely rich. But a lender wouldn't want to make such a loan precisely because the credit risk is high; the likely outcome is that the borrower will *not* succeed and the lender will not be paid back. Charging a higher interest rate just makes adverse selection worse for the lender; that is, it increases the likelihood that the lender is lending to a bad credit risk. The lender would therefore rather not make any loans at a higher interest rate; instead, it would engage in the first type of credit rationing and would turn down loans.

Financial institutions engage in the second type of credit rationing to guard against moral hazard: They grant loans to borrowers, but not loans as large as the borrowers want. Such credit rationing is necessary because the larger the loan, the greater the benefits from moral hazard. If a financial institution gives you a ₹1,000 loan, for example, you are likely to take actions that enable you to pay it back because you don't want to hurt your credit rating for the future. However, if the financial institution lends you ₹10 million, you are more likely to fly down to Rio to celebrate. The larger your loan, the greater your incentives to engage in activities that make it less likely that you will repay the loan. Because more borrowers repay their loans if the loan amounts are small, financial institutions ration credit by providing borrowers with smaller loans than they seek.

Managing Interest-Rate Risk

With the increased volatility of interest rates that occurred in the 1980s, financial institution managers became more concerned about their exposure to interest-rate risk, the riskiness of earnings and returns that is associated with changes in interest rates. Indeed, the S&L debacle, described in Chapter 18, made clearer the dangers of interest-rate risk when many S&Ls went out of business because they had not managed interest-rate risk properly. To see what interest-rate risk is all about, let's take a look at the balance sheet of the First National Bank:

First National Bank			
Assets		**Liabilities**	
Reserves and cash items	₹5 million	Checkable deposits	₹15 million
Securities		Money market	
Less than 1 year	₹5 million	deposit accounts	₹5 million
1 to 2 years	₹5 million	Savings deposits	₹15 million
Greater than 2 years	₹10 million	CDs	
Residential mortgages		Variable rate	₹10 million
Variable rate	₹10 million	Less than 1 year	₹15 million
Fixed rate (30-year)	₹10 million	1 to 2 years	₹5 million
Commercial loans		Greater than 2 years	₹5 million
Less than 1 year	₹15 million		
1 to 2 years	₹10 million	Borrowings	
Greater than 2 years	₹25 million	Less than 1 year	₹15 million
Physical capital	₹5 million	1 to 2 years	₹5 million
		Greater than 2 years	₹5 million
		Bank capital	₹5 million
Total	₹100 million	Total	₹100 million

The first step in assessing interest rate risk is for the bank manager to decide which assets and liabilities are rate-sensitive, that is, which have interest rates that will be reset (repriced) within the year. Note that rate-sensitive assets or liabilities can have interest rates repriced within the year either because the debt instrument matures within the year or because the repricing is done automatically, as with variable-rate mortgages.

For many assets and liabilities, deciding whether they are rate-sensitive is straightforward. In our example, the obviously rate-sensitive assets are securities with maturities of less than one year (₹5 million), variable-rate mortgages (₹10 million), and commercial loans with maturities of less than one year (₹15 million), for a total of ₹30 million. However, some assets that look like fixed-rate assets whose interest rates are not repriced within the year actually have a component that is rate-sensitive. For example, although fixed-rate residential mortgages may have a maturity of 30 years, homeowners can repay their mortgages early by selling their homes or repaying the mortgage in some other way. This means that within the year, a certain percentage of these fixed-rate mortgages will be paid off, and interest rates on this amount will be repriced. From past experience the bank manager knows that 20% of the fixed-rate residential mortgages are repaid within a year, which means that ₹2 million of these mortgages (20% of ₹10 million) must be considered rate-sensitive. The bank manager adds this ₹2 million to the ₹30 million of rate-sensitive assets already calculated, for a total of ₹32 million in rate-sensitive assets.

The bank manager now goes through a similar procedure to determine the total amount of rate-sensitive liabilities. The obviously rate-sensitive liabilities are money market deposit accounts (₹5 million), variable-rate CDs and CDs with less than one year to maturity (₹25 million), repo loans, and borrowings with maturities of less than one year (₹15 million), for a total of ₹45 million. Checkable deposits and savings deposits often have interest rates that can be changed at any time by the bank, although banks often like to keep their rates fixed for substantial periods. Thus, these liabilities are partially but not fully rate-sensitive. The bank manager estimates that 10% of checkable deposits (₹1.5 million) and 20% of savings deposits (₹3 million) should be considered rate-sensitive. Adding the ₹1.5 million and ₹3 million to the ₹45 million figure yields a total for rate-sensitive liabilities of ₹49.5 million.

Now the bank manager can analyze what will happen if interest rates rise by 1 percentage point, say, on average from 10% to 11%. The income on the assets rises by ₹320,000 (= 1% × ₹32 million of rate-sensitive assets), while the payments on the liabilities rise by ₹495,000 (= 1% × ₹49.5 million of rate-sensitive liabilities). The First National Bank's profits now decline by ₹175,000 = (₹320,000 − ₹495,000). Another way of thinking about this situation is with the net interest margin concept described in Chapter 16, which is interest income minus interest expense divided by bank assets. In this case, the 1% rise in interest rates has resulted in a decline of the net interest margin by 0.175% (= −₹175,000/₹100 million). Conversely, if interest rates fall by 1%, similar reasoning tells us that the First National Bank's income rises by ₹175,000 and its net interest margin rises by 0.175%. This example illustrates the following point: If a financial institution has more rate-sensitive liabilities than assets, a rise in interest rates will reduce the net interest margin and income, and a decline in interest rates will raise the net interest margin and income.

Income Gap Analysis

One simple and quick approach to measuring the sensitivity of bank income to changes in interest rates is **gap analysis** (also called **income gap analysis**), in which the amount of rate-sensitive liabilities is subtracted from the amount of rate-sensitive assets. This calculation, *GAP*, can be written as

$$GAP = RSA - RSL \tag{1}$$

where
$$RSA = \text{rate-sensitive assets}$$
$$RSL = \text{rate-sensitive liabilities}$$

In our example, the bank manager calculates GAP to be

$$GAP = ₹32 \text{ million} - ₹49.5 \text{ million} = -₹17.5 \text{ million}$$

Multiplying GAP times the change in the interest rate immediately reveals the effect on bank income:

$$\Delta I = GAP \times \Delta i \qquad (2)$$

where
$$\Delta I = \text{change in bank income}$$
$$\Delta i = \text{change in interest rates}$$

EXAMPLE 19.1

Income Gap Analysis

Using the −₹17.5 million gap calculated using Equation 1, what is the change in income if interest rates rise by 1%?

> Solution

The change in income is −₹175,000.

$$\Delta I = GAP \times \Delta i$$

where

$$GAP = RSA - RSL \qquad = -₹17.5 \text{ million}$$
$$\Delta i \quad = \text{ change in interest rate } = 0.01$$

Thus,

$$\Delta I = -₹17.5 \text{ million} \times 0.01 = -₹175,000$$

The analysis we just conducted is known as *basic gap analysis*, and it suffers from the problem that many of the assets and liabilities that are not classified as rate-sensitive have different maturities. One refinement to deal with this problem, the *maturity bucket approach*, is to measure the gap for several maturity subintervals, called maturity buckets, so that effects of interest-rate changes over a multiyear period can be calculated.

EXAMPLE 19.2

Income Gap Analysis

The manager of First National Bank notices that the bank balance sheet allows him to put assets and liabilities into more refined maturity buckets that allow him to estimate the potential change in income over the next one to two years. Rate-sensitive assets in this period consist of ₹5 million of securities maturing in one to two years, ₹10 million of commercial loans maturing in one to two years, and an additional ₹2 million (20% of fixed-rate mortgages) that the bank expects to be repaid. Rate-sensitive liabilities in this period consist of ₹5 million of one- to two-year CDs, ₹5 million of one- to two-year borrowings, ₹1.5 million of checkable deposits (the 10% of checkable deposits that the bank manager estimates are rate-sensitive in this period), and an additional ₹3 million of savings deposits (the 20% estimate of savings deposits). For the next one to two years, calculate the gap and the change in income if interest rates rise by 1%.

> **Solution**

The gap calculation for the one- to two-year period is ₹2.5 million.

$$GAP = RSA - RSL$$

where

RSA = rate-sensitive assets　　= ₹17 million

RSL = rate-sensitive liabilities = ₹14.5 million

Thus,

$$GAP = ₹17 \text{ million} - ₹14.5 \text{ million} = ₹2.5 \text{ million}$$

If interest rates remain 1% higher, then in the second year income will improve by ₹25,000.

$$\Delta I = GAP \times \Delta i$$

where

$GAP = RSA - RSL$　　　　　　= ₹2.5 million

Δi　= change in interest rate = 0.01

Thus,

$$\Delta I = ₹2.5 \text{ million} \times 0.01 = ₹25,000$$

By using the more refined maturity bucket approach, the bank manager can figure out what will happen to bank income over the next several years when there is a change in interest rates.

Duration Gap Analysis

The gap analysis we have examined so far focuses only on the effect of interest-rate changes on income. Clearly, owners and managers of financial institutions care not only about the effect of changes in interest rates on income but also about the effect of changes in interest rates on the market value of the net worth of the financial institution.[1]

An alternative method for measuring interest-rate risk, called **duration gap analysis,** examines the sensitivity of the market value of the financial institution's net worth to changes in interest rates. Duration analysis is based on Macaulay's concept of *duration*, which measures the average lifetime of a security's stream of payments (described in Chapter 3). Recall that duration is a useful concept because it provides a good approximation, particularly when interest-rate changes are small,

---

[1]Note that accounting net worth is calculated on a historical-cost (book-value) basis, meaning that the value of assets and liabilities is based on their initial price. However, book-value net worth does not give a complete picture of the true worth of the firm; the market value of net worth provides a more accurate measure. This is why duration gap analysis focuses on what happens to the market value of net worth, and not on book value, when interest rates change.

of the sensitivity of a security's market value to a change in its interest rate using the following formula:

$$\% \Delta P \approx -DUR \times \frac{\Delta i}{1 + i} \tag{3}$$

where $\% \Delta P = (P_{t+1} - P_t)/P_t =$ percent change in market value of the security
$DUR =$ duration
$i =$ interest rate

After having determined the duration of all assets and liabilities on the bank's balance sheet, the bank manager could use this formula to calculate how the market value of each asset and liability changes when there is a change in interest rates and then calculate the effect on net worth. There is, however, an easier way to go about doing this, derived from the basic fact about duration we learned in Chapter 3: Duration is additive; that is, the duration of a portfolio of securities is the weighted average of the durations of the individual securities, with the weights reflecting the proportion of the portfolio invested in each. What this means is that the bank manager can figure out the effect that interest-rate changes will have on the market value of net worth by calculating the average duration for assets and for liabilities and then using those figures to estimate the effects of interest-rate changes. To see how a bank manager would do this, let's return to the balance sheet of the First National Bank. The bank manager has already used the procedures outlined in Chapter 3 to calculate the duration of each asset and liability, as listed in Table 19.1. For each asset, the manager then calculates the weighted duration by multiplying the duration times the amount of the asset divided by total assets, which in this case is ₹100 million. For example, in the case of securities with maturities of less than one year, the manager multiplies the 0.4 year of duration times ₹5 million divided by ₹100 million to get a weighted duration of 0.02. (Note that physical assets have no cash payments, so they have a duration of zero years.) Doing this for all the assets and adding them up, the bank manager gets a figure for the average duration of the assets of 2.70 years.

The manager follows a similar procedure for the liabilities, noting that total liabilities excluding capital are ₹95 million. For example, the weighted duration for checkable deposits is determined by multiplying the 2.0-year duration by ₹15 million divided by ₹95 million to get 0.32. Adding up these weighted durations, the manager obtains an average duration of liabilities of 1.05 years.

EXAMPLE 19.3

Duration Gap Analysis

The bank manager wants to know what happens when interest rates rise from 10% to 11%. The total asset value is ₹100 million, and the total liability value is ₹95 million. Use Equation 3 to calculate the change in the market value of the assets and liabilities.

> **Solution**
With a total asset value of ₹100 million, the market value of assets falls by ₹2.5 million (₹100 million × 0.025 = ₹2.5 million).

$$\% \Delta P \approx -DUR \times \frac{\Delta i}{1 + i}$$

where

DUR = duration   = 2.70
Δi = change in interest rate = $0.11 - 0.10 = 0.01$
i = interest rate   = 0.10

Thus,

$$\% \Delta P \approx -2.70 \times \frac{0.01}{1 + 0.10} = -0.025 = -2.5\%$$

With total liabilities of ₹95 million, the market value of liabilities falls by ₹0.9 million (₹95 million × 0.009 = −₹0.9 million).

$$\% \Delta P \approx -DUR \times \frac{\Delta i}{1 + i}$$

where

DUR = duration   = 1.05
Δi = change in interest rate = $0.11 - 0.10 = 0.01$
i = interest rate   = 0.10

Thus,

$$\% \Delta P \approx -1.05 \times \frac{0.01}{1 + 0.10} = -0.009 = -0.94\%$$

The result is that the net worth of the bank would decline by ₹1.6 million (−₹2.5 million − (−₹0.9 million) = −₹2.5 million + ₹0.94 million = −₹1.5 million).

The bank manager could have obtained the answer even more quickly by calculating what is called a *duration gap*, which is defined as follows:

$$DUR_{gap} = DUR_a - \left(\frac{L}{A} \times DUR_l \right) \tag{4}$$

where
DUR_a = average duration of assets
DUR_l = average duration of liabilities
L = market value of liabilities
A = market value of assets

TABLE 19.1 **Duration of the First National Bank's Assets and Liabilities**

	Amount (₹ millions)	Duration (years)	Weighted Duration (years)
Assets			
Reserves and cash items	5	0.0	0.00
Securities			
Less than 1 year	5	0.4	0.02
1 to 2 years	5	1.6	0.08
Greater than 2 years	10	7.0	0.70

	Amount (₹ millions)	Duration (years)	Weighted Duration (years)
Residential mortgages			
Variable rate	10	0.5	0.05
Fixed rate (30-year)	10	6.0	0.60
Commercial loans			
Less than 1 year	15	0.7	0.11
1 to 2 years	10	1.4	0.14
Greater than 2 years	25	4.0	1.00
Physical capital	5	0.0	0.00
Average duration			2.70
Liabilities			
Checkable deposits	15	2.0	0.32
Money market deposit accounts	5	0.1	0.01
Savings deposits	15	1.0	0.16
CDs			
Variable rate	10	0.5	0.05
Less than 1 year	15	0.2	0.03
1 to 2 years	5	1.2	0.06
Greater than 2 years	5	2.7	0.14
Fed funds	5	0.0	0.00
Borrowings			
Less than 1 year	15	0.3	0.04
1 to 2 years	5	1.3	0.07
Greater than 2 years	5	3.1	0.16
Average duration			1.05

EXAMPLE 19.4

Gap Analysis

Based on the information provided in Example 3, use Equation 4 to determine the duration gap for First National Bank.

> **Solution**

The duration gap for First National Bank is 1.72 years.

$$DUR_{gap} = DUR_a - \left(\frac{L}{A} \times DUR_l \right)$$

where

DUR_a = average duration of assets = 2.70

L = market value of liabilities = 95

A = market value of assets = 100

DUR_l = average duration of liabilities = 1.05

Thus,

$$DUR_{gap} = 2.70 - \left(\frac{95}{100} \times 1.05 \right) = 1.70 \text{ years}$$

EXAMPLE 19.5

Duration Gap Analysis

What is the change in the market value of net worth as a percentage of assets if interest rates rise from 10% to 11%? (Use Equation 5.)

> **Solution**

A rise in interest rates from 10% to 11% would lead to a change in the market value of net worth as a percentage of assets of −1.6%.

$$\frac{\Delta NW}{A} = -DUR_{gap} \times \frac{\Delta i}{1 + i}$$

where

$$
\begin{aligned}
DUR_{gap} &= \text{duration gap} & = 1.7 \\
\Delta i &= \text{change in interest rate} &= 0.11 - 0.10 = 0.01 \\
i &= \text{interest rate} & = 0.10
\end{aligned}
$$

Thus,

$$\frac{\Delta NW}{A} = -1.7 \times \frac{0.01}{1 + 0.10} = -0.015 = -1.5\%$$

To estimate what will happen if interest rates change, the bank manager uses the DUR_{gap} calculation in Equation 4 to obtain the change in the market value of net worth as a percentage of total assets. In other words, the change in the market value of net worth as a percentage of assets is calculated as

$$\frac{\Delta NW}{A} \approx -DUR_{gap} \times \frac{\Delta i}{1 + i} \tag{5}$$

With assets totaling ₹100 million, Example 19.5 indicates a fall in the market value of net worth of ₹1.5 million, which is the same amount that we found in Example 19.3.

As our examples make clear, both income gap analysis and duration gap analysis indicate that the First National Bank will suffer from a rise in interest rates. Indeed, in this example, we have seen that a rise in interest rates from 10% to 11% will cause the market value of net worth to fall by ₹1.5 million, which is one-third the initial amount of bank capital. Thus, the bank manager realizes that the bank faces substantial interest-rate risk because a rise in interest rates could cause it to lose a lot of its capital. Clearly, income gap analysis and duration gap analysis are useful tools for telling a financial institution manager the institution's degree of exposure to interest-rate risk.

CASE

Interest Rate Risk in Banking Book in India

GO ONLINE

Access **https://www.rbi.org. in/scripts/bs_viewcontent. aspx?Id=3308** to study the Draft Guidelines on Governance, Measurement and Management of Interest Rate Risk in Banking Books.

The Interest Rate Risk (IRR) is the risk where changes in market interest rates affect a bank's financial position. The changes in interest rates impact a bank's earnings (i.e. reported profits) through changes in its Net Interest Income (NII) and also impact Market Value of Equity (MVE) or Net Worth through changes in the economic value of its rate sensitive assets, liabilities and off-balance sheet positions. The interest rate risks, when viewed from these two perspectives, are known as 'earnings perspective' and 'economic value perspective', respectively. Generally, the former is measured using the Traditional Gap Analysis (TGA) and the latter is measured by using more sophisticated methods like Duration Gap Analysis (DGA). The present RBI guidelines on IRR require banks to carry out both the analyses.

The focus of the TGA is to measure the level of a bank's exposure to interest rate risk in terms of sensitivity of its NII to interest rate movements over a period of one year. It involves bucketing of all rate sensitive assets (RSA) and rate sensitive liabilities (RSL) and off balance sheet items as per residual maturity/ re-pricing date in various time bands, and computing Earnings at Risk (EaR) i.e. loss of income under different interest rate scenarios over a time horizon of one year.

The focus of the DGA is to measure the level of a bank's exposure to interest rate risk in terms of sensitivity of MVE to interest rate movements. The DGA involves bucketing of all RSA and RSL as per residual maturity/ re-pricing dates in various time bands and computing the Modified Duration Gap (MDG). The RSA and RSL include the rate sensitive off balance sheet asset and liabilities. MDG can be used to evaluate the impact on the MVE of the bank under different interest rate scenarios.

The RBI guidelines on Asset liability Management (ALM) system dated February 10, 1999 require banks to perform Traditional Gap Analysis (TGA). The gap analysis measures mismatches between rate sensitive assets and rate sensitive liabilities by grouping them into various time buckets. Banks are required to set prudential limits on individual gaps with the approval of their Board/Management Committee. Banks are also required to perform a DGA.

Banks are required to set appropriate internal limits on Earnings at Risk (EaR) and on the volatility in the Market Value of Equity with the approval of its Board / Risk Management Committee of the Board. These limits may be linked to MVE for DGA and the NII (for TGA). Further, the Board / Asset Liability Management Committee (ALCO) must also periodically review the above limits after assessing various scenarios of interest rates and the resultant volatility of earnings in terms of Net Interest Income and volatility in net worth.

The extant guidelines provide detailed guidance to banks to bucket various positions in different time bands depending on their interest rate risk sensitivity. For certain types of deposits, like current deposits or savings bank deposits which are essentially Non Maturity Deposits (NMDs), banks are required to estimate behavioural patterns and place them into appropriate buckets. Banks, which are not able to estimate these behavioural patterns, are required to follow the standardised approach.

Interest Rate Risk in Banking Book

Interest Rate Risk in Banking Book (IRRBB) refers to the current or prospective risk to a bank's capital and earnings arising from adverse movements in interest rates that affect banking book positions. When interest rates change, the present value and timing of future cash flows change. This in turn changes the underlying value of a bank's assets, liabilities and off-balance sheet items and hence its economic value. Changes in interest rates also affect a bank's earnings by altering interest rate-sensitive income and expenses, affecting its net interest income (NII). Excessive IRRBB can pose a significant threat to a bank's current capital base and/or future earnings if not managed appropriately.

Capital requirements for Interest Rate Risk

Banks are required to compute capital requirements for interest rate risk in trading book positions, and the resultant risk weighted assets are added to banks' total risk weighted assets. As a part of Pillar 2 of Basel III Capital regulations, banks are required to identify the risks associated with the changing interest rates on its on-balance sheet and off-balance sheet exposures in the banking book from both, short-term and long-term perspective. It is also mentioned that banks can decide, with the approval of the Board, on the appropriate level of interest rate risk in the banking book, which they would like to carry keeping in view their capital level, interest rate management skills and the ability to re-balance the banking book portfolios quickly in case of adverse movement in the interest rates.

A level of interest rate risk, which generates a drop in the MVE of more than 20 per cent with an interest rate shock of 200 basis points, is treated as excessive, and such banks may be required by the RBI to hold additional capital against IRRBB as determined during the Supervisory Review and Evaluation Process (SREP). Banks, which have IRRBB exposure equivalent to less than 20 per cent drop in the MVE may be required to hold additional capital if the level of interest rate risk is considered, by the RBI, to be high in relation to their capital level or the quality of interest rate risk management framework obtaining in the bank. While banks may on their own decide to hold additional capital towards IRRBB keeping in view the potential drop in their MVE, the IRR management skills and the ability to re-balance the portfolios quickly in case of adverse movement in the interest rates, the amount of exact capital add-on, if considered necessary, may have to be decided by the RBI as part of the SREP, in consultation with the bank concerned.

Source: https://www.rbi.org.in/scripts/bs_viewcontent.aspx?Id=3308

Example of a Nonbanking Financial Institution

So far we have focused on an example involving a banking institution that has borrowed short and lent long so that when interest rates rise, both income and the net worth of the institution fall. It is important to recognize that income gap and duration gap analyses apply equally to other financial institutions. Furthermore, it is important for you to see that some financial institutions have income gaps and duration gaps that are opposite in sign to those of banks, so that when interest rates rise, both income and net worth rise rather than fall. To get a more complete picture of income gap and duration gap analyses, let us look at a nonbank financial institution, the Friendly Finance Company, which specializes in making consumer loans.

The Friendly Finance Company has the following balance sheet:

Friendly Finance Company			
Assets		**Liabilities**	
Cash and deposits	₹3 million	Commercial paper	₹40 million
Securities		Bank loans	
Less than 1 year	₹5 million	Less than 1 year	₹3 million
1 to 2 years	₹1 million	1 to 2 years	₹2 million
Greater than 2 years	₹1 million	Greater than 2 years	₹5 million
Consumer loans		Long-term bonds and	
Less than 1 year	₹50 million	other long-term debt	₹40 million
1 to 2 years	₹20 million	Capital	₹10 million
Greater than 2 years	₹15 million		
Physical capital	₹5 million		
Total	₹100 million	Total	₹100 million

The manager of the Friendly Finance Company calculates the rate-sensitive assets to be equal to the ₹5 million of securities with maturities of less than one year plus the ₹50 million of consumer loans with maturities of less than one year, for a total of ₹55 million of rate-sensitive assets. The manager then calculates the rate-sensitive liabilities to be equal to the ₹40 million of commercial paper, all of which has a maturity of less than one year, plus the ₹3 million of bank loans maturing in less than a year, for a total of ₹43 million. The calculation of the income gap is then

$$GAP = RSA - RSL = ₹55 \text{ million} - ₹43 \text{ million} = ₹12 \text{ million}$$

To calculate the effect on income if interest rates rise by 1%, the manager multiplies the GAP of ₹12 million times the change in the interest rate to get the following:

$$\Delta I = GAP \times \Delta i = ₹12 \text{ million} \times 1\% = ₹120,000$$

Thus, the manager finds that the finance company's income will rise by ₹120,000 when interest rates rise by 1%. The reason that the company has benefited from the interest-rate rise, in contrast to the First National Bank, whose profits suffer from the rise in interest rates, is that the Friendly Finance Company has a positive income gap because it has more rate-sensitive assets than liabilities.

Like the bank manager, the manager of the Friendly Finance Company is also interested in what happens to the market value of the net worth of the company when interest rates rise by 1%. So the manager calculates the weighted duration of each item in the balance sheet, adds them up as in Table 19.2, and obtains a duration for the assets of 1.14 years and for the liabilities of 2.77 years. The duration gap is then calculated to be

$$DUR_{gap} = DUR_a - \left(\frac{L}{A} \times DUR_l\right) = 1.14 - \left(\frac{90}{100} \times 2.77\right) = -1.35 \text{ years}$$

TABLE 19.2   **Duration of the Friendly Finance Company's Assets and Liabilities**

	Amount (₹ millions)	Duration (years)	Weighted Duration (years)
Assets			
Cash and deposits	3	0.0	0.00
Securities			
Less than 1 year	5	0.5	0.03
1 to 2 years	1	1.7	0.02
Greater than 2 years	1	9.0	0.09
Consumer loans			
Less than 1 year	50	0.5	0.25
1 to 2 years	20	1.5	0.30
Greater than 2 years	15	3.0	0.45
Physical capital	5	0.0	0.00
Average duration			1.14
Liabilities			
Commercial paper	40	0.2	0.09
Bank loans			
Less than 1 year	3	0.3	0.01
1 to 2 years	2	1.6	0.04
Greater than 2 years	5	3.5	0.19
Long-term bonds and other long-term debt	40	5.5	2.44
Average duration			2.77

Since the Friendly Finance Company has a negative duration gap, the manager realizes that a rise in interest rates by 1 percentage point from 10% to 11% will increase the market value of net worth of the firm. The manager checks this by calculating the change in the market value of net worth as a percentage of assets:

$$\frac{\Delta NW}{A} = -DUR_{gap} \times \frac{\Delta i}{1 + i} = -(-1.35) \times \frac{0.01}{1 + 0.10} = 0.012 = 1.2\%$$

With assets of ₹100 million, this calculation indicates that net worth will rise in market value by ₹1.2 million.

Even though the income gap and duration gap analyses indicate that the Friendly Finance Company gains from a rise in interest rates, the manager realizes that if interest rates go in the other direction, the company will suffer a fall in income and market value of net worth. Thus, the finance company manager, like the bank manager, realizes that the institution is subject to substantial interest-rate risk.

Some Problems with Income Gap and Duration Gap Analyses

Although you might think that income gap and duration gap analyses are complicated enough, further complications make a financial institution manager's job even harder.

One assumption that we have been using in our discussion of income gap and duration gap analyses is that when the level of interest rates changes, interest rates on all maturities change by exactly the same amount. That is the same as saying that we conducted our analysis under the assumption that the slope of the yield curve remains unchanged. Indeed, the situation is even worse for duration gap analysis because the duration gap is calculated assuming that interest rates for all maturities are the same—in other words, the yield curve is assumed to be flat. As our discussion of the term structure of interest rates in Chapter 5 indicated, however, the yield curve is not flat, and the slope of the yield curve fluctuates and has a tendency to change when the level of the interest rate changes. Thus, to get a truly accurate assessment of interest-rate risk, a financial institution manager has to assess what might happen to the slope of the yield curve when the level of the interest rate changes and then take this information into account when assessing interest-rate risk. In addition, duration gap analysis is based on the approximation in Equation 3 and thus only works well for small changes in interest rates.

A problem with income gap analysis is that, as we have seen, the financial institution manager must make estimates of the proportion of supposedly fixed-rate assets and liabilities that may be rate-sensitive. This involves estimates of the likelihood of prepayment of loans or customer shifts out of deposits when interest rates change. Such guesses are not easy to make, and as a result, the financial institution manager's estimates of income gaps may not be very accurate. A similar problem occurs in calculating durations of assets and liabilities because many of the cash payments are uncertain. Thus, the estimate of the duration gap might not be accurate either.

Do these problems mean that managers of banks and other financial institutions should give up on gap analysis as a tool for measuring interest rate risk? Financial institutions do use more sophisticated approaches to measuring interest-rate risk, such as scenario analysis and value-at-risk analysis, which make greater use of computers to more accurately measure changes in prices of assets when interest rates change. Income gap and duration gap analyses, however, still provide simple frameworks to help financial institution managers to get a first assessment of interest-rate risk, and thus they are useful tools in the financial institution managers' toolkit.

THE PRACTICING MANAGER

Strategies for Managing Interest-Rate Risk

Once financial institution managers have done the income gap and duration gap analyses for their institutions, they must decide which alternative strategies to pursue. If the manager of the First National Bank firmly believes that interest rates will fall in the future, he or she may be willing to take no action knowing that the bank has more rate-sensitive liabilities than rate-sensitive assets and so will benefit from the expected interest rate decline. However, the bank manager also realizes that the First National Bank is subject to substantial interest-rate risk because there is always a possibility that interest rates will rise rather than fall, and as we have seen, this outcome could bankrupt the bank. The manager might try to shorten the duration of the bank's assets to increase their rate sensitivity either by purchasing assets of shorter maturity or by converting fixed-rate loans into adjustable-rate loans. Alternatively, the bank manager could lengthen the duration of the liabilities. With these adjustments to the bank's assets and liabilities, the bank would be less affected by interest-rate swings.

For example, the bank manager might decide to eliminate the income gap by increasing the amount of rate-sensitive assets to ₹49.5 million to equal the ₹49.5 million of rate-sensitive liabilities. Or the manager could reduce rate-sensitive liabilities to ₹32 million so that they equal rate-sensitive assets. In either case, the income gap would now be zero, so a change in interest rates would have no effect on bank profits in the coming year.

Alternatively, the bank manager might decide to immunize the market value of the bank's net worth completely from interest-rate risk by adjusting assets and liabilities so that the duration gap is equal to zero. To do this, the manager can set DUR_{gap} equal to zero in Equation 4 and solve for DUR_a:

$$DUR_a = \frac{L}{A} \times DUR_l = \frac{95}{100} \times 1.05 = 1.00$$

These calculations reveal that the manager should reduce the average duration of the bank's assets to 1 year. To check that the duration gap is set equal to zero, the calculation is

$$DUR_{gap} = 1 - \left(\frac{95}{100} \times 1.05 \right) = 0$$

In this case, using Equation 5, the market value of net worth would remain unchanged when interest rates change. Alternatively, the bank manager could calculate the value of the duration of the liabilities that would produce a duration gap of zero. To do this would involve setting DUR_{gap} equal to zero in Equation 4 and solving for DUR_l:

$$DUR_l = DUR_a \times \frac{A}{L} = 2.70 \times \frac{100}{95} = 2.84$$

This calculation reveals that the interest-rate risk could also be eliminated by increasing the average duration of the bank's liabilities to 2.84 years. The manager again checks that the duration gap is set equal to zero by calculating

$$DUR_{gap} = 2.70 - \left(\frac{95}{100} \times 2.84 \right) = 0$$

One problem with eliminating a financial institution's interest-rate risk by altering the balance sheet is that doing so might be very costly in the short run. The financial institution may be locked into assets and liabilities of particular durations because of its field of expertise. Fortunately, recently developed financial instruments, such as financial futures, options, and interest-rate swaps, help financial institutions manage their interest-rate risk without requiring them to rearrange their balance sheets. We discuss these instruments and how they can be used to manage interest-rate risk in the next chapter.

SUMMARY

1. The concepts of adverse selection and moral hazard explain the origin of many credit risk management principles involving loan activities, including screening and monitoring, development of long-term customer relationships, loan commitments, collateral, compensating balances, and credit rationing.

2. With the increased volatility of interest rates that occurred in recent years, financial institutions became more concerned about their exposure to interest-rate risk. Income gap and duration gap analyses tell a financial institution if it has fewer rate-sensitive assets than liabilities (in which case a rise in interest rates will reduce income and a fall in interest rates will raise it) or more rate-sensitive assets than liabilities (in which case a rise in interest rates will raise income and a fall in interest rates will reduce it). Financial institutions can manage interest-rate risk by modifying their balance sheets and by making use of new financial instruments.

KEY TERMS

compensating balances, p. 486
credit rationing, p. 486

duration gap analysis, p. 490
gap analysis (income gap analysis), p. 488

loan commitment, p. 485
secured loans, p. 485

QUESTIONS

1. Can a financial institution keep borrowers from engaging in risky activities if there are no restrictive covenants written into the loan agreement?

2. Why are secured loans an important method of lending for financial institutions?

3. "If more customers want to borrow funds at the prevailing interest rate, a financial institution can increase its profits by raising interest rates on its loans." Is this statement true, false, or uncertain? Explain your answer.

4. Why is being nosy a desirable trait for a banker?

5. A bank almost always insists that the firms it lends to keep compensating balances at the bank. Why?

6 "Because diversification is a desirable strategy for avoiding risk, it never makes sense for a financial institution to specialize in making specific types of loans." Is this statement true, false, or uncertain? Explain your answer.

QUANTITATIVE PROBLEMS

1. A bank issues a ₹100,000 variable-rate 30-year mortgage with a nominal annual rate of 4.5%. If the required rate drops to 4.0% after the first six months, what is the impact on the interest income for the first 12 months?

2. A bank issues a ₹100,000 fixed-rate 30-year mortgage with a nominal annual rate of 4.5%. If the required rate drops to 4.0% immediately after the mortgage is issued, what is the impact on the value of the mortgage?

3. Calculate the duration of a ₹100,000 fixed-rate 30-year mortgage with a nominal annual rate of 7.0%. What is the expected percentage change in value if the required rate drops to 6.5% immediately after the mortgage is issued?

4. The value of a ₹100,000 fixed-rate 30-year mortgage falls to ₹89,537 when interest rates move from 5% to 6%. What is the approximate duration of the mortgage?

5. Calculate the duration of a commercial loan. The face value of the loan is ₹2,000,000. It requires simple interest yearly, with an APR of 8%. The loan is due in four years. The current market rate for such loans is 8%.

6. A bank's balance sheet contains interest-sensitive assets of ₹280 million and interest-sensitive liabilities of ₹465 million. Calculate the income gap.

7. Calculate the income gap for a financial institution with rate-sensitive assets of ₹20 million and rate-sensitive liabilities of ₹48 million. If interest rates rise from 4% to 4.8%, what is the expected change in income?

8. Calculate the income gap given the following items:
   - ₹8 million in reserves
   - ₹25 million in variable-rate mortgages
   - ₹4 million in checkable deposits
   - ₹2 million in savings deposits
   - ₹6 million of two-year CDs

9. The following financial statement is for the current year. From the past, you know that 10% of fixed-rate mortgages prepay each year. You also estimate that 10% of checkable deposits and 20% of savings accounts are rate-sensitive.

   What is the current income gap for Second National Bank? What will happen to the bank's current net interest income if rates fall by 75 basis points?

Second National Bank			
Assets		**Liabilities**	
Reserves	₹1,500,000	Checkable deposits	₹15,000,000
Securities		Money market deposits	₹5,500,000
< 1 year	₹6,000,000	Savings accounts	₹8,000,000
1 to 2 years	₹8,000,000	CDs	
> 2 years	₹12,000,000	Variable rate	₹15,000,000
Residential mortgages		< 1 year	₹22,000,000
Variable rate	₹7,000,000	1 to 2 years	₹5,000,000
Fixed rate	₹13,000,000	> 2 years	₹2,500,000
Commercial loans		Federal funds	₹5,000,000
< 1 year	₹1,500,000	Borrowings	
1 to 2 years	₹18,500,000	< 1 year	₹12,000,000
> 2 years	₹30,000,000	1 to 2 years	₹3,000,000
Buildings, etc.	₹2,500,000	> 2 years	₹2,000,000
		Bank capital	₹5,000,000
Total	₹100,000,000	Total	₹100,000,000

10. HDFC has the following assets:

Asset	Value	Duration (in years)
T-bills	₹100,000,000	0.55
Consumer loans	₹40,000,000	2.35
Commercial loans	₹15,000,000	5.90

   What is HDFC's asset portfolio duration?

11. A bank added a bond to its portfolio. The bond has a duration of 12.3 years and cost ₹1,109. Just after buying the bond, the bank discovered that market interest rates are expected to rise from 8% to 8.75%. What is the expected change in the bond's value?

12. Calculate the change in the market value of assets and liabilities when the average duration of assets is 3.60, the average duration of liabilities 0.88, and interest rates increase from 5% to 5.5%.

13. Bank A has assets totaling ₹180 million with a duration of five years, and liabilities totaling ₹160 million with a duration of two years. If interest rates drop from 9% by 75 basis points, what is the change in the bank's capitalization ratio?

14. The manager for Bank B has the following assets and liabilities to manage:

Asset	Value	Duration (years)
Bonds	₹75,000,000	9.00
Consumer loans	₹875,000,000	2.00
Commercial loans	₹700,000,000	5.00

Liability	Value	Duration (years)
Demand deposits	₹300,000,000	1.00
Saving accounts	??	0.50

If the manager wants a duration gap of 3.00, what level of saving accounts should the bank raise? Assume that any difference between assets and liabilities is held as cash (duration = 0).

15. The following financial statement is for the current year. After you review the data, calculate the duration gap for the bank.

Second National Bank					
Assets		**Duration (in years)**	**Liabilities**		**Duration (in years)**
Reserves	₹5,000,000	0.00	Checkable deposits	₹15,000,000	2.00
Securities			Money market deposits	5,000,000	0.10
< 1 year	5,000,000	0.40	Savings accounts	15,000,000	1.00
1 to 2 years	5,000,000	1.60	CDs		
> 2 years	10,000,000	7.00	Variable rate	10,000,000	0.50
Residential mortgages			< 1 year	15,000,000	0.20
Variable rate	10,000,000	0.50	1 to 2 years	5,000,000	1.20
Fixed rate	10,000,000	6.00	> 2 years	5,000,000	2.70
Commercial loans			Interbank loans	5,000,000	0.00
< 1 year	15,000,000	0.70	Borrowings		
1 to 2 years	10,000,000	1.40	< 1 year	10,000,000	0.30
> 2 years	25,000,000	4.00	1 to 2 years	5,000,000	1.30
Buildings, etc.	5,000,000	0.00	> 2 years	5,000,000	3.10
			Bank capital	5,000,000	
Total	₹100,000,000		Total	₹100,000,000	

For Problems 16–23, assume that the First National Bank initially has the balance sheet shown on page 567 and that interest rates are initially at 10%.

16. If the First National Bank sells ₹10 million of its securities with maturities greater than two years and replaces them with securities maturing in less than one year, what is the income gap for the bank? What will happen to profits next year if interest rates fall by 3 percentage points?

17. If the First National Bank decides to convert ₹5 million of its fixed-rate mortgages into variable-rate mortgages, what happens to its interest-rate risk? Explain with income gap and duration gap analyses.

18. If the manager of the First National Bank revises the estimate of the percentage of fixed-rate mortgages that are repaid within a year from 20% to 10%, what will be the revised estimate of the interest-rate risk the bank faces? What will happen to profits next year if interest rates fall by 2 percentage points?

19. If the manager of the First National Bank revises the estimate of the percentage of checkable deposits that are rate-sensitive from 10% to 25%, what will be the revised estimate of the interest-rate risk the bank faces? What will happen to profits next year if interest rates rise by 5 percentage points?

20. Given the estimates of duration in Table 19.1, what will happen to the bank's net worth if interest rates rise by 10 percentage points? Will the bank stay in business? Why or why not?

21. If the manager of the First National Bank revises the estimates of the duration of the bank's assets to four years and liabilities to two years, what is the effect on net worth if interest rates rise by 2 percentage points?

22. Given the estimates of duration in Problem 21, how should the bank alter the duration of its assets to immunize its net worth from interest-rate risk?

23. Given the estimates of duration in Problem 21, how should the bank alter the duration of its liabilities to immunize its net worth from interest-rate risk?

For Problems 24–29, assume that the Friendly Finance Company initially has the balance sheet shown on page 575 and that interest rates are initially at 8%.

24. If the manager of the Friendly Finance Company decides to sell off ₹10 million of the company's consumer loans, half maturing within one year and half maturing in greater than two years, and uses the resulting funds to buy ₹10 million of Treasury bills, what is the income gap for the company? What will happen to profits next year if interest rates fall by 5 percentage points? How could the Friendly Finance Company alter its balance sheet to immunize its income from this change in interest rates?

25. If the Friendly Finance Company raises an additional ₹20 million with commercial paper and uses the funds to make ₹20 million of consumer loans that mature in less than one year, what happens to its interest-rate risk? In this situation, what additional changes could it make in its balance sheet to eliminate the income gap?

26. Given the estimates of duration in Table 19.2, what will happen to the Friendly Finance Company's net worth if interest rates rise by 3 percentage points? Will the company stay in business? Why or why not?

27. If the manager of the Friendly Finance Company revises the estimates of the duration of the company's assets to two years and liabilities to four years, what is the effect on net worth if interest rates rise by 3 percentage points?

28. Given the estimates of duration found in Problem 27, how should the Friendly Finance Company alter the duration of its assets to immunize its net worth from interest-rate risk?

29. Given the estimates of duration in Problem 27, how should the Friendly Finance Company alter the duration of its liabilities to immunize its net worth from interest-rate risk?

WEB EXERCISES

Risk Management in Financial Institutions

1. This chapter discussed the need financial institutions have to control credit risk by lending to creditworthy borrowers. If you allow your credit to deteriorate, you may find yourself unable to borrow when you need to. Go to **http://quicken.intuit.com/support/help/managing-your-credit/winning-back-your-finances–how-to-increase-your-credit-score-in-6-months-/INF24303.html**. What factors affect your creditworthiness? What can you do to improve your appeal to lenders?

2. The FDIC is extremely concerned with risk management in banks. High-risk banks are more likely to fail and cost the FDIC money. The FDIC regularly examines banks and rates them using a system called CAMELS. Go to **http://www.frbsf.org/econrsrch/wklyltr/wklyltr99/el99-19.html**. What does the acronym CAMELS stand for? Discuss how CAMELS ratings are used in the supervisory process.

Hedging with Financial Derivatives

> PREVIEW

Starting in the 1970s and increasingly in the 1980s and 1990s, the world became a riskier place for financial institutions. Swings in interest rates widened, and the bond and stock markets went through some episodes of increased volatility. As a result of these developments, managers of financial institutions have become more concerned with reducing the risk their institutions face. Given the greater demand for risk reduction, the process of financial innovation described in Chapter 18 came to the rescue by producing new financial instruments that help

financial institution managers manage risk better. These instruments, called **financial derivatives,** have payoffs that are linked to previously issued securities and are extremely useful risk-reduction tools.

In this chapter we look at the most important financial derivatives that managers of financial institutions use to reduce risk: forward contracts, financial futures, options, and swaps. We examine not only how markets for each of these financial derivatives work but also how each can be used by financial institution managers to reduce risk.

Hedging

**GO
ONLINE**

Access **http://www.rmahq.org/**.
The Web site of the Risk
Management Association
reports useful information
such as annual statement
studies, online publications,
and so on.

Financial derivatives are so effective in reducing risk because they enable financial institutions to **hedge,** that is, engage in a financial transaction that reduces or eliminates risk. When a financial institution has bought an asset, it is said to have taken a **long position,** and this exposes the institution to risk if the returns on the asset are uncertain. On the other hand, if it has sold an asset that it has agreed to deliver to another party at a future date, it is said to have taken a **short position,** and this can also expose the institution to risk. Financial derivatives can be used to reduce risk by invoking the following basic principle of hedging: *Hedging risk involves engaging in a financial transaction that offsets a long position by taking an additional short position, or offsets a short position by taking an additional long position.* In other words, if a financial institution has *bought* a security and has therefore taken a long position, it conducts a hedge by contracting to *sell* that security (take a short position) at some future date. Alternatively, if it has taken a short position by *selling* a security that it needs to deliver at a future date, then it conducts a hedge by contracting to *buy* that security (take a long position) at a future date. We first look at how this principle can be applied using forward contracts.

Forward Markets

Forward contracts are agreements by two parties to engage in a financial transaction at a future (forward) point in time. Here we focus on forward contracts that are linked to debt instruments, called **interest-rate forward contracts;** later in the chapter we discuss forward contracts for foreign currencies.

Interest-Rate Forward Contracts

Interest-rate forward contracts involve the future sale or purchase of a debt instrument and have several dimensions: (1) specification of the actual debt instrument that will be delivered at a future date, (2) amount of the debt instrument to be delivered, (3) price (interest rate) on the debt instrument when it is delivered, and (4) date on which delivery will take place. An example of an interest-rate forward contract might be an agreement for the First National Bank to sell to the Rock Solid Insurance Company, one year from today, $5 million face value of the 6s of 2032 Treasury bonds (coupon bonds with a 6% coupon rate that mature in 2032) at a price that yields the same interest rate on these bonds as today's, say, 6%. Because Rock Solid will buy the securities at a future date, it has taken a long position, whereas the First National Bank, which will sell the securities, has taken a short position.

THE PRACTICING MANAGER

Hedging Interest-Rate Risk with Forward Contracts

To understand why the First National Bank might want to enter into this forward contract, suppose that you are the manager of the First National Bank and have previously bought $5 million of the 6s of 2032 Treasury bonds, which currently sell at par value and so their yield to maturity is also 6%. Because these are long-term bonds, you recognize that you are exposed to substantial interest-rate risk and worry that if interest rates rise in the future, the price of these bonds will fall, resulting in a substantial capital loss that may cost you your job. How do you hedge this risk?

Knowing the basic principle of hedging, you see that your long position in these bonds must be offset by an equal short position for the same bonds with a forward contract. That is, you need to contract to sell these bonds at a future date at the current par value price. As a result, you agree with another party, in this case, Rock Solid Insurance Company, to sell them the $5 million of the 6s of 2032 Treasury bonds at par one year from today. By entering into this forward contract, you have locked in the future price and so have eliminated the price risk First National Bank faces from interest-rate changes. In other words, you have successfully hedged against interest-rate risk.

Why would the Rock Solid Insurance Company want to enter into the forward contract with the First National Bank? Rock Solid expects to receive premiums of $5 million in one year's time that it will want to invest in the 6s of 2032 but worries that interest rates on these bonds will decline between now and next year. By using the forward contract, it is able to lock in the 6% interest rate on the Treasury bonds (which will be sold to it by the First National Bank).

Pros and Cons of Forward Contracts

The advantage of forward contracts is that they can be as flexible as the parties involved want them to be. This means that an institution like the First National Bank may be able to hedge completely the interest-rate risk for the exact security it is holding in its portfolio, just as it has in our example.

However, forward contracts suffer from two problems that severely limit their usefulness. The first is that it may be very hard for an institution like the First National Bank to find another party (called a *counterparty*) to make the contract with. There are brokers to facilitate the matching up of parties like the First National Bank with the Rock Solid Insurance Company, but few institutions may want to engage in a forward contract specifically for the 6s of 2032. This means that it may prove impossible to find a counterparty when a financial institution like the First National Bank wants to make a specific type of forward contract. Furthermore, even if the First National Bank finds a counterparty, it may not get as high a price as it wants because there may not be anyone else to make the deal with. A serious problem for the market in interest-rate forward contracts, then, is that it may be difficult to make the financial transaction or that it will have to be made at a disadvantageous price; in the parlance of the financial world, this market suffers from a *lack of liquidity*. (Note that this use of the term *liquidity* when it is applied to a market is somewhat broader than its use when it is applied to an asset. For an asset, liquidity refers to the ease with which the asset can be turned into cash, whereas for a market, liquidity refers to the ease of carrying out financial transactions.)

The second problem with forward contracts is that they are subject to default risk. Suppose that in one year's time, interest rates rise so that the price of the 6s of 2032 falls. The Rock Solid Insurance Company might then decide that it would like to default on the forward contract with the First National Bank because it can now buy the bonds at a price lower than the agreed price in the forward contract.

Or perhaps Rock Solid may not have been rock solid and will have gone bust during the year and so is no longer available to complete the terms of the forward contract. Because no outside organization is guaranteeing the contract, the only recourse is for the First National Bank to go to the courts to sue Rock Solid, but this process will be costly. Furthermore, if Rock Solid is already bankrupt, the First National Bank will suffer a loss; the bank can no longer sell the 6s of 2032 at the price it had agreed with Rock Solid but instead will have to sell at a price well below that because the price of these bonds has fallen.

The presence of default risk in forward contracts means that parties to these contracts must check each other out to be sure that the counterparty is both financially sound and likely to be honest and live up to its contractual obligations. Because this is a costly process and because all the adverse selection and moral hazard problems discussed in earlier chapters apply, default risk is a major barrier to the use of interest-rate forward contracts. When the default risk problem is combined with a lack of liquidity, we see that these contracts may be of limited usefulness to financial institutions. Although a market for interest-rate forward contracts exists, particularly in Treasury and mortgage-backed securities, it is not nearly as large as the financial futures market, to which we turn next.

Financial Futures Markets

Given the default risk and liquidity problems in the interest-rate forward market, another solution to hedging interest-rate risk was needed. This solution was provided by the development of financial futures contracts by the Chicago Board of Trade, starting in 1975.

Financial Futures Contracts

A **financial futures contract** is similar to an interest-rate forward contract in that it specifies that a financial instrument must be delivered by one party to another on a stated future date. However, it differs from an interest-rate forward contract in several ways that overcome some of the liquidity and default problems of forward markets.

To understand what financial futures contracts are all about, let's look at one of the most widely traded futures contracts, that for US Treasury bonds, which are traded on the Chicago Board of Trade. (An illustration of how prices on these contracts are quoted can be found in the Following the Financial News box, "Financial Futures.") The contract value is for $100,000 face value of bonds. Prices are quoted in points, with each point equal to $1,000, and the smallest change in price is 1/32 of a point ($31.25). This contract specifies that the bonds to be delivered must have at least 15 years to maturity at the delivery date (and must also not be callable, that is, redeemable by the Treasury at its option, in less than 15 years). If the Treasury bonds delivered to settle the futures contract have a coupon rate different from the 6% specified in the futures contract, the amount of bonds to be delivered is adjusted to reflect the difference in value between the delivered bonds and the 6% coupon bond. In line with the terminology used for forward contracts, parties who have bought a futures contract and thereby agreed to buy (take delivery) of the bonds are said to have taken a *long position,* and parties who have sold a futures contract and thereby agreed to sell (deliver) the bonds have taken a *short position.*

To make our understanding of this contract more concrete, let's consider what happens when you buy or sell one of these Treasury bond futures contracts. Let's say that on February 1, you sell one $100,000 June contract at a price of 115 (that is, $115,000). By selling this contract, you agree to deliver $100,000 face value of the long-term Treasury bonds to the contract's counterparty at the end of June for $115,000. By buying the contract at a price of 115, the buyer has agreed to pay $115,000 for the $100,000 face value of bonds when you deliver them at the end of June. If interest rates on long-term bonds rise so that when the contract matures at the end of June the price of these bonds has fallen to 110 ($110,000 per $100,000 of face value), the buyer of the contract will have lost $5,000 because he or she paid $115,000 for the bonds but can sell them only for the market price of $110,000. But you, the seller of the contract, will have gained $5,000 (less commission and expenses) because you can now sell the bonds to the buyer for $115,000 but have to pay only $110,000 for them in the market.

It is even easier to describe what happens to the parties who have purchased futures contracts and those who have sold futures contracts if we recognize the following fact: ***At the expiration date of a futures contract, the price of the contract converges to the price of the underlying asset to be delivered.*** To see why this is the case, consider what happens on the expiration date of the June contract at the end of June when the price of the underlying $100,000 face value Treasury bond is 110 ($110,000). If the futures contract is selling below 110, say, at 109, a trader can buy the contract for $109,000, take delivery of the bond, and immediately sell it for $110,000, thereby earning a quick profit of $1,000. Because earning this profit involves no risk, it is a great deal that everyone would like to get in on. That means that everyone will try to buy the contract, and as a result, its price will rise. Only when the price rises to 110 will the profit opportunity cease to

FOLLOWING THE FINANCIAL NEWS

Financial Futures

The prices for financial futures contracts for debt instruments are published daily in newspapers and Internet sites such as finance.yahoo.com. A typical entry, like the following one for the Chicago Board of Trade's $100,000 Treasury Bonds contract on June 19, 2013, would have the following information.

	Open	High	Low	Settle	Change	Open Interest
June	140-13	140-26	140-04	139-29	−21	10,288
Sept	139-17	139-27	137-12	138-00	−1-18	554,632

Prices are quoted with the number to the right of the hyphen in 1/32nds.

Open: Opening price; each point corresponds to $1,000 of face value—140 13/32 is $140,375 for the June contract.

High: Highest traded price that day—140 26/32 is $140,812 for the June contract.

Low: Lowest traded price that day—140 4/32 is $140,125 for the June contract.

Settle: Settlement price, the closing price that day—139, 29/32 is $139,906 for the June contract.

Chg: Change in the settlement price from the previous trading day— −21 1/32 is—$656.25 for the June contract.

Open Interest: Number of contracts outstanding—10,288 for the June contract, with a face value of $1.03 billion (10,288 × $100,000)

exist and the buying pressure disappear. Conversely, if the price of the futures contract is above 110, say, at 111, everyone will want to sell the contract. Now the sellers get $111,000 from selling the futures contract but have to pay only $110,000 for the Treasury bonds that they must deliver to the buyer of the contract, and the $1,000 difference is their profit. Because this profit involves no risk, traders will continue to sell the futures contract until its price falls back down to 110, at which price there are no longer any profits to be made. The elimination of riskless profit opportunities in the futures market is referred to as **arbitrage,** and it guarantees that the price of a futures contract at expiration equals the price of the underlying asset to be delivered.[1]

Armed with the fact that a futures contract at expiration equals the price of the underlying asset, it is even easier to see who profits and loses from such a contract when interest rates change. When interest rates have risen so that the price of the Treasury bond is 110 on the expiration day at the end of June, the June Treasury bond futures contract will also have a price of 110. Thus, if you bought the contract for 115 in February, you have a loss of 5 points, or $5,000 (5% of $100,000). But if you sold the futures contract at 115 in February, the decline in price to 110 means that you have a profit of 5 points, or $5,000.

Hedging with Financial Futures

As the manager of the First National Bank, you can also use financial futures to hedge the interest-rate risk on its holdings of $5 million of the 6s of 2032.

To see how to do this, suppose that in March 2014 the 6s of 2032 are the long-term bonds that would be delivered in a T-bond futures contract expiring one year in the future, in March 2015. Also suppose that the interest rate on these bonds is expected to remain at 6% over the next year so that both the 6s of 2032 and the futures contract are selling at par (i.e., the $5 million of bonds is selling for $5 million and the $100,000 futures contract is selling for $100,000). The basic principle of hedging indicates that you need to offset the long position in these bonds with a short position, so you have to sell the futures contract. But how many contracts should you sell? The number of contracts required to hedge the interest-rate risk is found by dividing the amount of the asset to be hedged by the rupee value of each contract, as is shown in Equation 1 below.

$$NC = VA/VC \qquad (1)$$

where
NC = number of contracts for the hedge
VA = value of the asset
VC = value of each contract

---

[1]In actuality, futures contracts sometimes set conditions for the timing and delivery of the underlying assets that cause the price of the contract at expiration to differ slightly from the price of the underlying assets. Because the difference in price is extremely small, we ignore it here.

EXAMPLE 20.1

Hedging with Interest-Rate Futures

The 6s of 2032 are the long-term bonds that would be delivered in the T-bond futures contract expiring one year in the future in March 2015. The interest rate on these bonds is expected to remain at 6% over the next year so that both the 6s of 2032 and the futures contract are selling at par. How many contracts must First National sell to remove its interest-rate risk exposure from its $5 million holdings of the 6s of 2032?*

➤ Solution

$$VA = \$5 \text{ million}$$
$$VC = \$100,000$$

Thus,

$$NC = 5 \text{ million}/100,000 = 50$$

You therefore hedge the interest-rate risk by selling 50 of the Treasury bond futures contracts.

Now suppose that over the next year, interest rates increase to 8% due to an increased threat of inflation. The value of the 6s of 2032 the First National Bank is holding will then fall to $4,039,640 in March 2015.** Thus, the loss from the long position in these bonds is $960,360, as shown below:

Value in March 2015 @ 8% interest rate	$4,039,640
Value in March 2014 @ 6% interest rate	−$5,000,000
Loss	−$960,360

However, the short position in the 50 futures contracts that obligates you to deliver $5 million of the 6s of 2032 in March 2015 has a value equal to the $5 million of these bonds on that date, after the interest rate has risen to 8%. This value is $4,039,640, as we have seen above. Yet when you sold the futures contract, the buyer was obligated to pay you $5 million on the maturity date. Thus, the gain from the short position on these contracts is also $960,360, as shown below:

Amount paid to you in March 2015, agreed in March 2014	$5,000,000
Cost of bonds delivered in March 2015 @ 8% interest rate	−$4,039,640
Gain	$960,360

Therefore, the net gain for the First National Bank is zero, showing that the hedge has been conducted successfully.

---

*In the real world, designing a hedge is somewhat more complicated than the example given here because the bond that is most likely to be delivered might not be a 6s of 2032.
**The value of the bonds can be calculated using a financial calculator as follows: $FV = \$5,000,000$, $PMT = \$300,000$, $I = 8\%$, $N = 19$, $PV = \$4,039,640$.

The hedge just described is called a **micro hedge** because the financial institution is hedging the interest-rate risk for a specific asset it is holding. A second type of hedge that financial institutions engage in is called a **macro hedge,** in which the hedge is for the institution's entire portfolio. For example, if a bank has a longer duration for its assets than its liabilities, we have seen in Chapter 19 that a rise in interest rates will cause the value of the bank to decline. By selling interest-rate futures contracts that will yield a profit when interest rates rise, the bank can offset the losses on its overall portfolio from an interest-rate rise and thereby hedge its interest-rate risk.[2]

Organization of Trading in Financial Futures Markets

Financial futures contracts are traded in the United States on organized exchanges such as the Chicago Board of Trade, the Chicago Mercantile Exchange, the New York Futures Exchange, the MidAmerica Commodity Exchange, and the Kansas City Board of Trade. These exchanges are highly competitive, and each organization tries to design contracts and set rules that will increase the amount of futures trading on its exchange.

The futures exchanges and all trades in financial futures in the United States are regulated by the Commodity Futures Trading Commission (CFTC), which was created in 1974 to take over the regulatory responsibilities for futures markets from the Department of Agriculture. The CFTC oversees futures trading and the futures exchanges to ensure that prices in the market are not being manipulated, and it also registers and audits the brokers, traders, and exchanges to prevent fraud and to ensure the financial soundness of the exchanges. In addition, the CFTC approves proposed futures contracts to make sure that they serve the public interest. The most widely traded financial futures contracts listed in the *Wall Street Journal* and the exchanges where they are traded (along with the number of contracts outstanding, called **open interest,** on July 2013) are listed in Table 20.1.

Given the globalization of other financial markets in recent years, it is not surprising that increased competition from abroad has been occurring in financial futures markets as well.

Interest Rate Derivatives in India

In the Over the Counter (OTC) interest rate derivatives (IRD) segment, interest rate swaps (IRS) and forward rate agreements (FRA) are permitted on various benchmarks where banks and primary dealers (PD) take hedging and trading positions. Other regulated entities like insurance companies, mutual funds, Non-Banking Finance Companies can participate in IRD for the purpose of hedging. The activity in IRS market has shown impressive growth with the average daily inter-bank trading volume (notional principal) at ₹88.60 billion in financial year 2014–15. In addition, there are exchange traded interest rate futures (IRF) which are also open to Foreign Portfolio Investors (FPI). Trading activity in the IRF market has picked up in the recent period with average daily trading volume of ₹19.18 billion during the financial year 2014–15.

---

[2]For more details and examples of how interest-rate risk can be hedged with financial futures, see the appendix to this chapter, which can be found on the book's Web site at www.pearsonhighered.com/mishkin_eakins.

TABLE 20.1 Widely Traded Financial Futures Contracts

Type of Contract	Contract Size	Exchange*	Open Interest (July 2013)
Interest-Rate Contracts			
Treasury bonds	$100,000	CME	576,609
Treasury notes	$100,000	CME	2,342,207
Five-year Treasury notes	$100,000	CME	1,611,675
Two-year Treasury notes	$200,000	CME	840,701
Fed funds	$5 million	CME	311,772
Eurodollar	$1 million	CME	8,933,577
Stock Index Contracts			
Standard & Poor's 500 Index	$250 × index	CME	165,532
DJ Industrial	$10 index	CBT	14,436
NASDAQ 100	$100 index	CME	405,306
Currency Contracts			
Yen	¥12,500,000	CME	172,270
Euro	€125,000	CME	227,631
Canadian dollar	C$100,000	CME	111,336
British pound	$62,500	CME	152,076
Swiss franc	SF 125,000	CME	36,147
Mexican peso	MXN 500,000	CME	101,051

*Exchange abbreviations: CBT, Chicago Board of Trade; CME, Chicago Mercantile Exchange.
Source: CME Group: www.cmegroup.com/market-data/volume-open-interest/index.html, as accessed on 17 March 2017 at 4pm.

Implementation of OTC Market Reforms

India is committed to implementing OTC derivatives reform measures recommended by G-20/Financial Stability Board and has initiated steps for adoption of these reforms. India was one of the few countries having a formal framework for regulation of OTC markets even before post-crisis, the focus shifted to this area globally. The ongoing efforts focus on improving transparency and reducing counterparty risk in the OTC derivatives markets and fostering development of robust market infrastructure for trading, settlement and reporting of transactions. Against this backdrop, the trade reporting arrangement for various OTC interest rate, foreign exchange and credit derivatives has since been completed. The arrangement covers the Rupee IRS/FRA, FX Forwards, Options and Swaps, Currency Swaps, IRS/FRA in foreign currencies and CDS. India is fully compliant under the G-20 commitment of reporting OTC derivative transactions. Central Counterparty (CCP) mechanism has been put in place for IRS, forex forward and swaps. In principle approval has been given to Clearing Corporation of India Limited (CCIL) to develop the anonymous trading platform with CCP facility for IRS trades.[3]

---

[3] Source: https://www.rbi.org.in/scripts/FS_Overview.aspx?fn=6.

Globalization of Financial Futures Markets

Because American futures exchanges were the first to develop financial futures, they dominated the trading of financial futures in the early 1980s. For example, in 1985 all of the top 10 futures contracts were traded on exchanges in the United States. With the rapid growth of financial futures markets and the resulting high profits made by the American exchanges, foreign exchanges saw a profit opportunity and began to enter this business. By the 1990s, Eurodollar contracts traded on the London International Financial Futures Exchange, Japanese government bond contracts and Euroyen contracts traded on the Tokyo Stock Exchange, French government bond contracts traded on the Marché à Terme International de France, and Nikkei 225 contracts traded on the Osaka Securities Exchange. All became among the most widely traded futures contracts in the world. Even developing countries are getting into the act. In 1996 seven developing countries (also referred to as *emerging market countries*) established futures exchanges, and this number is expected to double.

Foreign competition has also spurred knockoffs of the most popular financial futures contracts initially developed in the United States. These contracts traded on foreign exchanges are virtually identical to those traded in the United States and have the advantage that they can be traded when the American exchanges are closed. The movement to 24-hour-a-day trading in financial futures has been further stimulated by the development of the Globex electronic trading platform, which allows traders throughout the world to trade futures even when the exchanges are not officially open. Financial futures trading has thus become completely internationalized, and competition between U.S. and foreign exchanges is now intense.

Explaining the Success of Futures Markets

The tremendous success of the financial futures market in Treasury bonds is evident from the fact that the total open interest of Treasury bond contracts was 576,609 on July 19, 2013, for a total value of over \$57 billion (576,609 × \$100,000). Several differences can be noted between financial futures and forward contracts and in the organization of their markets that help explain why financial futures markets, like those for Treasury bonds, have been so successful.

Several features of futures contracts were designed to overcome the liquidity problem inherent in forward contracts. The first feature is that, in contrast to forward contracts, the quantities delivered and the delivery dates of futures contracts are standardized, making it more likely that different parties can be matched in the futures market, thereby increasing the liquidity of the market. In the case of the Treasury bond contract, the quantity delivered is \$100,000 face value of bonds, and the delivery dates are set to be the last business days of March, June, September, and December. The second feature is that after the futures contract has been bought or sold, it can be traded (bought or sold) again at any time until the delivery date. In contrast, once a forward contract is agreed on, it typically cannot be traded. The third feature is that in a futures contract, not just one specific type of Treasury bond is deliverable on the delivery date, as in a forward contract. Instead, any Treasury bond that matures in more than 15 years and is not callable for 15 years is eligible for delivery. Allowing continuous trading also increases the liquidity of the futures market, as does the ability to deliver a range of Treasury bonds rather than one specific bond.

Another reason why futures contracts specify that more than one bond is eligible for delivery is to limit the possibility that someone might corner the market and "squeeze" traders who have sold contracts. To corner the market, someone

> MINI-CASE

The Hunt Brothers and the Silver Crash

In early 1979, two Texas billionaires, W. Herbert Hunt and his brother, Nelson Bunker Hunt, decided that they were going to get into the silver market in a big way. Herbert stated his reasoning for purchasing silver as follows: "I became convinced that the economy of the United States was in a weakening condition. This reinforced my belief that investment in precious metals was wise . . . because of rampant inflation." Although the Hunts' stated reason for purchasing silver was that it was a good investment, others felt that their real motive was to establish a corner in the silver market. Along with other associates, several of them from the Saudi royal family, the Hunts purchased close to 300 million ounces of silver in the form of either actual bullion or silver futures contracts. The result was that the price of silver rose from $6 an ounce to over $50 an ounce by January 1980.

Once the regulators and the futures exchanges got wind of what the Hunts were up to, they decided to take action to eliminate the possibility of a corner by limiting to 2,000 the number of contracts that any single trader could hold. This limit, which was equivalent to 10 million ounces, was only a small fraction of what the Hunts were holding, and so they were forced to sell. The silver market collapsed soon afterward, with the price of silver declining back to below $10 an ounce. The losses to the Hunts were estimated to be in excess of $1 billion, and they soon found themselves in financial difficulty. They had to go into debt to the tune of $1.1 billion, mortgaging not only the family's holdings in the Placid Oil Company but also 75,000 head of cattle, a stable of thoroughbred horses, paintings, jewelry, and even such mundane items as irrigation pumps and lawn mowers. Eventually both Hunt brothers were forced into declaring personal bankruptcy, earning them the dubious distinction of declaring the largest personal bankruptcies ever in the United States.

Nelson and Herbert Hunt paid a heavy price for their excursion into the silver market, but at least Nelson retained his sense of humor. When asked right after the collapse of the silver market how he felt about his losses, he said, "A billion dollars isn't what it used to be."*

*Quotes are from G. Christian Hill, "Dynasty's Decline: The Current Question About the Hunts of Dallas: How Poor Are They?" *Wall Street Journal*, (November 14, 1984): c28.

buys up all the deliverable securities so that investors with a short position cannot obtain from anyone else the securities that they contractually must deliver on the delivery date. As a result, the person who has cornered the market can set exorbitant prices for the securities that investors with a short position must buy to fulfill their obligations under the futures contract. The person who has cornered the market makes a fortune, but investors with a short position take a terrific loss. Clearly, the possibility that corners might occur in the market will discourage people from taking a short position and might therefore decrease the size of the market. By allowing many different securities to be delivered, the futures contract makes it harder for anyone to corner the market because a much larger amount of securities would have to be purchased to establish the corner. Corners are more than a theoretical possibility, as the Mini-Case box "The Hunt Brothers and the Silver Crash" indicates, and are a concern to both regulators and the organized exchanges that design futures contracts.

Trading in the futures market has been organized differently from trading in forward markets to overcome the default risk problems arising in forward contracts. In both types, for every contract there must be a buyer who is taking a long position and a seller who is taking a short position. However, the buyer and seller of a futures contract make their contract not with each other but with the clearinghouse associated with the futures exchange. This setup means that the buyer of the futures contract does not need to worry about the financial health or trustworthiness of the seller, or vice versa, as in the forward market. As long as the clearinghouse is financially solid, buyers and sellers of futures contracts do not have to worry about default risk.

To make sure that the clearinghouse is financially sound and does not run into financial difficulties that might jeopardize its contracts, buyers or sellers of futures contracts must put an initial deposit, called a **margin requirement,** of perhaps $2,000 per Treasury bond contract into a margin account kept at their brokerage firm. Futures contracts are then **marked to market** every day. What this means is that at the end of every trading day, the change in the value of the futures contract is added to or subtracted from the margin account. Suppose that after buying the Treasury bond contract at a price of 115 on Wednesday morning, its closing price at the end of the day, the *settlement price*, falls to 114. You now have a loss of 1 point, or $1,000, on the contract, and the seller who sold you the contract has a gain of 1 point, or $1,000. The $1,000 gain is added to the seller's margin account, making a total of $3,000 in that account, and the $1,000 loss is subtracted from your account, so you now only have $1,000 in your account. If the amount in this margin account falls below the maintenance margin requirement (which can be the same as the initial requirement but is usually a little less), the trader is required to add money to the account. For example, if the maintenance margin requirement is also $2,000, you would have to add $1,000 to your account to bring it up to $2,000. Margin requirements and marking to market make it far less likely that a trader will default on a contract, thus protecting the futures exchange from losses.

A final advantage that futures markets have over forward markets is that most futures contracts do not result in delivery of the underlying asset on the expiration date, whereas forward contracts do. A trader who sold a futures contract is allowed to avoid delivery on the expiration date by making an offsetting purchase of a futures contract. Because the simultaneous holding of the long and short positions means that the trader would in effect be delivering the bonds to itself, under the exchange rules the trader is allowed to cancel both contracts. Allowing traders to cancel their contracts in this way lowers the cost of conducting trades in the futures market relative to the forward market in that a futures trader can avoid the costs of physical delivery, which is not so easy with forward contracts.

CASE

Business Growth in Futures & Options Segment

In India, the Securities Contract Regulation Act (SCRA) was amended in December 1999 to include derivatives within the definition of securities.

The passage of this Act made derivatives legal as long as they were traded on a recognized stock exchange. Exchange Traded Financial Derivatives were introduced in India, in June 2000, on the National Stock Exchange and the Bombay Stock Exchange.

The beginning was made with index futures contracts based on S&P CNX Nifty Index (Nifty) and BSE Sensitive Index (Sensex). Since then, the rise in the turnover of derivative contracts traded on NSE has been exponential. In 2016–17, the total turnover in the NSE derivatives market was ₹8,43,99,148.72 crores, (See Table 20.2)

NSE has around 99.5% of the market share of exchange traded financial derivatives market in India.

Stock futures and Index futures are two of the most popular contracts traded on NSE, having a market share of 59% and 29% (by turnover) respectively of the total derivatives market segment.

TABLE 20.2 Business Growth in FO Segment in India: NSE

Year	Index Futures		Vol Futures		Stock Futures		Index Options			Stock Options			Total		Average Daily Turnover* (₹ cr.)
	No. of Contracts	Turnover (₹ cr.)	No. of Contracts	Turnover (₹ cr.)	No. of Contracts	Turnover (₹ cr.)	No. of Contracts	Notional Turnover (₹ cr.)	Premium Turnover** (₹ cr.)	No. of Contracts	Notional Turnover (₹ cr.)	Premium Turnover** (₹ cr.)	No. of Contracts	Turnover* (₹ cr.)	
2000-01	90580	2365	–	–	–	–	–	–	–	–	–	–	90580	2365	11
2001-02	1025588	21483	–	–	1957856	51515	175900	3765	1299	1037529	25163	1305.23	4196873	101926	410
2002-03	2126763	43952	–	–	10676843	286533	442241	9246	112.70	3523062	100131	3033.97	16768909	439862	1752
2003-04	17191668	554446	–	–	32368342	1305939	1732414	52816	991.48	5583071	217207	8054.86	56886776	2130610	8388
2004-05	21635449	772147	–	–	47043066	1484056	3293558	121943	2356.98	5045112	168836	4948.95	77017185	2546982	10107
2005-06	58537886	1513755	–	–	80905493	2791697	12935116	338469	5770.52	5240776	180253	4895.23	157619271	4824174	19220
2006-07	81487424	2539574	–	–	104955401	3830967	25157438	791906	17650.87	5283310	193795	5904.31	216883573	7356242	29543
2007-08	156598579	3820667.27	–	–	203587952	7548563.23	55366038	1362110.88	29286.09	9460631	359136.55	13581.77	425013200	13090477.75	52153.30
2008-09	210428103	3570111.40	–	–	221577980	3479642.12	212088444	3731501.84	91715.58	13295970	229226.81	8250.53	657390497	11010482.20	45310.63
2009-10	178306889	3934388.67	–	–	145591240	5195246.64	341379523	8027964.20	124416.58	14016270	506065.18	15272.89	679293922	17363664.57	72392.07
2010-11	165023653	4356754.53	–	–	186041459	5495756.70	650638557	18365365.76	192637.87	32508393	1030344.21	20474.97	1034212062	29248221.09	115150.48
2011-12	146188740	3577998.41	–	–	158344617	4074843.03	864017736	25720031.34	253068.22	36494371	977031.13	19612.93	1205045464	31349731.74	125902.54
2012-13	96100385	2527130.76	–	–	147711691	4223872.32	820877149	22781574.14	184383.24	66778193	2000427.29	34288.56	1131467418	31533003.96	126638.47
2013-14	105252983	3083103.23	175-6	2193.24	170414186	4949231.72	928565175	27767341.25	244090.71	80174431	2409488.61	46428.41	1284442321	38211408.05	152236.69
2014-15	129303044	4107215.20	11274	2256.43	237604741	8291766.27	1578642963	39922663.48	265315.63	91479209	3282552.18	61732.59	1837041131	55606453.39	228833.14
2015-16	140538674	4557113.64	34	10.23	234243967	7828400.00	1623350486	48951990.60	351221.01	100299174	3488173.75	61118.39	2098610395	64825834.30	262452.77
2016-17	66635070	4335940.78	1	0.09	173860150	11123785.14	1067244916	72797285.69	350021.53	92106012	6107485.87	95570.09	1399746129	94370301.61	380525.41

Note:

* In case of Option Contracts "Turnover" represents "Notional Turnover"
* Premium Turnover is calculated w.e.f. September 01, 2015
* ADT is computed at segment level based on total trading days in the respective year across products.
* Daily turnover data is presented after rounding off.

Source: https://www.nseindia.com/products/content/derivatives/equities/historical_fo_bussinessgrowth.htm.

Hedging Foreign Exchange Risk with Forward and Futures Contracts

As we discussed in Chapter 15, foreign exchange rates have been highly volatile in recent years. The large fluctuations in exchange rates subject financial institutions and other businesses to significant foreign exchange risk because they generate substantial gains and losses. Luckily for financial institution managers, the financial derivatives discussed here—forward and financial futures contracts—can be used to hedge foreign exchange risk.

To understand how financial institution managers manage foreign exchange risk, let's suppose that in January the First National Bank's customer Frivolous Luxuries, Inc., is due a payment of 10 million euros in two months for $10 million worth of goods it has just sold in Germany. Frivolous Luxuries is concerned that if the value of the euro falls substantially from its current value of $1, the company might suffer a large loss because the 10 million euro payment will no longer be worth $10 million. So Sam, the CEO of Frivolous Luxuries, calls his friend Mona, the manager of the First National Bank, and asks her to hedge this foreign exchange risk for his company. Let's see how the bank manager does this using forward and financial futures contracts.

Hedging Foreign Exchange Risk with Forward Contracts

Forward markets in foreign exchange have been highly developed by commercial banks and investment banking operations that engage in extensive foreign exchange trading and so are widely used to hedge foreign exchange risk. Mona knows that she can use this market to hedge the foreign exchange risk for Frivolous Luxuries. Such a hedge is quite straightforward for her to execute. Because the payment of euros in two months means that at that time Sam would hold a long position in euros, Mona knows that the basic principle of hedging indicates that she should offset this long position by a short position. Thus, she just enters a forward contract that obligates her to sell 10 million euros two months from now in exchange for dollars at the current forward rate of $1 per euro.*

In two months, when Mona's customer receives the 10 million euros, the forward contract ensures that it is exchanged for dollars at an exchange rate of $1 per euro, thus yielding $10 million. No matter what happens to future exchange rates, Frivolous Luxuries will be guaranteed $10 million for the goods it sold in Germany. Mona calls her friend Sam to let him know that his company is now protected from any foreign exchange movements, and he thanks her for her help.

---

*The forward exchange rate will probably differ slightly from the current spot rate of $1 per euro because the interest rates in Europe and the United States may not be equal. In that case, as we saw in Equation A2 in the appendix to Chapter 15, the future expected exchange rate will not equal the current spot rate and neither will the forward rate. However, since interest differentials have typically been less than 6% at an annual rate (1% bimonthly), the expected appreciation or depreciation of the euro over a two-month period has always been less than 1%. Thus, the forward rate is always close to the current spot rate, and so our assumption in the example that the forward rate and the spot rate are the same is a reasonable one.

Hedging Foreign Exchange Risk with Futures Contracts

As an alternative, Mona could have used the currency futures market to hedge the foreign exchange risk. In this case, she would see that the Chicago Mercantile Exchange has a euro contract with a contract amount of 125,000 euros and a price of $1 per euro. To do the hedge, Mona must sell euros as with the forward contract, to the tune of 10 million euros of the March futures.

EXAMPLE 20.2

Hedging with Foreign Exchange Futures Contracts

How many of the Chicago Mercantile Exchange March euro contracts must Mona sell in order to hedge the 10 million euro payment due in March?

> Solution

Using Equation 1:

$VA = 10$ million euros

$VC = 125,000$ euros

Thus,

$$NC = 10 \text{ million}/125,000 = 80$$

Mona does the hedge by selling 80 of the CME euro contracts.

Given the $1 per euro price, the sale of the contract yields $80 \times 125,000$ euros $= $10 million. The futures hedge thus again enables her to lock in the exchange rate for Frivolous Luxuries so that it gets its payment of $10 million.

One advantage of using the futures market is that the contract size of 125,000 euros, worth $125,000, is quite a bit smaller than the minimum size of a forward contract, which is usually $1 million or more. However, in this case, the bank man ager is making a large enough transaction that she can use either the forward or the futures market. Her choice depends on whether the transaction costs are lower in one market than in the other. If the First National Bank is active in the forward market, that market would probably have the lower transaction costs, but if First National rarely deals in foreign exchange forward contracts, the bank manager may do better by sticking with the futures market.

Currency Futures in India

Exchange-traded currency futures are permitted in India. Such trading facilities are currently being offered by the National Stock Exchange, the Bombay Stock Exchange and the MCX-Stock Exchange. As the product is exchange traded, the conduct of currency futures trading facility is being regulated jointly by the Reserve Bank and the Securities and Exchange Board of India There are three sets of restrictions: on products, on participants and on participation. The access to the derivative markets is basically available for hedging. All economic agents–residents or non-residents-who have an exposure arising out of any permitted transaction have access to the derivative market–both OTC as well as exchange traded – on the strength of such underlying exposure.

Hedging of Currency Exposures by Corporates   In the recent period, the global financial markets have been going through a phase of low volatility and the Indian markets have been no exception to this trend. A supportive policy environment backed by accommodative monetary policy stance of the central banks of the advanced economies (AEs) and visible signs of pick-up in growth in some of the AEs have contributed, in a large measure, to reduction in volatility. On the flip side in India, there is emerging anecdotal evidence of reduced propensity to hedge foreign exchange exposures arising out of a sense of complacency. The unhedged exposures in respect of External Commercial Borrowings (ECBs)/ Foreign Currency Convertible Bonds (FCCBs) lead to large scale currency mismatches in view of the bulk amount borrowed by domestic corporates for longer tenors with limited or no natural hedges. Further, the increasing use of bond route for overseas borrowings exposes the domestic borrowers to greater roll-over risk. As per indicative data available with the RBI, the hedge ratio for ECBs/FCCBs declined sharply from about 34 per cent in FY 2013-14 to 24 per cent during April-August, 2014 with very low ratio of about 15 per cent in July-August 2014. Large scale currency mismatches could pose serious threat to the financial stability in case exchange rate encounters sudden depreciation pressure. It is absolutely essential that corporates should continue to be guided by sound hedging policies and the financing banks factor the risk of unhedged exposures in their credit assessment framework. Banks have expressed the difficulty faced by them in pricing the unhedged exposures of the corporates in an environment of low pick up in credit growth. Given the implications of large unhedged forex exposures on the financial stability, it is necessary for the banking industry to act in unison to bring about an awareness amongst the corporates about the need for adopting and implementing a well-deliberated hedging policy so that the Indian forex market is spared of regular episodes of extreme volatility.

Foreign Exchange Derivatives–Requirement of Underlying Exposure   The access to the OTC foreign exchange derivatives has been subject to production of documentary evidence in support of the underlying exposure except for hedging of probable exposures and special dispensations offered to SMEs, individuals and firms. The primary objective of the regulation has been to restrict the use of OTC foreign exchange derivatives by the corporate clients for hedging their exchange rate risks and not for trading in the instruments. Trading in derivatives requires sophisticated risk management skills and financial acumen which are not the natural strengths of corporate entities barring a few large corporates who are into treasury operations as an independent profit centre. Further, the trading activities of authorised dealer banks are subject to strict governance and regulatory standards, which the corporate entities even with sophisticated treasuries are not subjected to. The exchange rate being an important macroeconomic variable, unregulated trading in it has potential adverse consequences for macroeconomic and financial stability. The Reserve Bank is aware of active intra-day/short term trading by some corporate houses in the foreign exchange government securities market. In the past, the Reserve Bank has imposed restrictions on cancellation and rebooking of forward contracts by the corporates so as to curb their speculative trading that accentuates volatility of Rupee. As huge position taking by the corporates has the potential of destabilizing the market, particularly during periods of uncertainty, Reserve Bank would expect adherence to the spirit of its regulations by such non-bank entities.[4]

[4]*Reference*: https://www.rbi.org.in/scripts/FS_Overview.aspx?fn=5; https://www.rbi.org.in/scripts/FS_Speeches.aspx?Id=919&fn=5.

Stock Index Futures

As we have seen, financial futures markets can be useful in hedging interest-rate risk. However, financial institution managers, particularly those who manage mutual funds, pension funds, and insurance companies, also worry about **stock market risk,** the risk that occurs because stock prices fluctuate. Stock index futures were developed in 1982 to meet the need to manage stock market risk, and they have become among the most widely traded of all futures contracts.

Stock Index Futures Contracts

To understand stock index futures contracts, let's examine the Standard & Poor's 500 Index futures contract (shown in the Following the Financial News box, "Stock Index Futures"), the most widely traded stock index futures contract in the United States. (The S&P 500 Index measures the value of 500 of the most widely traded stocks.) Stock index futures contracts differ from most other financial futures contracts in that they are settled with a cash delivery rather than with the delivery of a security. Cash settlement gives these contracts the advantage of a high degree of liquidity and also rules out the possibility of anyone's cornering the market. In the case of the S&P 500 Index contract, at the final settlement date, the cash delivery due is $250 times the index, so if the index is at 1,000 on the final settlement date, $250,000 would be the amount due. The price quotes for this contract are also quoted in terms of index points, so a change of 1 point represents a change of $250 in the contract's value.

> **MINI-CASE**
>
> ## Program Trading and Portfolio Insurance: Were They to Blame for the Stock Market Crash of 1987?
>
> In the aftermath of the Black Monday crash on October 19, 1987, in which the stock market declined by over 20% in one day, trading strategies involving stock price index futures markets have been accused (especially by the Brady Commission, which was appointed by President Reagan to study the stock market) of being culprits in the market collapse. One such strategy, called program trading, involves computer-directed trading between the stock index futures and the stocks whose prices are reflected in the stock price index. Program trading is a form of arbitrage conducted to keep stock index futures and stock prices in line with each other. For example, when the price of the stock index futures contract is far below the prices of the underlying stocks in the index, program traders buy index futures, thereby increasing their price, and sell the stocks, thereby lowering their price. Critics of program trading assert that the sharp fall in stock index futures prices on Black Monday led to massive selling in the stock market to keep stock prices in line with the stock index futures prices.
>
> Some experts also blame portfolio insurance for amplifying the crash because they feel that when the stock market started to fall, uncertainty in the market increased, and the resulting increased desire to hedge stocks led to massive selling of stock index futures. The resulting large price declines in stock index futures contracts then led to massive selling of stocks by program traders to keep prices in line.
>
> Because they view program trading and portfolio insurance as causes of the October 1987 market collapse, critics of stock index futures have advocated restrictions on their trading. In response, certain brokerage firms, as well as organized exchanges, have placed limits on program trading. For example, the New York Stock Exchange has curbed computerized program trading when the Dow Jones Industrial Average moves by more than 50 points in one day. However, some prominent finance scholars (among them Nobel laureate Merton Miller of the University of Chicago) do not accept the hypothesis that program trading and portfolio insurance provoked the stock market crash. They believe that the prices of stock index futures primarily reflect the same economic forces that move stock prices—changes in the market's underlying assessment of the value of stocks.

> FOLLOWING THE FINANCIAL NEWS

Stock Index Futures

The prices for stock index futures contracts are published daily in newspapers and Internet sites such as finance.yahoo.com. A typical entry, like the following one for the Chicago Mercantile Exchange's S&P 500 Index contract on June 19, 2013, would have the following information:

	Open	High	Low	Settle	Change	Open Interest
June	1650.50	1652.50	1628.00	1629.60	−21.50	168,467
Sept	1646.80	1648.70	1620.60	1623.70	−21.50	130,647

Information for each contract is given in columns, as follows. (The June S&P 500 Index contract is used as an example.)

Open: Opening price; each point corresponds to $250 times the index—1650.50; that is, 1650.50 × $250 = $412,625 per contract.

High: Highest traded price that day—1652.50, or $413.125 per contract.

Low: Lowest traded price that day—1628.00, or $407,000 per contract.

Settle: Settlement price, the closing price that day—1629.60, or $407,400 per contract.

Chg: Change in the settlement price from the previous trading day— −21.50 points, or −$5,375 per contract.

Open Interest: Number of contracts outstanding—168,467, or a total value of $68.6 billion (= 168,467 × $407,400).

To understand what all this means, let's look at what happens when you buy or sell this futures contract. Suppose that on February 1, you sell one June contract at a price of 1,000 (that is, $250,000). By selling the contract, you agree to a delivery amount due of $250 times the S&P 500 Index on the expiration date at the end of June. By buying the contract at a price of 1,000, the buyer has agreed to pay $250,000 for the delivery amount due of $250 times the S&P 500 Index at the expiration date at the end of June. If the stock market falls so that the S&P 500 Index declines to 900 on the expiration date, the buyer of the contract will have lost $25,000 because he or she has agreed to pay $250,000 for the contract but has a delivery amount due of $225,000 (900 × $250). But you, the seller of the contract, will have a profit of $25,000 because you agreed to receive a $250,000 purchase price for the contract but have a delivery amount due of only $225,000. Because the amount payable and due are netted out, only $25,000 will change hands; you, the seller of the contract, receive $25,000 from the buyer.

THE PRACTICING MANAGER

Hedging with Stock Index Futures

Financial institution managers can use stock index futures contracts to reduce stock market risk.

EXAMPLE 20.3

Hedging with Stock Index Futures

Suppose that in March 2014, Mort, the portfolio manager of the Rock Solid Insurance Company, has a portfolio of stocks valued at $100 million that moves percentagewise one-for-one with the S&P Index. Suppose also that the March 2015 S&P 500 Index contracts are currently selling at a price of 1,000. How many of these contracts should Mort sell so that he hedges the stock market risk of this portfolio over the next year?

> **Solution**
Because Mort is holding a long position, using the basic principle of hedging, he must offset it by taking a short position in which he sells S&P futures. To calculate the number of contracts he needs to sell, he uses Equation 1.

$$VA = \$100 \text{ million}$$

$$VC = \$250 \times 1{,}000 = \$250{,}000$$

Thus,

$$NC = \$100 \text{ million}/\$250{,}000 = 400$$

Mort's hedge therefore involves selling 400 S&P March 2015 futures contracts.

If the S&P Index falls 10% to 900, the $100 million portfolio will suffer a $10 million loss. At the same time, however, Mort makes a profit of $100 \times \$250 = \$25{,}000$ per contract because he agreed to be paid $250,000 for each contract at a price of 1,000, but at a price of 900 on the expiration date he has a delivery amount of only $225,000 ($900 \times \$250$). Multiplied by 400 contracts, the $25,000 profit per contract yields a total profit of $10 million. The $10 million profit on the futures contract exactly offsets the loss on Rock Solid's stock portfolio, so Mort has been successful in hedging the stock market risk.

Why would Mort be willing to forego profits when the stock market rises? One reason is that he might be worried that a bear market was imminent, so he wants to protect Rock Solid's portfolio from the coming decline (and so protect his job).*

---

*For more details of how stock market risk can be hedged with futures options, see the appendix to this chapter, which can be found on the book's Web site at www.pearsonhighered.com/mishkin_eakins.

Options

Another vehicle for hedging interest-rate and stock market risk involves the use of options on financial instruments. **Options** are contracts that give the purchaser the option, or *right*, to buy or sell the underlying financial instrument at a specified price, called the **exercise price** or **strike price**, within a specific period of time (the *term to expiration*). The seller (sometimes called the *writer*) of the option is *obligated* to buy or sell the financial instrument to the purchaser if the owner of the option exercises the right to sell or buy. These option contract features are important enough to be emphasized: The *owner* or buyer of an option does not have to exercise the option; he or she can let the option expire without using it. Hence, the *owner* of an option is *not obligated* to take any action but rather has the *right* to exercise the contract if he or she so chooses. The *seller* of an option, by contrast, has no choice in the matter; he or she *must* buy or sell the financial instrument if the owner exercises the option.

Because the right to buy or sell a financial instrument at a specified price has value, the owner of an option is willing to pay an amount for it called a **premium.** There are two types of option contracts: **American options** can be exercised *at any time up to* the expiration date of the contract, and **European options** can be exercised only *on* the expiration date.

Option contracts are written on a number of financial instruments. Options on individual stocks are called **stock options,** and such options have existed for a long time. Option contracts on financial futures called **financial futures options,** or, more commonly, **futures options,** were developed in 1982 and have become the most widely traded option contracts.

You might wonder why option contracts are more likely to be written on financial futures than on underlying debt instruments such as bonds or certificates of deposit. As you saw earlier in the chapter, at the expiration date, the price of the futures contract and of the deliverable debt instrument will be the same because of arbitrage. So it would seem that investors should be indifferent about having the option written on the debt instrument or on the futures contract. However, financial futures contracts have been so well designed that their markets are often more liquid than the markets in the underlying debt instruments. Investors would rather have the option contract written on the more liquid instrument, in this case the futures contract. That explains why the most popular futures options are written on many of the same futures contracts listed in Table 20.1.

In the US, the regulation of option markets is split between the Securities and Exchange Commission (SEC), which regulates stock options, and the Commodity Futures Trading Commission (CFTC), which regulates futures options. Regulation focuses on ensuring that writers of options have enough capital to make good on their contractual obligations and on overseeing traders and exchanges to prevent fraud and ensure that the market is not being manipulated.

Option Contracts

A **call option** is a contract that gives the owner the right to *buy* a financial instrument at the exercise price within a specific period of time. A **put option** is a contract that gives the owner the right to *sell* a financial instrument at the exercise price within a specific period of time. Remembering which is a call option and which is a put option is not always easy. To keep them straight, just remember that having a *call* option to *buy a* financial instrument is the same as having the option to *call in* the instrument for delivery at a specified price. Having a *put* option to *sell* a financial instrument is the same as having the option to *put up* an instrument for the other party to buy.

Profits and Losses on Option and Futures Contracts

To understand option contracts more fully, let's first examine the option on the February Treasury bond futures contract in the following table.

Options on Treasury Bond Futures Contract
$100,000;Points and 64ths of 100%

	Calls-Settle			Puts-Settle		
Strike Price	Feb	Mar	Apr	Feb	Mar	Apr
110	1-39	1-52	1-29	0-02	0-15	0-49
111	0-45	1-05	0-57	0-08	0-32	1-13
112	0-09	0-34	0-32	0-36	0-61	...
113	0-02	0-13	0-16	1-28	1-40	...
114	0-01	0-04	0-07	...	2-31	...
115	0-01	0-01	0-03	...	3-28	...

If you buy this futures contract at a price of 115 (that is, $115,000), you have agreed to pay $115,000 for $100,000 face value of long-term Treasury bonds when they are delivered to you at the end of February. If you sold this futures contract at a price of 115, you agreed, in exchange for $115,000, to deliver $100,000 face value of the long-term Treasury bonds at the end of February. An option contract on the Treasury bond futures contract has several key features: (1) It has the same expiration date as the underlying futures contract, (2) it is an American option and so can be exercised at any time before the expiration date, and (3) the premium (price) of the option is quoted in points that are the same as in the futures contract, so each point corresponds to $1,000. If, for a premium of $2,000, you buy one call option contract on the February Treasury bond contract with an exercise price of 115, you have purchased the right to buy (call in) the February Treasury bond futures contract for a price of 115 ($115,000 per contract) at any time through the expiration date of this contract at the end of February. Similarly, when for $2,000 you buy a put option on the February Treasury bond contract with an exercise price of 115, you have the right to sell (put up) the February Treasury bond futures contract for a price of 115 ($115,000 per contract) at any time until the end of February.

Futures option contracts are somewhat complicated, so to explore how they work and how they can be used to hedge risk, let's first examine how profits and losses on the call option on the February Treasury bond futures contract occur. In November our friend Irving the investor buys, for a $2,000 premium, a call option on the $100,000 February Treasury bond futures contract with a strike price of 115. (We assume that if Irving exercises the option, it is on the expiration date at the end of February and not before.) On the expiration date at the end of February, suppose that the underlying Treasury bond for the futures contract has a price of 110. Recall that on the expiration date, arbitrage forces the price of the futures contract to converge to the price of the underlying bond, so it, too, has a price of 110 on the expiration date at the end of February. If Irving exercises the call option and buys the futures contract at an exercise price of 115, he will lose money by buying at 115 and selling at the lower market price of 110. Because Irving is smart, he will not exercise the option, but he will be out the $2,000 premium he paid. In such a situation, in which the price of the underlying financial instrument is below the exercise price, a call option is said to be "out of the money." At the price of 110 (less than the exercise price), Irving thus suffers a loss on the option contract of the $2,000 premium he paid. This loss is plotted as point A in panel (a) of Figure 20.1.

On the expiration date, if the price of the futures contract is 115, the call option is "at the money," and Irving is indifferent to whether he exercises his option to buy the futures contract or not, since exercising the option at 115 when the market price is also at 115 produces no gain or loss. Because he has paid the $2,000 premium, at the price of 115 his contract again has a net loss of $2,000, plotted as point B.

If the futures contract instead has a price of 120 on the expiration day, the option is "in the money," and Irving benefits from exercising the option: He would buy the futures contract at the exercise price of 115 and then sell it for 120, thereby earning a 5% gain ($5,000 profit) on the $100,000 Treasury bond contract. Because Irving paid a $2,000 premium for the option contract, however, his net profit is $3,000 ($5,000 − $2,000). The $3,000 profit at a price of 120 is plotted as point C. Similarly, if the price of the futures contract rose to 125, the option contract would yield a net profit of $8,000 ($10,000 from exercising the option minus the $2,000 premium), plotted as point D. Plotting these points, we get the kinked profit curve for the call option that we see in panel (a).

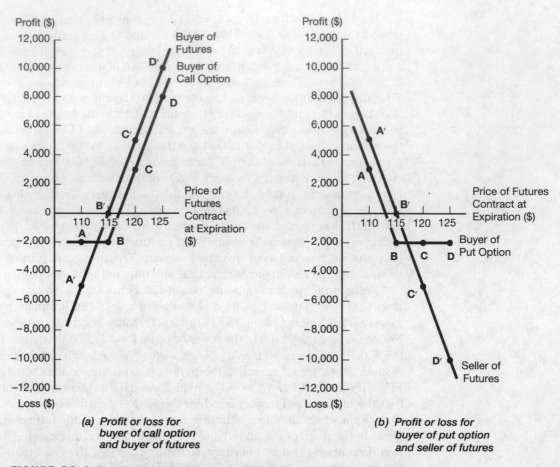

FIGURE 20.1 Profits and Losses on Options Versus Futures Contracts

The futures contract is the $100,000 February Treasury bond contract, and the option contracts are written on this futures contract with an exercise price of 115. Panel (a) shows the profits and losses for the buyer of the call option and the buyer of the futures contract, and panel (b) shows the profits and losses for the buyer of the put option and the seller of the futures contract.

Suppose that instead of purchasing the futures *option* contract in November, Irving decides instead to buy the $100,000 February Treasury bond *futures* contract at the price of 115. If the price of the bond on the expiration day at the end of February declines to 110, meaning that the price of the futures contract also falls to 110, Irving suffers a loss of 5 percentage points, or $5,000. The loss of $5,000 on the futures contract at a price of 110 is plotted as point A′ in panel (a). At a price of 115 on the expiration date, Irving would have a zero profit on the futures contract, plotted as point B′. At a price of 120, Irving would have a profit on the contract of 5 percentage points, or $5,000 (point C′), and at a price of 125, the profit would be 10 percentage points, or $10,000 (point D′). Plotting these points, we get the linear (straight-line) profit curve for the futures contract that appears in panel (a).

Now we can see the major difference between a futures contract and an option contract. As the profit curve for the futures contract in panel (a) indicates, the futures contract has a linear profit function: Profits grow by an equal dollar amount for every point increase in the price of the underlying financial instrument. By contrast, the kinked profit curve for the option contract is highly nonlinear, meaning that profits do not always grow by the same amount for a given change in the price of the underlying financial instrument. The reason for this nonlinearity is that the call option protects Irving from having losses that are greater than the amount of the $2,000 premium. In contrast, Irving's loss on the futures contract is $5,000 if the price on the expiration day falls to 110, and if the price falls even further, Irving's loss will be even greater. This insurance-like feature of option contracts explains why their purchase price is referred to as a premium. Once the underlying financial instrument's price rises above the exercise price, however, Irving's profits grow linearly. Irving has given up something by buying an option rather than a futures contract. As we see in panel (a), when the price of the underlying financial instrument rises above the exercise price, Irving's profits are always less than that on the futures contract by exactly the $2,000 premium he paid.

Panel (b) plots the results of the same profit calculations if Irving buys not a call but a put option (an option to sell) with an exercise price of 115 for a premium of $2,000 and if he sells the futures contract rather than buying one. In this case, if on the expiration date the Treasury bond futures have a price above the 115 exercise price, the put option is "out of the money." Irving would not want to exercise the put option and then have to sell the futures contract he owns as a result of exercising the put option at a price below the market price and lose money. He would not exercise his option, and he would be out only the $2,000 premium he paid. Once the price of the futures contract falls below the 115 exercise price, Irving benefits from exercising the put option because he can sell the futures contract at a price of 115 but can buy it at a price below this. In such a situation, in which the price of the underlying instrument is below the exercise price, the put option is "in the money," and profits rise linearly as the price of the futures contract falls. The profit function for the put option illustrated in panel (b) of Figure 20.1 is kinked, indicating that Irving is protected from losses greater than the amount of the premium he paid. The profit curve for the sale of the futures contract is just the negative of the profit for the futures contract in panel (a) and is therefore linear.

Panel (b) of Figure 20.1 confirms the conclusion from panel (a) that profits on option contracts are nonlinear but profits on futures contracts are linear.

Two other differences between futures and option contracts must be mentioned. The first is that the initial investment on the contracts differs. As we saw earlier, when a futures contract is purchased, the investor must put up a fixed amount, the margin requirement, in a margin account. But when an option contract is purchased, the initial investment is the premium that must be paid for the contract. The second important difference between the contracts is that the futures contract requires money to change hands daily when the contract is marked to market, whereas the option contract requires money to change hands only when it is exercised.

Factors Affecting the Prices of Option Premiums

Several interesting facts can be noted about how the premiums on option contracts are priced. The first fact is that when the strike (exercise) price for a contract is set at a higher level, the premium for the call option is lower and the premium for the put option is higher. For example, in going from a contract with a strike price of 112 to one with 115, the premium for a call option for the month of March might fall from 1 45/64 to 16/64, and the premium for the March put option might rise from 19/64 to 1 54/64.

Our understanding of the profit function for option contracts illustrated in Figure 20.1 helps explain this fact. As we saw in panel (a), a lower price for the underlying financial instrument (in this case a Treasury bond futures contract) relative to the option's exercise price results in lower profits on the call (buy) option. Thus, the higher the strike price, the lower the profits on the call option contract and the lower the premium that investors like Irving are willing to pay. Similarly, we saw in panel (b) that a lower price for the underlying financial instrument relative to the exercise price raises profits on the put (sell) option, so that a higher strike price increases profits and thus causes the premium to increase.

Second, as the period of time over which the option can be exercised (the term to expiration) gets longer, the premiums for both call and put options rise. For example, at a strike price of 112, the premium on a call option might increase from 1 45/64 in March to 1 50/64 in April and to 2 28/64 in May. Similarly, the premium on a put option might increase from 19/64 in March to 1 43/64 in April and to 2 22/64 in May. The fact that premiums increase with the term to expiration is also explained by the nonlinear profit function for option contracts. As the term to expiration lengthens, there is a greater chance that the price of the underlying financial instrument will be very high or very low by the expiration date. If the price becomes very high and goes well above the exercise price, the call (buy) option will yield a high profit; if the price becomes very low and goes well below the exercise price, the losses will be small because the owner of the call option will simply decide not to exercise the option. The possibility of greater variability of the underlying financial instrument as the term to expiration lengthens raises profits on average for the call option.

Similar reasoning tells us that the put (sell) option will become more valuable as the term to expiration increases because the possibility of greater price variability of the underlying financial instrument increases as the term to expiration increases. The greater chance of a low price increases the chance that profits on the put option will be very high. But the greater chance of a high price does not produce substantial losses for the put option, because the owner will again just decide not to exercise the option.

Another way of thinking about this reasoning is to recognize that option contracts have an element of "Heads, I win; tails, I don't lose too badly." The greater variability of where the prices might be by the expiration date increases the value of both kinds of options. Because a longer term to the expiration date leads to greater variability of where the prices might be by the expiration date, a longer term to expiration raises the value of the option contract.

The reasoning that we have just developed also explains another important fact about option premiums. When the volatility of the price of the underlying instrument is great, the premiums for both call and put options will be higher. Higher volatility of prices means that for a given expiration date, there will again be greater variability of where the prices might be by the expiration date. The "Heads, I win; tails, I don't lose too badly" property of options then means that the greater variability of possible prices by the expiration date increases average profits for the option and thus increases the premium that investors are willing to pay.

Summary

Our analysis of how profits on options are affected by price movements for the underlying financial instrument leads to the following conclusions about the factors that determine the premium on an option contract:

1. The higher the strike price, everything else being equal, the lower the premium on call (buy) options and the higher the premium on put (sell) options.

2. The greater the term to expiration, everything else being equal, the higher the premiums for both call and put options.
3. The greater the volatility of prices of the underlying financial instrument, everything else being equal, the higher the premiums for both call and put options.

The results we have derived here appear in more formal models, such as the Black-Scholes model, which analyze how the premiums on options are priced. You might study such models in other finance courses.

Hedging with Futures Options

Earlier in the chapter, we saw how a financial institution manager like Mona, the manager of the First National Bank, could hedge the interest-rate risk on its $5 million holdings of 6s of 2032 by selling $5 million of T-bond futures (50 contracts). A rise in interest rates and the resulting fall in bond prices and bond futures contracts would lead to profits on the bank's sale of the futures contracts that would exactly offset the losses on the 6s of 2032 the bank is holding.

As panel (b) of Figure 20.1 suggests, an alternative way for the manager to protect against a rise in interest rates and hence a decline in bond prices is to buy $5 million of put options written on the same Treasury bond futures. Because the size of the options contract is the same as the futures contract ($100,000 of bonds), the number of put options contracts bought is the same as the number of futures contracts sold, that is, 50. As long as the exercise price is not too far from the current price as in panel (b), the rise in interest rates and decline in bond prices will lead to profits on the futures and the futures put options, profits that will offset any losses on the $5 million of Treasury bonds.

The one problem with using options rather than futures is that the First National Bank will have to pay premiums on the options contracts, thereby lowering the bank's profits in order to hedge the interest-rate risk. Why might the bank manager be willing to use options rather than futures to conduct the hedge? The answer is that the option contract, unlike the futures contract, allows the First National Bank to gain if interest rates decline and bond prices rise. With the hedge using futures contracts, the First National Bank does not gain from increases in bond prices because the profits on the bonds it is holding are offset by the losses from the futures contracts it has sold. However, as panel (b) of Figure 20.1 indicates, the situation when the hedge is conducted with put options is quite different: Once bond prices rise above the exercise price, the bank does not suffer additional losses on the option contracts. At the same time, the value of the Treasury bonds the bank is holding will increase, thereby leading to a profit for the bank. Thus, using options rather than futures to conduct the micro hedge allows the bank to protect itself from rises in interest rates but still allows the bank to benefit from interest-rate declines (although the profit is reduced by the amount of the premium).

Similar reasoning indicates that the bank manager might prefer to use options to conduct the macro hedge to immunize the entire bank portfolio from interest rate risk. Again, the strategy of using options rather than futures has the disadvantage that the First National Bank has to pay the premiums on these contracts up front. By contrast, using options allows the bank to keep the gains from a decline in interest rates (which will raise the value of the bank's assets relative to its liabilities) because these gains will not be offset by large losses on the option contracts.

In the case of a macro hedge, there is another reason why the bank might prefer option contracts to futures contracts. Profits and losses on futures contracts can cause accounting problems for banks because such profits and losses are not allowed to be offset by unrealized changes in the value of the rest of the bank's portfolio. Consider the case when interest rates fall. If First National sells futures contracts to conduct the macro hedge, then when interest rates fall and the prices of the Treasury bond futures contracts rise, it will have large losses on these contracts. Of course, these losses are offset by unrealized profits in the rest of the bank's portfolio, but the bank is not allowed to offset these losses in its accounting statements. So even though the macro hedge is serving its intended purpose of immunizing the bank's portfolio from interest-rate risk, the bank would experience large accounting losses when interest rates fall. Indeed, bank managers have lost their jobs when perfectly sound hedges with interest-rate futures have led to large accounting losses. Not surprisingly, bank managers might shrink from using financial futures to conduct macro hedges for this reason.

Futures options, however, can come to the rescue of the managers of banks and other financial institutions. Suppose that First National conducted the macro hedge by buying put options instead of selling Treasury bond futures. Now if interest rates fall and bond prices rise well above the exercise price, the bank will not have large losses on the option contracts because it will just decide not to exercise its options. The bank will not suffer the accounting problems produced by hedging with financial futures. Because of the accounting advantages of using futures options to conduct macro hedges, option contracts have become important to financial institution managers as tools for hedging interest-rate risk.*

---

*For more details of how interest-rate risk can be hedged with futures options, see the appendix to this chapter, which can be found on the book's Web site at www.pearsonhighered.com/mishkin_eakins.

Interest-Rate Swaps

In addition to forwards, futures, and options, financial institutions use one other important financial derivative to manage risk. **Swaps** are financial contracts that obligate each party to the contract to exchange (swap) a set of payments it owns for another set of payments owned by another party. Swaps are of two basic kinds: **Currency swaps** involve the exchange of a set of payments in one currency for a set of payments in another currency. **Interest-rate swaps** involve the exchange of one set of interest payments for another set of interest payments, all denominated in the same currency. We focus on interest-rate swaps.

Interest-Rate Swap Contracts

Interest-rate swaps are an important tool for managing interest-rate risk, and they first appeared in the United States in 1982 when, as we have seen, there was an increase in the demand for financial instruments that could be used to reduce interest-rate risk. The most common type of interest-rate swap (called the *plain vanilla swap*) specifies (1) the interest rate on the payments that are being exchanged;

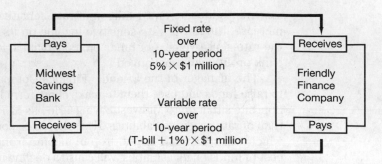

FIGURE 20.2 **Interest-Rate Swap Payments**

In this swap arrangement, with a notional principal of $1 million and a term of 10 years, the Midwest Savings Bank pays a fixed rate of 5% × $1 million to the Friendly Finance Company, which in turn agrees to pay the one-year Treasury bill rate plus 1% × $1 million to the Midwest Savings Bank.

(2) the type of interest payments (variable or fixed rate); (3) the amount of **notional principal,** which is the amount on which the interest is being paid; and (4) the time period over which the exchanges continue to be made. There are many other more complicated versions of swaps, including forward swaps and swap options (called *swaptions*), but here we will look only at the plain vanilla swap. Figure 20.2 illustrates an interest-rate swap between the Midwest Savings Bank and the Friendly Finance Company. Midwest Savings agrees to pay Friendly Finance a fixed rate of 5% on $1 million of notional principal for the next 10 years, and Friendly Finance agrees to pay Midwest Savings the one-year Treasury bill rate plus 1% on $1 million of notional principal for the same period. Thus, as shown in Figure 20.2, every year the Midwest Savings Bank would be paying the Friendly Finance Company 5% on $1 million while Friendly Finance would be paying Midwest Savings the one-year T-bill rate plus 1% on $1 million.

THE PRACTICING MANAGER

Hedging with Interest-Rate Swaps

You might wonder why the managers of the two financial institutions find it advantageous to enter into this swap agreement. The answer is that it may help both of them hedge interest-rate risk.

Suppose that the Midwest Savings Bank, which tends to borrow short term and then lend long term in the mortgage market, has $1 million less of rate-sensitive assets than it has of rate-sensitive liabilities. As we learned in Chapter 23, this situation means that as interest rates rise, the rise in the cost of funds (liabilities) is greater than the rise in interest payments it receives on its assets, many of which are fixed rate. The result of rising interest rates is thus a shrinking of Midwest Savings' net interest margin and a decline in its profitability. As we saw in Chapter 23, to avoid this interest-rate risk, the manager of Midwest Savings would like to convert $1 million of its fixed-rate assets into $1 million of rate-sensitive assets, in effect making rate-sensitive assets equal to rate-sensitive liabilities, thereby eliminating the gap. This is exactly what happens when she engages in the interest-rate swap. By taking $1 million of its fixed-rate income and exchanging it for $1 million of rate-sensitive Treasury bill income, she has converted income on $1 million of fixed-rate assets into income on $1 million of rate-sensitive assets. Now when interest rates increase, the rise in rate-sensitive income on its assets exactly matches the rise in the rate-sensitive cost of funds on its liabilities, leaving the net interest margin and bank profitability unchanged.

The manager of the Friendly Finance Company, which issues long-term bonds to raise funds and uses them to make short-term loans, finds that he is in exactly the opposite situation to Midwest Savings: He has $1 million more of rate-sensitive assets than of rate-sensitive liabilities. He is therefore concerned that a fall in interest rates, which will result in a larger drop in income from its assets than the decline in the cost of funds on its liabilities, will cause a decline in profits. By doing the interest-rate swap, the manager eliminates this interest-rate risk because he has converted $1 million of rate-sensitive income into $1 million of fixed-rate income. Now the manager of the Friendly Finance Company finds that when interest rates fall, the decline in rate-sensitive income is smaller and so is matched by the decline in the rate-sensitive cost of funds on its liabilities, leaving profitability unchanged.*

---

*For more details and examples of how interest-rate risk can be hedged with interest-rate swaps, see the appendix to this chapter, which can be found on the book's Web site at www.pearsonhighered.com/mishkin_eakins.

Advantages of Interest-Rate Swaps

To eliminate interest-rate risk, both the Midwest Savings Bank and the Friendly Finance Company could have rearranged their balance sheets by converting fixed-rate assets into rate-sensitive assets, and vice versa, instead of engaging in an interest-rate swap. However, this strategy would have been costly for both financial institutions for several reasons. The first is that financial institutions incur substantial transaction costs when they rearrange their balance sheets. Second, different financial institutions have informational advantages in making loans to certain customers who may prefer certain maturities. Thus, adjusting the balance sheet to eliminate interest-rate risk may result in a loss of these informational advantages, which the financial institution is unwilling to give up. Interest-rate swaps solve these problems for financial institutions because in effect they allow the institutions to convert fixed-rate assets into rate-sensitive assets without affecting the balance sheet. Large transaction costs are avoided, and the financial institutions can continue to make loans where they have an informational advantage.

We have seen that financial institutions can also hedge interest-rate risk with other financial derivatives such as futures contracts and futures options. Interest-rate swaps have one big advantage over hedging with these other derivatives: They can be written for very long horizons, sometimes as long as 20 years, whereas financial futures and futures options typically have much shorter horizons, not much more than a year. If a financial institution needs to hedge interest-rate risk for a long horizon, financial futures and option markets may not do it much good. Instead it can turn to the swap market.

Disadvantages of Interest-Rate Swaps

Although interest-rate swaps have important advantages that make them very popular with financial institutions, they also have disadvantages that limit their usefulness. Swap markets, like forward markets, can suffer from a lack of liquidity. Let's return to looking at the swap between the Midwest Savings Bank and the Friendly Finance Company. As with a forward contract, it might be difficult for the Midwest Savings Bank to link up with the Friendly Finance Company to arrange the swap. In addition, even if the Midwest Savings Bank could find a counterparty like the Friendly Finance Company, it might not be able to negotiate a good deal because it couldn't find any other institution to negotiate with.

Swap contracts also are subject to the same default risk that we encountered for forward contracts. If interest rates rise, the Friendly Finance Company would love to get out of the swap contract because the fixed-rate interest payments it receives are less than it could get in the open market. It might then default on the contract, exposing Midwest Savings to a loss. Alternatively, the Friendly Finance Company could go bust, meaning that the terms of the swap contract would not be fulfilled.

It is important to note that the default risk of swaps is not the same as the default risk on the full amount of the notional principal because the notional principal is never exchanged. If the Friendly Finance Company goes broke because $1 million of its one-year loans default and it cannot make its interest payment to Midwest Savings, Midwest Savings will stop sending its payment to Friendly Finance. If interest rates have declined, this will suit Midwest Savings just fine because it would rather keep the 5% fixed-rate interest payment, which is at a higher rate, than receive the rate-sensitive payment, which has declined. Thus, a default on a swap contract does not necessarily mean that there is a loss to the other party. Midwest Savings will suffer losses from a default only if interest rates have risen when the default occurs. Even then, the loss will be far smaller than the amount of the notional principal because interest payments are far smaller than the amount of the notional principal.[5]

Financial Intermediaries in Interest-Rate Swaps

As we have just seen, financial institutions do have to be aware of the possibility of losses from a default on swaps. As with a forward contract, each party to a swap must have a lot of information about the other party to make sure that the contract is likely to be fulfilled. The need for information about counterparties and the liquidity problems in swap markets could limit the usefulness of these markets. However, as we saw in Chapter 7, when informational and liquidity problems crop up in a market, financial intermediaries come to the rescue. That is exactly what happens in swap markets. Intermediaries such as investment banks and especially large commercial banks have the ability to acquire information cheaply about the creditworthiness and reliability of parties to swap contracts and are also able to match parties to a swap. Hence, large commercial banks and investment banks have set up swap markets in which they act as intermediaries.

Credit Derivatives

In recent years, a new type of derivative has come on the scene to hedge credit risk. Like other derivatives, **credit derivatives** offer payoffs linked to previously issued securities, but ones that bear credit risk. In the past 10 years, the markets in credit derivatives have grown at an astounding pace and the notional amounts of these

---

[5]The actual loss will equal the present value of the difference in the interest payments that the bank would have received if the swap were still in force as compared to interest payments it receives otherwise.

derivatives now number in the trillions of dollars. These credit derivatives take several forms.

Credit Options

Credit options work just like the options discussed earlier in the chapter: For a fee, the purchaser gains the right to receive profits that are tied either to the price of an underlying security or to an interest rate. Suppose you buy $1 million of General Motors bonds but worry that a potential slowdown in the sale of SUVs might lead a credit-rating agency to *downgrade* (lower the credit rating on) GM bonds. As we saw in Chapter 5, such a downgrade would cause the price of GM bonds to fall. To protect yourself, you could buy an option for, say, $15,000, to sell the $1 million of bonds at a strike price that is the same as the current price. With this strategy, you would not suffer any losses if the value of the GM bonds declined because you could exercise the option and sell them at the price you paid for them. In addition, you would be able to reap any gains that occurred if GM bonds rose in value.

A second type of credit option ties profits to changes in an interest rate, such as a credit spread (the interest rate on the average bond with a particular credit rating minus the interest rate on default-free bonds such as those issued by the U.S. Treasury). Suppose that your company, which has a Baa credit rating, plans to issue $10 million of one-year bonds in three months and expects to have a credit spread of 1 percentage point (i.e., it will pay an interest rate that is 1 percentage point higher than the one-year Treasury rate). You are concerned that the market might start to think that Baa companies in general will become riskier in the coming months. If this were to happen by the time you are ready to issue your bonds in three months, you would have to pay a higher interest rate than the 1 percentage point in excess of the Treasury rate, and your cost of issuing the bonds would increase. To protect yourself against these higher costs, you could buy for, say, $20,000 a credit option on $10 million of Baa bonds that would pay you the difference between the average Baa credit spread in the market minus the 1 percentage point credit spread on $10 million. If the credit spread jumps to 2 percentage points, you would receive $100,000 from the option (= [2% − 1%] × $10 million), which would exactly offset the $100,000 higher interest costs from the 1 percentage point higher interest rate you would have to pay on your $10 million of bonds.

Credit Swaps

Suppose you manage a bank in Houston called Oil Drillers' Bank (ODB), which specializes in lending to a particular industry in your local area, oil drilling companies. Another bank, Potato Farmers Bank (PFB), specializes in lending to potato farmers in Idaho. Both ODB and PFB have a problem because their loan portfolios are not sufficiently diversified. To protect ODB against a collapse in the oil market, which would result in defaults on most of its loans made to oil drillers, you could reach an agreement to have the loan payments on, say, $100 million worth of your loans to oil drillers paid to the PFB in exchange for PFB paying you the loan payments on $100 million of its loans to potato farmers. Such a transaction, in which risky payments on loans are swapped for each other, is called a **credit swap.** As a result of this swap, ODB and PFB have increased their diversification and lowered the overall risk of their loan portfolios because some of the loan payments to each bank are now coming from a different type of loan.

Another form of credit swap is, for arcane reasons, called a **credit default swap,** although it functions more like insurance. With a credit default swap, one party who wants to hedge credit risk pays a fixed payment on a regular basis, in return for a contingent payment that is triggered by a *credit event*, such as the bankruptcy of a particular firm or the downgrading of the firm's credit rating by a credit-rating agency. For example, you could use a credit default swap to hedge the $1 million of General Motors bonds that you are holding by arranging to pay an annual fee of $1,000 in exchange for a payment of $10,000 if the GM bonds' credit rating is lowered. If a credit event happens and GM's bonds are downgraded so that their price falls, you will receive a payment that will offset some of the loss you suffer if you sell the bonds at this lower price.

Credit-Linked Notes

Another type of credit derivative, the **credit-linked note,** is a combination of a bond and a credit option. Just like any corporate bond, the credit-linked note makes periodic coupon (interest) payments and a final payment of the face value of the bond at maturity. If a key financial variable specified in the note changes, however, the issuer of the note has the right (option) to lower the payments on the note. For example, General Motors could issue a credit-linked note that pays a 5% coupon rate, with the specification that if a national index of SUV sales falls by 10%, then GM has the right to lower the coupon rate by 2 percentage points to 3%. In this way, GM can lower its risk because when it is losing money as SUV sales fall, it can offset some of these losses by making smaller payments on its credit-linked notes.

CASE

Lessons from the Global Financial Crisis: When Are Financial Derivatives Likely to Be a Worldwide Time Bomb?

Although financial derivatives can be useful in hedging risk, the AIG blowup discussed in Chapter 8 illustrates that they can pose a real danger to the financial system. Indeed, Warren Buffet warned about the dangers of financial derivatives by characterizing them as "financial weapons of mass destruction." Particularly scary are the notional amounts of derivatives contracts—more than $500 trillion worldwide. What does the recent global financial crisis tell us about when financial derivatives are likely to be a time bomb that could bring down the world financial system?

Two major concerns surround financial derivatives. The first is that financial derivatives allow financial institutions to increase their leverage; that is, these institutions can, in effect, hold an amount of the underlying asset that is many times greater than the amount of money they have had to put up. Increasing their leverage enables them to take huge bets, which if they are wrong can bring down the institution. This is exactly what AIG did, to its great regret, when it plunged into the credit default swap market. Even more of a problem was that AIG's speculation in the credit default swap (CDS) market had the potential to bring down the whole financial system. An important lesson from the global financial crisis is that having one player take huge positions in a derivatives market is highly dangerous.

A second concern is that banks have holdings of huge notional amounts of financial derivatives, particularly interest-rate and currency swaps, that greatly exceed the amount of bank capital, and so these derivatives expose the banks to serious risk of failure. Banks are indeed major players in the financial derivatives markets, particularly in the interest-rate and currency swaps market, where our earlier analysis has shown that they are the natural market makers because they can act as intermediaries between two counterparties who would not make the swap without their involvement. However, looking at the notional amount of interest-rate and currency swaps at banks gives a very misleading picture of their risk exposure. Because banks act as intermediaries in the swap markets, they are typically exposed only to credit risk—a default by one of their counterparties. Furthermore, these swaps, unlike loans, do not involve payments of the notional amount but rather the much smaller payments that are based on the notional amounts. For example, in the case of a 7% interest rate, the payment is only $70,000 for a $1 million swap. Estimates of the credit exposure from swap contracts indicate that they are on the order of only 1% of the notional value of the contracts and that credit exposure at banks from derivatives is generally less than a quarter of their total credit exposure from loans. Banks' credit exposures from their derivative positions are thus not out of line with other credit exposures they face. Furthermore, an analysis by the GAO indicated that actual credit losses incurred by banks in their derivatives contracts have been very small, on the order of 0.2% of their gross credit exposure. Indeed, during the recent global financial crisis, in which the financial system was put under great stress, derivatives exposure at banks has not been a serious problem.

The conclusion is that recent events indicate that financial derivatives pose serious dangers to the financial system, but some of these dangers have been overplayed. The biggest danger occurs in trading activities of financial institutions, and this is particularly true for credit derivatives, as was illustrated by AIG's activities in the CDS market. As discussed in Chapter 18, regulators have been paying increased attention to this danger and are continuing to develop new disclosure requirements and regulatory guidelines for how derivatives trading should be done. Of particular concern is the need for financial institutions to disclose their exposure in derivatives contracts, so that regulators can make sure that a large institution is not playing too large a role in these markets and does not have too large an exposure to derivatives relative to its capital, as was the case for AIG. Another concern is that derivatives, particularly credit derivatives, need to have a better clearing mechanism so that the failure of one institution does not bring down many others whose net derivatives positions are small, even though they have many offsetting positions. Better clearing could be achieved either by having these derivatives traded in an organized exchange like a futures market or by having one clearing organization net out trades. Regulators such as the Federal Reserve Bank of New York have been active in making proposals along these lines.

The credit risk exposure posed by interest-rate derivatives, by contrast, seems to be manageable with standard methods of dealing with credit risk, both by managers of financial institutions and by the institutions' regulators.

New regulations for derivatives markets are sure to come in the wake of the global financial crisis. The industry has also had a wake-up call as to where the dangers in derivatives products might lie. Now the hope is that any time bomb arising from derivatives can be defused with appropriate effort on the part of markets and regulators.

SUMMARY

1. Interest-rate forward contracts, which are agreements to sell a debt instrument at a future (forward) point in time, can be used to hedge interest-rate risk. The advantage of forward contracts is that they are flexible, but the disadvantages are that they are subject to default risk and their market is illiquid.

2. A financial futures contract is similar to an interest-rate forward contract in that it specifies that a debt instrument must be delivered by one party to another on a stated future date. However, it has advantages over a forward contract in that it is not subject to default risk and is more liquid. Forward and futures contracts can be used by financial institutions to hedge against (protect) interest-rate risk.

3. Stock index futures are financial futures whose underlying financial instrument is a stock market index like the Standard and Poor's 500 Index. Stock index futures can be used to hedge stock market risk by reducing systematic risk in portfolios or by locking in stock prices.

4. An option contract gives the purchaser the right to buy (call option) or sell (put option) a security at the exercise (strike) price within a specific period of time. The profit function for options is nonlinear—profits do not always grow by the same amount for a given change in the price of the underlying financial instrument. The nonlinear profit function for options explains why their value (as reflected by the premium paid for them) is negatively related to the exercise price for call options, positively related to the exercise price for put options, positively related to the term to expiration for both call and put options, and positively related to the volatility of the prices of the underlying financial instrument for both call and put

options. Financial institutions use futures options to hedge interest-rate risk in a similar fashion to the way they use financial futures and forward contracts. Futures options may be preferred for macro hedges because they suffer from fewer accounting problems than financial futures.

5. Interest-rate swaps involve the exchange of one set of interest payments for another set of interest payments and have default risk and liquidity problems similar to those of forward contracts. As a result, interest-rate swaps often involve intermediaries such as large commercial banks and investment banks that make a market in swaps. Financial institutions find that interest-rate swaps are useful ways to hedge interest-rate risk. Interest-rate swaps have one big advantage over financial futures and options: They can be written for very long horizons.

6. Credit derivatives are a new type of derivatives that offer payoffs on previously issued securities that have credit risk. These derivatives—credit options, credit swaps, and credit-linked notes—can be used to hedge credit risk.

7. There are three concerns about the dangers of derivatives: They allow financial institutions to more easily increase their leverage and take big bets (by effectively enabling them to hold a larger amount of the underlying assets than the amount of money put down), they are too complex for managers of financial institutions to understand, and they expose financial institutions to large credit risks because the huge notional amounts of derivative contracts greatly exceed the capital of these institutions. The second two dangers seem to be overplayed, but the danger from increased leverage using derivatives is real.

KEY TERMS

American options, p. 523
arbitrage, p. 510
call option, p. 524
credit default swap, p. 535
credit derivatives, p. 533
credit-linked note, p. 535
credit options, p. 534
credit swap, p. 534
currency swaps, p. 530
European options, p. 523
exercise price (strike price), p. 523

financial derivatives, p. 505
financial futures contract, p. 508
financial futures options
   (futures options), p. 524
forward contracts, p. 506
hedge, p. 506
interest-rate forward contracts, p. 506
interest-rate swaps, p. 530
long position, p. 506
macro hedge, p. 511
margin requirement, p. 516

marked to market, p. 516
micro hedge, p. 511
notional principal, p. 531
open interest, p. 512
options, p. 523
premium, p. 523
put option, p. 524
short position, p. 506
stock market risk, p. 521
stock options, p. 523
swaps, p. 530

QUESTIONS

1. Why does a lower strike price imply that a call option will have a higher premium and a put option a lower premium?

2. If the finance company you manage has a gap of +$5 million (rate-sensitive assets greater than rate-sensitive liabilities by $5 million), describe an interest-rate swap that would eliminate the company's income gap.

QUANTITATIVE PROBLEMS

1. If the pension fund you manage expects to have an inflow of $120 million six months from now, what forward contract would you seek to enter into to lock in current interest rates?

2. If the portfolio you manage is holding $25 million of 6s of 2032 Treasury bonds with a price of 110, what forward contract would you enter into to hedge the interest-rate risk on these bonds over the coming year?

3. If at the expiration date, the deliverable Treasury bond is selling for 101 but the Treasury bond futures contract is selling for 102, what will happen to the futures price? Explain your answer.

4. If you buy a $100,000 February Treasury bond contract for 108 and the price of the deliverable Treasury bond at the expiration date is 102, what is your profit or loss on the contract?

5. Suppose that the pension you are managing is expecting an inflow of funds of $100 million next year and you want to make sure that you will earn the current interest rate of 8% when you invest the incoming funds in long-term bonds. How would you use the futures market to do this?

6. How would you use the options market to accomplish the same thing as in Problem 5? What are the advantages and disadvantages of using an options contract rather than a futures contract?

7. If you buy a put option on a $100,000 Treasury bond futures contract with an exercise price of 95 and the price of the Treasury bond is 120 at expiration, is the contract in the money, out of the money, or at the money? What is your profit or loss on the contract if the premium was $4,000?

8. Suppose that you buy a call option on a $100,000 Treasury bond futures contract with an exercise price of 110 for a premium of $1,500. If on expiration the futures contract has a price of 111, what is your profit or loss on the contract?

9. Explain why greater volatility or a longer term to maturity leads to a higher premium on both call and put options.

10. If the savings and loan you manage has a gap of −$42 million, describe an interest-rate swap that would eliminate the S&L's income risk from changes in interest rates.

11. If your company has a payment of 200 million euros due one year from now, how would you hedge the foreign exchange risk in this payment with 125,000 euros futures contracts?

12. If your company has to make a 10 million euros payment to a German company in June, three months from now, how would you hedge the foreign exchange risk in this payment with a 125,000 euros futures contract?

13. Suppose that your company will be receiving 30 million euros six months from now and the euro is currently selling for 1 euro per dollar. If you want to hedge the foreign exchange risk in this payment, what kind of forward contract would you want to enter into?

14. A hedger takes a short position in five T-bill futures contracts at the price of 98 5/32. Each contract is for $100,000 principal. When the position is closed, the price is 95 12/32. What is the gain or loss on this transaction?

15. A bank issues a $100,000 variable-rate 30-year mortgage with a nominal annual rate of 4.5%. If the required rate drops to 4.0% after the first six months, what is the impact on the interest income for the first 12 months? Assume the bank hedged this risk with a short position in a 181-day T-bill future. The original price was 97 26/32, and the final price was 98 1/32 on a $100,000 face value contract. Did this work?

16. Laura, a bond portfolio manager, administers a $10 million portfolio. The portfolio currently has a duration of 8.5 years. Laura wants to shorten the duration to 6 years using T-bill futures. T-bill futures have a duration of 0.25 years and are trading at $975 (face value = $1,000). How is this accomplished?

17. Futures are available on three-month T-bills with a contract size of $1 million. If you take a long position at 96.22 and later sell the contracts at 96.87, how much would the total net gain or loss be on this transaction?

18. Chicago Bank and Trust has $100 million in assets and $83 million in liabilities. The duration of the assets is 5.9 years, and the duration of the liabilities is 1.8 years. How many futures contracts does this bank need to fully hedge itself against interest-rate risk? The available Treasury bond futures contracts have a duration of 10 years, a face value of $1,000,000, and are selling for $979,000.

19. A bank issues a $3 million commercial mortgage with a nominal APR of 8%. The loan is fully amortized over 10 years, requiring monthly payments. The bank plans on selling the loan after two months. If the required nominal APR increases by 45 basis points when the loan is sold, what loss does the bank incur?

20. Assume the bank in the previous question partially hedges the mortgage by selling three 10-year T-note futures contracts at a price of 100 20/32. Each contract is for $1,000,000. After two months, the futures contract has fallen in price to 98 24/32. What was the gain or loss on the futures transaction?

21. Springer County Bank has assets totaling $180 million with a duration of five years, and liabilities totaling $160 million with a duration of two years. Bank management expects interest rates to fall from 9% to 8.25% shortly. A T-bond futures contract is available for hedging. Its duration is 6.5 years, and it is currently priced at 99 5/32. How many contracts does Springer need to hedge against the expected rate change? Assume each contract has a face value of $1,000,000.

22. From the previous question, rates do indeed fall as expected, and the T-bond contract is priced at 103 5/32. If Springer closes its futures position, what is the gain or loss? How well does this offset the approximate change in equity value?

23. A bank issues a $100,000 fixed-rate 30-year mortgage with a nominal annual rate of 4.5%. If the required rate drops to 4.0% immediately after the mortgage is issued, what is the impact on the value of the mortgage? Assume the bank hedged the position with a short position in two 10-year T-bond futures. The original price was 64 12/32 and expired at 67 16/32 on a $100,000 face value contract. What was the gain on the futures? What is the total impact on the bank?

24. A bank customer will be going to London in June to purchase $100,000 in new inventory. The current spot and futures exchange rates are as follows:

Exchange Rates (Dollars/Pound)

Period	Rate
Spot	1.5342
March	1.6212
June	1.6901
September	1.7549
December	1.8416

The customer enters into a position in June futures to fully hedge her position. When June arrives, the actual exchange rate is $1.725 per pound. How much did she save?

25. Consider a put contract on a T-bond with an exercise price of 101 12/32. The contract represents $100,000 of bond principal and had a premium of $750. The actual T-bond price falls to 98 16/32 at the expiration. What is the gain or loss on the position?

26. Consider a put contract on a T-bond with an exercise price of 101 12/32. The contract represents $100,000 of bond principal and has a premium of $750. The actual T-bond price is currently 100 1/32. How can you arbitrage this situation?

27. A banker commits to a two-year $5,000,000 commercial loan and expects to fulfill the agreement in 30 days. The interest rate will be determined at that time. Currently, rates are 7.5% for such loans. To hedge against rates falling, the banker buys a 30-day interest-rate floor with a floor rate of 7.5% on a notional amount of $10,000,000. After 30 days, actual rates fall to 7.2%. What is the expected interest income from the loan each year? How much did the option pay?

28. A trust manager for a $100,000,000 stock portfolio wants to minimize short-term downside risk using Dow put options. The options expire in 60 days, have a strike price of 9,700, and a premium of $50. The Dow is currently at 10,100. How many options should she use? Long or short? How much will this cost? If the portfolio is perfectly correlated with the Dow, what is the portfolio value when the option expires, including the premium paid?

29. A swap agreement calls for Durbin Industries to pay interest annually based on a rate of 1.5% over the one-year T-bill rate, currently 6%. In return, Durbin receives interest at a rate of 6% on a fixed-rate basis. The notional principal for the swap is $50,000. What is Durbin's net interest for the year after the agreement?

30. North-Northwest Bank (NNWB) has a differential advantage in issuing variable-rate mortgages but does not want the interest income risk associated with such loans. The bank currently has a portfolio of $25,000,000 in mortgages with an APR of prime +150 basis points, reset monthly. Prime is currently 4%. An investment bank has arranged for NNWB to swap into a fixed interest payment of 6.5% on a notional amount of $25,000,000 in return for its variable interest income. If NNWB agrees to this, what interest is received and given in the first month? What if prime suddenly increased 200 basis points?

WEB EXERCISES

Hedging with Financial Derivatives

1. The following site can be used to demonstrate how the features of an option affect the option's prices. Go to **http://www.hoadley.net/options/bs.htm**. Scroll down to the online options calculator. What happens to the price of an option under each of the following situations?

   a. The strike price increases.

   b. Interest rates increase.

   c. Volatility increases.

   d. The time until the option matures increases.

WEB APPENDICES

Please visit our Web site at **www.pearsonhighered.com/ mishkin_eakins** to read the Web appendix to Chapter 20:

- **Appendix:** More on Hedging with Financial Derivatives

Financial Crisis in Emerging Market Economies

> PREVIEW

Before 2007 the most prominent examples of severe financial crisis in recent times came from abroad. Particularly vulnerable were *emerging market economics*, which opened their markets to the outside world in the 1990s with high hopes of rapid economic growth and reduced poverty. Instead, however, many of these nations experienced financial crisis as debilitating as the Great Depression was in the United States.

Most dramatic were the Mexican crisis that began in 1994, the East Asian crisis that began in July 1997, and the Argentine crisis, which started in 2001. These events present a puzzle for economists: how can a developing country shift so dramatically

from a path of high growth—as did Mexico and particularly the East Asian countries of Thailand, Malaysia, Indonesia, the Philippines, and South Korea—to such a sharp decline in economic activity?

In this chapter we apply the asymmetric information theory of financial crisis developed in Chapter 8 to investigate the cause of frequent and devastating financial crisis in emerging market economies. First we explore the dynamics of financial crisis in emerging market economies. Then we apply the analysis to the events surrounding financial crisis in two of these economies in recent years and explore why these crisis caused such devastating contractions of economic activity.

Dynamics of Financial Crisis in Emerging Market Economies

The dynamics of financial crisis in **emerging market economies**—economies in an early stage of market development that have recently opened up to the flow of goods, services, and capital from the rest of the world—resemble those found in advanced countries such as the United States but with some important differences. Figure 21.1 outlines the sequence and stages of events in financial crisis in these emerging market economies that we will address in this section.

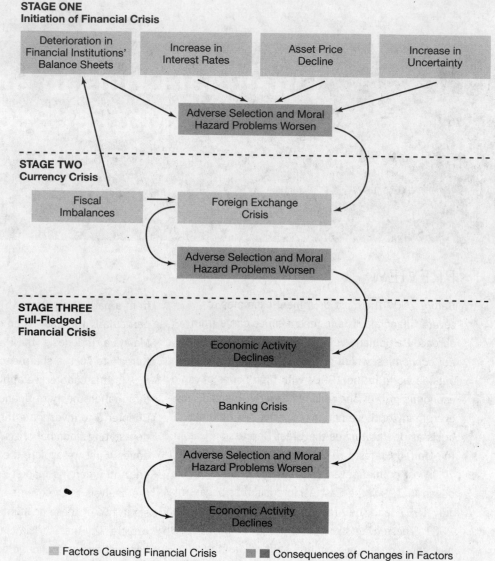

FIGURE 21.1 Sequence of Events in Emerging Market Financial Crisis

The solid arrows traces the sequence of events during a financial crisis. The sections separated by the dashed horizontal lines show the different stages of a financial crisis.

Stage One: Initiation of Financial Crisis

Crisis in advanced economies can be triggered by a number of factors. But in emerging market countries, financial crisis develop along the two basic paths—either the mismanagement of financial liberalization and globalization or severe fiscal imbalances. The first path of mismanagement of financial liberalization/globalization is the most common culprit, precipitating the crisis in Mexico in 1994 and many East Asian countries in 1997.

Path A: Credit Boom and Bust The seeds of a financial crisis in emerging market economies are often sown when countries liberalize their domestic financial systems by eliminating restrictions on financial institutions and markets, a process known as **financial liberalization,** and opening up their economies to flows of capital and financial firms from other nations, a process called **financial globalization.** Countries often begin the process with solid fiscal policy. In the run-up to crisis, Mexico ran a budget deficit of only 0.7% of GDP, a number to which most advanced countries would aspire. And the countries in East Asia even ran budget surpluses before their crisis struck.

It is often said that emerging market financial systems have a weak "credit culture" with ineffective screening and monitoring of borrowers and lax government supervision of banks. Credit booms that accompany financial liberalization in emerging market nations are typically marked by especially risky lending practices, sowing the seeds for enormous loan losses down the road. The financial globalization process adds fuel to the fire because it allows domestic banks to borrow abroad. Banks pay high interest rates to attract foreign capital and so can rapidly increase their lending. The capital inflow is further stimulated by government policies that fix the value of the domestic currency to the U.S. dollar, which provides foreign investors a sense of comfort.

Just as in advanced countries like the United States, the lending boom ends in a lending crash. Significant loan losses emerge from long periods of risky lending, weakening bank balance sheets and prompting banks to cut back on lending. The deterioration in bank balance sheets has an even greater negative impact on lending and economic activity than in advanced countries, which tend to have sophisticated securities markets and large nonbank financial sectors that can pick up the slack when banks falter. So as banks stop lending, there are really no other players to solve adverse selection and moral hazard problems (as shown by the arrow pointing from the first factor in the top row of Figure 21.1).

The story told so far suggests that a lending boom and crash are inevitable outcomes of financial liberalization and globalization in emerging market countries, but this is not the case. These events occur only when there is an institutional weakness that prevents the nation from successfully navigating the liberalization/globalization process. More specifically, if prudential regulation and supervision to limit excessive risk-taking were strong, the lending boom and bust would not happen. Why is regulation and supervision typically weak? The answer is the principal–agent problem, discussed in Chapter 7, which encourages powerful domestic business interests to pervert the financial liberalization process. Politicians and prudential supervisors are ultimately agents for voters-taxpayers (principals): that is, the goal of politicians and prudential supervisors is, or should be, to protect the taxpayers' interest. Taxpayers almost always bear the cost of bailing out the banking sector if losses occur.

Once financial markets have been liberalized, however, powerful business interests that own banks will want to prevent the supervisors from doing their jobs properly, and so prudential supervisors may not act in the public interest. Powerful business interests that contribute heavily to politicians' campaigns are often able to persuade politicians to weaken regulations that restrict their banks from engaging in high-risk/high-payoff strategies. After all, if bank owners achieve growth and expand bank lending rapidly, they stand to make a fortune. But if the bank gets in trouble, the government is likely to bail it out and the taxpayer foots the bill. In addition, these business interests can make sure that the supervisory agencies, even in the presence of tough regulations, lack the resources to effectively monitor banking institutions or to close them down.

Powerful business interests also have acted to prevent supervisors from doing their job properly in advanced countries like the United States. The weak institutional environment in emerging market countries adds to the perversion of the financial liberalization process. In emerging market economies, business interests are far more powerful than they are in advanced economies, where a better-educated public and a free press monitor (and punish) politicians and bureaucrats who are not acting in the public interest. Not surprisingly, then, the cost to society of the principal–agent problem we have been describing here is particularly high in emerging market economies.

Path B: Severe Fiscal Imbalances The financing of government spending can also place emerging market economies on a path toward financial crisis. The financial crisis in Argentina in 2001–2002 is of this type; other crisis, for example in Russia in 1998, Ecuador in 1999, and Turkey in 2001, also have some elements of this type of crisis.

When Willie Sutton, a famous bank robber, was asked why he robbed banks, he answered, "Because that's where the money is." Governments in emerging market countries sometimes have the same attitude. When they face large fiscal imbalances and cannot finance their debt, they often cajole or force domestic banks to purchase government debt. Investors who lose confidence in the ability of the government to repay this debt unload the bonds, which causes their prices to plummet. Banks that hold this debt then face a big hole on the asset side of their balance sheets, with a huge decline in their net worth. With less capital, these institutions must cut back on their lending and lending will decline. The situation can even be worse if the decline in bank capital leads to a bank panic in which many banks fail at the same time. The result of severe fiscal imbalances is therefore a weakening of the banking system, which leads to a worsening of adverse selection and moral hazard problems (as shown by the arrow from the first factor in the third row of Figure 21.1).

Additional Factors Other factors also often play a role in the first stage in crisis. For example, another precipitating factor in some crisis (such as the Mexican crisis) was a rise in interest rates from events abroad, such as a tightening of U.S. monetary policy. When interest rates rise, high-risk firms are most willing to pay the high interest rates, so the adverse selection problem is more severe. In addition, the high interest rates reduce firms' cash flows, forcing them to seek funds in external capital markets in which asymmetric problems are greater. Increases in interest rates abroad that raise domestic interest rates can then increase adverse selection and moral hazard problems (as shown by the arrow from the second factor in the top row of Figure 21.1).

Because asset markets are not as large in emerging market countries as they are in advanced countries, they play a less prominent role in financial crisis. Asset price declines in the stock market do, nevertheless, decrease the net worth of firms and so increase adverse selection problems. There is less collateral for lenders to seize and increased moral hazard problems because, given their decreased net worth, the owners of the firm have less to lose if they engage in riskier activities than they did before the crisis. Asset price declines can therefore worsen adverse selection and moral hazard problems directly and also indirectly by causing a deterioration in banks' balance sheets from asset write-downs (as shown by the arrow pointing from the third factor in the first row of Figure 21.1).

As in advanced countries, when an emerging market economy is in a recession or a prominent firm fails, people become more uncertain about the returns on investment projects. In emerging market countries, notoriously unstable political systems are another source of uncertainty. When uncertainty increases, it becomes hard for lenders to screen out good credit risks from bad and to monitor the activities of firms to whom they have loaned money, again worsening adverse selection and moral hazard problems (as shown by the arrow pointing from the last factor in the first row of Figure 21.1).

Stage Two: Currency Crisis

As the effects of any or all of the factors at the top of the diagram in Figure 21.1 build on each other, participants in the foreign exchange market sense an opportunity: they can make huge profits if they bet on a depreciation of the currency. As is discussed in in Chapter 14, a currency that is fixed against the U.S. dollar now becomes subject to a **speculative attack,** in which speculators engage in massive sales of the currency. As the currency sales flood the market, supply far outstrips the demand, the value of the currency collapses, and a currency crisis ensues (see the Stage Two section of Figure 21.1). High interest rates abroad, increases in uncertainty, and falling asset prices all play a role. The deterioration in bank balance sheets and severe fiscal imbalances, however, are the two key factors that trigger the speculative attacks and plunge the economies into a full-scale, vicious downward spiral of currency crisis, financial crisis, and meltdown.

Deterioration of Bank Balance Sheets Triggers Currency Crisis When banks and other financial institutions are in trouble, governments have a limited number of options. Defending their currencies by raising interest rates should encourage capital inflows, but if the government raises interest rates, banks must pay more to obtain funds. This increase in costs decreases bank profitability, which may lead them to insolvency. Thus when the banking system is in trouble, the government and central bank are now between a rock and a hard place: If they raise interest rates too much, they will destroy their already weakened banks and further weaken their economy. If they don't, they can't maintain the value of their currency.

Speculators in the market for foreign currency recognize the troubles in a country's financial sector and realize when the government's ability to raise interest rates and defend the currency is so costly that the government is likely to give up and allow the currency to depreciate. They will seize an almost sure-thing bet because the currency can only go downward in value. Speculators engage in a feeding frenzy and sell the currency in anticipation of its decline, which will provide them with huge profits. These sales rapidly use up the country's holdings of reserves of foreign currency because the country has to sell its reserves to buy the domestic currency and keep it from falling in value. Once the country's central bank has exhausted its holdings of foreign currency reserves, the cycle ends. It no longer has the resources to intervene in the foreign exchange market and must let the value of the domestic currency fall: that is, the government must allow a devaluation.

Severe Fiscal Imbalances Trigger Currency Crisis   We have seen that severe fiscal imbalances can lead to a deterioration of bank balance sheets and so can help produce a currency crisis along the lines described previously. Fiscal imbalances can also directly trigger a currency crisis. When government budget deficits spin out of control, foreign and domestic investors begin to suspect that the country may not be able to pay back its government debt and so will start pulling money out of the country and selling the domestic currency. Recognition that the fiscal situation is out of control thus results in a speculative attack against the currency, which eventually results in its collapse.

Stage Three: Full-Fledged Financial Crisis

In contrast to most advanced economies that typically denominate debt in domestic currency, emerging market economies denominate many debt contracts in foreign currency (usually U.S. dollars) leading to what is referred to as a **currency mismatch.** An unanticipated depreciation or devaluation of the domestic currency (for example, pesos) in emerging market countries increases the debt burden of domestic firms in terms of domestic currency. That is, it takes more pesos to pay back the dollarized debt. Since most firms price the goods and services they produce in the domestic currency, the firms' assets do not rise in value in terms of pesos, while their debt does. The depreciation of the domestic currency increases the value of debt relative to assets, and the firms' net worth declines. The decline in net worth then increases adverse selection and moral hazard problems described earlier. A decline in investment and economic activity then follows (as shown by the Stage Three section of Figure 21.1).

We now see how the institutional structure of debt markets in emerging market countries interacts with the currency devaluations to propel the economies into full-fledged financial crisis. A currency crisis, with its resulting depreciation of the currency, leads to a deterioration of firms' balance sheets that sharply increases adverse selection and moral hazard problems. Economists often call a concurrent currency crisis and financial crisis the "twin crisis."

The collapse of a currency also can lead to higher inflation. The central banks in most emerging market countries, in contrast to those in advanced countries, have little credibility as inflation fighters. Thus, a sharp depreciation of the currency after a currency crisis leads to immediate upward pressure on import prices. A dramatic rise in both actual and expected inflation will likely follow, which will cause domestic interest rates to rise. The resulting increase in interest payments causes reductions in firms' cash flow, which lead to increased asymmetric information problems since firms are now more dependent on external funds to finance their investment. This asymmetric information analysis suggests that the resulting increase in adverse selection and moral hazard problems leads to a reduction in investment and economic activity.

As shown in Figure 21.1, further deterioration in the economy occurs. The collapse in economic activity and the deterioration of cash flow and firm and household balance sheets means that many debtors are no longer able to pay off their debts, resulting in substantial losses for banks. Sharp rises in interest rates also have a negative effect on banks' profitability and balance sheets. Even more problematic for the banks is the sharp increase in the value of their foreign-currency-denominated liabilities after the devaluation. Thus, bank balance sheets are squeezed from both sides—the value of their assets falls as the value of their liabilities rises.

Under these circumstances, the banking system will often suffer a banking crisis in which many banks are likely to fail (as in the United States during the Great Depression). The banking crisis and the contributing factors in the credit markets explain a further worsening of adverse selection and moral hazard problems and a further collapse of lending and economic activity in the aftermath of the crisis.

We now apply the analysis here to study two of the many financial crisis that have struck emerging market economies in recent years.[1] First, we examine the crisis in South Korea in 1997–1998 because it illustrates the first path toward a financial crisis operating through mismanagement of the financial liberalization/globalization. Second, we look at the Argentine crisis of 2001–2002, which was triggered through the second path of severe fiscal imbalances.

CASE

Crisis in South Korea, 1997–1998

Before its crisis in 1997, South Korea was one of the great economic success stories in history. In 1960, seven years after the Korean War was over, the country was still extremely poor, with an annual income per person of less than $2,000 (in today's dollars), putting it on par with Somalia. During the postwar period, South Korea pursued an export-oriented strategy that helped it become one of the world's major economies. With an annual growth rate of nearly 8% from 1960 to 1997, it was one of the leaders in the "Asian miracle," the term used to refer to formerly poor countries now experiencing rapid economic growth. By 1997 South Korea's income per person had risen by more than a factor of ten.

South Korea's macroeconomic fundamentals were strong before the crisis. Figure 21.2 shows that in 1996 inflation was below 5%, while Figure 21.3 shows that real output growth was close to 7%, and unemployment was low (Figure 21.4). The government budget was in slight surplus, something that most advanced countries have been unable to achieve.

Financial Liberalization/Globalization Mismanaged

Starting in the early 1990s, the South Korean government removed many restrictive regulations on financial institutions to liberalize the country's financial markets and also embarked on the financial globalization process by opening up their capital markets to capital flows from abroad. This resulted in a lending boom in which bank credit

---

[1]For more detail on the South Korean and Argentine crisis as well as a discussion of other emerging market financial crisis, see Frederic S. Mishkin, *The Next Great Globalization: How Disadvantaged Nations Can Harness Their Financial Systems to Get Rich* (Princeton, NJ: Princeton University Press, 2006).

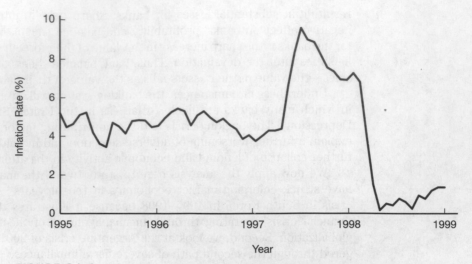

FIGURE 21.2 Inflation, South Korea, 1995–1999

Inflation was below 5% before the crisis but jumped to nearly 10% during the crisis.

Source: International Monetary Fund. *International Financial Statistics.* www.imfstatistics.org/imf/.

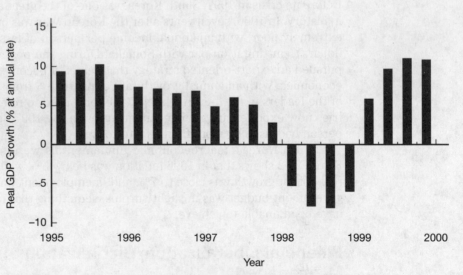

FIGURE 21.3 Real GDP Growth, South Korea, 1995–1999

Real GDP growth was close to 7% at an annual rate before the crisis but declined at over a 6% rate during the crisis.

Source: International Monetary Fund. *International Financial Statistics.* www.imfstatistics.org/imf/.

to the private nonfinancial business sector accelerated sharply, with lending fueled by massive foreign borrowing expanding at rates close to 20% per year. Because of weak bank regulator supervision and a lack of expertise in screening and monitoring borrowers at banking institutions, losses on loans began to mount, causing an erosion of banks' net worth (capital).

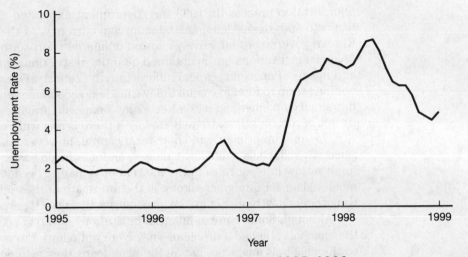

FIGURE 21.4 Unemployment, South Korea, 1995–1999

The unemployment rate was below 3% before the crisis but jumped to above 8% during the crisis.

Source: International Monetary Fund. *International Financial Statistics.* www.imfstatistics.org/imf/.

Perversion of the Financial Liberalization/Globalization Process: Chaebols and the South Korean Crisis

Powerful business interests often play an active role in the mismanagement of financial liberalization. Nowhere was this clearer than in South Korea before the financial crisis of the late 1990s, when large family-owned conglomerates known as chaebols dominated the economy with sales of nearly 50% of the country's GDP.

The chaebols were politically very powerful and deemed "too big to fail" by the government. With this implicit guarantee, the chaebols knew they would receive direct government assistance or direct credit if they got into trouble, but they could keep all of the profits if their bets paid off. Not surprisingly, chaebols borrowed like crazy and became highly leveraged.

In the 1990s, the chaebols weren't making any money. From 1993 to 1996, the return on assets for the top 30 chaebols was never much more than 3% (a comparable figure for U.S. corporations is 15%–20%). In 1996, right before the crisis hit, the rate of return on assets had fallen to 0.2%. Furthermore, only the top five chaebols had any profits, while the sixth to 30th chaebols never had a rate of return on assets much above 1% and in many years had negative rates of returns. With this poor profitability and the already high leverage, any banker would pull back on lending to these conglomerates *if* there were no government safety net. Because the banks knew the government would make good on the chaebols' loans if they were in default, banks continued to lend to the chaebols. This substantial financing from commercial banks, however, was not enough to feed the chaebols' insatiable appetite for more credit. The chaebols decided that the way out of their troubles was to pursue growth, and they needed massive amounts of funds to do it. Even with the vaunted South Korean national savings rate of over 30%, there was just not enough loanable funds to finance the chaebols' planned expansion. Where could they get it? The answer was in the international capital markets.

The chaebols encouraged the South Korean government to accelerate the process of opening up South Korean financial markets to foreign capital as part of the liberalization process. In 1993 the government expanded the ability of domestic banks to make loans denominated in foreign currency. At the same time, the South Korean government effectively allowed unlimited short-term foreign borrowing by financial institutions but maintained quantity restrictions on long-term borrowing as a means of managing capital inflows into the country. Opening up short term but not long term to foreign capital inflows made no economic sense. Short-term capital flows make an emerging market economy financially fragile: short-term capital can fly out of the country extremely rapidly if there is any whiff of a crisis.

Opening up primarily to short-term capital, however, made complete political sense: the chaebols needed the money, and it is much easier to borrow short-term funds at low interest rates in the international market because long-term lending is much riskier for foreign creditors. In the aftermath of these changes, South Korean banks opened 28 branches in foreign countries that gave them access to foreign funds.

Although South Korean financial institutions now had access to foreign capital, the chaebols still had a problem. They were not allowed to own commercial banks, so the chaebols might not get all the bank loans they needed. However, there was an existing type of financial institution specific to South Korea that *would* enable them to get the loans they needed: the merchant bank. Merchant banking corporations were wholesale financial institutions that engaged in underwriting securities, leasing, and short-term lending to the corporate sector. They obtained funds for these loans by issuing bonds and commercial paper and by borrowing from interbank and foreign markets. At the time of the Korean crisis, merchant banks were allowed to borrow abroad and were almost virtually unregulated. The chaebols saw their opportunity and convinced government officials to convert many finance companies (some already owned by the chaebols) into merchant banks. The merchant banks channeled massive amounts of funds to their chaebol owners, where they flowed into unproductive investments in steel, automobile production, and chemicals. When the loans went sour, the stage was set for a disastrous financial crisis.

Stock Market Decline and Failure of Firms Increase Uncertainty

The South Korean economy then experienced a negative shock to export prices that hurt the chaebols' already-thin profit margins and the small- and medium-sized firms that were tied to them. On January 23, 1997, a second major shock occurred, creating great uncertainty for the financial system: Hanbo, the 14th largest chaebol, declared bankruptcy. Indeed, the bankruptcy of Hanbo was just the beginning. Five more of the 30 largest chaebols declared bankruptcy before the year was over. As a result of the greater uncertainty created by these bankruptcies and the deteriorating condition of financial and nonfinancial balance sheets, the stock market declined sharply by more than 50% from its peak, as shown by Figure 21.5.

Adverse Selection and Moral Hazard Problems Worsen and the Economy Contracts

As we have seen, an increase in uncertainty and a decrease in net worth as a result of a stock market decline exacerbate asymmetric information problems. It becomes hard to screen out good from bad borrowers. The decline in net worth decreases the value of firms' collateral and increases their incentives to make risky investments because there is less equity to lose if the investments are unsuccessful. The increase in uncertainty and stock market declines that occurred before the crisis, along with

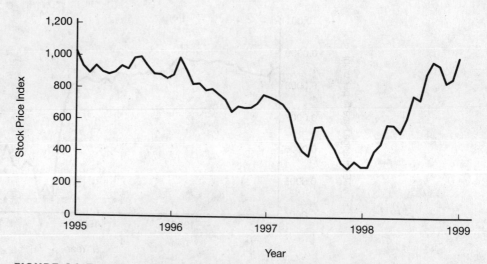

FIGURE 21.5 Stock Market Index, South Korea, 1995–1999

Stock prices fell by over 50% during the crisis.

Source: Global Financial Data, available at www.globalfinancialdata.com/.

the deterioration in banks' balance sheets, worsened adverse selection and moral hazard problems. As a result, lending declined and the economy weakened. The weakening of the economy, along with the deterioration of bank balance sheets, ripened the South Korean economy for the next stage, a currency crisis that would send the economy into a full-fledged financial crisis and a depression.

Currency Crisis Ensues

Given the weakness of balance sheets in the financial sector and the increased exposure of the economy to a sudden stop in capital inflows because of the large amount of short-term, external borrowing, a speculative attack on South Korea's currency was inevitable. With the collapse of the Thai baht in July 1997 and the announced closing of 42 finance companies in Thailand in early August 1997, contagion began to spread as participants in the market wondered whether similar problems existed in other East Asian countries. Soon speculators recognized that the banking sector in South Korea was in trouble. They knew the South Korean central bank could no longer defend the currency by raising interest rates because this would sink the already weakened banks. Speculators pulled out of the South Korean currency, the won, leading to a speculative attack.

Final Stage: Currency Crisis Triggers Full-Fledged Financial Crisis

The speculative attack then led to a sharp drop in the value of the won, by nearly 50%, as shown in Figure 21.6. Because both nonfinancial and financial firms had so much foreign-currency debt, the nearly 50% depreciation of the Korean won doubled the value of the foreign-denominated debt in terms of the domestic currency and therefore led to a severe erosion of net worth. This loss of net worth led to a severe increase in adverse selection and moral hazard problems in South Korean financial markets, for domestic and foreign lenders alike.

The deterioration in firms' cash flow and balance sheets worsened the banking crisis. Bank balance sheets were devastated when the banks paid off their

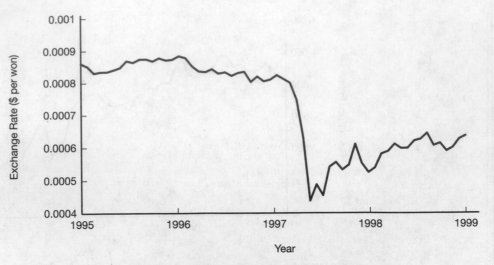

FIGURE 21.6 Value of South Korean Currency, 1995–1999

The Korean won lost nearly half its value during the crisis.

Source: International Monetary Fund. *International Financial Statistics.* www.imfstatistics.org/imf/.

foreign-currency borrowing with more Korean won and yet could not collect on the dollar-denominated loans they had made to domestic firms. In addition, the fact that financial institutions had been encouraged to make their foreign borrowing short term increased their liquidity problems because banks had to pay these loans back so quickly. The government stepped in to guarantee all bank deposits and prevent a bank panic, but the loss of capital meant that banks had to curtail their lending.

Real GDP fell in 1998 at over a 6% rate, as shown in Figure 21.3, and unemployment rose sharply (refer to Figure 21.4). In this situation, we might expect the inflation rate to fall as well. Inflation, however, did not fall; instead it rose, as we showed in Figure 21.2. The currency crisis is behind this key difference. Specifically, the collapse of the South Korean currency after the successful speculative attack on the currency raised import prices, which directly fed into inflation, and weakened the credibility of the Bank of Korea as an inflation fighter. The rise in import prices led to a price shock, while the weakened credibility of the Bank of Korea led to a rise in expected inflation, with inflation climbing sharply from around the 5% level to near 10%.

Market interest rates soared to over 20% by the end of 1997 (Figure 21.7) to compensate for the high inflation. They also rose because the Bank of Korea pursued a tight monetary policy in line with recommendations from the International Monetary Fund. High interest rates led to a drop in cash flows, which forced firms to obtain external funds and increased adverse selection and moral hazard problems in the credit markets. The increase in asymmetric information problems in the credit markets, along with the direct effect of higher interest rates on investment decisions, led to a further contraction in investment spending, providing another reason that economic activity fell.

Recovery Commences

In 1998 the South Korean government responded very aggressively to the crisis by implementing a series of financial reforms that helped restore confidence in the financial system. Financial markets began to recover, which helped stimulate lending, and the economy began to recover.

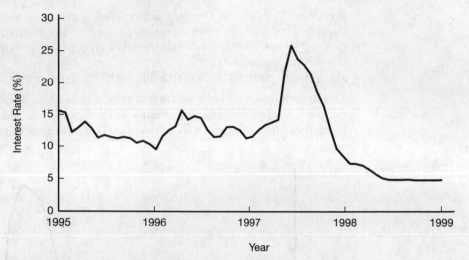

FIGURE 21.7 Interest Rates, South Korea, 1995–1999

Market interest rates soared to over 20% during the crisis.

Source: International Monetary Fund. *International Financial Statistics.* www.imfstatistics.org/imf/.

The South Korean financial crisis inflicted a high human cost, too. The ranks of the poor swelled from six million to over ten million, suicide and divorce rates jumped by nearly 50%, drug addiction rates climbed by 35%, and the crime rate rose by over 15%.

CASE

The Argentine Financial Crisis, 2001–2002

Argentina's financial crisis was triggered by severe fiscal imbalances that we will now examine.

Severe Fiscal Imbalances

In contrast to Mexico and the East Asian countries, Argentina had a well-supervised banking system, and a lending boom did not occur before the crisis. The banks were in surprisingly good shape before the crisis, even though a severe recession had begun in 1998. Unfortunately, however, Argentina has always had difficulty controlling its budgets. In Argentina, the provinces (similar to states in the United States) control a large percentage of public spending, but the responsibility for raising the revenue is left primarily to the federal government. With this system, the provinces have incentives to spend beyond their means and then call on the federal government periodically to assume responsibility for their debt. As a result, Argentina is perennially in deficit.

The recession starting in 1998 made the situation even worse because it led to declining tax revenues and a widening gap between government expenditures and taxes. The subsequent severe fiscal imbalances were so large that the government had trouble getting both domestic residents and foreigners to buy enough of its bonds, so it coerced banks into absorbing large amounts of government debt. By 2001 investors were losing confidence in the ability of the Argentine government to repay this debt. The price of the debt plummeted, leaving big holes in the banks' balance sheets. What had once been considered one of the best-supervised and strongest banking systems among emerging market countries was now losing deposits.

Adverse Selection and Moral Hazard Problems Worsen

The deterioration of bank balance sheets and the loss of deposits led the banks to cut back on their lending. As a result, adverse selection and moral hazard problems worsened and lending began to decline. The resulting weakening of the economy

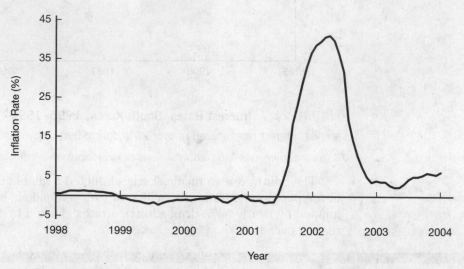

FIGURE 21.8 Inflation, Argentina, 1998–2004

Inflation surged to over 40% during the crisis.

Source: International Monetary Fund. *International Financial Statistics.* www.imfstatistics.org/imf/.

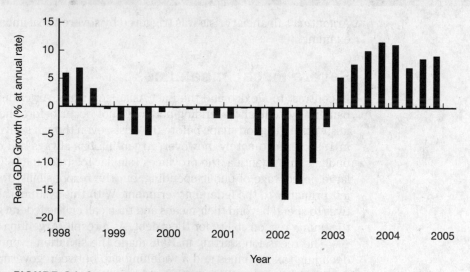

FIGURE 21.9 Real GDP Growth, Argentina, 1998–2004

Real GDP growth collapsed during the crisis, declining at an annual rate of over 15%.

Source: International Monetary Fund. *International Financial Statistics.* www.imfstatistics.org/imf/.

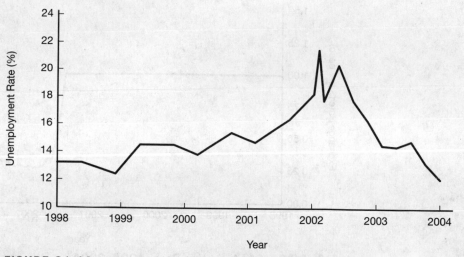

FIGURE 21.10 Unemployment Rate, Argentina, 1998–2004

The unemployment rate climbed to above 20% during the crisis.

Source: Global Financial Data, available at www.globalfinancialdata.com/.

and deterioration of bank balance sheets set the stage for the next stage of the crisis, a bank panic.

Bank Panic Begins

In October 2001, negotiations between the central government and the provinces to improve the fiscal situation broke down, and tax revenues continued to fall as the economy declined. Default on government bonds was now inevitable. As a result, a full-fledged bank panic began in November, with deposit outflows running nearly $1 billion a day. At the beginning of December, the government was forced to close the banks temporarily and impose a restriction called the *corralito* (small fence), under which depositors could withdraw only $250 in cash per week. The corralito was particularly devastating for the poor, who were highly dependent on cash to conduct their daily transactions. The social fabric of Argentine society began to unravel. Nearly 30 people died in violent riots.

Currency Crisis Ensues

The bank panic signaled that the government could no longer allow interest rates to remain high in order to prop up the value of the peso and preserve the currency board, an arrangement in which it fixed the value of one Argentine peso to equal one U.S. dollar by agreeing to buy and sell pesos at that exchange rate (discussed in Chapter 15). Raising interest rates to preserve the currency board was no longer an option because it would have meant destroying the already weakened banks. The public now recognized that the peso would have to decline in value in the near future, so a speculative attack began in which people sold pesos for dollars. In addition, the government's dire fiscal position made it unable to pay back its debt, providing another reason for the investors to pull money out of the country, leading to further peso sales.

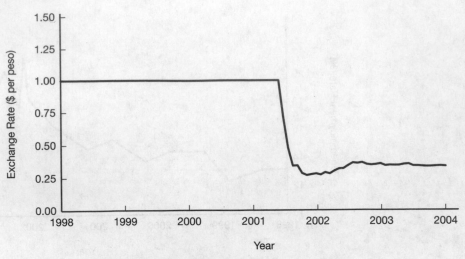

FIGURE 21.11 **Argentine Peso, 1998–2004**

The Argentine peso fell from $1.00 before the crisis to under $0.30 by June 2002.

Source: International Monetary Fund. *International Financial Statistics.* www.imfstatistics.org/imf/.

On December 23, 2001, the government announced the inevitable: a suspension of external debt payments for at least 60 days. Then on January 2, 2002, the government abandoned the currency board.

Currency Crisis Triggers Full-Fledged Financial Crisis

The peso now went into free fall, dropping from a value of $1.00 to less than $0.30 by June 2002 and then stabilizing at around $0.33 thereafter, as shown by Figure 21.11. Because Argentina had a higher percentage of debt denominated in dollars than any of the other crisis countries, the effects of the peso collapse on balance sheets were particularly devastating. With the peso falling to one-third of its value before the crisis, all dollar-denominated debt tripled in peso terms. Since Argentina's tradable sector was small, most businesses' production was priced in pesos. If they had to pay back their dollar debt, almost all firms would become insolvent. In this environment, financial markets could not function because net worth would not be available to mitigate adverse selection and moral hazard problems.

Given the losses on the defaulted government debt and the rising loan losses, Argentine banks found their balance sheets in a precarious state. Further, the run on the banks had led to huge deposit outflows. Lacking resources to make new loans, the banks could no longer solve adverse selection and moral hazard problems. The government bond default and conditions in Argentine financial markets also meant that foreigners were unwilling to lend and were actually pulling their money out of the country.

With the financial system in jeopardy, financial flows came to a grinding halt. The resulting curtailment of lending then led to a further contraction of economic activity. The corralito also played an important role in weakening the economy. By making it more difficult to get cash, it caused a sharp slowdown in the underground economy, which is large in Argentina and runs primarily on cash.

Just as in South Korea, the collapse of the Argentine currency after the successful speculative attack on the currency raised import prices, which directly fed into

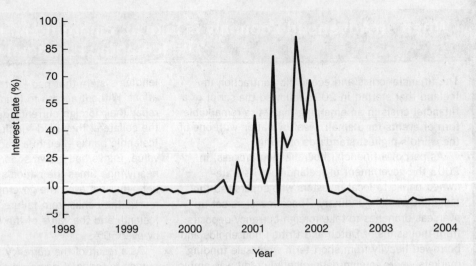

FIGURE 21.12 Interest Rates, Argentina, 1998–2004

Interest rates rose to nearly 100% during the crisis.

Source: International Monetary Fund. *International Financial Statistics.* www.imfstatistics.org/imf/.

inflation, and weakened the credibility of the Argentine central bank to keep inflation under control. Indeed, Argentina's history of very high inflation meant that there was an even larger rise in expected inflation in Argentina than in South Korea. Inflation in Argentina rose as high as 40% at an annual rate, as shown in Figure 21.8. Because the rise in actual inflation was accompanied by a rise in expected inflation, interest rates went to even higher levels, as indicated in Figure 21.12. The higher interest payments led to a decline in the cash flow of both households and businesses, which now had to seek external funds to finance their investments. Given the uncertainty in financial markets, asymmetric information problems were particularly severe, and this meant investment could not be funded. Households and businesses cut back their spending further. As our aggregate demand and supply analysis predicts, the Argentine economy plummeted. In the first quarter of 2002, Figure 21.9 shows that output was falling at an annual rate of more than 15% and Figure 21.10 demonstrates that unemployment shot up to near 20%. The increase in poverty was dramatic: the percentage of the Argentine population in poverty rose to almost 50% in 2002. Argentina was experiencing the worst depression in its history—one every bit as bad as, and maybe even worse than, the U.S. Great Depression.

Recovery Begins

With the financial crisis receding and a boom in the demand for Argentina's commodity exports, the economy recovered, and by the end of 2003 economic growth was running at an annual rate of around 10%, and Figure 21.10 demonstrates that unemployment had fallen below 15%. Inflation also fell to below 5%, as shown by Figure 21.8.

Although we have drawn a strong distinction between financial crisis in emerging market economies and those in advanced economies, there have been financial crisis in advanced economies that have more in common with financial crisis in emerging market economies. This is illustrated by the Global box, "When an Advanced Economy Is Like an Emerging Market Economy: The Icelandic Financial Crisis of 2008."

When an Advanced Economy Is Like an Emerging Market Economy: The Icelandic Financial Crisis of 2008

The financial crisis and economic contraction in Iceland that started in 2008 followed the script of a financial crisis in an emerging market, a remarkable turn of events for a small, wealthy nation with one of the world's highest standards of living.

As part of a financial liberalization process, in 2003 the government of Iceland sold its state-owned banks to local investors who supersized the Icelandic banking industry. These investors set up overseas branches to take foreign-currency deposits from thousands of Dutch and British households and borrowed heavily from short-term wholesale funding markets where foreign-denominated credit was ample and cheap. They channeled the funds to local investment firms, many of which had ties to the bank owners themselves. Not surprisingly, many of the funds went into high-risk investments like equities and real estate. Iceland's stock market value ballooned to 250% of GDP, and firms, households, and banks borrowed heavily in foreign currencies, leading to a severe currency mismatch, as had occurred in many emerging market countries. Meanwhile, Iceland's regulatory system provided ineffective supervision of bank risk taking.

In October 2008 the failure of the U.S. investment bank Lehman Brothers shut down the wholesale lending system that had kept the Icelandic banks afloat. Without access to funding, the banks couldn't repay their foreign currency debts, and much of the collateral they held—including shares in other Icelandic banks—fell to a fraction of its previous value. Banks had grown so large—their assets were nearly nine times the nation's gross domestic product—that not even the government could credibly rescue the banks from failure. Foreign capital fled Iceland, and the value of the Icelandic krona tumbled by over 50%.

As a result of the currency collapse, the debt burden in terms of domestic currency more than doubled, destroying a large part of Icelandic firms' and households' net worth, leading to a full-scale financial crisis. The economy went into a severe recession with the unemployment rate tripling, real wages falling, and the government incurring huge budget deficits. Relationships with foreign creditors became tense, with the United Kingdom even freezing assets of Icelandic firms under an antiterrorism law. Many Icelandic people returned to traditional jobs in fishing and agricultural industries, where citizens could find a silver lining: the collapse of the Icelandic currency made exports of Iceland's famous cod fish, Arctic char, and Atlantic salmon more affordable to foreigners.

India and the Global Financial Crisis

The global financial crisis, contrary to the 'decoupling theory' fashionable at the time, did affect India. The reasons for India being impacted by the global financial crisis, are to be found in its rapid and growing integration into the global economy. India's integration into the world economy, measured by the two-way trade (merchandize exports plus imports), as a proportion of GDP, had been rapid and had grown from 21.2% in 1997–1998 to 34.7% in 2007–2008. More significant than trade globalization was India's financial integration, measured by the ratio of total external transactions (gross current account flows plus gross capital flows) to GDP. The latter ratio had more than doubled from 46.8% in 1997–1998 to 117.4% in 2007–2008. Further, the investment-led growth of the Indian corporate sector was financed by external funding, due to mainly domestic funds being expensive.

The contagion spread to emerging economies, and to India too. Output growth in India which averaged 9.5% per annum during the three year period 2005–2008 dropped to 6.8% in the crisis year of 2008–2009. The deceleration in growth was seen across all three sectors, i.e. agriculture, industry and services. Domestic aggregate demand moderated due to a sharp deceleration in growth of private consumption demand. Exports which grew at 25% during 2005–2008 decelerated to 12.2% in the crisis year 2008–2009 following weakening global demand, and further declined by 2.2% in 2009–2010. The reversal of capital flows, which had exceeded the current account deficit prior to 2008–2009, led to net capital flows being significantly short of the current account deficit. This put downward pressure on the rupee and the exchange rate depreciated from ₹39.37 per dollar in January 2008 to ₹51.23 per dollar in March 2009.

As regards to inflation, it remained highly volatile during 2008–2009. WPI inflation, which had remained at 5.3% in the preceding 5 years (2003–2008), rose to a high of 12.9% in August 2008 and declined sharply thereafter to below 1% by the end of the year, before turning negative since June 2009. The negative inflation essentially reflected the impact of the high base of the previous year. Within WPI, essential commodities continued to exhibit high inflation.

Contagion of the Crisis

The crisis spread to India through various channels—the financial channel, the real channel, as also, through the confidence channel.

Financial channel contagion: With the global liquidity being squeezed, Indian corporates and banks were affected. To face such liquidity squeeze, corporates shifted their credit demand to the domestic banking sector. Moreover, they withdrew their investments from the domestic money market mutual funds. The latter, thus, were faced with redemption pressures; so were the non-banking financial companies (NBFCs) where the MFs had invested a significant portion of their funds. Money and credit markets were both affected.

Foreign exchange markets were affected in several ways. As part of the global deleveraging process, there was significant reversal of capital flows. Corporates, who had significant external obligations, were converting funds raised locally into foreign currency. The RBI's forex market interventions to manage the rupee volatility further led to liquidity tightening.

Real channel contagion: The slump in the demand for Indian exports of goods, as also services, especially from the United States, European Union and the Middle East, led to the contagion through the real channel.

Confidence channels: The crisis also spread through the confidence channel. With the global liquidity situation remaining tight in the period immediately following the Lehman failure in mid-September 2008, the finacial system became risk-averse and banks became cautious about their lending.

Response to the Crisis

Both the Government of India and RBI responded to the crisis in a coordinated fashion. While the government's response comprised of a fiscal stimulus, the RBI responded through measures including monetary accommodation and counter cyclical regulatory forbearance.

Monetary Response

The RBI responded by reversing its monetary policy stance of monetary tightening that it had followed hitherto due to heightened inflationary pressures. With inflationary pressures easing, as also with the reduction in growth, the RBI moved towards monetary easing. The RBI targeted three objectives: first, to maintain a comfortable rupee liquidity position; second, to augment foreign exchange liquidity; and third, to maintain a policy framework that would keep credit delivery on track so as to arrest the moderation in growth (Subbarao, 2009, 7–8).

The policy packages, initiated from mid-September 2008, included both conventional and unconventional measures. Conventional measures included reduction in policy rates, reduction in the quantum of bank reserves impounded by the central bank and liberalized refinance facilities for export credit.

The reverse repo rate was reduced by 425 basis points from 9% to 4.75% and the reverse repo rate by 275 basis points from 6% to 3.25%. However, post the crisis, the reverse repo rate (the lower band of the LAF corridor) began to be used as the operational policy rate, whereas, in the period prior to mid-September 2008, the repo rate (the upper band of the LAF corridor) was the operational policy rate. The effective policy rate, thus, had seen a larger cut of 575 basis points from 9% in mid-September 2008 to 3.25% in 2009. This was mirrored in the money market interest rates (weighted average of call, market repo and CBLO) falling from 9.3% in September 2008 to 3.8% in March 2009.

The cash reserve ratio (CRR) was reduced from 9% (September 2008) to 5% by early January 2009 injecting nearly ₹160,000 crore of primary liquidity in the system. Other measures taken by the RBI in response to the global financial crisis included cuts in the statutory liquidity ratio (SLR), opening of new refinancing windows, refinance to SIDBI and EXIM Banks, and clawing back of prudential norms in regard to provisioning and risk weights. The measures to improve forex liquidity included increase in interest rate ceilings on non-resident foreign currency deposits, easing of restrictions on external commercial borrowings and on short-term trade credits and allowing non-banking financial companies and housing finance companies access to foreign borrowing.

The unconventional measures taken by the RBI included a rupee-dollar swap facility for Indian banks to give them comfort in managing their short-term foreign funding requirements, an exclusive refinance window as also a special purpose vehicle for supporting non-banking financial companies, and expanding the lendable resources available to apex finance institutions for refinancing credit extended to small industries, housing and exports.

Taken together, the measures put in place since mid-September 2008 ensured that the Indian financial markets continued to function in an orderly manner. The cumulative amount of primary liquidity potentially available to the financial system through these measures was over $75 bn or 7% of GDP. This sizeable easing had ensured a comfortable liquidity position starting mid-November 2008 as evidenced by a number of indicators including the weighted-average call money rate, the overnight money market rate and the yield on the 10-year benchmark government security.

Government's Fiscal Stimulus

The government of India had tried to put into effect a road map to fiscal sustainability through the Fiscal Responsibility and Budget Management (FRBM) Act in 2003. However, following the crisis and recognising its potential deep impact, the central government invoked the emergency provisions of the FRBM Act to seek relaxation from the fiscal targets and launched two fiscal stimulus packages in December 2008 and January 2009. These fiscal stimulus packages, together amounting to about 3% of GDP, included additional public spending, particularly capital expenditure, government guaranteed funds for infrastructure spending, cuts in indirect taxes, expanded guarantee cover for credit to micro and small enterprises, and additional support to exporters. These stimulus packages came on top of an already announced expanded safety-net for rural poor, a farm loan waiver package and salary increases for government staff, all of which stimulated demand too.

As a result of the fiscal stimulus, government consumption demand increased by 20.2%. The contribution of government consumption expenditure to overall growth, accordingly, increased to 32.5% from an average contribution of 5.9% in the preceding five years.

The result of the fiscal stimulus package was a deterioration in the government's fiscal indicators. The Central Government's fiscal deficit more than doubled from 2.7% of GDP in 2007–2008 to 6% in 2008–2009; the revenue deficit reached 4.4% of GDP, while the primary balance again turned into deficit in 2008–2009, after recording surpluses during the preceding two years. Net market borrowings during 2008–2009 almost trebled from the budgeted ₹113,000 crore to ₹329,649 in the revised estimates (actual borrowings were ₹298,536 crore as per RBI records). In view of the renewed fiscal deterioration, the credit rating agency Standard and Poor's changed its outlook on long-term sovereign credit rating from stable to negative, while reaffirming the "BBB-" rating.

Though the Government of India and RBI worked in close coordination, the financial crisis brought to the fore questions regarding the co-ordination between monetary policy and fiscal/debt management policies, in particular, whether in respect of fiscal-monetary co-ordination, fiscal dominance or monetary dominance will prevail.

In the recent years, India's integration with the global economy has increased. A 1% decrease in the world growth rate is now associated with a 0.42% decrease in India's growth rates. As such, any deflationary impulses in the global arena will affect India considerably. Noting this, the Economic Survey 2015–2016 notes that India would need to reduce its dependence on foreign demand, and find and activate domestic sources to keep up its growth momentum (Government of India, 7–8).

References:

Duvvuri, Subbarao, " Impact of the Global Financial Crisis on India Collateral Damage and Response", Speech delivered at the Symposium on "The Global Economic Crisis and Challenges for the Asian Economy in a Changing World" organized by the Institute for International Monetary Affairs, Tokyo, February 18, 2009, https://rbidocs.rbi.org.in/rdocs/Speeches/PDFs/Speech%20-%20as%20sent-%20 Modified%20_4_.pdf

Duvvuri, Subbarao, "India and the Global Financial Crisis: What Have We Learnt?", Text of the K R Narayanan Oration at the South Asia Research Centre of the Australian National University, Canberra, 23 June 2011, http://www.bis.org/review/r110629a.pdf

Rakesh Mohan, "Global financial crisis-causes, impact, policy responses and lessons", Speech given at the 7th Annual India Business Forum Conference, London Business School, London, 23 April 2009, http://www.bis.org/review/r090506d.pdf

Reserve Bank of India, Annual Report 2009, https://www.rbi.org.in/scripts/AnnualReportPublications. aspx?Id=888

Reserve Bank of India, Report on Currency and Finance 2009-2012, Fiscal and Monetary Coordination, 2012, https://rbidocs.rbi.org.in/rdocs/Publications/PDFs/0RCF040313_F0912.pdf

Government of India, Economic Survey 2015-16, http://indiabudget.nic.in/budget2016-2017/es2015-16/ echapvol1-01.pdf

Preventing Emerging Market Financial Crisis

The experience with financial crisis in emerging market economies described in this chapter suggests a number of government policies that can help make financial crisis in emerging market countries less likely.[2]

Beef Up Prudential Regulation and Supervision of Banks

As we have seen, the banking sector sits at the root of financial crisis in emerging market economies. To prevent crisis, therefore, governments must improve prudential regulation and supervision of banks to limit their risk taking. First, regulators should ensure that banks hold ample capital to cushion the losses from economic shocks and to give bank owners, who have more to loose, an incentive to pursue safer investments.

Prudential supervision can also promote a safer and sounder banking system by ensuring that banks have proper risk management procedures in place, including (1) good risk measurement and monitoring systems, (2) policies to limit activities that present significant risks, and (3) internal controls to prevent fraud or unauthorized activities by employees. As the South Korea example indicates, regulation should also ban commercial businesses from owning banking institutions. When commercial businesses own banks, they are likely to use them to channel lending to themselves, as the chaebols in South Korea did, leading to risky lending that can provoke a banking crisis.

For prudential supervision to work, prudential supervisors must have adequate resources to do their jobs. This is a particularly serious problem in emerging market countries where prudential supervisors earn low salaries and lack basic tools such as computers. Because politicians often pressure prudential supervisors to discourage them from being "too tough" on banks that make political contributions (or outright bribes), a more independent regulatory and supervisory agency can better withstand political influence, increasing the likelihood that they will do their jobs and limit bank risk taking.

Encourage Disclosure and Market-Based Discipline

The public sector, acting through prudential regulators and supervisors, will always struggle to control risk taking by financial institutions. Financial institutions have incentives to hide information from bank supervisors in order to avoid restrictions on their activities, and they can become quite adept and crafty at masking risk. Also, supervisors may be corrupt or give in to political pressure and so may not do their jobs properly.

To eliminate these problems, financial markets need to discipline financial institutions from taking on too much risk. Government regulations to promote disclosure by banking and other financial institutions of their balance sheet positions,

---

[2]For a more extensive discussion of reforms to prevent financial crisis in emerging market countries, see Chapter 9, "Preventing Financial Crisis," in Frederic S. Mishkin, *The Next Great Globalization: How Disadvantaged Nations Can Harness Their Financial Systems to Get Rich* (Princeton, NJ: Princeton University Press, 2006), 137–163.

therefore, are needed to encourage these institutions to hold more capital because depositors and creditors will be unwilling to put their money into an institution that is thinly capitalized. Regulations to promote disclosure of banks' activities will also limit risk taking because depositors and creditors will pull their money out of institutions that are engaging in these risky activities.

Limit Currency Mismatch

As we have seen, emerging market financial systems can become very vulnerable to a decline in the value of the nation's currency. Often, firms in these countries borrow in foreign currency, even though their products and assets are priced in domestic currency. A collapse of the currency causes debt denominated in foreign currency to become particularly burdensome because it has to be paid back in more expensive foreign currency, thereby causing a deterioration in firms' balance sheets that helps lead to a financial crisis. Governments can limit currency mismatch by implementing regulations or taxes that discourage the issuance of debt denominated in foreign currency by nonfinancial firms. Regulation of banks can also limit bank borrowing in foreign currencies.

Moving to a flexible exchange rate regime in which exchange rates fluctuate, can also discourage borrowing in foreign currencies because there is now more risk in doing so. Monetary policy that promotes price stability also helps by making the domestic currency less subject to decreases in its value as a result of high inflation, thus making it more desirable for firms to borrow in domestic rather than foreign currency.

Sequence Financial Liberalization

Although financial liberalization can be highly beneficial in the long run, our analysis of financial crisis in emerging market economies in this chapter shows that if this process is not managed properly, it can be disastrous. If the proper bank regulatory/supervisory structure and disclosure requirements are not in place when liberalization occurs, the constraints on risk-taking behavior will be far too weak.

To avoid financial crisis, policy makers need to put in place the proper institutional infrastructure before liberalizing their financial systems. Crucial to avoiding financial crisis is implementation of the policies described previously, which involve having strong prudential regulation and supervision and limiting currency mismatch. Because implementing these policies takes time, financial liberalization may have to be phased in gradually, with some restrictions on credit issuance imposed along the way.

SUMMARY

1. Financial crisis in emerging market countries develop along two basic paths: one involving the mismanagement of financial liberalization/globalization that weakens bank balance sheets and the other involving severe fiscal imbalances. Both lead to a speculative attack on the currency and eventually to a currency crisis in which there is a sharp decline in the value of the domestic currency. The decline in the value of the domestic currency causes a sharp rise in the debt burden of domestic firms, which leads to a decline in firms' net worth, as well as increases in inflation and interest rates. Adverse selection and moral hazard problems then worsen, leading to a collapse of lending and economic activity. The worsening economic conditions and increases in interest rates result in substantial losses for banks, leading to a banking crisis, which further depresses lending and aggregate economic activity.

2. The financial crisis in South Korea follows the pattern described previously. It started with a mismanagement of financial liberalization and globalization,

followed by a stock market crash and a failure of firms that increased uncertainty, a worsening of adverse selection problems, a currency crisis, and then a full-fledged financial crisis. The financial crisis led to a sharp contraction in economic activity and a rise in inflation, as well as a weakening of the social fabric.

3. In contrast to the crisis in South Korea, the Argentine financial crisis started with severe fiscal imbalances. The recession, which had been going on since 1998, along with the deterioration of bank balance sheets when the fiscal imbalances led to losses from government bonds, which the banks had on their balance sheets, led to a worsening of adverse selection and moral hazard problems, a bank panic, a currency crisis, and then a full-fledged financial crisis. As in South Korea, the financial crisis led to a decline in economic activity and a rise in inflation in Argentina, but the economic contraction and rise in inflation was even worse because Argentina's central bank lacked credibility as an inflation fighter.

4. India, despite its banking system not being exposed to toxic sub-prime assets, as also having limited external demand, was impacted by the global financial crisis. This was due to its deep integration with the global economy—trade integration, financial integration, and also dependence of its corporate investment-led growth on external funding. Output growth as well as export growth declined, a reversal of capital flows led to a pressure on the exchange rate, which depreciated significantly. The contagion of the crisis took place through the various channels—financial channel, real channel, and also confidence channels. The Government of India and the RBI responded through fiscal stimulus and monetary measures (both conventional and unconventional) to avert the crisis and mitigate its impact.

5. Policies to prevent financial crisis in emerging market economies include improving prudential regulation and supervision, limiting currency mismatch, and sequencing of financial liberalization.

KEY TERMS

currency mismatch, p. 546
emerging market economies, p. 542
financial globalization, p. 543
financial liberalization, p. 543
speculative attack, p. 545

QUESTIONS

1. What are the two basic causes of financial crisis in emerging market economies?

2. Why might financial liberalization and globalization lead to financial crisis in emerging market economies?

3. Why might severe fiscal imbalances lead to financial crisis in emerging market economies?

4. What other factors can initiate financial crisis in emerging market economies?

5. What events can ignite a currency crisis?

6. Why do currency crisis make financial crisis in emerging market economies even more severe?

7. How did the financial crisis in South Korea and Argentina affect aggregate demand, short-run aggregate supply, and output and inflation?

8. What can emerging market countries do to strengthen prudential regulation and supervision of their banking systems? How would these steps help avoid future financial crisis?

9. How can emerging market economies avoid the problems of currency mismatch?

10. Why might emerging market economies want to implement financial liberalization and globalization gradually rather than all at once?

Guide to Commonly Used Symbols

Symbol	Page Where Introduced	Term
Δ	60	change in a variable
π^e	47	expected inflation
σ	67	standard deviation
B^d	72	demand for bonds
B^s	72	supply of bonds
C	43	yearly coupon payment
D	69	demand curve
DUR	58	duration
DUR_{GAP}	494	duration gap
E	340	exchange (spot) rate
$(E^e_{t+1} - E_t)/E_t$	347	expected appreciation of domestic currency
EM	409	equity multiplier
GAP	488	income gap
i	42	interest rate (yield to maturity)
i^D	371	interest rate on dollar assets
i^F	380	interest rate on foreign assets
i_r	47	real interest rate
P_t	51	price of a security at time t
R	51	return
R^D		expected return on dollar deposits
R^F		expected return on foreign deposits
ROA	404	return on assets
ROE	404	return on equity
RSA	489	rate-sensitive assets
RSL	489	rate-sensitive liabilities
S	71	supply curve

Glossary

advances: See *discount loans*.

adverse selection: The problem created by asymmetric information before a transaction occurs: the people who are the most undesirable from the other party's point of view are the ones who are most likely to want to engage in the financial transaction. 26

agency problem: A moral hazard problem that occurs when the one party (the agents) act in their own interest rather than in the interest of the other party (the principal) due to differing sets of incentives. 173

agency theory: The analysis of how asymmetric information problems affect economic behavior. 140

American depository receipts (ADR): A receipt for foreign stocks held by a trustee. The receipts trade on U.S. stock exchanges instead of the actual stock. 353

American option: An option that can be exercised at any time up to the expiration date of the contract. 523

amortized: Paid off in stages over a period of time. Each payment on a loan consists of the accrued interest and an amount that is applied to repay the principal. When all of the payments have been made, the loan is paid off (fully amortized). 39

anchor currency: The currency to which a country fixes its exchange rate. 370

annuity: An insurance product that provides a fixed stream of payments. 393

appreciation: Increase in a currency's value. 340

arbitrage: Elimination of a riskless profit opportunity in a market. 120

ask price: The price market makers sell the stock for. 318

asset: A financial claim or piece of property that is a store of value. 2, 66

asset management: The acquisition of assets that have a low rate of default and diversification of asset holdings to increase profits. 398

asset market approach: Determining asset prices using stocks of assets rather than flows. 73

asset-price bubble: An increase in asset prices that are driven above their fundamental economic values by investor psychology. 168, 238

asset transformation: The process by which financial intermediaries turn risky assets into safer assets for investors by creating and selling assets with risk characteristics that people are comfortable with and then use the funds they acquire by selling these assets to purchase other assets that may have far more risk. 25

asymmetric information: The inequality of knowledge that each party to a transaction has about the other party. 26

audits: Certification by accounting firms that a business is adhering to standard accounting principles. 143

automated banking machine (ABM): An electronic machine that combines in one location an ATM, an Internet connection to the bank's website, and a telephone link to customer service. 454

automated teller machine (ATM): An electronic machine that allows customers to get cash, make deposits, transfer funds from one account to another, and check balances. 453

balance of payments: A bookkeeping system for recording all payments that have a direct bearing on the movement of funds between a country and all other countries. 367

balance-of-payments crisis: A foreign exchange crisis stemming from problems in a country's balance of payments. 381

balance sheet: A list of the assets and liabilities of a bank (or firm) that balances: total assets equal total liabilities plus capital. 392

bank failure: A situation in which a bank cannot satisfy its obligation to pay its depositors and other creditors and so goes out of business. 419

bank panic: The simultaneous failure of many banks, as during a financial crisis. 169

bank supervision: Overseeing who operates banks and how they are operated. 425

banker's acceptance: A short-term promissory note drawn by a company to pay for goods on which a bank guarantees payment at maturity. Usually used in international trade. 287

banks: Financial institutions that accept deposits and make loans (such as commercial banks, savings and loan associations, and credit unions). 8

Basel Accord: An agreement that requires that banks hold as capital at least 8% of their risk-weighted assets. 425

Basel Committee on Banking Supervision: A committee that meets under the auspices of the Bank for International Settlements in Basel, Switzerland, and that sets bank regulatory standards. 425

behavioral finance: The field of study that applies concepts from other social sciences, such as anthropology, sociology, and particularly psychology, to understand the behavior of securities prices. 131

bid price: The price market makers pay for the stocks. 318

Board of Governors of the Federal Reserve System: A board with seven governors (including the chair) that plays an essential role in decision making within the Federal Reserve System. 200

bond: A debt security that promises to make payments periodically for a specified period of time. 2

bond indenture: Document accompanying a bond that spells out the details of the bond issue, such as covenants and sinking fund provisions. It states the lender's rights and privileges and the borrower's obligations. 301

book entry: A system of tracking securities ownership where no certificate is issued. Instead, the security issuer keeps records, usually electronically, of who holds outstanding securities. 280

branches: Additional offices of banks that conduct banking operations. 466

Bretton Woods system: The international monetary system in use from 1945 to 1971 in which exchange rates were fixed and the U.S. dollar was freely convertible into gold (by foreign governments and central banks only). 370

brokers: Agents for investors who match buyers with sellers. 19

bubble: A situation in which the price of an asset differs from its fundamental market value. 130, 238

call option: An option contract that provides the right to buy a security at a specified price. 524

call provision: A right, usually included in the terms of a bond, that gives the issuer the ability to repurchase outstanding bonds before they mature. 301

capital: Wealth, either financial or physical, that is employed to produce more wealth. 17

capital account: An account that describes the flow of capital between the United States and other countries. 368

capital adequacy management: Managing the amount of capital the bank should maintain and then acquiring the needed capital. 398

capital controls: Restrictions on the free movement of capital across the borders. 373

capital market: A financial market in which longer-term debt (maturity of greater than one year) and equity instruments are traded. 20

capital mobility: A situation in which foreigners can easily purchase a country's assets and the country's residents can easily purchase foreign assets. 373

captive finance company: A finance company that is owned by a retailer and makes loans to finance the purchase of goods from the retailer.

cash flow: The difference between cash receipts and cash expenditures. 37

central bank: The government agency that oversees the banking system and is responsible for the amount of money and credit supplied in the economy; in the United States, the Federal Reserve System. 7

Central Liquidity Facility (CLF): The lender of last resort for credit unions, created in 1978 by the Financial Institutions Reform Act.

collateral: Property that is pledged to the lender to guarantee payment in the event that the borrower should be unable to make debt payments. 145

collateralized debt obligation (CDO): Securities that pay out cash flows from subprime mortgage-backed securities. 173

common bond membership: A requirement that all members of credit unions share some common bond, such as working for the same employer.

common stock: A security that gives the holder an ownership interest in the issuing firm. This ownership interest includes the right to any residual cash flows and the right to vote on major corporate issues. 3

common stockholders: Individuals who have an ownership interest in a firm, with rights to receive dividends and vote on major corporate issues. 315

compensating balance: A required minimum amount of funds that a firm receiving a loan must keep in a checking account at the bank. 486

conflicts of Interest: A manifestation of moral hazard in which one party in a financial contract has incentives to act in its own interest, rather than in the interests of the other party. 28, 155

costly state verification: Monitoring a firm's activities, an expensive process in both time and money. 148

coupon bond: A credit market instrument that pays the owner a fixed interest payment every year until the maturity date, when a specified final amount is paid. 39

coupon rate: The dollar amount of the yearly coupon payment expressed as a percentage of the face value of a coupon bond. 39, 295

credit-rating agencies: Investment advisory firms that rate the quality of corporate and municipal bonds in terms of the probability of default. 90

credit boom: A lending spree when financial institutions expand their lending at a rapid pace. 168

credit default swap: A transaction in which one party who wants to hedge credit risk pays a fixed payment on a regular basis, in return for a contingent payment that is triggered by a credit event such as the bankruptcy of a particular firm or the downgrading of the firm's credit rating by a credit rating agency. 174, 306, 535

credit derivatives: Derivatives that have payoffs to previously issued securities, but ones which bear credit risk. 533

credit-linked note: A type of credit derivative that is a combination of a bond and a credit option. 535

credit options: Options in which for a fee, the purchaser has the right to get profits that are tied either to the price of an underlying risky security or to an interest rate. 534

credit rationing: A lender's refusing to make loans even though borrowers are willing to pay the stated interest rate or even a higher rate or restricting the size of loans to less than the amount being sought. 486

credit risk: The risk arising from the possibility that the borrower will default. 398

credit spread: risk premium: the interest rate on bonds with default risks relative to the interest rate on default-free bonds like U.S. Treasury bonds. 172

credit swap: A transaction in which risky payments on loans are swapped for each other. 534

Credit Union National Association (CUNA): A central credit union facility that encourages establishing credit unions and provides information to its members.

Credit Union National Extension Bureau (CUNEB): A central credit union facility established in 1921 that was later replaced by the Credit Union National Association.

creditor: A lender or holder of debt. 153

currency board: A monetary regime in which the domestic currency is backed 100% by a foreign currency (say, dollars) and in which the note-issuing authority, whether the central bank or the government, establishes a fixed exchange rate to this foreign currency and stands ready to exchange domestic currency at this rate whenever the public requests it. 378

currency swap: A swap that involves the exchange of a set of payments in another currency. 530

currency union: A situation in which a group of countries decide to adopt a common currency. (Also called a monetary union.) 376

current account: An account that shows international transactions involving currently produced goods and services. 367

current yield: An approximation of the yield to maturity that equals the yearly coupon payment divided by the price of a coupon bond. 46, 307

dealers: People who link buyers with sellers by buying and selling securities at stated prices. 19

debt deflation: A situation in which a substantial decline in the price level sets in, leading to a further deterioration in firms' net worth because of the increased burden of indebtedness. 169

default: A situation in which the party issuing a debt instrument is unable to make interest payments or pay off the amount owed when the instrument matures. 88

default-free bonds: Bonds with no default risk, such as U.S. government bonds. 89

default risk: The risk that a loan customer may fail to repay a loan as promised. 88

deleveraging: When financial institutions cut back on their lending because they have less capital. 168

demand curve: A curve depicting the relationship between quantity demanded and price when all other economic variables are held constant. 69

demand deposit: A deposit held by a bank that must be paid to the depositor on demand. Demand deposits are more commonly called *checking accounts*. 392

deposit facility: The European Central Bank's standing facility in which banks are paid a fixed interest rate 100 basis points below the target financing rate. 243

deposit outflows: Losses of deposits when depositors make withdrawals or demand payment. 398

deposit rate ceilings: Restrictions on the maximum interest rates payable on deposits. 459

depreciation: Decrease in a currency's value. 340

devaluation: Resetting of the par value of a currency at a lower level. 372

dirty float: An exchange rate regime in which exchange rates fluctuate from day to day, but central banks attempt to influence their countries' exchange rate by buying and selling currencies. 370

discount: When the bond sells for less than the par value. 310

discount bond: A credit market instrument that is bought at a price below its face value and whose face value is repaid at the maturity date; it does not make any interest payments. Also known as a *zero-coupon bond*. 39

discount yield: See *yield on a discount basis*.

discounting: Reduction in the value of a security at purchase such that when it matures at full value, the investor receives a fair return. 270

disintermediation: A reduction in the flow of funds into the banking system that causes the amount of financial intermediation to decline. 459

diversification: Investing in a collection (portfolio) of assets whose returns do not always move together, with the result that overall risk is lower than for individual assets. 26

dividends: Periodic payments made by equities to shareholders. 18

dollarization: A monetary strategy in which a country abandons its currency altogether and adopts that of another country, typically the U.S. dollar. 379

dual mandate: A central bank mandate in which there are two equal objectives, price stability and maximum employment. 222

duration: The average lifetime of a debt security's stream of payments. 56

duration gap analysis: A measurement of the sensitivity of the market value of a bank's assets and liabilities to changes in interest rates. 490

e-cash: A form of electronic money used on the Internet to pay for goods and services. 455

econometric model: A model whose equations are estimated using statistical procedures. 83

economies of scale: Savings that can be achieved through increased size. 24, 139

economies of scope: Increased business that can be achieved by offering many products in one easy-to-reach location. 28, 155

efficient market hypothesis: The hypothesis that prices of securities in financial markets fully reflect all available information. 118

e-finance: A new means of delivering financial services electronically. 8

electronic money (or e-money): Money that exists only in electronic form and substitutes for cash as well. 465

emerging market economies: Economies in an earlier stage of market development that have recently opened up to the flow of goods, services, and capital from the rest of the world. 542

equities: Claims to share in the net income and assets of a corporation (such as common stock). 18

equity capital: See *net worth*.

equity multiplier: The amount of assets per dollar of equity capital. 404

Eurobonds: Bonds denominated in a currency other than that of the country in which they are sold. 22

Eurocurrencies: Foreign currencies deposited in banks outside the home country. 22

Eurodollars: U.S. dollars that are deposited in foreign banks outside of the United States or in foreign branches of U.S. banks. 22

European option: An option that can be exercised only at the expiration date of the contract. 523

excess demand: A situation in which quantity demanded is greater than quantity supplied. 72

excess reserves: Reserves in excess of required reserves. 210

excess supply: A situation in which quantity supplied is greater than quantity demanded. 72

exchange rate: The price of one currency in terms of another. 338

exchanges: Secondary markets in which buyers and sellers of securities (or their agents or brokers) meet in one central location to conduct trades. 19

exercise price: The price at which the purchaser of an option has the right to buy or sell the underlying financial instrument. Also known as the *strike price*. 523

expectations theory: The theory that the interest rate on a long-term bond will equal an average of the short-term interest rates that people expect to occur over the life of the long-term bond. 98

expected return: The return on an asset expected over the next period. 66

face value: The specified final amount repaid at the maturity date of a coupon bond. Also called *par value*. 39

factoring: The sale of accounts receivable to another firm, which takes responsibility for collections.

fair-value accounting: An accounting principle in which assets are valued in the balance sheet at what they would sell for in the market. 432

Federal Credit Union Act: Law passed in 1934 that allowed federal chartering of credit unions in all states.

federal funds rate: The interest rate on overnight loans of deposits at the Federal Reserve. 200

Federal Home Loan Bank Act of 1932: Law that created the Federal Home Loan Bank Board and a network of regional home loan banks.

Federal Home Loan Bank Board (FHLBB): Agency responsible for regulating and controlling savings and loan institutions, abolished by FIRREA in 1989.

Federal Open Market Committee (FOMC): The committee that makes decisions regarding the conduct of open market operations; composed of the seven members of the Board of Governors of the Federal Reserve System, the president of the Federal Reserve Bank of New York, and the presidents of four other Federal Reserve banks on a rotating basis. 190

Federal Reserve banks: The 12 district banks in the Federal Reserve system. 200

Federal Reserve System (the Fed): The central banking authority responsible for monetary policy in the United States. 200

Federal Savings and Loan Insurance Corporation (FSLIC): An agency that provided deposit insurance to savings and loans similar to the Federal Deposit Insurance Corporation that insures banks. FSLIC was eliminated in 1989.

financial crisis: A major disruption in financial markets, characterized by sharp declines in asset prices and the failures of many financial and nonfinancial firms. 6, 166

financial derivatives: Instruments that have payoffs that are linked to previously issued securities and are extremely useful risk-reduction tools. 444

financial engineering: The process of researching and developing new financial products and services that would meet customer needs and prove profitable. 451

financial frictions: Asymmetric information problems that act as a barrier to financial markets channeling funds efficiently from savers to households and firms with productive investment opportunities, 166

financial futures contract: A futures contract in which the standardized commodity is a particular type of financial instrument. 508

financial futures options: Options in which the underlying instrument is a futures contract. Also called *futures options*. 524

financial globalization: The process of opening up to flows of capital and financial firms from other nations. 543

financial guarantee: A contract that guarantees that bond purchasers will be paid both principal and interest in the event the issuer defaults on the obligation. 305

financial innovation: The development of new financial products and services. 8, 166

Financial Institutions Reform Act: Law passed in 1978 that created the Central Liquidity Facility as the lender of last resort for credit unions.

Financial Institutions Reform, Recovery, and Enforcement Act: Law passed in 1989 to stop losses in the savings and loan industry. It reversed much of the deregulation included in the Garn–St Germain Act of 1982.

financial instrument: See *security*.

financial intermediaries: Institutions (such as banks, insurance companies, mutual funds, pension funds, and finance companies) that borrow funds from people who have saved and then make loans to others. 7

financial intermediation: The process of indirect finance whereby financial intermediaries link lender-savers and borrower-spenders. 24

financial liberalization: The elimination of restrictions on financial markets. 166

financial markets: Markets in which funds are transferred from people who have a surplus of available funds to people who have a shortage of available funds. 2

financial panic: The widespread collapse of financial markets and intermediaries in an economy. 33

financial supervision: Oversight of who operates financial institutions and how they are operated. (Also called *prudential supervision*.) 422

fire sales: The quick sale of assets to raise necessary funds. 169

Fisher effect: The outcome that when expected inflation occurs, interest rates will rise; named after economist Irving Fisher. 80

fixed exchange rate regime: Policy under which central banks buy and sell their own currencies to keep their exchange rates fixed at a certain level. 370

fixed-payment loan: A credit market instrument that provides a borrower with an amount of money that is repaid by making a fixed payment periodically (usually monthly) for a set number of years. 39

floating exchange rate regime: An exchange rate regime in which the value of currencies are allowed to fluctuate against one another. 370

foreign bonds: Bonds sold in a foreign country and denominated in that country's currency. 20

foreign exchange intervention: An international financial transaction in which a central bank buys or sells currency to influence foreign exchange rates. 363

foreign exchange market: The market in which exchange rates are determined. 5, 338

foreign exchange rate: See *exchange rate*.

forward contract: An agreement by two parties to engage in a financial transaction at a future (forward) point in time. 506

forward exchange rate: The exchange rate for a forward (future) transaction. 340

forward rate: The interest rate predicted by pure expectations theory of the term structure of interest rates to prevail in the future. 111

forward transaction: An exchange rate transaction that involves the exchange of bank deposits denominated in different currencies at some specified future date. 340

free-rider problem: The problem that occurs when people who do not pay for information take advantage of the information that other people have paid for. 142

fully amortized loan: A fixed payment loan in which the lender provides the borrower with an amount of funds that must be repaid by making the same payment every period, consisting of part of the principal and interest for a set number of years. 39

futures contract: A contract in which the seller agrees to provide a certain standardized commodity to the buyer on a specific future date at an agreed-on price. 452

futures options: See *financial futures options*.

gap analysis: A measurement of the sensitivity of bank profits to changes in interest rates, calculated by subtracting the amount of rate-sensitive liabilities minus rate-sensitive assets. Also called *income gap analysis*. 488

generalized dividend model: Calculates that the price of stock is determined only by the present value of the dividends. 322

Glass-Steagall Act: Law that made it illegal for commercial banks to underwrite securities for sale to the public. 436

goal independence: The ability of the central bank to set the goals of monetary policy. 200

Gordon growth model: A simplified model to compute the value of a stock by assuming constant dividend growth. 322

haircuts: Requirements that borrowers have more collateral than the amount of the loan. 177

hedge: To protect oneself against risk. 452, 506

hierarchical mandate: A mandate for the central bank that puts the goal of price stability first, but as long as it is achieved other goals can be pursued. 222

impossible trinity: See *policy trilemma*.

income gap analysis: See *gap analysis*.

inflation targeting: A monetary policy strategy that involves public announcement of a medium-term numerical target for inflation. 224

initial public offering (IPO): A corporation's first sale of securities to the public. 156, 295

installment credit: A loan that requires the borrower to make a series of equal payments over some fixed length of time.

instrument independence: The ability of the central bank to set monetary policy instruments. 200

interest rate: The cost of borrowing or the price paid for the rental of funds (usually expressed as a percentage per year). 2

interest-rate forward contracts: Forward contracts that are linked to debt instruments. 506

interest-rate risk: The possible reduction in returns that is associated with changes in interest rates. 54, 311

interest-rate swap: A financial contract that allows one party to exchange (swap) a set of interest payments for another set of interest payments owned by another party. 530

intermediate target: Any number of variables, such as monetary aggregates or interest rates, that have a direct effect on employment and price level and that the Fed seeks to influence. 242

intermediate-term: With reference to a debt instrument, having a maturity of between one and 10 years. 18

International Monetary Fund (IMF): The international organization created by the Bretton Woods agreement whose objective is to promote the growth of world trade by making loans to countries experiencing balance-of-payments difficulties. 370

international reserves: Central bank holdings of assets denominated in foreign currencies. 363

inverted yield curve: A yield curve that is downward sloping. 96

investment banks: Firms that assist in the initial sale of securities in the primary market. 19

January effect: An abnormal rise in stock prices from December to January. 125

junk bonds: Bonds rated lower than BBB by bond-rating agencies. Junk bonds are not investment grade and are considered speculative. They usually have a high yield to compensate investors for their high risk. 91, 455

large, complex banking organizations (LCBOs): Large companies that provide banking as well as many other financial services.

law of one price: The principle that if two or more countries produce an identical good, the price of this good should be the same no matter which country produces it. 342

leasing: An arrangement whereby one party obtains the right to use an asset for a fee paid to another party for a predetermined length of time.

leverage cycle: A lending boom and then a lending crash. 437

leverage ratio: A bank's capital divided by its assets. 424

liabilities: IOUs or debts. 16

liability management: The acquisition of funds at low cost to increase profits. 398

liquid: Easily converted into cash. 19

liquid market: A market in which securities can be bought and sold quickly and with low transaction costs. 271

liquidity: The relative ease and speed with which an asset can be converted into cash. 66

liquidity management: The decision made by a bank to maintain sufficient liquid assets to meet the bank's obligations to depositors. 243

liquidity premium theory: The theory that the interest rate on a long-term bond will equal an average of short-term interest rates expected to occur over the life of the long-term bond plus a positive term (liquidity) premium. 104

liquidity risk: The risk that a firm may run out of cash needed to pay bills and to keep the firm operating.

liquidity services: Services that make it easier for customers to conduct transactions. 25

loan commitment: A bank's commitment (for a specified future period of time) to provide a firm with loans up to a given amount at an interest rate that is tied to some market interest rate. 407

loan sale: The sale under a contract (also called a *secondary loan participation*) of all or part of the cash stream from a specific loan, thereby removing the loan from the bank's balance sheet. 407

London interbank bid rate (LIBID): The rate of interest large international banks charge on overnight loans among themselves. 288

London interbank offer rate (LIBOR): The interest rate charged on short-term funds bought or sold between large international banks. 288

long position: A contractual obligation to take delivery of an underlying financial instrument. 506

long-term: With reference to a debt instrument, having a maturity of 10 years or more. 18

macro hedge: A hedge of interest-rate risk for a financial institution's entire portfolio. 511

macroprudential regulation: Regulatory policy to affect what is happening in credit markets in the aggregate. 241

macroprudential supervision: Supervision that focuses on the safety and soundness of the financial system in the aggregate. 437

managed float regime: The current international financial environment in which exchange rates fluctuate from day to day, but central banks attempt to influence their countries' exchange rates by buying and selling currencies. Also known as a *dirty float*. 370

margin requirement: A sum of money that must be kept in an account (the margin account) at a brokerage firm. 516

mark-to-market accounting: An accounting method in which assets are valued in the balance sheets at what they would sell for in the market. 432

marked to market: Repriced and settled in the margin account at the end of every trading day to reflect any change in the value of the futures contract. 516

market equilibrium: A situation occurring when the quantity that people are willing to buy (demand) equals the quantity that people are willing to sell (supply). 72

market fundamentals: Items that have a direct effect on future income streams of the security. 130

market segmentation theory: A theory of the term structure that sees markets for different maturity bonds as completely separated and segmented such that the interest rate for bonds of a given maturity is determined solely by supply and demand for bonds of that maturity. 103

maturity: Time to the expiration date (maturity date) of a debt instrument. 18

mean reversion: The phenomenon that stocks with low returns today tend to have high returns in the future, and vice versa. 126

micro hedge: A hedge for a specific asset. 511

microprudential supervision: Supervision that focuses on the safety and soundness of individual financial institutions. 436

monetary base: The sum of the Fed's monetary liabilities (currency in circulation and reserves) and the U.S. Treasury's monetary liabilities (Treasury currency in circulation, primarily coins). 212

monetary neutrality: A proposition that in the long run, a percentage rise in the money supply is matched by the same percentage rise in the price level, leaving unchanged the real money supply and all other economic variables such as interest rates.

monetary policy: The management of the money supply and interest rates. 7

monetary union: A situation in which a group of countries decide to adopt a common currency. (Also called a *currency union*.) 376

money: Anything that is generally accepted in payment for goods or services or in the repayment of debts. Also called *money supply*. 7

money market: A financial market in which only short-term debt instruments (maturity of less than one year) are traded. 20

money market mutual funds: Funds that accumulate investment dollars from a large group of people and then invest in short-term securities such as Treasury bills and commercial paper. 31, 269, 459

money supply: See *money*.

moral hazard: The risk that one party to a transaction will engage in behavior that is undesirable from the other party's point of view. 26

mutual bank: A bank owned by the depositors.

National Association of Securities Dealers Automated Quotation System (NASDAQ): A computerized network that links dealers around the country together and provides price quotes on over-the-counter securities. 317

National Credit Union Act of 1970: Law that established the National Credit Union Administration (NCUA), an independent agency charged with the task of regulating and supervising federally chartered credit unions and state-chartered credit unions that receive federal deposit insurance.

natural rate of unemployment: The rate of unemployment consistent with full employment at which the demand for labor equals the supply of labor. 220

negotiable certificates of deposit: A bank-issued short-term security that is traded and that documents a deposit and specifies the interest rate and the maturity date. 288

net interest margin (NIM): The difference between interest income and interest expense as a percentage of assets. 412

net worth: The difference between a firm's assets (what it owns or is owed) and its liabilities (what it owes). Also called *equity capital*. 146

nominal anchor: A nominal variable such as the inflation rate, an exchange rate, or the money supply that monetary policy makers use to tie down the price level. 217

nominal interest rate: An interest rate that is not adjusted for inflation. 47

nonbank banks: Limited-service banks that either do not make commercial loans or do not take in deposits.

nonconventional monetary policy tools: Three non-interest-rate tools used to stimulate the economy: (1) liquidity provision, (2) asset purchases, and (3) commitment to future monetary policy actions. 214

notional principal: The amount on which interest is being paid in a swap arrangement. 531

off-balance-sheet activities: Bank activities that involve trading financial instruments and the generation of income from fees and loan sales, all of which affect bank profits but are not visible on bank balance sheets. 407, 424

open interest: The number of contracts outstanding. 512

open market operations: The buying and selling of government securities in the open market that affect both interest rates and the amount of reserves in the banking system. 211, 213

operating expenses: The expenses incurred from a bank's ongoing operations. 411

operating income: The income earned on a bank's ongoing operations. 410

options: Contracts that give the purchaser the option (right) to buy or sell the underlying financial instrument at a specified price, called the *exercise price* or *strike price*, within a specific period of time (the *term to expiration*). 523

over-the-counter (OTC) market: A secondary market in which dealers at different locations who have an inventory of securities stand ready to buy and sell securities to anyone who comes to them and is willing to accept their prices. 19

passbook savings account: An interest-bearing savings account held at a commercial bank.

pecking order hypothesis: The hypothesis that the larger and more established is a corporation, the more likely it will be to issue securities to raise funds. 145

perpetuity: A perpetual bond with no maturity date and no repayment of principal that makes periodic fixed payments forever. 44

policy instrument: A variable that is very responsive to the central bank's tools and indicates the stance of monetary policy (also called an *operating instrument*). 243

policy trilemma: A country cannot pursue the following three policies at the same time: (1) free capital mobility; (2) a fixed exchange rate; and (3) independent monetary policy. (Also called *impossible trinity*.) 373

political business cycle: A business cycle caused by expansionary policies before an election. 197

portfolio: A collection of assets. 26

potential output: The level of output that is produced at the natural rate of unemployment. Also called *natural rate of output*. 220

preferred habitat theory: A theory that assumes that investors have a preference for bonds of one maturity over another, a particular bond maturity (preferred habitat) in which they prefer to invest. 104

preferred stock: Stock on which a fixed dividend must be paid before common dividends are distributed. It often does not mature and usually does not give the holder voting rights in the company. 315

premium: The amount paid for an option contract. 310, 523

present discounted value: See *present value*. 37

present value: Today's value of a payment to be received in the future when the interest rate is i. Also called *present discounted value*. 37

price earnings ratio (PE): A measure of how much the market is willing to pay for $1 of earnings from a firm. 324

price stability: Low and stable inflation. 216

primary dealers: Government securities dealers, operating out of private firms or commercial banks, with whom the Fed's open market desk trades. 269

primary market: A financial market in which new issues of a security are sold to initial buyers. 18

principal-agent problem: A moral hazard problem that occurs when the managers in control (the agents) act in their own interest rather than in the interest of the owners (the principals) due to differing sets of incentives. 146, 173

proprietary trading: Financial institutions that trade with their own money. 444

put option: An option contract that provides the right to sell a security at a specified price. 298

quotas: Restrictions on the quantity of foreign goods that can be imported. 345

random walk: The movements of a variable whose future changes cannot be predicted because, given today's value, the variable is just as likely to fall as to rise. 122

rate of capital gain: The change in a security's price relative to the initial purchase price. 52

rate of return: See *return*.

real exchange rate: The rate at which domestic goods can be exchanged for foreign goods, meaning the price of domestic goods relative to foreign goods denominated in domestic currency. 343

real interest rate: The interest rate adjusted for expected changes in the price level (inflation) so that it more accurately reflects the true cost of borrowing. 47

real terms: Terms reflecting actual goods and services one can buy. 48

registered bonds: Bonds requiring that their owners register with the company to receive interest payments. Registered bonds have largely replaced bearer bonds, which did not require registration. 301

Regulation Z: The requirement that lenders disclose the full cost of a loan to the borrower; also known as the "truth in lending" regulation.

regulatory arbitrage: An attempt to avoid regulatory capital requirements by keeping assets on banks' books that have the same risk-based capital requirement but are relatively risky, while taking off their books low-risk assets. 425

reinvestment risk: The interest-rate risk associated with the fact that the proceeds of short-term investments must be reinvested at a future interest rate that is uncertain. 54

repossession: The taking of an asset that has been pledged as collateral for a loan when the borrower defaults.

repurchase agreement: A form of loan in which the borrower simultaneously contracts to sell securities and contracts to repurchase them, either on demand or on a specified date. 177

required reserve ratio: The fraction of deposits that the Fed requires to be kept as reserves. 393

required reserves: Reserves that are held to meet Fed requirements that a certain fraction of bank deposits be kept as reserves. 393

reserve currency: A currency such as the U.S. dollar that is used by other countries to denominate the assets they hold as international reserves. 371

reserve for loan losses: An account that offsets the loan accounts on a lender's books that reflects the lender's projected losses due to default.

reserve requirements: Regulations making it obligatory for depository institutions to keep a certain fraction of their deposits in accounts with the Fed. 393

reserves: Banks' holding of deposits in accounts with the Fed, plus currency that is physically held by banks (vault cash). 393

Resolution Trust Corporation (RTC): A temporary agency created by FIRREA that was responsible for liquidating the assets of failed savings and loans.

restrictive covenants: Provisions that specify certain activities that a borrower can and cannot engage in. 138, 301

return: The payments to the owner of a security plus the change in the security's value, expressed as a fraction of its purchase price; more precisely called the *rate of return*. 49

return on assets (ROA): Net profit after taxes per dollar of assets. 404

return on equity (ROE): Net profit after taxes per dollar of equity capital. 404

revaluation: Resetting of the par value of a currency at a higher level. 373

risk: The degree of uncertainty associated with the return on an asset. 25, 66

risk premium: The spread between the interest rate on bonds with default risk and the interest rate on default-free bonds. 89

risk sharing: The process by which financial intermediaries create and sell assets with risk characteristics that people are comfortable with and then use the funds they acquire by selling these assets to purchase other assets that may have far more risk. 25

risk structure of interest rates: The relationship among the various interest rates on bonds with the same term to maturity. 87

roll over: To renew a debt when it matures.

secondary market: A financial market in which securities that have previously been issued can be resold. 18

secured debt: Debt guaranteed by collateral. 138

secured loan: A loan guaranteed by collateral. 485

securitization: The process of transforming illiquid financial assets into marketable capital market instruments. 173, 457

securitized mortgage: See *mortgage-backed-security*.

security: A claim on the borrower's future income that is sold by the borrower to the lender. Also called a *financial instrument*. 2

Separate Trading of Registered Interest and Principal Securities (STRIPS): Securities that have their periodic interest payments separated from the final maturity payment and the two cash flows are sold to different investors. 299

shadow banking system: A system in which bank lending is replaced by lending via the securities market. 177, 451

share draft account: Accounts at credit unions that are similar to checking accounts at banks.

shelf registration: An arrangement with the Securities and Exchange Commission that allows a single registration document to be filed that permits multiple securities issues.

short position: A contractual obligation to deliver an underlying financial instrument. 506

short sale: An arrangement with a broker to borrow and sell securities. The borrowed securities are replaced with securities purchased later. Short sales let investors earn profits from falling securities prices. 132

short-term: With reference to a debt instrument, having a maturity of one year or less. 18

simple loan: A credit market instrument providing the borrower with an amount of funds that must be repaid to the lender at the maturity date along with an additional payment (interest). 37

sinking fund: Fund created by a provision in many bond contracts that requires the issuer to set aside each year a portion of the final maturity payment so that investors can be certain that the funds will be available at maturity. 302

smart card: A more sophisticated stored-value card that contains its own computer chip so that it can be loaded with digital cash from the owner's bank account whenever needed. 455

special drawing rights (SDRs): A paper substitute for gold issued by the International Monetary Fund that functions as international reserves.

speculative attack: A situation in which speculators engage in massive sales of a currency. 545

spinning: When an investment bank allocates hot, but underpriced, initial public offerings (IPOs), shares of newly issued stock, to executives of other companies in return for their companies' future business with the investment banks. 156

spot exchange rate: The exchange rate for the immediate (two-day) transaction. 340

spot rate: The interest rate at a given moment. 111

spot transaction: The immediate exchange of bank deposits denominated in different currencies. 340

standard deviation: A statistical indicator of an asset's risk. 67

state-owned banks: Banks that are owned by governments. 154

sterilized foreign exchange intervention: A foreign exchange intervention with an offsetting open market operation that leaves the monetary base unchanged. 365

stock: A security that is a claim on the earnings and assets of a corporation. 3

stock market risk: The risk associated with fluctuations in stock prices. 521

stock option: An option on an individual stock. 523

stress testing: Calculating losses under dire scenarios. 430

strike price: See *exercise price*.

structured credit products: Securities that are derived from cash flows of underlying assets and are tailored to have particular risk characteristics that appeal to investors with different preferences. 173

subprime mortgages: Mortgage loans made to borrowers who do not qualify for loans at the usual rate of interest due to a poor credit history. 173

supply curve: A curve depicting the relationship between quantity supplied and price when all other economic variables are held constant. 71

swap: A financial contract that obligates one party to exchange (swap) a set of payments it owns for a set of payments owned by another party. 530

sweep account: An arrangement in which any balances above a certain amount in a corporation's checking account at the end of a business day are "swept out" of the account and invested in overnight repos that pay the corporation interest. 460

systemic: Financial firms who pose a risk to the overall financial system because their failure would cause widespread damage. 444

tariffs: Taxes on imported goods. 345

term structure of interest rates: The relationship among interest rates on bonds with different terms to maturity. 87

theory of efficient capital markets: The theory that prices of securities in financial markets fully reflect all available information. 118

theory of portfolio choice: The theory that tells how much of an asset people want to hold in their portfolio. 69

theory of purchasing power parity (PPP): The theory that exchange rates between any two currencies will adjust to reflect changes in the price levels of the two countries. 342

time-inconsistency problem: The problem that occurs when monetary policy makers conduct monetary policy in a discretionary way and pursue expansionary policies that are attractive in the short run but lead to bad long-run outcomes. 218

too-big-to-fail problem: Quandary in which regulators are reluctant to close down large financial institutions and impose losses on to their depositors and creditors because doing so might precipitate a financial crisis. 423

trade association: A group of credit unions organized to provide a variety of services to a large number of credit unions.

trade balance: The difference between merchandise exports and imports. 367

transaction costs: The time and money spent trying to exchange financial assets, goods, or services. 24

Treasury bills (T-bills): Securities sold by the federal government with initial maturities of less than one year. They are often considered the lowest-risk security available.

underwriting: Guaranteeing prices on securities to corporations and then selling the securities to the public. 19

unexploited profit opportunity: A situation in which an investor can earn a higher-than-normal return. 120

unsecured debt: Debt not guaranteed by collateral. 138

unsterilized foreign exchange intervention: A foreign exchange intervention in which a central bank allows the purchase or sale of domestic currency to affect the monetary base. 365

U.S. Central Credit Union: A central bank for credit unions that was organized in 1974 and provides banking services to the state central credit unions.

usury: Charging an excessive or inordinate interest rate on a loan.

value at risk (VaR) calculations: Measurements of the size of the loss on a trading portfolio that might happen, say 1% of the time, over a particular period such as two weeks. 430

vault cash: Currency that is physically held by banks and stored in vaults overnight. 393

venture capital firm: A financial intermediary that pools the resources of its partners and uses the funds to help entrepreneurs start up new businesses. 148

virtual bank: A bank that has no building but rather exists only in cyberspace. 454

wealth: All resources owned by an individual, including all assets. 66

wholesale market: Market where extremely large transactions occur, as for money market funds or foreign currency. 265

World Bank: The International Bank for Reconstruction and Development, an international organization that provides long-term loans to assist developing countries in building dams, roads, and other physical capital that would contribute to their economic development. 370

World Trade Organization (WTO): The organization that monitors rules for the conduct of trade between countries (tariffs and quotas). 371

yield curve: A plot of the interest rates for particular types of bonds with different terms to maturity. 96

yield to maturity: The interest rate that equates the present value of payments received from a credit market instrument with its value today. 40

zero-coupon bond: See *discount bond*. 39

Index